THE HUMAN JOURNEY

READINGS IN THE HUMANITIES

MAX REICHARD   DEL MCGINNIS

Pearson
Custom
Publishing

Cover photo: Courtesy of NASA.

Printed in the United States of America

10 9 8 7 6 5 4 3 2

Please visit our website at www.pearsoncustom.com

ISBN 0–536–58129–0

BA 990502

PEARSON CUSTOM PUBLISHING
160 Gould Street/Needham Heights, MA 02494
A Pearson Education Company

COPYRIGHT ACKNOWLEDGMENTS

DEDICATION

To all our students at Delgado Community College who shared the sentiment: "I learned things in Humanities that I didn't know I wanted to know."

In the Beginning was the Word
And the Word was with God
And the Word was God

The Gospel According to John

What has been overlooked is the irrational, the inconsistent, the droll, even the insane, which nature, inexhaustibly operative, implants in an individual, seemingly for her own amusement.

Albert Einstein

Man cannot live without a sense of the sacred. But . . . for *technique* nothing is sacred, there is no mystery, no taboo . . . . Technique worships nothing, respects nothing. It has a single role: to strip off externals, to bring everything to light, and by rational use to transform everything into means.

Jacques Ellul, La Technique

Reason is God's crowning gift to man.

Sophocles, Antigone

TABLE OF CONTENTS

ILLUSTRATIONS

PREFACE

THE HUMAN JOURNEY

A human life is a journey of discovery, and the choice of direction is, to a great extent, our own. Of course one can simply sleepwalk through life, making few conscious choices, demonstrating behavior that the determinists confidently predict. But even when we conform, we are choosing, whether consciously or not.

Humanities affirm free will and therefore self direction. Students choose to attend college because they want to learn, and they should enroll in the introductory humanities course for the same reason. For such students, the humanities course offers the opportunity to discover ideas and at the same time to assess their own values.

While our choices are our own, we will make little progress on our journey without learning what others have written. All great writers have also been great readers, and all great thinkers build on knowledge discovered by others. Hence the history of humankind is itself a journey. Each generation begins where the previous generations have led, and each generation modifies the direction of previous generations. Certainly a reassessment is needed as we approach the coming millennium, for Earth's ecosystem is steadily being destroyed by our technologies.

As we seek a proper course, we need to learn from not only the traditions of Western thinkers but from other traditions as well. As Joseph Campbell says, the tenets of Buddhism have much to teach us, as do those of Native Americans, whose reverence for the life-sustaining planet supersedes considerations of individual needs and wants.

While this text focuses on writings from the Western tradition, it also contains works from non-Western cultures. Readings have been selected to provide differing viewpoints on human values by some of the foremost thinkers and writers, past and present.

To the instructor, we offer the same advice as we offered the student. That is to say, we have found from personal experience that the instructor learns as much as the students in the introductory humanities course. This is because instructors in humanities are drawn from various disciplines. Ours, for example, are history and English. In some areas, then, we speak with some authority; in others, we are eager learners along with the students.

This diversity of subject matter is one of the reasons the course needs guest lecturers and films to supplement the text. Another reason for using audio-visual aids is to study art and music of major historical periods. In our course, we also include class visits to an art museum and attendance at a live musical performance, theater, film, and art galleries.

This is the second edition of *The Human Journey: Readings in the Humanities*. The first edition was developed by Max Reichard; the second edition is a collaboration with Del McGinnis, who also teaches the course.

The reader is divided into six chapters. The first chapter introduces Western philosophy in historical perspective. Chapter II provides a discussion of critical thinking and its limits; the readings are themselves examples of good critical thinking. Chapter III, Art and Nature, provides only the briefest introduction to the arts, since words are not the medium of either music or the visual arts. This chapter must therefore be supplemented with visits to art galleries, museums, and live musical performances. Chapter IV makes a case for understanding morality in its historical interplay with faith. Three plays are included in Chapter V, as well as introductions to other drama and films. The final chapter explores the concept of myth and its relationship to historical consciousness.

The book was designed to be read in the order presented; however, an argument may be made for dealing with myth after Chapter II. Each chapter has an introductory essay with explicit or implied questions as a guide to the readings.

Max Reichard and Del McGinnis

ABOUT THE AUTHORS

Max Reichard is Professor of History at Delgado Community College in New Orleans and holds the Ph.D. in History from Washington University.

Del (Adelaide) McGinnis is Professor of English at Delgado Community College and holds the Ph.D. in English from Tulane University.

In spring 1991, the Introduction to Humanities course at Delgado Community College won the second-place Multicultural Humanities Award from the American Association of Community and Junior Colleges, out of 48 entries. This text provides the readings for the syllabus of that course.

HISTORICAL OUTLINE OF IMPORTANT FIGURES AND ACHIEVEMENTS

Ancient Egyptian and Hebrew Period

25th c. B.C. -	Great Pyramids and Sphinx
19th c. B.C. -	Abraham becomes Father of the Hebrews.
17th-13th c. -	Hebrews in Egypt; led away by Moses.
15th c. B.C. -	Height of Egyptian power; Pharaohs Tutmose III and Akenaton (believed in one God)
14th c. B.C. -	King Tut (boy king)
13th c. B.C. -	Ramses II

Classical Greek Period

9th c. B.C. -	Homer, Greek poet: *The Iliad* (depicts Trojan War) and *The Odyssey*.
7th c. B.C. -	Sappho, Greek poet of Lesbos (a woman)
6th c. B.C. -	Buddha (Siddhartha Gautoma) founds Buddhism in India.
5th c. B.C. -	Tragic Dramatists: Aeschylus (*Prometheus Bound*), Sophocles (*Oedipus Rex, Antigone*)
4th c. B.C. -	Comic Dramatist: Aristophanes (*The Clouds*) Greek Philosophers: Socrates, Plato (*The Republic*)
4th c. B.C. -	Aristotle: Philosopher, biologist, tutor of Alexander the Great

Classical Roman Period Through Medieval Period

1st c. A.D. -	Jesus Christ and followers found Christianity.
7th c. A.D. -	Mohammed founds the Moslem religion (Islam).
13th c. A.D. -	Thomas Aquinas (rational proofs of God's existence)

Renaissance (Revival of Greek Learning: 15th-17th centuries)

Artists

Leonardo da Vinci (d. 1519): painter and inventor from Milan, Italy ("Mona Lisa," "The Last Supper")

Michelangelo Buonarroti (d. 1564): sculptor, painter from Florence (""David," Sistine Chapel Ceiling)

Sanzio Raphael (d. 1520): Italian painter ("Sistine Madonna")

Scientists

Nicholas Copernicus (d. 1543): Polish astronomer who challenged the view of earth as center of universe

Galilei Galileo (d. 1642): Italian astronomer who affirmed Copernican view of earth; forced to recant.

Political Thinker

Nicholo Machiavelli: Italian (d. 1527)

The Baroque Period and the Enlightenment

Artists

Peter Rubens (d. 1640): Dutch Baroque painter
Rembrandt (d. 1669): Dutch Baroque painter of portraits

Musicians

Johann Sebastian Bach (d. 1750): German Baroque Musician
Antonio Vivaldi (d. 1743): Italian Baroque Musician
Wolfgang Amadeus Mozart (d. 1791): Austrian musician of "classical period," late 18th c., along with Haydn

Political Writers

Adam Smith (d. 1790): Scottish economist of capitalism
Jean Jacques Rousseau (d. 1778): French philosopher who influenced the French revolution and the Romantic era
Benjamin Franklin (d. 1790): American statesman, deist
Thomas Jefferson (d. 1826): American president; wrote the Declaration of Independence; also a deist

Scientist

Sir Isaac Newton (d. 1727): English mathematician, scientist, and philosopher

Romantic Age (19th century)

Artists

Francisco Goya (d. 1828): Spanish painter, satirist
Vincent Van Gogh (d. 1890): Dutch painter with bold style
Paul Gauguin (d. 1903): French painter; Tahitian subjects
Claude Monet (d. 1926): French impressionist painter
Edgar Degas (d. 1917): Impressionist painter, sculptor
August Rodin (d. 1917): French impressionist sculptor
Mary Cassatt (d. 1926): American impressionist painter

Musicians

Ludwig Van Beethoven (d. 1827): German composer
Frederic Chopin (d. 1849): Polish/French composer (piano)
Claude Debussy (d. 1918): French impressionist musician

Writers

Walt Whitman (d. 1892): American poet who used free verse
Emily Dickinson (d. 1886): American poet (pre-modern)
Henry David Thoreau (d. 1862): American writer (*Walden*)
Mark Twain (d. 1910): American novelist (anti-romantic)
Anton Chekhov (d. 1904): Russian dramatist (realist)
Soren Kierkegaard (d. 1885): Danish philosopher
Friedrich Nietzsche (d. 1900): German philosopher

Leaders

Abraham Lincoln (d. 1865): American President
Queen Victoria (d. 1901): British Queen (Victorian Era)

Scientist

Charles Darwin (d. 1882): English biologist of evolution

Modern Era (20th Century)

Artists

Pablo Picasso (d. 1974): Spanish painter (cubism)
Henri Matisse (d. 1954): French painter (at Nice)
Diego Rivera (d. 1957): Mexican muralist
Salvador Dali: Spanish surrealist painter
Georgia O'Keeffe (d. 1986): American minimalist

Musicians

George Gershwin (d. 1937): American ("Rhapsody in Blue")
Jelly Roll Morton (d. 1941): American jazz composer
Scott Joplin (d. 1917): American ragtime piano composer
Charlie Parker (d. 1955): American jazz musician

Writers

James Joyce (d. 1941): Irish novelist; wrote *Ulysses*
William Faulkner (d. 1962): Mississippi novelist
T. S. Eliot (d. 1965): American-British poet
Langston Hughes (d. 1967): Black American poet

Scientists

Sigmund Freud (d. 1919): Austrian psychoanalyst
Carl Jung (d. 1961): Swiss psychologist
Albert Einstein (d. 1955): German scientist

Philosophers

Jean Paul Sartre (d. 1980): French existentialist
Albert Camus (d. 1960): French existentialist
Joseph Campbell (d. 1988): American mythologist

Leaders

Mohandas Gandhi (d. 1948): led India to independence
Martin Luther King, Jr. (d. 1968): Civil rights leader

GREEK GODS AND HEROS

THE PRINCIPAL GODS

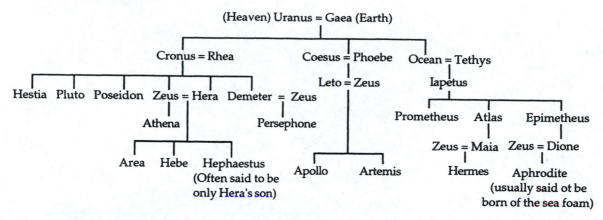

(Heaven) Uranus = Gaea (Earth)

Cronus = Rhea   Coesus = Phoebe   Ocean = Tethys

Hestia Pluto Poseidon Zeus = Hera Demeter = Zeus   Leto = Zeus   Iapetus

Athena   Persephone

Area Hebe Hephaestus
(Often said to be
only Hera's son)

Apollo   Artemis

Prometheus Atlas Epimetheus

Zeus = Maia Zeus = Dione

Hermes   Aphrodite
(usually said ot be
born of the sea foam)

THE ROYAL HOUSE OF THEBES AND THE ATREIDAE

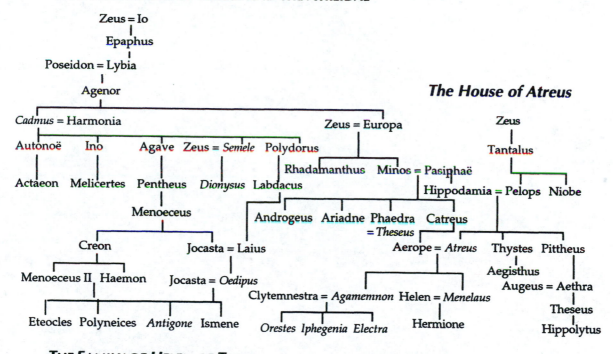

Zeus = Io

Epaphus

Poseidon = Lybia

Agenor

The House of Atreus

Cadmus = Harmonia   Zeus = Europa   Zeus

Autonoë Ino Agave Zeus = *Semele* Polydorus   Tantalus

Rhadamanthus Minos = Pasiphaë

Actaeon Melicertes Pentheus *Dionysus* Labdacus   Hippodamia = Pelops Niobe

Menoeceus   Androgeus Ariadne Phaedra Catreus
                                        = *Theseus*

Creon   Jocasta = Laius   Aerope = *Atreus* Thystes Pittheus

Menoeceus II Haemon Jocasta = *Oedipus*   Aegisthus
                                                          Augeus = Aethra

Eteocles Polyneices *Antigone* Ismene   Clytemnestra = *Agamemnon* Helen = *Menelaus*   Theseus

                    Orestes Iphegenia Electra   Hermione   Hippolytus

THE FAMILY OF HELEN OF TROY

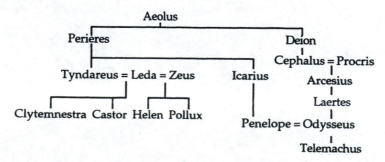

Aeolus

Periéres   Deion

                    Cephalus = Procris

Tyndareus = Leda = Zeus   Icarius   Arcesius

                            Laertes

Clytemnestra Castor Helen Pollux   Penelope = Odysseus

                            Telemachus

I.

THE WESTERN HUMANITIES

THE CAVE

The Cave by Peter Reichard, 1989.
Reprinted by permission of Peter Reichard.

INTRODUCTION

The great British philosopher, Alfred North Whitehead, once said that Western philosophy "consists of a series of footnotes to Plato." Plato (427 B.C.-347 B.C.), then, is a good beginning for our introduction not only to philosophy but to the humanities. In *The Allegory of the Cave* you are introduced to the ideas of Plato and the philosopher, Socrates (470-399 B.C.). Both are historical figures. They lived and died and in between they knew each other well. They are two different people; however, Plato always puts what he wants to say into the mouth of someone else — usually that of Socrates.

He also likes to have Socrates in a dialectic of questions-answers-logical resolutions called dialogues. The "Allegory of the Cave" is the seventh book of a very long dialogue called *The Republic*. The author is Plato. He is speaking to us. But you may forget this sometimes because Socrates gets the credit for leading the dialectic in the dialogue. Indeed, Socrates appears more rational and wise than he probably was. But what Plato is communicating is not only his and Socrates' ideas, but a method of dealing with ideas. And Socrates actually did engage people on the streets of Athens in this sort of dialogue.

The Republic is the most famous of Plato's dialogues. Here Socrates explores a vision of an ideal human community where the philosopher plays the central role. In the "Allegory of the Cave" Socrates discusses the responsibility of the philosopher in bringing "light" to the rest of mankind. The light is knowledge of reality. As we will see in a later reading, *Unless Philosophers Become Kings*, Plato took this responsibility very seriously. But Socrates is probably more interesting as a seeker, as a man of questions about the human journey through life, than he is as a problem solver. Socrates reminds us that pursuing the truth is dangerous because the consequences may leave us hurt and bewildered.

If it seems the readings overemphasize the Classical Age, a period of history 2500 years ago, Karl Jaspers' (1883-1969) essay, *The Axial Age of Human History*, may help us to understand why. Jaspers believed the period 800 B.C.-200 B.C. was a turning point in the history of all mankind. Something extraordinary happened at the same time in at least three major areas of the world: the Eastern Mediterranean; China; and India. Whether we agree with the details of Jaspers' argument or not, it is hard to deny the influence of the Axial Age on our literature and art, our history and philosophy, our concepts of good and bad, our political values and forms of government, our myths about love, freedom, happiness and the good life.

The Axial Age, Jaspers argues, involved for the first time a struggle between *logos* (reason) and *mythos* (myth; or the mysterious). A fuller discussion of *logos* follows in the introduction to Chapter II. The apparent victory of *logos* in the Axial Age is a good thing for all of mankind, according to Jaspers. Not everyone agrees with that conclusion — the philosopher Nietzsche directly questions it in some later readings. Nevertheless, the *struggle* between *logos* and *mythos* defines culture and civilization (at least in the West) for the next 2000 years. Indeed, that struggle forms the theme of the readings in this text.

MAX REICHARD

THE HUMANITIES: A SEARCH FOR MEANING

The definition of the humanities is suffering from conceptual confusion which is likely to be made worse by the emphasis on high technology. Two thousand years ago Cicero defined *humanities* as liberal education. Today, the cognate terms, "humanities" and "humanitarianism," are used interchangeably in public discourse and even in higher education. The mix-up suggests a cultural confusion that extends to the purpose of the humanities in our lives.

A distinction must be made or we will give up some important insights into what makes us human. For example, the humanitarian impulse will deny, or at least try to put off death. The humanities, steeped in death, recognize that man's consciousness of mortality distinguishes him from all other living things.

Humanities refers to the study of man — his thoughts, values and moral perspectives. The tradition of the humanities — literature, history, philosophy, and the appreciation of the arts — demands that we search for the meaning and purpose of life. The search does not depend on some magic formula or technique, but on hard-headed, disciplined thought and reflection.

Humanitarianism, on the other hand, is based on a generous impulse; the welfare of mankind. It suggests a particular value system — for example, that it is good to provide for people in economic need. It is action oriented and partly rooted in our feelings of sympathy and partly in the ethos of modern technology, the belief in reforming man. In the age of technology, the humanitarian impulse is distorted by the assumption that there is a solution to every human problem, that all problems can be solved with the appropriate technique, that we can eliminate tragedy and, perhaps, even mortality. This superficial approach to humanitarianism is not new; however, the tools and technology available to implement it are more sophisticated, insidious in their promise, and even sinister in their potential. The humanitarianism-as-a-quick-fix impulse demands that human emotions be pacified and homogenized and that their validity be measured by some standard or norm. It forces focus on the self and promotes detachment from commitment, passion, and involvement with a larger community. That is directly in conflict with the tradition of the humanities.

The distinction becomes clearer with an example from the *The Book of Job*. In his day Job had his humanitarian comforters, who essentially told him: "Job you're OK, I'm OK, God's OK. Just admit your secret sins, and prosperity will follow." Job, however, rejected the attempt to make his moral struggle irrelevant and to bring God down to some prosaic human level. Job was depressed. But, given what had happened to him, was depression not realistic?

Today, under the impulse of our humanitarian concern for Job's pain, we would want to eliminate the symptom (the pain) of Job's plight with drugs or some other modern therapy. In the process, might we not separate Job from reality, from the right to experience fully what it means to be human, from the depth of feeling and experience that comes with suffering? That is, would we not undermine Job's dignity and worth as a human being? The humanitarian impulse is part of a larger progressive movement that has emphasized the worth of all human beings; however, the means used to achieve a good end are often dehumanizing. For example, consider the 1980's formulation of a new verb: parenting. Given our insecurities about being good parents, a formula looks attractive. The problem here is not the humanitarian impulse to help people be better parents, but the focus on technique, which by its nature becomes a fascination and an end in itself. "Parenting" removes us from the artless cycle of life and nature. It makes being a parent something we learn from an "expert." No mystery, no ambiguity. Parenting becomes the means of control: over self, over another, over a *relationship*.

Technique. We have publications, films, and seminars on how to have a fulfilling life, how to have sex, how to get in touch with our feelings, how to listen, how to be a parent, how to love — how to be a human being. Some of this may be useful; much of this is mindless and, perhaps, harmless. Much of it comes from pop psychology — an incongruous combination of "humanist" and "behaviorist" psychology. The emphasis on technique, however, is a symptom of a larger cultural crisis, of turning to simplistic formulas to solve the complexities, perplexities, and ambiguities of human existence.

Why is it happening? Certainly the incoherence of values, the sense of impermanence, the need for order all contribute to the crisis. A simple formula provides a principle of authority; a technique gives the impression of order. A formula eliminates the need for choice, it eliminates cognitive dissonance, it gives us something secure. The humanitarian impulse — with its efficient techniques in organizing, communicating, and persuading — is leaving people without confidence to face the complexities and difficulties life brings to us all. People have come to believe that they cannot live with conflict, ambiguity, and anxiety.

The humanities demonstrate the opposite. History, literature, and art demonstrate man at his best, as most human when struggling with dissonance and disorder. For example the movie, *Prince of the City*, explores our human dilemma in choosing between conflicting values. A reviewer wrote, "No attempt has been made in this film to provide a pat psychological motive for [the hero's] actions. The viewer's own perceptions will suffice." That is, the movie does not tell us how we should think or feel. "It is precisely this unwillingness to simplify . . . which makes *Prince* as a work equal to the staggering ambiguity and ultimate incomprehensibility of life itself."

The humanities do not provide easy answers for being happy. The humanities approach happiness obliquely. From deep study of the humanities, we come to realize that there are no neat mechanisms for happiness, that happiness is worth seeking, and that we are blessed when we have a hold of it — however temporary it may be. Some people talk about "human potential" as if there were a simple technique for achieving it, and once achieved, happiness is assured. The humanities demonstrate clearly that the highest human potential and the most profound insights are often achieved at the cost of "happiness."

To gain perspective, we might go back to the Civil War, which holds endless fascination as human drama and tragedy. The central figure of this tragic and momentous event is Abraham Lincoln. He personifies human tragedy in a general sense and personifies the historical tragedy of America's coming of age.

Put another way, Lincoln as a historical persona represents tragedy, and as a personality he embodies tragedy. Lincoln suffered, and through his suffering he gained insight into himself and into his country. In modern therapeutic terms, he was a depressive personality. Happily, he lived before human engineers began dictating who is normal or what techniques we should use to make people normal. Lincoln suffered. Was that good? The question is absurd. The question is not whether suffering is good, but as Job showed long ago, given the inevitability of suffering, how do we face it?

We may not know what went on inside Lincoln's mind, what fears tore him apart, what personal concepts of good and evil struggled in his soul. But, as the main character of our country's central drama, he teaches us that a moral point of view transcends time, historical moment, and cultural place. He was the instrument, indeed the driving force, of the tragedy we call the Civil War. As the Greeks taught us long ago, tragedy is not only the fate of man, but also a necessary means for man to look at himself and at his world with clear eyes, with moral judgement, with sensitivity to the conflicts and ambiguities of life, to make choices and to live with the consequences of choices made.

All the private hell that Lincoln endured before and during the War suggests a relationship between the inner conflicts within a person and the external conflicts within a community. That relationship suggests another — the relationship between private morality and public virtue. Today there continues to be a healthy concern about ethics and public virtue: the emphasis on "character" in public officials; the world-wide fears about the environment and nuclear destruction; the search for quality in education, in public service, and in our everyday surroundings. Ethics and morality are universal ideals because ethics and morality transcend the everyday meaninglessness of existence and give form and direction to a society — particularly one that pretends to democratic ideals.

If there has to be a rationale for the humanities, then it is not how to be happy, but how to make choices; to choose to live with pain, and conflict, and ambiguity; to know how to choose one value over another.

The study of our ethical and moral heritage, of the history of men, women, and events, of values and myths, of how different people have expressed moral sensibility and outrage in literature and art, is necessary to us as individual human beings and to us as citizens sharing a common civic responsibility, aspiring to a common virtue based on democratic ideals.

Dr. McGinnis, in her essay which follows, also addresses the distinction between the humanities and humanitarianism. If she and I have some differences — and we do as any thinking individuals will — they include Dr. McGinnis's view of the role of humanitarianism in our world. She is more optimistic than I that we will choose the right course. I am more pessimistic, not as convinced that there is a right course. Regardless, as Dr. McGinnis suggests, we must make choices and we must engage in dialogue about how and why we make those choices. Nothing is more human.

DEL McGINNIS

WHAT MAKES US HUMAN?

Humans are the only creatures that we know of that are capable of self analysis. Yet most people spend little time or effort asking the probing questions of philosophers ("lovers of knowledge"). One reason for this may be that facing our mortality is too painful. It takes courage to confront questions that make us uncomfortable.

Why ask such questions, then? Isn't comfort one of the aims of life? Of course it is. But other aims should receive higher priority than comfort — aims such as honesty, creativity, and discovery of truth. The pursuit of comfort can be dangerous, for it can shut out everything else in life. Before we know it, our lives become a frantic struggle to pay off our credit cards — not in order to cover our basic needs but to provide for our "comforts." It's not easy to live a balanced life in the land of TV commercials and shopping malls.

Philosophy — along with the humanities as a whole — attempts to examine what being human is all about. How do we differ from the apes, which scientists tell us share 99 percent of our genetic makeup? The chief difference lies in our brain capacity.

In an age of computers, the human brain is still the greatest computer of all. With 100 billion neurons and 100 trillion neural connections — according to Carl Sagan — the brain never even comes close to being fully used. For example, while the autistic savant on whom the movie "Rain Man" was based cannot ascribe meaning to experience, he can correctly describe the weather every day of his life past infancy; he can also match the day of the week with any date — past or future for thousands of years — without error. No one can explain how he does this.

And yet all of us have mental powers that are even greater than those of the savant, for we possess the ability to reason, analyze, ascribe meaning, judge value, feel emotions, and create. The computer-like powers of the savant amaze us, but we tend to take our own minds for granted. It has been estimated that even the most knowledgeable humans use less than half their brain capacity. It's up to us to make sure those capabilities do not atrophy from disuse.

To be sure, the questions asked by the philosophers can make us uncomfortable, but they are a central part of our humanity. For example, why do we die? Why do strong animals feed on weaker ones? And why do innocent children sometimes suffer from painful birth defects or incurable diseases?

But asking questions also opens up new possibilities. For every child who dies of an incurable disease, hundreds die of simple malnutrition. The resources are available to save these children, but priorities have to be reassigned. In a democracy, every vote counts. If we turn the channel to something pleasant every time starving Kurds or Africans are shown, or every time a program deals with the burning rain forests or the thinning ozone layer, we may not be prepared to choose correctly in the voting booth. The future of mankind may very well depend on how democracies allocate their resources today.

In case this sounds like a challenge to Dr. Reichard's essay above, let me clarify where he and I agree. Real humanitarianism is an outgrowth of man's highest moral instincts, those feelings of love, compassion, and generosity that lead us to treat other people with kindness and respect. But the superficial approach that Dr. Reichard refers to — the insistence on "positive thinking" in every situation — does indeed run counter to the humanities. Suffering of the innocents demands our grief, and wrong choices require acknowledgement of guilt. We are as intensely alive when we grieve as when we experience the fulfillment of our desires.

Athletes know well the phrase, "no pain, no gain." That rule applies to the thinker as well. Knowledge does not come easily. Reading often requires great effort, and arriving at difficult moral choices requires struggle. But the gain in understanding is infinitely worth the effort. The struggle goes on as long as we live, and so does the reward. Knowledge is its own reward.

PLATO (427?-347 B.C.)

A Greek philosopher of Athens, Plato preserved the teachings of Socrates in dialogue form in books such as The Republic. *Plato's views regarding human nature and the search for the spiritual ideal he termed "the good" have greatly influenced Western thought.*

ALLEGORY OF THE CAVE (BOOK VII, THE REPUBLIC)

Socrates:

And now, I said, let me show in a figure how far our nature is enlightened or unenlightened: Behold I human beings living in an underground den, which has a mouth open toward the light and reaching all along the den; here they have been from their childhood, and have their legs and necks chained so that they cannot move, and can only see before them, being prevented by the chains from turning round their heads. Above and behind them a fire is blazing at a distance, and between the fire and the prisoners there is a raised way; and you will see, if you look, a low wall built along the way, like the screen which marionette-players have in front of them, over which they show the puppets.

I see.

And do you see, I said, men passing along the wall carrying all sorts of vessels, and statues and figures of animals made of wood and stone and various materials, which appear over the wall? Some of them are talking, others silent.

You have shown me a strange image, and they are strange prisoners.

Like ourselves, I replied, and they see only their own shadows, or the shadows of one another, which the fire throws on the opposite wall of the cave?

True, he said; how could they see anything but the shadows if they were never allowed to move their heads?

And of the objects which are being carried in likewise they would only see the shadows?

Yes, he said.

And if they were able to converse with one another, would they not suppose that they were naming what was actually before them?

Very true.

And suppose further that the prison had an echo which came from the other side, would they not be sure to fancy when one of the passers-by spoke that the voice which they heard came from the passing shadow?

No question, he replied.

To them, I said, the truth would be literally nothing but the shadows of the images.

That is certain.

And now look again, and see what will naturally follow if the prisoners are released and disabused of their error. At first, when any of them is liberated and compelled suddenly to stand up and turn his neck round and walk and look toward the light, he will suffer sharp pains; the glare will distress him — and he will be unable to see the realities of which in his former state he had seen the shadows; and then conceive someone saying to him, that what he saw before was an illusion, but that now, when he is approaching nearer to being and his eye is turned toward more real existence, he has a clearer vision — what will be his reply? And you may further imagine that his instructor is pointing to the objects as they pass and requiring him to name them — will he not be perplexed? Will he not fancy that the shadows which he formerly saw are truer than the objects which are now shown to him?

Far truer.

And if he is compelled to look straight at the light, will he not have a pain in his eyes which will make him turn away to take refuge in the objects of vision which he can see, and which he will conceive to be in reality clearer than the things which are now being shown to him?

True, he said.

And suppose once more, that he is reluctantly dragged up a steep and rugged ascent, and held fast until he is forced into the presence of the sun himself, is he not likely to be pained and irritated? When he approaches the light his eyes will be dazzled, and he will not be able to see anything at all of what are now called realities.

Not all in a moment, he said.

He will require to grow accustomed to the sight of the upper world. And first he will see the shadows best, next the reflections of men and other objects in the water, and then the objects themselves; then he will gaze upon the light of the moon and the stars and the spangled heaven; and he will see the sky and the stars by night better than the sun or the light of the sun by day?

Certainly.

Last of all he will be able to see the sun, and not mere reflections of him in the water, but he will see him in his own proper place, and not in another; and he will contemplate him as he is.

Certainly.

He will then proceed to argue that this is he who gives the season and the years, and is the guardian of all that is in the visible world, and in a certain way the cause of all things which he and his fellows have been accustomed to behold?

Clearly, he said, he would first see the sun and then reason about him.

And when he remembered his old habitation, and the wisdom of the den and his fellow-prisoners, do you not suppose that he would felicitate himself on the change, and pity them?

Certainly, he would.

And if they were in the habit of conferring honors among themselves on those who were quickest to observe the passing shadows and to remark which of them went before, and which followed after, and which were together; and who were therefore best able to draw conclusions as to the future, do you think that he would care for such honors and glories, or envy the possessors of them? Would he not say with Homer,

"Better to be the poor servant of a poor master,"

and to endure anything, rather than think as they do and live after their manner?

Yes, he said, I think that he would rather suffer anything than entertain these false notions and live in this miserable manner.

Imagine once more, I said, such a one coming suddenly out of the sun to be replaced in his old situation; would he not be certain to have his eyes full of darkness?

To be sure, he said.

And if there were a contest, and he had to compete in measuring the shadows with the prisoners who had never moved out of the den, while his sight was still weak, and before his eyes had become steady (and the time which would be needed to acquire this new habit of sight might be very considerable), would he not be ridiculous? Men would say of him that up he went and down he came without his eyes; and that it was better not even to think of ascending; and if anyone tried to loose another and lead him up to the light, let them only catch the offender, and they would put him to death.

No question, he said.

This entire allegory, I said, you may now append, dear Glaucon, to the previous argument; the prison-house is the world of sight, the light of the fire is the sun, and you will not misapprehend me if you interpret the journey upward to be the ascent of the soul into the intellectual world according to my poor belief, which, at your desire, I have expressed — whether rightly or wrongly, God knows. But, whether true or false, my opinion is that in the world of knowledge the idea of good appears last of all, and is seen only with an effort; and, when seen, is also inferred to be the universal author of all things beautiful and right, parent of light and of the lord of light in this visible world, and the immediate source of reason and truth in the intellectual; and that this is the power upon which he who would act rationally either in public or private life must have his eye fixed.

I agree, he said, as far as I am able to understand you.

Moreover, I said, you must not wonder that those who attain to this beatific vision are unwilling to descend to human affairs; for their souls are ever hastening into the upper world where they desire to dwell; which desire of theirs is very natural, if our allegory may be trusted.

Yes, very natural.

And is there anything surprising in one who passes from divine contemplations to the evil state of man, misbehaving himself in a ridiculous manner; if, while his eyes are blinking and before he has become accustomed to the surrounding darkness, he is compelled to fight in courts of law, or in other places, about the images or the shadows of images of justice, and is endeavoring to meet the conceptions of those who have never yet seen absolute justice?

Anything but surprising, he replied.

Anyone who has common-sense will remember that the bewilderments of the eyes are of two kinds, and arise from two causes, either from coming out of the light or from going into the light, which is true of the mind's eye, quite as much as of the bodily eye; and he who remembers this when he sees anyone whose vision is perplexed and weak, will not be too ready to laugh; he will first ask whether that soul of man has come out of the brighter life, and is unable to see because unaccustomed to the dark, or having turned from darkness to the day is dazzled by excess of light. And he will count the one happy in his condition and state of being, and he will pity the other; or, if he have a mind to laugh at the soul which comes from below into the light, there will be more reason in this than in the laugh which greets him who returns from above out of the light into the den.

That, he said, is a very just distinction.

But then, if I am right, certain professors of education must be wrong when they say that they can put a knowledge into the soul which was not there before, like sight into blind eyes.

They undoubtedly say this, he replied.

Whereas, our argument shows that the power and capacity of learning exists in the soul already; and that just as the eye was unable to turn from darkness to light without the whole body, so too the instrument of knowledge can only by the movement of the whole soul be turned from the world of becoming into that of being, and learn by degrees to endure the sight of being, and of the brightest and best of being, or, in other words, of the good.

Very true.

And must there not be some art which will effect conversion in the easiest and quickest manner; not implanting the faculty of sight, for that exists already, but has been turned in the wrong direction, and is looking away from the truth?

Yes, he said, such an art may be presumed.

And whereas the other so-called virtues of the soul seem to be akin to bodily qualities, for even when they are not originally innate they can be implanted later by habit and exercise, the virtue of wisdom more than anything else contains a divine element which always remains, and by this conversion is rendered useful and profitable; or, on the other hand, hurtful and useless. Did you never observe the narrow intelligence flashing from the keen eye of a clever rogue — how eager he is, how clearly his paltry soul sees the way to his end; he is the reverse of blind, but his keen eyesight is forced into the service of evil, and he is mischievous in proportion to his cleverness?

Very true, he said.

But what if there had been a circumcision of such natures in the days of their youth; and they had been severed from those sensual pleasures, such as eating and drinking, which, like leaden weights, were attached to them at their birth, and which drag them down and turn the vision of their souls upon the things that are below — if, I say, they had been released from these impediments and turned in the opposite direction, the very same faculty in them would have seen the truth as keenly as they see what their eyes are turned to now.

Very likely.

Yes, I said; and there is another thing which is likely, or rather a necessary inference from what has preceded, that neither the uneducated and uninformed of the truth, nor yet those who never make an end of their education, will be able ministers of the State; not the former, because they have no single aim of duty which is the rule of all their actions, private as well as public; nor the latter, because they will not act at all except upon compulsion, fancying that they are already dwelling apart in the islands of the blessed.

Very true, he replied.

Then, I said, the business of us who are the founders of the State will be to compel the best minds to attain that knowledge which we have already shown to be the greatest of all — they must continue to ascend until they arrive at the good; but when they have ascended and seen enough we must not allow them to do as they do now.

What do you mean?

I mean that they remain in the upper world: but this must not be allowed; they must be made to descend again among the prisoners in the den, and partake of their labors and honors, whether they are worth having or not.

But is not this unjust? he said; ought we to give them a worse life, when they might have a better?

You have again forgotten, my friend, I said, the intention of the legislator, who did not aim at making any one class in the State happy above the rest; the happiness was to be in the whole State, and he held the citizens together by persuasion and necessity, making them benefactors of the State, and therefore benefactors of one another; to this end he created them, not to please themselves, but to be his instruments in binding up the State.

True, he said, I had forgotten.

Observe, Glaucon, that there will be no injustice in compelling our philosophers to have a care and providence of others; we shall explain to them that in other States, men of their class are not obliged to share in the toils of politics: and this is reasonable, for they grow up at their own sweet will, and the government would rather not have them. Being self-taught, they cannot be expected to show any gratitude for a culture which they have never received. But we have brought you into the world to be rulers of the hive, kings of yourselves and of the other citizens, and have educated you far better and more perfectly than they have been educated, and you are better able to share in the double duty. Wherefore each of you, when his turn comes, must go down to the general underground abode, and get the habit of seeing in the dark. When you have acquired the habit, you will see ten thousand times better than the inhabitants of the den, and you will know what the several images are, and what they represent, because you have seen the beautiful and just and good in their truth. And thus our State, which is also yours, will be a reality, and not a dream only, and will be administered in a spirit unlike that of other States, in which men fight with one another about shadows only and are distracted in the struggle for power, which in their eyes is a great good. Whereas the truth is that the State in which the rulers are most reluctant to govern is always the best and most quietly governed, and the State in which they are most eager, the worst.

Quite true, he replied.

And will our pupils, when they bear this, refuse to take their turn at the toils of State, when they are allowed to spend the greater part of their time with one another in the heavenly light?

Impossible, he answered; for they are just men, and the commands which we impose upon them are just; there can be no doubt that every one of them will take office as a stern necessity, and not after the fashion of our present rulers of State.

Yes, my friend, I said; and there lies the point. You must contrive for your future rulers another and a better life than that of a ruler, and then you may have a well-ordered State; for only in the State which offers this, will they rule who are truly rich, not in silver and gold, but in virtue and wisdom, which are the true blessings of life. Whereas, if they go to the administration of public affairs, poor and hungering after their own private advantage, thinking that hence they are to snatch the chief good, order there can never be; for they will be fighting about office, and the civil and domestic broils which thus arise will be the ruin of the rulers themselves and of the whole State.

Most true, he replied.

And the only life which looks down upon the life of political ambition is that of true philosophy. Do you know of any other?

Indeed, I do not, he said.

And those who govern ought not to be lovers of the task? For, if they are, there will be rival lovers, and they will fight.

No question.

Who, then, are those whom we shall compel to be guardians? Surely they will be the men who are wisest about affairs of State, and by whom the State is best administered, and who at the same time have other honors and another and a better life than that of politics?

They are the men, and I will choose them, he replied. And now shall we consider in what way such guardians will be produced, and how they are to be brought from darkness to light — as some are said to have ascended from the world below to the gods?

By all means, he replied.

The process, I said, is not the turning over of an oyster shell,[1] but the turning round of a soul passing from a day which is little better than night to the true day of being, that is, the ascent from below, which we affirm to be true philosophy?

KARL JASPERS (1883-1969)

German psychiatrist and existentialist philosopher Karl Jaspers was greatly influenced by Kierkegaard and Nietzsche, but his views correspond more closely to Kierkegaard's, seeking spiritual meaning in a seemingly chaotic world. Jaspers' penetrating historical perspective sheds light on human development in "The Axial Age of Human History."

THE AXIAL AGE OF HUMAN HISTORY

A Base for the Unity of Mankind

Philosophy strives to interpret history as a single totality. In the West, the philosophy of history developed on the foundation of the Christian faith. In great works from St. Augustine to

---

[1] An allusion to a game in which two parties fled or pursued according as an oyster-shell which was thrown into the air fell with the dark or light side uppermost.

Hegel, history is seen as the work of God and God's acts of revelation define the decisive epoches. So late a thinker as Hegel could write: "All history moves toward Christ and begins with Christ. The coming of the son of God is the axis of world history."

But such a view of universal history can be valid only for Christians; Christianity is but one faith, not *the* faith of mankind. Through a specific historical development beginning in late antiquity, Christianity has become the faith of the Western world; but even in the West, the Christian has not allowed his religion to determine his view of history as human experience: even for him, a statement of faith is not a statement about the actual course of history, and sacred history remains in essence different and separate from profane history. The believing Christian can examine the Christian tradition just as he might examine any other object of his experience.

If there does exist such a thing as an axis or turning point in history, it must be based on observable or recorded fact; and it must be valid for all men, including Christians. Such an axis would be that point in history where man first discovered the notion of himself that he has realized since, the point in time where there occurred that shaping of man's being which has produced the most important results. And the existence of this turning point would have to be, if not absolutely demonstrable, at least convincing on an empirical basis for Europeans, for Asiatics, and for all men, without the need to appeal to the criterion of a definite religious doctrine. Only thus could it provide a common frame of historical self-understanding.

Such a historical axis, or turning point, seems to be situated in the years around 500 BCE, in the intellectual development that took place between 800 and 200 BCE. There lies, it appears to me, the most crucial turning point in history; it was then that man as he is today was born. Let us, for the sake of brevity, refer to this period as the "axial age."

Many extraordinary developments were crowded into this epoch. In China lived Confucius and Lao-tse, and all the characteristic Chinese philosophical tendencies were born; such thinkers as Mo Ti, Chuant-tze, Liadsi, and innumerable others were at work; in India it was the period of the Upanishads, of Buddha, and, just as in China, every philosophical possibility was then developed, including skepticism, materialism, sophistry, and nihilism; in Iran, Zoroaster taught the dramatic cosmology of the struggle between Good and Evil; in Palestine, it was the age of the Prophets from Elijah to Isaiah, Jeremiah, the Deuteronomiah; in Greece it was the age of Homer, of the philosophers Parmenides, Heraclitus, and Plato, of the dramatists, of Thucydides and Archimedes. All the great developments that these names suggest occurred in those few centuries — and almost simultaneously in China, India, and the West, though none of these three worlds was aware of the others.

The new element that appeared in this epoch was that man became aware of existence as a whole, of his self, and of his limitations. He experienced the awesomeness of the world and his own weakness. He raised radical questions and, in his quest for liberation and redemption, came face to face with the abyss. While gaining consciousness of his limitation, he set himself the highest aims; he experienced the absolute in the depth of selfhood and in the clarity of transcendence.

Man became aware of consciousness itself; the fact of thought became itself an object of thought. Spiritual battles arose, in which men strove to convince others by the communication of ideas, reasons, experiences. Contradictory possibilities were explored. Discussion, partisanship, the splitting-up of the intellectual sphere into antithetical tendencies that yet remained closely related by their very opposition — all this produced an unrest bordering on spiritual chaos.

The age produced the basic categories within which we still carry on our thinking, and the beginnings of the world religions by which man has lived until today. In every sense, a step was made towards the universal.

Opinions, customs, conditions that had been unconsciously accepted were now scrutinized, questioned, dissolved. The world became a retort in which the substance of tradition, still living and real, was brought to consciousness and thereby transformed.

The age of myth — age of the static and self-evident — came to an end, and there began the battle of rationality and practical experience against myth (*logos* versus *mythos*); the battle for the transcendence of the one God against the demons who did not exist; the battle of an aroused ethical sense against the false gods. Religion was informed with ethics, and thus the idea of divinity was enhanced. The myth became the vehicle of a language that expressed something entirely different from what the myth had originally meant; the myth became parable. Myths were transformed and given new depth; and during this transition period, new myths were still produced even while the myth as a whole was being destroyed. The mythical world slowly receded, but it remained, in the beliefs of the masses, the background of all life (and therefore it could triumph again in later periods over wide areas).

This whole transformation of man's condition may be called a spiritualization. An impulse surging up from the unexplored depths of life loosened the mainstays of existence, transforming stable polarities into antinomies and conflicts. Man was no longer self-sufficient. He had become unsure of himself, and thus open to new and boundless possibilities. He could hear and understand what until then no one had questioned or even noticed. Wonders were made manifest. Along with his world and his ego, Being itself now became perceptible to man, but not finally: the question remained. And his highest upsurge ended in new questions.

For the first time there were philosophers. Men dared to rely on themselves as individuals. Hermits and wandering thinkers in China, ascetics in India, philosophers in Greece, prophets in Israel — they all belong together, however much they may differ in faith, content, and inner orientation. Man was now able to set his inner life in opposition to the whole world; he discovered in himself the principle through which he could rise above both himself and the world.

In speculative thought man soared to the level of Being, which he grasped without duality; subject and object disappeared, and opposites became one. The objective formulations of speculative thought express, ambiguously and in a manner open to misunderstanding, what man in his highest flights experiences as a discovery of himself within the whole of Being, or a *unio mystica*, a merging with the godhead, or else a transformation of the self into an instrument of God's will, or a consciousness of the self as transcending the arbitrary particularity of the *hic et nunc*.

Imprisoned in a body fettered by passions, separated from the light and only dimly aware of himself, man longs for liberation and redemption; and he finds that he can achieve liberation and redemption in the world, whether it is by an ascent to the Idea; or in *ataraxia* — passive resignation; or by immersion in thought; or in the knowledge of himself and the world as Atman, the Universal Self; or in the experience of Nirvana; or in harmony with the Tao — the cosmic order; or in surrender to the will of God. There are, it is true, great differences among the various faiths, but they all alike come to serve as instruments by which man transcends himself, by which he becomes aware of his own being within the whole of Being, and by which he enters upon pathways that he must travel as an individual. It becomes possible for him to renounce the goods of the world and retire to the desert, the woods, the mountains; he can become a hermit and discover the creative power of solitude, and return to the world as philosopher, sage, prophet. What took place in this axial age was the discovery of what was later to be called reason and personality.

The conquests of individuals did not become the property of all; the distance between the heights of human possibility and the crowd was enormous. But what the individual became, changed everything indirectly; humanity as a whole took a leap forward.

Even sociological conditions in China, India, and around the Mediterranean show similarities during this age. There is an abundance of small states and cities, and a battle of all against all, making at first for astonishing prosperity, a development of power and wealth. In China, under the impotent empire of the Chou dynasty, cities and petty states flourished; the over-all political process consisted of the aggrandizement of small states by the subjection of other small states. In Greece and the Near East there existed an independent life of independent social units, even, in part, for those under the dominion of the Persians. In India there were many independent states and cities.

With the three worlds, travel and tumult created intellectual movement. Previously the world had known relatively stable conditions under which, despite catastrophes, everything repeated itself, horizons were restricted, and intellectual movement was gentle and very slow, unconscious and hence not understood. Now out of constant tension came tumultuous and swift movement, leading to revolution; and this was on the conscious plane.

The Chinese philosophers, Confucius and Mo Ti and others, roamed the country gathering together in famous places favorable to intellectual life. They established schools which the Sinologists call academies, like those of the Sophists and philosophers in Hellas; or else, like Buddha, they spent their lives wandering from town to town.

Men became conscious of history; an extraordinary age was beginning, but men felt and knew that an endless past had gone before. Thus at the very outset of this awakening of the truly human spirit, man was already preoccupied with memories, conscious of lateness, even of decadence.

Now men wished to take the course of events into their hand: to restore conditions that had existed in the past, or to create new conditions. History was conceived as a series of stages: either as a process of steady deterioration, or as a cycle, or as an ascent. Thinkers began to speculate on how men could best live together, how their lives could best be administered and governed. Ideas of reform inspired political activity. Philosophers wandered from state to state, acted as counselors and teachers, were despised or courted, argued with one another. There is a sociological analogy between Confucius' failure at the court of Wei and Plato's failure in Syracuse, and between the school of Confucius and the academy of Plato, in both of which future statesmen were trained.

This long epoch represents no simple transcending development. It was both destructive and creative, and its potentialities were never fully realized. The highest possibilities realized in individuals did not become common property because the mass of men could not follow. What started out as freedom of movement ended as anarchy. When the creative power of the epoch was lost the same thing happened in all three worlds: a petrifaction of dogmas and a general leveling; out of a disorder that had become intolerable there grew an urge toward a new stability, toward the restoration of static conditions of life.

The process of constant change first came to a stop in the political sphere. Great, all-encompassing empires came into being almost simultaneously in China (Chin Shih-Huang Ti), in India (the Maurya dynasty), and in the West (the Hellenistic empires and Rome). Everywhere collapse brought initial gain in the form of a highly systematized order. But nowhere was the relation to what had gone before completely extinguished; the achievements and figures of the Axial age became models and objects of veneration: the Han dynasty in China established Confucianism, Asoka established Buddhism in India, and the Augustan age in Rome set up the conscious Greco-Roman cultural tradition.

The universal empires that developed at the end of the axial age were considered to be established for all eternity. But their stability was illusory; although these empires lasted a long time measured by the political standards of the axial age, all ultimately declined and disintegrated, and the subsequent millennia have brought enormous changes. Since the end of the axial age, political history has been a history of the decline of great empires and the founding of new ones.

In order to establish the truth of a historical conception, it is not enough to glance at a few facts, as I have done. An accumulation of historical analysis must increasingly clarify the thesis, or else it must be abandoned. The observations I have made are intended merely to invite further exploration.

Assuming, however, that this idea of an axial age is true in the main, it seems to illuminate the whole of world history in such a way that something resembling a structure emerges. I shall attempt briefly to indicate this structure:

1. Age-old high civilizations everywhere end with the axial age. The axial age smelts them down, takes them over, submerges them, whether by internal revolution or foreign conquest. Much that existed before the axial age was indeed magnificent — for example, the cultures of Babylonia, Egypt, or the Indus, and the primitive culture of China — but all this has something unawakened about it. The old cultures survived only in those elements that were assimilated by the new beginning and became part of the axial age.

    Measured by the radiant humanity of the axial age, a strange veil lies over the receding ancient cultures, as though in them man had not yet truly come to himself; this remains true despite such impressive, isolated impulses — therefore without general or future influence — as can be found, for example, in an Egyptian literary document, the well-known "Dialogue of a Man Weary of Life with his Soul," or in the Babylonian penitential psalms or the epic of Gilgamesh. The axial age continued to venerate the monumental in religion and religious art, and the corresponding monumental phenomena in the political realm — the great authoritarian states and legal systems. These things were even regarded as prototypes — by Confucius and Plato, for example — but if so, it was in a new conception that informed them with the spirit of the new age.

    Thus the imperial idea, which at the end of the axial age achieved new force and, politically speaking, ended the age, was inherited from the old monolithic civilizations. But whereas the imperial idea had originally been the culture-creating principle, it now served to entomb and stabilize a declining culture. It is as if the principle which had once served to drive humanity upward, and which had been a despotic principle *de facto*, now broke though in the form of a *conscious* despotism that congealed and preserved like frost.

2. Mankind is still living by what happened in the axial age, by what it created and what it thought. In all its later flights mankind returns to that age and gathers new fire. The return to this beginning is the ever-recurring event in China, India, and the West; the renaissances that have brought new spiritual surges have consisted in the recollection and reawakening of the possibilities of the axial age.

3. Although the axial age began within a relatively limited area of the globe, its historical effect was universal. Those peoples that did not participate in the developments of that age have remained "primitive peoples," continuing the unhistorical lives that they had been leading for tens or hundreds of thousands of years. Men living outside of the three worlds of the axial age either remained apart from the stream of history or were drawn into it by coming into contact with one or the other of the three intellectual centers of radiation, as was the case, for example, with the Germanic and Slavic peoples in the West, and the Japanese, the Malays, and the Siamese in the East. Some primitive peoples died out as a result of this contact. All men living after the axial age were either relegated to the status of primitive peoples or took part in the fundamental new world process. Once history had begun, the life of primitive peoples took on the character of an enduring prehistory, which became increasingly restricted in area and has only recently definitively ended.

4. When the three worlds that experienced the axial age meet with one another, a profound understanding is possible. They recognize when they meet that their concerns are the same. Despite great distances, each deeply affects the others. To be sure, there is not truth common to all three that can be put into objective statement — this exists only in science, with its

conscious and compelling methodology, which can be disseminated without change throughout the world and to which all men are called to contribute — but, even so, the authentic and unconditional truth that is lived historically by men of different origins is reciprocally seen and heard.

To summarize: out of the vision of the axial age grow the questions and criteria through which we approach all previous and all subsequent development. The high civilizations that went before lose their distinct contours, and the peoples who were their vehicles become invisible as they merge into the movement of the axial age. Prehistoric peoples remain prehistorical until they are absorbed in the historical movement that spreads out from the axial age — or until they die out. The axial age assimilates everything else. From that age history gains the only structure and unity that survives, or that has survived up to now.

The fact of the threefold axial age is a kind of miracle, in the sense that any really adequate explanation lies beyond our recent scientific horizon. And in any case, the hidden meaning of this phenomenon cannot be found empirically, as if it were a meaning that someone had consciously sought to create. Rather, to inquire after this meaning is to ask: what are we to make of this fact, what does it give to us? If, in attempting to answer these questions, expressions may occur that make it appear as if we were thinking of some plan of providence, they are to be understood only as metaphors.

a.   Really to see the axial age, to gain it as a foundation for our universal view of history, means: to gain something that is common to all mankind above and beyond all differences of faith. It is one thing to see the unity of history only from the background of one's own faith; it is quite another to conceive the unity of history in communication with every other human background, combining one's own consciousness with that which is foreign to one. In this sense, it may be said of the centuries between 800 and 200 BCE that they constitute the empirically ascertainable axis of history for *all* men.

The transcendental history of Christian revealed faith knows creation, fall, the steps of revelation, prophecies, the coming of God's son, redemption, and last judgment. As the faith of a historical group of men, it remains intact. But it is not on the basis of revelation that men can come together; the basis of solidarity can only be experience. Revelation is the form of a particular historical faith; experience is accessible to man as man. Through our experience of history we — all men — can know in common the reality of the universal transformation of mankind that took place in the axial age. This transformation was, to be sure, limited to China, India, and the West, but, although there was at first no contact among these three worlds, it laid the basis for universal history, it drew the minds of all men into it.

b.   The threefold historical form of the great advance of the axial age is something like a summons to boundless communication. To see and to understand others helps us toward the greatest clarity concerning ourselves, helps us to overcome that narrowness which is the danger in every self-enclosed history, and to make a leap into the distance. This venture in boundless communication is once again the secret of achieving humanity, not in the prehistoric past but in ourselves.

The call to such communication — which arises from the very fact that our historical origins are threefold — is the strongest force opposing the fallacy that any faith enjoys exclusive possession of the truth. For faith must always be conditioned by historical existence; it cannot, like scientific truth, be stated universally for all. The claim to extensive truth — that weapon of fanaticism, of human pride, of self-deception through will for power, that scourge of the West in particular, with its secularization in dogmatic philosophies and so-called scientific *Weltanhavungen* — can be overcome precisely by the knowledge that God has revealed himself historically in many ways and opened up many paths to himself. It is as if God, speaking the language of universal history, were warning us against exclusive claims.

c. If the axial age takes on significance according to the depth of our immersion in it, the question arises: is this age and its creations a criterion for all that has happened since? Even if we disregard the quantitative aspect, the geographical scope of political events, the preeminence that intellectual manifestations have enjoyed through the centuries, do we not find that the austere greatness, the creative clarity, the depth of meaning, the élan toward new intellectual worlds manifested in the axial age constitute the intellectual summit of all history up until now? For all their greatness and uniqueness, does not Virgil pale before Homer, and Augustus before Solon?

Surely any mechanical answer would be false. What has come later has assuredly its own value, which was not present in that which went before, a maturity of its own, a sublime splendor, a spiritual depth, above all in its "exceptional" manifestations.

We cannot organize history into a hierarchy simply by setting up some universal idea and drawing automatic inferences from it. But the conception of the axial age may lead us to question what came later, perhaps even to form a prejudice against it — and this may lead us to a recognition of that which is truly new and great and which does not belong to the axial age. For example: the student of philosophy who has spent months with the Greeks may find in St. Augustine a liberation from too much coolness and impersonality, since Augustine raises questions of conscience that were unknown to the Greeks but have been with us ever since; but then a period spent in the study of Augustine may impel him to return to the Greeks, in order to cleanse himself from the mounting impurity. Nowhere on earth is there an ultimate truth, a perfect salvation.

The axial age was shattered. History continued.

I hold only this as certain: whether we adopt or reject this thesis, the conception of an axial age affects our contemporary consciousness of our situation and of our history in fundamental ways which I have been able to intimate only partially. What is involved in nothing less than the question of how the unity of mankind can become concrete for each of us, of whatever tradition.

II.

THE CRITICAL MIND

The Head of *David* (detail), by Michelangelo Buonarroti
Marble: in Florence, Italy
Gabbinetto Fotografico — Soprintendenza
Gallerie — Fotostudio Quattrone Mario.

INTRODUCTION

When men and women first started asking the question why, philosophy was born. As we have come to define the term, however, philosophy means a systematic search for knowledge and wisdom. For that task certain tools were necessary: reason, logic, analysis, judgement, evaluation. These are the tools of the critical, reflective mind. In Western Civilization the development of these tools and our emphasis on critical thinking is credited to the ancient, "classical" Greeks. In particular, we honor three Hellenic (Greek) philosophers for their contribution: Socrates (470–399 B.C.), Plato (427–347 B.C.), and Aristotle (384–322 B.C.). Socrates was the teacher of Plato, through whose writings (dialogues) we know Socrates. Plato was the teacher of Aristotle, who openly rejected much of Platonic thought.

What was classical Greece? It was a Mediterranean culture, made up of many city-states which dotted the rim of the Mediterranean Sea with the center on the Aegean Sea and its unofficial capital, the city of Athens. Greeks were bound by a common language (and alphabet) and some common ideals, including a political life based on the "city" (polis). The historian, Herodotus (484–425), spoke of "our Hellenism, our being of the same stock and the same speech, our common shrines and rituals, our similar customs."

For Socrates, Plato, and Aristotle, politics played a central role in defining Greek civilization as well as the purpose of life for each Greek citizen. The Greeks emphasized that the good life was only possible in the *polis*, the city, the community in which one was a citizen. They made little distinction between government and society. The *polis* in fact was a moral community united by a common way of life. The Greeks therefore glorified public lives and the public discourse which made up the social life of the *polis*.

As Aristotle suggested, humans were set apart from animals by the capacity for *logos* (rational speech or argument). More precisely, Aristotle defined *logos* as a public conversation or dialogue on what is good (or evil), on what is just (or unjust), and so on. This dialogue must occur within the community, in the public life of the *polis*. But if the *polis* was to be a moral community it had to have purpose as well. That purpose was fulfilled when citizens acted (*praxis*) cooperatively and virtuously after engaging in public, rational discourse or dialogue (*logos*).

Logos and *praxis* were essentials of the politics of the polis. They gave the people meaning, purpose, and identity. Participation was essential. Our word "idiot" comes from the Greek word *idios* referring to those people who did not or could not participate in public life. The Greek *polis* was a forum where community expressed itself, where the people expressed those qualities and virtues which distinguished them from animals. The Greeks, then, built a community on *logos* (public, rational discourse) and *praxis* (cooperative action). Each individual, as part of a *polis*, could thereby demonstrate his full humanity.

To think, to reflect, and to act is to be human. Whatever we may add to this fundamental tenet of Hellenic culture, however unpalatable certain aspects of Greek politics are to us today (e.g., women and slaves could not participate in *logos*), nevertheless, Western literature, Western history, and the Western sense of identity were fired, shaped, and hardened in the forge of Hellenic philosophy.

The readings that follow are, in various ways, examples of critical thinking and rational argument. In his "Confusing Levels of Abstraction," Neil Postman reminds us that reasoning usually happens within a particular context and that it is useful to step outside of that context and observe it from a new perspective. For example, we take the U.S. Constitution for granted because it is familiar, it has worked well for two centuries, it seems self-evidently "right." But 200 years ago it was a radical departure from conventional wisdom, providing an example of Postman's suggestion that sometimes the solution to a problem is to "get beyond and outside our own assumptions." Indeed the success of America's Founding Fathers is testimony to Aristotle's argument that we achieve our highest potential through *logos* and *praxis*.

"Homer's Contest" gives a somewhat different view of the "rational" Greeks than the one above. Friedrich Nietzsche (1844–1900) explores the pre-Homeric world as a "womb" of Hellenic culture. He finds that ambition for fame and glory consumed the best of the ancient Greeks. And so Greeks promoted contests of all types, including wrestling and reciting poetry, presenting dramas and engaging in dialogue. But what happens when one man rises *significantly* above all the rest? Is there a place for him? What happens to Socrates?

In the *Apology*, Plato's dialogue about the trial of Socrates, we may feel that Socrates is provided as a model of what we do to our "best men," our heroes. Why did the Athenians put Socrates to death? Because he was stubborn in sticking to his ideals? Didn't Socrates admit that he was a troublemaker, a "gadfly"? Didn't he say that he would continue to disturb the peace? Doesn't a society have a right to protect itself, to silence someone like Socrates? And is Socrates not excessively arrogant?

"The Problem of Socrates," Nietzsche's essay from his book, *Twilight of the Idols*, questions not only Socrates but his dialectic method. It continues the argument developed in *Homer's Contest*, suggesting that Socrates' pride in himself as a dialectician was no small vice. Is Nietzsche doing what Postman says all good thinkers should do?

Walker Percy (1916–1990) was a modern American novelist and Christian existentialist philosopher. Trained as a medical doctor, he gave up medicine to explore the nature of man and of language; he began writing novels in his forties after settling in Covington, Louisiana on the outskirts of metropolitan New Orleans. In "The Mystery of Language" Percy asks us to change our frame of reference in order to comprehend that most human of capacities: language. Percy suggests we cannot understand language by the normal, scientific method which involves the observation of cause and effect. Language is the key to the *mystery* of man. In recent years Percy has argued that the study of language demands a "scientific" study of soul and mind, a merging of philosophy and religion. How is this possible? Because, Percy says, the soul and the mind are linked to the physical (that is, observable) world through language. Language, he argues, is the key to explaining what connects the creative and spiritual aspects of the mind to the physical needs of the body.

In our final reading John Brodie, a great football player from the 1960's and 1970's, talks about intuition and communication: *I Experience A Kind of Clarity*. Is playing football a way of knowing? Or is it just a modern version of a brutal Homeric Contest? Is it possible, through a game like football (or through running), to achieve a new level of consciousness or self-awareness? Why is it so difficult for Brodie to put his experiences into *words* — as Percy would have us do — to connect the creative and spiritual to the physical? Does Brodie have to put it into words or is not the game his means of expression, of communication? As Brodie played it, is football an art? In the next section we can explore the nature of art.

A FURTHER THOUGHT

Percy emphasizes language as words, as symbols, as the way we choose to name things. But if language is the key to our soul, then language is not just a left brain function (logic and reason) but also a right brain function (intuition and creativity). It involves accents of pitch, rhythm, and voice inflection, there is tone and timbre, and there is "body" language. Losing one's language (mother tongue) or replacing it and relearning a new language must, then, have a powerful effect on our sense of self, on our ability to "see" what a one-language person cannot see because for him "his language" is empty of meaning. Perhaps, then, one may argue for Black English as a primary language, precisely because the marketplace has dictated that it should be replaced by Standard English if African Americans using Black English are to become part of the American mainstream. Here is the rub: in order to become part of the mainstream (whether you are born to Black English, Spanish or some other "foreign" tongue) you have to give up your way of talking, moving, acting, looking, communicating; you have to *be* in a standard way.

What are we willing to give up to gain "success"? To be "standard" is to have lost yourself, to have denied the Self, to "be" dead. Language empowers us, allows us to define ourselves. Language is the key to transcending the norm and to affirming the self as Self. So, when I give up my mother tongue am I giving up myself?

Have we come back to the ancient Greeks' belief that through our use of language (dialogue), each one of us demonstrates our full humanity?

NEIL POSTMAN

Author of Teaching as a Subversive Activity *(1969) and* Teaching as a Conserving Activity *(1979), Postman is Professor of English and Media Ecology at New York University.*

CONFUSING LEVELS OF ABSTRACTION

Many years ago, mathematics and logicians were confounded by a certain paradox for which their intellectual habits could produce no solutions. The paradox, which had been known about for centuries, is easily stated in the following way: A Cretan says, "All Cretans are liars." If the statement is true, then it is also false (because at least one Cretan, the speaker, has told the truth). We have a proposition, in other words, that is both true and false at the same time, which is terrifying to mathematicians and logicians. Bertrand Russell and Alfred North Whitehead solved this paradox in their great work, published in 1913, *Principia Mathematica.* They called their solution The Theory of Logical Types, and it, also, may be easily stated: A class of things must not be considered a member of that class. Or, to quote Russell and Whitehead, "Whatever involves *all* of a collection must not be one of that collection." And so, a particular statement by one Cretan about all of the statements made by Cretans is not itself to be considered part of what he is talking about. It is of a different logical type, a different order of things. To confuse them would be like confusing the word *finger* with a finger itself, so that if I asked you to count the number of fingers on your hand, you would (if you were confused) say six — five fingers plus the name of the class of things.

To take another example: There is no paradox in the statement "Never say never" because the first never is not at the same level of abstraction as the second, the first *never* referring to all statements, the second to particular ones.

Now, all of this has made mathematics and logicians reasonably happy, but what about the rest of us? It does not happen very often, not even on the isle of Crete, that a Cretan will approach anybody and announce, "All Cretans are liars." And as for fingers, not even a deranged logician will say he has six fingers on each hand — five plus the class of things. And yet, for all that, The Theory of Logical Types has some practical implications for reducing our stupid and crazy talk. For one thing, it provides us with a certain awareness of the different types of statements we customarily make. For example, we make statements about things and processes in the world, such as, "The temperature is now ninety degrees." And we make statements about our *reactions* to things and processes in the world, such as, "It is hot." If you think that those two statements are virtually the same, you are on a path that is bound to lead to some interesting stupid talk. Whether or not a thermometer registers ninety degrees is an issue that can be settled by anyone who knows how to read a thermometer. But whether or not something is "hot" depends on who is being heated. To a Laplander, a temperature of fifty-eight degrees may be "hot," to a south African it may be "cold." The statement "It is hot (or cold)" is a statement about what is going on inside one's body. The statement "The temperature is now ninety degrees (or fifty-eight degrees)" is a statement about what is going on outside one's body. Alfred Korzybski provided us with two terms which are useful in talking about these different types of statements: *Extensional* statements are those which try to point to observable processes that are occurring outside our skins. *Intentional* statements are those which point to processes occurring inside our skins.

This distinction is by no means trivial. As I mentioned earlier, more than a few arguments and misunderstandings are generated by people who have confused the two types of statements and who, therefore, look in the wrong direction for verification of what they are saying. I can never prove to a Laplander that fifty-eight degrees is "cool," but I can prove to him that it is fifty-eight degrees. In other words, there is no paradox in two different people's concluding that the weather is both "hot" and "cold" at the same time. As long as they know that each of them is talking about a different reality, their conversation can proceed in a fairly orderly way.

In addition to the differing "horizontal" directions of our statements (inside and outside), there are differing "vertical" directions of our statements. For example, assuming you and I are talking about some event that has occurred, and that we are trying to describe it "objectively," we may still differ in the degree of specificity of our sentences. I may say, "Two vehicles collided." And you may say, "Two Chevy Impalas collided." We are both being extensional in our remarks, but you have included more details than I and, to that extent, come closer to depicting "reality." We may say that my level of abstraction is higher than yours. And as a general rule, the higher the level of abstraction, the less able it is to denote the color and texture and uniqueness of specific realities. I do not say — please note — the less "true" it is. The statement "$E=mc^2$," I am told, is about as "true" as a statement can be, but it is at such a high level of abstraction — it leaves out so many details — as to be virtually useless to all but a select few who use it for specialized purposes. Einstein himself remarked that the more "true" mathematics is, the less it has to do with reality. Nowhere can this be seen more clearly than in our attempts to apply statistical statements to "real" situations. There is, for example, an apocryphal story about a pregnant woman (let us call her Mrs. Green) who went to see her obstetrician in a state of agitation bordering on hysteria. She had read in a magazine that one out of every five babies born in the world is Chinese. She already had given birth to four children and feared that her next would be a victim of the inexorable laws of statistics. The point is that the statement "one out of every five babies in the world is Chinese" is "true," but it is at such a high level of abstraction that it bears no relation to the realities of any *particular* person. It is of a different logical type from any statement made about Mrs. Green's situation and what she, in particular, might expect.

Mrs. Green's problem is apocryphal, but her confusion is not. There are plenty of people who worry themselves to death because they have discovered that they are "below average" in some respect. And there is no shortage of people who falsely assess their own expectations and, indeed, merit, because they have determined they are "above average." For example, a person whose IQ score is "above average" ought not to assure that he or she will have a better chance of understanding a certain situation than a person whose IQ score is "below average." For one thing, a score on a test is a highly abstract statement in itself. For another, a statement about one's score in relation to a thousand other scores is a future abstraction — so far removed from one's performance in a particular situation as to be meaningless. The point is that statistical language of even the most rudimentary sort leaves out so many details that it is, almost literally, not about anything. There is nothing "personal" about it, and therefore it is best to regard it as being of a different logical type from statements about what is actually happening to people.

Generalizations about groups of people present a similar problem. It may be "true," for example, that Jews, as a class of people, have a higher income than Italians, but it does not follow that Al Schwartz, in particular, earns more than Dominick Alfieri, in particular. One of the roots of what may be called prejudice lies somewhere in our confusion over what may be "true" in a general sense and what may be "true" in a particular sense.

The Theory of Logical Types, then, is useful in helping us to sort out our different modalities of talk. There are statements about what we observe and statements about how we feel and statements about our statements (of which self-reflexiveness is an example) and statements about how we classify things — in a phrase, statements about different orders of "reality."

It does not always matter, of course, that we be aware of these distinctions. No one is more obnoxious than the fanatical semanticist who insists upon straightening everyone out even though they have no wish to be straightened. But, obviously, there are many situations in which people descend into argument, confusion, or despair because they are not aware of the differing types of statements being made. In these cases, knowledge of logical types, levels of abstraction, and extensionality-intensionality can be very useful.

But there is still another application to all of this that is even more useful. I am referring to our efforts at solving problems. The basic distinction that is required here is between "first-order" thinking and "second-order" thinking. (I am lifting these terms from a remarkable book, *Change*, by Paul Watzlawick, John Weakland, and Richard Fisch, in which the authors explain, in great detail, how to apply The Theory of Logical Types to the resolution of practical human problems.) The difference between first- and second-order thinking is a difference in the level of abstraction at which we perceive a problem. When we try to solve a problem through first-order thinking, we work within a framework of the system, accepting the assumptions on which the system is based. For instance, suppose you were given this problem to solve: Here is a number, VI. By the addition of one line, can you make it into seven? The answer is simple enough — VII. First-order perceptions are entirely adequate for such a problem. But now suppose you are given the following problem: Here is a number, IX. By the addition of one line, can you make it into a six? This problem does not yield to first-order thinking. If you try to solve it by rearranging the elements of the system, you will not come up with a solution. But if you go to another level of abstraction, if you step outside the system, so to speak, an answer suggests itself: SIX. People who cannot solve this problem have usually failed for the following reasons: They assume that IX is a Roman number, and only a Roman number. They assume that the answer must, therefore, be expressed in a Roman number. And they assume that "a line" must be a straight line. In other words, they have framed the problem in a certain way and have tried to solve it by staying within that frame. Second-order thinking means going outside the "frame" of a problem and drawing on resources not contained in the original "frame."

There are several different names for second-order thinking. Some have referred to it simply as "creative thinking." The authors of *Change* call it "reframing." Edward de Bono calls it *lateral thinking*, of which he gives the following example:

> There is made in Switzerland a pear brandy in which a whole pear is to be seen within the bottle. How did the pear get into the bottle? The usual guess is that the bottle neck has been closed after the pear has been put into the bottle. Others guess that the bottom of the bottle was added after the pear was inside. It is always assumed that since the pear is a fully grown pear, it must have been placed in the bottle as a fully grown pear. In fact if a branch bearing a tiny bud was inserted through the neck of the bottle then the pear would actually grow within the bottle and there would be no question of how it got inside.
>
> (*Lateral Thinking*, pp. 93 and 94)

One must grant that problems about Roman numbers and pears in bottles are not of the type which ordinarily worry people. But the process by which they are solved — going to another level of perception — can be of substantial practical value. For example, in some New York City public schools, the teachers have a great deal of trouble keeping their students inside the classrooms. Students wander through the hallways during class time, sometimes running, fighting and screaming, which is not only dangerous but also distracting to those inside the classrooms. Now, if you assume that a classroom is the only place where learning can occur and that those who are not in their classrooms are a "problem," you will spend all your energy trying to get the problems to go where the solution is. You will threaten, plead, and even call the police, none of which works very well. But suppose you "reframe" the problem. Suppose, for example, you say that the issue is not how to get the students into a room but how to get them to learn something. All sorts of possibilities will now become available. In one New York City school, the assistant principal came up with this solution: She announced that the school was instituting a radical educational plan, known as "the open hall policy." The plan made *staying in the halls* a legitimate educational activity. A few teachers were made available to talk with students about a variety of subjects, and thus the halls *became* the classroom. The screaming, running, and fighting stopped, and I have been told on good authority that other principals now visit this school to observe this startling educational innovation.

To take another example, in *Change*, Watzlawick and his associates suggest that people suffering from insomnia will often choose the worst possible path to sleep. They will tell themselves that their problem is "to get to sleep." But since sleep must come spontaneously or it does not come, to work at getting to sleep will defeat its purpose. They recommend a little reverse English: Tell yourself that your problem is to stay awake, and try to do so.

Another example: The New York State Thruway Authority faced the problem of an excessive number of speed-limit violations. They could have, at great expense, hired more troopers to track down the violators. Instead, they raised the speed limit, and thus eliminated much of the problem, with no increase in accident rate.

The point of all this is that a great deal of stupid talk can be eliminated if we can get beyond our own assumptions. We too often become tyrannized by the way we have framed a certain situation; that is, we allow a set of words and sentences to define for us the level of perception at which we will view a matter. But if we change our words, we may change the matter. And, therefore, the solution.

FRIEDRICH NIETZSCHE (1844-1900)

One of the most influential thinkers of any age, Nietzsche lived in Germany and left his mark on most European writers of the twentieth century. Nietzsche saw in the human will infinite possibilities. An apostle of passion, he attacked weakness, laziness, and passivity. The titles of some of his major works — Fear and Trembling, The Sickness unto Death — reflect his existentialist sensibilities, but his works are joyous expressions of his love of life.

FROM *HOMER'S CONTEST*

When one speaks of *humanity*, the idea is fundamental that this is something which separates and distinguishes man from nature. In reality, however, there is no such separation: "natural" qualities and those called truly "human" are inseparably grown together. Man, in his highest and noblest capacities, is wholly nature and embodies its uncanny dual character. Those of his abilities which are terrifying and considered inhuman may even be the fertile soil out of which alone all humanity can grow: impulse, deed, and work.

Thus the Greeks, the most humane men of ancient times, have a trait of cruelty, a tigerish lust to annihilate — a trait that is also very distinct in that grotesquely enlarged mirror image of the Hellenes, in Alexander the Great, but that really must strike fear into our hearts throughout their whole history and mythology, if we approach them with the flabby concept of modern "humanity." When Alexander has the feet of Batis, the brave defender of Gaza, pierced, and ties him alive to his carriage, to drag him about while his soldiers mock, that is a revolting caricature of Achilles, who maltreats Hector's corpse in a similar fashion at night; and even this trait is offensive to us and makes us shudder. Here we look into the abyss of hatred. With the same feeling we may also observe the mutual laceration, bloody and insatiable, of two Greek parties, for example, in the Corcyrean revolution. When the victor in a fight among the cities executes the entire male citizenry in accordance with the laws of war, and sells all the women and children into slavery, we see in the sanction of such a law that the Greeks considered it an earnest necessity to let their hatred flow forth fully; in such moments crowded and swollen feeling relieved itself: the tiger leaped out, voluptuous cruelty in his terrible eyes. Why must the Greek sculptor give form again and again to war and combat in innumerable repetitions: distended human bodies, their sinews tense with hatred or with the arrogance of triumph; writhing bodies, wounded; dying bodies, expiring? Why did the whole Greek world exult over the combat scenes of the *Iliad*? I fear that we do not understand these in a sufficiently "Greek" manner; indeed, that we should shudder if we were ever to understand them "in Greek."

But what lies *behind* the Homeric world, as the womb of everything Hellenic? For *in* that world the extraordinary artistic precision, calm, and purity of the lines raise us above the mere contents: through an artistic deception the colors seem lighter, milder, warmer; and in this colorful warm light the men appear better and more sympathetic. But what do we behold when, no longer led and protected by the hand of Homer, we stride back into the pre-Homeric world? Only night and terror and an imagination accustomed to the horrible. What kind of earthly existence do these revolting, terrible theogonic myths reflect? A life ruled only by the children of Night: strife, lust, deceit, old age, and death. Let us imagine the atmosphere of Hesiod's poem already hard to breathe, made still denser and darker, and without all the mollifications and purifications that streamed over Hellas from Delphi and from numerous abodes of the gods; let us mix this thickened Boeotian atmosphere with the gloomy voluptuousness of the Etruscans; then such a reality would wring from us a world of myth in which Uranos, Cronos, Zeus and the wars with the Titans would seem like a relief: in this brooding atmosphere, combat is salvation; the cruelty of victory is the pinnacle of life's jubilation.

Further, it was in truth from murder and the expiation of murder that the conception of Greek law developed; so, too, the nobler culture takes its first wreath of victory from the altar of the expiation of murder. After the wave of that bloody age comes a trough that cuts deep into Hellenic history. The names of Orpheus, Musaeus, and their cults reveal the consequences to which the uninterrupted spectacle of a world of struggle and cruelty was pressing: toward a disgust with existence, toward the conception of this existence as a punishment and penance, toward the belief in the identity of existence and guilt. But it is precisely these consequences that are not specifically Hellenic: in this respect, Greece is at one with India and the Orient in general. The Hellenic genius was ready with yet another answer to the question, "What is a life of struggle and victory for?" and gave that answer through the whole breadth of Greek history.

To understand it, we must start with the point that the Greek genius tolerated the terrible presence of this urge and considered it *justified*; while the Orphic movement contained the idea that a life with such an urge as its root was not worth living. Struggle and the joy of victory were recognized — and nothing distinguishes the Greek world from ours as much as the coloring so derived, of individual ethical concepts, for example, *Eris*[1] and envy. . . .

And not only Aristotle but the whole of Greek antiquity thinks differently from us about hatred and envy, and judges with Hesiod, who in one place calls one Eris evil — namely, the one that leads men into hostile fights of annihilation against one another — while praising another Eris as good — the one that, as jealousy, hatred, and envy, spurs men to activity: not to the activity of fights of annihilation but to the activity of fights which are *contests*. The Greek is envious, and he does not consider this quality a blemish but the gift of a *beneficent* godhead. What a gulf of ethical judgement lies between us and him! . . .

The greater and more sublime a Greek is, the brighter the flame of ambition that flares out of him, consuming everybody who runs on the same course. Aristotle once made a list of such

---

[1] "Discord."

hostile contests in the grand manner; the most striking of the examples is that even a dead man can still spur a live one to consuming jealousy. That is how Aristotle describes the relationship between Xenophanes of Colophon to Homer. We do not understand the full strength of Xenophanes' attack on the national hero of poetry, unless — as again later with Plato — we see that at its root lay an overwhelming craving to assume the place of the overthrown poet and to inherit his flame. Every great Hellene hands on the torch of the contest: every great virtue kindles a new greatness. When the young Themistocles could not sleep because he was thinking of the laurels of Miltiades, his urge, awakened so early, was finally set free in the long contest with Aristides, to become that remarkably unique, purely instinctive genius of his political activity, which Thucydides describes for us. How characteristic are question and answer when a noted opponent of Pericles is asked whether he or Pericles is the best wrestler in the city, and answers: "Even when I throw him down, he denies that he fell and attains his purpose, persuading even those who saw him fall."

If one wants to observe this conviction — wholly undistinguished in its most naive expression — that the contest is necessary to preserve the health of the state, then one should reflect on the original meaning of *ostracism*, for example, as it is pronounced by the Ephesians when they banish Hermodorous: "Among us, no one shall be the best: but if someone is, then let him be elsewhere and among others." Why should no one be the best? Because then the contest would come to an end and the eternal source of life for the Hellenistic state would be endangered. . . . Originally this curious institution is not a safety valve but a means of stimulation: the individual who towers above the rest is eliminated so that the contest of forces may reawaken — an idea that is hostile to the "exclusiveness" of genius in the modern sense and presupposes that in the natural order of things there are always *several* geniuses who spur each other to action, even as they hold each other within the limits of measure. That is the core of the Hellenic notion of the contest: it abominates the rule of one and fears its dangers; it desires, as a *protection* against the genius, another genius.

Every talent must unfold itself in fighting: that is the command of Hellenic popular pedagogy, whereas modern educators dread nothing more than the unleashing of so-called ambition. . . . And just as the youths were educated through contests, their educators were also engaged in contests with each other. The great musical masters, Pindar and Simonides, stood side by side, mistrustful and jealous; in the spirit of contest, the sophist, the advanced teacher of antiquity, meets another sophist; even the most universal type of instruction, through the drama, was metered out to the people only in the form of a tremendous wrestling among the great musical and dramatic artists. How wonderful! "Even the artist hates the artist." Whereas modern man fears nothing in an artist more than the emotion of any personal fight, the Greek knows the artist *only as engaged in a personal fight*. Precisely where modern man senses the weakness of a work of art, the Hellene seeks the source of its greatest strength. What, for example, is of special artistic significance in Plato's dialogues is for the most part the result of a contest with the art of the orators, the sophists, and the dramatists of his time, invented for the purpose of enabling him to say in the end: "Look, I can do it better than my great rivals can do; indeed, I can do it better than they. No Protagoras had invented myths as beautiful as mine; no dramatist such a vivid and captivating whole as my *Symposion*; no orator had written orations like those in my *Gorgias* — and now I repudiate all this entirely and condemn all imitative art. Only the contest made me a poet, a sophist, an orator." What a problem opens up before us when we inquire into the relationship of the contest to the conception of the work of art!

However, when we remove the contest from Greek life we immediately look into that pre-Homeric abyss of a terrifying savagery of hatred and the lust to annihilate. This phenomenon unfortunately appears quite frequently when a personality is suddenly removed from the contest by an extraordinarily brilliant deed and becomes *hors de concours* in his own judgement, as in that of his fellow citizens. The effect is almost without exception a terrifying one; and if one usually infers from this that the Greek was incapable of enduring fame and happiness, one should say more precisely that he was unable to endure fame without any further contest, or the happiness at the end of the contest. There is no clearer example than the last experiences of Miltiades. Placed on a solitary peak and elevated far above every fellow fighter by his incomparable success at Marathon, he feels a base, vengeful craving awaken in him against a Parian citizen with whom he has long had a feud. To satisfy this craving he misuses fame, state property, civic honor — and dishonors himself. . . . An ignominious death sets its seal on his brilliant heroic career and darkens it for all posterity. After the battle of Marathon the envy of the heavenly powers seizes him. And this divine envy is inflamed when it beholds a human being without a rival, unopposed, on a solitary peak of fame. Only the gods are beside him now — and therefore they are against him. They seduce him to a deed of *hybris*,[2] and under it he collapses.

Let us note well that, just as Miltiades perishes, the noblest Greek cities perish too, when through merit and good fortune they arrive at the temple of Nike from the racecourse. Athens, who had destroyed the independence of her allies and then severely punished the rebellions of her subjects; Sparta, who expressed her domination over Hellas after the battle of Aegospotamoi, in yet much harsher and crueler ways, have also, after the example of Miltiades, brought about their own destruction through deeds of *hybris*, as proof that without envy, jealousy, and ambition in the contest, the Hellenic city, like the Hellenic man, degenerates. He becomes evil and cruel: he becomes vengeful and godless; in short, he became "pre-Homeric". . . .

PLATO

APOLOGY

Socrates:

How you, O Athenians, have been affected by my accusers, I cannot tell; but I know that they almost made me forget who I was so persuasively did they speak; and yet they have hardly uttered a word of truth. But of the many falsehoods told by them, there was one which quite amazed me; — I mean when they said that you should be upon your guard and not allow yourselves to be deceived by the force of my eloquence. To say this, when they were certain to be detected as soon as I opened my lips and proved myself to be anything but a great speaker, did indeed appear to me most shameless — unless by the force of eloquence they mean the force of truth; for if such is their meaning, I admit that I am eloquent. But in how different a way from theirs! Well, as I was saying, they have scarcely spoken the truth at all; but from me you shall hear the whole truth: not, however, delivered after their manner in a set oration duly ornamented with words and phrases. No, by heaven, but I shall use the words and arguments which occur to me at the moment; for I am confident in the justice of my cause: at my time of life I ought not to be appearing before you, O men of Athens, in the character of a juvenile orator — let no one expect it of me. And I must beg of you to grant me a favour: — If I defend myself in my accustomed manner, and you hear me using the words which I have been in the habit of using in theatre at the tables of the money-changers, or anywhere else, I would ask you not to be surprised, and not to interrupt me on this account. For I am more than seventy years of age, and appearing now for the first time in a court of law, I am quite a stranger to the language of the place; and therefore I would have you regard me as if I were really a stranger, whom you would excuse if he spoke in his native tongue, and after the fashion of his country: — Am I making an unfair request of you? Never mind the manner, which may or may not be good; but think only of the truth of my words, and give heed to that: let the speaker speak truly and the judge decide justly.

---

[2] "Overbearing pride"

And first, I have to reply to the older charges and to my first accusers, and then I will go on to the later ones. For of old I have had many accusers, who have accused me falsely to you during many years; and I am more afraid of them than of Anytus and his associates, who are dangerous, too, in their own way. But far more dangerous are the others, who began when you were children, and took possession of your minds with their falsehoods, telling of one Socrates, a wise man, who speculated about the heaven above, and searched into the earth beneath, and made the worse appear the better cause. The disseminators of this tale are the accusers whom I dread; for their hearers are apt to fancy that such enquirers do not believe in the existence of the gods. And they are many and their charges against me are of ancient date and they were made by them in the days when you were more impressible than you are now — in childhood, or it may have been in youth — and the cause when heard went by default, for there was none to answer. And hardest of all, I do not know and cannot tell the names of my accusers; unless in the chance case of a Comic poet. All who from envy and malice have persuaded you — some of them having first convinced themselves — all this class of men are most difficult to deal with; for I cannot have them up here, and cross-examine them, and therefore I must simply fight with shadows in my own defense, and argue when there is no one who answers. I will ask you then to assume with me, as I was saying, that my opponents are of two kinds: one recent, the other ancient; and I hope that you will see the propriety of my answering the latter first, for these accusations you heard long before the others, and much oftener.

Well, then, I must make my defence, and endeavor to clear away in a short time, a slander which has lasted a long time. May I succeed, if to succeed be for my good and yours, or likely to avail me in my cause! The task is not an easy one; I quite understand the nature of it. And so leaving the event with God, in obedience to the law I will now make my defence.

I will begin at the beginning, and ask what is the accusation which has given rise to the slander of me, and in fact has encouraged Meletus to prefer this charge against me. Well, what do the slanderers say? They shall be my prosecutors, and I will sum up their words in an affidavit: "Socrates is an evildoer, and a curious person, who searches into things under the earth and in heaven, and he makes the worse appear the better cause; and he teaches the aforesaid doctrines to others." Such is the nature of the accusation: it is just what you have yourselves seen in the comedy of Aristophones,[3] who has introduced a man whom he calls Socrates, going about and saying that he walks in air, and talking a deal of nonsense concerning matters of which I do not pretend to know either much or little — not that I mean to speak disparagingly of any one who is a student of natural philosophy. I should be very sorry if Meletus could bring so grave a charge against me. But the simple truth is, O Athenians, that I have nothing to do with physical speculations. Very many of those here present are witnesses to the truth of this, and to them I appeal. Speak then, you who have heard me, and tell your neighbors whether any of you have ever known me hold forth in few words or in many upon such matters.... You hear their answer. And from what they say of this part of the charge you will be able to judge of the truth of the rest.

As little foundation is there for the report that I am a teacher, and take money; this accusation has no more truth in it than the other. Although, if a man were really able to instruct mankind, to receive money for giving instruction would, in my opinion, be an honour to him. There is Gorgias of Leontium, and Prodicus of Ceos, and Hippias of Elis, who go the round of the cities, and are able to persuade the young men to leave their own citizens by whom they might be taught for nothing, and come to them whom they not only pay, but are thankful if they may be allowed to pay them.

There is at this time a Parian philosopher residing in Athens, of whom I have heard; and I came to hear of him in this way: — I came across a man who has spent a world of money on the Sophists, Callias, the son of Hipponicus, and knowing that he had sons, I asked him: "Callias," I said, "if your two sons were foals or calves, there would be no difficulty in finding someone to

---

[3] Aristophanes, *Clouds*.

put over them; we should hire a trainer of horses, or a farmer probably, who would improve and perfect them in their own proper virtue and excellence; but as they are human beings, whom are you thinking of placing over them? Is there anyone who understands human and political virtue? You must have thought about the matter, for you have sons; is there any one?" "There is," he said. "Who is he?" said I; "and of what country? and what does he charge?" "Evenus the Parian," he replied; "he is the man, and his charge is five minae." Happy is Evenus, I said to myself, if he really has this wisdom, and teaches at such a moderate charge. Had I the same, I should have been very proud and conceited; but the truth is that I have no knowledge of the kind.

I dare say, Athenians, that some one among you will reply, "Yes, Socrates, but what is the origin of these accusations which are brought against you; there must have been something strange which you have been doing? All these rumors and this talk about you would never have arisen if you had been like other men: tell us, then, what is the cause of them, for we should be sorry to judge hastily of you." Now I regard this as a fair challenge, and I will endeavor to explain to you the reason why I am called wise and have such an evil fame. Please to attend then. And although some of you may think that I am joking, I declare that I will tell you the entire truth. Men of Athens, this reputation of mine has come of a certain sort of wisdom which I possess. If you ask me what kind of wisdom, I reply, wisdom such as may perhaps be attained by man, for to that extent I am inclined to believe that I am wise; whereas the persons of whom I was speaking have a superhuman wisdom, which I may fail to describe, because I have it not myself; and he who says that I have, speaks falsely, and is taking away my character. And here, O men of Athens, I must beg you not to interrupt me, even if I seem to say something extravagant. For the word which I will speak is not mine. I will refer you to a witness who is worthy of credit; that witness shall be the God of Delphi — he will tell you about my wisdom, if I have any, and of what sort it is. You must have known Chaerephon; he was early a friend of mine, and also a friend of yours, for he shared in the recent exile of the people, and returned with you. Well, Chaerephon, as you know, was very impetuous in all his doings, and he went to Delphi and boldly asked the oracle to tell him whether — as I was saying, I must beg you not to interrupt — he asked the oracle to tell him whether any one was wiser than I was, and the Pythian prophetess answered, that there was no man wiser. Chaerephon is dead himself; but his brother, who is in court, will confirm the truth of what I am saying.

Why do I mention this? Because I am going to explain to you why I have such an evil name. When I heard the answer, I said to myself, What can the god mean? and what is the interpretation of his riddle? for I know that I have no wisdom, small or great. What then can he mean when he says that I am the wisest of men? And yet he is a god, and cannot lie; that would be against his nature. After long consideration, I thought of a method of trying the question. I reflected that if I could only find a man wiser than myself, then I might go to the god with a refutation in my hand. I should say to him, "Here is a man who is wiser than I am; but you said that I was the wisest." Accordingly I went to one who had the reputation of wisdom, and observed him — his name I need not mention; he was a politician whom I selected for examination — and the result was as follows: When I began to talk with him, I could not help thinking that he was not really wise, although he was thought wise by many, and still wiser by himself; and there upon I tried to explain to him that he thought himself wise, but was not really wise; and the consequence was that he hated me, and his enmity was shared by several who were present and heard me. So I left him, saying to myself, as I went away: Well, although I do not suppose that either of us knows anything really beautiful and good, I am better off than he is — for he knows nothing, and thinks that he knows; I neither know nor think that I know. In this latter particular, then, I seem to have slightly the advantage of him. Then I went to another who had still higher pretensions to wisdom, and my conclusion was exactly the same. Whereupon I made another enemy of him, and of many others besides him.

Then I went to one man after another, being not unconscious of the enmity which I provoked, and I lamented and feared this: But necessity was laid upon me, — the word of God, I thought,

ought to be considered first. And I said to myself, Go I must to all who appear to know and find out the meaning of the oracle. And I swear to you, Athenians, by the dog I swear — for I must tell you the truth — the result of my mission was — just this: I found that the men most in repute were all but the most foolish, and that others less esteemed were really wiser and better. I will tell you the tale of my wanderings and of the "Herculean" labours, as I may call them, which I endured only to find at last the oracle irrefutable. After the politicians I went to the poets; tragic, dithyrambic, and all sorts. And there, I said to myself, you will be instantly detected; now you will find out that you are more ignorant than they are. Accordingly, I took them some of the most elaborate passages in their own writings, and asked what was the meaning of them — thinking that they would teach me something. Will you believe me? I am almost ashamed to confess the truth but I must say that there is hardly a person present who would not have talked better about their poetry than they did themselves. Then I knew that not by wisdom do poets write poetry but by a sort of genius and inspiration; they are like diviners or soothsayers who also say many fine things, but do not understand the meaning of them. The poets appeared to me to be much in the same case; and I further observed that upon the strength of their poetry they believed themselves to be the wisest of men in other things in which they were not wise. So I departed, conceiving myself to be superior to them for the same reason that I was superior to the politicians.

At last I went to the artisans, for I was conscious that I knew nothing at all, as I may say, and I was sure that they knew many fine things; and here I was not mistaken, for they did know many things of which I was ignorant, and in this they certainly were wiser than I was. But I observed that even the good artisans fell into the same error as the poets; because they were good workmen they thought that they also knew all sorts of high matters, and this defect in them overshadowed their wisdom; and therefore I asked myself on behalf of the oracle whether I would like to be as I was, neither having their knowledge nor their ignorance, or like them in both; and I made answer to myself and to the oracle that I was better off as I was.

This inquisition has led to my having many enemies of the worst and most dangerous kind, and has given occasion also to many calumnies. And I am called wise, for my hearers always imagine that I myself possess the wisdom which I find wanting in others: but the truth is, O men of Athens, that God only is wise; and by his answer he intends to show that the wisdom of men is worth little or nothing; he is not speaking of Socrates, he is only using my name by way of illustration, as if he said, He, O men, is the wisest, who, like Socrates, knows that his wisdom is in truth worth nothing. And so I go about the world, obedient to the god, and search and make enquiry into the wisdom of any one, whether citizen or stranger, who appears to be wise; and if he is not wise, then in vindication of the oracle I show him that he is not wise; and my occupation quite absorbs me, and I have no time to give either to any public matter of interest or to any concern of my own, but I am in utter poverty by reason of my devotion to the god.

There is another thing: — young men of the richer classes, who have not much to do, come about me of their own accord; they like to hear the pretenders examined, and they often immune me, and proceed to examine others; there are plenty of persons, as they quickly discover, who think that they know something, but really know little or nothing; and then those who are examined by them instead of being angry with themselves are angry with me. This confounded Socrates, they say; this villainous misleader of youth — and then if somebody asks them, Why, what evil does he practice or teach? they do not know, and cannot tell; but in order that they may not appear to be at a loss, they repeat the ready-made charges which are used against all philosophers about teaching things up in the clouds and under the earth, and having no gods, and making the worse appear the better cause; for they do not like to confess that their pretence of knowledge has been detected — which is the truth; and as they are numerous and ambitious and energetic, and are drawn up in battle array and have persuasive tongues, they have filled your ears with their loud and inveterate calumnies. And this is the reason why my three accusers, Meletus and Anytus and Lycon, have set upon me; Meletus, who has a quarrel with me on behalf of the poets; Anytus, on behalf of the craftsmen and politicians; Lycon, on behalf of the rhetoricians: and as I said at the beginning, I cannot expect to get rid of such a mass of calumny all in a moment. And this, O men of Athens, is the truth and the whole truth; I have concealed nothing, I have dissembled nothing. And yet, I know that my plainness of speech makes them hate me, and what is their hatred but a proof that I am speaking the truth? — Hence has arisen the prejudice against me; and this is the reason of it, as you will find out either in this or in any future enquiry.

I have said enough in my defense against the first class of my accusers; I turn to the second class. They are headed by Meletus, that good man and true lover of his country, as he calls himself. Against these, too, I must try to make a defense — Let their affidavit be read; it contains something of this kind: It says that Socrates is a doer of evil, who corrupts the youth; and who does not believe in the gods of the state, but has other new divinities of his own. Such is the charge; and now let us examine the particular counts. He says that I am a doer of evil, and corrupt the youth; but I say, O men of Athens, that Meletus is a doer of evil, in that he pretends to be in earnest when he is only in jest, and is so eager to bring men to trial from a pretended zeal and interest about matters in which he really never had the smallest interest. And the truth of this I will endeavor to prove to you.

Come hither, Meletus, and let me ask a question of you. You think a great deal about the improvement of youth?

Yes, I do.

Tell the judges, then, who is their improver; for you must know, as you have taken the pains to discover their corrupter, and are citing and accusing me before them. Speak, then, and tell the judges who their improver is. Observe, Meletus, that you are silent, and have nothing to say. But is not this rather disgraceful, and a very considerable proof of what I was saying, that you have no interest in the matter? Speak up, friend, and tell us who their improver is.

The laws.

But that, my good sir, is not my meaning. I want to know who the person is, who, in the first place, knows the laws.

The judges, Socrates, who are present in court.

What, do you mean to say, Meletus, that they are able to instruct and improve youth?

Certainly they are.

What, all of them, or some only and not others?

All of them.

By the goddess Herè, that is good news! There are plenty of improvers, then. And what do you say of the audience, — do they improve them?

Yes, they do.

And the senators?

Yes, the senators improve them.

But perhaps the members of the assembly corrupt them? — or do they too improve them?

They improve them.

Then every Athenian improves and elevates them; all with the exception of myself; and I alone am their corrupter? Is that what you affirm?

That is what I stoutly affirm.

I am very unfortunate if you are right. But suppose I ask you a question: How about horses? Does one man do them harm and all the world good? Is not the exact opposite the truth? One man is able to do them good, or at least not many; — the trainer of horses, that is to say, does them good, and others who have to do with them rather injure them? Is not that true, Meletus, of horses, or of any other animals? Most assuredly it is; whether you and Anytus say yes or no. Happy indeed would be the condition of youth if they had one corrupter only, and all the rest of the world were their improvers. But you, Meletus, have sufficiently shown that you never had a thought about the young: your carelessness is seen in your not caring about the very things which you bring against me.

And now, Meletus, I will ask you another question — by Zeus I will: Which is better, to live among bad citizens, or among good ones? Answer, friend, I say; the question is one which may be easily answered. Do not the good do their neighbors good, and the bad do them evil?

Certainly.

And is there anyone who would rather be injured than benefited by those who live with him? Answer, my good friend, the law requires you to answer — does anyone like to be injured?

Certainly not.

And when you accuse me of corrupting and deteriorating the youth, do you allege that I corrupt them intentionally or unintentionally?

Intentionally, I say.

But you have just admitted that the good do their neighbors good, and evil do them evil. Now, is that a truth which your superior wisdom has recognized thus early in life, and am I, at my age, in such darkness and ignorance as not to know that if a man with whom I have to live is corrupted by me, I am very likely to be harmed by him; and yet I corrupt him, and intentionally, too — so you say, although neither I nor any other human being is ever likely to be convinced by you. But either I do not corrupt them, or I corrupt them unintentionally; and on either view of the case you lie. If my offense is unintentional, the law has no cognizance of unintentional offences: you ought to have taken me privately, and warned and admonished me; for if I had been better advised I should have left off doing what I only did unintentionally — no doubt I should; but you would have nothing to say to me and refused to teach me. And now you bring me up in this court, which is a place not of instruction, but of punishment.

It will be very clear to you, Athenians, as I was saying, that Meletus has no care at all great or small, about the matter. But still I should like to know, Meletus, in what I am affirmed to corrupt the young. I suppose you mean, as I infer from your indictment, that I teach them not to acknowledge the gods which the state acknowledges, but some other new divinities or spiritual agencies in their stead. These are the lessons by which I corrupt the youth, as you say.

Yes, that I say emphatically.

Then, by the gods, Meletus, of whom we are speaking, tell me and the court, in somewhat plainer terms, what you mean! for I do not as yet understand whether you affirm that I teach other men to acknowledge some gods, and therefore that I do believe in gods, and am not an entire atheist — this you do not lay to my charge, — but only you say that they are not the same gods which the city recognizes — the charge is that they are different gods. Or, do you mean that I am an atheist simply, and a teacher of atheism?

I mean the latter — that you are a complete atheist.

What an extraordinary statement! Why do you think so, Meletus? Do you mean that I do not believe in the godhead of the sun or moon like other men?

I assure you, judges, that he does not: for he says that the sun is stone, and the moon earth.

Friend Meletus, you think that you are accusing Anaxagoras: and you have but a bad opinion of the judges, if you fancy them illiterate to such a degree as not to know that these doctrines are found in the books of Anaxagoras the Clazomenian, which are full of them. And so, forsooth, the youth are said to be taught them by Socrates, when they are not unfrequently shown exhibitions of them at the theatre (price of admission one drachma at the most); and they might pay their money, and laugh at Socrates if he pretends to father these extraordinary views. And so, Meletus, you really think that I do not believe in any god?

I swear by Zeus that you believe absolutely in none at all.

Nobody will believe you, Meletus, and I am pretty sure that you do not believe yourself. I cannot help thinking, men of Athens, that Meletus is reckless and impudent, and that he has written this indictment in a spirit of mere wantonness and youthful bravado. Has he not compounded a riddle, thinking to try me? He said to himself — I shall see whether the wise Socrates will discover my facetious contradiction, or whether I shall be able to deceive him and the rest of them. For he certainly does appear to me to contradict himself in the indictment as much as if he said that Socrates is guilty of not believing in the gods, and yet of believing in them — but this is not like a person who is in earnest.

I should like you, O men of Athens, to join me in examining what I conceive to be his inconsistency; and do you, Meletus, answer. And I must remind the audience of my request that they would not make a disturbance if I speak in my accustomed manner:

Did ever man, Meletus, believe in the existence of human things, and not of human beings? ... I wish, men of Athens, that he would answer, and not be always trying to get up an interruption. Did ever any man believe in horsemanship, and not in horses? or in flute-playing, and not in flute-players? No, my friend; I will answer to you and to the court, as you refuse to answer for yourself. There is no man who ever did. But now please to answer the next question: Can a man believe in spiritual and divine agencies, and not in spirits or demigods?

He cannot.

How lucky I am to have extracted that answer, by the assistance of the court! But then you swear in the indictment that I teach and believe in divine or spiritual agencies (new or old, no matter for that); at any rate, I believe in spiritual agencies, — so you say and swear in the affidavit; and yet if I believe in divine beings, how can I help believing in spirits or demigods; — must I not? To be sure I must; and therefore I may assume that your silence gives consent. Now what are spirits or demigods? are they not either   gods or the sons of gods?

Certainly they are.

But this is what I call the facetious riddle invented by you: the demigods or spirits are gods, and you say first that I do not believe in gods, and then again that I do believe in gods; that is, if I believe in demigods. For if the demigods are the illegitimate sons of gods, whether by the nymphs or by any other mothers, of whom they are said to be the sons — what human being will ever believe that there are no gods if they are the sons of gods? You might as well affirm the existence of mules, and deny that of horses and asses. Such nonsense, Meletus, could only have been intended by you to make trial of me. You have put this into the indictment because you had nothing real of which to accuse me. But no one who has a particle of understanding will ever be convinced by you that the same men can believe in divine and superhuman things, and yet not believe that there are gods and demigods and heroes.

I have said enough in answer to the charge of Meletus: any elaborate defense is unnecessary; but I know only too well how many are the enmities which I have incurred, and this is what will be my destruction if I am destroyed; — not Meletus, nor yet Anytus, but the envy and detraction of the world, which has been the death of many good men, and will probably be the death of many more; there is no danger of my being the last of them.

Some one will say: And are you not ashamed, Socrates, of a course of life which is likely to bring you to an untimely end? To him I may fairly answer: There you are mistaken; a man who is good for anything ought not to calculate the chance of living or dying; he ought only to consider whether in doing anything he is doing right or wrong — acting the part of a good man or of a bad. Whereas, upon your view, the heroes who fell at Troy were not good for much, and the son of Thetis above all, who altogether despised danger in comparison with disgrace; and when he was so eager to slay Hector, his goddess mother said to him, that if he avenged his companion Patroclus, and slew Hector, he would die himself — "Fate," she said, in these or the like words, "waits for you next after Hector"; he, receiving this warning, utterly despised danger and death, and instead of fearing them, feared rather to live in dishonor, and not to avenge his friend. "Let me die forthwith," he replies, "and be avenged of my enemy, rather than abide here by the beaked ships, a laughingstock and a burden of the earth." Had Achilles any thought of death and danger? For wherever a man's place is, whether the place which he has chosen or that in which he has been placed by a commander, there he ought to remain in the hour of danger; he should not think of death or of anything but of disgrace. And this, O men of Athens, is a true saying.

Strange, indeed, would be my conduct, O men of Athens, if I who, when I was ordered by the generals whom you chose to command me at Potidaea and Amphipolis and Delium, remained where they placed me, like any other man, facing death — if now, when, as I conceive and imagine, God orders me to fulfil the philosopher's mission of searching into myself and other men, I were to desert my post through fear of death, or any other fear; that would indeed be strange, and I might justly be arraigned in court for denying the existence of the gods, if I disobeyed the oracle because I was afraid of death, fancying that I was wise when I was not wise. For the fear of death is indeed the pretence of wisdom, and not real wisdom, being a pretence of knowing the unknown; and no one knows whether death, which men in their fear apprehend to be the greatest evil, may not be the greatest good. Is not this ignorance of a disgraceful sort, the ignorance which is the conceit that man knows what he does not know? And in this respect only I believe myself to differ from men in general, and may perhaps claim to be wiser than they are: — that whereas I know but little of the world below, I do not suppose that I know: but I do know that injustice and disobedience to a better, whether God or man, is evil and dishonorable, and I will never fear or avoid a possible good rather than a certain evil. And therefore if you let me go now, and are not convinced by Anytus, who said that since I had been prosecuted I must be put to death (or if not that I ought never to have been prosecuted at all); and that if I escape now, your sons will all be utterly ruined by listening to my words — if you say to me, Socrates, this time we will not mind Anytus, and you shall be let off, but upon one condition, that you are not to enquire and speculate in this way any more, and that if you are caught doing so again you shall die; — if this was the condition on which you let me go, I should reply: Men of Athens, I honour and love you; but I shall obey God rather than you, and while I have life and strength I shall never cease from the practice and teaching of philosophy exhorting anyone whom I meet and saying to him after my manner: You, my friend, — a citizen of the great and mighty and wise city of Athens, — are you not ashamed of heaping up the greatest amount of money and honour and reputation, and caring so little about wisdom and truth and the greatest improvement of the soul, which you never regard or heed at all? And if the person with whom I am arguing, says: Yes, but I do care; then I do not leave him or let him go at once; but I proceed to interrogate and examine and cross-examine him, and if I think that he has no virtue in him, but only says that he has, I reproach him with undervaluing the greater, and overvaluing the less. And I shall repeat the same words to every one whom I meet, young and old, citizen and alien, but especially to the citizens, inasmuch as they are my brethren. For know that this is the command of God; and I believe that no greater good has ever happened in the state than my service to the God. For I do nothing but go about persuading you all, old and young alike, not to take thought for your persons or your properties, but first and chiefly to care about the greatest improvement of the soul. I tell you that virtue is not given by money, but that from virtue comes money and every other good of man, public as well as private. This is my teaching, and if this is the doctrine which corrupts the youth, I am a mischievous person. But if anyone says that this is not my teaching, he is speaking an untruth. Wherefore, O men of Athens, I say to you, do as Anytus bids or not as Anytus bids, and either acquit me or not; but whichever you do, understand that I shall never alter my ways, not even if I have to die many times.

Men of Athens, do not interrupt, but hear me; there was an understanding between us that you should hear me to the end; I have something more to say, at which you may be inclined to cry out; but I believe that to hear me will be good for you, and therefore I beg that you will not cry out. I would have you know, that if you kill such a one as I am, you will injure yourselves more than you will injure me. Nothing will injure me, not Meletus nor yet Anytus — they cannot, for a bad man is not permitted to injure a better than himself. I do not deny that Anytus may, perhaps, kill him, or drive him into exile, or deprive him of civil rights; and he may imagine, and others may imagine, that he is inflicting a great injury upon him: but there I do not agree. For the evil of doing as he is doing — the evil of unjustly taking away the life of another — is greater far.

And now, Athenians, I am not going to argue for my own sake, as you may think, but for yours, that you may not sin against the God by condemning me, who am his gift to you. For if you kill me you will not easily find a successor to me, who, if I may use such a ludicrous figure of speech, am a sort of gadfly, given to the state by God; and the state is a great and noble steed who is tardy in his motions owing to his very size, and requires to be stirred into life. I am that gadfly which God has attached to the state, and all day long and in all places am always fastening upon you, arousing and persuading and reproaching you. You will not easily find another like me, and therefore I would advise you to spare me. I dare say that you may feel out of temper (like a person who is suddenly awakened from sleep), and you think that you might easily strike me dead as Anytus advises, and then you would sleep on for the remainder of your lives, unless God in his care of you sent you another gadfly. When I say that I am given to you by God, the proof of my mission is this: — if I had been like other men, I should not have neglected all my own concerns or patiently seen the neglect of them during all these years, and have been doing yours, coming to you individually like a father or elder brother, exhorting you to regard virtue; such conduct, I say, would be unlike human nature. If I had gained anything, or if my exhortations had been paid, there would have been some sense in my doing so; but now, as you will perceive, not even the impudence of my accusers dares to say that I have ever exacted or sought pay of anyone; of that they have no witness. And I have a sufficient witness to the truth of what I say — my poverty.

Someone may wonder why I go about in private giving advice and busying myself with the concerns of others, but do not venture to come forward in public and advise the state. I will tell you why. You have heard me speak at sundry times and in divers places of an oracle or sign which comes to me, and is the divinity which Meletus ridicules in the indictment. This sign, which is a kind of voice, first began to come to me when I was a child; it always forbids but never commands me to do anything which I am going to do. This is what deters me from being a politician. And rightly, as I think. For I am certain, O men of Athens, that if I had engaged in politics, I should have perished long ago, and done no good either to you or to myself. And do not be offended at my telling you the truth; for the truth is, that no man who goes to war with you or any other multitude, honestly striving against the many lawless and unrighteous deeds which are done in a state, will save his life; he who will fight for the right, if he would live even for a brief space, must have a private station and not a public one.

I can give you convincing evidence of what I say, not words only, but what you value far more — actions. Let me relate to you a passage of my own life which will prove to you that I should never have yielded to injustice from any fear of death, and that "as I should have refused to yield" I must have died at once. I will tell you a tale of the courts, not very interesting perhaps, but nevertheless true. The only office of state which I ever held, O men of Athens, was that of senator: the tribe Antiochis, which is my tribe, had the presidency at the trial of the generals who had not taken up the bodies of the slain after the battle of Arginusae; and you proposed to try them in a body, contrary to law, as you all thought afterwards; but at the time I was the only one of the Prytanes who was opposed to the illegality, and I gave my vote against you; and when the orators threatened to impeach and arrest me, and you called and shouted, I made up my mind that I would run the risk, having law and justice with me, rather than take part in your injustice because I feared imprisonment and death. This happened in the days of the democracy. But when the oligarchy of the Thirty was in power, they sent for me and four others into the rotunda, and bade us bring Leon the Salaminian from Salamis, as they wanted to put him to death. This was a specimen of the sort of commands which they were always giving with the view of implicating as many as possible in their crimes; and then I showed, not in word only but in deed, that, if I may be allowed to use such an expression, I cared not a straw for death, and that my great and only care was lest I should do an unrighteous or unholy thing. For the strong arm of that oppressive power did not frighten me into doing wrong; and when we came out of the rotunda the other four went to Salamis and fetched Leon, but I went quietly home. For which I might have lost my life, had not the power of the Thirty shortly afterwards come to an end. And many will witness to my words.

Now do you really imagine that I could have survived all these years, if I had led a public life, supposing that like a good man I had always maintained the right and had made justice, as I ought, the first thing? No indeed, men of Athens, neither I nor any other man. But I have been always the same in all my actions, public as well as private, and never have I yielded any base compliance to those who are slanderously termed my disciples, or to any other. Not that I have any regular disciples. But if anyone likes to come and hear me while I am pursuing my mission, whether he be young or old, he is not excluded. Nor do I converse only with those who pay; but anyone, whether he be rich or poor, may ask and answer me and listen to my words; and whether he turns out to be a bad man or a good one, neither result can be justly imputed to me; for I never taught or professed to teach him anything. And if anyone says that he has ever learned or heard anything from me in private which all the world has not heard, let me tell you that he is lying.

But I shall be asked, Why do people delight in continually conversing with you? I have told you already, Athenians, the whole truth about this matter: they like to hear the cross-examination of the pretenders to wisdom; there is amusement in it. Now this duty of cross-examining other men has been imposed upon me by God; and has been signified to me by oracles, visions, and in every way in which the will of divine power was ever intimated to anyone. This is true, O Athenians; or, if not true, would be soon refuted. If I am or have been corrupting the youth, those of them who are now grown up and become sensible that I gave them bad advice in the days of their youth should come forward as accusers, and take their revenge; or if they do not like to come themselves, some of their relatives, fathers, brothers, or other kinsmen, should say what evil their families have suffered at my hands. Now is their time. Many of them I see in the court. There is Crito, who is of the same age and of the same deem with myself, and there is Critobulus his son, whom I also see. Then again there is Lysanias of Sphettus, who is the father of Aeschines — he is present; and also there is Antiphon of Cephisus, who is the father of Epigenes; and there are the brothers of several who have associated with me. There is Nicostratus the son of Theosdotides, and the brother or Theodotus (now Theodotus himself is dead, and therefore he, at any rate, will not seek to stop him); and there is Paralus the son of Demodocus, who had a brother Theages; and Adeimantus the son of Ariston, whose brother Plato is present; and Aeantodorus, who is the brother of Apollodorus, whom I also see. I might mention a great many others, some of whom Meletus should have produced as witnesses in the course of his speech; and let him still produce them, if he has forgotten — I will make way for him. And let him say, if he has any testimony of the sort which he can produce. Nay, Athenians, the very opposite is the truth. For all these are ready to witness on behalf of the corrupter, of the injurer of their kindred, as Meletus and Anytus call me; not the corrupted youth only — there might have been a motive for that — but their uncorrupted elder relatives. Why should they too support me with their testimony? Why, indeed, except for the sake of truth and justice, and because they know that I am speaking the truth, and that Meletus is a liar.

Well, Athenians, this and the like of this is all the defence which I have to offer. Yet a word more. Perhaps there may be someone who is offended at me, when he calls to mind how he himself on a similar, or even a less serious occasion, prayed and entreated the judges with many tears, and how he produced his children in court, which was a moving spectacle, together with a host of relations and friends; where as I, who am probably in danger of my life, will do none of these things. The contrast may occur to his mind, and he may be set against me, and vote in anger because he is displeased at me on this account. Now if there be such a person among you, — mind, I do not say that there is, — to him I may fairly reply: My friend, I am a man, and like other men, a creature of flesh and blood, and not "of wood or stone," as Homer says; and I have a family, yes, and sons, O Athenians, three in number, one almost a man, and two others who are still young; and yet I will not bring any of them hither in order to petition you for an acquittal. And why not? Not from any self-assertion or want of respect for you. Whether I am or am not afraid of death is another question, of which I will not now speak. But, having regard to public opinion, I feel that such conduct would be discreditable to myself, and to you, and to the whole state. One who has reached my years, and who has a name for wisdom, ought not to demean himself. Whether this opinion of me be derived or not, at any rate the world has decided that Socrates is in some way superior to other men. And if those among you who are said to be superior in wisdom and courage, and any other virtue, demean themselves in this way, how shameful is their conduct! I have seen men of reputation, when they have been condemned behaving in the strangest manner: they seemed to fancy that they were going to suffer something dreadful if they died, and that they could be immortal if you only allowed them to live; and I think that such are a dishonor to the state, and that any stranger coming in would have said of them that the most eminent men of Athens, to whom the Athenians themselves give honour and command, are no better than women. And I say that these things ought not to be done by those of us who have a reputation; and if they are done, you ought not to permit them; you ought rather to show that you are far more disposed to condemn the man who gets up a doleful scene and makes the city ridiculous, than him who holds his peace.

But, setting aside the question of public opinion, there seems to be something wrong in asking a favour of a judge, and thus procuring an acquittal, instead of informing and convincing him. For his duty is, not to make a present of justice, but to give judgment; and he has sworn that he will judge according to the laws, and not according to his own good pleasure; and we ought not to encourage you, nor should you allow yourself to be encouraged, in this habit of perjury — there can be no piety in that. Do not then require me to do what I consider dishonorable and impious and wrong, especially now, when I am being tried for impiety on the indictment of Meletus. For if, O men of Athos, by force of persuasion and entreaty I could overpower your oaths, then I should be teaching you to believe that there are no gods, and in defending should simply convict myself of the charge of not believing in them. But that is not so — far otherwise. For I do believe that there are gods, and in a sense higher than that in which any of my accusers believe in them. And to you and to God I commit my cause, to be determined by you as is best for you and me.

* * *

There are many reasons why I am not grieved, O men of Athens, at the vote of condemnation. I expected it, and am only surprised that the votes are so nearly equal; for I had thought that the majority against me would have been in larger; but now, had thirty votes gone over to the other side, I should have been acquitted. And I may say, I think, that I have escaped Meletus. I may say more; for without the assistance of Anytus and Lycon, anyone may see that he would not have had a fifth part of the votes, as the law requires, in which case he would have incurred a fine of a thousand drachmae.

And so he proposes death as the penalty. And what shall I propose on my part, O men of Athens? Clearly that which is my due. And what is my due? What return shall be made to the man who has never had the wit to be idle during his whole life; but has been careless of what the many care for — wealth, and family interests, and military offices, and speaking in the assembly, and magistracies, and plots, and parties. Reflecting that I was really too honest a man to be a politician and live, I did not go where I could do no good to you or to myself; but where I could do the greatest good privately to every one of you, thither I went, and sought to persuade every man among you that he must look to himself, and seek virtue and wisdom before he looks to his private interests, and look to the state before he looks to the interests of the state; and that this should be the order which he observes in all his actions. What shall be done to such an one? Doubtless some good thing, O men of Athens, if he has his reward; and the good should be of a kind suitable to him. What would be a reward suitable to a poor man who is your benefactor, and who desires leisure that he may instruct you? There can be no reward so fitting as maintenance in the Prytaneum, O men of Athens, a reward which he deserves far more than the citizen who has won the prize at Olympia in the horse or chariot race, whether the chariots were drawn by two horses or by many. For I am in want, and he has enough; and he only gives you the appearance of happiness, and I give you the reality. And if I am to estimate the penalty fairly, I should say that maintenance in the Prytaneum is the just return.

Perhaps you think that I am braving you in what I am saying now, as in what I said before about the tears and prayers. But this is not so. I speak rather because I am convinced that I never intentionally wronged anyone, although I cannot convince you — the time has been too short; if there were a law at Athens, as there is in other cities, that a capital cause should not be decided in one day, then I believe that I should have convinced you. But I cannot in a moment refute great slanders; and, as I am convinced that I never wronged another, I will assuredly not wrong myself. I will not say of myself that I deserve any evil, or propose any penalty. Why should I? Because I am afraid of the penalty of death which Meletus proposes? When I do not know whether death is a good or an evil, why should I propose a penalty which would certainly be an evil? Shall I say imprisonment? And why should I live in prison, and be the slave of the magistrates of the year — of the Eleven? Or shall the penalty be a fine, and imprisonment until the fine is paid? There is the same objection. I should have to lie in prison, for money I have none, and cannot pay. And if I say exile (and this may possibly be the penalty which you will affix), I must indeed be blinded by the love of life, if I am so irrational as to expect that when you, who are my own citizens, cannot endure my discourses and words, and have found them so grievous and odious that you will have no more of them, others are likely to endure me. No indeed, men of Athens, that is not very likely. And what a life should I lead at my age, wandering from city to city, ever changing my place of exile, and always being driven out! For I am quite sure that wherever I go, there, as here, the young men will flock to me; and if I drive them away, their elders will drive me out at their request; and if I let them come, their fathers and friends will drive me out for their sakes.

Someone will say: Yes, Socrates, but cannot you hold your tongue, and then you may go into a foreign city, and no one will interfere with you? Now I have great difficulty in making you understand my answer to this. For if I tell you that to do as you say would be a disobedience to the God, and therefore that I cannot hold my tongue, you will not believe that I am serious; and if I say again that daily to discourse about virtue, and of those other things about which you hear me examining myself and others, is the greatest good of man, and that the unexamined life is not worth living, you are still less likely to believe me. Yet I say what is true, although a thing of which it is hard for me to persuade you. Also, I have never been accustomed to think that I deserve to suffer any harm. Had I money I might have estimated the offence at what I was able to pay, and not have been much the worse. But I have none, and therefore I must ask you to proportion the fine to my means. Well, perhaps I could afford a mina, and therefore I propose that penalty: Plato, Crito, Critobulus, and Apollodorus, my friends here, bid me say thirty minae, and they will be the sureties. Let thirty minae be the penalty; for which sum they will be ample security to you.

* * *

Not much time will be gained, O Athenians, in return for the evil name which you will get from the detractors of the city, who will say that you killed Socrates, a wise man; for they will call me wise, even although I am not wise, when they want to reproach you. If you had waited a little while, your desire would have been fulfilled in the course of nature. For I am far advanced in years, as you may perceive, and not far from death. I am speaking now not to all of you, but only to those who have condemned me to death. And I have another thing to say to them: You think that I was convicted because I had no words of the sort which would have procured my acquittal — I mean, if I had thought fit to leave nothing undone or unsaid. Not so; the deficiency which led to my conviction was not of words — certainly not. But I had not the boldness or impudence or inclination to address you as you would have liked me to do, weeping and wailing and lamenting, and saying and doing many things which you have been accustomed to hear from others, and which, as I maintain, are unworthy of me. I thought at the time that I ought not to do anything common or mean when in danger: nor do I now repent of the style of my defence; I would rather die having spoken after my manner, than speak in your manner and live. For neither in war nor yet at law ought I or any man to use every way of escaping death. Often in battle there can be no doubt that if a man will throw away his arms, and fall on his knees before his pursuers, he may escape death; and in other dangers there are other ways of escaping death, if a man is willing to say and do anything. The difficulty, my friends, is not to avoid death, but to avoid unrighteousness; for that runs faster than death. I am old and move slowly, and the slower runner has overtaken me, and my accusers are keen and quick, and the faster runner, who is unrighteousness, has overtaken them. And now I depart hence condemned by you to suffer the penalty of death, — they too go their ways condemned by the truth to suffer the penalty of villainy and wrong; and I must abide by my award — let them abide by theirs. I suppose that these things may be regarded as fated, — and I think that they are well.

And now, O men who have condemned me, I would fain prophesy to you; for I am about to die, and in the hour of death men are gifted with prophetic power. And I prophesy to you who are my murderers, that immediately after my departure punishment far heavier than you have inflicted on me will surely await you. Me you have killed because you wanted to escape the accuser, and not to give an account of your lives. But that will not be as you suppose; far otherwise. For I say that there will be more accusers of you than there are now; accusers whom hitherto I have restrained: and as they are younger they will be more inconsiderate with you, and you will be more offended at them. If you think by killing men you can prevent someone from censuring your evil lives, you are mistaken; that is not a way of escape which is either possible or honorable; the easiest and the noblest way is not to be disabling others, but to be improving yourselves. This is the prophecy which I utter before my departure to the judges who have condemned me.

Friends, who would have acquitted me, I would like also to talk with you about the thing which has come to pass, while the magistrates are busy, and before I go to the place at which I must die. Stay then a little, for we may as well talk with one another while there is time. You are my friends, and I should like to show you the meaning of this event which has happened to me. O my judges — for you I may truly call judges — I should like to tell you of a wonderful circumstance. Hitherto the divine faculty of which the internal oracle is the source has constantly been in the habit of opposing me even about trifles, if I was going to make a slip or error in any matter; and now as you see there has come upon me that which may be thought, and is generally believed to be, the last and worst evil. But the oracle made no sign of opposition, either when I was leaving my house in the morning, or when I was on my way to the court, or while I was speaking, at anything which I was going to say; and yet I have often been stopped in the middle of a speech, but now in nothing I either said or did touching the matter in hand has the oracle opposed me. What do I take to be the explanation of this silence? I will tell you. It is an intimation that what has happened to me is a good, and that those of us who think that death is an evil are in error. For the customary sign would surely have opposed me had I been going to evil and not to good.

Let us reflect in another way, and we shall see that there is great reason to hope that death is a good; for one of two things — either death is a state of nothingness and utter unconsciousness, or, as men say, there is a change and migration of the soul from this world to another. Now, if you suppose that there is no consciousness, but a sleep like the sleep of him who is undisturbed even by dreams, death will be an unspeakable gain. For if a person were to select the night in which his sleep was undisturbed even by dreams, and were to compare with this the other days and nights of his life, and then were to tell us how many days and nights he had passed in the course of his life better and more pleasantly than this one, I think that any man, I will not say a private man, but even the great king will not find many such days or nights, when compared with the others. Now if death be of such a nature, I say that to die is gain; for eternity is then only a single night. But if death is the journey to another place, and there, as men say, all the dead abide, what good, O my friends and judges, can be greater than this? If indeed when the pilgrim arrives in the world below, he is delivered from the professors of justice in this world, and finds the true judges who are said to give judgment there, Minos and Rhadamanthus and Aeacus and Triptolemus, and other sons of God who were righteous in their own life, that pilgrimage will be worth making. What would not a man give if he might converse with Orpheus and Musaeus and Hesiod and Homer? Nay, if this be true, let me die again and again. I myself, too, shall have a wonderful interest in there meeting and conversing with Palamedes, and Ajax the son of Telamon, and any other ancient hero who has suffered death through an unjust judgment; and there will be no small pleasure, as I think, in comparing my own sufferings with theirs. Above all, I shall then be able to continue my search into true and false knowledge; as in this world, so also in the next; and I shall find out who is wise, and who pretends to be wise, and is not. What would not a man give, O judges, to be able to examine the leader of the great Trojan expedition; or Odysseus or Sisyphus, or numberless others, men and women too! What infinite delight would there be in conversing with them and asking them questions! In another world they do not put a man to death for asking questions: assuredly not. For besides being happier than we are, they will be immortal, if what is said is true.

Wherefore, O judges, be of good cheer about death, and know of a certainty, that no evil can happen to a good man, either in life or after death. He and his are not neglected by the gods; nor has my own approaching end happened by mere chance. But I see clearly that the time had arrived when it was better for me to die and be released from trouble; wherefore the oracle gave no sign. For which reason, also, I am not angry with my condemners, or with my accusers; they have done me no harm, although they did not mean to do me any good; and for this I may gently blame them.

Still I have a favour to ask of them. When my sons are grown up, I would ask you, O my friends, to punish them; and I would have you trouble them, as I have troubled you, if they seem to care about riches, or anything, more than about virtue; or if they pretend to be something when they are really nothing. — then reprove them, as I have reproved you, for not caring about that for which they ought to care, and thinking that they are something when they are really nothing. And if you do this, both I and my sons will have received justice at your hands.

The hour of departure has arrived, and we go our ways — I to die, and you to live. Which is better God only knows.

FRIEDRICH NIETZSCHE

THE PROBLEM OF SOCRATES

1

Concerning life, the wisest men of all ages have judged alike: *it is no good.* Always and everywhere one has heard the same sound from their mouths — a sound full of doubt, full of melancholy, full of weariness of life, full of resistance to life. Even Socrates said, as he died: "To live — that means to be sick a long time: I owe Asclepius the Savior a rooster." Even Socrates was tired of it. What does that evidence? What does it evince? Formerly one would have said (— oh, it has been said, and loud enough, and especially by our pessimists): "At least something of all this must be true! The consensus of the sages evidences the truth." Shall we still talk like that today? *May* we? "At least something must be *sick* here," *we* retort. These wisest men of all ages — they should first be scrutinized closely. Were they all perhaps shaky on their legs? late? tottery? decadents? Could it be that wisdom appears on earth as a raven, inspired by a little whiff of carrion?

2

This irreverent thought that the great sages are *types of decline* first occurred to me precisely in a case where it is most strongly opposed by both scholarly and unscholarly prejudice: I recognized Socrates and Plato to be symptoms of degeneration, tools of the Greek dissolution, pseudo-Greek, anti-Greek (*Birth of Tragedy*, 1872). The consensus of the sages — I comprehended this ever more clearly — proves least of all that they were right in what they agreed on: it shows rather that they themselves, these wisest men, agreed in some *physiological* respect, and hence adopted the same negative attitude to life, *had to* adopt it. Judgments, judgments of value, concerning life, for it or against it, can, in the end, never be true: they have value only as symptoms, they are worthy of consideration only as symptoms; in themselves such judgments are stupidities. One must by all means stretch out one's fingers and make the attempt to grasp this amazing finesse, *that the value of life cannot be estimated*. Not by the living, for they are an interested party, even a bone of contention, and not judges; not by the dead, for a different reason. For a philosopher to see a problem in the value of life is thus an objection to him, a question mark concerning his wisdom, an un-wisdom. Indeed? All these great wise men — they were not only decadents but not wise at all? But I return to the problem of Socrates.

3

In origin, Socrates belonged to the lowest class: Socrates was plebs. We know, we can still see for ourselves, how ugly he was. But ugliness, in itself an objection, is among the Greeks almost a refutation. Was Socrates a Greek at all? Ugliness is often enough the expression of a development that has been crossed, *thwarted* by crossing. Or it appears as *declining* development. The anthropologists among the criminologists tell us that the typical criminal is ugly: *monstrum in fronte, monstrum in animo*. But the criminal is a decadent. Was Socrates a typical criminal? At least that would not be contradicted by the famous judgment of the physiognomist which sounded so offensive to the friends of Socrates. A foreigner who knew about faces once passed through Athens and told Socrates to his face that he *was a monstrum* — that he harbored in himself all the bad vices and appetites. And Socrates merely answered: "You know me, sir!"

4

Socrates' decadence is suggested not only by the admitted wantonness and anarchy of his instincts, but also by the hypertrophy of the logical faculty and that *sarcasm of the rachitic* which distinguishes him. Nor should we forget those auditory hallucinations which, as "the *diamonion* of Socrates," have been interpreted religiously. Everything in him is exaggerated, *buffo*, a caricature; everything is at the same time concealed, ulterior, subterranean. I seek to comprehend what idiosyncrasy begot that Socratic equation of reason, virtue, and happiness: that most bizarre of all equations, which moreover, is opposed to all the instincts of the earlier Greeks.

5

With Socrates, Greek taste changes in favor of dialectics. What really happened there? Above all, a *noble* taste is thus vanquished; with dialectics the plebs come to the top. Before Socrates, dialectic manners were repudiated in good society: they were considered bad manners, they were compromising. The young were warned against them. Furthermore, all such presentations of one's reasons were distrusted. Honest things, like honest men, do not carry their reasons in their hands like that. It is indecent to show all five fingers. What must first be proved is worth little. Wherever authority still forms part of good bearing, where one does not give reasons but commands, the dialectician is a kind of buffoon: one laughs at him, one does not take him seriously. Socrates was the buffoon who *got himself taken seriously:* what really happened there?

6

One chooses dialectic only when one has no other means. One knows that one arouses mistrust with it, that it is not very persuasive. Nothing is easier to erase than a dialectical effect: the experience of every meeting at which there are speeches proves this. It can only be *self-defense* for those who no longer have other weapons. One must have to *enforce* one's right: until one reaches that point, one makes no use of it. The Jews were dialecticians for that reason; Reynard the Fox was one — , and Socrates too?

7

Is the irony of Socrates an expression of revolt? Of plebeian *resentment?* Does he, as one oppressed, enjoy his own ferocity in the knife-thrusts of his syllogisms? Does he *avenge* himself on the noble people whom he fascinates? As a dialectician, one holds a merciless tool in one's hand; one can become a tyrant by means of it; one compromises those one conquers. The dialectician leaves it to his opponent to prove that he is no idiot: he makes one furious and helpless at the same time. The dialectician renders the intellect of his opponent powerless. Indeed? Is dialectic only a form of *revenge* in Socrates?

8

I have given to understand how it was that Socrates could repel: it is therefore all the more necessary to explain his fascination. That he discovered a new kind of *agon*,[4] that he became its first fencing master for the noble circles of Athens, is one point. He fascinated by appealing to the agonistic impulse of the Greeks — he introduced a variation into the wrestling match between young men and youths. Socrates was also a great *erotic*.

9

But Socrates guessed even more. He saw *through* his noble Athenians; he comprehended that his own case, his idiosyncrasy, was no longer exceptional. The same kind of degeneration was quietly developing everywhere: old Athens was coming to an end. And Socrates understood that all the world *needed* him — his means, his cure, his personal artifice of self-preservation. Everywhere the instincts were in anarchy; everywhere one was within five paces of excess: *monstrum in animo* was the general danger. "The impulses want to play the tyrant; one must invent a *counter-tyrant* who is stronger." When the physiognomist had revealed to Socrates who he was — a cave of bad appetites — the great master of irony let slip another word which is the key to his character. "This is true," he said, "but I mastered them all." *How* did Socrates become master over *himself?* His case was, at bottom, merely the extreme case, only the most striking instance of what was then beginning to be a universal distress: no one was any longer master over himself, the instincts turned *against* each other. He fascinated, being this extreme case; his awe-inspiring ugliness proclaimed him as such to all who could see: he fascinated, of course, even more as an answer, a solution, an apparent *cure* of this case.

10

When one finds it necessary to turn *reason* into a tyrant, as Socrates did, the danger cannot be slight that something else will play the tyrant. Rationality was then hit upon as the savior; neither Socrates nor his "patients" had any choice about being rational: it was *de rigeur*, it was their last resort. The fanaticism with which all Greek reflection throws itself upon rationality betrays a desperate situation; there was danger, there was but one choice: either to perish or — to be *absurdly rational*. The moralism of the Greek philosophers from Plato on is pathologically

---

[4]Contest

conditioned; so is their esteem of dialectics. Reason-virtue-happiness, that means merely that one must imitate Socrates and counter the dark appetites with a permanent daylight — the daylight of reason. One must be clever, clear, bright at any price; any concession to the instincts, to the unconscious, leads *downward*.

11

I have given to understand how it was that Socrates fascinated. He seemed to be a physician, a savior. Is it necessary to go on to demonstrate the error in his faith in "rationality at any price"? It is a self-deception on the part of philosophers and moralists if they believe that they are extricating themselves from decadence when they merely wage war against it. Extrication lies beyond their strength: what they choose as a means, as salvation, is itself but another expression of decadence; they change its expression, but they do not get rid of decadence itself. Socrates was a misunderstanding; *the whole improvement-morality, including Christian, was a misunderstanding.* The most blinding daylight; rationality at any price; life, bright, cold, cautious, conscious, without instinct, in opposition to the instincts — all this too was a mere disease, another disease, and by no means a return to "virtue," to "health," to happiness. To *have* to fight the instincts — that is the formula of decadence: as long as life is *ascending*, happiness equals instinct.

12

Did he himself still comprehend this, this most brilliant of all self-outwitters? Was this what he said to himself in the end, in the *wisdom* of his courage to die? Socrates *wanted* to die: not Athens, but he himself chose the hemlock; he forced Athens to sentence him. "Socrates is no physician," he said softly to himself; "here death alone is the physician. Socrates himself has merely been sick a long time."

WALKER PERCY (1916-1990)

A Christian existentialist philosopher and novelist, Walker Percy was trained as a medical doctor. He gave up the practice of medicine after a long bout with tuberculosis. He turned his attention to the philosophy of language and the spiritual quest for meaning in the modern world. In his most important nonfiction work, The Message in the Bottle: How Queer Man Is, How Queer Language Is, and What One Has to Do with the Other *(1983), Percy collected essays written between 1954 and 1975, including "The Mystery of Language."*

THE MYSTERY OF LANGUAGE

Language is an extremely mysterious phenomenon. By mysterious I do not mean that the events which take place in the brain during an exchange of language are complex and little understood — although this is true too. I mean, rather, that language, which at first sight appears to be the most familiar sort of occurrence, an occurrence which takes its place along with other occurrences in the world — billiard balls hitting other billiard balls, barkings of dogs, cryings of babies, sunrises, and rainfalls — is in reality utterly different from these events. The importance of a study of language, as opposed to a scientific study of a space-time event like a solar eclipse or rat behavior, is that as soon as one scratches the surface of the familiar and comes face to face with the nature of language, one also finds himself face to face with the nature of man.

If you were to ask the average educated American or Englishman or Pole, or anyone else acquainted with the scientific temper of the last two hundred years, what he conceived the nature of language to be, he would probably reply in more or less the following way:

When I speak a word or sentence and you understand me, I utter a series of peculiar little sounds by which I hope to convey to you the meaning I have in mind. The sounds leave my mouth and travel through the air as waves. The waves strike the tympanic membrane of your outer ear and the motion of the membrane is carried to the inner ear, where it is transformed into electrical impulses in the auditory nerve. This nerve impulse is transmitted to your brain, where a very complex series of events takes place, the upshot of which is that you "understand" the words; that is, you either respond to the words in the way I had hoped you would or the words arouse in you the same idea or expectation or fear I had in mind. Your understanding of my sounds depends upon your having heard them before, upon a common language. As a result of your having heard the word *ball* in association with the thing ball, there has occurred a change in your brain of such a character that when I say *ball* you understand me to mean ball.

This explanation of language is not, of course, entirely acceptable to a linguist or a psychologist. But it is the sort of explanation one would give to a question of this kind. It is the sort of explanation to be found in the *Book of Knowledge* and in a college psychology textbook. It may be less technical or a great deal more technical — no doubt modern philosophers of meaning would prefer the term *response* to *idea* in speaking of your understanding of my words — but, technical or not, we agree in general that something of the kind takes place. The essence of the process is a series of events in space-time: muscular events in the mouth, wave events in the air, electro-colloidal events in the nerve and brain.

The trouble is that this explanation misses the essential character of language. It is not merely an oversimplified explanation; it is not merely an incomplete or one-sided explanation. It has nothing at all to do with language considered as language.

What I wish to call attention to is not a new discovery, a new piece of research in psycholinguistics which revolutionizes our concept of language as the Michelson-Morley experiment revolutionized modern physics. It is rather the extraordinary sort of thing language is, which our theoretical view of the world completely obscures. This extraordinary character of language does not depend for its unveiling upon a piece of research but is there under our noses for all to see. The difficulty is that it is under our noses; it is too close and too familiar. Language, symbolization, is the stuff of which our knowledge and awareness of the world are made, the medium through which we see the world. Trying to see it is like trying to see the mirror by which we see everything else.

There is another difficulty. It is the fact that language cannot be explained in the ordinary terminology of explanations. The terminology of explanations is the native attitude of the modern mind toward that which it does not understand — and is its most admirable trait. That attitude is briefly this: Here is a phenomenon . . . how does it work? The answer is given as a series of space-time events. This is how C works; you see, this state of affairs A leads to this state of affairs B, and B leads to C. This attitude goes a long way toward an understanding of billiards, of cellular growth, of anthills and sunrises. But it cannot get hold of language.

All of the space-time events mentioned in connection with the production of speech do occur, and without them there would be no language. But language is something else besides these events. This does not mean that language cannot be understood but that we must use another frame of reference and another terminology. If one studies man at a so-to-speak sublanguage level, one studies him as one studies anything else, as a phenomenon which is susceptible of explanatory hypothesis. A psychologist timing human responses moves about in the same familiar world of observer and data-to-be-explained as the physiologist and the physicist. But as soon as one deals with language not as a sequence of stimuli and responses, not as a science of phonetics or comparative linguistics, but as the sort of thing language is, one finds himself immediately in uncharted territory.

The usual version of the nature of language, then, turns upon the assumption that human language is a marvelous development of a type of behavior found in lower animals. As Darwin expressed it, man is not the only animal that can use language to express what is passing in his mind: "The *Cebus azarae* monkey in Paraguay utters at least six distinct sounds which excite in other monkeys similar emotions." More recent investigations have shown that bees are capable of an extraordinary dance language by which they can communicate not only direction but distance.

This assumption is of course entirely reasonable. When we study the human ear or eye or brain we study it as a development in continuity with subhuman ears and eyes and brains. What other method is available to us? But it is here that the radical difference between the sort of thing that language is and the sort of thing that the transactions upon the billiard table are manifests itself to throw us into confusion. This method of finding our way to the nature of language, this assumption, does not work. It not only does not work; it ignores the central feature of human language.

The oversight and the inability to correct it have plagued philosophers of language for the past fifty years. To get to the heart of the difficulty we must first understand the difference between a sign and a symbol.

A sign is something that directs our attention to something else. If you or I or a dog or a cicada hears a clap of thunder, we will expect rain and seek cover. It will be seen at once that this sort of sign behavior fits in very well with the explanatory attitude mentioned above. The behavior of a man or animal responding to a natural sign (thunder) or an artificial sign (Pavlov's buzzer) can be explained readily as a series of space-time events takes place because of changes in the brain brought about by past association.

But what is a symbol? A symbol does not direct our attention to something else, as a sign does. It does not direct at all. It "means" something else. It somehow comes to contain within itself the thing it means. The word *ball* is a sign to my dog and a symbol to you. If I say *ball* to my dog, he will respond like a good Pavlovian organism and look under the sofa and fetch it. But if I say *ball* to you, you will simply look at me and, if you are patient, finally say. "What about it?" The dog responds to the word by looking for the thing; you conceive the ball through the word *ball*.

Now we can, if we like, say that the symbol is a kind of sign, and that when I say the word *ball*, the sound strikes your ear drum, arrives in your brain, and then calls out the idea of a ball. Modern semioticists do, in fact, try to explain a symbol as a kind of sign. But this doesn't work. As Susanne Langer has observed, this leaves out something, and this something is the most important thing of all.

The thing that is left out is the relation of denotation. The word *names* something. The symbol symbolizes something. Symbolization is qualitatively different from sign behavior; the thing that distinguishes man is his ability to symbolize his experience rather than simply respond to it. The word *ball* does all the things the psychologist says it does, makes its well-known journey from tongue to brain. But it does something else too: it names the thing.

So far we have covered ground which has been covered much more adequately by Susanne Langer and the great German philosopher of the symbol, Ernst Cassirer. The question I wish to raise here is this: What are we to make of this peculiar act of naming? If we can't construe it in terms of space-time events, as we construe other phenomena — solar eclipses, gland secretion, growth — then how can we construe it?

The longer we think about it, the more mysterious the simplest act of naming becomes. It is, we begin to realize, quite without precedent in all of natural history as we know it. But so, you might reply, is the emergence of the eye without precedent, so is sexual reproduction without precedent. These are nevertheless the same kinds of events which have gone before. We can to a degree understand biological phenomena in the same terms in which we understand physical phenomena, as a series of events and energy exchanges, with each event arising from and being conditioned by a previous event. This is not to say that biology can be reduced to physical terms but only that we can make a good deal of sense of it as a series of events and energy exchanges.

But naming is *generically* different. It stands apart from everything else that we know about the universe. The collision of two galaxies and the salivation of Pavlov's dog, different as they are,

are far more alike than either is like the simplest act of naming. Naming stands at a far greater distance from Pavlov's dog than the latter does from a galactic collision.

Just what is the act of denotation? What took place when the first man uttered a mouthy little sound and the second man understood it, not as a sign to be responded to, but as "meaning" something they beheld in common? The first creature who did this is almost by minimal empirical definition the first man. What happened is of all things on earth the one thing we should know best. It is the one thing we do most; it is the warp and woof of the fabric of our consciousness. And yet it is extremely difficult to look *at* instead of through and even more difficult to express once it is grasped.

Naming is unique in natural history because for the first time a being in the universe stands apart from the universe and affirms some other being to be what it is. In this act, for the first time in the history of the universe, "is" is spoken. What does this mean? If something important has happened, why can't we talk about it as we talk about everything else, in the familiar language of space-time events?

The trouble is that we are face to face with a phenomenon which we can't express by our ordinary phenomenal language. Yet we are obliged to deal with it; it happens, and we cannot dismiss it as a "semantical relation." We sense, moreover, that this phenomenon has the most radical consequences for our thinking about man. To refuse to deal with it because it is troublesome would be fatal. It is as if an astronomer developed a theory of planetary motion and said that his theory holds true of planets A, B, C, and D but that planet E is an exception. It makes zigzags instead of ellipses. Planet E is a scandal to good astronomy; therefore we disqualify planet E as failing to live up to the best standards of bodies in motion.

This is roughly the attitude of some modern semanticists and semioticists toward the act of naming. If the relation of symbol to thing symbolized be considered as anything other than a sign calling forth a response, then this relation is "wrong." Say whatever you like about a pencil, Korzybski used to say, but never say it is a pencil. The word is not the thing, said Chase; you can't eat the word *oyster*. According to some semanticists, the advent of symbolization is a major calamity in the history of the human race. Their predicament is not without its comic aspects. Here are scientists occupied with a subject matter of which they, the scientists, disapprove. For the sad fact is that we shall continue to say "This is a pencil" rather than "This object I shall refer to in the future by the sound *pencil*."

By the semanticists' own testimony we are face to face with extraordinary phenomenon — even though it be "wrong." But if, instead of deploring this act of naming as a calamity, we try to see it for what it is, what can we discover?

When I name an unknown thing or hear the name from you, a remarkable thing happens. In some sense or other, the thing is said to "be" its name or symbol. The semanticists are right: this round thing is certainly not the word *ball*. Yet unless it becomes, in some sense or other, the word *ball* in our consciousness, we will never know the ball! Cassirer's thesis was that everything we know we know through symbolic media, whether words, pictures, formulae, or theories. As Mrs. Langer put it, symbols are the vehicles of meaning.

The transformation of word into thing in our consciousness can be seen in the phenomenon of false onomatopoeia. The words *limber, flat, furry, fuzzy, round, yellow, sharp* sound like the things they signify, not because the actual sounds resemble the thing or quality, but because the sound has been transformed in our consciousness to "become" the thing signified. If you don't believe this, try repeating one of these words several dozen times: All at once it will lose its magic guise as symbol and become the poor drab vocable it really is.

This modern notion of the symbolic character of our awareness turns out to have a very old history, however. The Scholastics, who incidentally had a far more adequate theory of symbolic meaning in some respects than modern semioticists, used to say that man does not have a direct knowledge of essences as do the angels but only an indirect knowledge, a knowledge mediated by symbols. John of St. Thomas observed that symbols come to contain within themselves the thing symbolized *in alio esse*, in another mode of existence.

But what has this symbolic process got to do with the "is" I mentioned earlier, with the unprecedented affirmation of existence? We know that the little copula "is" is a very late comer in the evolution of languages. Many languages contain no form of the verb "to be." Certainly the most primitive sentence, a pointing at a particular thing and a naming, does not contain the copula. Nevertheless it is a *pairing*, an opposing of word and thing, an act the very essence of which is an "is-saying," all affirming of the thing to be what it is for both of us.

Once we have grasped the nature of symbolization, we may begin to see its significance for our view of man's place in the world. I am assuming that we share, to begin with, an empirical realistic view of the world, that we believe that there are such things as rocks, planets, trees, dogs, which can be at least partially known and partially explained by science, and that man takes his place somewhere in the scheme. The faculty of language, however, confers upon man a very peculiar position in this scheme — and not at all the position we establish in viewing him as a "higher organism."

The significance of language may be approached in the following way. In our ordinary theoretical view of the world, we see it as a process, a dynamic succession of energy states. There are subatomic particles and atoms and molecules in motion; there are gaseous bodies expanding or contracting; there are inorganic elements in chemical interaction; there are organisms in contact with an environment, responding and adapting accordingly; there are animals responding to each other by means of sign behavior.

This state of affairs we may think of as a number of terms in interaction, each with all the others. Each being is in the world, acting upon the world and itself being acted upon by the world.

But when a man appears and names a thing, when he says this is water and water is cool, something unprecedented takes place. What the third term, man, does is not merely enter into interaction with the others — though he does this too — but stand apart from two of the terms and say that one "is" the other. The two things which he pairs or identifies are the *word* he speaks or hears and the *thing* he sees before him.

This is not only an unprecedented happening; it is also, as the semanticists have noted, scandalous. A is clearly not B. But were it not for this cosmic blunder, man would not be man; he would never be capable of folly and he would never be capable of truth. Unless he says that A is B, he will never know A or B; he will only respond to them. A bee is not as foolish as man, but it also cannot tell the truth. All it can do is respond to its environment.

What are the consequences for our thinking about man? There are a great many consequences, epistemological, existential, religious, psychiatric. There is space here to mention only one, the effect it has on our *minimal* concept of man. I do not mean our concept of his origin and his destiny, which is, of course, the province of religion. I mean, rather, our working concept, as our minimal working concept of water is a compound of hydrogen and oxygen.

An awareness of the nature of language must have the greatest possible consequences for our minimal concept of man. For one thing it must reveal the ordinary secular concept of man held in the West as not merely inadequate but quite simply mistaken. I do not refer to the Christian idea of man as a composite of body and soul, a belief which is professed by some and given lip service by many but which can hardly be said to be a working assumption of secular learning. We see man — when I say we, I mean 95 per cent of those who attend American high schools and universities — as the highest of the organisms: He stands erect, he apposes thumb and forefinger, his language is far more complex than that of the most advanced *Cebus azarae*. But the difference is quantitative, not qualitative. Man is a higher organism, standing in direct continuity with rocks, soil, fungi, protozoa, and mammals.

This happens not to be true, however, and in a way it is unfortunate. I say unfortunate because it means the shattering of the old dream of the Enlightenment — that an objective-explanatory-causal science can discover and set forth all the knowledge of which man is capable. The dream is drawing to a close. The existentialists have taught us that what man is cannot be grasped by the sciences of man. The case is rather that man's science is one of the things that man does, a mode of existence. Another mode is speech. Man is not merely a higher organism responding to and controlling his environment. He is, in Heidegger's words, that being in the world whose calling it is to find a name for Being, to give testimony to it, and to provide for it a clearing.

MICHAEL MURPHY; PRESIDENT, ESALEN INSTITUTE
JOHN BRODIE; QUARTERBACK, SAN FRANCISCO 49ERS

I EXPERIENCED A KIND OF CLARITY

Murphy: There are hundreds of thousands, maybe millions of words written about football. There is a huge amount of talent assembled to describe the game on TV and radio and in sports magazines and newspapers. Supposedly, the best sportswriters are analyzing what the game means. Recently, there has been an abrasive and "realistic" approach like Howard Cosell's or in books like Jim Bouton's *Ball Four*. But it seems to me, from my seat on the five-yard line, that there is a lot to the game that has not been described by all these talented sportswriters and analysts. All of these people are missing something.

Brodie: Many fans feel the way you do. A great many football players do. I certainly do. There is a side to the game that really hasn't been described yet — that "hidden" side of sport you talk about in your book, things having to do with the psychological side of the game, with what we might call "energy flows," and the extraordinary states of mind performing athletes sometimes get into. I've been reluctant to talk to sportswriters about these things because I'm afraid they would reduce them to categories they were more familiar with.

Murphy: What are these writers and analysts looking at when they describe football?

Brodie: People tend to look at life — and at sport — through their own experience and mental categories. When a person looks at a game of football, he tends to see a reflection of his own life. If it's mainly violence and getting ahead and winning at all costs, he'll tend to see that in the game. Or if life is mainly statistics and numbers and measurements, he'll tend to see that — many people have an incredible interest in football statistics. People look at the game and project their own reality onto it.

Murphy: You could say that the two images that dominate our understanding of football now are the Beast and the Computer.

Brodie: But many of the players — most of the ones I know — resent those images. They know there is more to the game than that. And I think there are many fans who see past those images and get glimpses of something more.

Murphy: Can you give me some examples of the aspects that usually go unrecorded, some examples of the game's psychological side or what you call "energy flows"?

Brodie: Often, in the heat and excitement of a game, a player's perception and coordination will improve dramatically. At times, and with increasing frequency now, I experience a kind of clarity that I've never seen adequately described in a football story. Sometimes, for example, time seems to slow way down, in an uncanny way, as if everyone were moving in slow motion. It seems as if I have all the time in the world to watch the receivers run their patterns, and yet I know the defensive line is coming at me just as fast as ever. I know perfectly well how hard and fast those guys are coming and yet the whole thing seems like a movie or a dance in slow motion. It's beautiful.

Murphy: What happens to your performance in moments like that? Do you actually see what's happening more clearly?

Brodie: Yes. Of course, some of the players on the other team may be in a similar state! Then the game moves up a level.

Murphy: Are these things contagious? Sometimes it looks as if a whole team catches fire and starts doing things it couldn't do ordinarily. In the Washington Redskins game last year, something seemed to happen to the 49ers in the third quarter after you threw that touchdown pass to Gene Washington.

Brodie: We had to make something happen then. That's why I went with that play. With third down and one yard to go on your own 22-yard line in a close game — and a play-off game, which leaves you with no second chances — you wouldn't usually go with the particular call I made. After I came to the line of scrimmage and started my snap count, I saw the defense shift into a position that might not happen in the game again. I gave the team a basic pass audible and gave Gene a little signal we had worked out, faded back and threw him that pass. When I threw it I knew it was going to connect.

Murphy: When the play began it looked for a moment like the safety would make an interception. But then it seemed as if the ball went through or over his hands as he came in front of Washington.

Brodie: Pat Fischer, the cornerback, told the reporters after the game that the ball seemed to jump right over his hands as he went for it. When we studied the game films that week, it did look as if the ball kind of jumped over his hands into Gene's. Some of the guys said it was the wind — and maybe it was.

Murphy: What do you mean by maybe?

Brodie: What I mean is that our sense of that pass was so clear and our intentions so strong that the ball was bound to get there, come wind, cornerbacks, hell or high water.

Murphy: In "Golf in the Kingdom" I discuss the "energy streamers" that a golf ball rides on its way toward the hole. I mean those lines of force that seem to emanate from the golfer when he can visualize and execute his shot in a moment of high clarity. Is that the kind of thing you are talking about? I know there are golfers who have had the experience.

Brodie: I would have to say that such things seem to exist — or emerge when your state of mind is right. It has happened to me dozens of times. An intention carries a force, a thought is connected with an energy that can stretch itself out in a pass play or a golf shot or a base hit or during a 30-foot jump shot in basketball. I've seen it happen too many times to deny it.

Murphy: Is this something you can practice or develop? Can you learn to develop clarity during a game? Can you strengthen your intentions?

Brodie: Yes. Pressures that used to get me down don't affect me to the same extent now. I've learned to shed certain destructive attitudes when a game is under way. A player's effectiveness is directly related to his ability to be right there, doing that thing, in the moment. All the preparation he may have put into the game — all the game plans, analysis of movies, etc. — is no good if he can't put it into action when game time comes. He can't be worrying about the past or the future or the crowd or some other extraneous event. He must be able to respond in the here and now. This is an ability we all have potentially. I believe it is our natural state. But because most of us lose it as we grow up, we have to regain it.

Murphy: This sounds very much like Zen or other spiritual disciplines. It seems to me that in many ways sport is like a Western Yoga. I have heard mountain climbers, surfers, sky divers and skiers who talk a language that is almost mystical, and now I hear you talking the same way.

Brodie: Call it mystical if you like. For me it is simply one of the elementary facts of experience. Here-and-now awareness, clarity, strong intention, a person's "tone level" — these are things a lot of people who don't know anything about Yoga or mysticism talk about. The trouble is, people don't make them operative in their life as often as they could.

Murphy: But some of the things you seem to suggest, like a ball jumping over a defender's hands or time slowing down, go beyond ordinary experience. In the East, and in our Western religious traditions, there have been disciplines to develop these extraordinary powers and states of mind. But the modern Western world, for the most part, is lacking in such disciplines. They seem esoteric and alien to most of us. Maybe that is one of the reasons sportswriters and sports commentators find it difficult to comprehend the kinds of things you are talking about.

Brodie: Not only reporters find it difficult, but oftentimes coaches do too. If a player begins to develop methods for tuning in to these deeper levels, many coaches are likely to criticize or disregard them. A player often has to be big enough to transcend his coach's limitations. But then a coach has to deal with the team's owners and even with the fans and the media to some extent. The whole system works to build up certain attitudes about the way in which a team should be run. Take the computer for example: the way some teams worship it in the selection of players and the creation of their game plans, you would think it was God. But computer-made game plans often lead a team away from the game itself. A team with a fixed game plan can be a brittle team, if it can't relate to the here and now of a game. The computer can be a helpful tool, as long as you don't expect too much from it. The same thing is true for certain programs of physical exercise: exceptions have to be made for the experienced athlete who has discovered training methods suited to his own makeup. A good coach will let him use those methods, even if they deviate from the fixed procedures the coaching staff has set up.

Murphy: One of the problems coaches and players have — and it's a problem all of us have in talking about these things — is that our language about unusual powers and states of mind is so limited. We don't have commonly understood words to describe "energy flows" or what you call "being clear." These expressions don't make sense to a lot of people. I think the time has come to begin creating a language and an understanding about these dimensions of life.

Brodie: Athletics could be a place where this kind of insight is developed. Sport is one of the few activities in which many Americans spend a great deal of time developing their potentialities. It influences character, I think, as much as our schools and churches do. But, even so, it falls far below what it could be. It leaves out so much. I would love to see a sports team developed with a more fulfilling purpose.

One place in which you see the principle of self-knowledge work most clearly is with injuries. Two years ago I had a problem with my arm; I couldn't lift it above my shoulder — which is not good for a quarterback. Dealing with that sore arm led me into a process of self-discovery. Getting well meant more than getting the soreness out of my shoulder. I found out that my arm's condition was related to a very limited notion I had about myself and life. It wasn't enough anymore to simply play a better game of football. I had to change the way I perceived the world, the way I thought and felt, and the way I treated others. Life was a larger and more interesting affair than I had ever dreamed.

Murphy: Why do you still play football? Sixteen years is a long time.

Brodie: I play because I enjoy the game. After 16 years there is still an enormous satisfaction in it.

Murphy: And yet so many people see football only in terms of winning at any cost, knocking the hell out of the other guy. Is that the only reason you enjoy the game?

Brodie: No. It's important to win — there's nothing quite like it. It's important to go all out during a game. But there is a lot more to football than that. Involving yourself wholeheartedly, in the way we have been discussing, is a satisfaction in itself.

Murphy: I get the idea that you and Gene Washington have a special kind of communication when a game is under way. Can you say anything about that?

Brodie: Well, we room together, and we are good friends. We've worked out a series of signals that can change even after I've begun my snap count. But most of all, I guess, is that we read each other so well. He knows where I want him to be on a given pass play. Sometimes he will run a set pattern, but at other times he has to get to a place in the field any way he can.

Murphy: Could that place be marked with a set of coordinates, say at a particular yard line? Or is it better to say that you meet somewhere in the field of existence, in the field of your relationship, amidst all the flux on the playing field?

Brodie: I think the more poetic way says it better — it's a highly intuitive thing. Sometimes we call a pass for a particular spot on the field, maybe to get a first down. But at other times it's less defined than that and depends upon the communication we have. Sometimes I let the ball fly before Gene has made his final move, without a pass route being set exactly. That's where the intuition and communication come in. But then we don't know what the other team, what those cornerbacks and safety men, might do next. That's part of the fun of the game, not knowing what they are going to do. The game never stops. You can never really take anything for granted — at least in most games in the NFL. And that's what's wrong with game plans so often — because you don't know where those guys are going to be a second before something happens. You have to be ready for the sudden glimmer.

Murphy: Do you ever get the idea after one of those incredible pass completions that there was some destiny to the play, something more than skill involved? To me, as a slightly lunatic fan, there are times when it seems as if the script for a game has been written by God himself — or that it springs from someplace in the collective unconscious.

Brodie: I know the feeling, but I don't know that we should call that kind of explanation an objective fact.

Murphy: But isn't there a kind of communication, a kind of artistry, a kind of Being, if you will, that emerges during an inspired game? Something that isn't measured by grids or coordinates or statistics? Doesn't bringing forth this kind of quality depend upon something that one is not ordinarily aware of?

Brodie: Yes, that's a good way to say it. I was reading a statement by Alan Page (defensive tackle for the Minnesota Vikings, the NFL's most valuable player for 1971) the other day in which he described the comedown when a game is over. He said it was a weird feeling adjusting back to reality, to sanity — having to be a person again. I understand that feeling. Life can feel like a box after a game. You can get into another order of reality when you're playing, a reality that doesn't fit into the grids and coordinates that most people lay across life — including the categories coaches, fans and sportswriters lay on the game.

Murphy: When you are in a state like that you must be tuned in to an incredible number of energies and patterns, to all those players on both teams, to the crowd. In fact, when you begin your first offensive sequence, you seem to be deliberately tuning in to all of this. I sometimes get the sense that you are probing the situation before you work out your plan of attack. Are those opening minutes a time when you are learning what a game is going to be like?

Brodie: Yes, we are tuning into the situation. And centering ourselves, dropping the nervousness, getting the feel of the game. We may have to drop useless emotional buildup and other distractions.

Murphy: So you are saying you have to be both focused and sensitive. An effective quarterback has to have his radar working.

Brodie: I equate creativity with awareness. It's a matter of simple knowledge. The more I know, the more I can do.

Murphy: But knowing like this is more than the kind of knowing we are supposed to learn in school, more than verbal knowing or book knowing. It involves a tuning in to subtle energies and feelings and forces we can only come to through direct awareness. It involves the emotions and the spirit as well as the intellect — and the here and now, the complexities and subtleties of a given situation rather than preconceptions about it, or your rehearsals of it or what has been written in a book about it. It seems to me that this sort of knowing leads to a new kind of being.

Brodie: You might say that. Football players and athletes generally get into this kind of being or beingness — call it what you will — more often than is generally recognized. But they often lose it after a game or after a season is over. They often don't have a workable philosophy or understanding to support the kind of thing they get into while they are playing. They don't have the words for it. So after a game you see some of them coming down, making fools of themselves sometimes, coming way down in their tone level. But during the game they come way up. A missing ingredient for many people, I guess, is that they don't have a supporting philosophy or discipline for a better life.

Murphy: After hearing you talk I gather that top athletes are people who are accustomed to altering time, who are accustomed to a higher state of focus and concentration, who are accustomed to altered perceptions of many types and to going with the inner flow of things. But I don't see any of this on the sport pages. Or in the sport books you hear about, or on the radio and TV programs. Our culture seems to screen it all out, even though such experience is at the very heart of a game so many of us love.

Brodie: That's right. It's a case of experience being ahead of what we can say about it. Maybe if we could talk about it more clearly we could make it happen more. Sport is so important in creating values in America, it would be great if it could open up these inner dimensions for people. It's really what many coaches and players want to do, after all. They want sport to be more than winning at any cost, more than beating people up and making money and getting ahead over somebody else's dead body. But we have got to break out of this conspiracy to belittle sport and human nature.

Murphy: Some critics of the game would say that its violence destroys the very things you hope for.

Brodie: Violence is not the game's basic intention, even though some people think it is. The idea is not to hurt or damage somebody. But there is an intensity and a danger in football — as in life generally — which keep us alive and awake. It is a test of our awareness and ability. Like so much of life, it presents us with the choice of responding either with fear or with action and clarity.

Murphy: I have heard some people say that all of this talk about "higher possibilities" and building character is fine, but that you don't need football to do it, that the game is a poor instrument in fact for accomplishing these things.

Brodie: But that wouldn't stop us from playing or enjoying football. It is better to improve the game, I think, than to indulge in a lot of idle criticism of it. And when you look at its history you see that it has already gone through enormous changes. It is a much different game than it was in the 1920's and 30's. It's a more complex and artistic game now, with all the offensive and defensive plays, with the game plans and the variety of skills involved. Why shouldn't the game go on changing? I see no reason why we should fix the game of football where it is, after the change it has gone through already. Why shouldn't it be a place to develop the mental and spiritual dimensions we have been talking about?

III.

ART AND NATURE

The Survivor (linocut) by Elizabeth Catlett.
Reprinted by Permission of by Elizabeth Catlett.

INTRODUCTION

Art. The Arts. The *Beaux* Arts, the Fine Arts, the Liberal Arts. By definition we mean something that is the work of man and not of nature. Or at least Aristotle thought so. He defined art as something made through the power of reason; and, although art involves imagination and thought, its aim is to produce *some thing*. In the myth of Prometheus, the elevation of mankind from brute to civilized existence happens when mortals acquire useful arts as a means of controlling nature and planning for the future.

The relationship between Art and Nature is explored both by Plato and by Aristotle. In his *Laws*, Plato argues that the creations of man are a higher order than the "creations" of nature precisely because art involves human beings in a struggle between spirit (the soul) and matter (nature). Focusing on the activity of what we call the arts, Aristotle in his *Poetics* defines the artist as an imitator of nature or reality. So that even a dancer "by the rhythms of his attitudes, may represent men's characters, as well as what they do and suffer." He goes on to suggest a connection between the arts and the nature of man:

> Imitation is natural to man from childhood ... (he) learns first from imitation. And it is also natural for all to delight in works of imitation.

Perhaps the word *imitation* suggests something artificial to us. Perhaps we should use the word *empathy* instead: to feel something another human being feels; then to express the feeling through some medium; finally, to *communicate* the feeling so that the bonds of friendship and common purpose are strengthened.

Our own emphasis on *expression* in the 20th century has demanded absolute freedom for the artist from any restraints — by government, by style or traditional forms, by medium, or by the moral feelings of a community. Without restraints, with absolute freedom, can art have purpose? Can it communicate? Can it provide common ground?

Each artistic medium seems to demand a struggle between freedom and form, between spontaneity and discipline, between intuition and reason. Even a definition of music as broad as this, "music is patterned sound," involves form and limits as well as the freedom to improvise. Just as sculpture requires a space, so music requires silence. Just as a violin can create a large range of hi/lo vibrations that we call pitch, so a brushstroke on a canvas can create shadows and light. Just as the rhythms of an epic poem can evoke the beats and accents of primitive life, so with a few pencil lines Picasso can make us feel the movement, the vitality of modern life. As the melody of *La Marseillaise* can draw people together in ideals of liberty, equality, and fraternity, so the colors of Van Gogh's *Starry Night* express his intense individuality and forlornness.

The tension between freedom and form is essential to the creative process. For me, as a teacher and writer, words and language are my medium. They are the means to communication, to connecting the self to the outside world. How that world responds to "my" words contributes to the development of my self. That is, the creative process involves all of us. There is the craft (e.g., music, painting, teaching), there is the performer (musician, painter, teacher), and there is the audience (concert audience, art gallery crowd, class of students). Each craft has its own medium; each performer manipulates the elements of her craft in her way; and each audience brings individual life experiences to a creative process.

The common thread of that creative process is tension: tension between self and audience, between the craftsman and the community. The tension is necessary both for self and for the community. That's how we grow. Aristotle was right. The good life means harmony and balance. But we have lost the concrete, common sense origins of the metaphor — a balance scale. It is the symbol of justice, a metaphor for justice, precisely because a scale (or pendulum) sometimes moves to the right and sometimes to the left. But it moves. When things are out of balance *too much* there is NO TENSION, there is *no* movement; indeed, less movement than when things are

David, by Michelangelo Buonarroti.
Marble, in Florence, Italy.

Notre Dame Cathedral in Paris on the Isle of St. Louis.
Copyright by Publishers Photo Service

perfectly balanced. Since perfect balance is an ideal, we can only strive for it; in the process of this struggle we create *movement*. The more the scales are tipped in one extreme or the other, the less tension there is, the less life there is.

Have we resolved the relationship between nature and art? The tension between the two is based on the Promethean assumption: human life is best when it is the result of human intention, will, and reason. So according to this assumption, the artist's greatness lies in his ability to conceptualize, to plan, and finally to impose form on nature. Where, then, is the beauty and the mystery of creativity? Perhaps, suggests Milan Kundera in *The Unbearable Lightness of Being*, beauty (like love) happens by "mistake." So, he argues, the "beauty" of New York City is "unintentional"; it is a city "much richer and more varied than the excessively strict and composed beauty of human design" found in European cities. Is this overly romantic? No. It is a return to Plato's argument, but reversing it. Kundera argues for the primacy of Nature, of the Accidental Moment, of the Spontaneous and Fortuitous in our lives.

I hope that among the poems that follow, the reader will find one or two, unintentionally, somehow beautiful.

PLATO

ART AND NATURE (BOOK X, LAWS)

Ath.:	Athenian Stranger
Cle.:	Cleinas, a Cretan
Meg.:	Megillus, a Lacedaemonian

Ath. They say that the greatest and fairest things are the work of nature and of chance, the lesser of art, which, receiving from nature the greater and primeval creations, moulds and fashions all those lesser works which are generally termed artificial.

Cle. How is that?

Ath. I will explain my meaning still more clearly. They say that fire and water, and earth and air, all exist by nature and chance, and none of them by art, and that as to the bodies which come next in order — earth, and sun, and moon, and stars — they have been created by means of these absolutely inanimate existences. The elements are severally moved by chance and some inherent force according to certain affinities among them — of hot with cold, or of dry with moist, or of soft with hard, and according to all the other accidental admixtures of opposites which have been formed by necessity. After this fashion and in this manner the whole heaven has been created, and all that is in the heaven, as well as animals and all plants, and all the seasons come from these elements, not by the action of mind, as they say, or of any God, or from art, but as I was saying, by nature and chance only. Art sprang up afterwards and out of these, mortal and of mortal birth, and produced in play certain images and very partial imitations of the truth, having an affinity to one another, such as music and painting create and their companion arts. And there are other arts which have a serious purpose, and these cooperate with nature, such, for example, as medicine, and husbandry, and gymnastic. And they say that politics cooperate with nature, but in a less degree, and have more of art; also that legislation is entirely a work of art, and is based on assumptions which are not true.

Cle. How do you mean?

Ath. In the first place, my dear friend, these people would say that the Gods exist not by nature, but by art, and by the laws of states, which are different in different places, according to the agreement of those who make them; and that the honourable is one thing by nature and another thing by law, and that the principles of justice have no existence at all in nature, but that mankind are always disputing about them and altering them; and that the alterations which are made by art and by law have no basis in nature. but are of authority for the moment and at the time at which they are made — These, my friends, are the sayings of wise men, poets and prose writers, which find a way into the minds of youth. They are told by them that the highest right is might, and in this way the young fall into impieties, under the idea that the Gods are not such as the law bids them imagine; and hence arise factions, these philosophers inviting them to lead a true life according to nature, that is, to live in real dominion over others, and not in legal subjection to them.[1]

Cle. What a dreadful picture, Stranger, have you given, and how great is the injury which is thus inflicted on young men to the ruin both of states and families!

Ath. True, Cleinias; but then what should the lawgiver do when this evil is of long standing? Should he only rise up in the state and threaten all mankind, proclaiming that if they will not say and think that the Gods are such as the law ordains (and this may be extended generally to the honourable, the just, and to all the highest things, and to all that relates to virtue and vice), and if they will not make their actions conform to the copy which the law gives them, then he who refuses to obey the law shall die, or suffer stripes and bonds, or privation of citizenship, or in some cases be punished by loss of property and exile? Should he not rather, when he is making laws for men, at the same time infuse the spirit of persuasion into his words, and mitigate the severity of them as far as he can?

Cle. Why, Stranger, if such persuasion be at all possible, then a legislator who has anything in him ought never to weary of persuading men; he ought to leave nothing unsaid in support of the ancient opinion that there are Gods, and of all those other truths which you were just now mentioning; he ought to support the law and also art, and acknowledge that both alike exist by nature, and no less than nature, they are the creations of mind in accordance with right reason, as you appear to me to maintain, and I am disposed to agree with you in thinking.

Ath. Yes, my enthusiastic Cleinias; but are not these things when spoken to a multitude hard to be understood, not to mention that they take up a dismal length of time?

Cle. Why, Stranger, shall we, whose patience failed not when drinking or music were the themes of discourse, weary now of discoursing about the Gods, and about divine things? And the greatest help to rational legislation is that the laws when once written down are always at rest; they can be put to the test at any future time, and therefore, if on first hearing they seem difficult, there is no reason for apprehension about them, because any man however dull can go over them and consider them again and again; nor if they are tedious but useful, is there any reason or religion, as it seems to me, in any man refusing to maintain the principles of them to the utmost of his power.

Meg. Stranger, I like what Cleinias is saying.

---

[1] Cf. *Gorgias*.

Ath.   Yes, Megillus, and we should do as he proposes; for if impious discourses were not scattered, as I may say, throughout the world, there would have been no need for any vindication of the existence of the Gods — but seeing that they are spread far and wide, such arguments are needed; and who should come to the rescue of the greatest laws, when they are being undermined by bad men, but the legislator himself?

Meg.   There is no more proper champion of them.

Ath.   Well, then, tell me, Cleinias — for I must ask you to be my partner — does not he who talks in this way conceive fire and water and earth and air to be the first elements of all things?[2] Then he calls nature, and out of these he supposes the soul to be formed afterwards; and this is not a mere conjecture of ours about his meaning, but is what he really means.

Cle.   Very true.

Ath.   Then, by Heaven, we have discovered the source of this vain opinion of all those physical investigators, and I would have you examine their arguments with the utmost care, for their impiety is a very serious matter; they not only make a bad and mistaken use of argument, but they lead away the minds of others: that is my opinion of them.

Cle.   You are right; but I should like to know how this happens.

Ath.   I fear that the argument may seem singular.

Cle.   Do not hesitate, Stranger; I see that you are afraid of such a discussion carrying you beyond the limits of legislation. But if there be no other way of showing our agreement in the belief that there are Gods, of whom the law is said now to approve, let us take this way, my good sir.

Ath.   Then I suppose that I must repeat the singular argument of those who manufacture the soul according to their own impious notions; they affirm that which is the first cause of the generation and destruction of all things, to be not first, but last, and that which is last to be first, and hence they have fallen into error about the true nature of the Gods.

Cle.   Still I do not understand you.

Ath.   Nearly all of them, my friends, seem to be ignorant of the nature and power of the soul, especially in what relates to her origin: they do not know that she is among the first of things, and before all bodies, and is the chief author of their changes and transpositions. And if this is true, and if the soul is older than the body, must not the things which are of the soul's kindred be of necessity prior to those which appertain to the body?

Cle.   Certainly.

Ath.   Then thought and attention and mind and art — and law — will be prior to that which is hard and soft and heavy and light; and the great and primitive works and actions will be works of art; they will be the first, and after them will come nature and works of nature,

---

[2] Cf. *Timacus.*

which however is a wrong term for men to apply to them; these will follow, and will be under the government of art and mind.

Cle.   But why is the word "nature" wrong?

Ath.   Because those who use the term mean to say that nature is not the first creative power; but if the soul turns out to be the primeval element, and not fire or air, then in the truest sense and beyond other things the soul may be said to exist by nature; and this would be true if you proved that the soul is older than the body, but not otherwise.

Cle.   You are quite right.

ARISTOTLE (384-322 B.C.)

A Greek philosopher, logician, and biologist, Aristotle was the student of Plato, engaging in dialogue at the Athenian Academy of Plato for twenty years. Aristotle also tutored Alexander the Great for three years. In 335, he established the Lyceum in Athens, rivaling the Academy. Like Socrates before him, Aristotle valued logical thinking, applying it in all areas of life, including the assessment of moral values according to the "golden mean."

ON POETICS

13

The next points after what we have said above will be these:
(1) What is the poet to aim at, and what is he to avoid, in constructing his Plots? and (2) What are the conditions on which the tragic effect depends?

We assume that, for the finest form of Tragedy, the Plot must be not simple but complex; and further, that it must imitate actions arousing fear and pity, since that is the distinctive function of this kind of imitation. It follows, therefore, that there are three forms of Plot to be avoided. (1) A good man must not be seen passing from happiness to misery, or (2) a bad man from misery to happiness. The first situation is not fear-inspiring or piteous, but simply odious to us. The second is the most untragic that can be; it has no one of the requisites of Tragedy; it does not appeal either to the human feeling in us, or to our pity, or to our fears. Nor, on the other hand, should (3) an extremely bad man be seen falling from happiness into misery. Such a story may arouse the human feeling in us, but it will not move us to either pity or fear; pity is occasioned by undeserved misfortune, and fear by that of one like ourselves; so that there will be nothing either piteous or fear-inspiring in the situation. There remains, then, the intermediate kind of personage, a man not pre-eminently virtuous and just, whose misfortune, however, is brought upon him not by vice and depravity but by some error of judgement, of the number of those in the enjoyment of great reputation and prosperity; e. g. Oedipus, Thyestes, and the men of note of similar families. The perfect Plot, accordingly, must have a single, and not (as some tell us) a double issue; the change in the hero's fortunes must be not from misery to happiness, but on the contrary from happiness to misery; and the cause of it must lie not in any depravity, but in some great error on his part; the man himself being either such as we have described, or better, not worse, than that. Fact also confirms our theory. Though the poets began by accepting any tragic story that came to hand, in these days the finest tragedies are always on the story of some few houses, on that of Alcmeon, Oedipus, Orestes, Meleager, Thyestes, Telephus, or any others that may have been involved, as either agents or sufferers, in some deed of horror. The theoretically best tragedy, then, has a Plot of this description.

16

Discovery in general has been explained already. As for the species of Discovery, the first to be noted is (1) the least artistic form of it, of which the poets make most use through mere lack of invention, Discovery by signs or marks. Of these signs some are congenital, like the "lance-head which the Earth born have on them," or "stars," such as Carcinus brings in his Thyestes; others acquired after birth — these later being either marks on the body, e.g. scars, or external tokens, like necklaces, or (to take another sort of instance) the ark in the Discovery in Tyro. Even these, however, admit of two uses, a better and a worse; the scar of Ulysses is an instance; the Discovery of him through it is made in one way by the nurse and in another by the swineherds. (3) A third species is Discovery through memory, from a man's consciousness being awakened by something seen. (4) A fourth kind is Discovery through reasoning. (5) There is, too, a composite Discovery arising from bad reasoning on the side of the other party. An instance of it is in Ulysses the False Messenger: he said he should know the bow which he had not seen; but to suppose from that that he would know it again (as though he had once seen it) was bad reasoning. (6) The best of all Discoveries, however, is that arising from the incidents themselves, when the great surprise comes about through a probable incident, like that in the Oedipus of Sophocles. These last are the only Discoveries independent of the artifice of signs and necklaces. Next after them come Discoveries through reasoning.

17

At the time when he is constructing his Plots, and engaged on the Diction in which they are worked out, the poet should remember (1) to put the actual scenes as far as possible before his eyes. In this way, seeing everything with the vividness of an eye-witness as it were, he will devise what is appropriate, and be least likely to overlook incongruities. This is shown by what was censured in Carcinus, the return of Amphiaraus from the sanctuary; it would have passed unnoticed, if it had not been actually seen by the audience; but on the stage his play failed, the incongruity of the incident offending the spectators. (2) As far as may be, too, the poet should even act his story with the very gestures of his personages. Given the same natural qualifications, he who feels the emotions to be described will be the most convincing; distress and anger, for instance, are portrayed most truthfully by one who is feeling them at the moment. Hence it is that poetry demands a man with a special gift for it, or else one with a touch of madness in him; the former can easily assume the required mood, and the latter may be actually beside himself with emotion. (3) His story, again, whether already made or of his own making, he should first simplify and reduce to a universal form, before proceeding to lengthen it out by the insertion of episodes. The following will show how the universal element in Iphigenia, for instance, may be viewed: A certain maiden having been offered in sacrifice, and spirited away from her sacrificers into another land, where the custom was to sacrifice all strangers to the Goddess, she was made there the priestess of this rite. Long after that the brother of the priestess happened to come; the fact, however, of the oracle having for a certain reason bidden him go thither, and his object in going, are outside the Plot of the play. On his coming he was arrested, and about to be sacrificed, when he revealed who he was either as Euripides puts it, or (as suggested by Polyidus) by the not improbable exclamation, "So I too am doomed to be sacrificed, as my sister was"; and the disclosure led to his salvation. This done, the next thing, after the proper names have been fixed as a basis for the story, is to work in episodes or accessory incidents. One must mind, however, that the episodes are appropriate, like the fit of madness in Orestes, which led to his arrest, and the purifying, which brought about his salvation. In plays, then, the episodes are short; in epic poetry they serve to lengthen out the poem. The argument of the Odyssey is not a long one. A certain man has been abroad many years; Poseidon is ever on the watch for him, and he is all alone. Matters at home too have come to this, that his substance is being wasted and his son's death plotted by suitors to his wife. Then he arrives there himself after his grievous sufferings;

reveals himself, and falls on his enemies; and the end is his salvation and their death. This being all that is proper to the Odyssey, everything else in it is episode.

18

(4) There is a further point to be borne in mind. Every tragedy is in part Complication and in part Denouement; the incidents before the opening scene, and often certain also of those within the play, forming the Complication ; and the rest the Denouement. By Complication I mean all from the beginning of the story to the point just before the change in the hero's fortunes; by Denouement, all from the beginning of the change to the end. In the Lynceus of Theodectes, for instance, the Complication includes, together with the presupposed incidents, the seizure of the child and that in turn of the parents; and the Denouement all from the indictment for the murder to the end. Now it is right, when one speaks of a tragedy as the same or not the same as another, to do so on the ground before all else of their Plot, i.e. as having the same or not the same Complication and Denouement. Yet there are many dramatists who, after a good Complication, fail in the Denouement. But it is necessary for both points of construction to be always duly mastered. (5) There are four distinct species of Tragedy that being the number of the constituents also that have been mentioned: first, the complex Tragedy, which is all Peripety and Discovery; second, the Tragedy of suffering, e.g. the Ajaxes and Ixions; third, the Tragedy of character, e.g. The Phthiotides and Peleus. The fourth constituent is that of "Spectacle," exemplified in The Phorcides, in Prometheus, and in all plays with the scene laid in the nether world. The poet's aim, then, should be to combine every element of interest, if possible, or else the more important and the major part of them. This is now especially necessary owing to the unfair criticism to which the poet is subjected in these days. Just because there have been poets before him strong in the several species of tragedy, the critics now expect the one man to surpass that which was the strong point of each one of his predecessors. (6) One should also remember what has been said more than once, and not write a tragedy on an epic body of incident (i.e. one with a plurality of stories in it), by attempting to dramatize, for instance, the entire story of the Iliad. In the epic owing to its scale every part is treated at proper length; with a drama, however, on the same story the result is very disappointing. This is shown by the fact that all who have dramatized the fall of Ilium in its entirety, and not part by part, like Euripides, or the whole of the Niobe story, instead of a portion, like Aeschylus, either fail utterly or have but ill success on the stage; for that and that alone was enough to ruin even a play by Agathon. Yet in their Peripeties, as also in their simple plots, the poets I mean show wonderful skill in aiming at the kind of effect they desire a tragic situation that arouses the human feeling in one, like the clever villain (e.g. Sisyphus) deceived, or the brave wrongdoer worsted. This is probable, however, only in Agathon's sense, when he speaks of the probability of even improbabilities coming to pass. (7) The Chorus too should be regarded as one of the actors; it should be an integral part of the whole, and take a share in the action — that which it has in Sophocles, rather than in Euripides. With the later poets, however, the songs in a play of theirs have no more to do with the Plot of that than of any other tragedy. Hence it is that they are now singing intercalary pieces, a practice first introduced by Agathon. And yet what real difference is there between singing such intercalary pieces, and attempting to fit in a speech, or even a whole act, from one play into another?

19

The Plot and Characters having been discussed, it remains to consider the Diction and Thought. As for the Thought, we may assume what is said of it in our Art of Rhetoric, as it belongs more properly to that department of inquiry. The Thought of the personages is shown in everything to be effected by their language in every effort to prove or disprove, to arouse emotion (pity, fear, anger, and the like), or to maximize or minimize things. It is clear, also, that their mental procedure must be on the same lines in their actions likewise, whenever they wish them to arouse pity or horror, or to have a look of importance or probability. The only difference is that with the act the impression has to be made without explanation; whereas with the spoken word it has to be produced by the speaker, and result from his language. What, indeed, would be the good of the speaker, if things appeared in the required light even apart from anything he says?

As regards the Diction, one subject for inquiry under this head is the turns given to the language when spoken; e.g. the difference between command and prayer, simple statement and threat, question and answer, and so forth. The theory of such matters, however, belongs to Elocution and the professors of that art. Whether the poet knows these things or not, his art as a poet is never seriously criticized on that account. What fault can one see in Homer's "Sing of the wrath, Goddess," which Protagoras has criticized as being a command where a prayer was meant, since to bid one do or not do, he tells us, is a command? Let us pass over this, then, as appertaining to another art, and not to that of poetry.

25

As regards Problems and their Solutions, one may see the number and nature of the assumptions on which they proceed by viewing the matter in the following way. (1) The poet being an imitator just like the painter or other maker of likenesses, he must necessarily in all instances represent things in one or other of three aspects, either as they were or are, or as they are said or thought to be or to have been, or as they ought to be. (2) All this he does in language, with an admixture, it may be, of strange words and metaphors, as also of the various modified forms of words, since the use of these is conceded in poetry. (3) It is to be remembered, too, that there is not the same kind of correctness in poetry as in politics, or indeed any other art. There is, however, within the limits of poetry itself a possibility of two kinds of error, the one directly, the other only accidentally connected with the art. If the poet meant to describe the thing correctly, and failed through lack of power of expression, his art itself is at fault. But if it was through his having meant to describe it in some incorrect way (e.g. to make the horse in movement have both right legs thrown forward) that the technical error (one in a matter of, say, medicine or some other special science), or impossibilities of whatever kind they may be, have got into his description, his error in that case is not in the essentials of the poetic art. These, therefore, must be the premises of the Solutions in answer to the criticisms involved in the Problems.

I.   As to the criticisms relating to the poet's art itself. Any impossibilities there may be in his descriptions of things are faults. But from another point of view they are justifiable, if they serve the end of poetry itself if (to assume what we have said of that end) they make the effect of either that very portion of the work or some other portion more astounding. The Pursuit of Hector is an instance in point. If, however, the poetic end might have been as well or better attained without sacrifice of technical correctness in such matters, the impossibility is not to be justified, since the description should be, if it can, entirely free from error. One may ask, too, whether the error is in a matter directly or only accidentally connected with the poetic art; since it is a lesser error in an artist not to know, for instance, that the hind has no horns, than to produce an unrecognizable picture of one.

II.   If the poet's description be criticized as not true to fact, one may urge perhaps that the object ought to be as described an answer like that of Sophocles, who said that he drew men as they ought to be, and Euripides as they were. If the description, however, be neither true nor of the thing as it ought to be, the answer must be then, that it is in accordance with opinion. The tales about Gods, for instance, may be as wrong as Xenophanes thinks, neither true nor the better thing to say; but they are certainly in accordance with opinion. Of other statements in poetry one may perhaps say, not that they are better than the truth, but that the fact was so at the time; e.g. the description of the arms: "their spears stood upright, butt-end upon the ground"; for that was the usual way of fixing them then, as it is still with the Illyrians. As for the question whether something said or done in a poem is morally right or not, in dealing with that one should consider not only the intrinsic quality of the actual word or deed, but also the person who says or does it, the person to whom he says or does it, the time, the means, and the motive of the agent, whether he does it to attain a greater good, or to avoid a greater evil.

Speaking generally, one has to justify (1) the Impossible by reference to the requirements of poetry, or to the better, or to opinion. For the purposes of poetry a convincing possibility; and if men such as Zeuxis depicted by impossible, the answer is that it is better they should be like that, as the artist ought to improve on his model. (2) The Improbable one has to justify either by showing it to be in accordance with opinion, or by urging that at times it is not improbable; for there is a probability of things happening also against probability. (3) The contradictions found in the poet's language one should first test as one does an opponent's confutation in a dialectical argument, so as to see whether he means the same thing, in the same relation, and in the same sense, before admitting that he has contradicted either something he has said himself or what a man of sound sense assumes as true. But there is no possible apology for improbability of Plot or depravity of character, when they are not necessary and no use is made of them, like the improbability in the appearance of Aegeus in Medea and the baseness of Menelaus in Orestes.

The objections, then, of critics start with faults of five kinds: the allegation is always that something is either (1) impossible, (2) improbable, (3) corrupting, (4) contradictory, or (5) against technical correctness. The answers to these objections must be sought under one or other of the above-mentioned heads, which are twelve in number.

26

The question may be raised whether the epic or the tragic is the higher form of imitation. It may be argued that, if the less vulgar is the higher, and the less vulgar is always that which addresses the better public, an art addressing any and every one is of a very vulgar order. It is a belief that their public cannot see the meaning, unless they add something themselves, that causes the perpetual movements of the performers — bad flute-players, for instance, rolling about, if quoit-throwing is to be represented, and pulling at the conductor, if Scylla is the subject of the piece. Tragedy, then, is said to be an art of this order — to be in fact just what the later actors were in the eyes of their predecessors; for Mynniscus used to call Callippides "the aoe," because he thought he so overacted his parts; and a similar view was taken of Pindarus also. All Tragedy, however, is said to stand to the Epic as the newer to the older school of actors. The one, accordingly, is said to address a cultivated audience, which does not need the accompaniment of gesture; the other, an uncultivated one. If, therefore, Tragedy is a vulgar art, it must clearly be lower than the Epic.

The answer to this is twofold. In the first place, one may urge (1) that the censure does not touch the art of the dramatic poet, but only that of his interpreter; for it is quite possible to overdo the gesturing even in an epic recital, as did Sosistratus, and in a singing contest, as did Mnasitheus of Opus. (2) That one should not condemn all movement, unless one means to condemn even the dance, but only that of ignoble people, which is the point of the criticism passed on Callippides and in the present day on others, that their women are not like gentlewomen. (3) That Tragedy may produce its effect even without movement or action in just the same way as Epic poetry; for from the mere reading of a play its quality may be seen. So that, if it be superior in all other respects, this element of inferiority is no necessary part of it.

In the second place, one must remember (1) that Tragedy has everything that the Epic has (even the epic metre being admissible), together with a not inconsiderable addition in the shape of the music (a very real factor in the pleasure of the drama) and the Spectacle. (2) That its reality of presentation is felt in the play as read, as well as in the play as acted. (3) That the tragic imitation requires less space for the attainment of its end; which is a great advantage, since the more concentrated effect is more pleasurable than one with a large admixture of time to dilute it — consider the Oedipus of Sophocles, for instance, and the effect of expanding it into the number of lines of the *Iliad*. (4) That there is less unity in the imitation of the epic poets, as is proved by the fact that any one work of theirs supplies matter for several tragedies; the result being that, if they take what is really a single story, it seems curt when briefly told, and thin and waterish when on the scale of length usual with their verse. In saying that there is less unity in an epic, I mean an epic made up of a plurality of actions, in the same way as the *Iliad* and *Odyssey* have many such parts, each one of them in itself of some magnitude; yet the structure of the two Homeric poems is as perfect as can be, and the action in them is as nearly as possible one action. If, then, Tragedy is superior in these respects, and also, besides these, in its poetic effect (since the two forms of poetry should give us, not any or every pleasure, but the very special kind we have mentioned), it is clear that, as attaining the poetic effect better than the Epic, it will be the higher form of art.

So much for Tragedy and Epic poetry — for these two arts in general and their species; the number and nature of their constituent parts; the causes of success and failure in them; the Objections of the critics, and the Solutions in answer to them.

WILLIAM SHAKESPEARE (1564-1616)

Shakespeare, generally accepted to be the greatest writer in the English language, began his dramatic career as an actor in London in 1590. He had already fathered three children before he turned twenty-one. He wrote thirty-seven plays — including tragedies, comedies, romances, and history plays — and a large collection of sonnets. All his plays are in poetry, as was the tradition until the eighteenth century. The contributions of Shakespeare lie chiefly in his wide range of vivid characters and his rich and imaginative use of language.

SONNETS

Shall I compare thee to a summer's day?
Thou art more lovely and more temperate:
Rough winds do shake the darling buds of May,
And summer's lease hath all too short a date:
Sometimes too hot the eye of heaven shines,
And often is his gold complexion dimmed;
And every fair from fair sometime declines,
By chance, or nature's changing course untrimmed;
But thy eternal summer shall not fade,
Nor lose possession of that fair thou owest;
Nor shall death brag thou wander'st in his shade,
When in eternal lines to time thou growest.

    So long as men can breathe, or eyes can see,
    So long lives this, and this gives life to thee.

* * * * *

That time of year thou mayst in me behold
When yellow leaves, or none, or few, do hang
Upon those boughs which shake against the cold,
Bare ruined choirs where late the sweet birds sang.
In me thou seest the twilight of such day,
As after sunset fadeth in the west,
Which by and by black night doth take away,
Death's second self, that seals up all in rest.
In me thou seest the glowing of such fire
That on the ashes of his youth doth lie,
As the deathbed whereon it must expire,
Consumed with that which it was nourished by,
     This thou perceivest, which makes thy love more strong,
     To love that well which thou must leave ere long.

* * * * *

Some glory in their birth, some in their skill,
Some in their wealth, some in their bodies' force,
Some in their garments, though new-fangled ill,
Some in their hawks and hounds, some in their horse;
And every humour hath his adjunct pleasure,
Wherein it finds a joy above the rest:
But these particulars are not my measure;
All these I better in one general best.
Thy love is better than high birth to me,
Richer than wealth, prouder than garments' cost,
Of more delight than hawks or horses be;
And having thee, of all men's pride I boast:
Wretched in this alone, that thou mayst take
All this away, and me most wretched make.

* * * * *

They that have power to hurt, and will do none,
That do not do the things they most do show,
Who, moving others, are themselves as stone,
Unmoved, cold, and to temptation slow,
They rightly do inherit heaven's graces
And husband nature's riches from expense;
They are the Lords and owners of their faces,
Others, but stewards of their excellence.
The summer's flower is to the summer sweet,
Though to itself it only live and die,
But if that flower with base infection meet,
The basest weed outbraves his dignity:
For sweetest things turn sourest by their deeds:
Lilies that fester smell far worse than weeds.

* * * * *

Poor soul, the centre of my sinful earth —
Thrall to these rebel powers that thee array,
Why dost thou pine within and suffer dearth,
Painting thy outward walls so costly gay?
Why so large cost, having so short a lease,
Dost thou upon thy fading mansion spend?
Shall worms, inheritors of this excess,
Eat up thy charge? is this thy body's end?
Then, soul, live thou upon thy servant's loss,
And let that pine to aggravate thy store;
Buy terms divine in selling hours of dross;
Within be fed, without be rich no more:
So shalt thou feed on Death, that feeds on men,
And Death once dead, there's no more dying then.

* * * * *

My love is as a fever, longing still
For that which longer nurseth the disease,
Feeding on that which doth preserve the ill,
Th'uncertain sickly appetite to please.
My reason, the Physician to my love,
Angry that his prescriptions are not kept,
Hath left me, and I desperate now approve
Desire is death, which Physic did except.
Past cure I am, now Reason is past care,
And frantic-mad with evermore unrest;
My thoughts and my discourse as mad men's are,
At random from the truth vainly express'd;
For I have sworn thee fair and thought thee bright,
Who are as black as hell, as dark as night.

* * * * *

FROM *ROMEO & JULIET*

Act I, Scene 5

Romeo.   If I profane with my unworthiest hand
            This holy shrine, the gentle fine is this;
            My lips, two blushing pilgrims, ready stand
            To smooth that rough touch with a tender kiss.

Juliet.   Good pilgrim, you do wrong your hand too much,
            Which mannerly devotion shows in this;
            For saints have hands that pilgrims' hands do touch,
            And palm to palm is holy palmers' kiss.

Romeo.   Have not saints lips, and holy palmers too?

Juliet.   Ay, pilgrim, lips that they must use in prayer.

Romeo.   O, then, dear saint, let lips do what hands do;
              They pray, grant thou, lest faith turn to despair.

Juliet.   Saints do not move, though grant for prayers' sake.

Romeo.   Then move not, while my prayer's effect I take.

*　*　*　*　*

Thus from my lips, by yours, my sin is purged.
              (He kisses her.)

Act II, Scene 2

The Balcony Scene

Romeo.   But, soft! What light through yonder window breaks?
           It is the east, and Juliet is the sun.
           Arise, fair sun, and kill the envious moon,
           Who is already sick and pale with grief,
           That thou her maid art far more fair than she:
           Be not her maid, since she is envious;
           Her vestal livery is but sick and green
           And none but fools do wear it; cast it off.
           It is my lady, O, it is my love!
           O, that she knew she were!
           She speaks, yet she says nothing: what of that?
           Her eye discourses; I will answer it.

           I am too bold, 'tis not to me she speaks:
           Two of the fairest stars in all the heaven,
           Having some business, do entreat her eyes
           To twinkle in their spheres till they return.
           What if her eyes were there, they in her head?
           The brightness of her cheek would shame those stars,
           As daylight doth a lamp; her eyes in heaven
           Would through the airy region stream so bright
           That birds would sing and think it were not night.
           See, how she leans her cheek upon her hand!
           O, that I were a glove upon that hand,
           That I might touch that cheek!

Juliet.   Ay me!

Romeo *(aside)*.   She speaks:
           O, speak again, bright angel! for thou art
           As glorious to this night, being o'er my head,
           As is a wingèd messenger of heaven
           Unto the white-upturnèd wondering eyes

                Of mortals that fall back to gaze on him
                When he bestrides the lazy-pacing clouds
                And sails upon the bosom of the air.

Juliet.   O Romeo, Romeo! Wherefore art thou Romeo?
                Deny thy father and refuse thy name;
                Or, if thou wilt not, be but sworn my love,
                And I'll no longer be a Capulet.

Romeo (*aside*).   Shall I hear more, or shall I speak at this?

Juliet.   'Tis but thy name that is my enemy;
                Thou art thyself, though not a Montague.
                What's Montague? It is nor hand, nor foot,
                Nor arm, nor face, nor any other part
                Belonging to a man. O, be some other name!
                What's in a name? That which we call a rose
                By any other name would smell as sweet;
                So Romeo would, were he not Romeo called,
                Retain that dear perfection which he owes
                Without that title. Romeo, doff thy name,
                And for that name which is no part of thee
                Take all myself.

Romeo (*stepping forward*).   I take thee at thy word:
                Call me but love, and I'll be new baptized;
                Henceforth I never will be Romeo.

Juliet.   What man art thou thus bescreened in night
                So stumblest on my council?

Romeo.   By a name
                I know not how to tell thee who I am:
                My name, dear saint, is hateful to myself,
                Because it is an enemy to thee;
                Had I it written, I would tear the word.

Juliet.   My ears have not yet drunk a hundred words
                Of that tongue's utterance, yet I know the sound:
                Art thou not Romeo and a Montague?

Romeo.   Neither, fair saint, if either thee dislike.

Juliet.   How camest thou hither, tell me, and wherefore?
                The orchard walls are high and hard to climb,
                And the place death, considering who thou art,
                If any of my kinsmen find thee here.

Romeo.   With love's light wings did I o'erperch these walls;
                For stony limits cannot hold love out,
                And what love can do, that dares love attempt;

        Therefore thy kinsmen are no let to me.

Juliet.   If they do see thee, they will murder thee.

Romeo.   Alack, there lies more peril in thine eye
        Than twenty of their swords: look thou but sweet,
        And I am proof against their enmity.

Juliet.   I would not for the world they saw thee here.

Romeo.   I have night's cloak to hide me from their sight;
        And but thou love me, let them find me here:
        My life were better ended by their hate,
        Than death prorogued, wanting of thy love.

Juliet.   By whose direction found'st thou out this place?

Romeo.   By love, who first did prompt me to inquire;
        He lent me council and I lent him eyes.
        I am no pilot; yet, wert thou as far
        As that vast shore washed with the farthest sea,
        I would adventure for such merchandise.

Juliet.   Thou know'st the mask of night is on my face,
        Else would a maiden blush bepaint my cheek
        For that which thou hast heard me speak tonight.
        Fain would I dwell on form, fain, fain deny
        What I have spoke: but farewell compliment!
        Dost thou love me? I know thou wilt say "Ay."
        And I will take thy word: yet, if thou swear'st,
        Thou mayst prove false; at lovers' perjuries,
        They say, Jove laughs. O gentle Romeo,
        If thou dost love, pronounce it faithfully:
        Or if thou think'st I am too quickly won,
        I'll frown and be perverse and say thee nay,
        So thou wilt woo; but else, not for the world.
        In truth, fair Montague, I am too fond,
        And therefore thou mayst think my 'haviour light:
        But trust me gentleman, I'll prove more true
        Than those that have more cunning to be strange.
        I should have been more strange, I must confess,
        But that thou overheard'st, ere I was ware,
        My true love's passion; therefore pardon me,
        And not impute this yielding to light love,
        Which the dark night hath so discovered.

Romeo.   Lady, by yonder moon I swear
        That tips with silver all these fruit-tree tops.

Juliet.   O, swear not by the moon, the innocent moon,
                   That monthly changes in her circled orb,
                   Lest that thy love prove likewise variable.

Romeo.   What shall I swear by?

Juliet.   Do not swear at all;
                   Or, if thou wilt, swear by thy gracious self,
                   Which is the god of my idolatry,
                   And I'll believe thee.

Romeo.   If my heart's dear love-

Juliet.   Well, do not swear: although I joy in thee,
                   I have no joy of this contract tonight:
                   It is too rash, too unadvised, too sudden;
                   Too like the lightning, which doth cease to be
                   Ere one can say "It lightens." Sweet, good night!
                   This bud of love, by summer's ripening breath,
                   May prove a beautious flower when next we meet.
                   Good night, good night! As sweet repose and rest
                   Come to thy heart as that within my breast!

Romeo.   O, wilt thou leave me so unsatisfied?

Juliet.   What satisfaction canst thou have tonight?

Romeo.   The exchange of thy love's faithful vow for mine.

Juliet.   I gave thee mine before didst request it:
                   And yet I would it were to give again.

Romeo   Wouldst thou withdraw it? For what purpose, love?

Juliet.   But to be frank, and give it thee again.
                   And yet I wish but for the one thing I have:
                   My bounty is as boundless as the sea,
                   My love as deep; the more I give to thee,
                   The more I have, for both are infinite.
                       (Nurse *calls from within the room*)
                   I hear some noise within; dear love, adieu!
                   Anon, good nurse!
                        Sweet Montague, be true.
                       (*as she goes into her room*)
                   Stay but a little, I will come again.

Romeo.   O blessèd, blessèd night! I am afeard,
                   Being in night, all this is but a dream,
                   Too flattering-sweet to be substantial.

Scene from *Romeo and Juliet,* Franco Zeffirelli Productions.
Courtesy of Paramount Pictures.

Juliet (*returning*) Three words, dear Romeo, and good night indeed.
          If that thy bent of love be honorable,
          Thy purpose marriage, send me word tomorrow,
          By one that I'll procure to come to thee,
          Where and what time thou wilt perform the rite;
          And all my fortunes at thy foot I'll lay
          And follow thee my lord throughout the world.

Nurse (*calling from within*).
          Madam!

Juliet.   I come, anon.
          -But if thou mean'st not well,
          I do beseech thee-

Nurse (*from within*). Madam!

Juliet   By and by, I come:-
          To cease thy suit, and leave me to my grief:
          Tomorrow will I send.

Romeo   So thrive my soul-

Juliet.   A thousand times good night!
                    (*She goes*).

Romeo.   A thousand times the worse, to want thy light.
          Love goes toward love, as schoolboys from their books,
          But love from love, toward school with heavy looks.
          (*As he moves away,* Juliet *comes out again.*)

Juliet.   Hist!
          Romeo, hist! O, for a falconer's voice,
          To lure this tassel-gentle back again!
          Bondage is hoarse, and may not speak aloud;
          Else would I tear the cave where Echo lies,
          And make her airy tongue more hoarse than mine,
          With repetition of my Romeo's name.

Romeo.   It is my soul that calls upon my name:
          How silver-sweet sound lovers' tongues by night,
          Like softest music to attending ears!

Juliet.   Romeo!

Romeo.   My dear?

Juliet   At what o'clock tomorrow
          Shall I send to thee?

Romeo   At the hour of nine.

Juliet.   I will not fail: 'tis twenty years till then.
               I have forgot why I did call thee back.

Romeo.   Let me stand here till thou remember it.

Juliet.   I shall forget, to have thee still stand there,
               Remembering how I love thy company.

Romeo.   And I'll still stay, to have thee still forget,
               Forgetting any other home but this.

Juliet.   'Tis almost morning; I would have thee gone:
               and yet no further than a wanton's bird;
               Who lets it hop a little from her hand,
               Like a poor prisoner in his twisted gyves,
               And with a silk thread plucks it back again,
               So loving-jealous of his liberty.

Romeo.   I would I were thy bird.

Juliet   Sweet, so would I:
               Yet I should kill thee with much cherishing.
               Good night, good night! Parting is such sweet sorrow,
               That I shall say good night till it be morrow.
               (*She goes back into her room.*)

Romeo.   Sleep dwell upon thine eyes, peace in thy breast!
               Would I were sleep and peace, so sweet to rest!

               Hence will I to my ghostly father's cell,
               His help to crave, and my dear hap to tell.
               (*He leaves*)

ANONYMOUS

NOT JUST FOR THE RIDE

There was a young lady of Niger
Who smiled as she rode on a tiger:
   They came back from the ride
   with the lady inside
And the smile on the face of the tiger.

GA PEOPLE
(West Africa)

NAMING POEM

May good fortune come
May our stools be clean
May our brooms be clean
In a circle of unity
   have we met
When we dig a well
May we find water
When of this water we drink
May our shoulders find peace
The stranger who has come
On his mother's head be life
On his father's head be life
Behind his back may
   darkness be
Before his face may
   all be bright
May his head the world respect
And his brethren may he know
May we have forgiveness
   to forgive him
May he work and eat
When he sees he has
   not seen
When he hears he has
   not heard
In black he has come
In white may he return
May good fortune come

ANONYMOUS

RELATIVITY

There was a young lady named Bright,
Who traveled much faster than light,
   She started one way
   In the relative day,
And returned on the previous night.

AMADOU HAMPATÉ BA
(Fulani/West Africa)

THE BELOVED

Diko,
of light skin, of smooth hair and long;
her smells sweet and gentle
she never stinks of fish
she never breathes sweat
like gatherers of dry wood.
She has no bald patch on her head
like those who carry heavy loads.
Her teeth are white
her eyes are like
those of a new born fawn
that delights in the milk
that flows for the first time
from the antelope's udder.
Neither her heel nor her palm
are rough; but sweet to touch
like liver; or better still
the fluffy down of kopok.

SAPPHO (C. 620-575 B.C.)

The poet Sappho instructed girls on the island of Lesbos in the arts of music, singing, and graceful living. Many of her poems are addressed to certain of these young women whom Sappho loved intensely, particularly expressing her sadness at their departure. Because of the vibrant emotions expressed, the spontaneity of her words, and the music of her verse, she is sometimes called "The Tenth Muse."

LYRICS

TO ANAKTORIA, NOW A SOLDIER'S WIFE IN LYDIA

Some say cavalry and some would claim
infantry or a fleet of long oars
is the supreme sight on the black earth.
   I say it is

the girl you love. And easily proved.
Did not Helen, who was queen of mortal
beauty, choose as first among mankind
   the very scourge

Of Trojan honor? Haunted by Love
she forgot kinsmen, her own dear child,
and wandered off to a remote country.
   O weak and fitful

Woman bending before any man:
So Anaktoria, although you are
Far, do not forget your loving friends.
   And I for one

Would rather listen to your soft step
and see your radiant face — than watch
all the dazzling horsemen and armored
   Hoplites of Lydia.

PARALYSIS

Mother darling, I cannot work the loom
for the Cyprian[3] has almost crushed me,
broken me with love for a slender boy.

TO EROS

From all the offspring
of the earth and heaven
Love is the most precious.

---

[3] Aphrodite, who was born on the island of Cypros.

HOMAGE

Our slender Adonis is dying, Kytherea,
  tell us what to do.
Tear open your dresses, virgins, and
  batter your breasts!

TO THE QUEEN OF LOVE

Cyprian, come
and gently pour nectar in our
golden cups, and pour joy too
in all our hearts.

THE LYRIC POEM

Come, holy tortoise shell,
my lyre, and become a poem.

LIGHT VANISHING

The moon has gone down,
the Pleiades have set.
Night is half gone,
and life speeds by.
I lie in bed, alone.

THE BLAST OF LOVE

Like a windstorm
punishing the oak trees,
love shakes my heart.

SEIZURE

To me that man equals a god
as he sits before you and listens
closely to your sweet voice

and lovely laughter — which troubles
the heart in my ribs. For Brocheo,
when I look at you my voice fails,

my tongue is broken and thin fire
runs like a thief through my body.

My eyes are dead to light, my ears

pound, and sweat pours down over me.
I shudder, I am paler than grass,
and am intimate with dying — but

I must suffer everything, being poor.

WORLD

I could not hope
to touch the sky
with my two arms.

BEACH COLOR

The fuzzy flower of the golden broom
grew along the shore.

FULL MOON

The glow and beauty of the stars
are nothing near the splendid moon
when in her roundness she burns silver
about the world.

THEN

In gold sandals
dawn like a thief
fell upon me.

SHRILL SONG

When sun sprays the earth
with straight-falling flames,
a cricket rubs his wings,
scraping up thin sweet song.

THE HERALD

Nightingale, with your
lovely voice, you are
the herald of spring.

CONFESSION

But I love refinement, and the bright
and beautiful are for me the same
    as desire for sunlight.

EVENING STAR

Hesperos, of all stars,
is the most beautiful.

TO APHRODITE OF THE FLOWERS, AT KNOSSOS

Come to the holy temple of the virgins
where the pleasant grove of apple trees
circles an altar smoking with frankincense.

The roses leave shadow on the ground
and cool springs murmur through apple
    branches
where shuddering leaves pour down
    profound sleep.

In that meadow where horses have grown
glossy, and all spring flowers grow wild,
the anise shoots fill the air with
    aroma.

And there our queen Aphrodite pours
celestial nectar in the gold cups,
which she fills gracefully with
    sudden joy.

A LETTER TO ATTHIS I

My Atthis, although our dear Anaktoria
lives in distant Sardis,
she thinks of us constantly, and

of the life we shared in days when for her
you were a splendid goddess,
and your singing gave her deep joy.

Now she shines among Lydian women as
when the red-fingered moon
rises after sunset, erasing

stars around her, and pouring light equally
across the salt sea
and over densely flowered fields;

and lucent dew spread on the earth to
    quicken
roses and fragile thyme
and the sweet-blooming honey-lotus.

Now while our darling wanders she
    remembers lovely Atthis' love,
and longing sinks deep in her breast.

She cries loudly for us to come! We hear,
for the night's many tongues
carry her cry across the sea.

KING SOLOMON (10TH CENTURY B.C.)

The Song of Solomon, or Song of Songs, is a book in the old Testament usually ascribed, although uncertainly, to King Solomon, son of King David, who is remembered for his strong kingdom and his many wives.

THE SONG OF SONGS

According to many scholars, the *Song of Songs*, meaning the greatest of songs (1.1), contains in exquisite poetic form the sublime portrayal and praise of the mutual love of the Lord and his people. The Lord is the Lover and his people are the beloved. Describing this relationship in terms of human love, the author simply follows Israel's tradition. Isaiah (5.1-7, 54.4-8), Jeremiah (2.2f. 32), and Ezekiel (16; 23) all characterize the covenant between the Lord and Israel as a marriage. Isaiah the prophet sees the idolatry of Israel in the adultery of Gomer. He also represents the Lord speaking to Israel's heart (2.16) and changing her into a new spiritual people, purified by the Babylonian captivity and betrothed anew to her divine Lover "in justice and uprightness, in love and mercy" (2.21).

The author of the Song, using the same literary figure, paints a beautiful picture of the ideal Israel, the chosen people of the Old and New Testaments, whom the Lord led by degrees to an exalted spiritual union with himself in the bond of perfect love. When the Song is thus interpreted there is no reason for surprise at the tone of the poem, which employs in its descriptions the courtship and marriage customs of the author's time. Moreover, the poem is not an allegory in which each remark, e.g., in the dialogue of the lovers, has a higher meaning. It is a parable in which the true meaning of mutual love comes from the poem as a whole.

While the Song is thus commonly understood by some scholars, it is also possible to see in it an inspired portrayal of ideal human love. Here we would have from God a description of the sacredness and the depth of married union.

Although the poem is attributed to Solomon in the traditional title (1.1), the language and style of the work, among other considerations, point to a time after the end of the Babylonian Exile (538 B.C.) as that in which an unknown poet composed this masterpiece. The structure of the Song is difficult to analyze; here it is regarded as a lyric dialogue, with dramatic movement and interest.

The use of marriage as a symbol, characteristic of the Song, is found extensively also in the New Testament.

CHAPTER 1

Love's Desires

2B   Let him kiss me with kisses of his mouth!

1.2: The marginal letters indicate the speaker of the verses: *B*—Bride; *D*—Daughters of Jerusalem; *G*—Bridegroom. In verses 2-7 the bride and the daughters address the bridegroom who appears here as a king, but more often in the poem as a shepherd. King and shepherd are familiar figures of the Lord in the Sacred Scriptures. Cf. Psalms 23.1; Is 40.11; Jn 10.1-16.

More delightful is your love than wine!
3   Your name spoken is a spreading perfume —
       that is why the maidens love you.
4   Draw me! —

D   We will follow you eagerly!

B   Bring me, O king, to your chambers.

D   With you we rejoice and exult,
       we extol your love; it is beyond wine:
       how rightly you are loved!

Love's Boast

5B   I am as dark — but lovely,
         O daughters of Jerusalem —
      As the tents of Kedar,
         as the curtains of Salma.

6   Do not stare at me because I am
         swarthy,
      because the sun has burned me.
      My brothers have been angry with me;
         they charged me with the care of the
         vineyards:
      my own vineyard I have not cared for.

Love's Inquiry

7B   Tell me, you whom my heart loves,
         where you pasture your flock,
         where you give them rest at midday,
      Lest I be found wandering
         after the flocks of your companions.

8G   If you do not know,
         O most beautiful among women,
      Follow the tracks of the flock
         and pasture the young ones
         near the shepherds' camps.

Love's Vision

9G   To the steeds of Pharaoh's chariots
         would I liken you, my beloved:

10   Your cheeks lovely in pendants,
         your neck in jewels.
11   We will make pendants of gold for you,
         and silver ornaments.

Love's Union

12B For the king's banquet
         my nard gives forth its fragrance.
13   My lover is for me a sachet of myrrh
         to rest in my bosom.
14   My lover is for me a cluster of henna
         from the vineyards of Ein Gedi.

15G Ah, you are beautiful, my beloved,
         ah, you are beautiful; your eyes are
         doves!

16B Ah, you are beautiful, my lover — yes,
         you are lovely.
      Our couch, too, is verdant;
17   the beams of our house are cedars,
         our rafters, cypresses.

Chapter 2

1   If I am a flower of Sharon,
         a lily of the valley.

2G   As a lily among thorns,
         so is my beloved among women.
3B   As an apple tree among the trees of the
         woods,
         so is my lover among men.

      I delight to rest in his shadow,

1.5: *Daughters of Jerusalem:* the chorus whom the bride addresses and who ask her questions (5.9; 6.1), thus developing action within the poem. *Kedar:* a Syrian desert region whose name suggests blackness; tents were often made of black goat hair. *Curtains:* tent coverings of *Salma*, a region close to Kedar.

1.6: *Swarthy:* tanned by the sun from working in her brothers' vineyards. *My own vineyard:* the bride herself; cf. Is. 5.1-7, where Israel is designated as the vineyard and the Lord is the Lover.

1.7: Here and elsewhere in the Song (3.1; 5.8; 6.1) the bride expresses her desire to be in the company of her lover. These verses point to a certain tension in the poem. Openly at the end (8.5ff) does mutual possession of the lovers become final.

1.9: The bridegroom compares the girl's beauty to the rich adornment of the royal chariot of Pharaoh.

1.12: *Nard:* a precious perfume, a figure of the bride; cf. 4.14.

1.13: *Myrrh:* produced from aromatic resin of balsam or roses.

1.14: *Henna:* a plant which bears white scented flowers.

1.15: *Doves:* suggesting innocence and charm.

1.16: Though the meeting place of the lovers is but a shepherd's hut of green branches, it becomes a palace with beams of cedar and rafters of cypress when adorned with their love.

2.1: *Flower of Sharon:* probably the narcissus, which grows in the fertile Plain of Sharon lying between Mount Carmel and Jaffa on the Mediterranean coast.

and his fruit is sweet to my mouth.

4   He brings me into the banquet hall
    and his emblem over me is love

5   Strengthen me with raisin cakes,
    refresh me with apples,
    for I am faint with love.

6   His left hand is under my head
    and his right arm embraces me.

7   I adjure you, daughters of Jerusalem,
    by the gazelles and hinds of the field,
    Do not arouse, do not stir up love
    before its own time.

A Tryst in the Spring

8B Hark! my lover — here he comes
    springing across the mountains,
    leaping across the hills.

9   My lover is like a gazelle
    or a young stag.
    Here he stands behind our wall,
    gazing through the windows,
    peering through the lattices.

10 My lover speaks; he says to me,
    "Arise, my beloved, my beautiful one,
    and come!

11 For see, the winter is past,
    the rains are over and gone.

12 The flowers appear on the earth,
    the time of pruning the vines has
        come,
    and the song of the dove is heard in
        our land.

13 The fig tree puts forth its figs,
    and the vines, in bloom, give forth
        fragrance
    Arise, my beloved, my beautiful one,
    and come!

14 "O my dove in the clefts of the rock,
    in the secret recesses of the cliff,
    Let me see you,
    let me hear your voice,
    For your voice is sweet.
    and you are lovely."

15 Catch us the foxes, the little foxes
    that damage the vineyards; for our
        vineyards are in bloom!

16 My lover belongs to me and I to him;
    he browses among the lilies.

17 Until the day breathes cool and the
        shadows lengthen,
    roam, my lover,
    Like a gazelle or a young stag
    upon the mountains of Bether.

CHAPTER 3

Loss and Discovery

1B On my bed at night I sought him
    whom my heart loves —
    I sought him but I did not find him.

2   I will rise then and go about the city;
    in the streets and crossings I will seek

3   Him whom my heart loves.
    I sought him but I did not find him.
    The watchmen came upon me
    as they made their rounds of the city:
    Have you seen him whom my heart
        loves?

4   I had hardly left them
    when I found him whom my heart
        loves.
    I took hold of him and would not let
        him go

2.4: *The banquet hall:* the sweet things of the table, the embrace of the bride and bridegroom, express the delicacy of their affection and the intimacy of their love.

2.7: *By the gazelles and hinds:* the swiftness of these animals and the luster and soft expression of their eyes are suggestive of love; cf. Proverbs 5.19.

2.8: In this sudden change of scene, the bride pictures her lover hastening toward her dwelling until his voice is heard bidding her come to him.

2.14: The bride is addressed as though she were a dove in a mountain fastness out of sight and reach.

2.15: A snatch of song in answer to the request of v. 14; cf.8.123ff. *Foxes:* all who threaten to disturb the security of love symbolized by the vineyard.

2.17 Breathes *cool:* in the evening when the sun is going down. Cf. Genesis 3.8. *Bether:* a very obscure word; some interpret it in the sense of ruggedness; others, of spices; still others, of sacrifice (Genesis 15.10).

3.1: See the parallel in 5.2-8.

till I should bring him to the home of
   my mother,
to the room of my parent.

5   I adjure you, daughters of Jerusalem,
     by the gazelles and hinds of the field,
Do not arouse, do not stir up love before
    its own time.

Regal State of the Bridegroom

6D   What is this coming up from the desert,
     like a column of smoke
Laden with myrrh, with frankincense,
    and with the perfume of every exotic
     dust?

7   Ah, it is the litter of Solomon;
    sixty valiant men surround it,
    of the valiant men of Israel:

8   All of them expert with the sword,
    skilled in battle,
Each with his sword at his side.
against danger in the watches of the
    night.

9   King Solomon made himself a carriage
    of wood from Lebanon.

10   He made its columns of silver,
    its roof of gold,
Its seat of purple cloth,
    its framework inlaid with ivory.

11   Daughters of Jerusalem, come forth
    and look upon King Solomon
In the crown with which his mother has
    crowned him
on the day of his marriage,
on the day of the joy of his heart.

CHAPTER 4

The Charms of the Beloved

1G   Ah, you are beautiful, my beloved,
    ah, you are beautiful!
Your eyes are doves
    behind your veil.
Your hair is like a flock of goats
    streaming down the mountains of
     Gilead.

3.6: The lover is portrayed as King Solomon, escorted by sixty armed men, coming in royal procession to meet his bride.

2   Your teeth are like a flock of ewes to be
    shorn,
    which come up from the washing,
All of them big with twins,
    none of them thin and barren.

3   Your lips are like a scarlet strand;
    your mouth is lovely.
Your cheek is like a half-pomegranate
    behind your veil.

4   Your neck is like David's tower
    girt with battlements;
A thousand bucklers hang upon it,
    all the shields of valiant men.

5   Your breasts are like twin fawns,
    the young of a gazelle
    that browse among the lilies.

6   Until the day breathes cool and the
    shadows lengthen,
    I will go to the mountain of myrrh,
    to the hill of incense.

7   You are all-beautiful, my beloved,
    and there is no blemish in you.

8   Come from Lebanon, my bride,
    come from Lebanon, come!
Descend from the top of Amana,
    from the top of Senir and Hermon,
From the haunts of lions,
    from the leopards' mountains.

9   You have ravished my heart, my sister,
    my bride;

4.2: *Teeth:* praised for whiteness and regularity.

4.3: *Pomegranate:* a fruit somewhat like an orange, with a firm skin and deep red color. The girl's cheek is compared, in roundness and tint, to a half-pomegranate.

4.4: The ornaments about her neck are compared to the trophies on the city walls. Cf. 1 Kings 10.10.

4.6: *Mountain of myrrh. . . hill of incense:* spoken figuratively of the bride; cf 8, 14.

4.7: Cf St. Paul's description of the Church in Eph. 5.27.

4.8: *Amana . . . Senir and Hermon:* these rugged heights symbolize obstacles that would separate the lovers; cf. 2.14.

4.9: Sister: a term of endearment; it forms part of the conventional language of love used in this canticle.

you have ravished my heart with one
  glance of your eyes,
  with one bead of your necklace.
10   How beautiful is your love, my sister,
  my bride,
  how much more delightful is your
    love than wine,
  and the fragrance of your ointments
    than all spices!
11   Your lips drip honey, my bride,
  sweetmeats and milk are under your
    tongue;
  And the fragrance of your garments
    is the fragrance of Lebanon.

The Lover and His Garden

12G   You are an enclosed garden, my sister,
  my bride,
  an enclosed garden, a fountain sealed.
13   You are a park that puts forth
    pomegranates,
  with all choice fruits;
14   Nard and saffron, calamus and cin-
    namon,
  with all kinds of incense;
  Myrrh and aloes,
  with all the finest spices.
15   You are a garden fountain, a well of
    water
  flowing fresh from Lebanon.
16   Arise, north wind! Come, south wind!
  blow upon my garden
  that its perfumes may spread abroad.
  Let my lover come to his garden
  and eat its choice fruits.

CHAPTER 5

1G   I have come to my garden, my sister, my
  bride;
  I gather my myrrh and my spices,
  I eat my honey and my sweetmeats,
  I drink my wine and my milk.

D   Eat, friends; drink! Drink freely of
  love!

A Fruitless Search

2B   I was sleeping, but my heart kept vigil;
  I heard my lover knocking:
  "Open to me, my sister, my bride
  my dove, my perfect one.
  For my head is wet with dew,
  my locks with the moisture of the
    night."
3   I have taken off my robe,
  am I then to put it on?
  I have bathed my feet,
  am I then to soil them?

4   My lover put his hand through the
    opening;
  my heart trembled within me,
  and I grew faint when he spoke.
5   I rose to open to my lover,
  with my hands dripping myrrh
  With my fingers dripping choice myrrh
  upon the fittings of the lock.
6   I opened to my lover —
  but my lover had departed, gone.
  I sought him but I did not find him;
  I called to him but he did not answer
    me.

4.11: *Honey:* sweet words. Cf. Proverbs 5.3.

4.12: *Enclosed garden . . . fountain sealed:* reserved for the bridegroom alone. The bride's fidelity is implied.

4.14: These plants are all known for their sweet scents

4.16: The last two lines of the verse are spoken by the girl, inviting her lover to herself, the *garden.*

5.1: *Eat, friends; drink!:* the lovers are encouraged to enjoy the delights of their love, symbol of Christ's union with the Church.

5.2: A trial similar to that in 3.1ff.

5.3: The bride's hesitation is due, not to levity, but to strong emotion.

5.6: The disappearance of the lover seems to be a deliberate trial and test inflicted on the girl.

EMILY DICKINSON (1830-1886)

One of the greatest American poets, Emily Dickinson was not recognized in her lifetime. Only seven of her poems appeared in print before she died, all published anonymously. Unmarried, she lived with her brother and his wife in Amherst, Massachusetts. She was close to them and to a few friends. Her poems express deep feeling and question both God and nature. Her penetrating, concise use of language is unsurpassed in American literature.

AFTER GREAT PAIN, A FORMAL FEELING COMES

After great pain, a formal feeling comes —
The Nerves sit ceremonious, like Tombs —
The stiff Heart questions was it He, that bore,
And Yesterday, or Centuries before?

The Feet, mechanical, go round —
Of Ground, or Air, or Ought —
A Wooden way
Regardless grown,
A Quartz contentment, like a stone —

This is the Hour of Lead —
Remembered, if outlived,
As Freezing persons, recollect the Snow —
First — Chill — then Stupor — then the letting
     go —

A NARROW FELLOW IN THE GRASS

A narrow Fellow in the Grass
Occasionally rides —
You may have met Him — did you not
His notice sudden is —

The Grass divides as with a Comb —
A spotted shaft is seen —
And then it closes at your feet
And opens further on —

He likes a Boggy Acre
A Floor too cool for Corn —
Yet when a Boy, and Barefoot —
I more than once at Noon

Have passed, I thought, a Whip lash
Unbraiding in the Sun
When stooping to secure it
It wrinkled, and was gone —

Several of Nature's People

I know, and they know me —
I feel for them a transport
Of cordiality —

But never met this Fellow
Attended, or alone
Without a tighter breathing
And Zero at the Bone —

WHERE SHIPS OF PURPLE — GENTLY TOSS

Where Ships of Purple — gently toss —
On Seas of Daffodil —
Fantastic Sailors — mingle —
And then — the Wharf is still!

THE BRAIN IS WIDER THAN THE SKY

The Brain — is wider than the Sky —
For — put them side by side —
The one the other will contain
With ease — and You — beside —

The Brain is deeper than the sea —
For — hold them — Blue to Blue —
The one the other will absorb —
As Sponges — Buckets — do —

The Brain is just the weight of God —
For — Heft them — Pound for Pound —
And they will differ — if they do —
As Syllable from Sound —

MY LIFE CLOSED TWICE

My life closed twice before its close —
It yet remains to see
If Immortality unveil
A third event to me

So huge, so hopeless to conceive
As these that twice befell,
Parting is all we know of heaven,
And all we need of hell.

WILD NIGHTS! WILD NIGHTS!

Wild Nights — Wild Nights!
Were I with thee
Wild Nights should be
Our luxury!

Futile — the Winds —
To a Heart in port —

Done with the Compass —
Done with the Chart!

Rowing in Eden —
Ah, the Sea!
Might I but moor Tonight
In Thee!

MATTHEW ARNOLD (1822-1888)

A leading British poet, Matthew Arnold reflects in his poetry the loss of religious faith so common in the Victorian period following Darwin's promulgation of evolutionary theory. While "Dover Beach" suggests a beautiful feast for the eyes, the "grating roar" of the tide destroys the scene for the poet by reminding him of the unpleasant reality of a meaningless world.

DOVER BEACH

The sea is calm tonight,
The tide is full, the moon lies fair
Upon the straits; on the French coast the light
Gleams and is gone: the cliffs of England
    stand,
Glimmering and vast, out in the tranquil bay.
Come to the window, sweet is the night-air!
Only, from the long line of spray
Where the sea meets the moon-blanched land,
Listen! you hear the grating roar
Of pebbles which the waves draw back, and
    fling,
At their return, up the high strand,
Begin, and cease, and then again begin,
With tremulous cadence slow, and bring
The eternal note of sadness in.

Sophocles long ago
Heard it on the Aegean, and it brought
Into his mind the turbid ebb and flow
Of human misery; we
Find also in the sound a thought,
Hearing it by this distant northern sea.

The Sea of Faith
Was once, too, at the full, and round earth's
    shore
Lay like the folds of a bright girdle furled.
But now I only hear
Its melancholy, long, withdrawing roar,
Retreating, to the breath
Of the night-wind, down the vast edges drear
And naked shingles° of the world.

                        ° Pebbled beaches

Ah, love, let us be true
To one another! for the world, which seems
To lie before us like a land of dreams,
So various, so beautiful, so new,
Hath really neither joy, nor love, nor light,
Nor certitude, nor peace, nor help for pain,
And we are here as on a darkling plain
Swept with confused alarms of struggle and
    flight,
Where ignorant armies clash by night.

WALT WHITMAN (1819-1892)

Whitman was Romantic in his expansive vision of nature and human brotherhood and yet quite Modern in his verse form. The first to use free verse (that is, no rhyme and no meter), he defied the literary conventions of his day with the publication of Leaves of Grass in 1855. The influence of his free verse forms on modern poetry parallels the influence of his unconventional sexual views and behavior on moral attitudes.

WHEN I HEARD THE LEARN'D ASTRONOMER

When I heard the learn'd astronomer,
When the proofs, the figures, were ranged in columns before me,
When I was shown the charts and diagrams, to add, divide, and measure them,
When I sitting heard the astronomer where he lectured with much applause in the lecture-
    room,
How soon unaccountable I became tired and sick,
Till rising and gliding out I wandered off by myself,
In the mystical moist night-air, and from time to time,
Looked up in perfect silence at the stars.

JOHN MILTON (1608-1674)

Considered the second greatest poet in the English language, after Shakespeare, John Milton is best known for Paradise Lost, *a long narrative poem that follows the epic form of* The Odyssey *to tell the story of the casting out of Satan and the creation and fall of mankind, in the person of Adam and Eve. Milton was a devout Puritan who supported the Commonwealth government that overthrew the British monarchy. Upon the restoration of the Monarchy, Milton was jailed but later released, having become totally blind. Most of his poetry was dictated because of his blindness.*

WHEN I CONSIDER HOW MY LIGHT IS SPENT

When I consider how my light is spent[4]
  Ere half my days, in this dark world and wide,
  And that one talent[5] which is death to hide
  Lodged with me useless, though my soul more bent
To serve therewith my Maker, and present
  My true account, lest he returning chide,
  "Doth God exact day-labor, light denied?"
  I fondly° ask. But Patience, to prevent   foolishly
That murmur, soon replies, "God doth not need
  Either man's work or his own gifts. Who best
  Bear his mild yoke, they serve him best. His state
  Is kingly: thousands at his bidding speed,
  And post o'er land and ocean without rest;
  They also serve who only stand and wait."

---

[4] Milton was blind before he was fifty.
[5] A pun on Milton's talent as a poet and Christ's Parable of the Talents (Matt. 25: 14-30)

IV.

FAITH & MORALITY

Mask of Abraham
Plaster of Paris replica of an original altarpiece in a
medieval Roman Catholic Church in Kri žev či, Croatia.

INTRODUCTION

The humanities are "Western" — even while their values are universal — because the seeds of what Cicero called the *humanities* are planted in the classical period of Greek history and nourished by the religious beliefs and practices of three great religions: Judaism, Christianity, and Islam.

Both the Greeks and the Jews emphasized self-knowledge — the Greeks through reason and reflection, the Jews through faith and guilt. Jesus came along and taught love and redemption. Love God; love your neighbor; love yourself. The chief commandments. Why did Jesus include love of self? Because we have to be willing to accept failure (sin) as a stage for further growth. Not mindless existence, but a self-conscious growth leads to bliss, to a (eternal?) reward. Jesus, or at least the Greek/Jewish/Roman/Christian St. Paul, pulled together secular ethics and religious faith to create a new focus on man and his role on earth.

Philosophy (the love of wisdom) involves the pursuit of knowledge and understanding. And until the 20th century the pursuit focused on knowledge and understanding of the nature of man. What is man? Why is he here? What is his purpose, the end of his existence? If it is to pursue the Good then how do we know what is Good or Bad? And what is the *basis* of our decision?

In the *Book of Genesis* the story of Adam & Eve in the Garden of Eden gives us some simple answers. Not so easy to accept is the later *Book of Job* (5th century B.C.). We feel like saying: "Oh! Come on! No real person could be as accepting, as loving, as healthy and balanced as Job." Even Abraham's anguish over his decision to sacrifice his beloved son, Isaac, does not move us like the tale of Job. But is that, perhaps, because of the language, the style, the beauty of the *Book of Job*? Like *Prometheus Bound* the *Book of Job* explores the relationship between man and God, between divine right and the rights of man, between God's purpose for man and man's ability through his reason to know that purpose. But how different is Job's response from that of Prometheus? Ultimately, Job teaches us not how to *be good*, but how to accept faith, how to accept our need to make a commitment which we may not be able to understand fully.

The *Genesis* account of the anguish of Abraham may not stir us the way the *Book of Job* does, but Soren Kierkegaard's (1813-1855) exploration of that event in *Fear and Trembling* is startling. Using a poetic, difficult style of narrative, Kierkegaard's story of Abraham and Isaac and his penetration of the meaning of Abraham's faith seems to have forever changed the definition of faith in human history. Before Kierkegaard, religious faith in the Christian world required ceremony and sacrament, prayer and incantation, rules and regulations, dogma and theology, miracles, angels, and devils. After Kierkegaard, the very word, "faith," seems to have changed to accommodate his concept of the "leap of faith." For Kierkegaard faith is a leap from uncertainty to commitment. The leap implies trust and toleration of others and acceptance of absolute freedom and responsibility for self. There is no adherence to past authority, to rigid ritual, or to dead dogmas. There is always the potential for ridicule, despair, and the absurdity of a meaningless choice.

Kierkegaard placed a great burden on us. We are responsible for who we are. We create our own meaningful existence. We say, for example, that we "fall in love"; that is, we believe in a mystery for which there is no *logical* explanation. But we choose to act (or not act) anyway on that belief. Without certainty that we have chosen wisely (anguish) and with the possibility that our choice is absurd (because it may have no meaning or only the meaning we give to it through an improbable choice) we *nevertheless* believe, love, commit ourselves.

Most of us cannot grasp or accept the full implications of Kierkegaard's thought. The burden is too heavy. One German philosopher who did — and pushed beyond the limits set by Kierkegaard — was Friedrich Nietzsche (1844-1900). Although Nietzsche died when he was only 56, he was already completely insane by the time he was 45 years old. We have read two excerpts from his work already. What follows, the *Aphorisms and Maxims*, is not a systematic treatise (he hated systems) on faith or morality; rather we have a variety of snippets revealing his extraordinary willingness to question everything: God, art, philosophy, and, finally, sanity. The poem that follows, *Zemlja* (*Earth*), by Antun Šimić (1898-1925) was written shortly after World War I. It is an example of Central European (Croatian) literature influenced by Nietzsche. Šimić began writing as a devout Catholic and ended with antireligious "realism."

Between World War I and World War II there developed a literature built on Kierkegaard and Nietzsche which we call Existentialism. Existentialists emphasized the isolation of the individual, the absence of meaning in life, and the absurdity of conventional standards of belief and behavior. But they also affirmed the *necessity* for choice and the *necessity* for people, individually, to define themselves. Out of a demand for absolute freedom, out of a literature which claimed no purpose to man other than to be, Existentialists created new purpose and a new "form." The best known of the post World War II founders of this "philosophy" was Jean Paul Sartre (1905-1976), who talks about the chaos of his youthful Catholic faith: "the result was a disorder which became my particular order." Sartre represents atheistic existentialism: "There is no human nature, since there is no God to conceive it. " So, what is man? "Man is nothing else but what he makes of himself." Man, therefore, has a profound responsibility, and anguish comes from realizing that he cannot "escape the feeling of his total and deep responsibility." Unlike Aristotle, Sartre does not believe some men are brave and some cowardly, some good or some bad. Rather, he says, a "coward is responsible for his cowardice."

The courage to be what we are is precisely the theme of Paul Tillich's (1886-1965) work as a Christian Existentialist. In *Being and Courage* and in *The Courage of Despair* we find the reaffirmation of the relationship between faith and morality: "The act of accepting meaninglessness is in itself a meaningful act. It is an act of faith." Tillich is concerned about moral integrity. To be a full human being, one has to be consistently true to oneself and to other human beings. Isn't that a return to Jesus' great commandment: love self; love neighbor?

The existentialists deal with the question: What is the basis of our moral behavior? Related to that is a question they seem to find irrelevant as they find history nonrelevant: Where do we get the sanctions, or rules, or ideals of moral behavior? Existentialist emphasis on choice is good; however, we have to choose something, we need alternatives. Does that not imply knowledge of some beliefs and values? For example, the belief in individual worth; or the value of individual freedom.

For Socrates and Plato the answer to the first question was simple: "No evil can befall a good man." Do you agree? Glaucon challenges Socrates on that point with an allegory worthy of Socrates himself, *The Ring of Gyges*. Does Glaucon argue persuasively that even a "just" man will not act morally if he is invisible and society cannot restrain his behavior?

That brings us to the second question: In order to choose, do we need specific knowledge, indeed, moral education? Aristotle responds to that question systematically in four parts of his *Nicomachean Ethics*. In Book I, *The End of Human Activity*, he asks what is the ultimate end of all human striving. For the community it is to make "citizens . . . good and capable of noble acts" (later he will pursue that theme in his *Politics*). For the individual the end is happiness, the fulfillment of human life. How does Aristotle define happiness? What is the function of reason? of prosperity? of virtue? In Book X, *The Laws of Moral Education*, Aristotle rejects pleasure as the principle of happiness and argues for the serious life of moral action and pursuit of truth. But how is man to attain such a life? What kind of training is necessary? And what does Aristotle believe about the relationship between the nature of man and happiness?

In Book II, *Moral Virtue*, and in Book III, *Moral Responsibility*, Aristotle gives us his famous theory of the *media via*, the middle road. Each virtue, he argues, is the middle way between two extremes which are by definition vices. So, for example: courage is a virtue, it is the middle way between the extremes of rashness and cowardice; friendliness is a virtue, it avoids the extreme vices of obsequiousness and sulkiness. But are these mere formulas for virtue? Is a virtuous person someone who has a lukewarm moral personality? who is cold and calculating? Or does

Aristotle have another idea of the morally good man? For example, notice his emphasis on voluntary action, free will, free choice. Is his notion of moral responsibility not compatible with that of Tillich or even Sartre?

In pursuit of our discussion of faith and morality the value of Martin Luther King's (1929-1968) *Letter from Birmingham Jail* is King's powerful synthesis of three millenia of dialogue about beliefs and morals with a practical application, indeed a demand for action. In the tradition of *logos* and *praxis*, King creates a "tension in the mind" in order to get cooperative action; to get the American community to meet its moral responsibility to black citizens in particular but to all human beings in general. He evokes themes from many of our readings: the conflict between particular and universal laws in Antigone; the image of enlightenment in Plato's *Allegory of the Cave*; the despair of Langston Hughes' *Harlem*; the painful love of country expressed in Claude McKay's *America*; the hope and faith of Christian existence in Tillich's *The Courage of Despair*; the basic principles of moral responsibility in Aristotle's *Nicomachean Ethics*; the eloquence of Jefferson's *Declaration of Independence*; the basic commandments — love neighbor, love self.

All of the above is about the present and the past. Is there something the future can teach us about moral responsibility? In a provocative conclusion to his book, *The Human Prospect*, Robert Heilbronner, an MIT economist, asks us to consider the question: *What Has Posterity Done For Me?* Must we consider future generations? Is that a moral issue for us?

OLD TESTAMENT

THE BOOK OF JOB

The Book of Job *was written by an unknown author in the 5th century B.C.*

Job's History

THERE was a man in the land of Luz named Job. He was true and upright, and feared GOD, and avoided wrong. He had seven sons and three daughters born to him, and his possessions were seven thousand sheep, and three thousand camels, and five hundred yoke of oxen, and five hundred she-asses, a very large estate, so that the man was greater than all the Beni-Kedem.

His sons were accustomed often to feast at the house of each other; and would send and invite their sisters to eat and drink with them. But when the days of festivity had gone round, Job would send and sanctify them in the morning, and offer burnt-offerings for the whole, for Job reflected, "It may be my children have sinned, by not thanking GOD in their hearts."
Job continually behaved thus.

But a day came when the sons of GOD advanced to report themselves before the LORD, and the Accuser also was amongst them.
And when the LORD asked the Accuser, "Where do you come from?" the Accuser answered the LORD, and said:
"From flying over the earth, and travelling in it."
Then the LORD asked the Accuser, "Have you fixed your attention upon my servant Job? That there is not a man like him upon earth — honest and upright, who fears GOD and avoids wrong?"
The Accuser, however, answered the LORD and said, "Does Job reverence GOD for nothing? Have you not made a fence for him, and his family, and all that he has all round? You have

blessed the work of his hands, and his property has extended over the country. But perhaps if you stretched out your hand, and destroyed all he possesses, he would curse you to your face!"

The LORD consequently replied to the Accuser, "Whatever he has shall be in your power! except that you shall not exert your hand upon himself."

So the Accuser departed from the presence of the LORD.

Then another day arrived when his sons and daughters were eating and drinking wine in the house of their eldest brother, when a messenger came to Job and said, "The oxen were ploughing and the she-asses grazing near them, when the Shabim fell on and seized them, and have assaulted their attendants with the sword, and I alone have escaped to inform you."

Whilst he was speaking another came and said, "The fire of GOD has fallen from the skies, and has consumed the flocks and their attendants, and destroyed them, except myself, and I only have escaped to inform you!"

Whilst he was yet speaking another came, and said:

"The Kasdim collected in three troops, and rushed upon the camels, and seized them, and have assailed their attendants with the edge of the sword, except myself, and I only have escaped to tell you!"

While he was speaking another came, and said:

"Your sons and daughters were eating and drinking wine in their eldest brother's house, when a great storm came from over the Desert and seized the four corners of the house, and flung it down upon the youths, and killed them, except myself, and I alone have escaped to tell you!"

Then Job arose and tore his robe, and shaved his head, and threw himself upon the ground and worshipped, and said:

"I came naked from my mother's womb;
And naked I shall return.
The LORD gives and the LORD removes!
Let the name of the LORD be blessed!"
In this Job did not sin, nor accuse GOD of injustices.

Another day arrived when the sons of GOD reported themselves to the LORD, and the Accuser reported himself amongst them to the LORD; when the LORD asked the Accuser, "Where do you come from?"

And the Accuser answered the LORD and said, "From flying over the earth, and travelling in it."

The LORD then asked the Accuser, "Have you fixed your attention on My servant Job, that there is none like him on the earth, an honest and upright man, who fears GOD, and turns from wrong; who yet happily retains his virtues, although you induced Me to causelessly afflict him?"

The Accuser, however, replied to the LORD and said, "Skin to skin! A man will give all that he has for his life! Perhaps if you were to extend your hand now, and torture his bones and his flesh, he would curse you to your face."

So the LORD answered the Accuser and said to him, "Look! He is in your power, except that you shall regard his life."

The Accuser consequently went out from the presence of the LORD, and struck Job with a painful ulcerous inflammation, from the sole of his foot to the crown of his head. And he took a potsherd to scrape himself with, and he sat down amongst the ashes.

His wife, however, said to him, "Will you still stick to your virtues? Curse GOD; and die!"

But he replied to her, "You speak as one of the worthless women speak. We accepted comforts from GOD, so should we not also accept discomfort?"

In all that Job did not sin with his lips.

* * *

Now three friends of Job heard of all these troubles that had come upon him, so each came from his house — Eliphaz the Themanite, and Bildad the Shuhite, and Zophar the Namathite — and agreed to go and mourn with him, and comfort him; but when they from a distance raised their eyes and could not recognize him, they lifted up their voices and wept, and each tore his robe, and flung dust on their heads, and were stupefied, and sat with him for seven days and seven nights on the earth, but did not speak to him, for they saw that his despair was great.

Job's Lament

At length Job opened his mouth, and cursed his day; and Job exclaimed, and said:

Perish the day upon which I was born,
And the night it was said, "A man is
    conceived!"
Let that day be darkness itself,
Let not GOD look down from above
Nor shine upon it with His light!
Let death's gloomy shadow avenge,
Black clouds make their resting-place there;
And terrors in daytime affright.
Count it not in the course of the year,
Nor reckon along with the months!
Let solitude be in that night,
That in it no joy may be heard!
Let them curse it, who curse at the day,
Who are stripped for the serpent at dawn;
Let the stars of its dawning be dark,
Let it long for, but never have light,
And see not the eyelids of morn!
For it closed not the doors of the womb,
Nor hid my distress from my sight!
  Why died I not in the womb,
Or expired in the act of my birth?
Oh! why did the knees give support?
And why did the breasts that I sucked?
For then I had lain, and been still,
Then had rest and found ease for myself,
With the kings and the statesmen of earth,
Who build themselves desolate tombs;
Or with princes, along with their gold,
Who fill up their graves with their wealth;
Or had been like abortions concealed,
Like children that never see light,
Where the wicked must cease from their
    crimes,
Where the strong, when exhausted, have rest;
Where together the captives can lie,
And hear not their driver's fierce voice!
Where the small and the great are alike,
And the slave from his master is free!

Oh! why give the wretched the light,
And life to the bitter in soul —
Who long for, but cannot meet death,
And who dig more than for treasure for him!
Who delight, and will even exult,
And are glad when they find out the tomb!
To a man on a path that is lost,
And whose landmarks his GOD has
    confused?
For my sighing comes up with my food,
And my groanings like water poured out;
For the terror I feared has arrived,
And that which I dreaded has come!
I invited Peace, Quiet, and Rest,
But instead savage Tumult steps in!

The First Address of Eliphaz

Eliphaz the Themanite, however, replied and said:

If we speak you a word, will you fret?
But who can his excitement restrain?
Consider how many you taught,
And strengthened the hands of the weak!
Your speaking supported the faint,
And you strengthened the trembling knees;
But now it has come on yourself,
You stagger and grieve at its touch.
Was not your religion your trust,
And your trueness in action your hope?
Think — where are the innocent lost?
And where are the upright destroyed?
I see that the ploughers for vice,
And the sowers of wrong, reap the crop!
Undone by the blast sent from GOD
They waste in His tempest of wrath.
            * * *

He will save you six times from distress,
And in seven the woe will not touch;
In famine will free you from death,
And in war from the hand of the sword;
            * * *

Job's Reply to Eliphaz

But Job replied, and said:

Who will carefully weigh out my grief,
And poise all my woes in the scale?
For they outweigh the sand of the sea,
(My words are in consequence sharp.)
I am pierced by the Almighty's darts,
Whose poison my spirit drinks up,
And against me all God's terrors fight.

         * * *

I acknowledge that it is a truth
That no man can be just before GOD.
If one wished to contend against Him,
Not one in a thousand could speak.
Wise-hearted, Almighty in Force,
Who can resist Him with success
Who casts down the hills unawares,
O'erwhelms them in His anger and wrath.
And makes the supports of it rock;
At whose order the sun would not shine,
And He even can seal up the stars!
Who only can stretch out the skies,
And walk on the waves of the sea!
Who made the fixed star of the North,
The Bright-way and the Halls of the South;
Who does great and inscrutable things,
And wonders that no one can count!
He passes! But I see Him not!
He flits by, and I do not perceive!
When He snatches — who then can resist?
Who can say to Him — what would you do?
GOD turns not away from our wrath;
To Him the proud giants must bow.

   Then how could I answer to Him?
Or against Him arrange all my thoughts?
Were I right I could never debate,
But must humbly entreat to my judge.
If I called, and He answered to me,
Am I sure He would list to my voice?
Who sweeps me as though with a storm,
And strikes me with wounds without cause;
Who hinders me drawing my breath,
Who has gorged me with bitterest griefs;
As to Power? — How mighty He is!
As for Right? — Who dare witness for me?
Am I righteous? — My mouth would convict;
Am I honest? — I may be deceived!
I am honest! Know I not my soul?
And yet I despise my own life!
But this I assert as a fact,

He destroys both the good and the bad.
He kills as with some sudden lash,
And laughs at the victims who strike!
Gives the earth to the hand of the bad,
And muffles the mouth of the judge.
If it is not He? Then who does?

   But my days are more swift than a post!
They run forward, and never find rest;
Like the ships of the pirates sail off;
Like eagles that pounce on their prey!
If I say, "I care not for my woes,
I will loosen my face, and will smile!"
I am terrified still by my griefs,
For I know that you will not release!

   I know I am wicked myself;
Why then should I labor in vain?
If I wash myself white as the snow,
And make my hands clean with the soap,
You would plunge me again in a ditch,
And my clothing would shrink from myself.
For a man like myself could not speak,
Nor bring us together to plead,
For no one exists to decide,
And control both of us by his hand.
From me let him take off his rod!
And not by his terrors oppress,
For then I could speak and not fear,
But not in the state I now am!

   My body is weary of life;
I abandon myself to complaint;
I will speak in the grief of my mind!
And I beg of GOD not to convict.
Inform me for what you contend?
Is oppression a pleasure to you,
To despise the poor work of your hand;
And prosper the plans of the bad?
Have you only the eyes of a man
Or see but as mortals perceive?
Are your days like the days of mankind?
Or your years like the period of man?
That you hunt to find out my defects,
And seek to discover my sin,
When you know that I am not depraved
And that none can relieve from your hand?
It was your hand that formed me and made,
And compacted. — Then why now destroy?
Remember, you made me from clay,
That to dust you will make me return!
And did you not curdle like milk,
And fixed me together like cheese,
Then clothed me with skin, and with flesh,

And with bones and with muscles compact?
And gave me my Life, and my Reason.
Then last, fixed my Spirit in me?
Tho' you hid all these things in your heart,
I know the result was from you.
And that you would observe if I sinned;
And would not acquit from my guilt.
    If wicked, alas! then for me!
If righteous, I raise not my head!
Be content with my shame! See my woe,
Like a lion, he rises to seize!
And you are turned from me estranged;
Against me you heap up the proof,
Increasing your anger with me
And against me your armies are massed!
So why did you bring from the womb?
    Oh! would I had died, and none seen,
As tho' I had never had life,
And had gone from the womb to the grave!
Are not my days fading and few?
Oh! leave me a moment of rest,
Ere I go, whence I never return,
To the land of the black shadowed gloom,
To the land where the brightness is black,
Like the shadow of death,
Where there are no columns of light,
And whose brightness is black!

The First Address of Zophar

Zophar the Namathite, however, replied, and
said:

The number of words does answer not,
No man is made right by his lips;
For your chatter, should men become silent,
And your sneering should no one resent?
For you say: "My conduct was spotless,
And I have been pure in your sight!"
How I wish GOD would grant you a word,
And against you would open His lips!
And teach you the Wisdom Unseen,
For His Knowledge and power are wide,
It would teach you GOD pardons your faults.
Can you find GOD by your research,
Though intently you seek the Most High?
Mount to heaven! Yet what can you do?
Explore then the Grave. — What is found?
He extends beyond limits of earth,
And further than stretches the sea;
If He turns, and decides, and proclaims,

Who then can resist to His will?
For He knows when a mortal is vile;
Sees his vice — that himself does not know.
But man has a heart that is dull,
Man is born but a wild ass's colt.
Yet if you will order your heart,
And spread out your hands before Him,
If you throw out your faults from your grasp,
Nor let wickedness dwell in your tent,
You can lift up your face without shame,
You then can be bold, and not fear;
Your sufferings will then be forgot,
Or remembered like streams that are passed!
And your lifetime arise to its noon,
For your life will break out into dawn,
Bringing comfort, because there is hope,
And be shamed for your trust in the false,
And rest, and have nothing to fear,
And many will seek for your face;
But the eyes of the wicked will fail,
And to them shall no refuge remain,
For their hope is — their very last breath!

The Third Reply of Job

Job, however, answered:

No doubt but that you are the men,
And that wisdom will die with yourselves!
But I have a mind like your own,
And I am not inferior to you!
But who does not know things like these?
Yet I am a joke to my friends!
"Let him call to his God, and get a reply!"
The Upright and Just are despised!
Those resting in light scorn a lamp,
Which is prized by those feeling their steps.
    Yet the tents of the plunderers prosper,
And GOD makes the ruffians secure;
And GOD brings the wealth to the stores
Of those whose sole god is their power!
Even ask of the beasts to instruct
And the birds of the skies to inform,
Or the weeds of the earth who can teach,
Or the fish of the sea to relate,
Such rubbish as yours, who knows not?
For the hand of the LORD has done this,
In whose hand is the breath of all life,
With the soul that resides in each man.
But cannot the ear taste of words,
As the palate distinguishes food?

Let it be; "That the old man is wise
And that those of long days understand,"
Yet with Him reside wisdom and power,
With Him are reflection and thought,
Look! He throws down, and none can
    rebuild,
Shuts up, and no man can release;
He holds back the waters — they fly
He releases — and then the lands floods!
Both Strength and Perfection are his,
His are the Oppressor, and Oppressed!
He leads the contrivers to plunder;
But yet makes their punishment shine!
He expands the dominion of kinds,
And girdles their loins with might;
But yet lets the priesthoods be captured,
And the mightiest he overwhelms!
From the eloquent, he takes the lip,
And deprives the old men of their sense;
On princes he pours out contempt,
And loosens the belt of the great!
Uncovers the depths of the gloom,
Brings light to the shadow of death;
He nations exalts and depresses;
Or the nations extends and they last;
Yet takes sense from the heads of the earth,
And they wander in wastes without paths,
They grope in the dark without light,
And they stagger like men who are drunk.

Mine eyes have observed all these things,
I have heard, and my ears understood;
What you know, I know that myself,
I am no more a fool than are you.

Now, I will address the Most High,
And to GOD I will turn with my plea;
For you are but painters of falsehood!
And worthless physicians are you!
I wish you would keep yourself silent;
For that is your far wisest plan;
And listen to me while I reason
And attend to the plea of my lips!
Why will you talk folly for GOD?
Why utter your falsehoods as His?
For can you His Presence exalt?
Are you the defenders of GOD?
When He searches, will He approve you,
If you flatter, as you flatter men?
Be assured that He will reprove
If you flatter by falsehood His state.
And should you not reverence His Height?
And should not His dread fall on you?

Reflect, that your proverbs are dust,
And your maxims are mountains of mud!
Keep silent to me while I speak!
I, myself, let come on me what may!
I am mad, — with my flesh in my teeth,
And I put my life into my hand;
Let Him kill me; yet I do not care!
In His presence I plead for my course!
Perhaps He will save me Himself;
For villains dare not seek His face!
Listen, listen! to what I can say,
And I will explain to your ears,
For, how I arrange my defence,
I know my acquittal is sure!
Who is it against me will plead?
I then will be silent and die!
Oh! only grant two things for me,
Then I will not hide from your face;
Remove this affliction away,
And let not your terror o'erwhelm;
Then summon and I will respond,
Or let me speak — and you can reply.
Say what are my vices and sins?
Oh! teach me my frailties and faults.
For what do you hide up your face,
And think me a foeman of yours?
And why do you chase withered leaves,
Or hunt after stubble dried up?
That you write against me bitter things,
And clothe with the sins of my youth;
And fasten my feet in the stocks,
And watch to find my hidden ways,
And examine the marks of my feet?
And that here I am rotting away
Like a garment that moths have consumed!

Man — who is born of a woman,
For a few days, and those full of grief,
Who springs like a flower, and is cut,
Who flies like a shadow unfixed!
On such a thing why set your eyes,
And why call me to judgment with you?
To whom is it given to be pure?
Not one can exist without stain!
His years and his months are decreed;
You fix his impassable bound;
Then let him alone — let him rest,
Till he end, like a workman his day!
For the tree has a hope if cut down,
For it sprouts, and its shoot does not fail;
Though its roots have grown old in the earth,
And its stump may decay in the dust,

At the scent of the water it lives,
And its boughs grow, as planted anew;
But man dies, and he withers away!
And a mortal expires, and is gone!
Like the waters depart from a fladge,
And a torrent when scorched up and dried.
So man must recline and not rise,
Nor wake till the skies are no more,
Nor arouse from the depth of his sleep!
　Who will help me to rest in the grave?
To hide till your anger is passed?
And fix me a time for recall?
For if the dead man is recalled,
I would hope all the days of my war,
Until my discharge would arrive.
If you called me, then I would attend,
You could order the creature you made.
But now you are counting my steps,
And closely are watching my sins!
Seal up my defects in a bag,
And my passions sew up with a seam.
For a mountain falls down by degrees,
And a rock can decay from its place,
The stones are worn down by the brook,
And the dust is swept off by a flood,
But the hopes of mankind are destroyed.
You crush, and he goes off for ever!
His form fades, and you send him away!
He knows not, if his sons come to fame;
If they suffer he cannot console;
His body grieves but for himself,
And his mind for himself only mourns.

*　*　*

My spirit is writhing in pain
　My days flying fast to the grave!
Altho' my deriders withstand,
As an obstacle fixed in my sight!
Oh! fix now my bail for yourself;
But who will give bond on my part?
For you take common sense from their
　hearts,
And so you rely not on them,
To decide on the fate of their friend,
So the sight of their children shall fail.
I am placed as a proverb to men,
And become a contempt in their sight!
So with sadness my eyes are oppressed,
And my form is consumed to a shade.
The upright may wonder at this;
And the clean from pollution be roused;
But the righteous will hold on his way,

And the pure-handed add to his strength.
But all you, — turn round, and be off!
For wisdom I find not in you!
My days fly! My purposes fail!
The cherished ideas of my heart,
Can they change the night into day,
By light that proceeds from the dark?
When I measure my home in the grave,
And in darkness spread I out my bed;
When I call to my father, Corruption,
You, my Mother and Sister, the Worm,
But if so, then where is my hope?
And my hope, who can ever behold
When gone down with my frame to the
　grave,
If together we rest in the dust?

The Second Address of Bildad

However, Bildad the Shuhite answered, and
said:

Pray when will you stop in your talk?
Be sensible! Then we can speak.
Why are we regarded as beasts,
As something unclean in your sight?
He tears up his soul in his rage!
Should the earth be deserted for you?
And the rocks be removed from their place?
　Yes! the light of the bad is put out,
And the gleam from the flame of his fire!
And the light in his tent shall be dark,
And the lantern above it be quenched!
His vigorous stridings will halt,
And his tactics will lead to defeat,
For his feet will be caught in his net,
And himself bound about in his toils!
His heel will be caught in a hole,
A noose will be flung over him;
A rope be concealed in the earth;
And a trap for him laid on the road,
Be harassed by terrors all round,
And his feet shall be broken to bits!
A famine shall come on his strength,
And destruction shall fix to his flank
Devouring the skin of his limbs,
And the first-born of death gnaw his frame;
His guard will be driven from his tent,
And the King of the Terrors march in;
Who will dwell in his tent, no more his,
And lightning be poured on his home.
His root will be dried up below,

And his branches be withered above;
His memory will perish from earth;
And his fame not remain in the streets!
He be driven from dawn to the dark,
And hunted away from the world!
Without son, or grandson, in his tribe,
And none to survive in his home.
The Westerns will wonder at his day,
And the Easterns be seized with a fear,
    Yes! such are the homes of the bad!
Such the place not acknowledging GOD!

The Fifth Reply of Job

Job, however, replied, and said:

How long will you worry my life?
And make me feel crushed by your words?
You have libelled me fully ten times,
And are yet not ashamed to revile?
But grant it be true, I have sinned,
My errors remain with myself.
Why indeed should you swell up against
And reproach me, with my own disgrace?
Admit, that GOD has oppressed me,
And His lasso has flung round my neck,
That unanswered, I cry in distress,
And appeal — but I have not a judge!
That He blocks up the path I would go,
And spreads darkness over my roads;
Has stipped off my glory from me
And my turban has thrown from my head;
That He breaks me wherever I go,
And has pulled up my hopes like a tree;
That He kindled His fury at me,
That He treats me as one of His foes,
For His troops come advancing in mass,
Their rampart against me they pile,
And encamping, encompass my hall!

    My kinsmen have flown far away,
My companions are scattered abroad,
They cease to approach, and forget;
My guests and my maids think me strange,
They forget; I'm unknown in their sight!
My lad replies not if I call
To him I must soften my voice!
And my feelings are strange to my wife,
And I plead to the sons of my breast;
Even children regard me with scorn,
When I rise up they ridicule me;
I am loathed by my intimate friends

And those whom I loved turn away;
My bones pierce my skin and my flesh,
I possess but the skin of my teeth!
Oh pity me! pity me, friends!
For GOD's hand is heavy on me!
Like GOD would you persecute me,
Unsatisfied yet with my flesh?
    Who will help me to write out my tale?
Who will help to record in a book?
Or with pen made of iron, or lead,
Or cut deep on a rock for all time?
    For I know my defender does live,
And at last will rise over my dust,
And after this skin is destroyed
I shall yet in my flesh gaze on GOD!
Whom I shall gaze on for myself,
Mine eyes see Himself — no one else
Fulfilling the hopes of my breast!
While you cry, "Why did we pursue
When the root of the fact he had found?"
And you tremble yourselves at the sword,
For the sword is the fear of the bad,
When at last you discover my judge!

The Second Address of Zophar

Zophar the Namathite, however, answered and
said:

Because I am driven by my mind,
And I rush from the passion within,
Having heard an insulting reproof
I answer with spirited thought.
Know you not this from of old,
Since Adam was placed upon earth,
That the triumph of sinners is short
And the joys of the vile but an hour?
If he goes up as high as the skies
And his head reaches up to the clouds,
Like his dung he will perish for ever;
Those who saw him will ask, "Where is he?"
He will fly like a dream, nor be found,
And vanish like visions at night.
An eye-glance, — for it is no more,
And he never returns to his place!
His children shall flatter the low,
And their hands will repay for his sin.
His vices will fill up his bones,
And with him lie down in the dust!
Tho' vice has been sweet to his taste,
Concealing it under his tongue;

Tho' he fondled and never forsook
But retained in the roof of his mouth;
Yet the food in his bowels will turn
To the venom of asps in his breast.
He will vomit the plunder he gorged,
From his stomach his god will be cast!
He will suck in the poison of asps,
The sting of the adder will kill.
He shall not see the pools or the streams
Of the rivers of honey and oil,
Nor consume the reward of his work;
He carries the wealth, but owns not!
For he crushed and abandoned the weak,
Stole a house that he never had built,
For he never knew rest in his greed,
He never let slip his desire,
And nothing escaped from his knife:
His wealth, therefore, will not endure.
He has fear in amassing his hoard
That the hand of distress may approach.
While he goes to accomplish his greed
Fierce wrath is discharged upon him,
And is rained as he sits at his food!
If he flies from the weapon of iron,
He is shot by a bow made of steel!
A swift arrow comes up to his back,
And it goes to his gall, with its barb!
All darkness is stored up for him,
A fire unblown will consume;
It is bad for those left in his tent!
The skies will uncover his sins,
And against him the earth will rise up,
And the wealth of his house flow away
Like the floods in the day of a storm!
    Such from GOD is the fate of bad men!
And their portion appointed from GOD.

The Sixth Reply of Job

But Job answered and said:

Attentively list to my speech!
That may, perhaps, alter your mind.
Bear with me, while I, myself, speak,
And after I speak you can jeer.
Is my complaint made to a man?
And why should not my spirit be sharp?
Look at me! and be not surprised;
And place your hand over your mouth!
I'm amazed when I think of myself,
And trembling takes hold of my flesh!
    Say, why are the wicked in life?

Grow old, and are mighty in wealth?
Their offspring are sitting by them,
And playing about in their sight.
There is peace in their houses, not fear,
GOD brings no disturbance on them;
Their bull genders, and that without fail,
Their cow calves, without ever a slip;
Their children go out like a flock,
And their infants are skipping about;
They sing to the timbrel and harp,
And delight in the sound of the flute;
On pleasure they float all their days,
And easily go to the grave!
Tho' they say to GOD, "Get far from us!
We care not to learn of your ways!
For why should we serve the Most High?
What our wages for working for Him?"
    Do they not enjoy what is nice?
(Get from me you villainous thoughts!)
How seldom the villains' lamp fails,
Or upon them arrives a distress
Distributing griefs in its rage?
When are they as straw before wind,
Or like chaff that the tempest sweeps off?
"But GOD stores up grief for their sons?"
Let Him punish their sins on themselves,
Let their own eyes perceive the results,
And drink the wrath of the Most High!
What care they for their house after them
When their number of months has rushed
    by?
But who can teach knowledge to GOD,
When He is the judge of the highest?
    This one dies in perfection of strength,
Reclining at ease, and in peace;
With his buckets o'erflowing with milk,
And with marrow to moisten his bones;
That one dies with his soul full of grief,
And never with pleasure could eat.
Together they lie in the dust
And over them wallows the worm!
    Yes! I know of what are your thoughts
And the libels you frame against me!
You ask, "Where the house of the prince
And the hall where he spread out his bed?"
Why not ask those who pass on the road,
On whose evidence you would rely?
That the bad escape times of distress,
And are led from the dangerous day;
Who dare tell to his face of his ways?
Who repay to him what he has done?

He is carried away to his tomb
And a guard watches over his mound;
The clods of the valley are sweet,
And after him all will proceed
As unnumbered before him have gone!
　　Then why do you comfort in vain
Since your reasonings result in a lie?

The Third Address of Eliphaz

Eliphaz the Themanite, however, answered and said

Can a man be essential to GOD
As a man of skill may to his like?
Does your righteousness profit the Highest?
Does He gain by your course being straight?
For fear of you, will He debate,
Or with your will He go to a judge?
　　Now! Is not your wickedness great,
And your vices without any end?
For your brother you robbed of his pledge
And have stripped from the naked his rags;
You quenched not the weary with drink,
From the famishing held back his bread!
But the powerful — to him gave the land!
And the haughty-faced dwelt upon it!
You sent starving widows away,
And the arms of the fatherless broke!
So, therefore, unlooked for confound!
And darkness that you cannot see;
And torrents of water o'erwhelm!
　　Is not GOD in the Heavens on high,
Looking over the heads of the stars?
　　But you may ask, "What can GOD know?
Or distinguish behind the black gloom?
Black clouds are around, — He sees not;
For He walks in the sphere of the skies!"
　　You keep to the very old path
Which the vilest of mortals have trod;
Who were snatched off before their full time
Whose foundations were swept by a flood;
Who cried to GOD, "Get far away!"
And, "What gain is th' ALMIGHTY to us?
He fills up their houses with wealth."
(Begone your vile statements from me!)
No! The righteous look on and are glad,
And the virtuous laugh him to scorn;
"Our foeman," they cry, "is now wrecked,
And the fire will consume his remains."

Now make Him your friend and have peace;
To you the results will be good.
Accept, now, the Law from His mouth,
And fasten His words on your heart.
To the Mighty Constructor return,
Depravity drive from your tent,
And throw your gold into the dust,
　　— Yes, your ore from the rivers of Ophir!
And let the Most High be your wealth,
And the glitter of silver to you!
For then the ALMIGHTY will love,
And your face you can lift up to GOD!
He will hear you whenever you pray
And He will accomplish your vows;
And He will effect your intent,
And the light will shine over your ways!
Though He humbles; He can say, "Arise,"
When the eyes are cast down, then He saves,
Protecting the virtuous home,
Protecting your unsoiled hands!

The Seventh Reply of Job

Job, however, replied, and said:

Very bitter my thought is to-day!
But His hand overpowers my groans.
Who will help to discover and find?
I would go to the place where He dwells,
Arranging before Him my cause,
And with reasonings filling my mouth.
I would learn the replies He would give,
And understand what He would say.
Would He fight me with powerful speech?
No! But He would be gentle with me,
For the honest can reason with Him;
So my cause would triumphantly win!
　　Look! I go to the East; He is not!
To the West; — But I cannot perceive!
To the North, where He works — But find not!
To the South, where He hides; — But unseen!
Yet He knows the course that I go.
At the test, stand pure as gold;
I have fastened my feet in his steps,
Unwavering have I kept to His path;
Not shirking the law of His lips,
In my breast I have stored His commands!
But Him? — He is ONE! — Who can turn?
For what He desires, He does!

He will work out His objects with me;
But how many are there with Him?
So, excluded His presence, I faint;
I reflect, and I tremble at Him!
For GOD has deprived me of heart,
Th' ALMIGHTY brought trouble to me.
Why was I not cut off ere the dark,
And before I was covered with gloom?

Since Times are not hid from th' Almighty,
Why know not His friends His fixed days?
For there are movers of handmarks,
There are robbers of flocks as they graze;
They drive from the orphans their ass,
The widow's ox take as a pledge,
The wretched they turn from their path,
Till the poor of the land herd in troops,
And go like wild colts on the plains.
Their plunder begins at the dawn,
To seize for their followers food;
They reap in a field not their own,
And with violence pluck off the grapes;
The naked they leave without clothes
And without any cover from cold,
So they soak in the rain from the hills
And shelterless stick to the rock!
The infant they drag from the breast
And the clothes from the wretched as pledge,
Who without any covering go bare,
And who hungering carry their sheaves;
And who, in their barns, press the oil,
And tread out their wine — but have thirst!
In the city the murdered may groan,
And the soul of the tortured may roar,
But GOD pays no heed to their prayer!
And others revolt from the light,
Hate His ways nor will stay in His path.
The murderer detesting the light,
Who slaughters the wretched and poor,
And comes like a thief in the night.
The adulterer waits for the dark
When he thinks that no eye can observe,
And places a mask on his face.
With darkness he enters the home
He had marked for himself in the day,
That he dare not approach in the light,
Fearing dawn, as the shadow of death,
For it seems to his terrors like doom.
You say, "Swiftly he glides down a brook!
His lot will be cursed on the earth;
To his vineyard he never retains;

As drought and heat steal the snow-streams,
So will the grave those who sin.
Reft of love, and devoured by worms
The Villain is always forgot;
And the wicked will break like a stick,
For they injure the wretch without child,
To the widows they never do good!"
Yet He[1] strengthens the proud in his power,
Lifts him up when he thought not to live,
And gives to him confident strength,
Tho' His eyes can discover his ways.
They rise for their time; then depart;
And they curl up when perfectly ripe
And are cut like the ears of the corn!
And if not — let who will refute me
And fling to oblivion my speech?

* * *

The Eighth Reply of Job

Job, however, answered and said:

To the helpless — what help do you bring?

Have you strengthened the arm without
   force?
To the ignorant what do you teach
Or help by the lot that you know?
From whom have you stolen your speech,
And whose thoughts are sent out thro' you?

[2]GOD lives, tho' He turned from my plea,
And Th' Almighty, who bitters my soul!
So while ever breath lingers in me
And the spirit of GOD in my face,
No rubbish shall come from my lips
And my tongue shall not pour out deceit!
Curse me, if I justify you!

---

[1]That is, GOD does so. In the Hebrew writings the
Creator is often referred to without meaning, but is
understood by force of the context.

[2]Chapter xxvii., verse I. The first verse of chapter
xxvii., "And Job continued to take up his speech and
said," is not part of the original text, for it breaks the
sense. It has been added by some old copyist as an
endeavor to lessen the gap made by the part of
Bildad's speech erroneously inserted in Job's, from
verses 5 to 14 of chapter xxvi. I therefore relegate it
to a note, and let the fiery flow of Job's address run
on without interruption — F.F.

Till I die, I'll not turn from my right,
To my righteousness I will cling fast,
Nor the thought of my life be reproached!
Let my enemy be like the bad,
My opponent become like the vile!
For what hope has the rogue, tho' enriched,
When GOD is demanding his soul?
Will GOD refrain if he shrieks
When upon him the anguish has come?
In th' Almighty he did not delight
Or call upon GOD at all times.

    I could teach you the power of GOD
Nor conceal what is with the Most High;
But yourselves, all of you can see that,
Then why do you babble such stuff?

The Third Address of Zophar

[3]Zophar the Namathite, however, answered and said:

This is the lot of the wicked from GOD,
And the scoundrel's fate from the Most High!
His children increase for the sword,
And his offspring are not filled with bread.
His descendants are buried by death,
And his widows will never lament!
If he heaps up the silver like dust
And piles up his clothing like clay,
He may pile, but the righteous will wear,
And the virtuous inherit his wealth.
He builds up his house like a moth,
Or a watchman erecting a hut,
He lies down without loss and is rich,
When he opens his eyes, all is gone!
The terrors rush on him like streams,
He is ruined by thieves in the night.

---

[3] Verse 13. The reply of Zophar begins here, as the sense of the text up to the end of chapter xxvii, shows, though by the error of some old transcribers it is made to appear as if uttered by Job, although the import of it is totally opposed to his line of argument, and to his style, and makes him stultify his previous contention—that we do not see the good invariably rewarded and successful in this world, nor the bad always punished; but with terrible frequency the contrary. I shall therefore restore the proper heading to this speech, as suggested by Mr. A. Elzas in his "Book of Job": Trubner and Co., London — F.F.

The east wind will rise, and he flies,
And the whirlwind will sweep him from
  home
It unsparingly sweeps upon him
From its powerful blast he must fly;
After him it will clap with its hands
And whistle him out of his home!

    But for silver there yet is a vein
And a place where they wash out the gold;
And iron is obtained from the dust,
And copper is smelted from stone;
A mine is sunk down to the dark
And its secrets are fully explored;
In the black rock and shadow of death
A shaft is sunk down to descend
Without any rests for the feet,
The men hanging on to a swing
Who bring from earth's bowels their bread;
Whose basement they tear up with fire,
Whose rocks are the sapphire's home.
In its dust is discovered the gold,
In places unknown to the hawk,
Untraced by the vulture's keen eye.
Wild beasts would not travel that road,
Nor the lion would venture to go!
Yet man lays his hand to the flint,
He breaks up the roots of the hill;
He hews out his drives in the rocks,
And his eye searches everything rare.
He stops off the trickling streams,
And he brings out the hidden to light.

    But wisdom, where can he find,
Or where is the dwelling of sense?
Its origin man cannot know
Nor find in the land where we live.
Space answers, "With me it is not!"
And the Sea says, "It rests not in me!"
Nor for it can bullion be paid;
Nor payment in silver can buy!
Nor the ingots of Ophir be sold,
Or the brightest of diamonds and gems.
Unequalled by jewels of gold,
And unmatched by the glittering stone;
Nor can onyx and crystal be named
Or wisdom be purchased by pearls!
The topaz of Kush equals not
And the chasings on gold cannot buy!

    From where then can wisdom be got,
And where is the home of good sense,

If she hides from the eyes of all life,
And is hid from the birds of the skies?
Destruction and Death both declare.
We have heard of her fame with our ears;
But GOD, only, has looked on her ways
And He alone knows of her home!
For He looks to the ends of the earth,
Observing all under the skies;
When He fixes the weight of the wind
And measures the seas with a rule!
When He makes a decree for the rain
And a way for the thunderous flash:
He sees her, and makes a decree,
Applies her, and also approves,
And proclaims to mankind, "Be assured,
It is wisdom, to fear the Supreme;
And sense, to abandon the wrong!"

The Ninth Reply of Job

But Job proceeded to take up his contention,
and replied:

Who will make me as in former months,
As the times when GOD watched over me?
When His lamp brightly shone o'er my head,
And His light when I walked in the dark;
As I was in the days of my wealth,
When GOD counselled me in my tent;
And whilst the Almighty was mine,
And servants attended around;
When washing my footpath in cream,
When the rock poured me ponds full of oil;
When I went to the gate through the town,
When I spread out my seat in the square;
The children on seeing me hid,
And the elder men rose up and stood;
The princes broke off from their speech,
And laid their hand over their mouth;
The voice of the nobles was still,
And their tongue was held close to its roof.
And when the ear heard me, it blest,
And the eye that looked on me approved;
For I rescued the wretch who appealed
And the destitute who had no help!
The perishing brought me their thanks,
And I gladdened the poor widow's heart.
In goodness I dressed, and was clothed,
I made justice my robe and my crown!
And I became eyes to the blind,
And I, also, was feet to the lame;
And a father I was to the poor,

And the cause of the friendless I searched.
I broke the jaw teeth of the vile,
And tore the prey out of their mouth!
  So I thought I should die in my nest,
And add to my days like the sand!
That my roots would spread out to the
  streams,
And the dew drops would rest on my
  boughs;
And my honors be freshened for me,
And my bow keep its spring in my hand!
  Then they waited to listen to me,
And were silent to hear my advice;
When I had spoke, no one replied,
And upon them my sentences dropped.
And they waited for me as for rain,
And opened their mouths as for showers.
If I laughed at them, did they believe?
They turned not from the smile on my face!
I chose their course, sitting as chief,
And I stood as commander of troops.
I encouraged them when they despaired!

But they now are laughing at me
Who are lower in rank than myself,
Whose fathers I would have disdained
To put with the dogs of my flocks!
  What to me is the strength of their hands
Whose whole vigor has wasted away?
Gaunt with hunger and famine, they
  gnawed,
And raged yesterday in the wastes!
And plucking up cress in the bush
And the roots of the bracken for food!
They were chased away out of our midst;
They roared after them as to thieves;
They dwelt in the rents of ravines,
In holes in the dust, and in caves!
In the shelter of bushes they brayed,
And under the thorns they were wed!
Sons of tramps — yes, men with no name
They were driven away from the land.
  But I am become now their song,
And I am become their contempt!
They insult, and they wave me away,
And refrain not to spit in my face,
Since He loosened my nerve and depressed,
In my presence they throw off the rein.
On the right a mob rise at my feet,
They point and heap insults on me.
They roughen my paths to annoy,

And do mischief that profits them not.
They come on, as though thro' a breach,
With roaring they roll themselves up;
Their terrors are turned upon me.

My nobility flies like the wind,
And my power has passed like a cloud.
My life now is poured out from me
And times of depression have seized;
My bones shoot within me at night,
And their gnawing will not let me rest;
My clothes must be stripped off by force,
I am galled by the band of my coat.
I am flung out, as tho' I were dirt,
And become like to ashes and dust!

I shout, but they answer me not.
I stand up. But they look not on me!

How fiercely upon me you turn
To desolate by your strong hand!
You lift me to ride on the wind
And melt me away in a mist!
For I know you will bring me to death,
To the home fixed for all who may live!
Yet he lays not his hand on my wreck
Though I should be glad of my end!

I wept in their time of distress,
And troubled my mind for the poor.
Yet when I hoped good, evil came:
When hoping for light, came the gloom!
My bowels boil up and rest not;
I'm confronted by days of distress!
I am blackened, but not by the heat.
I rise in the public and roar;
I am come to be brother to snakes,
And mate with the daughters of woe!

My blackened skin peels off in strips,
And my bones are burnt up by the heat,
And my harp has become to me grief,
And my flute as the sobbing of tears!

Yet a treaty I made with my eyes
That I never would look on a maid;
Else what part could I have in HIGH GOD,
Or share in th' ALMIGHTY above?
Do not the depraved meet distress,
and to practise such vices estrange?
Would He not have looked on my ways,
And reckoned up every step?

Yet if I have walked with the vile
And my footsteps have run to seduce,
Let HIM weigh me in scales that are just;
Then GOD will acknowledge my truth!
If my eyes have turned towards that road,

And my heart has gone after my eyes,
And defilement has stuck to my hand,
Let me sow, what another will eat,
And my crops be pulled up by the roots!

If my heart was seducing a wife,
If I watched at the door of my friend,
For another then let my wife grind,
And strangers be lying with her!
For that is a cowardly crime
And a wrong for the judges to brand,
And a fire, consuming to Hell,
Which would root up the whole I produced.

If I refused right to my slave,
Or my waitress, disputing with me,
Then what could I do when GOD rose,
And when He inquired, what say?
He formed them in the breast like myself,
And constructed alike in the womb.

If I turned from the plea of the poor,
Or the eyes of the widow made fail;
If I ate of my morsel alone,
And the orphan shared not of the same;
— Like a father I nourished his youth;
Her, I helped from my own mother's breast

If I looked on a tramp without clothes,
Or the wretched without any cloak;
If his joints were not thankful to me
When warmed by the fleece of my sheep;
If I raised up my hand on the weak,
When I looked on my power in the Court;
Let my shoulder fall off from its blade,
And my arm at its socket be broke!
For the reverence of GOD was on me,
And I would not resist His decrees.

If my trust I have placed in my gold,
Or said, "I rely on my hoards";
If glad that my wealth was so great
And that treasure was found by my hand;
If I looked on the sun when it shone,
Or on the bright moon in her walk;
And in secret my heart was seduced,
And my hand I have kissed to her face,
That also I knew to be wrong,
A denial of GOD the SUPREME[4]
If I joyed at the death of my foe,

---

[4] Verses 38 to 40 must be inserted between verses 34 and 35 of the common reading, as they have been misplaced by some ancient transcriber, and destroy the proper form of Job's sublime defence as they are ordinarily printed.

If pleased when he met with distress,
Or gave up my palate to sin
By asking a curse on his life;
If the men of my tent ever said,
"Who will give us his meat in our need?"
No stranger lodged outside my court,
To the trav'ler my doors were unclosed;
Had I hidden, like Adam, my fault,
Concealing my sin in my breast,
As though I had fear of the crowd,
Dismayed by contempt of the mass,
And dare not go out of my door;
If my land has shrieked out against me
And its furrows together lament;
If I ate of its fruits without pay,
And sneered at its owner's demands,
Let thistles spring up, and not wheat,
And instead of the barley, vile weeds!
Who will grant me to listen to me?
How I wish the ALMIGHTY would speak,
Or my enemy write in a book!
I could carry it then on my back,
I could place on my head as a wreath,
I could tell Him the tale of my steps,
I would go up to Him like a prince!

THE END OF THE SPEECHES OF JOB

* * *

The Address of Jehovah

Then JEHOVAH answered to Job out of the whirlwind, and said:

Who is this that obscures reflection
By speeches on what he knows not?
Like a hero now gird up your loins
I will ask you, and you answer Me!
Where were you, when I founded the earth!
Inform! if you knew of My plan!
Who fixed its extent? Since you know!
Or who on it stretched out the line?
On what were its timberings laid;
Or who fixed its keystone on high?
When the stars of the morn sang together
And the sons of GOD shouted for joy?
When the sea was shut up within doors,
When it came with a rush from the womb,
When I gave it the fogs for a cloak.
And in darkness enwrapped it around;
And over it laid my decree,
And fixed it with bars and with doors,

And said, "So far you can come
Advance not — but there stay your proud
    waves!"
All your days have you governed the dawn,
Taught the morning to know her own place?
With her vesture of roseate bloom,
And draped in it as with a robe,
To seize on the wings of the earth,
And to drive off the bad from her face,
And to take from the wicked their light,[5]
And the arm they are lifting to wound?
    Have you gone to the springs of the Sea
Have you traversed the limits of Space
Have Death's portals been opened to you
Have you looked on the Gates of Despair?
Know you all that is done upon earth?
Explain — if you know of the whole!
    Where is the road to the dwelling of Light,
And where is of Darkness the home?
Can you guide us as far as their bounds,
Do you know the paths to their house?
You know! — for then you were born!
And the number of your days is extreme!
    Have you been to the countries of snow
And examined the treasure of hail
That I hoard for the time of distress,
For the day of encounter and war?
What path tread the rays of the Light
And how spread the winds over earth?
Who cut for the typhoon its course
And a road for the lightnings to shine?
    Who pours rain on the land without men,
On the desert where no man resides;
To satiate the desert and waste
And to cause a green meadow to grow?
And who is the father of the rain?
And the drops of the dew, who begot?
From whose belly comes out the ice,
And the frost of the skies who has made;
When the waters congeal like a stone,
And it captures the face of the deep
Did you fasten the Pleiades' chain?
Or scatter the Wandering-Fool?[6]
Do you guide the Signs of the Seasons?
Or console the North Star and his sons?

---

[5] "And to take from the wicked their light." That is, to take away darkness, which is the day of criminals, whose time of action is night.

[6] Supposed to be the constellation called now Orion.

Have you revealed Laws for the Skies,
Or settled the Laws of the Earth?
Can you lift up your voice to the clouds
And with water-floods cover yourself?
If you send lightnings out, will they go
And reply, "We are ready for you?"
   Who leads out the meteors with skill,
Or gives to the comets their sight?
Who skillfully numbers the clouds,
Who pours out the skins of the skies,
When the dust is converted to mud,
And together the clods of earth stick?
   Do you hunt for the lion his prey;
Or fill the young whelps of wild beasts,
When they lie cowering down in their dens,
And hide by themselves in their lairs?
Who prepares for the raven its food
When its young ones are shrieking aloud
And are worn out for want of their meat?

   Mark the birth time of goats of the rock,
And watch the birth-throes of gazelles!
And count the full period they breed,
And observe at the time they bring forth!
They contract, and their children leap out
They cast all their sorrows away!
Their children are hardy and strong,
And run off to reside by themselves.
   Who sent out the wild asses free?
From the zebra who loosened the chain?
Whose house I have fixed in the waste
And in the salt-marshes its home?
It laughs at the crowd of the town,
Regards not the call of the groom;
It feeds on the chance of the hills
And hunts after anything green!
   Do you wish for the Reem as your slave?
Would he lodge at the side of your crib?
If you harness the Reem to your plough
Will he harrow the plain after you?
Will you trust him because he is strong
And abandon your earnings to him?
Or trust him that he will come back
And pile up your grain in your barn?
   Would you trust to the loud clapping wing
Of the stork — to the ostrich, so strong,
Who abandons her eggs on the earth
And hatches them out on the dust;
And forgets that the footstep may crush
Or the beast of the pasture may break?

Who is hard to her young, as not hers,
And cares not if she labor in vain;
For GOD has withheld from her sense,
And gave her no mind to reflect;
Yet when she has risen to fly
She laughs at the rider and horse!
   Did you give his strength to the horse?
Clothe his neck with the quivering mane?
And make like a grasshopper leap
And snort in his terrible pride?
He paws on the plain, and is glad;
With his vigor he charges in fight,
Eats the ground in his fierceness and rage,
Unrestrained at the sound of the horn;
At the blast of the trumpet he neighs
And snorts for the battle from far,
For the thundering captains and cheers!
He laughs undismayed at its woes,
Nor shrinks from the face of the sword,
Tho' on him the arrows may pour
And the flash of the spear and the dart!
   By your intellect do swallows fly,
And spread out their wings for the South?
Does the eagle mount up at your word
And build up his nest on the peak,
And settle his home on the crag
And his foot on the ledge of a cliff,
From where he can spy out his prey,
Where his eyes can perceive it from far;
His fledglings there suck up the blood,
And his is where the slain bodies lie!

The LORD also continued, and said:

   Is the ALMIGHTY's Appellant content?
   Has the Critic of GOD a reply?

Then Job answered, and said:

   I was foolish, what can I reply?
   So my hand I lay over my mouth.
   I spoke once; — but will not speak again.
   Nay twice, but I will not repeat.

Jehovah's Second Address

Again JEHOVAH answered Job out of the
Whirlwind, and said:

   Then gird up your waist like a man;
   I will ask you, and you instruct Me;

How can you My judgments reverse;
Convict Me and set yourself free?
Or is your arm equal to GOD's,
And can your voice thunder like His?
Deck yourself now with glory and might
And clothe you in splendor and power;
Fling round you your anger and wrath
And examine the proud and o'erthrow!
Examine and humble the fierce,
Depressing the bad by their acts,
And hide them together in dust,
And blindfold their faces from light;
And I, then, will congratulate you
That your right hand can rescue yourself!

See Behemoth, My work, like yourself!
He feeds upon grass like an ox,
His power is placed in his loins,
And force in his obstinate breast;
Like a cedar he flashes his tail,
His thighs are a muscular plait,
His bones are as pieces of steel,
Like forgings of iron his frame:
He is chief of the products of GOD;
He who made, can destroy with His sword!
Then the mountains produce him his food,
Where all beasts of the field sport about;
Under willows he lies down to sleep,
In the shade of the reeds and the fens;
The willow tree's shade is his tent,
And the bush of the valley surrounds.
He fears not the furious flood!
He is calm, tho' streams rush in his face!
Who can catch him, when laid on the watch?
Or who run a rope through his nose?

Is Leviathan caught with a hook?
Can they tie down his tongue with a cord?
Or put a straw rope through his nose,
Or pierce through his jaws with a thorn?
Will he multiply pleadings to you,
Or address you in flattering words?
Will he write out a treaty with you
To be your perpetual slave?
Can you play with him, as with a bird,
Or put in a cage for your girls?
Can your friends make a feast off of him?
Or can he to merchants be sold?
Can you pierce with your prickling his skin,
Or his head with the spear used for fish?
Once touch him! you will not forget!
You never again will assail!

Why, to try for him would be in vain!

One drops, if but looking at him!
I will not relate of his limbs,
His courage, and power, and form!
Who dare open his mouth for a bit,
Or bring double bridle to him?
Who dare open the doors of his mouth
Surrounded with terrible teeth:
His back is the bosses of shields
Pressed close with the print of a seal,
Where everyone sticks to his mate,
And the wind cannot go in between!
For everyone holds in its place.
They grasp, and they cannot be split!
And when he is sneezing, light shines;
And his eyes are the eyelids of dawn!
And flashes come out of his mouth,
And sparkles of fire escape;
From his nostrils a vapor proceeds
Like flame from a furnace, or straw!
His breath is the burning of coals
And flames proceed out of his mouth!
His vigor sits down on his neck,
And terror precedes his advance!
The flakes of his flesh stick as one
So close that they cannot be moved!
His heart is as hard as a stone,
Yes! as hard as the stone of a mill!
When he rises, the brave are dismayed;
They stagger, as tho' in the waves!
If the sword reach, it will not pierce him,
Nor the spear, or the stone, or the dart!
He fancies that iron is straw,
And the steel to be mere rotten wood!
No arrows can turn him to flight!
Sling-stones he converts into chaff!
He thinks that the club is a rush!
And laughs at the shake of a spear!
And his sharp-pointed claws are beneath,
Supporting his course on the mud!
He makes the deep boil like a pot
And embroiders the water with foam,
And after his passage it shines!
It seems that the depths have turned grey!
On the dust there is nowhere his match
Who was made so as not to feel fear!
He gazes on all that is great;
He is king over all the wild beasts.

Who are you, who dare not arouse him,
Yet who dare resist Me to My face?
Who has worked for Me? — I will repay.

All under the heavens is Mine!

Then Job answered, and said:

"I know that your power is supreme,
And your purpose cannot be withstood!
Who am I? I hid fact without thought
And I spoke what I never could know

Of acts that I understood not,
When I said, `Hear, and then I will speak,
`I will question, and you must reply!'
I had heard of you once by my ear,
But now I have seen with my eyes,
So I am convinced, and repent
On the dust and in ashes reclined."

Now it occurred that after JEHOVAH had addressed these discourses to Job, that JEHOVAH said to Eliphaz the Themanite, "My anger burns against you and your two friends, for you have not reasoned correctly about Me, like My servant Job. So now choose for yourselves seven bullocks and seven rams, and go to My servant Job, and offer a sacrifice for yourselves, when My servant Job will pray for you, — for I will accept his presence, — so that I may not do any injury to you because you have not reasoned correctly about me, like my servant Job."

Consequently Eliphaz the Themanite, and Bildad the Shuhite, and Zophar the Namathite, went and did as the EVER LIVING commanded them, and the EVER LIVING accepted the presence of Job. Then the EVER LIVING removed the miseries of Job when he prayed for his friends, and the EVER LIVING gave Job twice as much as he had formerly. And his brothers and sisters came to him, with all his acquaintance, to congratulate him, and ate bread with him in his home, and condoled with him and comforted him over all the suffering that the LORD had laid upon him, and each of them gave him a lamb, and every one a ring of gold.

The EVER LIVING thus blessed Job more than formerly, and he possessed fourteen thousand sheep, six thousand camels, a thousand yoke of oxen and a thousand she-asses. He also had seven sons, and three daughters, and called the first of them Jemima, and the second Kezia, and the name of the third was Karenhepuk, and in all the country none were found so beautiful as the daughters of Job. Their father gave them fortunes as well as to their brothers.

Job lived after this a hundred and forty years, and saw his sons, and grandsons, and great-grandsons of the fourth generation. Then Job died, an old man, and satiated with years.

AESCHYLUS (525-456 B.C.)

Aeschylus, the first Greek dramatist to use dialogue and stage action, explored the relationship between human beings and the gods. In the character of Prometheus, a god who defied all-powerful Zeus, he gives us a model of courage and sacrificial love who is often compared with Christ.

FROM PROMETHEUS BOUND

Prometheus:
    An easy tale for one who has his foot
    Without the toils to teach and lecture him
    Who feels the actual ill. But I indeed
    Was well prepared for all befallen me.
    With intent I sinned, with intent — I hide it
      not:

    By helping men I gained myself these
      pangs.
    Yet thought I not by such a punishment
    To waste away amid these high-poised
      rocks,
    Doomed to this barren solitary peak.
    But ye, bewail not my now present woes,

But light down on the ground, and to the
    fate
In store for me give ear: so thoroughly
Shall ye know all. Yield to my asking,
    yield;

Bear so much part with the sufferer. Even
    thus
Winged trouble flits from each to each by
    turn.

THE BOOK OF GENESIS, CHAPTER 22

THE ANGUISH OF ABRAHAM

The Testing of Abraham

Some time after these events, God put Abraham to the test. He called to him, "Abraham!" "Ready!" he replied. Then God said: "Take your son Isaac, your only one, whom you love, and go to the land of Moriah. There you shall offer him up as a holocaust on a height that I will point out to you." Early the next morning Abraham saddled his donkey, took with him his son Isaac, and two of his servants as well, and with the wood that he had cut for the holocaust, set out for the place of which God had told him.

On the third day Abraham got sight of the place from afar. Then he said to his servants: "Both of you stay here with the donkey, while the boy and I go on over yonder. We will worship and then come back to you." Thereupon Abraham took the wood for the holocaust and laid it on his son Isaac's shoulders, while he himself carried the fire and the knife. As the two walked on together, Isaac spoke to his father Abraham. "Father!" he said. "Yes, son," he replied. Isaac continued, "Here are the fire and the wood, but where is the sheep for the holocaust?" "Son," Abraham answered, "God himself will provide the sheep for the holocaust." Then the two continued going forward.

When they came to the place of which God had told him, Abraham built an altar there and arranged the wood on it. Next he tied up his son Isaac, and put him on top of the wood on the altar. Then he reached out and took the knife to slaughter his son. But the Lord's messenger called to him from heaven, "Abraham, Abraham!" "Yes, Lord," he answered. "Do not lay your hand on the boy," said the messenger. "Do not do the least thing to him. I know now how devoted you are to God, since you did not withhold from me your own beloved son." As Abraham looked about, he spied a ram caught by its horns in the thicket. So he went and took the ram and offered it up as a holocaust in place of his son. Abraham named the site Yahweh-yireh; hence people now say, "On the mountain the Lord will see."

Again the Lord's messenger called to Abraham from heaven and said: "I swear by myself, declares the Lord, that because you acted as you did in not withholding from me your beloved son, I will bless you abundantly and make your descendants as countless as the stars of the sky and the sands of the seashore; your descendants shall take possession of the gates of their enemies, and in your descendants all the nations of the earth shall find blessing — all this because you obeyed my command."

Abraham then returned to his servants, and they set out together for Beer-Sheba, where Abraham made his home.

SÖREN KIERKEGAARD (1813-1855)

Born in Denmark, Kierkegaard became disillusioned with society and religion, while at the same time he longed for the religious faith that his intellect was unable to accept because his poetic and spiritual quest raised questions that contradicted the spirit of his age. His writings, unappreciated in his lifetime, were rediscovered in the post-World War I period and later developed by French existentialists Camus and Sartre. Unlike them, however, Kierkegaard chose to make the "leap of faith" that was required to maintain a personal commitment to Christianity in a world that seemed to lack any meaning.

FEAR AND TREMBLING[7]

Foreward

Not only in the world of commerce but also in the world of ideas our age has arranged a regular clearance sale. Everything may be had at such absurdly low prices that very soon the question will arise whether anyone cares to bid. Every waiter with a speculative turn who carefully marks the significant progress of modern philosophy, every lecturer in philosophy, every tutor, student, every sticker-and-quitter of philosophy — they are not content with doubting everything, but "go right on." It might, possibly, be ill-timed and inopportune to ask them whither they are bound; but it is no doubt polite and modest to take it for granted that they have doubted everything — else it were a curious statement for them to make that they were proceeding onward. So they have, all of them, completed that preliminary operation and, it would seem, with such ease that they do not think it necessary to waste a word about how they did it. The fact is, not even he who looked anxiously and with a troubled spirit for some little point of information ever found one, nor any instruction, nor even any little dietetic prescription, as to how one is to accomplish this enormous task. "But did not Descartes proceed in this fashion?" Descartes, indeed! that venerable, humble, honest thinker whose writings surely no one can read without deep emotion — Descartes did what he said, and said what he did. Alas, alas! that is a mighty rare thing in our times! But Descartes, as he says frequently enough, never uttered doubts concerning his faith. . . .

In our times, as was remarked, no one is content with faith, but "goes right on." The question as to whither they are proceeding may be a silly question; whereas it is a sign of urbanity and culture to assume that everyone has faith, to begin with, for else it were a curious statement for them to make, that they are proceeding further. In the olden days it was different. Then, faith was a task for a whole lifetime because it was held that proficiency in faith was not to be won within a few days or weeks. Hence, when the tried patriarch felt his end approaching, after having fought his battles and preserved his faith, he was still young enough at heart not to have forgotten the fear and trembling which disciplined his youth and which the mature man has under control, but which no one entirely outgrows — except insofar as he succeeds in "going on" as early as possible. The goal which those venerable men reached at last — at that spot everyone starts, in our times, in order to "proceed further." . . .

The Spirit of the Occasion

There lived a man who, when a child, had heard the beautiful Bible story of how God tempted Abraham and how he stood the test, how he maintained his faith and, against his expectations, received his son back again. As this man grew older, he read this same story with ever greater admiration; for now life had separated what had been united in the reverent simplicity of the child. And the older he grew, the more frequently his thoughts reverted to that

---

[7]S. V. III, 57-82.

story. His enthusiasm waxed stronger and stronger, and yet the story grew less and less clear to him. Finally he forgot everything else in thinking about it, and his soul contained but one wish, which was, to behold Abraham; and but one longing, which was, to have been witness to that event. His desire was, not to see the beautiful lands of the Orient, and not the splendor of the Promised Land, and not the reverent couple whose old age the Lord had blessed, and not the venerable figure of the aged patriarch, and not the God-given vigorous youth of Isaac — it would have been the same to him if the event had come to pass on some barren heath. But his wish was, to have been with Abraham on the three days' journey, when he rode with sorrow before him and with Isaac at his side. His wish was, to have been present at the moment when Abraham lifted up his eyes and saw Mount Moriah afar off; to have been present at the moment when he left his asses behind and wended his way up to the mountain alone with Isaac. For the mind of this man was busy, not with the delicate conceits of the imagination, but rather with his shuddering thought.

The man we speak of was no thinker, he felt no desire to go beyond his faith: it seemed to him the most glorious fate to be remembered as the Father of Faith, and a most enviable lot, to be possessed of that faith, even if no one knew it.

The man we speak of was no learned exegetist, he did not even understand Hebrew — who knows but a knowledge of Hebrew might have helped him to understand readily both the story and Abraham.[8]

I

And God tempted Abraham and said unto him: take Isaac, thine only son, whom thou lovest, and go to the land Moriah and sacrifice him there on a mountain which I shall show thee.[9]

It was in the early morning. Abraham arose betimes and had his asses saddled. He departed from his tent, and Isaac with him; but Sarah looked out of the window after them until they were out of sight. Silently they rode for three days; but on the fourth morning Abraham said not a word but lifted up his eyes and beheld Mount Moriah in the distance. He left his servants behind and, leading Isaac by the hand, he approached the mountain. But Abraham said to himself: "I shall surely not conceal from Isaac whither he is going." He stood still, he laid his hand on Isaac's head to bless him, and Isaac bowed down to receive his blessing. And Abraham's aspect was fatherly, his glance was mild, his speech admonishing. But Isaac understood him not, his soul could not rise to him; he embraced Abraham's knees, he besought him at his feet, he begged for his young life, for his beautiful hopes; he recalled the joy in Abraham's house when he was born, he reminded him of the sorrow and the loneliness [that would be after him]. Then did Abraham raise up the youth and lead him by the hand, and his words were full of consolation and admonishment. But Isaac understood him not. He ascended Mount Moriah, but Isaac understood him not. Then Abraham averted his face for a moment; but when Isaac looked again, his father's countenance was changed, his glance wild, his aspect terrible. He seized Isaac and threw him to the ground and said: "Thou foolish lad, believest thou I am thy father? An idol worshiper am I. Believest thou it is God's command? Nay, but my pleasure." Then Isaac trembled and cried out in his fear: "God in heaven, have pity on me, God of Abraham, show mercy to me, I have no father on earth, be thou then my father!" But Abraham said softly to himself: "Father in heaven, I thank thee. Better is it that he believes me inhuman than that he should lose his faith in thee."

When the child is to be weaned, his mother blackens her breast; for it were a pity if her breast should look sweet to him when he is not to have it. Then the child believes that her breast has changed; but his mother is ever the same, her glance is full of love and as tender is ever. Happy he who needed not worse means to wean his child!

---

[8] This is ironic, of course.
[9] Freely after Genesis 22.

II

It was in the early morning. Abraham arose betimes and embraced Sarah, the bride of his old age. And Sarah kissed Isaac who had taken the reproach from her — Isaac, her pride, her hope for all coming generations. Then the twain rode silently along their way, and Abraham's glance was fastened on the ground before him; until on the fourth day, when he lifted up his eyes and beheld Mount Moriah in the distance; but then his eyes again sought the ground. Without a word he put the fagots in order and bound Isaac, and without a word he unsheathed his knife. Then he beheld the ram God had chosen, and sacrificed him, and wended his way home. . . . From that day on Abraham grew old. He could not forget that God had required this of him. Isaac flourished as before, but Abraham's eye was dimmed; he saw happiness no more.

When the child has grown and is to be weaned, his mother will in maidenly fashion conceal her breast. Then the child has a mother no longer. Happy the child who lost not his mother in any other sense!

III

It was in the early morning. Abraham arose betimes: he kissed Sarah, the young mother, and Sarah kissed Isaac, her joy, her delight for all times. And Abraham rode on his way, lost in thought — he was thinking of Hagar and her son whom he had driven out into the wilderness. He ascended Mount Moriah and he drew the knife.

It was a calm evening when Abraham rode out alone, and he rode to Mount Moriah. There he cast himself down on his face and prayed to God to forgive him his sin in that he had been about to sacrifice his son Isaac, and in that the father had forgotten his duty toward his son. And yet oftener he rode on his lonely way, but he found no rest. He could not grasp that it was a sin that he had wanted to sacrifice to God his most precious possession, him for whom he would most gladly have died many times. But, if it was a sin, if he had not loved Isaac thus, then could he not grasp the possibility that he could be forgiven: for what sin more terrible?

When the child is to be weaned, the mother is not without sorrow that she and her child are to be separated more and more, that the child who had first lain under her heart, and afterward at any rate rested at her breast, is to be so near to her no more. So they sorrow together for that brief while. Happy he who kept his child so near to him and needed not to sorrow more!

IV

It was in the early morning. All was ready for the journey in the house of Abraham. He bade farewell to Sarah; and Eliezer, his faithful servant, accompanied him along the way for a little while and then turned back. They rode together in peace, Abraham and Isaac, until they came to Mount Moriah. And Abraham prepared everything for the sacrifice, calmly and mildly; but when his father turned aside in order to unsheath his knife, Isaac saw that Abraham's left hand was knit in despair and that a trembling shook his frame — but Abraham drew forth the knife.

Then they returned home again, and Sarah hastened to meet them; but Isaac had lost his faith. No one in all the world ever said a word about this, nor did Isaac speak to any man concerning what he had seen, and Abraham suspected not that anyone had seen it.

When the child is to be weaned, his mother has the stronger food ready lest the child perish. Happy he who has in readiness this stronger food!

Thus, and in many similar ways, thought the man whom I have mentioned about this event. And every time he returned, after a pilgrimage to Mount Moriah, he sank down in weariness, folding his hands and saying: "No one, in truth, was great as was Abraham, and who can understand him?"

A Panegyric on Abraham

If a consciousness of the eternal were not implanted in man; if the basis of all that exists were but a confusedly fermenting element which, convulsed by obscure passions, produced everything, both the great and the insignificant; if under everything there lay a bottomless void never to be filled — what else were life but despair? If that were the case, and if there were no sacred bonds between man and man; if one generation arose after another, as in the forest the leaves of one season succeed the leaves of another, or like the songs of birds which are taken up one after another; if the generations of man passed through the world like a ship passing through the sea and the wind over the desert — a fruitless and a vain thing; if eternal oblivion were ever greedily watching for its prey and there existed no power strong enough to wrest it from its clutches — how empty were life then, and how dismal! And therefore it is not thus; but, just as God created man and woman, he likewise called into being the hero and the poet or orator. The latter cannot perform the deeds of the hero — he can only admire and love him and rejoice in him. And yet he also is happy and not less so; for the hero is, as it were, his better self with which he has fallen in love, and he is glad he is not himself the hero, so that his love can express itself in admiration.

The poet is the genius of memory and does nothing but recall what has been done, can do nothing but admire what has been done. He adds nothing of his own, but he is jealous of what has been entrusted to him. He obeys the choice of his own heart; but once he has found what he has been seeking, he visits every man's door with his song and with his speech, so that all may admire the hero as he does and be proud of the hero as he is. This is his achievement, his humble work, this is his faithful service in the house of the hero. If thus, faithful to his love, he battles day and night against the guile of oblivion which wishes to lure the hero from him, then has he accomplished his task, then is he gathered to his hero who loves him as faithfully; for the poet is, as it were, the hero's better self, unsubstantial, to be sure, like a mere memory, but also transfigured as is a memory. Therefore shall no one be forgotten who has done great deeds; and even if there be delay, even if the cloud of misunderstanding obscure the hero to our vision, still his lover will come sometime; and the more time has passed, the more faithfully will he cleave to him.

No, no one shall be forgotten who was great in this world. But each hero was great in his own way, and each one was eminent in proportion to the great things he loved. For he who loved himself became great through himself, and he who loved others became great through his devotion, but he who loved God became greater than all of these. Every one of them shall be remembered; but each one became great in proportion to his trust. One became great by hoping for the possible; another, by hoping for the eternal; but he who hoped for the impossible, he became greater than all of these. Every one shall be remembered; but each one was great in proportion to the power he struggled with. For he who strove with the world became great by overcoming it; and he who struggled with himself by overcoming himself; but he who strove with God, he became the greatest of them all. Thus there have been struggles in the world, man against man, one against a thousand; but he who struggled with God, he became greatest of them all. Thus there was fighting on this earth, and there was he who conquered everything by his strength, and there was he who conquered God by his weakness. There was he who, trusting in himself, gained all; and there was he who, trusting in his strength, sacrificed everything; but he who believed in God was greater than all of these. There was he who was great through his strength, and he who was great through his wisdom, and he who was great through his hopes, and he who was great through his love; but Abraham was greater than all of these — great through the strength whose power is weakness, great through the wisdom whose secret is folly, great through the hope whose expression is madness, great through the love which is hatred of one's self.

Through the urging of his faith, Abraham left the land of his forefathers to become a stranger in the land of promise. He left one thing behind and took one thing along: he left his worldly wisdom behind and took with him faith. For else he would not have left the land of his fathers, but would have thought it an unreasonable demand. Through his faith he came to be a stranger in the land of promise, where there was nothing to remind him of all that had been dear to him, but where everything by its newness tempted his soul to longing [for the old]. And yet was he God's chosen, he in whom the Lord was well pleased! Indeed, had he been one cast off, one thrust out of God's mercy, then might he have comprehended it; but now it seemed like a mockery of him and of his faith. There have been others who lived in exile from the fatherland which they loved. They are not forgotten, nor is the song of lament forgotten in which they mournfully sought and found what they had lost. Of Abraham there exists no song of lamentation. It is human to complain; it is human to weep with the weeping; but it is greater to believe, and more blessed to consider him who has faith.

Through his faith Abraham received the promise that in his seed were to be blessed all races of mankind. Time passed, and it became most unlikely; yet Abraham had faith. Another man there was who also lived in hopes. Time passed, the evening of his life was approaching; neither was he paltry enough to have forgotten his hopes: neither shall he be forgotten by us! Then he sorrowed, and his sorrow did not deceive him, as life had done, but gave him all it could; for in the sweetness of sorrow he became possessed of his disappointed hopes. It is human to sorrow, it is human to sorrow with the sorrowing; but it is greater to have faith and more blessed to consider him who has faith.

No song of lamentation has come down to us from Abraham. He did not sadly count the days as time passed; he did not look at Sarah with suspicious eyes, whether she was becoming old; he did not stop the sun's course lest Sarah should grow old and his hope with her; he did not lull her with his songs of lamentation. Abraham grew old, and Sarah became a laughingstock to the people; and yet was he God's chosen and heir to the promise that in his seed were to be blessed all races of mankind. Were it, then, not better if he had not been God's chosen? For what is it to be God's chosen? Is it to have denied to one in one's youth all the wishes of youth in order to have them fulfilled after great labor in old age?

But Abraham had faith and steadfastly lived in hope. Had Abraham been less firm in his trust, then would he have given up that hope. He would have said to God: "So it is, perchance, not Thy will, after all, that this shall come to pass. I shall surrender my hope. It was my only one, it was my bliss. I am sincere, I conceal no secret grudge for that Thou didst deny it to me." He would not have remained forgotten; his example would have saved many a one; but he would not have become the Father of Faith. For it is great to surrender one's hope, but greater still to abide by it steadfastly after having surrendered it; for it is great to seize hold of the eternal hope, but greater still to abide steadfastly by one's worldly hopes after having surrendered them.

Then came the fullness of time. If Abraham had not had faith, then Sarah would probably have died of sorrow, and Abraham, dulled by his grief, would not have understood the fulfillment, but would have smiled about it as a dream of his youth. But Abraham had faith, and therefore he remained young; for he who always hopes for the best, him life will deceive, and he will grow old; and he who is always prepared for the worst, he will soon age; but he who has faith, he will preserve eternal youth. Praise, therefore, be to this story! For Sarah, though advanced in age, was young enough to wish for the pleasures of a mother, and Abraham, though gray of hair, was young enough to wish to become a father. In a superficial sense it may be considered miraculous that what they wished for came to pass, but in a deeper sense the miracle of faith is to be seen in Abraham's and Sarah's being young enough to wish, and their faith having preserved their wish and therewith their youth. The promise he had received was fulfilled, and he accepted it in faith, and it came to pass according to the promise and his faith, whereas Moses smote the rock with his staff but believed not.[10]

There was joy in Abraham's house when Sarah celebrated the day of her Golden Wedding.

But it was not to remain thus; for once more was Abraham to be tempted. He had struggled with that cunning power to which nothing is impossible, with that ever watchful enemy who

---

[10] Numbers 20. 12.

never sleeps, with that old man who outlives all — he had struggled with Time and had preserved his faith. And now all the terror of that fight was concentrated in one moment. "And God tempted Abraham, saying to him: take now thine only son Isaac, whom thou lovest, and get thee into the land of Moriah; and offer him there for a burnt offering upon one of the mountains which I will tell thee of."[11]

All was lost, then, and more terribly than if a son had never been given him! The Lord had only mocked Abraham, then! Miraculously he had realized the unreasonable hopes of Abraham; and now he wished to take away what he had given. A foolish hope it had been, but Abraham had not laughed, as did Sarah, when the promise had been made him. Now all was lost — the trusting hope of seventy years, the brief joy at the fulfillment of his hopes. Who, then, is he that snatches away the old man's staff, who that demands that he himself shall break it in two? Who is he that render disconsolate the gray hair of old age, who is he that demands that he himself shall do it? Is there no pity for the venerable old man, and none for the innocent child? And yet was Abraham God's chosen one, and yet was it the Lord that tempted him. And now all was to be lost! The glorious remembrance of him by a whole race, the promise of Abraham's seed — all that was but a whim, a passing fancy of the Lord, which Abraham was now to destroy forever! That glorious treasure, as old as the faith in Abraham's heart, and many, many years older than Isaac, the fruit of Abraham's life, sanctified by prayers, matured in struggles — the blessing on the lips of Abraham: this fruit was now to be plucked before the appointed time, and to remain without significance; for of what significance were it if Isaac was to be sacrificed? That sad and yet blessed hour when Abraham was to take leave from all that was dear to him, the hour when he would once more lift up his venerable head, when his face would shine like the countenance of the Lord, the hour when he would collect his whole soul for a blessing strong enough to render Isaac blessed all the days of his life — that hour was not to come! He was to say farewell to Isaac, to be sure, but in such wise that he himself was to remain behind; death was to part them, but in such wise that Isaac was to die. The old man was not in happiness to lay his hand on Isaac's head when the hour of death came, but, tired of life, he was to lay violent hands on Isaac. And it was God who tempted him. Woe, woe to the messenger who would have come before Abraham with such a command! Who would have dared to be the messenger of such dread tidings? But it was God that tempted Abraham.

But Abraham had faith, and had faith for this life. Indeed, had his faith been but concerning the life to come, then might he more easily have cast away all, in order to hasten out of this world which was not his. . . .

But Abraham had faith and doubted not, but trusted that the improbable would come to pass. If Abraham had doubted, then would he have undertaken something else, something great and noble; for what could Abraham have undertaken but was great and noble! He would have proceeded to Mount Moriah, he would have cloven the wood, and fired it, and unsheathed his knife — he would have cried out to God: "Disdain not this sacrifice; it is not, indeed, the best I have; for what is an old man against a child foretold of God; but it is the best I can give thee. Let Isaac never know that he must find consolation in his youth." He would have plunged the steel in his own breast. And he would have been admired throughout the world, and his name would not have been forgotten; but it is one thing to be admired and another to be a lodestar which guides one troubled in mind.

But Abraham had faith. He prayed not for mercy and that he might prevail upon the Lord: it was only when just retribution was to be visited upon Sodom and Gomorrah that Abraham ventured to beseech Him for mercy.

We read in Scripture; "And God did tempt Abraham, and said unto him, Abraham: and he said, Behold here I am."[12] You, whom I am now addressing, did you do likewise? When you saw

---

[11] Genesis 22. 2 f.
[12] Genesis 22. 1.

the dire dispensations of Providence approach threateningly, did you not then say to the mountains, Fall on me, and to the hills, Cover me?[13] Or, if you were stronger in faith, did not your step linger along the way, longing for the old accustomed paths, as it were? And when the voice called you, did you answer then, or not at all, and if you did, perchance in a low voice or whispering? Not thus Abraham, but gladly and cheerfully and trustingly and with a resonant voice he made answer: "Here am I." And we read further: "And Abraham rose up early in the morning."[14] He made haste as though for some joyous occasion, and early in the morning he was in the appointed place on Mount Moriah. He said nothing to Sarah, nothing to Eliezer, his steward; for who would have understood him? Did not his temptation by its very nature demand of him the vow of silence? "He laid the wood in order, and bound Isaac his son, and laid him on the altar upon the wood. And Abraham stretched forth his hand, and took the knife to slay his son." My listener! Many a father there has been who thought that with his child he lost the dearest of all there was in the world for him; yet assuredly no child ever was in that sense a pledge of God as was Isaac to Abraham. Many a father there has been who lost his child; but then it was God, the unchangeable and inscrutable will of the Almighty and His hand which took it. Not thus with Abraham. For him was reserved a more severe trial and Isaac's fate was put into Abraham's hand together with the knife. And there he stood, the old man, with his only hope! Yet did he not doubt, nor look anxiously to the left or right, nor challenge Heaven with his prayers. He knew it was God the Almighty who now put him to the test; he knew it was the greatest sacrifice which could be demanded of him; but he knew also that no sacrifice was too great which God demanded — and he unsheathed his knife.

Who strengthened Abraham's arm, who supported his right arm that it drooped not powerless? For he who contemplates this scene is unnerved. Who strengthened Abraham's soul so that his eyes grew not too dim to see either Isaac or the ram? For he who contemplates this scene will be struck with blindness. And yet it is rare enough that one is unnerved or is struck with blindness, and still more rare that one narrates worthily what there did take place between father and son. To be sure, we know well enough — it was but a trial!

If Abraham had doubted, when standing on Mount Moriah; if he had looked about him in perplexity; if he had accidentally discovered the ram before drawing his knife; if God had permitted him to sacrifice it instead of Isaac — then would he have returned home and all would have been as before; he would have had Sarah and would have kept Isaac; and yet how different all would have been! For then had his return been a flight, his salvation an accident, his reward disgrace, his future, perchance, perdition. Then would he have borne witness neither to his faith nor to God's mercy, but would have witnessed only to the terror of going to Mount Moriah. Then Abraham would not have been forgotten, nor either Mount Moriah. It would be mentioned, then, not as is Mount Ararat on which the Ark landed, but as a sign of terror, because it was there Abraham doubted.

Venerable patriarch Abraham! When you returned home from Mount Moriah you required no encomiums to console you for what you had lost; for, indeed, you did win all and still kept Isaac, as we all know. And the Lord did no more take him from your side, but you sat gladly at table with him in your tent as in the life to come you will, for all times. Venerable patriarch Abraham! Thousands of years have passed since those times, but still you need no late-born lover to snatch your memory from the power of oblivion, for every language remembers you — and yet do you reward your lover more gloriously than anyone, rendering him blessed in your bosom, and taking heart and eyes captive by the marvel of your deed. Venerable patriarch Abraham! Second father of the race! You who first perceived and bore witness to that unbounded passion which has but scorn for the terrible fight with the raging elements and the strength of

---

[13] Luke 23. 30.
[14] Genesis 22. 3 and 9.

brute creation, in order to struggle with God; you who first felt that sublimest of all passions, you who found the holy, pure, humble expression for the divine madness which was a marvel to the heathen — forgive him who would speak in your praise, in case he did it not fittingly. He spoke humbly, as if it concerned the desire of his heart; he spoke briefly, as is seemly; but he will never forget that you required a hundred years to obtain a son of your old age, against all expectations; that you had to draw the knife before being permitted to keep Isaac; he will never forget that in a hundred and thirty years you never got farther than to faith.

Preliminary Exploration

An old saying, derived from the world of experience, has it that "he who will not work shall not eat."[15] But, strange to say, this does not hold true in the world where it is thought applicable; for in the world of matter the law of imperfection prevails, and we see, again and again, that he also who will not work has bread to eat — indeed, that he who sleeps has a greater abundance of it than he who works. In the world of matter everything belongs to whosoever happens to possess it; it is thrall to the law of indifference, and he who happens to possess the Ring also has the Spirit of the Ring at his beck and call, whether now he be Noureddin or Aladdin,[16] and he who controls the treasures of this world, controls them howsoever he managed to do so. It is different in the world of spirit. There an eternal and divine order obtains, there the rain does not fall on the just and the unjust alike, nor does the sun shine on the good and the evil alike;[17] but there the saying does hold true that he who will not work shall not eat, and only he who was troubled shall find rest, and only he who descends into the nether world shall rescue his beloved, and only he who unsheathes his knife shall be given Isaac again. There he who will not work shall not eat but shall be deceived, as the gods deceived Orpheus with an immaterial figure instead of his beloved Euridice,[18] deceived him because he was lovesick and not courageous, deceived him because he was a player on the cithara rather than a man. There it avails not to have an Abraham for one's father,[19] or to have seventeen ancestors. But in that world the saying about Israel's maidens will hold true of him who will not work: he shall bring forth wind;[20] but he who will work shall give birth to his own father.

There is a kind of learning which would presumptuously introduce into the world of spirit the same law of indifference under which groans the world of matter. It is thought that to know about great men and great deeds is quite sufficient, and that other exertion is not necessary. And therefore this learning shall not eat, but shall perish of hunger while seeing all things transformed into gold by its touch. And what, forsooth, does this learning really know? There were many thousands of contemporaries, and countless men in after times who knew all about the triumphs of Miltiades; but there was only one whom they rendered sleepless.[21] There have existed countless generations that knew by heart, word for word, the story of Abraham; but how many lost their sleep over it?

Now the story of Abraham has the remarkable property of always being glorious, in however limited a sense it is understood; still, here also the point is whether one means to labor and exert one's self. Now, people do not care to labor and exert themselves, but will nevertheless to understand the story. They extol Abraham, but how? By expressing the matter in the most

---

[15]Cf. Thessalonians II 3.10.

[16]In *Aladdin*, Oehlenschlager's famous dramatic poem, Aladdin, "the cheerful son of nature," is contrasted with Noureddin, representing the gloom of doubt and night.

[17]Matthew 5.45.

[18] Cf. not the legend but Plato's *Symposion* 179 D.

[19] Matthew 3.9.

[20] Isaiah 26.18.

[21] Themistocles, that is; see Plutarch, *Lives, Themistocles* 3.3.

general terms and saying: "The great thing about him was that he loved God so ardently that he was willing to sacrifice to Him his most precious possession." That is very true; but "the most precious possession" is an indefinite expression. As one's thoughts, and one's mouth, run on one assumes, in a very easy fashion, the identity of Isaac and "the most precious possession" — and meanwhile he who is meditating may smoke his pipe and his audience comfortably stretch out their legs. If the rich youth whom Christ met on his way[22] had sold all his possessions and given all to the poor, we would extol him as we extol all which is great — aye, would not understand even him without labor; and yet, would he never have become an Abraham, notwithstanding his sacrificing the most precious possessions he had. That which people generally forget in the story of Abraham is his fear and anxiety; for as regards money, one is not ethically responsible for it, whereas for his son a father has the highest and most sacred responsibility. However, fear is a dreadful thing for timorous spirits, so they omit it. And yet they wish to speak of Abraham.

So they keep on speaking, and in the course of their speech, the two terms *Isaac* and *the most precious thing* are used alternately, and everything is in the best order. But now suppose that among the audience there was a man who suffered with sleeplessness — and then the most terrible and profound, the most tragic, and at the same time the most comic, misunderstanding is within the range of possibility. That is, suppose this man goes home and wishes to do as did Abraham; for his son is his most precious possession. If a certain preacher learned of this he would, perhaps, go to him; he would gather up all his spiritual dignity and exclaim: "Thou abominable creature, thou scum of humanity, what devil possessed thee to wish to murder thy son?" And this preacher, who had not felt any particular warmth, nor perspired while speaking about Abraham, this preacher would be astonished himself at the earnest wrath with which he thundered against that poor wretch; indeed, he would be pleased with himself, for never had he spoken with such power and unction, and he would have said to himself and his wife: "I am an orator, the only thing I have lacked so far was the occasion. Last Sunday, when speaking about Abraham, I did not feel thrilled in the least."

Now, if this same orator had just a bit of sense to spare, I believe he would lose it if the sinner would reply in a quiet and dignified manner: "Why, it was on this very same matter you preached last Sunday!" But however could the preacher have entertained such thoughts? Still, such was the case, and the preacher's mistake was merely not knowing what he was talking about. Ah, would that some poet might see his way clear to prefer such a situation to the stuff and nonsense of which novels and comedies are full! For the comic and the tragic here run parallel to infinity. The sermon probably was ridiculous enough in itself, but it became infinitely ridiculous through the very natural consequence it had. Or, suppose now the sinner was converted by this lecture without daring to raise any objection, and this zealous divine now went home elated, glad in the consciousness of being effective, not only in the pulpit but chiefly, and with irresistible power, as a spiritual guide, inspiring his congregation on Sunday, whilst on Monday he would place himself like a cherub with flaming sword before the man who, by his actions, tried to give the lie to the old saying that "the course of the world follows not the priest's word."

If, on the other hand, the sinner were not convinced of his error, his position would become tragic. He would probably be executed or else sent to the lunatic asylum — at any rate he would become a sufferer in this world; but in another sense I should think that Abraham rendered him happy; for he who toils, he shall not perish.

Now how shall we explain the contradiction contained in that sermon? Is it due to Abraham's having the reputation of being a great man — so that whatever he does is great, but if another should undertake to do the same it is a sin, a heinous sin? If this be the case I prefer not to participate in such thoughtless laudations. If faith cannot make it a sacred thing to wish to sacrifice one's son, then let the same judgment be visited on Abraham as on any other man. And if we perchance lack the courage to drive our thoughts to the logical conclusion and to say that

---

[22] Matthew 19.16f.

Abraham was a murderer, then it were better to acquire that courage, rather than to waste one's time on undeserved encomiums. The fact is, the ethical expression for what Abraham did is that he wanted to murder Isaac; the religious, that he wanted to sacrifice him. But precisely in this contradiction is contained the fear which may well rob one of one's sleep. And yet Abraham were not Abraham without this fear. Or, again, supposing Abraham did not do what is attributed to him; if his action was an entirely different one, based on conditions of those times, then let us forget him; for what is the use of calling to mind *that* past which can no longer become a present reality? — Or, the speaker had perhaps forgotten the essential fact that Isaac was the son. For if faith is eliminated, having been reduced to a mere nothing, then only the brutal fact remains that Abraham wanted to murder Isaac — which is easy for everybody to imitate who has not the faith — the faith, that is, which renders it most difficult for him. . . .

Love has its priests in the poets,[23] and one hears at times a poet's voice which worthily extols it. But not a word does one hear of faith. Who is there to speak in honor of that passion? Philosophy "goes right on." Theology sits at the window with painted visage and sues for philosophy's favor, offering it her charms. It is said to be difficult to understand the philosophy of Hegel; but to understand Abraham, why, that is an easy matter! To proceed further than Hegel is a wonderful feat, but to proceed further than Abraham, why, nothing is easier! Personally, I have devoted a considerable amount of time to a study of Hegelian philosophy and believe I understand it fairly well; in fact, I am rash enough to say that when, notwithstanding an effort, I am not able to understand him in some passages, it is because he is not entirely clear about the matter himself. All this intellectual effort I perform easily and naturally, and it does not cause my head to ache. On the other hand, whenever I attempt to think about Abraham, I am, as it were, overwhelmed. At every moment I am aware of the enormous paradox which forms the content of Abraham's life, at every moment I am repulsed, and my thought, notwithstanding its passionate attempts, cannot penetrate into it, cannot forge on the breadth of a hair. I strain every muscle in order to envisage the problem — and become a paralytic in the same moment.

I am by no means unacquainted with what has been admired as great and noble; my soul feels kinship with it, being satisfied, in all humility, that it was also my cause the hero espoused; and when contemplating his deed I say to myself: "*jam tua causa agitur.*"[24] I am able to *identify* myself with the hero; but I cannot do so with Abraham, for whenever I have reached his height I fall down again, since he confronts me as the paradox. It is by no means my intention to maintain that faith is something inferior, but, on the contrary, that it is the highest of all things; also that it is dishonest in philosophy to offer something else instead and to pour scorn on faith; but it ought to understand its own nature in order to know what it can offer. It should take away nothing; least of all, fool people out of something as if it were of no value. I am not unacquainted with the sufferings and dangers of life, but I do not fear them and cheerfully go forth to meet them. . . . But my courage is not, for all that, the courage of faith, and is as nothing compared with it. I cannot carry out the movement of faith: I cannot close my eyes and confidently plunge into the absurd — it is impossible for me; but neither do I boast of it. . . .

Now I wonder if every one of my contemporaries is really able to perform the movements of faith. Unless I am much mistaken they are, rather, inclined to be proud of making what they perhaps think me unable to do, viz., the imperfect movement. It is repugnant to my soul to do what is so often done, to speak inhumanly about great deeds, as if a few thousands of years were an immense space of time. I prefer to speak about them in a human way and as though they had been done but yesterday, to let the great deed itself be the distance which either inspires or condemns me. Now if I, in the capacity of tragic hero — for a higher flight I am unable to take — if I had been summoned to such an unordinary royal progress as was the one to Mount Moriah, I

---

[23] S. V. III, 84-87.
[24] Your cause, too, is at stake.

know very well what I would have done. I would not have been craven enough to remain at home; neither would I have dawdled on the way; nor would I have forgotten my knife — just to draw out the end a bit. But I am rather sure that I would have been promptly on the spot, with everything in order — in fact, would probably have been there before the appointed time, so as to have the business soon over with. But I know also what I would have done besides. In the moment I mounted my horse I would have said to myself: "Now all is lost, God demands Isaac, I shall sacrifice him, and with him all my joy — but for all that, God is love and will remain so for me; for in this world God and I cannot speak together; we have no language in common."

Possibly, one or the other of my contemporaries will be stupid enough, and jealous enough of great deeds, to wish to persuade himself and me that if I had acted thus I should have done something even greater than what Abraham did; for my sublime resignation was (he thinks) by far more ideal and poetic than Abraham's literal-minded action. And yet this is absolutely not so, for my sublime resignation was only a substitute for faith. I could not have made more than the infinite movement (of resignation) to find myself and again repose in myself. Nor would I have loved Isaac as Abraham loved him. The fact that I was resolute enough to resign is sufficient to prove my courage in a human sense, and the fact that I loved him with my whole heart is the very presupposition without which my action would be a crime; but still I did not love as did Abraham, for else I would have hesitated even in the last minute, without, for that matter, arriving too late on Mount Moriah. Also, I would have spoiled the whole business by my behavior; for if I had had Isaac restored to me I would have been embarrassed. That which was an easy matter for Abraham would have been difficult for me, I mean, to rejoice again in Isaac; for he who with all the energy of his soul *proprio motu et propriis auspiciis*[25] has made the infinite movement of resignation and can do no more, he will retain possession of Isaac only in his sorrow.

But what did Abraham? He arrived neither too early nor too late. He mounted his ass and rode slowly on his way. And all the while he had faith, believing that God would not demand Isaac of him, though ready all the while to sacrifice him, should it be demanded of him. He believed this on the strength of the absurd; for there was no question of human calculation any longer. And the absurdity consisted in God's, who yet made this demand of him, recalling his demand the very next moment. Abraham ascended the mountain and whilst the knife already gleamed in his hand he believed — that God would not demand Isaac of him. He was, to be sure, surprised at the outcome; but by a double movement he had returned at his first state of mind and therefore received Isaac back more gladly than the first time. . . .

On this height, then, stands Abraham. The last stage he loses sight of is that of infinite resignation. He does really proceed further; he arrives at faith. For all these caricatures of faith, wretched lukewarm sloth, which thinks: "Oh, there is no hurry, it is not necessary to worry before the time comes"; and miserable hopefulness, which says: "One cannot know what will happen, there might perhaps —"; all these caricatures belong to the sordid view of life and have already fallen under the infinite scorn of infinite resignation. Abraham, I am not able to understand; and in a certain sense I can learn nothing from him without being struck with wonder. They who flatter themselves that by merely considering the outcome of Abraham's story they will necessarily arrive at faith, they only deceive themselves and wish to cheat God out of the first movement of faith — it were tantamount to deriving worldly wisdom from the paradox. But who knows, one or the other of them may succeed in doing this; for our times are not satisfied with faith and not even with the miracle of changing water into wine — they "go right on," changing wine into water.

Is it not preferable to remain satisfied with faith, and is it not outrageous that everyone wishes to "go right on"? If people in our times decline to be satisfied with love, as is proclaimed from various sides, where will we finally land? In worldly shrewdness, in mean calculation, in paltriness and baseness, in all that which renders man's divine origin doubtful. Were it not better

---

[25] By his own impulse and on his own responsibility.

to stand fast in the faith, and better that he that standeth take heed lest he fall;[26] for the movement of faith must ever be made by virtue of the absurd, but, note well, in such wise that one does not lose the things of this world but wholly and entirely regains them.

As far as I am concerned, I am able to describe most excellently the movements of faith; but I cannot make them myself. When a person wishes to learn how to swim he can don a swimming belt suspended from the roof and then go through the motions, but that does not mean that he can swim. In the same fashion I too can go through the motions of faith, but when I am thrown into the water I swim, to be sure (for I am not a wader in the shallows), but I go through a different set of movements, to wit, those of infinity, whereas faith does the opposite, to wit, makes the movements to regain the finite after having made those of infinite resignation. Blessed is he who can make these movements, for he performs a marvelous feat, and I shall never weary of admiring him, whether now it be Abraham himself or the slave in Abraham's house, whether it be a professor of philosophy or a poor servant girl; it is all the same to me, for I have regard only to the movements. But these movements I watch closely, and I will not be deceived, whether by myself or by anyone else. The knights of infinite resignation are easily recognized, for their gait is dancing and bold. But they who possess the jewel of faith frequently deceive one because their bearing is curiously like that of a class of people heartily despised by infinite resignation as well as by faith — the Philistines.

Let me admit frankly that I have not in my experience encountered any certain specimen of this type; but I do not refuse to admit that, as far as I know, every other person may be such a specimen. At the same time I will say that I have searched vainly for years. It is the custom of scientists to travel around the globe to see rivers and mountains, new stars, gay-colored birds, misshapen fish, ridiculous races of men. They abandon themselves to a bovine stupor which gapes at existence and believe they have seen something worth-while. All this does not interest me; but if I knew where there lived such a knight of faith I would journey to him on foot, for that marvel occupies my thoughts exclusively. Not a moment would I leave him out of sight, but would watch how he makes the movements, and I would consider myself provided for life and would divide my time between watching him and myself practicing the movements, and would thus use all my time in admiring him.

As I said, I have not met with such a one, but I can easily imagine him. Here he is. I make his acquaintance and am introduced to him. The first moment I lay my eyes on him I push him back, leaping back myself. I hold up my hands in amazement and say to myself: "Good Lord! that person? Is it really he — why, he looks like a parish beadle!" But it is really he. I become more closely acquainted with him, watching his every movement to see whether some trifling incongruous movement of his has escaped me, some trace, perchance, of a signaling from the infinite, a glance, a look, a gesture, a melancholy air, or a smile, which might betray the presence of infinite resignation contrasting with the finite.

But no! I examine his figure from top to toe to discover whether there be anywhere a chink through which the infinite might be seen to peer forth. But no! he is of a piece, all through. And how about his footing? Vigorous, altogether that of finiteness, no citizen dressed in his very best, prepared to spend his Sunday afternoon in the park, treads the ground more firmly. He belongs altogether to this world, no Philistine more so. There is no trace of the somewhat exclusive and haughty demeanor which marks off the knight of infinite resignation. He takes pleasure in all things, is interested in everything, and perseveres in whatever he does with the zest characteristic of persons wholly given to worldly things. He attends to his business and when one sees him, one might think he was a clerk who had lost his soul in doing double bookkeeping, he is so exact. He takes a day off on Sundays. He goes to church. But no hint of anything supernatural or any other sign of the incommensurable betrays him, and if one did not know him it would be

---

[26] Cf. I Corinthians 10.12.

impossible to distinguish him in the congregation, for his brisk and manly singing proves only that he has a pair of good lungs.

In the afternoon he walks out to the forest. He takes delight in all he sees, in the crowds of men and women, the new omnibuses, the Sound — if one met him on the promenade one might think he was some shopkeeper who was having a good time, so simple is his joy; for he is not a poet, and in vain have I tried to lure him into betraying some sign of the poet's detachment. Toward evening he walks home again, with a gait as steady as that of a mail carrier. On his way he happens to wonder whether his wife will have some little special warm dish ready for him when he comes home — as she surely has — as, for instance, a roasted lamb's head garnished with greens. And if he met one minded like him he is very likely to continue talking about this dish with him till they reach the East Gate and to talk about it with a zest befitting a *chef*. As it happens, he has not four shillings to spare, and yet he firmly believes that his wife surely has that dish ready for him. If she has, it would be an enviable sight for distinguished people, and an inspiring one for common folks, to see him eat, for he has an appetite greater than Esau's. His wife has not prepared it — and strange, he remains altogether the same.

Again, on his way he passes a building lot and there meets another man. They fall to talking, and in a trice he erects a building, freely disposing of everything necessary. And the stranger will leave him with the impression that he has been talking with a capitalist — the fact being that the knight of my admiration is busy with the thought that if it really came to the point he would unquestionably have the means wherewithal at his disposal.

Now he is lying on his elbows in the window and looking over the square on which he lives. All that happens there, if it be only a rat creeping into a gutter hole, or children playing together — everything engages his attention, and yet his mind is at rest as though it were the mind of a girl of sixteen. He smokes his pipe in the evening, and to look at him you would swear it was the greengrocer from across the street who is lounging at the window in the evening twilight. Thus he shows as much unconcern as any worthless happy-go-lucky fellow; and yet every moment he lives he purchases his leisure at the highest price, for he makes not the least movement except by virtue of the absurd; and yet, yet — indeed, I might become furious with anger, if for no other reason than that of envy — and yet this man has performed, and is performing every moment, the movement of infinity. . . . He has resigned everything absolutely and then again seized hold of it all on the strength of the absurd. . . .

But this miracle may so easily deceive one that it will be best if I describe the movements in a given case which may illustrate their aspect in contact with reality; and that is the important point. Suppose, then, a young swain falls in love with a princess, and all his life is bound up in this love. But circumstances are such that it is out of the question to think of marrying her, an impossibility to translate his dreams into reality. The slaves of paltriness, the frogs in the sloughs of life, they will shout, of course: "Such a love is folly, the rich brewer's widow is quite as good and solid a match." Let them but croak. The knight of infinite resignation does not follow their advice, he does not surrender his love, not for all the riches in the world. He is no fool, he first makes sure that this love really is the contents of his life, for his soul is too sound and too proud to waste itself on a mere intoxication. He is no coward, he is not afraid to let his love insinuate itself into his most secret and most remote thoughts, to let it wind itself in innumerable coils about every fiber of his consciousness — if he is disappointed in his love he will never be able to extricate himself again. He feels a delicious pleasure in letting love thrill his every nerve, and yet his soul is solemn as is that of him who has drained a cup of poison and who now feels the venom mingle with every drop of his blood, poised in that moment between life and death.

Having thus imbibed love, and being wholly absorbed in it, he does not lack the courage to try and dare all. He surveys the whole situation, he calls together his swift thoughts which like tame pigeons obey his every beck, he gives the signal, and they dart in all directions. But when they return, everyone bearing a message of sorrow, and explain to him that it is impossible, then he becomes silent, he dismisses them, he remains alone; and then he makes the movement. Now if what I say here is to have any significance, it is of prime importance that the movement be made in a normal fashion. The knight of resignation is supposed to have sufficient energy to concentrate the entire contents of his life and the realization of existing conditions into one single wish. But if one lacks this concentration, this devotion to a single thought; if his soul from the very beginning is scattered on a number of objects, he will never be able to make the movement — he will be as worldly wise in the conduct of his life as the financier who invests his capital in a number of securities to win on the one if he should lose on the other; that is, he is no knight. Furthermore, the knight is supposed to possess sufficient energy to concentrate all his thought into a single act of consciousness. If he lacks this concentration he will only run errands in life and will never be able to assume the attitude of infinite resignation; for the very minute he approaches it he will suddenly discover that he forgot something so that he must remain behind. The next minute, thinks he, it will be attainable again, and so it is; but such inhibitions will never allow him to make the movement but will, rather, tend to let him sink ever deeper into the mire.

Our knight, then, performs the movement — which movement? Is he intent on forgetting the whole affair, which, too, would presuppose much concentration? No, for the knight does not contradict himself, and it is a contradiction to forget the main contents of one's life and still remain the same person. And he has no desire to become another person; neither does he consider such a desire to smack of greatness. Only lower natures forget themselves and become something different. Thus the butterfly has forgotten that it once was a caterpillar — who knows but it may forget altogether that it once was a butterfly and turn into a fish! Deeper natures never forget themselves and never change their essential qualities. So the knight remembers all; but precisely this remembrance is painful. Nevertheless, in his infinite resignation he has become reconciled with existence. His love for the princess has become for him the expression of an eternal love, has assumed a religious character, has been transfigured into a love for the eternal being which, to be sure, denied him the fulfillment of his love, yet reconciled him again by presenting him with the abiding consciousness of his love's being preserved in an everlasting form of which no reality can rob him. . . .

Now, he is no longer interested in what the princess may do and precisely this proves that he has made the movement of infinite resignation correctly. In fact, this is a good criterion for detecting whether a person's movement is sincere or just make-believe. Take a person who believes that he too has resigned, but lo! time passed, the princess did something on her part, for example, married a prince, and then his soul lost the elasticity of its resignation. This ought to show him that he did not make the movement correctly, for he who has resigned absolutely is sufficient unto himself. The knight does not cancel his resignation, but preserves his love as fresh and young as it was at the first moment, he never lets go of it just because his resignation is absolute. Whatever the princess does cannot disturb him, for it is only the lower natures who have the law for their actions in some other person, i.e., have the premises of their actions outside of themselves. . . .

Infinite resignation is the last stage which goes before faith, so that everyone who has not made the movement of infinite resignation cannot have faith; for only through absolute resignation do I become conscious of my eternal worth, and only then can there arise the problem of again grasping hold of this world by virtue of faith.

We will now suppose the knight of faith in the same case. He does precisely as the other knight, he absolutely resigns the love which is the contents of his life, he is reconciled to the pain; but then the miraculous happens, he makes one more movement, strange beyond comparison, saying: "And still I believe that I shall marry her — marry her by virtue of the absurd, by virtue of the act that to God nothing is impossible." Now the absurd is not one of the categories which belong to the understanding proper. It is not identical with the improbable, the unforeseen, the unexpected. The very moment our knight resigned himself he made sure of the absolute impossibility, in any human sense, of his love. This was the result reached by his reflections, and he had sufficient energy to make them. In a transcendent sense, however, by his very resignation, the attainment of his end is not impossible; but this very act of again taking possession of his love is at the same time a relinquishment of it. Nevertheless this kind of possession is by no means an absurdity to the intellect; for the intellect all the while continues to be right, as it is aware that in the world of finalities, in which reason rules, his love was and is an impossibility. The knight of faith realizes this fully as well. Hence, the only thing which can save him is recourse to the absurd, and this recourse he has through his faith. That is, he clearly recognizes the impossibility, and in the same moment he believes the absurd; for if he imagined he had faith, without at the same time recognizing, with all the passion his soul is capable of, that his love is impossible, he would be merely deceiving himself, and his testimony would be of no value, since he had not arrived even at the stage of absolute resignation. . . .

This last movement, the paradoxical movement of faith, I cannot make, whether or no it be my duty, although I desire nothing more ardently than to be able to make it. It must be left to a person's discretion whether he cares to make this confession; and at any rate, it is a matter between him and the Eternal Being, who is the object of his faith, whether an amicable adjustment can be effected. But what every person can do is to make the movement of absolute resignation, and I for my part would not hesitate to declare him a coward who imagines he cannot perform it. It is a different matter with faith. But what no person has a right to is to delude others into the belief that faith is something of no great significance, or that it is an easy matter, whereas it is the greatest and most difficult of all things.

But the story of Abraham is generally interpreted in a different way. God's mercy is praised which restored Isaac to him — it was but a trial! A trial. This word may mean much or little, and yet the whole of it passes off as quickly as the story is told: one mounts a winged horse; in the same instant one arrives on Mount Moriah, and presto one sees the ram. It is not remembered that Abraham only rode on an ass which travels but slowly, that it was a three days' journey for him, and that he required some additional time to collect the firewood, to bind Isaac, and to whet his knife.

And yet one extols Abraham. He who is to preach the sermon may sleep comfortably until a quarter of an hour before he is to preach it, and the listener may comfortably sleep during the sermon, for everything is made easy enough, without much exertion either to preacher or listener. But now suppose a man was present who suffered with sleeplessness and who went home and sat in a corner and reflected as follows: "The whole lasted but a minute, you need only wait a little while, and then the ram will be shown and the trial will be over." Now if the preacher should find him in this frame of mind, I believe he would confront him in all his dignity and say to him: "Wretch that thou art, to let thy soul lapse into such folly; miracles do not happen, all life is a trial." And as he proceeded he would grow more and more passionate, and would become ever more satisfied with himself; and whereas he had not noticed any congestion in his head whilst preaching about Abraham, he now feels the veins on his forehead swell. Yet who knows but he would stand aghast if the sinner should answer him in a quiet and dignified manner that it was precisely this about which he preached the Sunday before.

Let us then either waive the whole story of Abraham, or else learn to stand in awe of the enormous paradox which constitutes his significance for us, so that we may learn to understand that our age, like every age, may rejoice if it has faith. If the story of Abraham is not a mere nothing, an illusion, or if it is just used for show and as a pastime, the mistake cannot by any means be in the sinner's wishing to do likewise; but it is necessary to find out how great was the deed which Abraham performed in order that the man may judge for himself whether he has the courage and the mission to do likewise. The comical contradiction in the procedure of the preacher was his reduction of the story of Abraham to insignificance whilst rebuking the other man for doing the very same thing.

But should we then cease to speak about Abraham? I certainly think not. But if I were to speak about him, I would first of all describe the terrors of his trial. To that end, leach-like, I would suck all the suffering and distress out of the anguish of a father in order to be able to describe what Abraham suffered whilst yet preserving his faith. I would remind the hearer that the journey lasted three days and a goodly part of the fourth — in fact, these three and a half days ought to become infinitely longer than the few thousand years which separate me from Abraham. I would remind him, as I think right, that every person is still permitted to turn about before trying his strength on this formidable task; in fact, that he may return every instant in repentance. Provided this is done, I fear for nothing. Nor do I fear to awaken great desire among people to attempt to emulate Abraham. But to get out a cheap edition of Abraham and yet forbid everyone to do as he did, that I call ridiculous.[27]

FRIEDRICH NIETZSCHE

APHORISMS AND MAXIMS

[37]

You run *ahead*? Are you doing it as a shepherd? Or as an exception? A third case would be the fugitive. *First* question of conscience.

[38]

Are you genuine? Or merely an actor? A representative? Or that which is represented? In the end, perhaps you are merely a copy of an actor. *Second* question of conscience.

[39]

The disappointed one speaks. I searched for great human beings; I always found only the *apes* of their ideals.

[40]

Are you one who looks on? Or one who lends a hand? Or one who looks away and walks off? *Third* question of conscience.

[41]

Do you want to walk along? Or walk ahead? Or walk by yourself? One must know *what* one wants and *that* one wants. *Fourth* question of conscience.

[42]

Those were steps for me, and I have climbed up over them: to that end I had to pass over them. Yet they thought that I wanted to retire on them.

[146]

The artist's sense of truth. Regarding truths, the artist has a weaker morality than the thinker. He definitely does not want to be deprived of the splendid and profound interpretations of life, and he resists sober, simple methods and results. Apparently he fights for the higher dignity and significance of man; in truth, he does not want to give up the most effective presuppositions of his art: the fantastic, mythical, uncertain, extreme, the sense for the symbolic, the overestimation of the person, the faith in some miraculous element in the genius. Thus he considers the continued existence of his kind of creation more important than scientific devotion to the truth in every form, however plain.

[170]

Artists' ambition. The Greek artists, for example, the tragedians, wrote in order to triumph. Their whole art is unthinkable without the contest: Hesiod's good Eris, ambition, gave wings to their genius. Now this ambition demanded above all that their work attain the highest excellence in their own eyes, as they understood excellence, without consideration for any prevailing taste or public opinion concerning excellence in a work of art. Thus Aeschylus and Euripides remained unsuccessful for a long time, until they had finally educated judges of art who appraised their work by the standards they themselves applied.

---

[27] The above, with the omissions indicated, constitutes about one third of *Fear and Trembling*.

[224]

Ennoblement through degeneration. History teaches that the best-preserved tribe among a people is the one in which most men have a living communal sense as a consequence of sharing their customary and indisputable principles — in other words, in consequence of a common faith. Here the good, robust *mores* thrive; here the subordination of the individual is learned and the character receives firmness, first as a gift, and then is further cultivated. The danger to these strong communities founded on homogeneous individuals who have character is growing stupidity, which is gradually increased by heredity, and which, in any case, follows all stability like a shadow. It is the individuals who have fewer ties and are much more uncertain and morally weaker upon whom *spiritual progress* depends in such communities; they are the men who make new and manifold experiments. Innumerable men of this sort perish because of their weakness without any very visible effect; but in general, especially if they have descendants, they loosen up and from time to time inflict a wound on the stable element of a community. Precisely in this wounded and weakened spot the whole structure is *inoculated*, as it were, with something new; but its over-all strength must be sufficient to accept this new element into its blood and assimilate it. Those who degenerate are of the highest importance wherever progress is to take place; every great progress must be preceded by a partial weakening. The strongest natures *hold fast* to to the type; the weaker ones help to *develop it further*.

It is somewhat the same with the individual: rarely is degeneration, a crippling, even a vice or any physical or moral damage, unaccompanied by some gain on the other side. The sicker man in a warlike and restless tribe, for example, may have more occasion to be by himself and may thus become calmer and wiser; the one-eyed will have one stronger eye; the blind will see more deeply within, and in any case have a keener sense of hearing. So the famous *struggle for existence* does not seem to me to be the only point of view from which to explain the progress or the strengthening of

a human being or a race. Rather, two things must come together: first, the increase of stable power through close spiritual ties such as faith and communal feeling; then, the possibility of reaching higher goals through the appearance of degeneral types and, as a consequence, a partial weakening and wounding of the stable power.

[97]

One becomes moral — not because one is moral. Submission to morality can be slavish or vain or selfish or resigned or obtusely enthusiastic or thoughtless or an act of desperation, like submission to a prince; in itself it is nothing moral.

[101]

Doubtful. To accept a faith just because it is customary, means to be dishonest, to be cowardly, to be lazy. And do dishonesty, cowardice, and laziness then appear as the presupposition of morality?

[123]

Reason. How did reason come into the world? As is fitting, in an irrational manner, by accident. One will have to guess at it as at a riddle.

[164]

Perhaps premature. . . . There is no morality that alone makes moral, and every ethic that affirms itself exclusively kills too much good strength and costs humanity too dearly. The deviants, who are so frequently the inventive and fruitful ones, shall no longer be sacrificed; it shall not even be considered infamous to deviate from morality, in thought and deed; numerous new experiments of life and society shall be made; a tremendous burden of bad conscience shall be removed from the world — these most general aims should be recognized and promoted by all who are honest and seek truth.

[206]

The impossible class. Poor, gay, and independent — that is possible together. Poor, gay and a slave — that is possible too. And I would not know what better to say to the workers in factory slavery — provided they don't consider it altogether shameful to be used up as they are, like the gears of a machine, and in a sense as stopgaps of human inventiveness.

Phew! to believe that higher pay could abolish the *essence* of their misery — I mean their impersonal serfdom! Phew! to be talked into thinking that an increase in this impersonality, within the machine-like workings of a new society, could transform the shame of slavery into a virtue! Phew! to have a price for which one remains a person no longer but becomes a gear!

Are you co-conspirators in the current folly of nations, who want above all to produce as much as possible and to be as rich as possible? It would be your affair to present them with the counter-calculation: what vast sums of *inner* worth are thrown away for such an external goal. But where is your inner worth when you no longer know what it means to breathe freely? when you no longer have the slightest control over yourselves? when you all too frequently become sick of yourselves, as of a stale drink? when you listen to the newspapers and leer at your rich neighbor, made lustful by the rapid rise and fall of power, money, and opinions? when you no longer have any faith in philosophy, which wears rags, and in the candor of those who have no wants? when the voluntary idyllic life of poverty, without occupation or marriage, which might well suit the more spiritual among you, has become a laughingstock to you? Do your ears ring from the pipes of the socialistic pied pipers, who want to make you wanton with mad hopes? who bid you be *prepared* and nothing else, prepared from today to tomorrow so that you wait and wait for something from the outside, and live in every other respect as you have lived before — until this waiting turns into hunger and thirst and fever and madness, and finally the day of the *bestia triumphnans* rises in all its glory?

Against all this, everyone should think in his heart: Sooner emigrate and in savage fresh regions seek to become *master* of the world, and above all master of myself; keep changing location as long as a single sign of slavery still beckons to me; not avoid adventure and war

and be prepared for death if the worst accidents befall — but no more of this indecent serfdom, no more of this becoming sour and poisonous and conspiratorial! This would be the right state of mind: the workers in Europe should declare that henceforth *as a class* they are a human impossibility, and not only, as is customary, a harsh and purposeless establishment. They should introduce an era of a vast swarming out from the European beehive, the like of which has never been experienced, and with this act of emigration in the grand manner protest against the machine, against capital, and against the choice with which they are now threatened, of becoming *of necessity* either slaves of these states or slaves of a revolutionary party. Let Europe relieve itself of the fourth part of its inhabitants! . . . What at home began to degenerate into dangerous discontent and criminal tendencies will, once outside, gain a wild and beautiful naturalness and be called heroism. . . .

[297]

Corruption. The surest way to corrupt a youth is to instruct him to hold in higher esteem those who think alike than those who think differently.

[125]

The madman. Have you not heard of that madman who lit a lantern in the bright morning hours, ran to the market place, and cried incessantly, "I seek God! I seek God!" As many of those who do not believe in God were standing around just then, he provoked much laughter. Why, did he get lost? said one. Did he lose his way like a child? said another. Or is he hiding? Is he afraid of us? Has he gone on a voyage? or emigrated? Thus they yelled and laughed. The madman jumped into their midst and pierced them with his glances.

"Whither is God" he cried. "I shall tell you. *We have killed him* — you and I. All of us are his murderers. But how have we done this? How were we able to drink up the sea? Who gave us the sponge to wipe away the entire horizon? What did we do when we unchained this earth from its sun? Whither is it moving now? Whither are we moving now? Away from all suns? Are we not plunging continually? Backward, sideward, forward, in all direction? Is there any up or down left? Are we not straying as through an infinite nothing? Do we not feel the breath of empty space? Has it not become colder? Is not night and more night coming on all the while? Must not lanterns be lit in the morning? Do we not hear anything yet of the noise of the gravediggers who are burying God? Do we not smell anything yet of God's decomposition? Gods too decompose. God is dead. God remains dead. And we have killed him. How shall we, the murderers of all murderers, comfort ourselves? What was holiest and most powerful of all that the world has yet owned has bled to death under our knives. Who will wipe this blood off us? What water is there for us to clean ourselves? What festivals of atonement, what sacred games shall we have to invent? Is not the greatness of this deed too great for us? Must not we ourselves become gods simply to seem worthy of it? There has never been a greater deed; and whoever will be born after

us — for the sake of this deed he will be part of a higher history than all history hitherto."

Here the madman fell silent and looked again at his listeners; and they too were silent and stared at him in astonishment. At last he threw his lantern on the ground, and it broke and went out. "I come too early," he said then; "my time has not come yet. This tremendous event is still on its way, still wandering — it has not yet reached the ears of man. Lightning and thunder require time, the light of the stars requires time, deeds require time even after they are done, before they can be seen and heard. This deed is still more distant from them than the most distant stars — *and yet they have done it themselves.*"

It has been related further that on the same day the madman entered divers churches and there sang his *requiem aeternam deo*. Led out and called to account, he is said to have replied each time, "What are these churches now if they are not the tombs and sepulchers of God?"

Guernica by Pablo Picasso.
Giraudon/Art Resource, N.Y. Copyright 1992 ARS, N.Y./SPADEM.

JEAN PAUL SARTRE (1905-1980)

A French novelist, playwright, philosopher, and essayist, Sartre was the foremost spokesman for existentialism. During World War II he spent nine months in a German prison; afterward he worked in the French underground against the Nazi occupation. His companion was the feminist writer Simone de Beauvoir. In 1964 Sartre refused the Nobel Prize for literature, saying he did not wish to compromise his independence.

EXISTENTIALISM IS A HUMANISM

My purpose here is to offer a defence of existentialism against several reproaches that have been laid against it.

First, it has been reproached as an invitation to people to dwell in quietism of despair. For if every way to a solution is barred, one would have to regard any action in this world as entirely ineffective, and one would arrive finally at a contemplative philosophy. Moreover, since contemplation is a luxury, this would be only another bourgeois philosophy. This is, especially, the reproach made by the Communists.

From another quarter we are reproached for having underlined all that is ignominious in the human situation, for depicting what is mean, sordid or base to the neglect of certain things that possess charm and beauty and belong to the brighter side of human nature: for example, according to the Catholic critic, Mlle. Mercier, we forget how an infant smiles. Both from this side and from the other we are also reproached for leaving out of account the solidarity of mankind and considering man in isolation. And this, say the Communists, is because we base our doctrine upon pure subjectivity — upon the Cartesian "I think": which is the moment in which solitary man attains to himself; a position from which it is impossible to regain solidarity with other men who exist outside of the self. The *ego* cannot reach them through the *cogito*.

From the Christian side, we are reproached as people who deny the reality and seriousness of human affairs. For since we ignore the commandments of God and all values prescribed as eternal, nothing remains but what is strictly voluntary. Everyone can do what he likes, and will be incapable, from such a point of view, of condemning either the point of view or the action of anyone else.

It is to these various reproaches that I shall endeavor to reply today; that is why I have entitled this brief exposition "Existentialism is a Humanism." Many may be surprised at the mention of humanism in this connection, but we shall try to see in what sense we understand it. In any case, we can begin by saying that existentialism, in our sense of the word, is a doctrine that does render human life possible; a doctrine, also, which affirms that every truth and every action imply both an environment and a human subjectivity. The essential charge laid against us is, of course, that of over-emphasis upon the evil side of human life. I have lately been told of a lady who, whenever she lets slip a vulgar expression in a moment of nervousness, excuses herself by exclaiming, "I believe I am becoming an existentialist." So it appears that ugliness is being identified with existentialism. That is why some people say we are "naturalistic," and if we are, it is strange to see how much we scandalize and horrify them, for no one seems to be much frightened or humiliated nowadays by what is properly called naturalism. Those who can quite well keep down a novel by Zola such as *La Terre* are sickened as soon as they read an existentialist novel. Those who appeal to the wisdom of the people — which is a sad wisdom — find ours sadder still. And yet, what could be more disillusioned than such sayings as "Charity begins at home" or "Promote a rogue and he'll sue you for damage, knock him down and he'll do you homage"? We all know how many common sayings can be quoted to this effect, and they all mean much the same — that you must not oppose the powers that be; that you must not fight against superior force; must not meddle in matters that are above your station. Or that any action not in accordance with some tradition is mere romanticism; or that any undertaking which has not the support of proven experience is foredoomed to frustration; and that since experience has shown men to be invariably inclined to evil, there must be firm rules to restrain them, otherwise we shall have anarchy. It is, however, the people who are forever mouthing these dismal proverbs and, whenever they are told of some more or less repulsive action, say "How like human nature!" — it is these very people, always harping upon realism, who complain that existentialism is too gloomy a view of things. Indeed their excessive protests make me suspect that what is annoying them is not so much our pessimism, but, much more likely, our optimism. For at bottom, what is alarming in the doctrine that I am about to try to explain to you is — is it not? — that it confronts man with a possibility of choice. To verify this, let us review the whole question upon the strictly philosophic level. What, then, is this that we call existentialism?

Most of those who are making use of this word would be highly confused if required to explain its meaning. For since it has become fashionable, people cheerfully declare that this musician or that painter is "existentialist." A columnist in *Clartés* signs himself "The Existentialist," and, indeed, the word is now so loosely applied to so many things that it no longer means anything at all. It would appear that, for the lack of any novel doctrine such as that of surrealism, all those who are eager to join in the latest scandal or movement now seize upon this philosophy in which, however, they can find nothing to their purpose. For in truth this is of all teachings the least scandalous and the most austere: it is intended strictly for technicians and philosophers. All the same, it can easily be defined.

The question is only complicated because there are two kinds of existentialists. There are, on the one hand, the Christians, amongst whom I shall name Jaspers and Gabriel Marcel, both professed Catholics; and on the other the existential atheists, amongst whom we must place Heidegger as well as the French existentialists — and myself. What they have in common is simply the fact that they believe that *existence* comes before *essence* — or, if you will, that we must begin from the subjective. What exactly do we mean by that?

If one considers an article of manufacture — as, for example, a book or a paper-knife — one sees that it has been made by an artisan who had a conception of it; and he has paid attention, equally, to the conception of a paper-knife and to the pre-existent technique of production which is a part of that conception and is, at bottom, a formula. Thus the paper-knife is at the same time an article producible in a certain manner and one which, on the other hand, serves a definite purpose, for one cannot suppose that a man would produce a paper-knife without knowing what it was for. Let us say, then, of the paper-knife that its essence — that is to say the sum of the formulae and the qualities which made its production and its definition possible — precedes its existence. The presence of such-and-such a paper-knife or book is thus determined before my eyes. Here, then, we are viewing the world from a technical standpoint, and we can say that production precedes existence.

When we think of God as the creator, we are thinking of him, most of the time, as a supernal artisan. Whatever doctrine we may be considering, whether it be a doctrine like that of Descartes, or of Leibnitz himself, we always imply that the will follows, more or less, from the understanding or at least accompanies it, so that when God creates he knows precisely what he is creating. Thus, the conception of man in the mind of God is comparable to that of the paper-knife in the mind of the artisan: God makes man according to a procedure and a conception, exactly as the artisan manufactures a paper-knife, following a definition and a formula. Thus each individual man is the realization of a certain conception which dwells in the divine understanding. In the philosophic atheism of the eighteenth century, the notion of God is suppressed, but not, for all that, the idea that essence is prior to existence; something of that idea we still find everywhere, in Diderot, in Voltaire and even in Kant. Man possesses a human nature; that "human nature," which is the conception of human being, is found in every man; which means that each man is a particular example of a universal conception, the conception of Man. In Kant, this universality goes so far that the wild man of the woods, man in the state of nature and the bourgeois are all contained in the same definition and have the same fundamental qualities. Here again, the essence of man precedes that historic existence which we confront in experience.

Atheistic existentialism, of which I am a representative, declares with greater consistency that if God does not exist there is at least one being whose existence comes before its essence, a being which exists before it can be defined by any conception of it. That being is man or, as Heidegger has it, the human reality. What do we mean by saying that existence precedes essence? We mean that man first of all exists, encounters himself, surges up in the world — and defines himself afterwards. If man as the existentialist sees him is not definable, it is because to begin with be is nothing. He will not be anything until later, and then he will be what he makes of himself. Thus, there is no human nature, because there is no God to have a conception of it. Man simply is. Not that he is simply what he conceives himself to be, but he is what he wills, and as be conceives himself after already existing — as he wills to be after that leap towards existence. Man is nothing else but that which he makes of himself. That is the first principle of existentialism. Add this is what people call its "subjectivity," using the word as a reproach against us. But what do we mean to say by this, but that man is of a greater dignity than a stone or a table? For we mean to say that man primarily exists — that man is, before all else, something which propels itself towards a future and is aware that it is doing so. Man is, indeed, a project which possesses a subjective life, instead of being a kind of moss, or a fungus or a cauliflower. Before that projection of the self nothing exists; not even in the heaven of intelligence: man will only attain existence when he is what he purposes to be. Not, however, what he may wish to be. For what we usually understand by wishing or willing is a conscious decision taken — much more often than not — after we have made ourselves what we are. I may wish to join a party, to write a book or to marry — but in such a case what is usually called my will is probably a manifestation of a prior and more spontaneous decision. If, however, it is true that existence is prior to essence, man is responsible for what he is. Thus, the first effect of existentialism is that it puts every man in possession of himself as he is, and places the entire responsibility for his existence squarely upon his own shoulders. And, when we say that man is responsible for himself, we do not mean that he is responsible only for his own individuality, but that he is responsible for all men. The word "subjectivism" is to be understood in two senses, and our adversaries play upon only one of them. Subjectivism means, on the one hand, the freedom of the individual subject and, on the other, that man cannot pass beyond human subjectivity. It is the latter which is the deeper meaning of existentialism. When we say that man chooses himself, we do mean that every one of us must choose himself; but by that we also mean that in choosing for himself he chooses for all men. For in effect, of all the actions a man may take in order to create himself as he wills to be, there is not one which is not creative, at the same time, of an image of man such as he believes he ought to be. To choose between this or that is at the same time to affirm the value of that which is chosen; for we are unable ever to choose the worse. What we choose is always the better; and nothing can be better for us unless it is better for all. If, moreover, existence precedes essence and we will to exist at the same time as we fashion our image, that image is valid for all and for the entire epoch in which we find ourselves. Our responsibility is thus much greater than we had supposed, for it concerns mankind as a whole. If I am a worker, for instance, I may choose to join a Christian rather than a Communist trade union. And if, by that membership, I choose to signify that resignation is, after all, the attitude that best becomes a man, that man's kingdom is not upon this earth, I do not commit myself alone to that view. Resignation is my will for everyone, and my action is, in consequence, a commitment on behalf of all mankind. Or if, to take a more personal case, I decide to marry and to have children, even though this decision proceeds simply from my situation, from my passion or my desire, I am thereby committing not only myself, but humanity as a whole, to the practice of monogamy. I am thus responsible for myself and for all men, and I am creating a certain image of man as I would have him to be. In fashioning myself I fashion man.

This may enable us to understand what is meant by such terms — perhaps a little grandiloquent — as anguish, abandonment and despair. As you will soon see, it is very simple. First, what do we mean by anguish? The existentialist frankly states that man is in anguish. His meaning is as follows — When a man commits himself to anything, fully realizing that he is not only choosing what he will be, but is thereby at the same time a legislator deciding for the whole of mankind — in such a moment a man cannot escape from the sense of complete and profound responsibility. There are many, indeed, who show no such anxiety. But we affirm that they are merely disguising their anguish or are in flight from it. Certainly, many people think that in what they are doing they commit no one but themselves to anything: and if you ask them, "What would happen if everyone did so?" they shrug their shoulders and reply, "Everyone does not do so." But in truth, one ought always to ask oneself what would happen if everyone did as one is doing; nor can one escape from that disturbing thought except by a kind of self-deception. The man who lies in self-excuse, by saying "Everyone will not do it" must be ill at ease in his conscience, for the act of lying implies the universal value which it denies By its very disguise his anguish reveals itself. This is the anguish that Kierkegaard called "the anguish of Abraham." You know the story: An angel commanded Abraham to sacrifice his son: and obedience was obligatory, if it really was an angel who had appeared and said, "Thou, Abraham, shalt sacrifice thy son." But anyone in such a case would wonder, first, whether it was indeed an angel and secondly, whether I am really Abraham. Where are the proofs? A certain mad woman who suffered from hallucinations said that people were telephoning to her, and giving her orders. The doctor asked, "But who is it that speaks to you?" She replied: "He says it is God." And what, indeed, could prove to her that it was God? If an angel appears to me, what is the proof that it is an angel; or, if I hear voices, who can prove that they proceed from heaven and not from hell, or from my own subconsciousness or some pathological condition? Who can prove that they are really addressed to me?

Who, then, can prove that I am the proper person to impose, by my own choice, my conception of man upon mankind? I shall never find any proof whatever; there will be no sign to convince me of it. If a voice speaks to me, it is still I myself who must decide whether the voice is or is not that of an angel. If I regard a certain course of action as good, it is only I who choose to say that it is good and not bad. There is nothing to show that I am Abraham: nevertheless I also am obliged at every instant to perform actions which are examples. Everything happens to every man as though the whole human race had its eyes fixed upon what he is doing and regulated its conduct accordingly. So every man ought to say, "Am I really a man who has the right to act in such a manner that humanity regulates itself by what I do?" If a man does not say that, he is dissembling his anguish. Clearly, the anguish with which we are concerned here is not one that could lead to quietism or inaction. It is anguish pure and simple, of the kind well known to all those who have borne responsibilities. When, for instance, a military leader takes upon himself the responsibility for an attack and sends a number of men to their death, he chooses to do it and at bottom he alone chooses. No doubt he acts under a higher command, but its orders, which are more general, require interpretation by him and upon that interpretation depends the life of ten, fourteen or twenty men. In making the decision, he cannot but feel a certain anguish. All leaders know that anguish. It does not prevent their acting, on the contrary it is the very condition of their action, for the action presupposes that there is a plurality of possibilities, and in choosing one of these, they realize that it has value only because it is chosen. Now it is anguish of that kind which existentialism describes, and moreover, as we shall see, makes explicit through direct responsibility towards other men who are concerned. Far from being a screen which could separate us from action, it is a condition of action itself.

And when we speak of "abandonment" — a favorite word of Heidegger — we only mean to say that God does not exist, and that it is necessary to draw the consequences of his absence right to the end. The existentialist is strongly opposed to a certain type of secular moralism which seeks to suppress God at the least possible expense. Towards 1880, when the French professors endeavored to formulate a secular morality, they said something like this: — God is a useless and costly hypothesis, so we will do without it. However, if we are to have morality, a society and a law-abiding world, it is essential that certain values should be taken seriously; they must have an *à priori* existence ascribed to them. It must be considered obligatory *à priori* to be honest, not to lie, not to beat one's wife, to bring up children and so forth; so we are going to do a little work on this subject, which will enable us to show that these values exist all the same, inscribed in an intelligible heaven although, of course, there is no God. In other words — and this is, I believe, the purport of all that we in France call radicalism — nothing will be changed if God does not exist; we shall rediscover the same norms of honesty, progress and humanity, and we shall have disposed of God as an out-of-date hypothesis which will die away quietly of itself. The existentialist, on the contrary, finds it extremely embarrassing that God does not exist, for there disappears with Him all possibility of finding values in an intelligible heaven. There can no longer be any good *à priori* , since there is no infinite and perfect consciousness to think it. It is nowhere written that "the good" exists, that one must be honest or must not lie, since we are now upon the plane where there are only men. Dostoevsky once wrote "If God did not exist, everything would be permitted"; and that, for existentialism, is the starting point. Everything is indeed permitted if God does not exist, and man is in consequence forlorn, for he cannot find anything to depend upon either within or outside himself. He discovers forthwith, that he is without excuse. For if indeed existence precedes essence, one will never be able to explain one's action by reference to a given and specific human nature; in other words, there is no determinism — man is free, man *is* freedom. Nor, on the other hand, if God does not exist, are we provided with any values or commands that could legitimize our behavior. Thus we have neither behind us, nor before us in a luminous realm of values, any means of justification or excuse. We are left alone, without excuse. That is what I mean when I say that man is condemned to be free. Condemned, because he did not create himself, yet is nevertheless at liberty, and from the moment that he is thrown into this world he is responsible for everything he does. The existentialist does not believe in the power of passion. He will never regard a grand passion as a destructive torrent upon which a man is swept into certain actions as by fate, and which, therefore, is an excuse for them. He thinks that man is responsible for his passion. Neither will an existentialist think that a man can find help through some sign being vouchsafed upon earth for his orientation: for he thinks that the man himself interprets the sign as he chooses. He thinks that every man, without any support or help whatever, is condemned at every instant to invent man. As Ponge has written in a very fine article, "Man is the future of man." That is exactly true. Only, if one took this to mean that the future is laid up in Heaven, that God knows what it is, it would be false, for then it would no longer even be a future. If, however, it means that, whatever man may now appear to be, there is a future to be fashioned, a virgin future that awaits him — then it is a true saying. But in the present, one is forsaken.

As an example by which you may the better understand this state of abandonment, I will refer to the case of a pupil of mine, who sought me out in the following circumstances. His father was quarrelling with his mother and was also inclined to be a "collaborator"; his elder brother had been killed in the German offensive of 1940 and this young man, with a sentiment somewhat primitive but generous, burned to avenge him. His mother was living alone with him, deeply afflicted by the semi-treason of his father and by the death of her eldest son, and her one consolation was in this young man. But he, at this moment, had the choice between going to England to join the Free French Forces or of staying near his mother and helping her to live. He fully realized that this woman lived only for him and that his disappearance — or perhaps his death — would plunge her into despair. He also realized that, concretely and in fact, every action he performed on his mother's behalf would be sure of effect in the sense of aiding her to live, whereas anything he did in order to go and fight would be an ambiguous action which might vanish like water into sand and serve no purpose. For instance, to set out for England he would have to wait indefinitely in a Spanish camp on the way through Spain; or, on arriving in England or in Algiers he might be put into an office to fill up forms. Consequently, he found himself confronted by two very different modes of action; the one concrete, immediate, but directed towards only one individual; and the other an action addressed to an end infinitely greater, a national collectivity, but for that very reason ambiguous — and it might be frustrated on the way. At the same time, he was hesitating between two kinds of morality; on the one side the morality of sympathy, of personal devotion and, on the other side, a morality of wider scope but of more debatable validity. He had to choose between those two. What could help him to choose? Could the Christian doctrine? No. Christian doctrine says: Act with charity, love your neighbor, deny yourself for others, choose the way which is hardest, and so forth. But which is the harder road? To whom does one owe the more brotherly love, the patriot or the mother? Which is the more useful aim, the general one of fighting in and for the whole community, or the precise aim of helping one particular person to live? Who can give an answer to that à priori? No one. Nor is it given in any ethical scripture. The Kantian ethic says, Never regard another as a means, but always as an end. Very well: if I remain with my mother, I shall be regarding her as the end and not as a means: but by the same token I am in danger of treating as means those who are fighting on my behalf; and the converse is also true, that if I go to the aid of the combatants I shall he treating them as the end at the risk of treating my mother as a means.

If values are uncertain, if they are still too abstract to determine the particular, concrete case under consideration, nothing remains but to trust in our instincts. That is what this young man tried to do; and when I saw him he said, "In the end, it is feeling that counts; the direction in which it is really pushing me is the one I ought to choose. If I feel that I love my mother enough to sacrifice everything else for her — my will to be avenged, all my longings for action and adventure — then I stay with her. If, on the contrary, I feel that my love for her is not enough, I go." But how does one estimate the strength of a feeling? The value of his feeling for his mother was determined precisely by the fact that he was standing by her. I may say that I love a certain friend enough to sacrifice such or such a sum of money for him, but I cannot prove that unless I have done it. I may say, "I love my mother enough to remain with her," if actually I have remained with her. I can only estimate the strength of this affection if I have performed an action by which it is defined and ratified. But if I then appeal to this affection to justify my action, I find myself drawn into a vicious circle.

Moreover, as Gide has very well said, a sentiment which is play-acting and one which is vital are two things that are hardly distinguishable one from another. To decide that I love my mother by staying beside her, and to play a comedy the upshot of which is that I do so — these are nearly the same thing. In other words, feeling is formed by the deeds that one does; therefore I cannot consult it as a guide to action. And that is to say that I can neither seek within myself for an authentic impulse to action, nor can I expect, from some ethic, formulae that will enable me to act. You may say that the youth did, at least, go to a professor to ask for advice. But if you seek counsel — from a priest, for example — you have selected that priest; and at bottom you already knew, more or less, what he would advise. In other words, to choose an adviser is nevertheless to commit oneself by that choice. If you are a Christian, you will say, Consult a priest; but there are collaborationists, priests who are resisters and priests who wait for the tide to turn: which will you choose? Had this young man chosen a priest of the resistance, or one of the collaboration, he would have decided beforehand the kind of advice he was to receive. Similarly, in coming to me, he knew what advice I should give him, and I had but one reply to make. You are free, therefore choose — that to say, invent. No rule of general morality can show you what you ought to do; no signs are vouchsafed in this world. The Catholics will reply: "Oh, but they are!" Very well; still it is I myself, in every case, who have to interpret the signs. While I was imprisoned, I made the acquaintance of a somewhat remarkable man, a Jesuit, who had become a member of that order in the following manner. In his life he had suffered a succession of rather severe setbacks. His father had died when he was a child, leaving him in poverty, and he had been awarded a free scholarship in a religious institution, where he had been made continually to feel that be was accepted for charity's sake, and, in consequence, he had been denied several of those distinctions and honours which gratify children. Later, about the age of eighteen, be came to grief in a sentimental affair; and finally, at twenty-two — this was a trifle in itself, but it was the last drop that overflowed his cup — he failed in his military examination. This young man, then, could regard himself as a total failure: it was a sign — but a sign of what? He might have taken refuge in bitterness or despair. But he took it — very cleverly for him — as a sign that he was not intended for secular successes, and that only the attainments of religion, those of sanctity and of faith, were accessible to him. He interpreted his record as a message from God, and became a member of the Order. Who can doubt but that this decision as to the meaning of the sign was his, and his alone? One could have drawn quite different conclusions from such a series of reverses — as, for example, that he had better become a carpenter or a revolutionary. For the decipherment of the sign, however, he bears the entire responsibility. That is what "abandonment" implies, that we ourselves decide our being. And with this abandonment goes anguish.

As for "despair," the meaning of this expression is extremely simple. It merely means that we limit ourselves to a reliance upon that which is within our wills, or within the sum of the probabilities which render our action feasible. Whenever one wills anything, there are always these elements of probability. If I am counting upon a visit from a friend, who may be coming by train or by tram, I presuppose that the train will arrive at the appointed time, or that the tram will not be derailed. I remain in the realm of possibilities; but one does not rely upon any possibilities beyond those that are strictly concerned in one's action. Beyond the point at which the possibilities under consideration cease to affect my action, I ought to disinterest myself. For there is no God and no prevenient design, which can adapt the world and all its possibilities to my will. When Descartes said, "Conquer yourself rather than the world," what he meant was, at bottom, the same — that we should act without hope.

Marxists, to whom I have said this, have answered: "Your action is limited, obviously, by your death; but you can rely upon the help of others. That is, you can count both upon what the others are doing to help you elsewhere, as in China and in Russia, and upon what they will do later, after your death, to take up your action and carry it forward to its final accomplishment which will be the revolution. Moreover you must rely upon this; not to do so is immoral." To this I rejoin, first, that I shall always count upon my comrades-in-arms in the struggle, in so far as they are committed, as I am, to a definite, common cause; and in the unity of a party or a group which I can more or less control — that is, in which I am enrolled as a militant and whose movements at every moment are known to me. In that respect, to rely upon the unity and the will of the party is exactly like my reckoning that the train will run to time or that the tram will not be derailed. But I cannot count upon men whom I do not know, I cannot base my confidence upon human goodness or upon man's interest in the good of society, seeing that man is free and that there is no human nature which I can take as foundational. I do not know where the Russian revolution will lead. I can admire it and take it as an example in so far as it is evident, today, that the proletariat plays a part in Russia which it has attained in no other nation. But I cannot affirm that this will necessarily lead to the triumph of the proletariat: I must confine myself to what I can see. Nor can I be sure that comrades-in-arms will take up my work after my death and carry it to the maximum perfection, seeing that those men are free agents and will freely decide, tomorrow, what man is then to be. Tomorrow, after my death, some men may decide to establish Fascism, and the others may be so cowardly or so slack as to let them do so. If so, Fascism will then be the truth of man, and so much the worse for us. In reality, things will be such as men have decided they shall be. Does that mean that I should abandon myself to quietism? No. First I ought to commit myself and then act my commitment, according to the time-honored formula that "one need not hope in order to undertake one's work." Nor does this mean that I should not belong to a party, but only that I should be without illusion and that I should do what I can. For instance, ask myself "Will the social ideal as such, ever become a reality?" I cannot tell, I only know that whatever may be in my power to make it so, I shall do; beyond that, I can count upon nothing.

Quietism is the attitude of people who say, "let others do what I cannot do". The doctrine I am presenting before you is precisely the opposite of this, since it declares that there is no reality except in action. It goes further, indeed, and adds, "Man is nothing else but what he purposes, he exists only in so far as he realizes himself, he is therefore nothing else but the sum of his actions, nothing else but what his life is." Hence we can well understand why some people are horrified by our teaching. For many have but one resource to sustain them in their misery, and that is to think, "Circumstances have been against me, I was worthy to be something much better than I have been. I admit I have never had a great love or a great friendship; but that is because I never met a man or a woman who were worthy of it; if I have not written any very good books, it is because I had not the leisure to do so; or, if I have had no children to whom I could devote myself it is because I did not find the man I could have lived with. So there remains within me a wide range of abilities, inclinations and potentialities, unused but perfectly viable, which endow me with a worthiness that could never be inferred from the mere history of my actions." But in reality and for the existentialist, there is no love apart from the deeds of love; no potentiality of love other than that which is manifested in loving; there is no genius other than that which is expressed in works of art. The genius of Proust is the totality of the works of Proust; the genius of Racine is the series of his tragedies, outside of which there is nothing. Why should we attribute to Racine the capacity to write yet another tragedy when that is precisely what he did not write? In life, a man commits himself, draws his own portrait and there is nothing but that portrait. No doubt this thought may seem comfortless to one who has not made a success of his life. On the other hand, it puts everyone in a position to understand that reality alone is reliable; that dreams, expectations and hopes serve to define a man only as deceptive dreams, abortive hopes, expectations unfulfilled; that is to say, they define him negatively, not positively. Nevertheless, when one says, "you are nothing else but what you live," it does not imply that an artist is to be judged solely by his works of art, for a thousand other things contribute no less to his definition as a man. What we mean to say is that a man is no other than a series of undertakings, that he is the sum, the organization, the set of relations that constitute these undertakings.

In the light of all this, what people reproach us with is not, after all, our pessimism, but the sternness of our optimism. If people condemn our works of fiction, in which we describe characters that are base, weak, cowardly and sometimes even frankly evil, it is not only because those characters are base, weak, cowardly or evil. For suppose that, like Zola, we showed that the behavior of these characters was caused by their heredity, or by the action of their environment upon them, or by determining factors, psychic or organic. People would be reassured, they would say, "You see, that is what we are like, no one can do anything about it." But the existentialist, when he portrays a coward, shows him as responsible for his cowardice. He is not like that on account of a cowardly heart or lungs or cerebrum, he has not become like that through his physiological organism; he is like that because he has made himself into a coward by his actions. There is no such thing as a cowardly temperament. There are nervous temperaments; there is what is called impoverished blood, and there are also rich temperaments. But the man whose blood is poor is not a coward for all that, for what produces cowardice is the act of giving up or giving way; and a temperament is not an action. A coward is defined by the deed that he has done. What people feel obscurely, and with horror, is that the coward as we present him is guilty of being a coward. What people would prefer would be to be born either a coward or a hero. One of the charges most often laid against the *Chemins de la Liberté* is something like this — "But, after all, these people being so base, how can you make them into heroes?" That objection is really rather comic, for it implies that people are born heroes: and that is, at bottom, what such people would like to think; If you are born cowards, you can be quite content. you can do nothing about it and you will be cowards all your lives whatever you do; and if you are born heroes you can again be quite content; you will be heroes all your lives eating and drinking heroically. Whereas the existentialist says that the coward makes himself cowardly, the hero makes himself heroic; and that there is always a possibility for the coward to give up cowardice and for the hero to stop being a hero. What counts is the total commitment, and it is not by a particular case or particular action that you are committed altogether.

We have now, I think, dealt with a certain number of the reproaches against existentialism. You have seen that it cannot be regarded as a philosophy of quietism since it defines man by his action; nor as a pessimistic description of man, for no doctrine is more optimistic, the destiny of man is placed within himself. Nor is it an attempt to discourage man from action since it tells him that there is no hope except in his action, and that the one thing which permits him to have life is the deed. Upon this level therefore, what we are considering is an ethic of action and self-commitment. However, we are still reproached, upon these few data, for confining man within his individual subjectivity. There again people badly misunderstand us.

Our point of departure is, indeed, the subjectivity of the individual, and that for strictly philosophic reasons. It is not because we are bourgeois, but because we seek to base our teaching upon the truth, and not upon a collection of fine theories, full of hope but lacking real foundations. And at the point of departure there cannot be any other truth than this, *I think, therefore I am*, which is the absolute truth of consciousness as it attains to itself. Every theory which begins with man, outside of this moment of self-attainment, is a theory which thereby suppresses the truth, for outside of the Cartesian *cogito*, all objects are no more than probable, and any doctrine of probabilities which is not attached to a truth will crumble into nothing. In order to define the probable, one must possess the true. Before there can be any truth whatever, then, there must be an absolute truth, and there is such a truth which is simple, easily attained and within the reach of everybody; it consists in one's immediate sense of one's self.

In the second place, this theory alone is compatible with the dignity of man, it is the only one which does not make man into an object. All kinds of materialism lead one to treat every man including oneself as an object — that is, as a set of pre-determined reactions, in no way different from the patterns of qualities and phenomena which constitute a table, or a chair or a stone. Our aim is precisely to establish the human kingdom as a pattern of values in distinction from the material world. But the subjectivity which we thus postulate as the standard of truth is no narrowly individual subjectivism, for as we have demonstrated, it is not only one's own self that one discovers in the *cogito*, but those of others too. Contrary to the philosophy of Descartes, contrary to that of Kant, when we say "I think" we are attaining to ourselves in the presence of the other, and we are just as certain of the other as we are of ourselves. Thus the man who discovers himself directly in the *cogito* also discovers all the others, and discovers them as the condition of his own existence. He recognizes that he cannot be anything (in the sense in which one says one is spiritual, or that one is wicked or jealous) unless others recognize him as such. I cannot obtain any truth whatsoever about myself, except through the mediation of another. The other is indispensable to my existence, and equally so to any knowledge I can have of myself. Under these conditions, the intimate discovery of myself is at the same time the revelation of the other as a freedom which confronts mine, and which cannot think or will without doing so either for or against me. Thus, at once, we find ourselves in a world which is, let us say, that of "inter-subjectivity." It is in this world that man has to decide what he is and what others are.

Furthermore, although it is impossible to find in each and every man a universal essence that can be called human nature, there is nevertheless a human universality of *condition*. It is not by chance that the thinkers of today are so much more ready to speak of the condition than of the nature of man. By his condition they understand, with more or less clarity, all the *limitations* which *à priori* define man's fundamental situation in the universe. His historical situations are variable: man may be born a slave in a pagan society, or may be a feudal baron, or a proletarian. But what never vary are the necessities of being in the world, of having to labor and to die there. These limitations are neither subjective nor objective, or rather there is both a subjective and an objective aspect of them. Objective, because we meet with them everywhere and they are everywhere recognizable: and subjective because they are *lived* and are nothing if man does not live them — if, that is to say, he does not freely determine himself and his existence — in relation to them. And, diverse though man's purposes may be, at least none of them is wholly foreign to me, since every human purpose presents itself as an attempt either to surpass these limitations, or to widen them, or else to deny or to accommodate oneself to them. Consequently every purpose, however individual it may be, is of universal value. Every purpose, even that of a Chinese, an Indian or a Negro, can be understood by a European. To say it can be understood, means that the European of 1945 may be striving out of a certain situation towards the same limitations in the same way, and that he may reconceive in himself the purpose of the Chinese, of the Indian or the African. In every purpose there is universality, in this sense that every purpose is comprehensible to every man. Not that this or that purpose defines man for ever, but that it may be entertained again and again. There is always some way of understanding an idiot, a child, a primitive man or a foreigner if one has sufficient information. In this sense we may say that there is a human universality, but it is not something given; it is being perpetually made. I make this universality in choosing myself; I also make it by understanding the purpose of any other man, of whatever epoch. This absoluteness of the act of choice does not alter the relativity of each epoch.

What is at the very heart and center of existentialism, is the absolute character of the free commitment, by which every man realizes himself in realizing a type of humanity — a commitment always understandable, to no matter whom in no matter what epoch — and its bearing upon the relativity of the cultural pattern which may result from such absolute commitment. One must observe equally the relativity of Cartesianism and the absolute character of the Cartesian commitment. In this sense you may say, if you like, that every one of us makes the absolute by breathing, by eating, by sleeping or by behaving in any fashion whatsoever. There is no difference between free being — being as self-committal, as existence choosing its essence — and absolute being. And there is no difference whatever between being as an absolute, temporarily localized — that is, localized in history — and universally intelligible being.

This does not completely refute the charge of subjectivism. Indeed that objection appears in several other forms, of which the first is as follows. People say to us, "Then it does not matter what you do," and they say this in various ways. First they tax us with anarchy, then they say, "You cannot judge others, for there is no reason for preferring one purpose to another"; finally, they may say, "Everything being merely voluntary in this choice of yours, you give away with one hand what you pretend to gain with the other." These three are not very serious objections. As to the first, to say that it does not matter what you choose is not correct. In one sense choice is possible, but what is not possible is not to choose. I can always choose, but I must know that if I do not choose, that is still a choice. This, although it may appear merely formal, is of great importance as a limit to fantasy and caprice. For, when I confront a real situation — for example, that I am a sexual being, able to have relations with a being of the other sex and able to have children — I am obliged to choose my attitude to it, and in every respect I bear the responsibility of the choice which, in committing myself, also commits the whole of humanity. Even if my choice is determined by no *à priori* value whatever, it can have nothing to do with caprice; and if anyone thinks that this is only Gide's theory of the *acte gratuit* over again, he has failed to see the enormous difference between this theory and that of Gide. Gide does not know what a situation is, his "act" is one of pure caprice. In our view, on the contrary, man finds himself in an organized situation in which he is himself involved: his choice involves mankind in its entirety, and he cannot avoid choosing. Either he must remain single, or he must marry without having children, or he must marry and have children. In any case, and whichever he may choose, it is impossible for him, in respect of this situation, not to take complete responsibility. Doubtless he chooses without reference to any pre-established values, but it is unjust to tax him with caprice. Rather let us say that the moral choice is comparable to the construction of a work of art.

But here I must at once digress to make it quite clear that we are not propounding an aesthetic morality, for our adversaries are disingenuous enough to reproach us even with that. I mention the work of art only by way of comparison. That being understood, does anyone reproach an artist, when he paints a picture, for not following rules established *à priori*? Does one ever ask what is the picture that he ought to paint? As everyone knows, there is no pre-defined picture for him to make; the artist applies himself to the composition of a picture, and the picture that ought to be made is precisely that which he will have made. As everyone knows, there are no aesthetic values *à priori* , but there are values which will appear in due course in the coherence of the picture, in the relation between the will to create and the finished work. No one can tell what the painting of tomorrow will be like; one cannot judge a painting until it is done. What has that to do with morality? We are in the same creative situation. We never speak of a work of art as irresponsible; when we are discussing a canvas by Picasso, we understand very well that the composition became what it is at the time when he was painting it, and that his works are part and parcel of his entire life.

It is the same upon the plane of morality. There is this in common between art and morality, that in both we have to do with creation and invention. We cannot decide *à priori* what it is that should be done. I think it was made sufficiently clear to you in the case of that student who came to see me, that to whatever ethical system he might appeal, the Kantian or any other, he could find no sort of guidance whatever; he was obliged to invent the law for himself. Certainly we cannot say that this man, in choosing to remain with his mother — that is, in taking sentiment, personal devotion and concrete charity as his moral foundations — would be making an irresponsible choice, nor could we do so if he preferred the sacrifice of going away to England. Man makes himself; he is not found ready-made; he makes himself by the choice of his morality, and he cannot but choose a morality, such is the pressure of circumstances upon him. We define man only in relation to his commitments; it is therefore absurd to reproach us for irresponsibility in our choice.

In the second place, people say to us, "You are unable to judge others." This is true in one sense and false in another. It is true in this sense, that whenever a man chooses his purpose and his commitment in all clearness and in all sincerity, whatever that purpose may be, it is impossible for him to prefer another. It is true in the sense that we do not believe in progress. Progress implies amelioration; but man is always the same, facing a situation which is always changing, and choice remains always a choice in the situation. The moral problem has not changed since the time when it was a choice between slavery and anti-slavery — from the time of the war of Secession, for example, until the present moment when one chooses between the M.R.P. [*Mouvement Republicain Populaire*] and the Communists.

We can judge, nevertheless, for, as I have said, one chooses in view of others, and in view of others one chooses himself. One can judge, first — and perhaps this is not a judgment of value, but it is a logical judgment — that in certain cases choice is founded upon an error, and in others upon the truth. One can judge a man by saying that he deceives himself. Since we have defined the situation of man as one of free choice, without excuse and without help, any man who takes refuge behind the excuse of his passions, or by inventing some deterministic doctrine, is a self-deceiver. One may object: "But why should he not choose to deceive himself?" I reply that it is not for me to judge him morally, but I define his self-deception as an error. Here one cannot avoid pronouncing a judgment of truth. The self-deception is evidently a falsehood, because it is a dissimulation of man's complete liberty of commitment. Upon this same level, I say that it is also a self-deception if I choose to declare that certain values are incumbent upon me; I am in contradiction with myself if I will these values and at the same time say that they impose themselves upon me. If anyone says to me, "And what if I wish to deceive myself?" I answer, "There is no reason why you should not, but I declare that you are doing so, and that the attitude of strict consistency alone is that of good, faith." Furthermore, I can pronounce a moral judgment. For I declare that freedom, in respect of concrete circumstances, can have no other end and aim but itself; and when once a man has seen that values depend upon himself, in that state of forsakenness he can will only one thing, and that is freedom as the foundation of all values. That does not mean that he wills it in the abstract: it simply means that the actions of men of good faith have, as their ultimate significance, the quest of freedom itself as such. A man who belongs to some communist or revolutionary society wills certain concrete ends, which imply the will to freedom, but that freedom is willed in community. We will freedom for freedom's sake, in and through particular circumstances. And in thus willing freedom, we discover that it depends entirely upon the freedom of others and that the freedom of others depends upon our own. Obviously, freedom as the definition of a man does not depend upon others, but as soon as there is a commitment, I am obliged to will the liberty of others at the same time as my own. I cannot make liberty my aim unless I make that of others equally my aim. Consequently, when I recognize, as entirely authentic, that man is a being whose existence precedes his essence, and that he is a free being who cannot, in any circumstances, but will his freedom, at the same time I realize that I cannot not will the freedom of others. Thus, in the name of that will to freedom which is implied in freedom itself, I can form judgments upon those who seek to hide from themselves the wholly voluntary nature of their existence and its complete freedom. Those who hide from this total freedom, in a guise of solemnity or with deterministic excuses, I shall call cowards. Others, who try to show that their existence is necessary, when it is merely an accident of the appearance of the human race on earth — I shall call scum. But neither cowards nor scum can be identified except upon the plane of strict authenticity. Thus, although the content of morality is variable, a certain form of this morality is universal. Kant declared that freedom is a will both to itself and to the freedom of others. Agreed: but he thinks that the formal and the universal suffice for the constitution of a morality. We think, on the contrary, that principles that are too abstract break down when we come to defining action. To take once again the case of that student; by what authority, in the name of what golden rule of morality, do you think he could have decided, in perfect peace of mind, either to abandon his mother or to remain with her? There are no means of judging. The content is always concrete, and therefore unpredictable; it has always to be invented. The one thing that counts, is to know whether the invention is made in the name of freedom.

Let us, for example, examine the two following cases, and you will see how far they are similar in spite of their difference. Let us take *The Mill on the Floss*. We find here a certain young woman, Maggie Tulliver, who is an incarnation of the value of passion and is aware of it. She is in love with a young man, Stephen, who is engaged to another, an insignificant young woman. This Maggie Tulliver, instead of heedlessly seeking her own happiness, chooses in the name of human solidarity to sacrifice herself and to give up the man she loves. On the other hand, La Sanseverina in Stendhal's *Chartreuse de Parme*, behaving that it is passion which endows man with his real value, would have declared that a grand passion justifies its sacrifices, and must be preferred to the banality of such conjugal love as would unite Stephen to the little goose he was engaged to marry. It is the latter that she would have chosen to sacrifice in realizing her own happiness, and, as Stendhal shows, she would also sacrifice herself upon the plane of passion if life made that demand upon her. Here we are facing two clearly opposed moralities; but I claim that they are equivalent, seeing that in both cases the overruling aim is freedom. You can imagine two attitudes exactly similar in effect, in that one girl might prefer, in resignation, to give up her lover while the other preferred, in fulfillment of sexual desire, to ignore the prior engagement of the man she loved; and, externally, these two cases might appear the same as the two we have just cited, while being in fact entirely different. The attitude of La Sanseverina is much nearer to that of Maggie Tulliver than to one of careless greed. Thus, you see, the second objection is at once true and false. One can choose anything, but only if it is upon the plane of free commitment.

The third objection, stated by saying, "You take with one hand what you give with the other," means, at bottom, "your values are not serious, since you choose them yourselves." To that I can only say that I am very sorry that it should be so; but if I have excluded God the Father, there must be somebody to invent values. We have to take things as they are. And moreover, to say that we invent values means neither more nor less than this; that there is no sense in life *à priori*. Life is nothing until it is lived; but it is yours to make sense of, and the value of it is nothing else but the sense that you choose. Therefore, you can see that there is a possibility of creating a human community. I have been reproached for suggesting that existentialism is a form of humanism: people have said to me, "But you have written in your *Nausée* that the humanists are wrong, you have even ridiculed a certain type of humanism, why do you now go back upon that?" In reality, the word humanism has two very different meanings. One may understand by humanism a theory which upholds man as the end-in-itself and as the supreme value. Humanism in this sense appears, for instance, in Cocteau's story *Round the World in 80 Hours*, in which one of the characters declares, because he is flying over mountains in an airplane, "Man is magnificent!" This signifies that although I, personally, have not built airplanes I have the benefit of those particular inventions and that I personally, being a man, can consider myself responsible for, and honored by, achievements that are peculiar to some men. It is to assume that we can ascribe value to man according to the most distinguished deeds of certain men. That kind of humanism is absurd, for only the dog or the horse would be in a position to pronounce a general judgment upon man and declare that he is magnificent, which they have never been such fools as to do — at least, not as far as I know. But neither is it admissible that a man should pronounce judgment upon Man. Existentialism dispenses with any judgment of this sort: an existentialist will never take man as the end, since man is still to be determined. And we have no right to believe that humanity is something to which we could set up a cult, after the manner of Auguste Comte. The cult of humanity ends in Comtian humanism, shut-in upon itself, and — this must be said — in Fascism. We do not want a humanism like that.

But there is another sense of the word, of which the fundamental meaning is this: Man is all the time outside of himself: it is in projecting and losing himself beyond himself that he makes man to exist; and, on the other hand, it is by pursuing transcendent aims that he himself is able to exist. Since man is thus self-surpassing, and can grasp objects only in relation to his self-surpassing, he is himself the heart and center of his transcendence. There is no other universe except the human universe, the universe of human subjectivity. This relation of transcendence as constitutive of man (not in the sense that God is transcendent, but in the sense of self-surpassing) with subjectivity (in such a sense that man is not shut up in himself but forever present in a human universe) — it is this that we call existential humanism. This is humanism, because we remind man that there is no legislator but himself; that he himself, thus abandoned, must decide for himself; also because we show that it is not by turning back upon himself, but always by seeking, beyond himself, an aim which is one of liberation or of some particular realization, that man can realize himself as truly human.

You can see from these few reflections that nothing could be more unjust than the objections people raise against us. Existentialism is nothing else but an attempt to draw the full conclusions from a consistently atheistic position. Its intention is not in the least that of plunging men into despair. And if by despair one means — as the Christians do — any attitude of unbelief, the despair of the existentialists is something different. Existentialism is not theist in the sense that it would exhaust itself in demonstrations of the non-existence of God. It declares, rather, that even if God existed that would make no difference from its point of view. Not that we believe God does exist, but we think that the real problem is not that of His existence; what man needs is to find himself again and to understand that nothing can save him from himself, not even a valid proof of the existence of God. In this sense existentialism is optimistic. It is a doctrine of action, and it is only by self-deception, by confusing their own despair with ours that Christians can describe us as without hope.

ALBERT CAMUS (1913-1960)

Born in Algeria, Camus (pronounced Camoo) moved to France, where he was closely associated with Sartre until Sartre became a Communist. Camus wrote a number of novels, including The Stranger *and* The Plaque, *portraying at the same time the absurdity of existence and the heroism of the man of courage. Some argue that Camus is not an existentialist; indeed he did prefer the term "absurd" to "existential." Nevertheless, his view of the human condition in a meaningless universe is essentially the same as that of the existentialists.*

THE MYTH OF SISYPHUS

The gods had condemned Sisyphus to ceaselessly rolling a rock to the top of a mountain, whence the stone would fall back of its own weight. They had thought with some reason that there is no more dreadful punishment than futile and hopeless labor.

If one believes Homer, Sisyphus was the wisest and most prudent of mortals. According to another tradition, however, he was disposed to practice the profession of highwayman. I see no contradiction in this. Opinions differ as to the reasons why he became the futile laborer of the underworld. To begin with, he is accused of a certain levity in regard to the gods. He stole their secrets. Aegina, the daughter of Aesopus, was carried off by Jupiter. The father was shocked by that disappearance and complained to Sisyphus. He, who knew of the abduction, offered to tell about it on condition that Aesopus would give water to the citadel of Corinth. To the celestial thunderbolts he preferred the benediction of water. He was punished for this in the underworld. Homer tells us also that Sisyphus had put Death in chains. Pluto could not endure the sight of his deserted, silent empire. He dispatched the god of war, who liberated Death from the hands of her conqueror.

It is said also that Sisyphus, being near to death, rashly wanted to test his wife's love. He ordered her to cast his unburied body into the middle of the public square. Sisyphus woke up in the underworld. And there, annoyed by an obedience so contrary to human love, he obtained from Pluto permission to return to earth in order to chastise his wife. But when he had seen again the face of this world, enjoyed water and sun, warm stones and the sea, he no longer wanted to go back to the infernal darkness. Recalls, signs of anger, warnings were of no avail. Many years more he lived facing the curve of the gulf, the sparkling sea, and the smiles of earth. A decree of the gods was necessary. Mercury came and seized the impudent man by the collar and, snatching him from his joys, led him forcibly back to the underworld, where his rock was ready for him.

You have already grasped that Sisyphus is the absurd hero. He is, as much through his passions as through his torture. His scorn of the gods, his hatred of death, and his passion for life won him that unspeakable penalty in which the whole being is exerted toward accomplishing nothing. This is the price that must be paid for the passions of this earth. Nothing is told us about Sisyphus in the underworld. Myths are made for the imagination to breathe life into them. As for this myth, one sees merely the whole effort of a body straining to raise the huge stone, to roll it and push it up a slope a hundred times over; one sees the face screwed up, the cheek tight against the stone, the shoulder bracing the clay-covered mass, the foot wedging it, the fresh start with arms outstretched, the wholly human security of two earth-clotted hands. At the very end of his long effort measured by skyless space and time without depth, the purpose is achieved. Then Sisyphus watches the stone rush down in a few moments toward that lower world whence he will have to push it up again toward the summit. He goes back down to the plain.

It is during that return, that pause, that Sisyphus interests me. A face that toils so close to stones is already stone itself! I see that man going back down with a heavy yet measured step toward the torment of which he will never know the end. That hour like a breathing-space which returns as surely as his suffering, that is the hour of consciousness. At each of those moments when he leaves the heights and gradually sinks toward the lairs of the gods, he is superior to his fate. He is stronger than his rock.

If this myth is tragic, that is because its hero is conscious. Where would his torture be, indeed, if at every step the hope of succeeding upheld him? The workman of today works every day in his life at the same tasks, and this fate is no less absurd. But it is tragic only at the rare moments when it becomes conscious. Sisyphus, proletarian of the gods, powerless and rebellious, knows the whole extent of his wretched condition: it is what he thinks of during his descent. The lucidity that was to constitute his torture at the same time crowns his victory. There is no fate that cannot be surmounted by scorn.

* * * * *

If the descent is thus sometimes performed in sorrow, it can also take place in joy. This word is not too much. Again I fancy Sisyphus returning toward his rock, and the sorrow was in the beginning. When the images of earth cling too tightly to memory, when the call of happiness becomes too insistent, it happens that melancholy rises in man's heart: this is the rock's victory, this is the rock itself. The boundless grief is too heavy to bear. These are our nights of Gethsemane. But crushing truths perish from being acknowledged. Thus, Oedipus at the outset obeys fate without knowing it. But from the moment he knows, his tragedy begins. Yet at the same moment, blind and desperate, he realizes that the only bond linking him to the world is the cool hand of a girl. Then a tremendous remark rings out: "Despite so many ordeals, my advanced age and the nobility of my soul make me conclude that all is well." Sophocles' Oedipus, like Dostoevsky's Kirilov, thus gives the recipe for the absurd victory. Ancient wisdom confirms modern heroism.

One does not discover the absurd without being tempted to write a manual of happiness. "What! by such narrow ways — ?" There is but one world, however. Happiness and the absurd are two sons of the same earth. They are inseparable. It would be a mistake to say that happiness necessarily springs from the absurd discovery. It happens as well that the feeling of the absurd springs from happiness. "I conclude that all is well," says Oedipus, and that remark is sacred. It echoes in the wild and limited universe of man. It teaches that all is not, has not been, exhausted. It drives out of this world a god who had come into it with dissatisfaction and a preference for futile sufferings. It makes of fate a human matter, which must be settled among men.

All Sisyphus' silent joy is contained therein. His fate belongs to him. His rock is his thing. Likewise, the absurd man, when he contemplates his torment, silences all the idols. In the universe suddenly restored to its silence, the myriad wondering little voices of the earth rise up. Unconscious, secret calls, invitations from all the faces, they are the necessary reverse and price of victory. There is no sun without shadow, and it is essential to know the night. The absurd man says yes and his effort will henceforth be unceasing. If there is a personal fate, there is no higher destiny, or at least there is but one which he concludes is inevitable and despicable. For the rest, he knows himself to be the master of his days. At that subtle moment when man glances backward over his life, Sisyphus returning toward his rock, in that slight pivoting he contemplates that series of unrelated actions which becomes his fate, created by him, combined under his memory's eye and soon sealed by his death. Thus, convinced of the wholly human origin of all that is human, a blind man eager to see who knows that the night has no end, he is still on the go. The rock is still rolling.

I leave Sisyphus at the foot of the mountain! One always finds one's burden again. But Sisyphus teaches the higher fidelity that negates the gods and raises rocks. He too concludes that all is well. This universe henceforth without a master seems to him neither sterile nor futile. Each atom of that stone, each mineral flake of that night-filled mountain, in itself forms a world. The struggle itself toward the heights is enough to fill a man's heart. One must imagine Sisyphus happy.

ANTUN BRANKO ŠIMIĆ (1889-1925)

Born in Drinovci, Hercegovina (near Medjugorija) of a Croatian family, Šimić attended Catholic schools in his birthplace and Zagreb. He was a strict Catholic until World War I, when he became anti-religious, and under the influence of Central European writers like Nietzsche began emphasizing an anti-modern classical realism in literature. As editor of a number of journals, he became known to Yugo-Slavs as an enfant terrible of Croatian literature, and his anti-modernist poetry made a strong imprint on 20th-century South Slav literature.

ZEMLJA (EARTH)

For many centuries good people believed in heaven.
A place of brief residence was earth to them.
To be exchanged for life eternal.

For many centuries people went to heaven.
Flying millions of miles beyond the stars.
Like birds their souls soared from earth to eternity.

But beliefs die, each in turn.
And we have realized there is no heaven.
No upward soaring, no resurrection.
Earth is our home for all eternity.

On earth we stay forever.
We — animals and plants — are all one family:
The stone is but a distant brother.
Death makes us all alike.

ca. 1920

PAUL TILLICH (1886-1965)

The German-American philosopher and theologian Paul Tillich was greatly influenced by Nietzsche. As a Lutheran minister, he served the dying in World War I Germany. Later he was dismissed from his position as university professor for criticizing Hitler. He moved to the United States knowing no English. As a professor at Harvard and the University of Chicago, he rejected the literal interpretations of religion in favor of mythological language.

BEING AND COURAGE

I have chosen as my lecture topic a concept in which theological, sociological, and philosophical problems converge, the concept of "courage." Few concepts are as useful for the analysis of the human situation. Courage is an ethical reality, but it is rooted in the whole breadth of human existence and ultimately in the structure of being itself. It must be considered ontologically in order to be understood ethically.

This becomes manifest in one of the earliest philosophical discussions of courage, in Plato's dialogue *Laches*. In the course of the dialogue several preliminary definitions are rejected. Then Nikias, the well-known general, tries again. As a military leader he should know what courage is and he should be able to define it. But his definition, like the others, proves to be inadequate. If courage, as he asserts, is the knowledge of "what is to be dreaded and what dared," then the question tends to become universal, for in order to answer it one must have "a knowledge concerning all goods and all evils under all circumstances." But this definition contradicts the previous statement that courage is only a part of virtue. "Thus," Socrates concludes, "we have failed to discover what courage really is." And this failure is quite serious within the frame of Socratic thinking. According to Socrates virtue is knowledge, and ignorance about what courage is makes any action in accordance with the true nature of courage impossible. But this Socratic failure is more important than most of the seemingly successful definitions of courage (even those of Plato himself and of Aristotle). For the failure to find a definition of courage as a virtue among other virtues reveals a basic problem of human existence. It shows that an understanding of courage presupposes an understanding of man and of his world, its structures and values. Only he who knows this knows what to affirm and what to negate. The ethical question of the nature of courage leads inescapably to the ontological question of the nature of being. And the procedure can be reversed. The ontological question of the nature of being can be asked as the ethical question of the nature of courage. Courage can show us what being is, and being can show us what courage is. Therefore the first chapter of this book is about "Being and Courage." Although there is no chance that I shall succeed where Socrates failed, the courage of risking an almost unavoidable failure may help to keep the Socratic problem alive.

* * *

The title of this book, *The Courage to Be*, unites both meanings of the concept of courage, the ethical and the ontological. Courage as a human act, as a matter of valuation, is an ethical concept. Courage as the universal and essential self-affirmation of one's being is an ontological concept. The courage to be is the ethical act in which man affirms his own being in spite of those elements of his existence which conflict with his essential self-affirmation.

Looking at the history of Western thought one finds the two meanings of courage indicated almost everywhere, explicitly or implicitly. Since we have to deal in separate chapters with the Stoic and NeoStoic ideas of courage I shall restrict myself at this point to the interpretation of courage in the line of thought which leads from Plato to Thomas Aquinas. In Plato's *Republic* courage is related to that element of the soul which is called *thymós* (the spirited, courageous element), and both are related to that level of society which is called *phýlakes* (guardians). Thymós lies between the intellectual and the sensual element in man. It is the unreflective striving toward what is noble. As such it has a central position in the structure of the soul, it bridges the cleavage between reason and desire. At least it could do so. Actually the main trend of Platonic thought and the tradition of Plato's school were dualistic, emphasizing the conflict between the reasonable and the sensual. The bridge was not used. As late as Descartes and Kant, the elimination of the "middle" of man's being (the *thymoeidés*) had ethical and ontological consequences. It was responsible for Kant's moral rigor and Descartes' division of being into thought and extension. The sociological context in which this development occurred is well known. The Platonic *phýlakes* are the armed aristocracy, the representatives of what is noble and graceful. Out of them the bearers of wisdom arise, adding wisdom to courage. But this aristocracy and its values disintegrated. The later ancient world as well as the modern bourgeoisie have lost them; in their place appear the bearers of enlightened reason and technically organized and directed masses. But it is remarkable that Plato himself saw the thymoeidés as an essential function of man's being, an ethical value and sociological quality.

The aristocratic element in the doctrine of courage was preserved as well as restricted by Aristotle. The motive for withstanding pain and death courageously is, according to him, that it is noble to do so and base not to do so (Nic. Eth. iii. 9). The courageous man acts "for the sake of what is noble, for that is the aim of virtue" (iii. 7). "Noble," in these and other passages, is the translation of *kalós* and "base" the translation of *aischrós*, words which usually are rendered by "beautiful" and "ugly." A beautiful or noble deed is a deed to be praised. Courage does what is to be praised and rejects what is to be despised. One praises that in which a being fulfills its potentialities or actualizes its perfections. Courage is the affirmation of one's essential nature, one's inner aim or entelechy, but it is an affirmation which has in itself the character of "in spite of." It includes the possible and, in some cases, the unavoidable sacrifice of elements which also belong to one's being but which, if not sacrificed, would prevent us from reaching our actual fulfillment. This sacrifice may include pleasure, happiness, even one's own existence. In any case it is praiseworthy, because in the act of courage the most essential part of our being prevails against the less essential. It is the beauty and goodness of courage that the good and the beautiful are actualized in it. Therefore it is noble.

Perfection for Aristotle (as well as for Plato) is realized in degrees, natural, personal, and social; and courage as the affirmation of one's essential being is more conspicuous in some of these degrees than in others. Since the greatest test of courage is the readiness to make the greatest sacrifice, the sacrifice of one's life, and since the soldier is required by his profession to be always ready for this sacrifice, the soldier's courage was and somehow remained the outstanding example of courage. The Greek word for courage, *andreía* (manliness) and the Latin word *fortitudo* (strength) indicate the military connotation of courage. As long as the aristocracy was the group which carried arms the aristocratic and the military connotations of courage merged. When the aristocratic tradition disintegrated and courage could be defined as the universal knowledge of what is good and evil, wisdom and courage converged and true courage became distinguished from the soldier's courage. The courage of the dying Socrates was rational-democratic, not heroic-aristocratic.

But the aristocratic line was revived in the early Middle Ages. Courage became again characteristic of nobility. The knight is he who represents courage as a soldier and as a nobleman. He has what was called *hohe Mut*, the high, noble, and courageous spirit. The German language has two words for courageous, *tapfer* and *mutig*. Tapfer originally means firm, weighty, important, pointing to the power of being in the upper strata of feudal society. Mutig is derived from *Mut*, the movement of the soul suggested by the English word "mood." Thus words like *Schwermut, Hochmut, Kleinmut* (the heavy, the high, the small "spirit"). Mut is a matter of the "heart," the personal center. Therefore mutig can be rendered by *beherzt* (as the French-English "courage" is derived from the French *coeur*, heart). While Mut has preserved this larger sense, *Tapferkeit* became more and more the special virtue of the soldier — who ceased to be identical with the knight and the nobleman. It is obvious that the terms *Mut* and courage directly introduce the ontological question, while *Tapferkeit* and fortitude in their present meanings are without such connotations. The title of these lectures could not have been "The Fortitude to Be" (*Die Tapferkeit zum Sein*); it had to read "The Courage to Be" (*Der Mut zum Sein*). These linguistic remarks reveal the medieval situation with respect to the concept of courage, and with it the tension between the heroic-aristocratic ethics of the early Middle Ages on the one hand and on the other the rational-democratic ethics which are a heritage of the Christian-humanistic tradition and again came to the fore at the end of the Middle Ages.

This situation is classically expressed in Thomas Aquinas' doctrine of courage. Thomas realizes and discusses the duality in the meaning of courage. Courage is strength of mind, capable of conquering whatever threatens the attainment of the highest good. It is united with wisdom, the virtue which represents the unity of the four cardinal virtues (the two others being temperance and justice). A keen analysis could show that the four are not of equal standing. Courage, united with wisdom, includes temperance in relation to oneself as well as justice in relation to others. The question then is whether courage or wisdom is the more comprehensive virtue. The answer is dependent on the outcome of the famous discussion about the priority of intellect or will in the essence of being, and consequently, in the human personality. Since Thomas decides unambiguously for the intellect, as a necessary consequence he subordinates courage to wisdom. A decision for the priority of the will would point to a greater, though not a total, independence of courage in its relation to wisdom. The difference between the two lines of thought is decisive for the valuation of "venturing courage" (in religious terms, the "risk of faith"). Under the dominance of wisdom courage is essentially the "strength of mind" which makes obedience to the dictates of reason (or revelation) possible, while venturing courage participates in the creation of wisdom. The obvious danger of the first view is uncreative stagnation, as we find in a good deal of Catholic and some rationalistic thought, while the equally obvious danger of the second view is undirected willfulness, as we find in some Protestant and much Existentialist thinking.

*   *   *

Nietzsche is the most impressive and effective representative of what could be called a "philosophy of life." Life in this term is the process in which the power of being actualizes itself. But in actualizing itself it overcomes that in life which, although belonging to life, negates life. One could call it the will which contradicts the will to power. In his *Zarathustra*, in the chapter called "The Preachers of Death" (Pt. 1, chap. 9), Nietzsche points to the different ways in which life is tempted to accept its own negation: "They meet an invalid, or an old man, or a corpse — and immediately they say: 'Life is refuted!' But they only are refuted, and their eye, which seeth only one aspect of existence."[28] Life has many aspects, it is ambiguous. Nietzsche has described its ambiguity most typically in the last fragment of the collection of fragments which is called the *Will to Power*. Courage is the power of life to affirm itself in spite of this ambiguity, while the negation of life because of its negativity is an expression of cowardice. On this basis Nietzsche develops a prophecy and philosophy of courage in opposition to the mediocrity and decadence of life in the period whose coming he saw.

*   *   *

Like the earlier philosophers Nietzsche in *Zarathustra* considered the "warrior" (whom he distinguishes from the mere soldier) an outstanding example of courage. "'What is good?' ye ask. To be brave is good" (I, 10), not to be interested in long life, not to want to be spared, and all this just because of the love for life. The death of the warrior and of the mature man shall not be a reproach to the earth (I, 21). Self-affirmation is the affirmation of life and of the death which belongs to life.

Virtue for Nietzsche as for Spinoza is self-affirmation. In the chapter on "The Virtuous" Nietzsche writes: "It is your dearest Self, your virtue. The ring's thirst is in you: to reach itself again struggleth every ring, and turneth itself" (II, 27). This analogy describes better than any definition the meaning of self-affirmation in the philosophy of life: The Self has itself, but at the same time it tries to reach itself. Here Spinoza's *conatus* becomes dynamic, as, generally speaking, one could say that Nietzsche is a revival of Spinoza in dynamic terms: "Life" in Nietzsche replaces "substance" in Spinoza. And this is true not only of Nietzsche but of most of the philosophers of life. The truth of virtue is that the Self is in it "and not an outward thing." That *your* very Self be in your action, as the mother is in the child: let that be *your* formula of virtue! (II, 27.) Insofar as courage is the affirmation of one's self it is virtue altogether. The self whose self-affirmation is virtue and courage is the self which surpasses itself: "And this secret spake Life herself unto me. 'Behold,' said she, 'I am that *which must ever surpass itself*:'" (II, 34). By italicizing the last words Nietzsche indicates that he wants to give a definition of the essential nature of life. ". . . There doth Life sacrifice itself — for power!" he continues, and shows in these words that for him self-affirmation includes self-negation, not for the sake of negation but for the sake of the greatest possible affirmation, for what he calls "power." Life creates and life loves what it has created — but soon it must turn against it: "so willeth my [Life's] will." Therefore it is wrong to speak of "will to existence" or even of "will to life"; one must speak of "will to power," i.e. to more life.

---

[28] *The Complete Works of Friedrich Nietzsche*, ed. Oscar Levy (London, T. N. Foulis, 1911) Vol. 11, trans. Thomas Common.

soul banishes "everything cowardly; it says: bad — that is cowardly" (III, 54) But in order to reach such a nobility it is necessary to obey and to command and to obey while commanding. This obedience which is included in commanding is the opposite of submissiveness. The latter is the cowardice which does not dare to risk itself. The submissive self is the opposite of the self-affirming self, even if it is submissive to a God. It wants to escape the pain of hurting and being hurt. The obedient self, on the contrary, is the self which commands itself and "risketh itself thereby" (II, 34). In commanding itself it becomes its own judge and its own victim. It commands itself according to the law of life, the law of self-transcendence. The will which commands itself is the creative will. It makes a whole out of fragments and riddles of life. It does not look back, it stands beyond a bad conscience, it rejects the "spirit of revenge" which is the innermost nature of self-accusation and of the consciousness of guilt, it transcends reconciliation, for it is the will to power (II, 42). In doing all this the courageous self is united with life itself and its secret (II, 34).

We may conclude our discussion of Nietzsche's ontology of courage with the following quotation: "Have ye courage, O my brethren? . . . *Not* the courage before witnesses, but anchorite and eagle courage, which not even a God any longer beholdeth? . . . He hath heart who knoweth fear but *vanquisheth* it; who seeth the abyss, but with *pride*. He who seeth the abyss but with eagle's eyes — he who with eagle's talons *graspeth* the abyss: he hath courage" (IV, 73, sec. 4).

These words reveal the other side of Nietzsche, that in him which makes him an Existentialist, the courage to look into the abyss of nonbeing in the complete loneliness of him who accepts the message that "God is dead." About this side we shall have more to say in the following chapters. At this point we must close our historical survey, which was not meant to be a history of the idea of courage. It had a double purpose. It was supposed to show that in the history of Western thought from Plato's *Laches* to Nietzsche's *Zarathustra* the ontological problem of courage has attracted creative philosophy, partly because the moral character of courage remains incomprehensible without its ontological character, partly because the experience of courage proved to be an outstanding key for the ontological approach to reality. And further, the historical survey is meant to present conceptual material for the systematic treatment of the problem of courage, above all the concept of ontological self-affirmation in its basic character and its different interpretations.

THE COURAGE OF DESPAIR IN CONTEMPORARY ART AND LITERATURE

The courage of despair, the experience of meaninglessness, and the self-affirmation in spite of them are manifest in the Existentialists of the 20th century. Meaninglessness is the problem of all of them. The anxiety of doubt and meaninglessness is, as we have seen, the anxiety of our period. The anxiety of fate and death and the anxiety of guilt and condemnation are implied but they are not decisive. When Heidegger speaks about the anticipation of one's own death it is not the question of immortality which concerns him but the question of what the anticipation of death means for the human situation. When Kierkegaard deals with the problem of guilt it is not the theological question of sin and forgiveness that moves him but the question of what the possibility of personal existence is in the light of personal guilt. The problem of meaning troubles recent Existentialists even when they speak of finitude and guilt.

The decisive event which underlies the search for meaning and the despair of it in the 20th century is the loss of God in the 19th century. Feuerbach explained God away in terms of the infinite desire of the human heart; Marx explained him away in terms of an ideological attempt to rise above the given reality; Nietzsche as a weakening of the will to live. The result is the pronouncement "God is dead," and with him the whole system of values and meanings in which one lived. This is felt both as a loss and as a liberation. It drives one either to nihilism or to the courage which takes nonbeing into itself. There is probably nobody who has influenced modern Existentialism as much as Nietzsche and there is probably nobody who has presented the will to be oneself more consistently and more absurdly. In him the feeling of meaninglessness became despairing and self-destructive.

On this basis Existentialism, that is the great art, literature, and philosophy of the 20th century, reveals the courage to face things as they are and to express the anxiety of meaninglessness. It is creative courage which appears in the creative expressions of despair. Sartre calls one of his most powerful plays *No Exit*, a classical formula for the situation of despair. But he himself has an exit: he can say "no exit," thus taking the situation of meaninglessness upon himself. T. S. Eliot called his first great poem "The Wasteland." He described the decomposition of civilization, the lack of conviction and direction, the poverty and hysteria of the modern consciousness (as one of his critics has analyzed it). But it is the beautifully cultivated garden of a great poem which describes the meaninglessness of the Wasteland and expresses the courage of despair.

In Kafka's novels *The Castle* and *The Trial* the unapproachable remoteness of the source of meaning and the obscurity of the source of justice and mercy are expressed in language which is pure and classical. The courage to take upon oneself the loneliness of such creativity and the horror of such visions is an outstanding expression of the courage to be as oneself. Man is separated from the sources of courage — but not completely: he is still able to face and to accept his own separation. In Auden's *The Age of Anxiety* the courage to take upon oneself the anxiety in a world which has lost the meaning is as obvious as the profound experience of this loss: the two poles which are united in the phrase "courage of despair" receive equal emphasis. In Sartre's *The Age of Reason* the hero faces a situation in which his passionate desire to be himself drives him to the rejection of every human commitment. He refuses to accept anything which could limit his freedom. Nothing has ultimate meaning for him, neither love nor friendship nor politics. The only immovable point is the unlimited freedom to change, to preserve freedom without content. He represents one of the most extreme forms of the courage to be as oneself, the courage to be a self which is free from any bond and which pays the price of complete emptiness. In the invention of such a figure Sartre proves his courage of despair. From the opposite side, the same problem is faced in the novel *The Stranger* by Camus, who stands on the boundary line of Existentialism but who sees the problem of meaninglessness as sharply as the Existentialists. His hero is a man without subjectivity. He is not extraordinary in any respect. He acts as any ordinary official in a small position would act. He is a stranger because he nowhere achieves an existential relation to himself or to his world. Whatever happens to him has no reality and meaning to him: a love which is not a real love, a trial which is not a real trial, an execution which has no justification in reality. There is neither guilt nor forgiveness, neither despair nor courage in him. He is described not as a person but as a psychological process which is completely conditioned, whether he works or loves or kills or eats or sleeps. He is an object among objects, without meaning for himself and therefore unable to find meaning in his world. He represents that destiny of absolute objectivation against which Existentialists fight. He represents it in the most radical way, without reconciliation. The courage to create this figure equals the courage with which Kafka has created the figure of Mr. K.

A glimpse at the theater confirms this picture. The theater, especially in the United States, is full of images of meaninglessness and despair. In some plays nothing else is shown (as in Arthur Miller's *Death of a Salesman*); in others the negativity is less unconditional (as in Tennessee Williams' *A Streetcar Named Desire*). But it seldom becomes positivity: even comparatively positive solutions are undermined by doubt and by awareness of the ambiguity of all solutions. It is astonishing that these plays are attended by large crowds in a country whose prevailing courage is the courage to be as a part in a system of democratic conformity. What does this mean for the situation of America and with it of mankind as a whole? One can easily play down the importance of this phenomenon. One can point to the unquestionable fact that even the largest crowds of theatergoers are an infinitely small percentage of the American population. One can dismiss the significance of the attraction the Existentialist theater has for many by calling it an imported fashion, doomed to disappear very soon. This is possibly but not necessarily so. It may be that the comparatively few (few even if one adds to them all the cynics and despairing ones in our institutions of higher learning) are a vanguard which precedes a great change in the spiritual and social-psychological situation. It may be that the limits of the courage to be as a part have become visible to more people than the increasing conformity shows. If this is the meaning of the appeal that Existentialism has on the stage, one should observe it carefully and prevent it from becoming the forerunner of collectivist forms of the courage to be as a part — a threat which history has abundantly proved to exist.

The combination of the experience of meaninglessness and of the courage to be as oneself is the key to the development of visual art since the turn of the century. In expressionism and surrealism the surface structures of reality are disrupted. The categories which constitute ordinary experience have lost their power. The category of substance is lost: solid objects are twisted like ropes; the causal interdependence of things is disregarded: things appear in a complete contingency; temporal sequences are without significance, it does not matter whether an event has happened before or after another event; the spatial dimensions are reduced or dissolved into a horrifying infinity. The organic structures of life are cut into pieces which are arbitrarily (from the biological, not the artistic, point of view) recomposed: limbs are dispersed, colors are separated from their natural carriers. The psychological process (this refers to literature more than to art) is reversed: one lives from the future to the past, and this without rhythm or any kind of meaningful organization. The world of anxiety is a world in which the categories, the structures of reality, have lost their validity. Every body would be dizzy if causality suddenly ceased to be valid. In Existentialist art (as I like to call it) causality has lost its validity.

Modern art has been attacked as a forerunner of totalitarian systems. The answer that all totalitarian systems have started their careers by attacking modern art is insufficient, for one could say that the totalitarian systems fought modern art just because they tried to resist the meaninglessness expressed in it. The real answer lies deeper. Modern art is not propaganda but revelation. It shows that the reality of our existence is as it is. It does not cover up the reality in which we are living. The question therefore is this: Is the revelation of a situation propaganda for it? If this were the case all art would have to become dishonest beautification. The art propagated by both totalitarianism and democratic conformism is dishonest beautification. It is an idealized naturalism which is preferred because it removes every danger of art becoming critical and revolutionary. The creators of modern art have been able to see the meaninglessness of our existence; they participated in its despair. At the same time they have had the courage to face it and to express it in their pictures and sculptures. They had the courage to be as themselves.

* * *

The faith which makes the courage of despair possible is the acceptance of the power of being, even in the grip of nonbeing. Even in the despair about meaning being affirms itself through us. The act of accepting meaninglessness is in itself a meaningful act. It is an act of faith.

PLATO

THE RING OF GYGES

Glaucon:

Now that those who practise justice do so involuntarily and because they have not the power to be unjust will best appear if we imagine something of this kind: having given both to the just and the unjust power to do what they will, let us watch and see whither desire will lead them; then we shall discover in the very act the just and unjust man to be proceeding along the same road, following their interest, which all natures deem to be their good, and are only diverted into the path of justice by the force of law. The liberty which we are supposing may be most completely given to them in the form of such a power as is said to have been possessed by Gyges the ancestor of Croesus the Lydian. According to the tradition, Gyges was a shepherd in the service of the king of Lydia; there was a great storm, and an earthquake made an opening in the earth at the place where he was feeding his flock. Amazed at the sight, he descended into the opening, where, among other marvels, he beheld a hollow brazen horse, having doors, at which he stooping and looking in saw a dead body of stature, as appeared to him, more than human, and having nothing on but a gold ring; this he took from the finger of the dead and reascended. Now the shepherds met together, according to custom, that they might send their monthly report about the flocks to the king; into their assembly he came having the ring on his finger, and as he was sitting among them he chanced to turn the collet of the ring inside his hand, when instantly he became invisible to the rest of the company and they began to speak of him as if he were no longer present. He was astonished at this, and again touching the ring he turned the collet outwards and reappeared; he made several trials of the ring, and always with the same result — when he turned the collet inwards he seduced the queen, and with her help conspired against the king and slew him, and took the kingdom. Suppose now that there were two such magic rings, and the just put on one of them and the unjust the other; no man can be imagined to be of such an iron nature that he would stand fast in justice. No man would keep his hands off what was not his own when he could safely take what he liked out of the market, or go into houses and lie with anyone at his pleasure, or kill or release from prison whom he would, and in all respects be like a God among men. Then the actions of the just would be as the actions of the unjust; they would both come at last to the same point. And this we may truly affirm to be a great proof that a man is just, not willingly or because he thinks that justice is any good to him individually, but of necessity, for wherever any one thinks that he can safely be unjust, there he is unjust. For all men believe in their hearts that injustice is far more profitable to the individual than justice, and he who argues as I have been supposing, will say that they are right. If you could imagine anyone obtaining this power of becoming invisible, and never doing any wrong or touching what was another's he would be thought by the lookers-on to be a most wretched idiot, although they would praise him to one another's faces, and keep up appearances with one another from a fear that they too might suffer injustice.

ARISTOTLE

NICOMACHEAN ETHICS

Book II. Moral Virtue

1. EXCELLENCE, then, being of these two kinds, intellectual and moral, intellectual excellence owes its birth and growth mainly to instruction, and so requires time and experience, while moral excellence is the result of habit or custom (εθος), and has accordingly in our language received a name formed by a slight change from εθος.[29]

From this it is plain that none of the moral excellences or virtues is implanted in us by nature; for that which is by nature cannot be altered by training. For instance, a stone naturally tends to fall downwards, and you could not train it to rise upwards, though you tried to do so by

---

[29] εθος, customs; ηθος, character; ηθικη αρετη, moral excellence; we have no similar sequence, but the Latin *mos, mores*, from which "morality" comes, covers both εθος and εθος

throwing it up ten thousand times, nor could you train fire to move downwards, nor accustom anything which naturally behaves in one way to behave in any other way.

The virtues[30] then, come neither by nature nor against nature, but nature gives the capacity for acquiring them, and this is developed by training.

Again, where we do things by nature we power first, and put this power forth in act afterwards: as we plainly see in the case of the senses; for it is not by constantly seeing and hearing that we acquire those faculties, but, on the contrary, we had the power first and then used it, instead of acquiring the power by the use. But the virtues we acquire by doing the acts, as is the case with the arts too. We learn an art by doing that which we wish to do when we have learned it; we become builders by building, and harpers by harping. And so by doing just acts we become just, and by doing acts of temperance and courage we become temperate and courageous.

This is attested, too, by what occurs in states; for the legislators make their citizens good by training; i.e. this is the wish of all legislators, and those who do not succeed in this miss their aim, and it is this that distinguishes a good from a bad constitution.

Again, both virtues and vices result from and are formed by the same acts in which they manifest themselves, as is the case with the arts also. It is by harping that good harpers and bad harpers alike are produced: and so with builders and the rest; by building well they will become good builders, and bad builders by building badly. Indeed, if it were not so, they would not want anybody to teach them, but would all be born either good or bad at their trades. And it is just the same with the virtues also. It is by our conduct in our intercourse with other men that we become just or unjust, and by acting in circumstances of danger, and training ourselves to feel fear or confidence, that we become courageous or cowardly. So, too, with our animal appetites and the passion of anger; for by behaving in this way or in that on the occasions with which these passions are concerned, some become temperate and gentle. And others profligate and ill-tempered. In a word, the several habits or characters are formed by the same kind of acts as those which they produce.

Hence we ought to make sure that our acts be of a certain kind; for the resulting character varies as they vary. It makes no small difference, therefore, whether a man be trained from his youth up in this way or in that, but a great difference, or rather all the difference.

2. But our present inquiry has not, like the rest, a merely speculative aim; we are not inquiring merely in order to know what excellence or virtue is, but in order to become good; for otherwise it would profit us nothing. We must ask therefore about these acts, and see of what kind they are to be; for, as we said, it is they that determine our habits or character.

First of all, then, that they must be in accordance with right reason is a common characteristic of them, which we shall here take for granted, reserving for future discussion the question what this right reason is, and how it is related to the other excellences.

But let it be understood, before we go on, that all reasoning on matters of practice must be in outline merely, and not scientifically exact; for, as we said at starting the kind of reasoning to be demanded varies with the subject in hand; and in practical matters and questions of expediency there are no invariable laws, any more than in questions of health.

And if our general conclusions are thus inexact, still more inexact is all reasoning about particular cases; for these fall under no system of scientifically established rules or traditional maxims, but the agent must always consider for himself what the special occasion requires, just as in medicine or navigation.

But though this is the case we must try to render what help we can.

First of all, then, we must observe that in matters of this sort, to fall short and to exceed are alike fatal. This is plain (to illustrate what we cannot see by what we can see) in the case of

---

[30] It is with the moral virtues that this and the three following books are exclusively concerned, the discussion of the intellectual virtues being postponed to Book VI.

strength and health. Too much and too little exercise alike destroy strength, and to take too much meat and drink, or to take too little, is equally ruinous to health, but the fitting amount produces and increases and preserves them. Just so, then, is it with temperance also, and courage, and the other virtues. The man who shuns and fears everything and never makes a stand, becomes a coward; while the man who fears nothing at all, but will face anything, becomes foolhardy. So, too, the man who takes his fill of any kind of pleasure, and abstains from none, is a profligate, but the man who shuns all (like him whom we call a "boor") is devoid of sensibility. For temperance and courage are destroyed both by excess and defect, but preserved by moderation.

But habits or types of character are not only produced and preserved and destroyed by the same occasions and the same means, but they will also manifest themselves in the same circumstances. This is the case with palpable things like strength. Strength is produced by taking plenty of nourishment and doing plenty of hard work, and the strong man, in turn, has the greatest capacity for these. And the case is the same with the virtues: by abstaining from pleasure we become temperate, and when we have become temperate we are best able to abstain. And so with courage: by habituating ourselves to despise danger, and to face it, we become courageous; and when we have become courageous, we are best able to face danger.

3. The pleasure or pain that accompanies the acts must be taken as a test of the formed habit or character.

He who abstains from the pleasures of the body and rejoices in the abstinence is temperate, while he who is vexed at having to abstain is profligate; and again, he who faces danger with pleasure, or, at any rate, without pain, is courageous, but he to whom this is painful is a coward.

For moral virtue or excellence is closely concerned with pleasure and pain. It is pleasure that moves us to do what is base, and pain that moves us to refrain from what is noble. And therefore, as Plato says, man needs to be so trained from his youth up as to find pleasure and pain in the right objects. This is what sound education means.

Another reason why virtue has to do with pleasure and pain, is that it has to do with actions and passions or affections; but every affection and every act is accompanied by pleasure or pain.

The fact is further attested by the employment of pleasure and pain in correction; they have a kind of curative property, and a cure is effected by administering the opposite of the disease.

Again, as we said before, every type of character [or habit or formed faculty] is essentially relative to, and concerned with, those things that form it for good or for ill; but it is through pleasure and pain that bad characters are formed — that is to say, through pursuing and avoiding the wrong pleasures and pains, or pursuing and avoiding them at the wrong time, or in the wrong manner, or in any other of the various ways of going wrong that may be distinguished.

And hence some people go so far as to define the virtues as a kind of impassive or neutral state of mind. But they err in stating this absolutely, instead of qualifying it by the addition of the right and wrong manner, time, etc.

We may lay down, therefore, that this kind of excellence (i.e., moral excellence) makes us do what is best in matters of pleasure and pain, while vice or badness has the contrary effect.

The following considerations will throw additional light on the point.

There are three kinds of things that move us to choose, and three that move us to avoid them: on the one hand, the beautiful or noble, the advantageous, the pleasant; on the other hand, the ugly or base, the hurtful, the painful. Now, the good man is apt to go right, and the bad man to go wrong, about them all, but especially about pleasure: for pleasure is not only common to man with animals, but also accompanies all pursuit or choice; since the noble, and the advantageous also, are pleasant in idea.

Again, the feeling of pleasure has been fostered in us all from our infancy by our training, and has thus become so engrained in our life that it can scarce be washed out.[31] And, indeed, we

---

[31] Actions and the accompanying feelings of pleasure and pain have so grown together, that it is impossible to separate the former and judge them apart: cf. X. 4, 11.

all more or less make pleasure our test in judging of actions. For this reason too, then, our whole inquiry must be concerned with these matters; since to be pleased and pained in the right or the wrong way has great influence on our actions.

And lastly, as Heraclitus says, it is harder to fight with pleasure than with wrath, and virtue, like art, is always more concerned with what is harder; for the harder the task the better is success. For this reason also, then, both (moral) virtue or excellence and the science of the state must always be concerned with pleasures and pains; for he that behaves rightly with regard to them will be good, and he that behaves badly will be bad.

We will take it as established, then, that (moral) excellence or virtue has to do with pleasures and pains; and that the acts which produce it develop it, and also, when differently done, destroy it; and that it manifests itself in the same acts which produced it.

4. But here we may be asked what we mean by saying that men can become just and temperate only by doing what is just and temperate: surely, it may be said, if their acts are just and temperate, they themselves are already just and temperate, as they are grammarians and musicians if they do what is grammatical and musical.

We may answer, I think, firstly, that this is not quite the case even with the arts. A man may do something grammatical (or write something correctly) by chance, or at the prompting of another person: he will not be grammatical till he not only does something grammatical, but also does it grammatically (or like a grammatical person), i.e., in virtue of his own knowledge of grammar.

But, secondly, the virtues are not in this point analogous to the arts. The products of art have their excellence in themselves, and so it is enough if when produced they are of a certain quality; but in the case of the virtues, a man is not said to act justly or temperately (or like a just or temperate man) if what he does merely be of a certain sort — he must also be in a certain state of mind when he does it; i.e., first of all, he must know what he is doing; secondly, he must choose it, and choose it for itself; and, thirdly, his act must be the expression of a formed and stable character. Now, of these conditions, only one, the knowledge, is necessary for the possession of any art; but for the possession of the virtues knowledge is of little or no avail, while the other conditions that result from repeatedly doing what is just and temperate are not a little important, but all-important.

The thing that is done, therefore, is called just or temperate when it is such as the just or temperate man would do; but the man who does it is not just or temperate, unless he also does it in the spirit of the just or the temperate man.

It is right, then, to say that by doing what is just a man becomes just, and temperate by doing what is temperate, while without doing thus he has no chance of ever becoming good.

But most men, instead of doing thus, fly to theories, and fancy that they are philosophizing and that this will make them good, like a sick man who listens attentively to what the doctor says and then disobeys all his orders. This sort of philosophizing will no more produce a healthy habit of mind than this sort of treatment will produce a health habit of body.

5. We have next to inquire what excellence or virtue is.

Everything psychical is either (1) a passion or emotion, or (2) a power or faculty, or (3) a habit or trained faculty; and so virtue must be one of these three. By (1) a passion or emotion we mean appetite, anger, fear, confidence, envy, joy, love, hate, longing, emulation, pity, or generally that which is accompanied by pleasure or pain; (2) a power or faculty is that in respect of which we are said to be capable of being affected in any of these ways, as, for instance, that in respect of which we are able to be angered or pained or to pity; and (3) a habit or trained faculty is that in respect of which we are well or ill regulated or disposed in the matter of our affections; as, for instance, in the matter of being angered, we are ill regulated if we are too violent or too slack, but if we are moderate in our anger we are well regulated. And so with the rest.

Now, the virtues are not emotions, nor are the vices — (1) because we are not called good or bad in respect of our emotions, but are called so in respect of our virtues or vices; (2) because we are neither praised nor blamed in respect of our emotions (a man is not praised for being afraid or angry, nor blamed for being angry simply, but for being angry in a particular way), but we are praised or blamed in respect of our virtues or vices; (3) because we may be angered or frightened without deliberate choice, but the virtues are a kind of deliberate choice, or at least are impossible without it; and (4) because in respect of our emotions we are said to be moved, but in respect of our virtues and vices we are not said to be moved, but to be regulated or disposed in this way or in that.

For these same reasons also they are not powers or faculties; for we are not called either good or bad for being merely capable of emotion, nor are we either promised or blamed for this. And further, while nature gives us our powers or faculties, she does not make us either good or bad. (This point, however, we have already treated.)

If, then, the virtues be neither emotions nor faculties, it only remains for them to be habit or trained faculties.

6. We have thus found the genus to which virtue belongs; but we want to know, not only that it is a trained faculty, but also what species of trained faculty it is.

We may safely assert that the virtue or excellence of a thing causes that thing both to be itself in good condition and to perform its function well. The excellence of the eye, for instance, makes both the eye and its work good; for it is by the excellence of the eye that we see well. So the proper excellence of the horse makes a horse what he should be, and makes him good at running, and carrying his rider, and standing a charge.

If, then, this holds good in all cases, the proper excellence or virtue of man will be a habit or trained faculty that makes a man good and makes him perform his function well.

How this is to be done we have already said, but we may exhibit the same conclusion in another way, by inquiring what the nature of this virtue is.

Now, if we have any quantity, whether continuous or discrete,[32] it is possible to take either a larger [or too large], or a smaller [or too small], or an equal [or fair] amount, and that either absolutely or relatively to our own needs.

By an equal or fair amount I understand a mean amount, or one that lies between excess and deficiency.

By the absolute mean, or mean relatively to the thing itself, I understand that which is equidistant from both extremes, and this is one and the same for all.

By the mean relatively to us I understand that which is neither too much nor too little for us; and this is not one and the same for all.

For instance, if ten be larger [or too large] and two be smaller [or too small], if we take six we take the mean relatively to the thing itself [or the arithmetical mean]; for it exceeds one extreme by the same amount by which it is exceeded by the other extreme: and this is the mean in arithmetical proportion.

But the mean relatively to us cannot be found in this way. If ten pounds of food is too much for a given man to eat, and two pounds too little, it does not follow that the trainer will order him six pounds: for that also may perhaps be too much for the man in question, or too little; too little for Milo, too much for the beginner. The same holds true in running and wrestling.

And so we may say generally that a master in any art avoids what is too much and what is too little, and seeks for the mean and chooses it — not the absolute but the relative mean.

Every art or science, then, perfects its work in this way, looking to the mean and bringing its work up to this standard; so that people are wont to say of a good work that nothing could be taken from it or added to it, implying that excellence is destroyed by excess or deficiency, but accrued by observing the mean. And good artists, as we say, do in fact keep their eyes fixed on this in all that they do.

---

[32] A line (or a generous emotion) is a "continuous quantity"; you can part it where you please: a rouleau of sovereigns is a "discrete quantity," made up of definite parts, and primarily separable into them.

Virtue therefore, since like nature it is more exact and better than any art, must also aim at the mean — virtue of course meaning moral virtue or excellence; for it has to do with passions and actions, and it is these that admit of excess and deficiency and the mean. For instance, it is possible to feel fear, confidence, desire, anger, pity, and generally to be affected pleasantly and painfully, either too much or too little, in either came wrongly; but to be thus affected at the right times, and on the right occasions, and towards the right persons, and with the right object, and in the right fashion, is the mean course and the best course, and these are characteristics of virtue. And in the same way our outward acts also admit of excess and deficiency, and the mean or due amount.

Virtue, then, has to deal with feelings or passions and with outward acts, in which excess is wrong and deficiency also is blamed, but the mean amount is praised and is right — both of which are characteristics of virtue.

Virtue, then, is a kind of moderation inasmuch as it aims at the mean or moderate amount.

Again, there are many ways of going wrong (for evil is infinite in nature, to use a Pythagorean figure, while good is finite), but only one way of going right; so that the one is easy and the other hard — easy to miss the mark and hard to hit. On this account also, then, excess and deficiency are characteristic of vice, hitting the mean is characteristic of virtue:

"Goodness is simple, ill takes any shape."

Virtue, then, is a habit or trained faculty of choice, the characteristic of which lies in observing the mean relatively to the persons concerned, and which is guided by reason, i.e., by the judgment of the prudent man.

And it is a moderation, firstly, inasmuch as it comes in the middle or mean between two vices, one on the side of excess, the other on the side of defect; and, secondly, inasmuch as, while these vices fall short of or exceed the due measure in feeling and in action, it finds and chooses the mean, middling, or moderate amount.

Regarded in its essence, therefore, or according to the definition of its nature, virtue is a moderation or middle state, but viewed in its relation to what is best and right it is the extreme of perfection.

But it is not all actions nor all passions, that admit of moderation; there are some whose very names imply badness, as malevolence, shamelessness, envy, and, among acts, adultery, theft, murder. These and all other like things are blamed as being bad in themselves, and not merely in their excess or deficiency. It is impossible therefore to go right in them; they are always wrong: rightness and wrongness in such things (e.g., in adultery) does not depend upon whether it is the right person and occasion and manner, but the mere doing of any one of them is wrong.

It would be equally absurd to look for moderation or excess or deficiency in unjust cowardly or profligate conduct; for then there would be moderation in excess or deficiency, and excess in excess, and deficiency in deficiency.

The fact is that just as there can be no excess or deficiency in temperance or courage because the mean or moderate amount is, in a sense, an extreme, so in these kinds of conduct also there can be no moderation or excess or deficiency, but the acts are wrong however they be done. For, to put it generally, there cannot be moderation in excess or deficiency, nor excess or deficiency in moderation.

7. But it is not enough to make these general statements (about virtue and vice): we must go on and apply them to particulars [i.e., to the several virtues and vices]. For in reasoning about matters of conduct general statements are too vague, and do not convey so much truth as particular propositions. It is with particulars that conduct is concerned: our statements, therefore, when applied to these particulars, should be found to hold good.

These particulars then (i.e., the several virtues and vices and the several acts and affections with which they deal), we will take from the following table.

Moderation in the feelings of fear and confidence is courage: of those that exceed, he that exceeds in fearlessness has no name (as often happens), but he that exceeds in confidence is foolhardy, while he that exceeds in fear, but is deficient in confidence, is cowardly.

Moderation in respect of certain pleasures and also (though to a less extent) certain pains is temperance, while excess is profligacy. But defectiveness in the matter of these pleasures is hardly ever found, and so this sort of people also have as yet received no name: let us put them down as "void of sensibility."

In the matter of giving and taking money, moderation is liberality, excess and deficiency are prodigality and illiberality. But these two vices exceed and fall short in contrary ways: the prodigal exceeds in spending, but falls short in taking; while the illiberal man exceeds in taking, but falls short in spending.

(For the present we are but giving an outline or summary, and aim at nothing more; we shall afterward treat these points in greater detail.)

But, besides these, there are other dispositions in the matter of money: there is a moderation which is called magnificence (for the magnificent is not the same as the liberal man: the former deals with large sums, the latter with small), and an excess which is called bad taste or vulgarity, and a deficiency which is called meanness; and these vices differ from those which are opposed to liberality: how they differ will be explained later.

With respect to honour and disgrace, there is a moderation which is high-mindedness, an excess which may be called vanity, and a deficiency which is little-mindedness.

But just as we said that liberality is related to magnificence, differing only in that it deals with small sums, so here there is a virtue related to high-mindedness and differing only in that it is concerned with small instead of great honours. A man may have a due desire for honour, and also more or less than a due desire: he that carries this degree to excess is called ambitious, he that has not enough of it is called unambitious, but he that has the due amount has no name. There are also no abstract names for the characters, except "ambition," corresponding to ambitious. And on this account those who occupy the extremes lay claim to the middle place. And in common parlance, too, the moderate man is sometimes called ambitious and sometimes unambitious, and sometimes the ambitious man is praised and sometimes the unambitious. Why this is we will explain afterwards; for the present we will follow out our plan and enumerate the other types of character.

In the matter of anger also we find excess and deficiency and moderation. The characters themselves hardly have recognized names, but as the moderate man is here called gentle, we will call his character, gentleness; of those who go into extremes, we may take the term wrathful for him who exceeds, with wrathfulness for the vice, and wrathless for him who is deficient, with wrathlessness for his character.

Besides these, there are three kinds of moderation, bearing some resemblance to one another, and yet different. They all have to do with intercourse in speech and action, but they differ in that one has to do with the truthfulness of this intercourse, while the other two have to do with its pleasantness — one of the two with pleasantness in matters of amusement, the other with pleasantness in all the relations of life. We must therefore speak of these qualities also in order that we may the more plainly see how, in all cases, moderation is praiseworthy, while the extreme courses are neither right nor praiseworthy, but blamable.

In these cases also names are for the most part wanting, but we must try, here as elsewhere, to coin names ourselves, in order to make our argument clear and easy to follow.

In the matter of truth, then, let us call him who observes the mean a true (or truthful) person, and observance of the mean truth (or truthfulness): pretence, when it exaggerates, may be called boasting, and the person a boaster; when it understates, let the names be irony and ironical.

With regard to pleasantness in amusement, he who observes the mean may be called witty, and his character wittiness; excess may be called buffoonery, and the man a buffoon; while boorish may stand for the person who is deficient, and boorishness for his character.

With regard to pleasantness in the other affairs of life, he who makes himself properly pleasant may be called friendly, and his moderation friendliness; he that exceeds may be called obsequious if he has no ulterior motive, but a flatterer if he has an eye to his own advantage; he that is deficient in this respect, and always makes himself disagreeable, may be called a quarrelsome or peevish fellow.

Moreover, in mere emotions[33] and in our conduct with regard to them, there are ways of observing the mean; for instance, shame is not a virtue, but yet the modest man is praised. For in these matters also we speak of this man as observing the mean, of that man as going beyond it as the shame-faced man whom the least thing makes shy, while he who is deficient in the feeling, or lacks it altogether, is called shameless; but the term modest (α δημων) is applied to him who observes the mean.

Righteous indignation, again, hits the mean between envy and malevolence. These have to do with feelings of pleasure and pain at what happens to our neighbors. A man is called righteously indignant when he feels pain at the sight of undeserved prosperity, but your envious man goes beyond him and is pained by the sight of any one in prosperity, while the malevolent man is so far from being pained that he actually exults in the sight of prosperous iniquity.

But we shall have another opportunity of discussing these matters.

As for justice, the term is used in more senses than one; we will, therefore, after disposing of the above questions, distinguish these various senses, and show how each of these kinds of justice is a kind of moderation.

And then we will treat of the intellectual virtues in the same way.

8. There are, as we said, three classes of disposition, viz. two kinds of vice, one marked by excess, the other by deficiency, and one kind of virtue, the observance of the mean.

Now, the extreme dispositions are opposed both to the mean or moderate disposition and to one another, while the moderate disposition is opposed to both the extremes. Just as a quantity which is equal to a given quantity is also greater when compared with a less, and less when compared with a greater quantity, so the mean or moderate dispositions exceed as compared with the defective dispositions, and fall short as compared with the excessive dispositions, both in feeling and in action; e.g., the courageous man seems foolhardy as compared with the coward, and cowardly as compared with the foolhardy; and similarly the temperate man appears profligate in comparison with the insensible, and insensible in comparison with the profligate man; and the liberal man appears prodigal by the side of the illiberal man, and illiberal by the side of the prodigal man.

And so the extreme characters try to displace the mean or moderate character, and each represents him as falling into the opposite extreme, the coward calling the courageous man foolhardy, the foolhardy calling him coward, and so on in other cases.

But while the mean and the extremes are thus opposed to one another, the extremes are still more contrary to each other than to the mean; for they are further removed from one another than from the mean, as that which is greater than a given magnitude is further from that which is less, and that which is less is further from that which is greater, than either the greater or the less is from that which is the given magnitude.

Sometimes, again, an extreme, when compared with the mean, has a sort of resemblance to it, as foolhardiness to courage, or prodigality to liberality; but there is the greatest possible dissimilarity between the extremes.

Again, "things that are as far as possible removed from each other" is the accepted definition of contraries, so that the further things are removed from each other the more contrary they are.

In comparison with the mean, however, it is sometimes the deficiency that is the more opposed, and sometimes the excess; e.g., foolhardiness, which is excess, is not so much opposed

---

[33] i.e., which do not issue in act like those hitherto mentioned.

to courage as cowardice, which is deficiency; but insensibility, which is lack of feeling, is not so much opposed to temperance as profligacy, which is excess.

The reasons for this are two. One is the reason derived from the nature of the matter itself: since one extreme is, in fact, nearer and more similar to the mean, we naturally do not oppose it to the mean so strongly as the other; e.g., as foolhardiness seems more similar to courage and nearer to it, and cowardice more dissimilar, we speak of cowardice as the opposite rather than the other: for that which is further removed from the mean seems to be more opposed to it.

This, then, is one reason, derived from the nature of the thing itself. Another reason lies in ourselves: and it is this — those things to which we happen to be more prone by nature appear to be more opposed to the mean: e.g. our natural inclination is rather towards indulgence in pleasure, and so we more easily fall into profligate than into regular habits: those courses, then, in which we are more apt to run to great lengths are spoken of as more opposed to the mean; and thus profligacy, which is an excess, is more opposed to temperance than the deficiency is.

9. We have sufficiently explained, then, that moral virtue is moderation or observance of the mean, and in what sense, viz. (1) as holding a middle position between two vices, one on the side of excess, and the other on the side of deficiency, and (2) as aiming at the mean or moderate amount both in feeling and in action.

And on this account it is a hard time to be good; for finding the middle or the mean in each case is a hard thing, just as finding the middle or centre of a circle is a thing that is not within the power of everybody, but only of him who has the requisite knowledge.

Thus any one can be angry — that is quite easy; any one can give money away or spend it: but to do these things to the right person, to the right extent, at the right time, with the right object, and in the right manner, is not what everybody can do, and is by no means easy; and that is the reason why right doing is rare and praiseworthy and noble.

He that aims at the mean, then, should first of all strive to avoid that extreme which is more opposed to it, as Calypso bids Ulysses —

"Keep your ship clear of yonder spray and surf." For of the extremes one is more dangerous, the other less. Since then it is hard to hit the mean precisely, we must "row when we cannot sail," as the proverb has it, and choose the least of two evils; and that will be best effected in the way we have described.

And secondly we must consider, each for himself, what we are most prone to — for different natures are inclined to different things — which we may learn by the pleasure or pain we feel. And then we must bend ourselves in the opposite direction; for by keeping well away from error we shall fall into the middle course, as we straighten a bent stick by bending it the other way.

But in all cases we must be especially on our guard against pleasant things, and against pleasure; for we can scarce judge her impartially. And so, in our behaviour towards her, we should imitate the behaviour of the old counsellors towards Helen, and in all cases repeat their saying: if we dismiss her we shall be less likely to go wrong.

This then, in outline, is the course by which we shall best be able to hit the mean.

But it is a hard task, we must admit, especially in a particular case. It is not easy to determine, for instance, how and with whom one ought to be angry, and upon what grounds, and for how long; for public opinion sometimes praises those who fall short and calls them gentle, and sometimes applies the term manly to those who show a harsh temper.

In fact, a slight error, whether on the side of excess or deficiency, is not blamed, but only a considerable effort for then there can be no mistake. But it is hardly possible to determine by reasoning how far or to what extent a man must err in order to incur blame; and indeed matters that fall within the scope of perception never can be so determined. Such matters lie within the region of particulars, and can only be determined by perception.

So much then is plain, that the middle character is in all cases to be praised, but that we ought to incline sometimes towards excess, sometimes towards deficiency; for in this way we shall most easily hit the mean and attain to right doing.

Book III. Chapters 1-5. The Will.

1. VIRTUE, as we have seen, has to do with feelings and actions. Now, praise[34] or blame is given only to what is voluntary; that which is involuntary receives pardon, and sometimes even pity.

It seems, therefore, that a clear distinction between the voluntary and the involuntary is necessary for those who are investigating the nature of virtue, and will also help legislators in assigning rewards and punishments.

That is generally held to be involuntary which is done under compulsion or through ignorance.

"Done under compulsion" means that the cause is external, the agent or patient contributing nothing towards it; as, for instance, if he were carried somewhere by a whirlwind or by men whom he could not resist.

But there is some question about acts done in order to avoid a greater evil, or to obtain some noble end; e.g., if a tyrant were to order you to do something disgraceful, having your parents or children in his power, who were to live if you did it, but to die if you did not — it is a matter of dispute whether such acts are involuntary or voluntary.

Throwing a cargo overboard in a storm is a somewhat analogous case. No one voluntarily throws away his property if nothing is to come of it,[35] but any sensible person would do so to save the life of himself and the crew.

Acts of this kind, then, are of a mixed nature, but they more nearly resemble voluntary acts. For they are desired or chosen at the time when they are done, and the end or motive of an act is that which is in view at the time. In applying the terms voluntary and involuntary, therefore, we must consider the state of the agent's mind at the time. Now, he wills the act at the time; for the cause which sets the limbs going lies in the agent in such cases, and where the cause lies in the agent, it rests with him to do or not to do.

Such acts, then, are voluntary, though in themselves [or apart from these qualifying circumstances] we may allow them to be involuntary; for no one would choose anything of this kind on its own account.

And, in fact, for actions of this sort men are sometimes praised,[36] e.g., when they endure something disgraceful or painful in order to secure some great and noble result: but in the contrary case they are blamed; for no worthy person would endure the extremity of disgrace when there was no noble result in view, or but a trifling one.

But in some cases we do not praise, but pardon, i.e., when a man is induced to do a wrong act by pressure which is too strong for human nature and which no one could bear. Though there are some cases of this kind, I think, where the plea of compulsion is inadmissible,[37] and where, rather than do the act, a man ought to suffer death in its most painful form; for instance, the circumstances which "compelled" Alcmaeon in Euripides[38] to kill his mother seem absurd.

---

[34] It must be remembered that "virtue" is synonymous with "praiseworthy habit." I. 1, 20; II. 9, 9.

[35] ἁπλῶ, "without qualification:" no one chooses loss of property simply, but loss of property with saving of life is what all sensible people would choose.

[36] Which shows that the acts are regarded as voluntary.

[37] ονκ εστιν αναγκασφηναι, "compulsion is impossible." If the act was compulsory it was not my act, I cannot be blamed: there are some acts, says Aristotle, for which we could not forgive a man, for which whatever the circumstances, we must blame him; therefore no circumstances can compel him, or compulsion is impossible. The argument is, in fact, "I ought not, therefore I cannot (am able not to do it),"—like Kant's, "I ought, therefore I can." But, if valid at all, it is valid universally, and the conclusion should be that the body only can be compelled, and not the will—that a compulsory act is impossible.

[38] The play alluded to seems to be entirely lost.

It is sometimes hard to decide whether we ought to do this deed to avoid this evil, or whether we ought to endure this evil rather than do this deed; but it is still harder to abide by our decisions: for generally the evil which we wish to avoid is something painful, the deed we are pressed to do is something disgraceful; and hence we are blamed or praised according as we do or do not allow ourselves to be compelled.

What kinds of acts, then, are to be called compulsory?

I think our answer must be that, in the first place, when the cause lies outside and the agent has no part in it, the act is called, without qualification, "compulsory" [and therefore involuntary]; but that, in the second place, when an act that would not be voluntarily done for its own sake is chosen now in preference to this given alternative, the cause lying in the agent, such an act must be called "involuntary in itself," or "in the abstract," but "now, and in preference to this alternative, voluntary." But an act of the latter kind is rather of the nature of a voluntary act: for acts fall within the sphere of particulars; and here the particular thing that is done is voluntary.

It is scarcely possible, however, to lay down rules for determining which of two alternatives is to be preferred; for there are many differences in the particular cases.

It might, perhaps, be urged that acts whose motive is something pleasant or something noble are compulsory, for here we are constrained by something outside us.

But if this were so, all our acts would be compulsory; for these are the motives of every act of every man.[39]

Again, acting under compulsion and against one's will is painful, but action whose motive is something pleasant or noble involves pleasure.[40]

It is absurd, then, to blame things outside us instead of our own readiness to yield to their allurements, and, while we claim our noble acts as our own, to set down our disgraceful actions to "pleasant things outside us."

Compulsory, then, it appears, is that of which the cause is external, the person compelled contributing nothing thereto.

What is done through ignorance is always "not-voluntary," but is "involuntary"[41] when the agent is pained afterwards and sorry when he finds what he has done.[42] For when a man, who has done something through ignorance, is not vexed at what he has done, you cannot indeed say that he did it voluntarily, as he did not know what he was doing, but neither can you say that he did it involuntarily or unwillingly, since he is not sorry.

A man who has acted through ignorance, then, if he is sorry afterwards, is held to have done the deed involuntarily or unwillingly; if he is not sorry afterwards we may say (to mark the distinction) he did the deed "not-voluntarily"; for, as the case is different, it is better to have a distinct name.

Acting through ignorance, however, seems to be different from acting in ignorance. For instance, when a man is drunk or in a rage he is not thought to act through ignorance, but through intoxication or rage, and yet not knowingly, but in ignorance.

Every vicious man, indeed, is ignorant of what ought to be done and what ought not to be done, and it is this kind of error that makes men unjust and bad generally. But the term

---

[39] Therefore, strictly speaking, a "compulsory act" is a contradiction in terms; the real question is, "What is an act?"

[40] Therefore, since these are the motives of every act, all voluntary action involves pleasure. If we add "when successful," this quite agrees with Aristotle's theory of pleasure in Book, VII, and X.

[41] i. e., not merely "not-willed," but done "unwillingly," or against the agent's will. Unfortunately our usage recognizes no such distinction between "not-voluntary" and "involuntary."

[42] εν μεταμελεια, lit. "when the act involves change of mind." This, under the circumstances, can only mean that the agent who willed the act, not seeing the true nature of it at the time, is sorry afterwards, when he comes to see what he has done.

"involuntary" is not properly applied to cases in which a man is ignorant of what is fitting. The ignorance that makes an act involuntary is not this ignorance of the principles which should determine preference (this constitutes vice), — not, I say, this ignorance of the universal (for we blame a man for this), but ignorance of the particular occasion and circumstances of the act. These are the grounds of pity and pardon; for he who is ignorant of any of these particulars acts involuntarily.

It may be as well, then, to specify what these particulars are, and how many. They are — first, the doer; secondly, the deed; and, thirdly, the circumstance or occasion of it; sometimes also that wherewith (e.g., the instrument with which) it is done, and that for the sake of which it is done (e.g., for protection), and the way in which it is done (e.g., gently or violently.)

Now, a man cannot (unless he be mad) be ignorant of all these particulars; for instance, he evidently cannot be ignorant of the doer: for how can he not know himself?

But a man may be ignorant of what he is doing; e.g., a man who has said something will sometimes plead that the words escaped him unawares, or that he did not know that the subject was forbidden (as Æschylus pleaded in the case of the Mysteries); or a man might plead that when he discharged the weapon he only intended to show the working of it, as the prisoner did in the catapult case. Again, a man might mistake his son for an enemy, as Merope did, or a sharp spear for one with a button, or a heavy stone for a pumice-stone. Again, one might kill a man with a blow intended to save him, or strike a serious blow when one only wished to show how a blow should be delivered (as boxers do when they spar with open hands).

Ignorance, then, being possible with regard to all these circumstances, he who is ignorant of any of them is held to have acted involuntarily, and especially when he is ignorant of the most important particulars, which are generally taken to be the occasion and the result.

Besides this, however, the agent must be grieved and sorry for what he has done, if the act thus ignorantly committed is to be called involuntary [not merely not-voluntary].

But now, having found that an act is involuntary when done under compulsion or through ignorance, we may conclude that a voluntary act is one which is originated by the doer with knowledge of the particular circumstances of the act.

For I venture to think that it is incorrect to say that acts done through anger or desire are involuntary.

In the first place, if this be so we can no longer allow that any of the other animals act voluntarily, nor even children.

Again, does the saying mean that none of the acts which we do through desire or anger are voluntary, or that the noble ones are voluntary and the disgraceful ones involuntary? Interpreted in the latter sense, it is surely ridiculous, as one man is the author of both.

If we take the former interpretation, it is absurd, I think, to say that we ought to desire a thing, and also to say that its pursuit is involuntary; but in fact, there are things at which we ought to be angry, and things which we ought to desire, e.g., health and learning.

Again, it seems that what is done unwillingly is painful, while what is done through desire is pleasant.

Again, what difference is there, in respect of involuntariness, between wrong deeds done upon calculation and wrong deeds done in anger? Both alike are to be avoided, and our unreasoning passions or feelings seem to be just as much our own [as our reasonings or calculations].

But the fact is that all human actions proceed either from anger or from desire: to make all such actions involuntary, therefore, would be too absurd.

2. Now that we have distinguished voluntary from involuntary facts, our next task is to discuss choice, or purpose. For it seems to be most intimately connected with virtue, and to be a surer test of character than action itself.

It seems that choosing is willing, but that the two terms are not identical, willing being the wider. For children and other animals have will but not choice or purpose; and acts done upon the spur of the moment are said to be voluntary, but not to be done with deliberate purpose.

Those who say that choice is appetite, or anger, or wish, or an opinion of some sort, do not seem to give a correct account of it.

In the first place, choice is not shared by irrational creatures, but appetite and anger are.

Again, the incontinent man acts from appetite and not from choice or purpose, the continent man from purpose and not from appetite.

Again, appetite may be contrary to purpose, but one appetite cannot be contrary to another appetite.

Again, the object of appetite (or aversion) is the pleasant or the painful, but the object of purpose (as such) is neither painful nor pleasant.

Still less can purpose be anger (ϑψμο); for acts done in anger seem to be least of all done of purpose or deliberate choice.

Nor yet is it wish, through it seem very like; for we cannot purposely or deliberately choose the impossible, and a man who should say that he did would be thought a fool; but we may wish for the impossible, e.g., to escape death.

Again, while we may wish what never could be effected by our own agency (e.g., the success of a particular actor or athlete), we never purpose or deliberately choose such things, but only those that we think may be effected by our own agency.

Again, we are more properly said to wish the end, to choose the means; e.g., we wish to be healthy, but we choose what will make us healthy: we wish to be happy, and confess the wish, but it would not be correct to say we purpose or deliberately choose to be happy; for we may say roundly that purpose or choice deals with what is in our power.

Nor can it be opinion; for, in the first place, anything may be matter of opinion — what is unalterable and impossible no less than what is in our power; and, in the second place, we distinguish opinion according as it is true or false, not according as it is good or bad, as we do with purpose or choice.

We may say, then, that purpose is not the same as opinion in general; nor, indeed, does any one maintain this.

But, further, it is not identical with a particular kind of opinion. For our choice of good or evil makes us morally good or bad, holding certain opinions does not.

Again, we choose to take this or to avoid it, and so on; we opine what its nature is, or what it is good for, or in what way; but we cannot opine to take or to avoid.

Again, we commend a purpose for its rightness rather than its correctness, an opinion for its truth.

Again, we choose a thing when we know well that it is good; we may have an opinion about a thing of which we know nothing.

Again, it seems that those who are best at choosing are not always the best at forming opinions, but that some who have an excellent judgment fail, through depravity, to choose what they ought.

It may be said that choice or purpose must be preceded or accompanied by an opinion or judgment; but this makes no difference: our question is not that, but whether they are identical.

What, then, is choice or purpose, since it is none of these?

It seems, as we add, that what is chosen or purposed is willed, but that what is willed is not always chosen or purposed.

The required differentia, I think, is "after previous deliberation." For choice or purpose implies calculation and reasoning. The name itself, too, seems to indicate this, implying that something is chosen before or in preference to other things.

3. Now, as to deliberation, do we deliberate about everything, and may anything whatever be matter for deliberation, or are there some things about which deliberation is impossible?

By "matter for deliberation" we should understand, I think, not what a fool or a maniac, but what a rational being would deliberate about.

Now, no one deliberates about eternal or unalterable things, e.g., the system of the heavenly bodies, or the incommensurability of the side and the diagonal of a square.

Again, no one deliberates about things which change, but always change in the same way (whether the cause of change be necessity, or nature, or any other agency), e.g., the solstices and the sunrise; nor about things that are quite irregular, like drought and wet; nor about matters of chance, like the finding of a treasure.

Again, even human affairs are not always matter of deliberation; e.g., what would be the best constitution for Scythia is a question that no Spartan would deliberate about.

The reason why we do not deliberate about these things is that none of them are things that we can ourselves effect.

But the things that we do deliberate about are matters of conduct that are within our control. And these are the only things that remain; for besides nature and necessity and chance, the only remaining cause of change is reason and human agency in general. Though we must add that men severally deliberate about what they can themselves do.

A further limitation is that where there is exact and absolute knowledge, there is no room for deliberation; e.g., writing: for there is no doubt how the letters should be formed.

We deliberate, then, about things that are brought about by our own agency, but not always in the same way; e.g., about medicine and money-making, and about navigation more than about gymnastic, inasmuch as it is not yet reduced to so perfect a system, and so on; but more about matters of art than matters of science, as there is more doubt about them.

Matters of deliberation, then, are matters in which there are rules that generally hold good, but in which the result cannot be predicted, i.e., in which there is an element of uncertainty. In important matters we call in advisers, distrusting our own powers of judgment.

It is not about ends, but about means that we deliberate. A physician does not deliberate whether he shall heal, nor an orator whether he shall persuade, nor a statesman whether he shall make a good system of laws, nor a man in any other profession about his end; but, having some particular end in view, we consider how and by what means this end can be attained; and if it appears that it can be attained by various means, we farther consider which is the easiest and best; but if it can only be attained by one means, we consider how it is to be attained by this means, and how this means itself is to be secured, and so on, until we come to the first link in the chain of causes, which is last in the order of discovery.

For in deliberation we seem to inquire and to analyze in the way described, just as we analyze a geometrical figure in order to learn how to construct it (and though inquiry is not always deliberation — mathematical inquiry, for instance, is not — deliberation is always inquiry); that which is last in the analysis coming first in the order of construction.

If we come upon something impossible, we give up the plan; e.g., if it needs money, and money cannot be gotten: but if it appear possible, we set to work. By possible I mean something that can be done by *us*; and what can be done by our friends can in a manner be done by us; for it is we who set our friends to work.

Sometimes we have to find out instruments, sometimes how to use them; and so on with the rest: sometimes we have to find out what agency will produce the desired effect, sometimes how or through whom this agency is to be set at work.

Now, it appears that a man, as we have already said, originates his acts; that he deliberates about that which he can do himself, and that what he does is done for the sake of something else. From this it follows that he does not deliberate about the end, but about the means to the end.

Again, he does not deliberate about particular facts, e.g., whether this be a loaf, or whether it be properly baked: these are matters of immediate perception. And if he goes on deliberating forever he will never come to a conclusion.

The object of deliberation and the object of choice or purpose are the same, except that the latter is already fixed and determined; when we say, "this is chosen" or "purposed," we mean that it has been selected after deliberation. For we always stop in our inquiry how to do a thing when we have traced back the chain of causes to ourselves, and to the commanding part of ourselves; for this is the part that chooses.

This may be illustrated by the ancient constitutions which Homer describes; for there the kings announce to the people what they have chosen.

Since, then, a thing is said to be chosen or purposed when, being in our power, it is desired after deliberation, choice or purpose may be deferred as deliberate desire for something in our power; for we first deliberate, and then, having made our decision thereupon, we desire in accordance with deliberation.

Let this stand, then, for an account in outline of choice or purpose, and of what it deals with, viz. means to ends.

4. Wish, we have already said, is for the end; but whereas some hold that the object of wish is the good, others hold that it is what seems good.

Those who maintain that the object of wish[43] is the good have to admit that what those wish for who choose wrongly is not object of wish (for if so it would be good; but it may so happen that it was bad); on the other hand, those who maintain that the object of wish is what seems good have to admit that there is nothing, which is naturally object of wish, but that each wishes for what seems good to him — different and even contrary things seeming good to different people.

As neither of these alternatives quite satisfies us, perhaps we had better say that the good is the real object of wish (without any qualifying epithet), but that what seems good is object of wish to each man. The good man, then, wishes for the real object of wish; but what the bad man wishes for may be anything whatever; just as, with regard to the body, those who are in good condition find those things healthy that are really healthy, while those who are diseased find other things healthy (and it is just the same with things bitter, sweet, hot, heavy, etc.): for the good or ideal man judges each case correctly, and in each case what is true seems true to him.

For, corresponding to each of our trained faculties, there is a special form of the noble and the pleasant, and perhaps there is nothing so distinctive of this good or ideal man than the power he has of discerning these special forms in each case, being himself, as it were, their standard and measure.

What misleads people seems to be in most cases pleasure; it seems to be a good thing, even when it is not. So they choose what is pleasant as good, and shun pain as evil.

5. We have seen that, while we wish for the end, we deliberate upon and choose the means thereto.

Actions that are concerned with means, then, will be guided by choice, and so will be voluntary.

But the acts in which the virtues are manifested are concerned with means.[44]

Therefore virtue depends upon ourselves: and vice likewise. For where it lies with us to do, it lies with us not to do. Where we can say no, we can say yes. If then the doing a deed, which is noble, lies with us, the not doing it, which is disgraceful, lies with us; and if the not doing, which is noble, lies with us, the doing, which is disgraceful, also lies with us. But if the doing and

---

[43] Βοψλητον. This word hovers between two senses, (1) wished for, (2) to be wished for, just as eros hovers between (1) desired, (2) desirable. The difficulty, as here put, turns entirely upon the equivocation; but at bottom lies the fundamental question, whether there be a common human nature, such that we can say, "This kind of life in man's real life."

[44] Each virtuous act is desired and chosen as a means to realizing a particular virtue, and this again is desired as a part or constituent of, and so as a means to, that perfect self-realization which is happiness: cf. 3, 15.

likewise the not doing of noble or base deeds lies with us, and if this is, as we found, identical with being good or bad, then it follows that it lies with us to be worthy or worthless men.

And so the saying —

"None would be wicked, none would not be blessed,"

seems partly false and partly true: no one indeed is blessed against his will; but vice is voluntary.

If we deny this, we must dispute the statements made just now, and must contend that man is not the originator and the parent of his actions, as of his children.

But if those statements commend themselves to us, and if we are unable to trace our acts to any other sources than those that depend upon ourselves, then that whose source is within us must itself depend upon us and be voluntary.

This seems to be attested, moreover, by each one of us in private life, and also by the legislators; for they correct and punish those that do evil (except when it is done under compulsion, or through ignorance for which the agent is not responsible), and honour those that do noble deeds, evidently intending to encourage the one sort and discourage the other. But no one encourages us to do that which does not depend on ourselves, and which is not voluntary: it would be useless to be persuaded not to feel heat or pain or hunger and so on, as we should fool them all the same.

I say "ignorance for which the agent is not responsible," for the ignorance itself is punished by the law, if the agent appears to be responsible for his ignorance, e.g., for an offence committed in a fit of drunkenness the penalty is doubled: for the origin of the offence lies in the man himself; he might have avoided the intoxication, which was the cause of his ignorance. Again, ignorance of any of the ordinances of the law, which a man ought to know and easily can know, does not avert punishment. And so in other cases, where ignorance seems to be the result of negligence, the offender is punished, since it lay with him to remove this ignorance; for he might have taken the requisite trouble.

It may be objected that it was the man's character not to take the trouble.

We reply that men are themselves responsible for acquiring such a character by a dissolute life, and for being unjust or profligate in consequence of repeated acts of wrong, or of spending their time in drinking and so on. For it is repeated acts of a particular kind that give a man a particular character.

This is shown by the way in which men train it themselves for any kind of contest or performance: they practice continually.

Not to know, then, that repeated acts of this or that kind produce a corresponding character or habit, shows an utter want of sense.

Moreover, it is absurd to say that he who acts unjustly does not wish to be unjust, or that he who behaves profligately does not wish to be profligate.

If then a man knowingly does acts which must make him unjust, he will be voluntarily unjust; but it does not follow that, if he wishes it, he can cease to be unjust and be just, any more than he who is sick can, if he wishes it, be whole. And it may be that he is voluntarily sick, through living incontinently and disobeying the doctor. At one time, then, he had the option not to be sick, but he no longer has it now that he has thrown away his health. When you have discharged a stone it is no longer in your power to call it back; but nevertheless the throwing and casting away of that stone rests with you; for the beginning of its flight depended upon you.[45]

Just so the unjust or the profligate man at the beginning was free not to acquire this character, and therefore he is voluntarily unjust or profligate; but now that he has acquired it, he is no longer free to put it off.

---

[45] My act is mine, and does not cease to be mine because I would undo it if I could; and so, further, since we made the habits whose bonds we cannot now unloose, we are responsible, not merely for the acts which made them, but also for the acts which they now produce "in spite of us"; what constrains us is ourselves.

But it is not only our mental or moral vices that are voluntary; bodily vices also are sometimes voluntary, and then are censured. We do not censure natural ugliness, but we do censure that which is due to negligence and want of exercise. And so with weakness and infirmity: we should never reproach a man who was born blind, or had lost his sight in an illness or by a blow — we should rather pity him; but we should all censure a man who had blinded himself by excessive drinking or any other kind of profligacy.

We see, then, that of the vices of the body it is those that depend on ourselves that are censured, while those that do not depend on ourselves are not censured. And if this be so, then in other fields also those vices that are blamed must depend upon ourselves.

Some people may perhaps object to this.

"All men," they may say, "desire that which appears good to them, but cannot control this appearance; a man's character, whatever it be, decides what shall appear to him to be the end."

If, I answer, each man be in some way responsible for his habits or character, then in some way he must be responsible for this appearance also.

But if this be not the case, then a man is not responsible for, or is not the cause of, his own evil doing, but it is through ignorance of the end that he does evil, fancying that thereby he will secure the greatest good: and the striving towards the true end does not depend on our own choice, but a man must be born with a gift of sight, so to speak, if he is to discriminate rightly and to choose what is really good: and he is truly well-born who is by nature richly endowed with this gift; for, as it is the greatest and the fairest gift, which we cannot acquire or learn from another, but must keep all our lives just as nature gave it to us, to be well and nobly born in this respect is to be well-born in the truest and completest sense.

Now, even supposing this to be true, how will virtue be any more voluntary than vice?

For whether it be nature or anything else that determines what shall appear to be the end, it is determined in the same way for both alike, for the good man as for the bad, and both alike refer all their acts of whatever kind to it.

And so whether we hold that it is not merely nature that decides what appears to each to be the end (whatever that be), but that the man himself contributes something; or whether we hold that the end is fixed by nature, but that virtue is voluntary, inasmuch as the good man voluntarily takes the steps to that end — in either case vice will be just as voluntary as virtue; for self is active in the bad man just as much as in the good man, in choosing the particular acts at least, if not in determining the end.

If then, as is generally allowed, the virtues are voluntary (for we do, in fact, in some way help to make our character, and, by being of a certain character, give a certain complexion to our idea of the end), the vices also must be voluntary; for all this applies equally to them.

We have thus described in outline the nature of the virtues in general, viz., that they are forms of moderation or modes of observing the mean, and that they are habits or trained faculties; and we have shown what produces them, and how they themselves issue in the performance of the same acts which produce them, and that they depend on ourselves and are voluntary, and that they follow the guidance of right reason.

But our particular acts are not voluntary in the same sense as our habits.

We are masters of our acts from beginning to end, when we know the particular circumstances; but we are masters of the beginnings only of our habits or characters, while their growth by gradual steps is imperceptible, like the growth of disease. Inasmuch, however, as it lay with us to employ or not to employ our faculties in this way, the resulting characters are on that account voluntary.

6. Now let us take up each of the virtues again in turn, and say what it is, and what its subject is, and how it deals with it; and in doing this, we shall at the same time see how many they are.

First of all, let us take courage.

We have already said that it is moderation or observance of the mean with respect to feelings of fear and confidence.

Now, fear evidently is excited by fearful things, and these are, roughly speaking, evil things; and so fear is sometimes defined as "expectation of evil."

Fear, then, is excited by evil of any kind, e.g., by disgrace, poverty, disease, friendlessness, death; but it does not appear that every kind gives scope for courage. There are things which we actually ought to fear, which it is noble to fear and base not to fear, e.g., disgrace. He who fears disgrace is an honourable man, with a due sense of shame, while he who fears it not is shameless (though some people stretch the word courageous so far as to apply it to him; for he has a certain resemblance to the courageous man, courage also being a kind of fearlessness). Poverty, perhaps, we ought not to fear, nor disease, nor generally those things that are not the result of vice, and do not depend upon ourselves. But still to be fearless in regard to these things is not strictly courage; though here also the term is sometimes applied in virtue of a certain resemblance. There are people, for instance, who, though cowardly in the presence of the dangers of war, are yet liberal and bold in the spending of money.

On the other hand, a man is not to be called cowardly for fearing outrage to his children or his wife, or for dreading envy and things of that kind, nor courageous for being unmoved by the prospect of a whipping.

In what kind of terrors, then, does the courageous man display his quality? Surely in the greatest; for no one is more able to endure what is terrible. But of all things the most terrible is death; for death is our limit, and when a man is once dead it seems that there is no longer either good or evil for him.

It would seem, however, that even death does not on all occasions give scope for courage, e.g., death by water or by disease.

On what occasions then? Surely on the noblest occasions: and those are the occasions which occur in war; for they involve the greatest and the noblest danger.

This is confirmed by the honours which courage receives in free states and at the hands of princes.

The term courageous, then, in the strict sense, will be applied to him who fearlessly faces an honourable death; and such emergencies mostly occur in war.

Of course the courageous man is fearless in the presence of illness also, and at sea, but in a different way from the sailors; for the sailors, because of their experience, are full of hope when the landsmen are already despairing of their lives and filled with aversion at the thought of such a death.

Moreover, the circumstances which especially call out courage are those in which prowess may be displayed, or in which death is noble; but in these forms of death there is neither nobility nor room for prowess.

7. Fear is not excited in all men by the same things, but yet we commonly speak of fearful things that surpass man's power to face. Such things, then, inspire fear in every rational man. But the fearful things that a man may face differ in importance and in being more or less fearful (and so with the things that inspire confidence). Now, the courageous man always keeps his presence of mind (so far as a man can). So though he will fear these fearful things, he will endure them as he ought and as reason bids him, for the sake of that which is noble; for this is the end or aim of virtue.

But it is possible to fear these things too much or too little, and again to take as fearful what is not really so. And thus men err sometimes by fearing the wrong things, sometimes by fearing in the wrong manner or at the wrong time, and so on.

And all this applies equally to things that inspire confidence.

He, then, that endures and fears what he ought from the right motive, and in the right manner, and at the right time, and similarly feels confidence, is courageous.

For the courageous man regulates both his feeling and his action according to the merits of each case and as reason bids him.

But the end or motive of every manifestation of a habit or exercise of a trained faculty is the end or motive of the habit or trained faculty itself.

Now, to the courageous man courage is essentially a fair or noble thing.

Therefore the end or motive of his courage is also noble; for everything takes its character from its end.

It is from a noble motive, therefore, that the courageous man endures and acts courageously in each particular case.[46]

Of the characters that run to excess, he that exceeds in fearlessness has no name (and this is often the case, as we have said before); but a man would be either a maniac or quite insensible to pain who should fear nothing, not even earthquakes and breakers, as they say is the case with the Celts.

He that is over-confident in the presence of fearful things is called foolhardy. But the foolhardy man is generally thought to be really a braggart, and to pretend a courage which he has not. He wishes therefore to seem what the courageous man really is in the presence of danger; so he imitates him where he can. And so your foolhardy man is generally a coward at bottom: he blusters so long as he can, but does not stand his ground when there is something to fear.

MARTIN LUTHER KING, JR.

The "Negro Revolution" of the 1950s and early 1960s, which in the public mind had its beginning in The 1954 Supreme Court decision desegregating public schools, generally followed two paths: lawsuits pressed in state and federal courts, and the direct action programs of such organizations as the National Association for the Advancement of Colored People (NAACP), Congress of Racial Equality (CORE), and the Southern Christian Leadership Conference (SCLC). The Reverend Martin Luther King, Jr., who urged the tactic of passive resistance — Negroes, he said, should meet "physical force with an even stronger force, namely, soul force" — assumed the presidency of the SCLC and leadership of the new nonviolent protest movement. King and his followers chose Birmingham, Alabama, as the target of their antisegregation drive of 1963. King explained the choice: "If Birmingham could be cracked, the direction of the entire nonviolent movement in the South could take a significant turn." While King's group was pressing a boycott that crippled business and forced Birmingham businessmen to negotiate a desegregation agreement, Attorney General Robert F. Kennedy acted to secure the immediate registration of more than 2,000 Birmingham Negroes previously denied voting rights. Federal courts upheld the right of Negroes to nonviolent protest in Birmingham and elsewhere, but not before King had been arrested and jailed. The following letter (reprinted here in part), written from his cell on April 16, 1963, contained King's answer to charges by a group of eight Birmingham clergymen that he was in their city as an "outside agitator." King was assassinated five years later.

LETTER FROM BIRMINGHAM JAIL (1963)[47]

My Dear Fellow Clergymen:

While confined here in the Birmingham City Jail, I came across your recent statement calling my present activities "unwise and untimely." Seldom do I pause to answer criticism of my work and ideas. If I sought to answer all the criticisms that cross my desk, my secretaries would have little time for anything other than such correspondence in the course of the day, and I would have

---

[46] The courageous man desires the courageous act for the same reason for which he desires the virtue itself, viz. simply because it is noble: see note on § 2.

[47] Source: *Christian Century*, June 12, 1963.

no time for constructive work. But since I feel that you are men of genuine good will and that your criticisms are sincerely set forth, I want to try to answer your statement in what I hope will be patient and reasonable terms.

I think I should indicate why I am here in Birmingham, since you have been influenced by the view which argues against "outsiders coming in." I have the honor of serving as president of the Southern Christian Leadership Conference, an organization operating in every southern state, with headquarters in Atlanta, Georgia. We have some eighty-five affiliated organizations across the South, and one of them is the Alabama Christian Movement for Human Rights. Frequently we share staff, educational and financial resources with our affiliates. Several months ago the affiliate here in Birmingham asked us to be on call to engage in a nonviolent direct-action program if such were deemed necessary. We readily consented, and when the hour came we lived up to our promise. So I, along with several members of my staff, am here because I was invited here. I am here because I have organizational ties here.

But more basically, I am in Birmingham because injustice is here. Just as the prophets of the eighth century B.C. left their villages and carried their "thus saith the Lord" far beyond the boundaries of their home towns, and just as the Apostle Paul left his village of Tarsus and carried the gospel of Jesus Christ to the far corners of the Greco-Roman world, so am I compelled to carry the gospel of freedom beyond my own home town. Like Paul, I must constantly respond to the Macedonian call for aid.

Moreover, I am cognizant of the interrelatedness of all communities and states. I cannot sit idly by in Atlanta and not be concerned about what happens in Birmingham. Injustice anywhere is a threat to justice everywhere. We are caught in an inescapable network of mutuality, tied in a single garment of destiny. Whatever affects one directly, affects all indirectly. Never again can we afford to live with the narrow, provincial "outside agitator" idea. Anyone who lives inside the United States can never be considered an outsider anywhere within its bounds.

You deplore the demonstrations taking place in Birmingham. But your statement, I am sorry to say, fails to express a similar concern for the conditions that brought about the demonstrations. I am sure that none of you would want to rest content with the superficial kind of social analysis that deals merely with effects and does not grapple with underlying causes. It is unfortunate that demonstrations are taking place in Birmingham, but it is even more unfortunate that the city's white power structure left the Negro community with no alternative.

In any nonviolent campaign there are four basic steps: collection of the facts to determine whether injustices exist; negotiation; self-purification; and direct action. We have gone through all these steps in Birmingham. There can be no gainsaying the fact that racial injustice engulfs this community. Birmingham is probably the most thoroughly segregated city in the United States. Its ugly record of brutality is widely known. Negroes have experienced grossly unjust treatment in the courts. There have been more unsolved bombings of Negro homes and churches in Birmingham than in any other city in the nation. These are the hard, brutal facts of the case. On the basis of these conditions, Negro leaders sought to negotiate with the city fathers. But the latter consistently refused to engage in good-faith negotiation.

Then, last September, came the opportunity to talk with leaders of Birmingham's economic community. In the course of the negotiations, certain promises were made by the merchants--for example, to remove the stores' humiliating racial signs. On the basis of these promises, the Reverend Fred Shuttlesworth and the leaders of the Alabama Christian Movement for Human Rights agreed to a moratorium on all demonstrations. As the weeks and months went by, we realized that we were the victims of a broken promise. A few signs, briefly removed, returned; the others remained.

As in so many past experiences, our hopes had been blasted, and the shadow of deep disappointment settled upon us. We had no alternative except to prepare for direct action, whereby we would present our very bodies as a means of laying our case before the conscience of the local and the national community. Mindful of the difficulties involved, we decided to undertake a process of self-purification. We began a series of workshops on nonviolence, and we repeatedly asked ourselves: "Are you able to accept blows without retaliating?" "Are you able to endure the ordeal of jail?" We decided to schedule our direct-action program for the Easter season, realizing that except for Christmas, this is the main shopping period of the year. Knowing that a strong economic-withdrawal program would be the by-product of direct action, we felt that this would be the best time to bring pressure to bear on the merchants for the needed change.

Then it occurred to us that Birmingham's mayoralty election was coming up in March, and we speedily decided to postpone action until after election day. When we discovered that the Commissioner of Public Safety, Eugene "Bull" Connor, had piled up enough votes to be in the run-off, we decided again to postpone action until the day after the run-off so that the demonstrations could not be used to cloud the issues. Like many others, we waited to see Mr. Connor defeated, and to this end we endured postponement after postponement. Having aided in this community need, we felt that our direct-action program could be delayed no longer.

You may well ask: "Why direct action? Why sit-ins, marches and so forth? Isn't negotiation a better path?" You are quite right in calling for negotiation. Indeed, this is the very purpose of direct action. Nonviolent direct action seeks to create such a crisis and foster such a tension that a community which has constantly refused to negotiate is forced to confront the issue. It seeks so to dramatize the issue that it can no longer be ignored. My citing the creation of tension as part of the work of the nonviolent-resister may sound rather shocking. But I must confess that I am not afraid of the word "tension." I have earnestly opposed violent tension, but there is a type of constructive, nonviolent tension which is necessary for growth. Just as Socrates felt that it was necessary to create a tension in the mind so that individuals could rise from the bondage of myths and half-truths to the unfettered realm of creative analysis and objective appraisal, so must we see the need for nonviolent gadflies to create the kind of tension in society that will help men rise from the dark depths of prejudice and racism to the majestic heights of understanding and brotherhood.

The purpose of our direct-action program is to create a situation so crisis-packed that it will inevitably open the door to negotiation. I therefore concur with you in your call for negotiation. Too long has our beloved Southland been bogged down in a tragic effort to live in monologue rather than dialogue.

One of the basic points in your statement is that the action that I and my associates have taken in Birmingham is untimely. Some have asked: "Why didn't you give the new city administration time to act?" The only answer that I can give to this query is that the new Birmingham administration must be prodded about as much as the outgoing one, before it will act. We are sadly mistaken if we feel that the election of Albert Boutwell as mayor will bring the millennium to Birmingham. While Mr. Boutwell is a much more gentle person than Mr. Connor, they are both segregationists, dedicated to maintenance of the status quo. I have hope that Mr. Boutwell will be reasonable enough to see the futility of massive resistance to desegregation. But he will not see this without pressure from devotees of civil rights. My friends, I must say to you that we have not made a single gain in civil rights without determined legal and nonviolent pressure. Lamentably, it is an historical fact that privileged groups seldom give up their privileges voluntarily. Individuals may see the moral light and voluntarily give up their unjust posture; but, as Reinhold Niebuhr has reminded us, groups tend to be more immoral than individuals.

We know through painful experience that freedom is never voluntarily given by the oppressor; it must be demanded by the oppressed. Frankly, I have yet to engage in a direct-action campaign that was "well timed" in the view of those who have not suffered unduly from the disease of segregation. For years now I have heard the word "Wait!" It rings in the ear of every Negro with piercing familiarity. This "Wait!" has almost always meant "Never." We must come to see, with one of our distinguished jurists, that "justice too long delayed is justice denied."

We have waited for more than 340 years for our constitutional and God-given rights. The nations of Asia and Africa are moving with jetlike speed toward gaining political independence, but we still creep at horse-and-buggy pace toward gaining a cup of coffee at a lunch counter. Perhaps it is easy for those who have never felt the stinging darts of segregation to say, "Wait." But when you have seen vicious mobs lynch your mothers and fathers at will and drown your sisters and brothers at whim; when you have seen hate-filled policemen curse, kick and even kill your black brothers and sisters; when you see the vast majority of your twenty million Negro brothers smothering in an airtight cage of poverty in the midst of an affluent society; when you suddenly find your tongue twisted and your speech stammering as you seek to explain to your six-year-old daughter why she can't go to the public amusement park that has just been advertised on television, and see tears welling up in her eyes when she is told that Funtown is closed to colored children, and see ominous clouds of inferiority beginning to form in her little mental sky, and see her beginning to distort her personality by developing an unconscious bitterness toward white people; when you have to concoct an answer for a five-year-old son who is asking: "Daddy, why do white people treat colored people so mean?"; when you take a cross-country drive and find it necessary to sleep night after night in the uncomfortable corners of your automobile because no motel will accept you; when you are humiliated day in and day out by nagging signs reading "white" and "colored"; when your first name becomes "nigger," your middle name becomes "boy" (however old you are) and your last name becomes "John," and your wife and mother are never given the respected title "Mrs."; when you are harried by day and haunted by night by the fact that you are a Negro, living constantly at tiptoe stance, never quite knowing what to expect next, and are plagued with inner fears and outer resentments; when you are forever fighting a degenerating sense of "nobodiness"—then you will understand why we find it difficult to wait. There comes a time when the cup of endurance runs over, and men are no longer willing to be plunged into the abyss of despair. I hope, sirs, you can understand our legitimate and unavoidable impatience.

You express a great deal of anxiety over our willingness to break laws. This is certainly a legitimate concern. Since we so diligently urge people to obey the Supreme Court's decision of 1954 outlawing segregation in the public schools, at first glance it may seem rather paradoxical for us consciously to break laws. One may well ask: "How can you advocate breaking some laws and obeying others?" The answer lies in the fact that there are two types of laws: just and unjust. I would be the first to advocate obeying just laws. One has not only a legal but a moral responsibility to obey just laws. Conversely, one has a moral responsibility to disobey unjust laws. I would agree with St. Augustine that "an unjust law is no law at all."

Now, what is the difference between the two? How does one determine whether a law is just or unjust? A just law is a man-made code that squares with the moral law or the law of God. An unjust law is a code that is out of harmony with the moral law. To put it in the terms of St. Thomas Aquinas: An unjust law is a human law that is not rooted in eternal law and natural law. Any law that uplifts human personality is just. Any law that degrades human personality is unjust. All segregation statutes are unjust because segregation distorts the soul and damages the personality. It gives the segregator a false sense of superiority and the segregated a false sense of inferiority. Segregation, to use the terminology of the Jewish philosopher Martin Buber, substitutes an "I—it" relationship for an "I—thou" relationship and ends up relegating persons to the status of things. Hence segregation is not only politically, economically and sociologically unsound, it is morally wrong and sinful. Paul Tillich has said that sin is separation. Is not segregation an existential expression of man's tragic separation, his awful estrangement, his terrible sinfulness? Thus it is that I can urge men to obey the 1954 decision of the Supreme Court, for it is morally right; and I can urge them to disobey segregation ordinances, for they are morally wrong.

Let us consider a more concrete example of just and unjust laws. An unjust law is a code that a numerical or power majority group compels a minority group to obey but does not make binding on itself. This is *difference* made legal. By the same token, a just law is a code that a majority compels a minority to follow and that it is willing to follow itself. This is *sameness* made legal.

Let me give another explanation. A law is unjust if it is inflicted on a minority that, as a result of being denied the right to vote, had no part in enacting or devising the law. Who can say that the legislature of Alabama which set up that state's segregation laws was democratically elected? Throughout Alabama all sorts of devious methods are used to prevent Negroes from becoming registered voters, and there are some counties in which, even though Negroes constitute a majority of the population, not a single Negro is registered. Can any law enacted under such circumstances be considered democratically structured?

Sometimes a law is just on its face and unjust in its application. For instance, I have been arrested on a charge of parading without a permit. Now, there is nothing wrong in having an ordinance which requires a permit for a parade. But such an ordinance becomes unjust when it is used to maintain segregation and to deny citizens the First-Amendment privilege of peaceful assembly and protest.

I hope you are able to see the distinction I am trying to point out. In no sense do I advocate evading or defying the law, as would the rabid segregationist. That would lead to anarchy. One who breaks an unjust law must do so openly, lovingly, and with a willingness to accept the penalty. I submit that an individual who breaks a law that conscience tells him is unjust, and who willingly accepts the penalty of imprisonment in order to arouse the conscience of the community over its injustice, is in reality expressing the highest respect for law.

Of course, there is nothing new about this kind of civil disobedience. It was evidenced sublimely in the refusal of Shadrach, Meshach and Abednego to obey the laws of Nebuchadnezzar, on the ground that a higher moral law was at stake. It was practiced superbly by the early Christians, who were willing to face hungry lions and the excruciating pain of chopping blocks rather than submit to certain unjust laws of the Roman Empire. To a degree, academic freedom is a reality today because Socrates practiced civil disobedience. In our own nation, the Boston Tea Party represented a massive act of civil disobedience.

We should never forget that everything Adolf Hitler did in Germany was "legal" and everything the Hungarian freedom fighters did in Hungary was "illegal." It was "illegal" to aid and comfort a Jew in Hitler's Germany. Even so, I am sure that, had I lived in Germany at the time, I would have aided and comforted my Jewish brothers. If today I lived in a Communist country where certain principles dear to the Christian faith are suppressed, I would openly advocate disobeying that country's antireligious laws.

I must make two honest confessions to you, my Christian and Jewish brothers. First, I must confess that over the past few years I have been gravely disappointed with the white moderate. I have almost reached the regrettable conclusion that the Negro's great stumbling block in his stride toward freedom is not the White Citizen's Councilor or the Ku Klux Klanner, but the white moderate, who is more devoted to "order" than to justice; who prefers a negative peace which is the absence of tension to a positive peace which is the presence of justice; who constantly says: "I agree with you in the goal you seek, but I cannot agree with your methods of direct action"; who paternalistically believes he can set the timetable for another man's freedom; who lives by a mythical concept of time and who constantly advises the Negro to wait for a "more convenient season." Shallow understanding from people of good will is more frustrating than absolute misunderstanding from people of ill will. Lukewarm acceptance is much more bewildering than outright rejection.

I had hoped that the white moderate would understand that law and order exist for the purpose of establishing justice and that when they fail in this purpose they become the dangerously structured dams that block the flow of social progress. I had hoped that the white moderate would understand that the present tension in the south is a necessary phase of the transition from an obnoxious negative peace, in which the Negro passively accepted his unjust plight, to a substantive and positive peace, in which all men will respect the dignity and worth of human personality. Actually, we who engage in nonviolent direct action are not the creators of tension. We merely bring to the surface the hidden tension that is already alive. We bring it out in the open, where it can be seen and dealt with. Like a boil that can never be cured so long as it is covered up but must be opened with all its ugliness to the natural medicines of air and light, injustice must be exposed, with all the tension its exposure creates, to the light of human conscience and the air of national opinion before it can be cured.

In your statement you assert that our actions, even though peaceful, must be condemned because they precipitate violence. But is this a logical assertion? Isn't this like condemning a robbed man because his possession of money precipitated the evil act of robbery? Isn't this like condemning Socrates because his unswerving commitment to truth and his philosophical inquiries precipitated the act by the misguided populace in which they made him drink hemlock? Isn't this like condemning Jesus because his unique God-consciousness and never-ceasing devotion to God's will precipitated the evil act of crucifixion? We must come to see that, as the federal courts have consistently affirmed, it is wrong to urge an individual to cease his efforts to gain his basic constitutional rights because the quest may precipitate violence. Society must protect the robbed and punish the robber.

I had also hoped that the white moderate would reject the myth concerning time in relation to the struggle for freedom. I have just received a letter from a white brother in Texas. He writes: "All Christians know that the colored people will receive equal rights eventually, but it is possible that you are in too great a religious hurry. It has taken Christianity almost two thousand years to accomplish what it has. The teachings of Christ take time to come to earth." Such an attitude stems from a tragic misconception of time, from the strangely irrational notion that there is something in the very flow of time that will inevitably cure all ills. Actually, time itself is neutral; it can be used either destructively or constructively. More and more I feel that the people of ill will have used time much more effectively than have the people of good will. We will have to repent in this generation not merely for the hateful words and actions of the bad people but for the appalling silence of the good people. Human progress never rolls in on wheels of inevitability; it comes through the tireless efforts of men willing to be co-workers with God, and without this hard work, time itself becomes an ally of the forces of social stagnation. We must use time creatively, in the knowledge that the time is always ripe to do right. Now is the time to make real the promise of democracy and transform our pending national elegy into a creative psalm of brotherhood. Now is the time to lift our national policy from the quicksand of racial injustice to the solid rock of human dignity.

You speak of our activity in Birmingham as extreme. At first I was rather disappointed that fellow clergymen would see my nonviolent efforts as those of an extremist. I began thinking about the fact that I stand in the middle of two opposing forces in the Negro community. One is a force of complacency, made up in part of Negroes who, as a result of long years of oppression, are so drained of self-respect and a sense of "somebodiness" that they have adjusted to segregation; and in part of a few middle-class Negroes who, because of a degree of academic and economic security and because in some ways they profit by segregation, have become insensitive to the problems of the masses. The other force is one of bitterness and hatred, and it comes perilously close to advocating violence. It is expressed in the various black nationalist groups that are springing up across the nation, the largest and best-known being Elijah Muhammad's Muslim movement. Nourished by the Negro's frustration over the continued existence of racial discrimination, this movement is made up of people who have lost faith in America, who have absolutely repudiated Christianity, and who have concluded that the white man is an incorrigible "devil."

I have tried to stand between these two forces, saying that we need emulate neither the "do-nothingism" of the complacent nor the hatred and despair of the black nationalist. For there is the more excellent way of love and nonviolent protest. I am grateful to God that, through the influence of the Negro church, the way of nonviolence became an integral part of our struggle.

If this philosophy had not emerged, by now many streets of the South would, I am convinced, be flowing with blood. And I am further convinced that if our white brothers dismiss as "rabble-rousers" and "outside agitators" those of us who employ nonviolent direct action, and if they refuse to support our nonviolent efforts, millions of Negroes will, out of frustration and despair, seek solace and security in black-nationalist ideologies—a development that would inevitably lead to a frightening racial nightmare.

Oppressed people cannot remain oppressed forever. The yearning for freedom eventually manifests itself, and that is what has happened to the American Negro. Something within has reminded him of his birthright of freedom, and something without has reminded him that it can be gained. Consciously or unconsciously, he has been caught up by the *Zeitgeist*, and with his black brother of Africa and his brown and yellow brothers of Asia, South America and the Caribbean, the United States Negro is moving with a sense of great urgency toward the promised land of racial justice. If one recognized this vital urge that has engulfed the Negro community, one should readily understand why public demonstrations are taking place. The Negro has many pent-up resentments and latent frustrations, and he must release them. So let him march; let him make prayer pilgrimages to the city hall; let him go on freedom rides—and try to understand why he must do so. If his repressed emotions are not released in nonviolent ways, they will seek expression through violence; this is not a threat but a fact of history. So I have not said to my people: "Get rid of your discontent." Rather, I have tried to say that this normal and healthy discontent can be channeled into the creative outlet of nonviolent direct action. And now this approach is being termed extremist.

But though I was initially disappointed at being categorized as an extremist, as I continued to think about the matter I gradually gained a measure of satisfaction from the label. Was not Jesus an extremist for love? — "Love your enemies, bless them that curse you, do good to them that hate you, and pray for them which despitefully use you, and persecute you." Was not Amos an extremist for justice? — "Let justice roll down like waters and righteousness like an ever-flowing stream." Was not Paul an extremist for the Christian gospel? — "I bear in my body the marks of the Lord Jesus." Was not Martin Luther an extremist?" — Here I stand; I cannot do otherwise, so help me God." And John Bunyan — "I will stay in jail to the end of my days before I make a butchery of my conscience." And Abraham Lincoln: — "This nation cannot survive half slave and half free." And Thomas Jefferson — "We hold these truths to be self-evident, that all men are created equal . . . ." So the question is not whether we will be extremists, but what kind of extremists we will be. Will we be extremists for hate or love? Will we be extremists for the preservation of injustice or for the extension of justice? In that dramatic scene on Calvary's hill three men were crucified. We must never forget that all three were crucified for the same crime—the crime of extremism. Two were extremists for immorality, and thus fell below their environment. The other, Jesus Christ, was an extremist for love, truth and goodness, and thereby rose above his environment. Perhaps the South, the nation and the world are in dire need of creative extremists.

I had hoped that the white moderate would see this need. Perhaps I was too optimistic; perhaps I expected too much. I suppose I should have realized that few members of the oppressor race can understand the deep groans and passionate yearnings of the oppressed race, and still fewer have the vision to see that injustice must be rooted out by strong, persistent and determined action. I am thankful, however, that some of our white brothers in the South have grasped the meaning of this social revolution and committed themselves to it. They are still all too few in quantity, but they are big in quality. Some—such as Ralph McGill, Lillian Smith, Harry Golden, James McBride Dabbs, Ann Braden and Sarah Patton Boyle—have written about our struggle in eloquent and prophetic terms. Others have marched with us down nameless streets of the South. They have languished in filthy, roach-infested jails, suffering the abuse and brutality of policemen who view them as "dirty nigger-lovers." Unlike so many of their moderate brothers and sisters, they have recognized the urgency of the moment and sensed the need for powerful "action" antidotes to combat the disease of segregation.

Let me take note of my other major disappointment. I have been so greatly disappointed with the white church and its leadership. Of course, there are some notable exceptions. I am not unmindful of the fact that each of you has taken some significant stands on this issue. I commend you, Reverend Stallings, for your Christian stand on this past Sunday, in welcoming Negroes to your worship service on a nonsegregated basis. I commend the Catholic leaders of this state for integrating Spring Hill College several years ago.

But despite these notable exceptions, I must honestly reiterate that I have been disappointed with the church. I do not say this as one of those negative critics who can always find something wrong with the church. I say this as a minister of the gospel, who loves the church; who was nurtured in its bosom; who has been sustained by its spiritual blessings and who will remain true to it as long as the cord of life shall lengthen.

When I was suddenly catapulted into the leadership of the bus protest in Montgomery, Alabama, a few years ago, I felt we would be supported by the white church. I felt that the white ministers, priests and rabbis of the South would be among our strongest allies. Instead, some have been outright opponents, refusing to understand the freedom movement and misrepresenting its leaders; all too many others have been more cautious than courageous and have remained silent behind the anesthetizing security of stained-glass windows.

In spite of my shattered dreams, I came to Birmingham with the hope that the white religious leadership of this community would see the justice of our cause and, with deep moral concern, would serve as the channel through which our just grievances could reach the power structure. I had hoped that each of you would understand. But again I have been disappointed.

I have heard numerous southern religious leaders admonish their worshippers to comply with a desgregation decision because it is the law, but I have longed to hear white ministers declare: "Follow this decree because integration is morally right and because the Negro is your brother." In the midst of blatant injustices inflicted upon the Negro, I have watched white churchmen stand on the sideline and mouth pious irrelevancies and sanctimonious trivialities. In the midst of a mighty struggle to rid our nation of racial and economic injustice, I have heard many ministers say: "Those are social issues, with which the gospel has no real concern." And I have watched many churches commit themselves to a completely otherworldly religion which makes a strange, un-Biblical distinction between body and soul, between the sacred and the secular.

I have traveled the length and breadth of Alabama, Mississippi and all the other southern states. On sweltering summer days and crisp autumn mornings I have looked at the South's beautiful churches with their lofty spires pointing heavenward. I have beheld the impressive outlines of her massive religious-education buildings. Over and over I have found myself asking: "What kind of people worship here? Who is their God? Where were their voices when the lips of Governor Barnett dripped with words of interposition and nullification? Where were they when Governor Wallace gave a clarion call for defiance and hatred? Where were their voices of support when bruised and weary Negro men and women decided to rise from the dark dungeons of complacency to the bright hills of creative protest?"

Yes, these questions are still in my mind. In deep disappointment I have wept over the laxity of the church. But be assured that my tears have been tears of love. There can be no deep disappointment where there is not deep love. Yes, I love the church. How could I do otherwise? I am in the rather unique position of being the son, the grandson and the great-grandson of preachers. Yet, I see the church as the body of Christ. But, oh! How we have blemished and scarred that body through social neglect and through fear of being nonconformists.

There was a time when the church was very powerful--in the time when the early Christians rejoiced at being deemed worthy to suffer for what they believed. In those days the church was not merely a thermometer that recorded the ideas and principles of popular opinion; it was a thermostat that transformed the mores of society. Whenever the early Christians entered a town, the people in power became disturbed and immediately sought to convict the Christians for being "disturbers of the peace" and "outside agitators." But the Christians pressed on, in the conviction that they were "a colony of heaven," called to obey God rather than man. Small in number, they were big in commitment. They were too God-intoxicated to be "astronomically intimidated." By their effort and example they brought an end to such ancient evils as infanticide and gladiatorial contests.

Things are different now. So often the contemporary church is a weak, ineffectual voice with an uncertain sound. So often it is an archdefender of the status quo. Far from being disturbed by the presence of the church, the power structure of the average community is consoled by the church's silent—and often even vocal—sanction of things as they are.

But the judgment of God is upon the church as never before. If today's church does not recapture the sacrificial spirit of the early church, it will lose its authenticity, forfeit the loyalty of millions, and be dismissed as an irrelevant social club with no meaning for the twentieth century. Every day I meet young people whose disappointment with the church has turned into outright disgust.

Perhaps I have once again been too optimistic. Is organized religion too inextricably bound to the status quo to save our nation and the world? Perhaps I must turn my faith to the inner spiritual church, the church within the church, as the true *ekklesia* and the hope of the world. But again I am thankful to God that some noble souls from the ranks of organized religion have broken loose from the paralyzing chains of conformity and joined us as active partners in the struggle for freedom. They have left their secure congregations and walked the streets of Albany, Georgia, with us. They have gone down the highways of the South on tortuous rides for freedom. Yes, they have gone to jail with us. Some have been dismissed from their churches, have lost the support of their bishops and fellow ministers. But they have acted in the faith that right defeated is stronger than evil triumphant. Their witness has been the spiritual salt that has preserved the true meaning of the gospel in these troubled times. They have carved a tunnel of hope through the dark mountain of disappointment.

I hope the church as a whole will meet the challenge of this decisive hour. But even if the church does not come to the aid of justice, I have no despair about the future. I have no fear about the outcome of our struggle in Birmingham, even if our motives are at present misunderstood. We will reach the goal of freedom in Birmingham and all over the nation, because the goal of America is freedom. Abused and scorned though we may be, our destiny is tied up with America's destiny. Before the pilgrims landed at Plymouth, we were here. Before the pen of Jefferson etched the majestic words of the Declaration of Independence across the pages of history, we were here. For more than two centuries our forebears labored in this country without wages; they made cotton king; they built the homes of their masters while suffering gross injustice and shameful humiliation--and yet out of a bottomless vitality they continued to thrive and develop. If the inexpressible cruelties of slavery could not stop us, the opposition we now face will surely fail. We will win our freedom because the sacred heritage of our nation and the eternal will of God are embodied in our echoing demands.

Before closing I feel impelled to mention one other point in your statement that has troubled me profoundly. You warmly commended the Birmingham police force for keeping "order" and "preventing violence." I doubt that you would have so warmly commended the police force if you had seen its dogs sinking their teeth into unarmed, non-violent Negroes. I doubt that you would so quickly commend the policemen if you were to observe their ugly and inhumane treatment of Negroes here in the city jail; if you were to watch them push and curse old Negro women and young Negro girls; if you were to see them slap and kick old Negro men and young boys; if you were to observe them, as they did on two occasions, refuse to give us food because we wanted to sing our grace together. I cannot join you in your praise of the Birmingham police department.

It is true that the police have exercised a degree of discipline in handling the demonstrators. In this sense they have conducted themselves rather "nonviolently" in public. But for what purpose? To preserve the evil system of segregation. Over the past few years I have consistently preached that nonviolence demands that the means we use must be as pure as the ends we seek. I have tried to make clear that it is wrong to use immoral means to attain moral ends. But now I must affirm that it is just as wrong, or perhaps even more so, to use moral means to preserve immoral ends. Perhaps Mr. Connor and his policemen have been rather nonviolent in public, as was Chief Pritchett in Albany, Georgia, but they have used the moral means of nonviolence to maintain the immoral end of racial injustice. As T. S. Eliot has said: "The last temptation is the greatest treason: To do the right deed for the wrong reason."

I wish you had commended the Negro sit-inners and demonstrators of Birmingham for their sublime courage, their willingness to suffer and their amazing discipline in the midst of great provocation. One day the South will recognize its real heroes. They will be the James Merediths, with the noble sense of purpose that enables them to face jeering and hostile mobs, and with the agonizing loneliness that characterizes the life of the pioneer. They will be old, oppressed, battered Negro women, symbolized in a seventy-two-year-old woman in Montgomery, Alabama, who rose up with a sense of dignity and with her people decided not to ride segregated buses, and who responded with ungrammatical profundity to one who inquired about her weariness: "My feets is tired, but my soul is at rest." They will be the young high school and college students, the young ministers of the gospel and a host of their elders, courageously and nonviolently sitting in at lunch counters and willingly going to jail for conscience's sake. One day the South will know that when these disinherited children of God sat down at lunch counters, they were in reality standing up for what is best in the American dream and for the most sacred values in our Judaeo-Christian heritage, thereby bringing our nation back to those great wells of democracy which were dug deep by the founding fathers in their formulation of the Constitution and the Declaration of Independence.

Never before have I written so long a letter. I'm afraid it is much too long to take your precious time. I can assure you that it would have been much shorter if I had been writing from a comfortable desk, but what else can one do when he is alone in a narrow jail cell, other than write long letters, think long thoughts and pray long prayers?

If I have said anything in this letter that overstates the truth and indicates an unreasonable impatience, I beg you to forgive me. If I have said anything that understates the truth and indicates my having a patience that allows me to settle for anything less than brotherhood, I beg God to forgive me.

I hope this letter finds you strong in the faith. I also hope that circumstances will soon make it possible for me to meet each of you, not as an integrationist or a civil-rights leader but as a fellow clergyman and a Christian brother. Let us all hope that the dark clouds of racial prejudice will soon pass away and the deep fog of misunderstanding will be lifted from our fear-drenched communities, and in some not too distant tomorrow the radiant stars of love and brotherhood will shine over our great nation with all their scintillating beauty.

Yours for the cause of Peace and Brotherhood,

Martin Luther King, Jr.

ROBERT L. HEILBRONER (BORN 1919)

An economist, author, and university professor, Robert Heilbroner wrote The Great Ascent: The Struggle for Economic Development in Our Time *(1963) and* The Limits of American Capitalism. *As suggested by these titles, Heilbroner is a self-styled "radical conservative."*

WHAT HAS POSTERITY EVER DONE FOR ME?

Will MANKIND survive? Who knows? The question I want to put is more searching: Who cares? It is clear that most of us today do not care—or at least do not care enough. How many of us would be willing to give up some minor convenience—say, the use of aerosols—in the hope that this might extend the life of man on earth by a hundred years? Suppose we also knew with a high degree of certainty that humankind could not survive a thousand years unless we gave up our wasteful diet of meat, abandoned all pleasure driving, cut back on every use of energy that was not essential to the maintenance of a bare minimum. Would we care enough for posterity to pay the price of its survival?

I doubt it. A thousand years is unimaginably distant. Even a century far exceeds our powers of empathetic imagination. By the year 2075, I shall probably have been dead for three quarters of a century. My children will also likely be dead, and my grandchildren, if I have any, will be in their dotage. What does it matter to me, then, what life will be like in 2075, much less 3075? Why should I lift a finger to affect events that will have no more meaning for me seventy-five years after my death than those that happened seventy-five years before I was born?

There is no rational answer to that terrible question. No argument based on reason will lead me to care for posterity or to lift a finger in its behalf. Indeed, by every rational consideration, precisely the opposite answer is thrust upon us with irresistible force. As a Distinguished Professor of political economy at the University of London has written in the current winter issue of *Business and Society Review:*

> Suppose that, as a result of using up all the world's resources, human life did come to an end. So what? What is so desirable about an indefinite continuation of the human species, religious convictions apart? It may well be that nearly everybody who is already here on earth would be reluctant to die, and that everybody has an instinctive fear of death. But one must not confuse this with the notion that, in any meaningful sense, generations who are yet unborn can be said to be better off if they are born than if they are not.

Thus speaks the voice of rationality. It is echoed in the book *The Economic Growth Controversy* by a Distinguished Younger Economist from the Massachusetts Institute of Technology:

> . . .Geological time [has been] made comprehensible to our finite human minds by the statement that the 4.5 billion years of the earth's history [are] equivalent to once around the world in an SST. . . . Man got on eight miles before the end, and industrial man got on six feet before the end. . . . Today we are having a debate about the extent to which man ought to maximize the length of time that he is on the airplane.
>
> According to what the scientists now think, the sun is gradually expanding and 12 billion years from now the earth will be swallowed up by the sun. This means that our airplane has time to go round three more times. Do we want man to be on it for all three times around the world? Are we interested in man being

on for another eight miles? Are we interested in man being on for another six feet? Or are we only interested in man for a fraction of a millimeter—our lifetimes?

That led me to think: Do I care what happens a thousand years from now? . . . Do I care when man gets off the airplane? I think I basically [have come] to the conclusion that I don't care whether man is on the airplane for another eight feet, or if man is on the airplane another three times around the world.

Is this an outrageous position? I must confess it outrages me. But this is not because the economists' arguments are "wrong"—indeed, within their rational framework they are indisputably right. It is because their position reveals the limitations—worse, the suicidal dangers—of what we call "rational argument" when we confront questions that can only be decided by an appeal to an entirely different faculty from that of cool reason. More than that, I suspect that if there is cause to fear for man's survival it is because the calculus of logic and reason will be applied to problems where they have as little validity, even as little bearing, as the calculus of feeling or sentiment applied to the solution of a problem in Euclidean geometry.

If reason cannot give us a compelling argument to care for posterity—and to care desperately and totally—what can? For an answer, I turn to another distinguished economist whose fame originated in his profound examination of moral conduct. In 1759, Adam Smith published "The Theory of Moral Sentiments," in which he posed a question very much like ours, but to which he gave an answer very different from that of his latter-day descendants.

Suppose, asked Smith, that "a man of humanity" in Europe were to learn of a fearful earthquake in China—an earthquake that swallowed up its millions of inhabitants. How would that man react? He would, Smith mused, "make many melancholy reflections upon the precariousness of human life, and the vanity of all the labors of man, which could thus be annihilated in a moment. He would, too, perhaps, if he was a man of speculation, enter into many reasonings concerning the effects which this disaster might produce upon the commerce of Europe, and the trade and business of the world in general." Yet, when this fine philosophizing was over, would our "man of humanity" care much about the catastrophe in distant China? He would not. As Smith tells us, he would "pursue his business or his pleasure, take his repose or his diversion, with the same ease and tranquillity as if nothing had happened."

But now suppose, Smith says, that our man were told he was to lose his little finger on the morrow. A very different reaction would attend the contemplation of this "frivolous disaster." Our man of humanity would be reduced to a tormented state, tossing all night with fear and dread—whereas "provided he never saw them, he will snore with the most profound security over the ruin of a hundred millions of his brethren."

Next, Smith puts the critical question: Since the hurt to his finger bulks so large and the catastrophe in China so small, does this mean that a man of humanity, given the choice, would prefer the extinction of a hundred million Chinese in order to save his little finger? Smith is unequivocal in his answer. "Human nature startles at the thought," he cries, "and the world in its greatest depravity and corruption never produced such a villain as would be capable of entertaining it."

But what stays our hand? Since we are all such creatures of self-interest (and is not Smith the very patron saint of the motive of self-interest?), what moves us to give precedence to the rights of humanity over those of our own immediate well-being? The answer, says Smith, is the presence within us all of a "man within the breast," an inner creature of conscience whose insistent voice brooks no disobedience: "It is the love of what is honorable and noble, of the grandeur and dignity, and superiority of our own characters."

It does not matter whether Smith's eighteenth-century view of human nature in general or morality in particular appeals to the modern temper. What matters is that he has put the question that tests us to the quick. For it is one thing to appraise matters of life and death by the principles of rational self-interest and quite another *to take responsibility for our choice*. I cannot imagine the Distinguished Professor from the University of London personally consigning humanity to oblivion with the same equanimity with which he writes off its demise. I am certain that if the Distinguished Younger Economist from M.I.T. were made responsible for determining the precise length of stay of humanity on the SST, he would agonize over the problem and end up by exacting every last possible inch for mankind's journey.

Of course, there are moral dilemmas to be faced even if one takes one's stand on the "survivalist" principle. Mankind cannot expect to continue on earth indefinitely if we do not curb population growth, thereby consigning billions or tens of billions to the oblivion of nonbirth. Yet, in this case, we sacrifice some portion of life-to-come in order that life itself may be preserved. This essential commitment to life's continuance gives us the moral authority to take measures, perhaps very harsh measures, whose justification cannot be found in the precepts of rationality, but must be sought in the unbearable anguish we feel if we imagine ourselves as the executioners of mankind.

This anguish may well be those "religious convictions," to use the phrase our London economist so casually tosses away. Perhaps to our secular cast of mind, the anguish can be more easily accepted as the furious power of the biogenetic force we see expressed in every living organism. Whatever its source, when we ask if mankind "should" survive, it is only here that we can find a rationale that gives us the affirmation we seek.

This is not to say we will discover a religious affirmation naturally welling up within us as we career toward Armageddon. We know very little about how to convince men by recourse to reason and nothing about how to convert them to religion. A hundred faiths contend for believers today, a few perhaps capable of generating that sense of caring for human salvation on earth. But, in truth, we do not know if "religion" will win out. An appreciation of the magnitude of the sacrifices required to perpetuate life may well tempt us to opt for "rationality"—to enjoy life while it is still to be enjoyed on relatively easy terms, to write mankind a shorter ticket on the SST so that some of us may enjoy the next millimeter of the trip in first-class seats.

V.

DRAMA

Wooden Mask, West Africa.
(Private Collection, Max Reichard).

INTRODUCTION

Our discussion of Existentialism points in many directions. Existentialists make it clear that we must deal with the question of self-consciousness. From a moral perspective, "self-conscious" relates to shame, to guilt, to the awareness that something is right and wrong. "Conscious" and "conscience" have the same Latin root: *scio* (I know). Self-conscious, then, means to be self-aware, to know ourselves, to accept responsibility for ourselves. In *The Unbearable Lightness of Being*, Milan Kundera suggests that we cannot escape from ourselves, that loving and being loved by another person cannot be an unconscious act, that we cannot love and be loved the way a dog "loves" or the way we "love" a dog.

If self-awareness, including a moral consciousness of right and wrong, is an inescapable part of our existence as human beings, then, perhaps, it is also our responsibility to pursue all paths to self-knowledge, to self-consciousness.

Nowhere is that task set out for us more clearly than in the art form we call drama.

* * *

Drama compels us to look at ourselves and our society. It allows us to confront our mortality: as Zorba the Greek says, "We all end up the same—food for worms." And drama is ubiquitous; it is literally omnipresent in some American households where television/video machines are everywhere and are never turned off. Drama entertains us. It allows us to see ourselves through the eyes of others; it gives us opportunities to walk in the shoes of people with lives and values very different from ours. When Iago, Shakespeare's evil genius in *Othello*, describes himself, we momentarily recognize ourselves—our arrogance and racism, our envy of what others have, our hearts of darkness.

The origins of this art form, DRAMA, seem to be the 5th century (B.C.) of Hellenic (classical Greek) culture. Building on folklore, myth, poetic form, and religious festivals, the Greeks created "classical" theater—a place where a community, the audience, would meet characters publicly acting out an intentional art form. Beginning with Aeschylus (525 B.C. -456 B.C.) Greek tragedy is procreated. He first used dialogue and stage action. And he developed dramatic devices to explore the suffering and joy in man's relationship to God. In *Prometheus Bound* he dramatizes that tension by staging the myth of Prometheus, the Greek hero, who was cruelly punished by the god Zeus for bringing culture to man. In Greek mythology, Prometheus was the benefactor of mankind who defied the supreme power at the cost of great and long suffering. In his tragic drama, Aeschylus gets us to think about some enduring questions: Is might right? Is it proper for man to rely on his human powers of reason against the power of God? When is man to obey and when to revolt? Can we reconcile human freedom and divine rule?

The tragic playwright Sophocles (496 B.C. - 406 B.C.) developed the dramatic techniques of Aeschylus even further. He is appreciated particularly for the construction of his plots: A rapid introduction to the characters and theme and then a quick building of the climax. In Sophocles we have a playwright who uses the knowledge his audience has about Greek history, culture, and heroic myths to set the tragic action. By creating tension between what the audience knows about the fate of a noble hero and what the character knows, Sophocles creates irony as a principle of dramatic structure. In his *Poetics*, Aristotle defined the tragic hero as one with whom the audience can identify. The suffering of the hero rises from some great error, most often hubris. Moreover, Aristotle praised Sophocles' use of the chorus as "one of the actors; it should be an integral part of the whole and take a share in the action."

Sophocles may have written 120 plays; we have only seven. Three of his most famous form a trilogy—a tragic narrative of a family's lives and deaths: *Oedipus The King* (430 B.C.), *Oedipus at Colonnus* (407 B.C.), and *Antigone* (441 B.C.). All three plays deal with *hubris* or arrogant, excessive pride. For the Greeks, like the later Christians, excessive pride was the cardinal sin. Hubris was seen as antagonistic to a virtuous life, to making right choices, and to the performance of right action. In *Antigone*, Sophocles uses hubris as a setting for a conflict between universal (natural) or higher law and particular (social) or man's law. The struggle and conflict in *Antigone* is reminiscent of the tension Martin Luther King discusses in his "Letter from Birmingham Jail" almost 2500 years later. We must have laws to protect society from anarchy and chaos. But how much power can the state have in limiting or controlling the rights and beliefs of individuals and in forbidding expressions of those beliefs?

Antigone is also of interest to us because the conflict and tension in the drama come from the struggle between a man and a woman. Sophocles seems to be reminding us that there are certain moral questions and problems which are timeless.

From the beginning of tragedy as a dramatic art, it has depended on its structure, particularly the use of irony, to communicate certain universal, timeless ideas about the human condition, to get us to empathize with characters whom we admire, pity, envy, detest, and otherwise empathize with or reject. Moreover, until at least the 20th century, drama has emphasized that we have alternatives, choices, the freedom to choose within a moral order. Drama also reminds us of the mysterious and sacred in life; it helps us to recognize complex truths. Drama gives human beings the opportunity to confront reality—even if that means simply to accept the ambiguities in life.

In between the simple, classical dramas of Sophocles and the modern moral dilemmas of 20th century playwrights like Arthur Miller (*Death of a Salesman*) and Tennessee Williams (*A Streetcar Named Desire*), are the tragedies, comedies, drama-histories, and poetry of William Shakespeare. Clearly Shakespeare believes there is a social, political, and moral order which must be understood and upheld. His tragedies focus on the relationship between what we as human beings are and what we can be. Shakespeare's tragedies explore the ethical foundations of society and politics. They investigate the relationship between what we say we value and how we actually behave. They are a reflection of the turbulent world of Elizabethan England when many assumptions about God, King, and Country were being challenged.

In some of his most famous lines Shakespeare has Prince Hamlet say:

> What a piece of work is man.
> How noble in reason.
> How infinite in faculty ....
> How like a god ....
> And yet, to me what is
>   this quintessence of dust?

What a romantic vision of man Shakespeare gives us! Our lives are full of tension: divinity and dust, hope and death, love and hate, growth and decline, virtue and villainy. But death, like sex, is rebirth. In *Romeo and Juliet* Shakespeare seems to be saying that in a world of uncertainties, death is certain and true love is absolute. Commitment to another, to something higher than mere physical existence, to a noble love, is a form of divinity. That is, pure love is too good for this world; it lives forever in the next.

In *Othello* Shakespeare plays with the tension in his 17th century audience's values: the racial self-consciousness and belief of Englishmen that their culture was superior to all others juxtaposed against the virtues of nobility and courage; the beauty, innocence, simplicity, and unquestioning love of the "fair" (= beautiful; white) Desdemona juxtaposed against the noble Moor, Othello—worldly, powerful, and racially an outsider (black African), representing the best and worst that a man can aspire to.

Both Othello and Shakespeare's audience are conscious of Othello's "blackness" and of its being a characteristic less than desirable in Elizabethan or Viennese society. The character of Othello, however, is so noble and virtuous that he not only becomes a great leader of men but also wins the prize of prizes, the hand of the lovely, fair Desdemona. This relationship allows Shakespeare to explore the hypocrisy of his society, as well as to penetrate the heart of darkness in every human being.

Although Shakespeare is known for his earthy language, a variety of remarks in this play suggests that he and his audience were aware of the popular English stereotypes of Africans as sexually aggressive. Shakespeare knew that his audience would react to a play that creates a sexual union between a Black man and a White woman. He did not condemn such a union; rather he used it to create ironic tension. Shakespeare played on the theme of white and black sexuality, showing how even the most noble of men, the most noble of loves, could be perverted and destroyed by the poisons of pride, jealousy, and self-doubt. At the play's climax, when the hero has his moment of self-recognition, when Othello recognizes—too late—his hubris, he characterizes himself as "dirt." Shakespeare reveals his genius: he has juxtaposed the Elizabethans' concept of blackness (evil, darkness, dirt) with the view of whiteness (goodness, light, angelic purity). He juxtaposed the characters as well: inner blackness and inner whiteness. In a sense, Shakespeare used his audience's racism to explore universal themes about all of us as human beings, regardless of time, culture, beliefs, or skin pigmentation.

Verdi's opera version of the play, *Otello*, is even more like a classic Greek tragedy because the plot is more singularly focused on the tragic hero and because the music seems to carry the action much faster to its climax. Franco Zeffirelli brings the full power and passion of both Shakespeare and Verdi to his film, *Otello*.

Modern drama is more "realistic" than Renaissance drama. We have prose rather than poetry, and ordinary "heroes" (protagonists) rather than nobility. In Susan Glaspell's *Trifles*, two rural housewives make a moral choice comparable to that of Antigone, except that their moral duty is less clear in an age of relative values, and the stakes are less significant.

Likewise, in the film, *Zorba the Greek* we have no Greek tragedy. We have no tragic hero. We have "personalities." Using Friedrich Nietzsche's mythic categories we can analyze the film's delightful character, Alexis Zorba, as a Dionysian: pleasure-loving, spontaneous, living by his wits and intuition, excessive, unreliable, with little past, no plans for the future. In contrast, we have the young English writer, an Apollonian personality: critical, rational, orderly, detached, disciplined, unable to be vulnerable, missing, as Zorba said, what we all need, "a little bit of madness."

The personalities of the two female characters in *Zorba* are less clearly defined. The women serve, literally and figuratively, the needs of the male characters. Some questions may occur to you in viewing this film: Are the two women central to the plot? Are they persons in their own right or are they "sex objects"? Was the film, made in 1965, even conscious of these questions? The film brings together many themes in Western drama and in the humanities. The tension between the individual and the community; between freedom and order. The connections in life between love, sex, and death. The pursuit of the ideal of happiness and the acceptance of the now, of what we have at this moment. The importance of friendship and of loving others for what they are and not what we would have them be. *Zorba* urges us to open ourselves up, to take some risks: "life is trouble, only death is not." We are reminded that some things are not for sale: "In work I am your man—but in things like [dancing and] playing [music] I am my own .... I am free." We are even warned of "thinking too much." And in the final scene, unlike much of serious, modern drama, the film gives us a positive sense of our potential as human beings. We can fail and start again; we can love; we can accept the love of others; we can accept and love ourselves and be free.

* * *

Perhaps drama is the most important of the arts today, because it is the most accessible. It provides common ground for people of varied backgrounds and values to meet and to experience human feelings and ideas in some sort of community. We have developed this art form, as Aristotle suggested in his theory of tragedy, to allow ourselves to be purified, cleansed of our own weaknesses, self-doubts, bitter thoughts, and arrogant pride. Drama gives us the opportunity to explore our self-consciousness, our identity; it fortifies us to continue the struggle for moral integrity.

SOPHOCLES (497-406 B.C.)

Living at the height of Athens' glory, Sophocles was a versatile actor as well as winning playwright. In the annual drama contests at the festival of Dionysus, Sophocles always won first or second place each time he participated. His powerful tragedies depict a chaotic universe in which blind fate, in the form of the gods, ruled supreme. Yet he did not lose his sense of life's beauty, and his tragic insight leads to a kind of serenity in his most admirable characters, such as Oedipus and Antigone.

The play Antigone *is third in a trilogy, with* Oedipus Rex *and* Oedipus at Colonus *preceding it. The background is given in the conversation between Antigone and Ismene in the opening scene. Fated to marry his mother and kill his own father, without realizing it until later, Antigone's father Oedipus was tragically heroic in his search for the bitter truth. Antigone also displays courage as she takes responsibility for her brother's burial. Central to her motivation is the belief that a soul must be buried to find rest in the afterlife.*

ANTIGONE

Characters

Antigone (an-TIG-o-nee)   Choragus (ko-RAY-gus)
Ismene (is-MEE-nee)   A Sentry
Creon (KREE-ahn)   A Messenger
Haimon (HAY-mon)   Chorus

Time: Dawn of the day after the repulse of the Argive army from the assault of Thebes.

Prologue

(Antigone and Ismene enter from the central door of the Palace.)

Antigone: Ismene, dear sister,
             You would think that we had already suffered enough
             For the curse of Oedipus: (ED-i-pus)
             I cannot imagine any grief
             That you and I have not gone through. And now—
             Have they told you of the new decree of our King Creon?

Ismene: I have heard nothing: I know
             That two sisters lost two brothers, a double death
             In a single hour; and I know that the Argive army
             Fled in the night; but beyond this, nothing.

Antigone: I thought so. And that is why I wanted you
             To come out here with me. There is something we must do.

Ismene: Why do you speak so strangely?

Antigone: Listen, Ismene:
             Creon buried our brother Eteocles (e-TEE-uk-kleez)
             With military honors, gave him a soldier's funeral,

And it was right that he should: but Polyneices, (poly-NICE-eez)
Who fought as bravely and died as miserably—
They say that Creon has sworn
No one shall bury him, no one mourn for him.
But his body must lie in the fields, a sweet treasure
For carrion birds to find as they search for food.
That is what they say, and our good Creon is coming here
To announce it publicly; and the penalty—
Stoning to death in the public square!
                        There it is,
And now you can prove what you are:
A true sister, or a traitor to your family.

Ismene: Antigone, you are mad! What could I possibly do?

Antigone: You must decide whether you will help me or not.

Ismene: I do not understand you. Help you in what?

Antigone: Ismene, I am going to bury him. Will you come?

Ismene: Bury him! You have just said the new law forbids it.

Antigone: He is my brother. And he is your brother, too.

Ismene: But think of the danger! Think what Creon will do!

Antigone: Creon is not strong enough to stand in my way.

Ismene: Ah Sister!
Oedipus died, everyone hating him
For what his own search brought to light, his eyes
Ripped out by his own hand, and Jocasta died, (jo-CAST-uh)
His mother and wife at once: she twisted the cords
That strangled her life; and our two brothers died.
Each killed by the other's sword. And we are left:
But oh. Antigone,
Think how much more terrible than these
Our own death would be if we should go against Creon
And do what he has forbidden! We are only women.
We cannot fight with men. Antigone!
The law is strong, we must give in to the law
In this thing, and in worse. I beg the dead
To forgive me, but I am helpless. I must yield
To those in authority. And I think it is dangerous business
To be always meddling.

Antigone: If that is what you think.
I should not want you, even if you asked to come.
You have made your choice, you can be what you want to be.
But I will bury him; and if I must die,

I say that this crime is holy: I shall lie down
With him in death. and I shall be as dear
To him as life is to me.
                    It is the dead,
Not the living, who make the longest demands:
We die for ever. . .
                    You may do as you like,
Since apparently the laws of the gods mean nothing to you.

Ismene: They mean a great deal to me; but I have no strength
            To break laws that were made for the public good.

Antigone: That must be your excuse, I suppose. But as for me,
            I will bury the brother I love.

Ismene: Antigone,
            I am so afraid for you!

Antigone: You need not be:
            You have yourself to consider, after all.

Ismene: But no one must hear of this, you must tell no one!
            I will keep it a secret, I promise!

Antigone: Oh tell it! Tell everyone!
            Think how they'll hate you when it all comes out
            If they learn that you knew about it all the time!

Ismene: So fiery! You should be cold with fear.

Antigone: Perhaps. But I am doing only what I must.

Ismene: But can you do it? I say that you cannot.

Antigone: Very well: when my strength gives out, I shall do no more.

Ismene: Impossible things should not be tried at all.

Antigone: Go away, Ismene:
            I shall be hating you soon, and the dead will too.
            For your words are hateful. Leave me my foolish plan:
            I am not afraid of the danger: if it means death.
            It will not be the worst of deaths—death without honor.

Ismene: Go then, if you feel that you must.
            You are unwise,
            But a loyal friend indeed to those who love you.

(Exit into the Palace. Antigone goes off, L. Enter the Chorus.)

Parados

Chorus: Now the long blade of the sun, lying
Level east to west, touches with glory
Thebes of the Seven Gates. Open, unlidded
Eye of golden day! O marching light
Across the eddy and rush of Dirce's stream,
Striking the white shields of the enemy
Thrown headlong backward from the blaze of morning!

Choragos: Polyneices their commander
Roused them with windy phrases,
He the wild eagle screaming
Insults above our land,
His wings their shields of snow,
His crest their marshalled helms.

Chorus: Against our seven gates, in a yawning ring
The famished spears came onward in the night:
But before his jaws were sated with our blood,
Or pinefire took the garland of our towers,
He was thrown back; and as he turned, great Thebes—
No tender victim for his noisy power
Rose like a dragon behind him, shouting war.

Choragos: For God hates utterly
The bray of bragging tongues;
And when he beheld their smiling,
Their swagger of golden helms,
The frown of his thunder blasted
Their first man from our walls.

Chorus: We heard his shout of triumph high in the air
Turn to a scream, far out in a flaming arc
He fell with his windy torch, and the earth struck him.
And others storming in fury no less than his
Found shock of death in the dusty joy of battle.

Choragos: Seven captains at seven gates
Yielded their clanging arms to the god
That bends the battle-line and breaks it.
These two only, brothers in blood,
Face to face in matchless rage,
Mirroring each the other's death,
Clashed in long combat.

Chorus: But now in the beautiful morning of victory
Let Thebes of the many chariots sing for joy!
With hearts for dancing we'll take leave of war:
Our temples shall be sweet with hymns of praise,
And the long night shall echo with our chorus.

Scene I

Choragos: But now at last our new King is coming:
             Creon of Thebes, Menoikeus' son.
             In this auspicious dawn of his reign
             What are the new complexities
             That shifting Fate has woven for him?
             What is his counsel? Why has he summoned
             The old men to hear him?

(Enter Creon from the Palace, C. He addresses the Chorus from the top step.)

Creon: Gentlemen: I have the honor to inform you that our Ship of State, which recent
             storms have threatened to destroy, has come safely to harbor at last, guided by the
             merciful wisdom of Heaven. I have summoned you here this morning because I
             know that I can depend upon you: your devotion to King Laios was absolute: you
             never hesitated in your devotion to our late ruler Oedipus; and when Oedipus
             died, your loyalty was transferred to his children. Unfortunately, as you know, his
             two sons, the princes Eteocles and Polyneices, have killed each other in battle: and
             I, as the next in blood, have succeeded to the full power of the throne.

             I am aware, of course, that no Ruler can expect complete loyalty from his subjects
             until he has been tested in office. Nevertheless, I say to you at the very outset that I
             have nothing but contempt for the kind of Governor who is afraid, for whatever
             reason, to follow the course that he knows is best for the State; and as for the man
             who sets private friendship above the public welfare—I have no use for him, either.
             I call God to witness that if I saw my country headed for ruin, I should not be
             afraid to speak out plainly: and I need hardly remind you that I would never have
             any dealings with an enemy of the people. No one values friendship more highly
             than I: but we must remember that friends made at the risk of wrecking our Ship
             are not real friends at all.

             These are my principles, at any rate, and that is why I have made the following
             decision concerning the sons of Oedipus: Eteocles, who died as a man should die,
             fighting for his country, is to be buried with full military honors, with all the
             ceremony that is usual when the greatest heroes die; but his brother Polyneices,
             who broke his exile to come back with fire and sword against his native city and
             the shrines of his father's gods, whose one idea was to spill the blood of his blood
             and sell his own people into slavery—Polyneices, I say, is to have no burial: no
             man is to touch him or say the least prayer for him: he shall lie on the plain,
             unburied: and the birds and the scavenging dogs can do with him whatever they
             like.

             This is my command, and you can see the wisdom behind it. As long as I am King,
             no traitor is going to be honored with the loyal man. But whoever shows by word
             and deed that he is on the side of the State—he shall have my respect while he is
             living, and my reverence when he is dead.

Choragos: If that is your will, Creon, son of Menoikeus,
             You have the right to enforce it: we are yours.

Creon: That is my will. Take care that you do your part.

Choragos: We are old men: let the younger ones carry it out.

Creon: I do not mean that: the sentries have been appointed.

Choragos: Then what is it that you would have us do?

Creon: You will give no support to whoever breaks this law.

Choragos: Only a crazy man is in love with death!

Creon: And death it is; yet money talks, and the wisest
                Have sometimes been known to count a few coins too many.

                (Enter Sentry from L.)

Sentry: I'll not say that I'm out of breath from running, King, because every time I stopped
                to think about what I have to tell you, I felt like going back. And all the time a voice
                kept saying, "You fool, don't you know you're walking straight into trouble?": and
                then another voice: "Yes, but if you let somebody else get the news to Creon first, it
                will be even worse than that for you!" But good sense won out, at least I hope it
                was good sense, and here I am with a story that makes no sense at all: but I'll tell it
                anyhow, because, as they say, what's going to happen happens to happen, and—

Creon: Come to the point. What have you to say?

Sentry: I did not do it. I did not see who did it. You must not punish me for what someone
                else has done.

Creon: A comprehensive defense! More effective, perhaps if I knew its purpose. Come:
                what is it?

Sentry: A dreadful thing . . . I don't know how to put it—

Creon: Out with it!

Sentry: Well. then:
                The dead man—
                            Polyneices—

                (Pause. The Sentry is overcome, fumbles for words, Creon waits impassively.)

                            out there—
                                someone,—
                New dust on the slimy flesh!

                (Pause. No sign from Creon.)

                Someone has given it burial that way, and
                Gone. . .

(Long pause. Creon finally speaks with deadly control.)

Creon: And the man who dared do this?

Sentry: I swear I
Do not know! You must believe me!
                    Listen:
The ground was dry, not a sign of digging, no.
Not a wheeltrack in the dust, no trace of anyone.
It was when they relieved us this morning: and one of them,
The corporal, pointed to it.
                    There it was,
The strangest—
                    Look:
The body, just mounded over with light dust: you see?
Not buried really, but as if they'd covered it
Just enough for the ghost's peace. And no sign
Of dogs or any wild animal that had been there.

And then what a scene there was! Every man of us
Accusing the other: we all proved the other man did it,
We all had proof that we could not have done it.
We were ready to take hot iron in our hands,
Walk through fire, swear by all the gods,
It was not I!
I do not know who it was, but it was not I!

(Creon's rage has been mounting steadily. But the Sentry is too intent upon his story to notice it.)

And then, when this came to nothing, someone said
A thing that silenced us and made us stare
Down at the ground: you had to be told the news.
And one of us had to do it! We threw the dice,
And the bad luck fell to me. So here I am.
Nobody likes the man who brings bad news.

Choragos: I have been wondering, King: can it be that the gods
have done this?

Creon: *(furiously)*: Stop!
Must you doddering wrecks
Go out of your heads entirely? "The gods!"
Intolerable!
The gods favor this corpse? Why? How had he served them?
Tried to loot their temples, burn their images,
Yes, and the whole State, and its laws with it!
Is it your senile opinion that the gods love to honor bad men?
A pious thought!—
                    No, from the very beginning
There have been those who have whispered together.

Stiff-necked anarchists, putting their heads together,
Scheming against me in alleys. These are the men.
And they have bribed my own guard to do this thing.

(Senteniously.)

Money!
There's nothing in the world so demoralizing as money.
Down go your cities,
Homes gone, men gone, honest hearts corrupted,
Crookedness of all kings, and all for money!
(To Sentry)   Buy you—!
I swear by God and by the throne of God,
The man who has done this thing shall pay for it!
Find the man, bring him here to me, or your death
Will be the least of your problems: I'll string you up
Alive, and there will be certain ways to make you
Discover your employer before you die:
And the process may teach you a lesson you seem to have missed:
The dearest profit is sometimes all too dear:
That depends on the source. Do you understand me?
A fortune won is often misfortune.

Sentry: King, may I speak?

Creon: Your very voice distresses me.

Sentry: Are you sure that it is my voice, and not your conscience?

Creon: By God, he wants to analyze me now!

Sentry: It is not what I say, but what has been done, that hurts you.

Creon: You talk too much.

Sentry: Maybe, but I've done nothing.

Creon: Sold your soul for some silver: that's all you've done.

Sentry: How dreadful it is when the right judge judges wrong!

Creon: Your figures of speech
May entertain you now; but unless you bring me the man,
You will get little profit from them in the end.

(Exit Creon into the Palace.)

Sentry: "Bring me the man"—!
I'd like nothing better than bringing him the man!
But bring him or not, you have seen the last of me here.
At any rate, I am safe!

(Exit Sentry)

Ode I

Chorus: Numberless are the world's wonders, but none
           More wonderful than man, the stormy gray sea
           Yields to his prows, the huge crests bear him high;
           Earth, holy and inexhaustible, is graven
           With shining furrows where his plows have gone
           Year after year, the timeless labor of stallions.

           The lightboned birds and beasts that cling to cover.
           The lithe fish lighting their reaches of dim water,
           All are taken, tamed in the net of his mind:
           The lion on the hill, the wild horse windy-maned,
           Resigned to him; and his blunt yoke has broken
           The sultry shoulders of the mountain bull.

           Words also, and thought as rapid as air,
           He fashions to his good use; statecraft is his,
           And his the skill that deflects the arrows of snow,
           The spears of winter rain: from every wind
           He has made himself secure—from all but one:
           In the late wind of death he cannot stand.

           O clear intelligence, force beyond all measure!
           O fate of man, working both good and evil!
           When the laws are kept, how proudly his city stands!
           When the laws are broken, what of his city then?
           Never may the anarchic man find rest at my hearth.
           Never be it said that my thoughts are his thoughts.

Scene II

           (Re-enter Sentry leading Antigone.)

Choragos: What does this mean? Surely this captive woman
           Is the Princess, Antigone. Why should she be taken?

Sentry: Here is the one who did it! We caught her
           In the very act of burying him.—Where is Creon?

Choragos: Just coming from the house.

           (Enter Creon, C.)

Creon: What has happened?
           Why have you come back so soon?

Sentry: (expansively) O King.
           A man should never be too sure of anything: I would have sworn
           That you'd not see me here again: your anger
           Frightened me so, and the things you threatened me with;
           But how could I tell then

That I'd be able to solve the case so soon?

No dice-throwing this time: I was only too glad to come!

Here is the woman, she is the guilty one:
We found her trying to bury him.
Take her, then: question her; judge her as you will.
I am through with the whole thing now, and glad of it.

Creon: But this is Antigone! Why have you brought her here?

Sentry: She was burying him, I tell you!

Creon: *(severely)*:   Is this the truth?

Sentry: I saw her with my own eyes. Can I say more?

Creon: The details: come, tell me quickly!

Sentry: It was like this:
After those terrible threats of yours, King,
We went back and brushed the dust away from the body.
The flesh was soft by now, and stinking,
So we sat on a hill windward and kept guard.
No napping this time. We kept each other awake.
But nothing happened until the white round sun
Whirled in the center of the round sky over us:
Then, suddenly,
A storm of dust roared up from the earth, and the sky
Went out, the plain vanished with all its trees
In the stinging dark. We closed our eyes and endured it.
The whirlwind lasted a long time, but it passed:
And then we looked, and there was Antigone,
I have seen
A mother bird come back to a stripped nest, heard
Her crying bitterly a broken note or two
For the young ones stolen. Just so, when this girl
Found the bare corpse, and all her love's work wasted,
She wept, and cried on heaven to damn the hands
That had done this thing.
                    And then she brought more dust
And sprinkled wine three times for her brother's ghost.

We ran and took her at once. She was not afraid,
Not even when we charged her with what she had done.
She denied nothing.
                    And this was a comfort to me,
And some uneasiness: for it is a good thing
To escape from death, but it is no great pleasure
To bring death to a friend.
                    Yet I always say
There is nothing so comfortable as your own safe skin!

Creon: *(slowly, dangerously)*: And you, Antigone,
You with your head hanging — do you confess this thing?

Antigone: I do. I deny nothing.

Creon *(to Sentry)*:   You may go. *(Exit Sentry)*
(to Antigone): Tell me, tell me briefly:
Had you heard my proclamation touching this matter?

Antigone: It was public. Could I help hearing it?

Creon: And yet you dared defy the law.

Antigone: I dared.
It was not God's proclamation. That final justice
That rules the world below makes no such laws.
Your edict, King, was strong,
But all your strength is weakness itself against
The immortal unrecorded laws of God.
They are not merely now: they were, and shall be.
Operative for ever, beyond man utterly.
I knew I must die, even without your decree:
I am only mortal. And if I must die
Now, before it is my time to die.
Surely this is no hardship: can anyone
Living, as I live, with evil all about me,
Think Death less than a friend? This death of mine
Is of no importance; but if I had left my brother
Lying in death unburied, I should have suffered.
Now I do not.
You smile at me. Ah Creon,
Think me a fool, if you like: but it may well be
That a fool convicts me of folly.

Choragos: Like father, like daughter: both headstrong, deaf to
reason! She has never learned to yield.

Creon: She has much to learn.
The inflexible heart breaks first, the toughest iron
Cracks first, and the wildest horses bend their necks
At the pull of the smallest curb.
Pride? In a slave?
This girl is guilty of a double insolence,
Breaking the given laws and boasting of it.
Who is the man here,
She or I, if this crime goes unpunished?
Sister's child, or more than sister's child,
Or closer yet in blood—she and her sister
Win bitter death for this!
(to Servants) Go, some of you.
Arrest Ismene. I accuse her equally.
Bring her: you will find her sniffling in the house there.

Her mind's a traitor: crimes kept in the dark
Cry for light, and the guardian brain shudders,
But how much worse than this
Is brazen boasting of barefaced anarchy!

Antigone: Creon, what more do you want than my death?

Creon: Nothing.
That gives me everything.

Antigone: Then I beg you: kill me.
This talking is a great weariness: your words
Are distasteful to me, and I am sure that mine
Seem so to you. And yet they should not seem so:
I should have praise and honor for what I have done.
All these men here would praise me
Were their lips not frozen shut with fear of you.

(Bitterly)

Ah the good fortune of kings.
Licensed to say and do whatever they please!

Creon: You are alone here in that opinion.

Antigone: No, they are with me. But they keep their tongues in leash.

Creon: Maybe. But you are guilty, and they are not.

Antigone: There is no guilt in reverence for the dead.

Creon: But Eteocles—was he not your brother too?

Antigone: My brother too.

Creon: And you insult his memory?

Antigone   (softly): The dead man would not say that I insult it.

Creon: He would: for you honor a traitor as much as him.

Antigone: His own brother, traitor or not, and equal in blood.

Creon: He made war on his country. Eteocles defended it.

Antigone: Nevertheless, there are honors due all the dead.

Creon: But not the same for the wicked as for the just.

Antigone: Ah Creon, Creon
Which of us can say what the gods hold wicked?

Creon: An enemy is an enemy, even dead.

Antigone: It is my nature to join in love, not hate.

Creon: *(finally losing patience)*: Go join them, then: if you must have
              your love,
              Find it in hell!

Choragos: But see, Ismene comes:

              (Enter Ismene, guarded.)

              Those tears are sisterly, the cloud
              That shadows her eyes rains down gentle sorrow.

Creon: You too, Ismene.
              Snake in my ordered house, sucking my blood
              Stealthily—and all the time I never knew
              That these two sisters were aiming at my throne!
                              Ismene.
              Do you confess your share in this crime, or deny it?
              Answer me.

Ismene: Yes, if she will let me say so. I am guilty.

Antigone   *(coldly)*: No, Ismene, you have no right to say so.
              You would not help me, and I will not have you help me.

Ismene: But now I know what you meant; and I am here
              To join you, to take my share of punishment.

Antigone: The dead man and the gods who rule the dead
              Know whose act this was. Words are not friends.

Ismene: Do you refuse me, Antigone? I want to die with you:
              I too have a duty that I must discharge to the dead.

Antigone: You shall not lessen my death by sharing it.

Ismene: What do I care for life when you are dead?

Antigone: Ask Creon. You're always hanging on his opinions.

Ismene: You are laughing at me. Why, Antigone?

Antigone: It's a joyless laughter, Ismene.

Ismene: But can I do nothing?

Antigone: Yes. Save yourself. I shall not envy you.
              There are those who will praise you; I shall have honor, too.

Ismene: But we are equally guilty!

Antigone: No more, Ismene.
You are alive, but I belong to Death.

Creon   (to the Chorus): Gentlemen, I beg you to observe these
                 girls: One has just now lost her mind; the other,
                 It seems, has never had a mind at all.

Ismene: Grief teaches the steadiest minds to waver, King.

Creon: Yours certainly did, when you assumed guilt with the
                 guilty!

Ismene: But how could I go on living without her?

Creon: You are.
                 She is already dead.

Ismene: But your own son's bride!

Creon: There are places enough for him to push his plow.
                 I want no wicked women for my sons!

Ismene: O dearest Haimon, how your father wrongs you!

Creon: I've had enough of your childish talk of marriage!

Choragos: Do you really intend to steal this girl from your son?

Creon: No: Death will do that for me.

Choragos: Then she must die?

Creon   (ironically): You dazzle me.
                              —But enough of this talk!

                 (to Guards)

                 You, there, take them away and guard them well:
                 For they are but women, and even brave men run
                 When they see Death coming.

                 (Exeunt Ismene, Antigone, and Guards.)

Ode II

The Chorus sings of the woes of the Labdacidae (descendents of Labdacus: Laius, Oedipus, and Oedipus' children). Once a house has been cursed by heaven, the curse continues to bring evil, generation after generation. Now the last flower of that house is to be destroyed. The power of Zeus is without limit; he lives forever. Man hopes for much, but he is blind. The old saying is true that Fate brings misfortune under the disguise of happiness—then woe descends.

I have seen this gathering sorrow from time long past
From upon Oedipus' children: generation from generation
Takes the compulsive rage of the enemy god.
So lately this last flower of Oedipus' line
Drank the sunlight! But now a passionate word
And handful of dust have closed up all its beauty.

Scene III

Choragos: But here is Haimon, King, the last of all your sons,
Is it grief for Antigone that brings him here,
And bitterness at being robbed of his bride?

(Enter Haimon.)

Creon: We shall soon see, and no need of diviners.
                —Son.
You have heard my final judgment on that girl:
Have you come here hating me, or have you come
With deference and with love, whatever I do?

Haimon: I am your son, Father. You are my guide.
You make things clear for me, and I obey you.
No marriage means more to me than your continuing wisdom.

Creon: Good. That is the way to behave: subordinate
Everything else, my son, to your father's will.
This is what a man prays for, that he may get
Sons attentive and dutiful in his house,
Each one hating his father's enemies,
Honoring his father's friends. But if his sons
Fail him, if they turn out unprofitably,
What has he fathered but trouble for himself
And amusement for the malicious?
                So you are right
Not to lose your head over this woman.
Your pleasure with her would soon grow cold, Haimon.
And then you'd have a hellcat in bed and elsewhere.
Let her find her husband in Hell!
Of all the people in this city, only she
Has had contempt for my law and broken it.
Do you want me to show myself weak before the people?
Or to break my sworn word? No, and I will not.
The woman dies.
I suppose she'll plead "family ties." Well, let her.
If I permit my own family to rebel,
How shall I earn the world's obedience?
Show me the man who keeps his house in hand;
He's fit for public authority.
                I'll have no dealings
With law-breakers, critics of the government:
Whoever is chosen to govern should be obeyed—

Must be obeyed, in all things, great and small,
Just and unjust! O Haimon,
The man who knows how to obey, and that man only,
Knows how to give commands when the time comes.
You can depend on him, no matter how fast
The spears come: he's a good soldier, he'll stick it out.
Anarchy, anarchy! Show me a greater evil!
This is why cities tumble and the great houses rain down.
This is what scatters armies!

No, no: good lives are made so by discipline.
We keep the laws then, and the lawmakers,
And no woman shall seduce us. If we must lose,
Let's lose to a man, at least! Is a woman stronger than we?

Choragos: Unless time has rusted my wits,
What you say, King, is said with point and dignity.

Haimon: (boyishly earnest): Father:
Reason is God's crowning gift to man, and you are right
To warn me against losing mine. I cannot say—
I hope that I shall never want to say!—that you
Have reasoned badly. Yet there are other men
Who can reason, too; and their opinions might be helpful.
You are not in a position to know everything
That people say or do, or what they feel:
Your temper terrifies them—everyone
Will tell you only what you like to hear.
But I, at any rate, can listen; and I have heard them
Muttering and whispering in the dark about this girl.
They say no woman has ever, so unreasonably,
Died so shameful a death for a generous act:
"She covered her brother's body. Is this indecent?
She kept him from dogs and vultures. Is this a crime?
Death?—She should have all the honor that we can give her!"

This is the way they talk out there in the city.

You must believe me:
Nothing is closer to me than your happiness.
What could be closer? Must not any son
Value his father's fortune as his father does his?
I beg you, do not be unchangeable:
Do not believe that you alone can be right.
The man who thinks that,
The man who maintains that only he has the power
To reason correctly, the gift to speak, the soul—
A man like that, when you know him, turns out empty.

It is not reason never to yield to reason!
In good time you can see how some trees bend.

And because they bend, even their twigs are safe,
While stubborn trees are torn up, roots and all.
And the same thing happens in sailing:
Make your sheet fast, never slacken—and over you go,
Head over heels and under, and there's your voyage.
Forget you are angry! Let yourself be moved!
I know I am young, but please let me say this:
The ideal condition
Would be, I admit, that men should be right by instinct:
But since we are all too likely to be astray,
The reasonable thing is to learn from those who can teach.

Choragos: You will do well to listen to him, King.
If what he says is sensible. And you, Haimon.
Must listen to your father—Both speak well.

Creon: You consider it right for a man of my years and experience
To go to school to a boy?

Haimon: It is not right
If I am wrong. But if I am young, and right,
What does my age matter?

Creon: You think it right to stand up for an anarchist?

Haimon: Not at all. I pay no respect to criminals.

Creon: Then she is not a criminal?

Haimon: The City would deny it, to a man.

Creon: And the City proposes to teach me how to rule?

Haimon: Who is it that's talking like a boy now?

Creon: My voice is the one voice giving orders in this City!

Haimon: It is no City if it takes orders from one voice.

Creon: The State is the King!

Haimon: Yes, if the State is a desert.

(Pause)

Creon: This boy, it seems has sold out to a woman.

Haimon: If you are a woman: my concern is only for you.

Creon: So? Your "concern!" In a public brawl with your father!

Haimon: How about you, in a public brawl with justice?

Creon: With justice, when all that I do is within my rights?

Haimon: You have no right to trample on God's right.

Creon: *(completely out of control):* Fool, adolescent fool! Taken in
                by a woman!

Haimon: You'll never see me taken in by anything vile.

Creon: Every word you say is for her!

Haimon: *(quietly, darkly):* And for you.
                And for me. And for the gods under the earth.

Creon: You'll never marry her while she lives.

Haimon: Then she must die. But her death will cause another.

Creon: Another?
                Have you lost your senses? Is this an open threat?

Haimon: There is no threat in speaking to emptiness.

Creon: I swear you'll regret this superior tone of yours!
                You are the empty one!

Haimon: If you were not my father,
                I'd say you were perverse.

Creon: You girlstruck fool, don't play at words with me!

Haimon: I am sorry. You prefer silence.

Creon: Now, by God—!
                I swear by all the gods in heaven above us,
                You'll watch it, I swear you shall!

                (to the Servants) Bring her out!
                Bring the woman out! Let her die before his eyes,
                Here, this instant, with her bridegroom beside her!

Haimon: Not here, no: she will not die here, King.
                And you will never see my face again.
                Go on raving as long as you've a friend to endure you.

                (Exit Haimon.)

Choragos: Gone, gone.
                Creon, a young man in a rage is dangerous!

Creon: Let him do, or dream to do, more than a man can.
                He shall not save these girls from death.

Choragos: These girls?
You have sentenced them both?

Creon: No, you are right.
I will not kill the one whose hands are clean.

Choragos: But Antigone?

Creon: (*somberly*): I will carry her far away
Out there in the wilderness, and lock her
Living in a vault of stone. She shall have food.
As the custom is, to absolve the State of her death.
And there let her pray to the gods of hell:
They are her only gods:
Perhaps they will show her an escape from death,
Or she may learn,
                though late,
That piety shown the dead is pity in vain.

(*Exit Creon.*)

Ode III

Chorus: Love, unconquerable
Waster of rich men, keeper
Of warm lights and all-night vigil
In the soft face of a girl:
Sea-wanderer, forest-visitor!
Even the pure Immortals cannot escape you,
And mortal man, in his one day's dusk,
Trembles before your glory.
Surely you swerve upon ruin
The just man's consenting heart,
As here you have made bright anger
Strike between father and son—
And none has conquered but Love!
A girl's glance working the will of heaven:
Pleasure to her alone who mocks us,
Merciless Aphrodite.

Scene IV

(*As Antigone enters guarded*)

Choragos: But I can no longer stand in awe of this,
Nor, seeing what I see, keep back my tears.
Here is Antigone, passing to that chamber
Where ill find sleep at last.

Antigone: Look upon me, friends, and pity me
Turning back at the night's edge to say
Good-bye to the sun that shines for me no longer;
Now sleepy Death

Summons me down to Acheron, that cold shore:
There is no bridesong there, nor any music.

Chorus: Yet not unpraised, not without a kind of honor,
You walk at last into the underworld:
Untouched by sickness, broken by no sword.
What woman has ever found your way to death?

Antigone: How often I have heard the story of Niobe,
Tantalus' wretched daughter, how the stone
Clung fast about her, ivy-close: and they say
The rain falls endlessly
And shifting soft snow; her tears are never done.
I feel the loneliness of her death in mine.

Chorus: But she was born of heaven, and you
Are woman, woman-born. If her death is yours,
A mortal woman's, is this not for you
Glory in our world and in the world beyond?

Antigone: You laugh at me. Ah, friends, friends,
Can you not wait until I am dead? O Thebes,
O men many-charioted, in love with Fortune,
Dear springs of Dirce, sacred Thebes, grove,
Be witnesses for me, denied all pity,
Unjustly judged! And think a word of love
For her whose path turns
Under dark earth, where there are no more tears.

Chorus: You have passed beyond human daring and come at last
Into a place of stone where justice sits.
I cannot tell
What shape of your father's guilt appears in this.

Antigone: You have touched it at last: that bridal bed
Unspeakable, horror of son and mother mingling:
Their crime, infection of all our family!
O Oedipus, father and brother!
Your marriage strikes from the grave to murder mine.
I have been a stranger here in my own land:
All my life
The blasphemy of my birth has followed me.

Chorus: Reverence is a virtue, but strength
Lives in established law: that must prevail.
You have made your choice.
Your death is the doing of your conscious hand.

Antigone: Then let me go, since all your words are bitter.
And the very light of the sun is cold to me.
Lead me to my vigil, where I must have
Neither love nor lamentation, no song, but silence.

(Creon interrupts impatiently.)

Creon: If dirges and planned lamentations could put off death,
Man would be singing forever.

(to the Servants)   Take her, go!
You know your orders: take her to the vault
And leave her alone there. And if she lives or dies,
That's her affair, not ours: our hands are clean.

Antigone: O tomb, vaulted bride-bed in eternal rock,
Soon I shall be with my own again
Where Persephone welcomes the thin ghosts underground:
And I shall see my father again, and you, mother,
And dearest Polyneices—
                dearest indeed
To me since it was my hand
That washed him clean and poured the ritual wine:
And my reward is death before my time!

And yet, as men's hearts know, I have done no wrong,
I have not sinned before God. Or if I have,
I shall know the truth in death. But if the guilt
Lies upon Creon who judged me, then, I pray,
May his punishment equal my own.

Choragos: O passionate heart,
Unyielding, tormented still by the same winds!

Creon: Her guards shall have good cause to regret their delaying.

Antigone: Ah! That voice is like the voice of death!

Creon: I can give you no reason to think you are mistaken.

Antigone: Thebes, and you my father's gods,
And rulers of Thebes, you see me now, the last
Unhappy daughter of a line of kings,
Your kings, led away to death. You will remember
What things I suffer, and at what men's hands,
Because I would not transgress the laws of heaven.

(to the Guards, simply)

Come: let us wait no loner.

(Exit Antigone, L., guarded.)

Ode IV

The Chorus refers to others who suffered cruel misfortunes: the son of Dryas, the sons of Phineus, and Danae.

Scene V

The blind prophet Teiresias (ti-REE-see-us), led by a boy, enters. He has come to warn Creon that the unburied body of Polyneices has offended the gods—the sacrifices are not being accepted and the birds of augury scream and fight with rage. Creon accuses him of having accepted bribes to recommend burying Polyneices. Teiresias continues, telling Creon it will not be long before a child of his dies because Creon is keeping from Hades one who belongs there (Polyneices), and is sending to Hades one who belongs in the sunlight (Antigone). Refusing to stay for a reply, Teiresias tells Creon to vent his anger on younger men. After the boy has led Teiresias out, the leader of the Chorus tells Creon that the old prophet has never been wrong. Creon becomes frightened and decides, reluctantly, to take the advice of the Chorus, which is to bury Polyneices and free Antigone. Telling his servants to bring axes, he leads them to the cave holding Antigone.

The Chorus sings a hymn of praise to Bacchus and joyfully asks him to come to the aid of the city.

A messenger comes in and tells the Chorus that Creon, once blessed for having saved the city of Thebes from attack, by having been its only ruler, and by having princely children, has now lost all. Haimon has committed suicide. Eurydice (u-RID-uh-see), Creon's wife, enters, having heard of Haimon's death, and asks the messenger for more information. He says that he went with Creon to the body of Polyneices, which, after prayers, was given a proper burial. They then went to the cave where Antigone was imprisoned and were greeted by lamentations from Haimon. Inside they found that Antigone had hanged herself, and Haimon was clinging to her body. When Creon called to him, he cursed his father and drew his sword to kill him, but Creon rushed forward and he missed. Angry with himself, he leaned against his sword, driving it into his side. He died clinging to Antigone's body. Without saying anything Eurydice goes back into the house. The messenger believes she has gone to lament in private, but the Chorus feels her silence to be ominous. The messenger follows her. Creon enters, lamenting the death of his son, admitting it was caused by his own folly. The messenger returns from the house to tell Creon that Eurydice is dead. The doors of the palace are opened and the body of Eurydice is revealed. The messenger says that before she stabbed herself, she cursed Creon for causing the death of both their sons.

Creon:	It is right that it should be. I alone am guilty.
	I know it, and I say it. Lead me in,
	Quickly, friends.
	I have neither life nor substance. Lead me in.

Choragos:	You are right, if there can be right in so much wrong.
	The briefest way is best in a world of sorrow.

Creon:	Let it come,
	Let death come quickly, and be kind to me.
	I would not ever see the sun again.

Choragos:	All that will come when it will: but we, meanwhile,
	Have much to do. Leave the future to itself.

Creon:	All my heart was in that prayer!

Choragos:	Then do not pray any more: the sky is deaf.
Creon:	Lead me away, I have been rash and foolish. I have killed my son and my wife. I look for comfort; my comfort lies here dead. Whatever my hands have touched has come to nothing. Fate has brought all my pride to a thought of dust.

(As Creon is being led into the house, the Choragos advances and speaks directly to the audience.)

Choragos:	There is no happiness where there is no wisdom; No wisdom but in submission to the gods. Big words are always punished, And proud men in old age learn to be wise.

ANTON CHEKHOV (1860-1904)

Checkhov was a Russian physician and humanist who explored new techniques in his drama and short stories. His works explore life realistically, showing the drabness, materialism, and selfishness of life among the middle classes. Yet his subtle irony and humor make his works entertaining as well as enlightening.

THE BRUTE

A Joke in One Act

English Version by ERIC BENTLEY

Characters

MRS. POPOV, widow and landowner, small, with dimpled cheeks.
MR. GREGORY S. SMIRNOV, gentleman farmer, middle-aged.
LUKA, Mrs. Popov's footman, an old man.
GARDENER
COACHMAN
HIRED MEN

The drawing room of a country house. MRS. POPOV, in deep mourning, is staring hard at a photograph. LUKA is with her.

Luka:	It's not right, ma'am, you're killing yourself. The cook has gone off with the maid to pick berries. The cat's having a high old time in the yard catching birds. Every living thing is happy. But you stay moping here in the house like it was a convent, taking no pleasure in nothing. I mean it, ma'am! It must be a full year since you set foot out of doors.
Mrs. Popov:	I must never set foot out of doors again, Luka. Never! I have nothing to set foot out of doors for. My life is done. He is in his grave. I have buried myself alive in this house. We are both in our graves.

Luka: You're off again, ma'am. I just won't listen to you no more. Mr. Popov is dead, but what can we do about that? It's God's doing. God's will be done. You've cried over him, you've done your share of mourning, haven't you? There's a limit to everything. You can't go on weeping and wailing forever. My old lady died, for that matter, and I wept and wailed over her a whole month long. Well, that was it. I couldn't weep and wail all my life, she just wasn't worth it. (*He sighs.*) As for the neighbours, you've forgotten all about them, ma'am. You don't visit them and you don't let them visit you. You and I are like a pair of spiders—excuse the expression, ma'am — here we are in this house like a pair of spiders, we never see the light of day. And it isn't like there was no nice people around either. The whole county's swarming with 'em. There's a regiment quartered at Riblov, and the officers are so good-looking! The girls can't take their eyes off them—There's a ball at the camp every Friday — The military band plays most every day of the week — What do you say, ma'am? You're young, you're pretty, you could enjoy yourself! Ten years from now you may want to strut and show your feathers to the officers, and it'll be too late.

Mrs. Popov (*firmly*) You must never bring this subject up again, Luka. Since Popov died, life has been an empty dream to me, you know that. You may think I am alive. Poor ignorant Luka! You are wrong. I am dead. I'm in my grave. Never more shall I see the light of day, never strip from my body this ... raiment of death! Are you listening, Luka? Let his ghost learn how I love him! Yes, *I* know, and *you* know, he was often unfair to me, he was cruel to me, and he was unfaithful to me. What of it? I shall be faithful to him, that's all. I will show him how I can love. Hereafter, in a better world than this, he will welcome me back, the same loyal girl I always was.

Luka: Instead of carrying on this way, ma'am, you should go out in the garden and take a bit of a walk, ma'am. Or why not harness Toby and take a drive? Call on a couple of the neighbours, ma'am?

Mrs. Popov: (*breaking down*) Oh, Luka!

Luka: Yes, ma'am? What have I said, ma'am? Oh dear!

Mrs. Popov: Toby! You said Toby! He adored that horse. When he drove me out to the Korchagins and the Viasovs, it was always with Toby! He was a wonderful driver, do you remember, Luka? So graceful! So strong! I can see him now, pulling at those reins with all his might and main! Toby! Luka, tell them to give Toby an extra portion of oats today.

Luka: Yes, ma'am.

(*A bell rings.*)

Mrs. Popov: Who is that? Tell them I'm not at home.

Luka: Very good, ma'am. (*Exit.*)

Mrs. Popov: (*gazing again at the photograph*). You shall see, my Popov, how a wife can love and forgive. Till death do us part. Longer than that. Till death re-unite us forever! (*Suddenly a titter breaks through her tears.*) Aren't you ashamed of yourself, Popov?

Here's your little wife, being good, being faithful, so faithful she's locked up here waiting for her own funeral, while you—doesn't it make you ashamed, you naughty boy? You were terrible, you know. You were unfaithful, and you made those awful scenes about it, you stormed out and left me alone for weeks—

(Enter Luka.)

Luka: *(upset).* There's someone asking for you, ma'am. Says he must—

Mrs. Popov: I suppose you told him that since my husband's death I see no one?

Luka: Yes, ma'am. I did, ma'am. But he wouldn't listen, ma'am. He says it's urgent.

Mrs. Popov: *(shrilly).* I see no one!!

Luka: He won't take no for an answer, ma'am. He just curses and swears and comes in anyway. He's a perfect monster, ma'am. He's in the dining room right now.

Mrs. Popov: In the dining room, is he? I'll give him his come uppance. Bring him in here this minute.

(Exit Luka.)

(Suddenly sad again.) Why do they do this to me? Why? Insulting my grief, intruding on my solitude? *(She sighs.)* I'm afraid I'll have to enter a convent. I will, I must enter a convent!

(Enter Mr. Smirnov and Luka.)

Smirnov: *(to Luka).* Dolt! Idiot! You talk too much! *(Seeing Mrs. Popov. With dignity.)* May I have the honour of introducing myself, madam? Gregory S. Smirnov, landowner and lieutenant of artillery, retired. Forgive me, madam, if I disturb your peace and quiet, but my business is both urgent and weighty.

Mrs. Popov: *(declining to offer him her hand).* What is it you wish, sir?

Smirnov: At the time of his death, your late husband—with whom I had the honour to be acquainted, ma'am—was in my debt to the tune of twelve hundred rubles. I have two notes to prove it. Tomorrow, ma'am, I must pay the interest on a bank loan. I have therefore no alternative, ma'am, but to ask you to pay me the money today.

Mrs. Popov: Twelve hundred rubles? But what did my husband owe it to you for?

Smirnov: He used to buy his oats from me, madam.

Mrs. Popov: *(to Luka, with a sigh).* Remember what I said, Luka: tell them to give Toby an extra portion of oats today!

(Exit Luka.)

My dear Mr.—what was the name again?

Smirnov: Smirnov, ma'am.

Mrs. Popov: My dear Mr. Smirnov, if Mr. Popov owed you money, you shall be paid—to the last ruble, to the last kopeck. But today—you must excuse me, Mr.—what was it?

Smirnov: Smirnov, ma'am.

Mrs. Popov: Today, Mr. Smirnov, I have no ready cash in the house.

(Smirnov starts to speak.)

                Tomorrow, Mr. Smirnov, no, the day after tomorrow, all will be well. My steward will be back from town. I shall see that he pays what is owing. Today, no. In any case, today is exactly seven months from Mr. Popov's death. On such a day you will understand that I am in no mood to think of money.

Smirnov: Madam, if you don't pay up now, you can carry me out feet foremost. They'll seize my estate.

Mrs. Popov: You can have your money.

(He starts to thank her.)

                Tomorrow.

(He again starts to speak.)

                That is: the day after tomorrow.

Smirnov: I don't need the money the day after tomorrow. I need it today.

Mrs. Popov: I'm sorry, Mr.—

Smirnov: *(shouting)*. Smirnov!

Mrs. Popov: *(sweetly)*. Yes, of course. But you can't have it today.

Smirnov: But I can't wait for it any longer!

Mrs. Popov: Be sensible, Mr. Smirnov. How can I pay you if I don't have it?

Smirnov: You don't have it?

Mrs. Popov: I don't have it.

Smirnov: Sure?

Mrs. Popov: Positive.

Smirnov: Very well. I'll make a note to that effect. *(Shrugging.)* And then they want me to keep cool. I meet the tax commissioner on the street, and he says, 'Why are you always in such a bad humour, Smirnov?' Bad humour! How can I help it, in God's name? I need money, I need it desperately. Take yesterday: I leave home at the crack of dawn, I call on all my debtors. Not a one of them pays up. Footsore and weary, I creep at midnight into some little dive, and try to snatch a few winks of sleep on the floor by the vodka barrel. Then today, I come here, fifty miles from home, saying to myself, 'At last, at last, I can be sure of something,' and you're not in the mood! You give me a mood! Christ, how can I help getting all worked up?

Mrs. Popov: I thought I'd made it clear, Mr. Smirnov, that you'll get your money the minute my steward is back from town?

Smirnov: What the hell do I care about your steward? Pardon the expression, ma'am. But it was you I came to see.

Mrs. Popov: What language! What a tone to take to a lady! I refuse to hear another word. (*Quickly, exit.*)

Smirnov: Not in the mood, huh? 'Exactly seven month since Popov's death,' huh? How about me? (*Shouting after her.*) Is there this interest to pay, or isn't there? I'm asking you a question: is there this interest to pay, or isn't there? So your husband died, and you're not in the mood, and your steward's gone off some place, and so forth and so on, but what I can do about all that, huh? What do you think I should do? Take a running jump and shove my head through the wall? Take off in a balloon? You don't know my other debtors. I call on Gruzdeff. Not at home. I look for Yaroshevitch. He's hiding out. I find Kooritsin. He kicks up a row, and I have to throw him through the window. I work my way right down the list. Not a kopeck. Then I come to you, and God damn it to hell, if you'll pardon the expression, you're not in the mood! (*Quietly, as he realizes he's talking to air.*) I've spoiled them all, that's what, I've let them play me for a sucker. Well, I'll show them. I'll show this one. I'll stay right here till she pays up. Ugh! (*He shudders with rage.*) I'm in a rage! I'm in a positively towering rage! Every nerve in my body is trembling at forty to the dozen! I can't breathe, I feel ill, I think I'm going to faint, hey, you there!

(*Enter Luka.*)

Luka: Yes, sir? Is there anything you wish, sir?

Smirnov: Water! Water!! No, make it vodka.

(*Exit Luka.*)

Consider the logic of it. A fellow creature is desperately in need of cash, so desperately in need that he has to seriously contemplate hanging himself, and this woman, this mere chit of a girl, won't pay up, and why not? Because, forsooth, she isn't in the mood! Oh, the logic of women! Come to that, I never have liked them, I could do without the whole sex. Talk to a woman? I'd rather sit on a barrel of dynamite, the very thought gives me gooseflesh. Women! Creatures of poetry and romance! Just to see one in the distance gets me mad. My legs start twitching with rage. I feel like yelling for help.

(*Enter Luka, handing Smirnov a glass of water.*)

Luka: Mrs. Popov is indisposed, sir. She is seeing no one.

Smirnov: Get out.

(Exit Luka.)

Indisposed, is she? Seeing no one, huh? Well, she can see me or not, but I'll be here, I'd be right here till she pays up. If you're sick for a week, I'll be here for a week. If you're sick for a year, I'll be here for a year. You won't get around *me* with your widow's weeds and your schoolgirl dimples. I know all about dimples. *(Shouting through the window.)* Semyon, let the horses out of those shafts, we're not leaving, we're staying, and tell them to give the horses some oats, yes, oats, you fool, what do you think? *(Walking away from the window.)* What a mess, what an unholy mess! I didn't sleep last night, the heat is terrific today, not a damn one of 'em has paid up, and here's this—this skirt in mourning that's not in the mood! My head aches, where's that— *(He drinks from the glass.)* Water, ugh! You there!

(Enter Luka.)

Luka: Yes, sir. You wish for something, sir?

Smirnov: Where's that confounded vodka I asked for?

(Exit Luka.)

(Smirnov sits and looks himself over.) Oof! A fine figure of a man I am! Unwashed, uncombed, unshaven, straw on my vest, dust all over me. The little woman must've taken me for a highwayman. *(Yawns.)* I suppose it wouldn't be considered polite to barge into a drawing room in this state, but who cares? I'm not a visitor, I'm a creditor—most unwelcome of guests, second only to Death.

(Enter Luka.)

Luka: *(handing him the vodka)*. If I may say so, sir, you take too many liberties, sir.

Smirnov: What?!

Luka: Oh, nothing, sir, nothing.

Smirnov: Who in hell do you think you're talking to? Shut your mouth!

Luka: *(aside)*. There's an evil spirit abroad. The Devil must have sent him. Oh! *(Exit Luka.)*

Smirnov: What a rage I'm in! I'll grind the whole world to powder. Oh, I feel ill again. You there!

(Enter Mrs. Popov)

Mrs. Popov: *(looking at the floor)*. In the solitude of my rural retreat, Mr. Smirnov, I've long since grown unaccustomed to the sound of the human voice. Above all, I cannot bear shouting. I must beg you not to break the silence.

Smirnov: Very well. Pay me my money and I'll go.

Mrs. Popov: I told you before, and I tell you again, Mr. Smirnov, I have no cash, you'll have to wait till the day after tomorrow. Can I express myself more plainly?

Smirnov: And I told *you* before, and I tell *you* again, that I need the money today, that the day after tomorrow is too late, and that if you don't pay, and pay now, I'll have to hang myself in the morning!

Mrs. Popov: But I have no cash. This is quite a puzzle.

Smirnov: You won't pay, huh?

Mrs. Popov: I *can't* pay, Mr. Smirnov.

Smirnov: In that case, I'm going to sit here and wait. (*Sits down.*) You'll pay up the day after tomorrow? Very good. Till the day after tomorrow, here I sit. (*Pause. He jumps up.*) Now look, do I have to pay that interest tomorrow, or don't I? Or do you think I'm joking?

Mrs. Popov: I must ask you not to raise your voice, Mr. Smirnov. This is not a stable.

Smirnov: Who said it was? Do I have to pay the interest tomorrow or not?

Mrs. Popov: Mr. Smirnov, do you know how to behave in he presence of a lady?

Smirnov: No, madam, I do not know how to behave in the presence of a lady.

Mrs. Popov: Just what I thought. I look at you, and I say: ugh! I hear you talk, and I say to myself: 'That man doesn't know how to talk to a lady.'

Smirnov: You'd like me to come simpering to you in French, I suppose. *Enchante, madame! Merci beaucoup* for not paying zee money, *madame! Pardonnez-moi* if I 'ave disturbed you, *madame!* How *charmante* you look in mourning, *madame!'*

Mrs. Popov: Now you're being silly, Mr. Smirnov.

Smirnov: (*Mimicking*). 'Now you're being silly, Mr. Smirnov. You don't know how to talk to a lady, Mr. Smirnov.' Look here, Mrs. Popov, I've known more women than you've known pussy cats. I've fought three duels on their account. I've jilted twelve, and been jilted by nine others. Oh, yes, Mrs. Popov, I've played the fool in my time, whispered sweet nothings, bowed and scraped and endeavoured to please. Don't tell me I don't know what it is to love, to pine away with longing, to have the blues, to melt like butter, to be weak as water. I was full of tender emotion. I was carried away with passion. I squandered half my fortune on the sex. I chattered about women's emancipation. But there's an end to everything, dear madam. Burning eyes, dark eyelashes, ripe, red lips, dimpled cheeks, heaving bosoms, soft whisperings, the moon above, the lake below—I don't give a rap for that sort of nonsense any more, Mrs. Popov. I've found out about women. Present company excepted, they're liars. Their behaviour is mere play acting; their conversation is sheer gossip. Yes, dear lady, women, young or old, are false, petty, vain, cruel, malicious, unreasonable. As for intelligence, any sparrow could give them points. Appearances, I admit, can be deceptive. In appearance, a woman may be all poetry and romance, goddess and angel, muslin and fluff. To look at her exterior is to be transported to heaven. But I have looked at her interior, Mrs. Popov, and what did I find there—in her very soul? A crocodile. (*He has gripped the back of the chair so firmly that it snaps.*) And, what is more revolting, a crocodile with an illusion, a crocodile that imagines tender sentiments are its own special province, a crocodile that thinks itself queen of the realm of love! Whereas, in sober fact, dear madam, if a woman can love anything except a lapdog you can hang me by the feet on that nail. For a man, love is suffering, love is sacrifice. A woman just swishes her train around and tightens her grip on your nose. Now, you're a woman, aren't you, Mrs. Popov? You must be an expert on some of this. Tell me, quite frankly, did you ever know a woman to be faithful, for instance? Or even sincere? Only old hags, huh? Though some women are old hags from birth. But as for the others? You're right: a faithful woman is a freak of nature—like a cat with horns.

Mrs. Popov: Who *is* faithful, then? Who *have* you cast for the faithful lover? Not man?

Smirnov: Right first time, Mrs. Popov: man.

Mrs. Popov: (*going off into a peal of bitter laughter*). Man! Man is faithful! that's a new one! (*Fiercely.*) What right do you have to say this, Mrs. Smirnov? Men faithful? Let me tell you something. Of all the men I have ever known my late husband Popov was the best. I loved him, and there are women who know how to love, Mr. Smirnov. I gave him my youth, my happiness, my life, my fortune. I worshipped the ground he trod on—and what happened? The best of men was unfaithful to me, Mr. Smirnov. Not once in a while. All the time. After he died, I found his desk drawer full of love letters. While he was alive, he was always going away for the week-end. He squandered my money. He made love to other women before my very eyes. But, in spite of all, Mr. Smirnov, I was faithful. Unto death. And beyond. I am still faithful, Mr. Smirnov! Buried alive in this house, I shall wear mourning till the day I, too, am called to my eternal rest.

Smirnov: (*laughing scornfully*). Expect me to believe that? As if I couldn't see through all this hocus-pocus. Buried alive! Till you're called to your eternal rest! Till when? Till some little poet—or some little subaltern with his first moustache—comes riding by and asks: 'Can that be the house of the mysterious Tamara who for love of her late husband has buried herself alive, vowing to see no man?' Ha!

Mrs. Popov: (*flaring up*). How dare you? How dare you insinuate—?

Smirnov: You may have buried yourself alive, Mrs. Popov, but you haven't forgotten to powder your nose.

Mrs. Popov: (*incoherent*). How dare you? How—?

Smirnov: Who's raising his voice now? just because I call a spade a spade. Because I shoot straight from the shoulder. Well, don't shout at me, I'm not your steward.

Mrs. Popov: I'm not shouting, you're shouting! Oh, leave me alone!

Smirnov: Pay me the money, and I will.

Mrs. Popov: You'll get no money out of me!

Smirnov: Oh, so that's it!

Mrs. Popov: Not a ruble, not a kopeck. Get out! Leave me alone!

Smirnov: Not being your husband, I must ask you not to make scenes with me. *(He sits.)* I don't like scenes.

Mrs. Popov: *(choking with rage).* You're sitting down?

Smirnov: Correct, I'm sitting down.

Mrs. Popov: I asked you to leave!

Smirnov: Then give me the money. *(Aside.)* Oh, what a rage I'm in, what a rage!

Mrs. Popov: The impudence of the man! I won't talk to you a moment longer. Get out. *(Pause.)* Are you going?

Smirnov: No.

Mrs. Popov: No?!

Smirnov: No.

Mrs. Popov: On your head be it. Luka!

(Enter Luka.)

Show the gentleman out, Luka.

Luka: *(approaching).* I'm afraid, sir, I'll have to ask you, um, to leave, sir, now, um—

Smirnov: *(jumping up).* Shut your mouth, you old idiot! Who do you think you're talking to? I'll make mincemeat of you.

Luka: *(clutching his heart).* Mercy on us! Holy saints above! *(He falls into an armchair.)* I'm taken sick! I can't breathe!!

Mrs. Popov: Then where's Dasha? Dasha! Dasha! Come here at once! *(She rings.)*

Luka: They gone picking berries, ma'am, I'm alone here—Water, water, I'm taken sick!

Mrs. Popov: *(to Smirnov).* Get out, you!

Smirnov: Can't you even be polite with me, Mrs. Popov?

Mrs. Popov: *(clenching her fists and stamping her feet).* With you? You're a wild animal, you were never house-broken!

Smirnov: What? What did you say?

Mrs. Popov: I said you were a wild animal, you were never house-broken.

Smirnov: *(advancing upon her).* And what right do you have to talk to me like that?

Mrs. Popov: Like what?

Smirnov: You have insulted me, madam.

Mrs. Popov: What of it? Do you think I'm scared of you?

Smirnov: So you think you can get away with it because you're a woman. A creature of poetry and romance, huh? Well, it doesn't go down with me. I hereby challenge you to a duel.

Luka: Mercy on us! Holy saints alive! Water!

Smirnov: I propose we shoot it out.

Mrs. Popov: Trying to scare me again? Just because you have big fists and a voice like a bull? You're a brute.

Smirnov: No one insults Gregory S. Smirnov with impunity! And I don't care if you are a female.

Mrs. Popov: *(trying to outshout him).* Brute, brute, brute!

Smirnov: The sexes are equal, are they? Fine: then it's just prejudice to expect men alone to pay for insults. I hereby challenge—

Mrs. Popov: *(screaming).* All right! You want to shoot it out? All right! Let's shoot it out!

Smirnov: And let it be here and now!

Mrs. Popov: Here and now! All right! I'll have Popov's pistols here in one minute! *(Walks away, then turns.)* Putting one of Popov's bullets through your silly head will be a pleasure! Au revoir. *(Exit.)*

Smirnov: I'll bring her down like a duck, a sitting duck. I'm not one of your little poets, I'm no little subaltern with his first moustache. No, sir, there's no weaker sex where I'm concerned!

Luka: Sir! Master! *(He goes down on his knees.)* Take pity on a poor old man, and do me a favour: go away. It was bad enough before, you nearly scared me to death. But a duel—!

Smirnov: *(ignoring him).* A duel! That's equality of the sexes for you! That's women's emancipation! Just as a matter of principle I'll bring her down like a duck. But what a woman! 'Putting one of Popov's bullets through your silly head . . .' Her cheeks were flushed, her eyes were gleaming! And, by God, she's accepted the challenge! I never knew a woman like this before!

Luka: Sir! Master! Please go away! I'll always pray for you!

Smirnov: *(again ignoring him)*. What a woman! Phew!! She's no sour puss, she's no cry baby. She's fire and brimstone. She's a human cannon ball. What a shame I have to kill her!

Luka: *(weeping)*. Please, kind sir, please, go away!

Smirnov: *(as before)*. I like her, isn't that funny? With those dimples and all? I like her. I'm even prepared to consider letting her off that debt. And where's my rage? It's gone. I never knew a woman like this before.

(Enter Mrs. Popov —with pistols.)

Mrs. Popov: *(boldly)*. Pistols, Mr. Smirnov! *(Matter of fact.)* But before we start, you'd better show me how it's done, I'm not too familiar with these things. In fact I never gave a pistol a second look.

Luka: Lord, have mercy on us, I must go hunt up the gardener and the coachman. Why has this catastrophe fallen upon us, O Lord? *(Exit.)*

Smirnov: *(examining the pistols)*. Well, it's like this. There are several makes: one is the Mortimer, with capsules, especially constructed for dueling. What you have here are Smith and Wesson triple-action revolvers, with extractor, first-rate job, worth ninety rubles at the very least. You hold it this way. *(Aside.)* My God, what eyes she has! They're setting me on fire.

Mrs. Popov: This way?

Smirnov: Yes, that's right. You cock the trigger, take aim like this, head up, and out like this. Then you just press with this finger here, and it's all over. The main thing is, keep cool, take slow aim, and don't let your arm jump.

Mrs. Popov: I see. And if it's inconvenient to do the job here, we can go out in the garden.

Smirnov: Very good. Of course, I should warn you: I'll be firing in the air.

Mrs. Popov: What? This is the end. Why?

Smirnov: Oh, well—because—for private reasons.

Mrs. Popov: Scared, huh? *(She laughs heartily.)* Now don't you try to get out of it, Mr. Smirnov. My blood is up. I won't be happy till I've drilled a hole through that skull of yours. Follow me. What's the matter? Scared?

Smirnov: That's right. I'm scared.

Mrs. Popov: Oh, come on, what's the matter with you?

Smirnov: Well, um, Mrs. Popov, I, um, I like you.

Mrs. Popov: *(laughing bitterly).* Good God! He likes me, does he? The gall of the man. *(Showing him the door.)* You may leave, Mr. Smirnov.

Smirnov: *(quietly puts the gun down, takes his hat, and walks to the door. Then he stops and the pair look at each other without a word. Then, approaching gingerly).* Listen, Mrs. Popov. Are you still mad at me? I'm in the devil of a temper myself, of course. But then, you see—what I mean is—it's this way—the fact is— *(Roaring.)* Well, is it my fault, damn it, if I like you? *(Clutches the back of a chair. It breaks.)* Christ, what fragile furniture you have here. I like you. Know what I mean? I could fall in love with you.

Mrs. Popov: I hate you. Get out!

Smirnov: What a woman! I never saw, anything like it. Oh, I'm lost, I'm done for, I'm a mouse in a trap.

Mrs. Popov: Leave this house, or I shoot!

Smirnov: Shoot away! What bliss to die of a shot that was fired by that little velvet hand! To die gazing into those enchanting eyes. I'm out of my mind. I know: you must decide at once. Think for one second, then decide. Because if I leave now, I'll never be back. Decide! I'm a pretty decent chap. Landed gentleman, I should say. Ten thousand a year. Good stable. Throw a kopeck up in the air, and I'll put a bullet through it. Will you marry me?

Mrs. Popov: *(indignant, brandishing the gun).* We'll shoot it out! Get going! Take your pistol!

Smirnov: I'm out of my mind. I don't understand anything any more. *(Shouting.)* You there! That vodka!

Mrs. Popov: No excuses! No delays! We'll shoot it out!

Smirnov: I'm out of my mind. I'm falling in love. I have fallen in love. *(He takes her hand vigorously; she squeals.)* I love you. *(He goes down on his knees.)* I love you as I've never loved before. I jilted twelve, and was jilted by nine others. But I didn't love a one of them as I love you. I'm full of tender emotion. I'm melting like butter. I'm weak as water. I'm on my knees like a fool, and I offer you my hand. It's a shame, it's a disgrace. I haven't been in love in five years. I took a vow against it. And now, all of a sudden, to be swept off my feet, it's a scandal. I offer you my hand, dear lady. Will you or won't you? You won't? Then don't! *(He rises and walks toward the door.)*

Mrs. Popov: I didn't say anything.

Smirnov: *(stopping).* What?

Mrs. Popov: Oh, nothing, you can go. Well, no, just a minute. No, you can go. Go! I detest you! But, just a moment. Oh, if you knew how furious I feel! *(Throws the gun on the table.)*

My fingers have gone to sleep holding that horrid thing. (*She is tearing her handkerchief to shreds.*) And what are you standing around for? Get out of here!

Smirnov: Goodbye.

Mrs. Popov: Go, go, go! (*Shouting.*) Where are you going? Wait a minute! No, no, it's all right, just go. I'm fighting mad. Don't come near me, don't come near me!

Smirnov: (*who is coming near her*). I'm pretty disgusted with myself— falling in love like a kid, going down on my knees like some moongazing whippersnapper, the very thought gives me gooseflesh. (*Rudely.*) I love you. But it doesn't make sense. Tomorrow, I have to pay that interest, and we've already started mowing. (*He puts his arm about her waist.*) I shall never forgive myself for this.

Mrs. Popov: Take your hands off me, I hate you! Let's shoot it out!

(*A long kiss. Enter Luka with an axe, the gardener with a rake, the coachman with a pitchfork, hired men with sticks.*)

Luka: (*seeing the kiss*). Mercy on us! Holy saints above!

Mrs. Popov: (*dropping her eyes*). Luka, tell them in the stable that Toby is *not* to have any oats today.

SUSAN GLASPELL (1882-1948)

Susan Glaspell, an American writer of drama and fiction, was founder of the Provincetown Players. Her play Alison's House, based on the life of Emily Dickinson, won the Pulitzer prize in 1930. Trifles is the dramatic version of her short story "A Jury of Her Peers."

TRIFLES

Characters

SHERIFF
COUNTY ATTORNEY
MR. HALE
MRS. HALE
MRS. PETERS

Scene

The kitchen in the now abandoned farm-house of John Wright, a gloomy kitchen, and left without having been put in order--unwashed pans under the sink, a loaf of bread outside the bread-box, a dish-towel on the table--other signs of incompleted work. At the rear the outer door opens and the Sheriff comes in followed by the County Attorney and Hale. The Sheriff and Hale are men in middle life, the County Attorney is a young man; all are much bundled up and go at once to the stove. They are followed by the two women--the Sheriff's wife first, she is a slight wiry woman, with a thin nervous face. Mrs. Hale is larger *and would ordinarily be called more comfortable looking, but she is disturbed now and looks fearfully about as she enters. The women have come in slowly, and stand close together near the door.*

County Attorney: *(rubbing his hands)* This feels good. Come up to the fire, ladies.

Mrs. Peters: *(after taking a step forward)* I'm not—cold.

Sheriff: *(unbuttoning his overcoat and stepping away from the stove as if to mark the beginning of official business)* Now, Mr. Hale, before we move things about, you explain to Mr. Henderson just what you saw when you came here yesterday morning.

County Attorney: By the way, has anything been moved? Are things just as you left them yesterday?

Sheriff: *(looking about)* It's just the same. When it dropped below zero last night I thought I'd better send Frank out this morning to make a fire for us—no use getting pneumonia with a big case on, but I told him not to touch anything except the stove—and you know Frank.

County Attorney: Somebody should have been left here yesterday.

Sheriff: Oh—yesterday. When I had to send Frank to Morris Center for that man who went crazy—I want you to know I had my hands full yesterday. I knew you could get back from Omaha by today and as long as I went over everything here myself—

County Attorney: Well, Mr. Hale, tell just what happened when you came here yesterday morning.

Hale: Harry and I had started to town with a load of potatoes. We came along the road from my place and as I got here I said, "I'm going to see if I can't get John Wright to go in with me on a party telephone." I spoke to Wright about it once before and he put me off, saying folks talked too much anyway, and all he asked was peace and quiet—I guess you know about how much he talked himself; but I thought maybe if I went to the house and talked about it before his wife, though I said to Harry that I didn't know as what his wife wanted made much difference to John—

County Attorney: Let's talk about that later, Mr. Hale. I do want to talk about that, but tell now just what happened when you got to the house.

Hale: I didn't hear or see anything; I knocked at the door, and still it was all quiet inside. I knew they must be up, it was past eight o'clock. So I knocked again, and I thought I heard somebody say "Come in." I wasn't sure, I'm not sure yet, but I opened the door—this door *(indicating the door by which the two women are still standing)* and there in that rocker—*(pointing to it)* sat Mrs. Wright.

(They all look at the rocker.)

County Attorney: What—was she doing?

Hale: She was rockin' back and forth. She had her apron in her hand and was kind of—pleating it.

County Attorney: And how did she—look?

Hale: Well, she looked queer.

County Attorney: How do you mean—queer?

Hale: Well, as if she didn't know what she was going to do next. And kind of done up.

County Attorney: How did she seem to feel about your coming?

Hale: Why, I don't think she minded—one way or other. She didn't pay much attention. I said, "How do, Mrs. Wright, it's cold, ain't it?" And she said "Is it?" —and went on kind of pleating at her apron. Well, I was surprised; she didn't ask me to come up to the stove, or to set down, but just sat there, not even looking at me, so I said, "I want to see John." And then she—laughed. I guess you would call it a laugh. I thought of Harry and the team outside, so I said a little sharp: "Can't I see John?" "No," she says, kind o' dull like. "Ain't he home?" says I. "Yes," says she, "he's home." "Then why can't I see him?" I asked her, out of patience. "'Cause he's dead," says she. "Dead?" says I. She just nodded her head, not getting a bit excited, but rockin' back and forth. "Why—where is he?" says I, not knowing what to say. She just pointed upstairs—like that (*himself pointing to the room above*). I got up, with the idea of going up there. I walked from there to here—then I says, "Why, what did he die of?" "He died of a rope around his neck," says she, and just went on pleatin' at her apron. Well, I went out and called Harry. I thought I might—need help. We went upstairs and there he was lyin'—

County Attorney: I think I'd rather have you go into that upstairs, where you can point it all out. Just go on now with the rest of the story.

Hale: Well, my first thought was to get that rope off. It looked . . . (*Stops, his face twitches.*) . . . but Harry, he went up to him, and he said, "No, he's dead all right, and we'd better not touch anything." So we went back down stairs. She was still sitting that same way. "Has anybody been notified?" I asked. "No," says she, unconcerned. "Who did this, Mrs. Wright?" said Harry. He said it business-like —and she stopped pleatin' of her apron. "I don't know," she says. "You don't know?" says Harry. "No," says she. "Weren't you sleepin' in the bed with him?" says Harry. "Yes," says she, "but I was on the inside." "Somebody slipped a rope round his neck and strangled him and you didn't wake up?" says Harry. "I didn't wake up," she said after him. We must'a looked as if we didn't see how that could be, for after a minute she said, "I sleep sound." Harry was going to ask her more questions, but I said maybe we ought to let her tell her story first to the coroner, or the sheriff, so Harry went fast as he could to Rivers' place, where there's a telephone.

County Attorney: And what did Mrs. Wright do when she knew that you had gone for the coroner?

Hale: She moved from that chair to this over here . . . (*Pointing to a small chair in the corner.*) . . . and just sat there with her hands held together and looking down. I got a feeling that I ought to make some conversation, so I said I had come in to see if John wanted to put in a telephone, and at that she started to laugh, and then she stopped and looked at me—scared. (*The County Attorney, who has had his notebook out, makes a note.*) I dunno, maybe it wasn't scared. I wouldn't like to say it was. Soon Harry got back, and then Dr. Lloyd came, and you, Mr. Peters, and so I guess that's all I know that you don't.

County Attorney: (*looking around*) I guess we'll go upstairs first—and then out to the barn and around there. (*To the Sheriff.*) You're convinced that there was nothing important here—nothing that would point to any motive?

Sheriff: Nothing here but kitchen things. (*The County Attorney, after again looking around the kitchen, opens the door of a cupboard closet. He gets up on a chair and looks on a shelf. Pulls his hand away, sticky.*)

County Attorney: Here's a nice mess.

(*The women draw nearer.*)

Mrs. Peters: (*to the other woman*) Oh, her fruit; it did freeze. (*To the Lawyer.*) She worried about that when it turned so cold. She said the fire'd go out and her jars would break.

Sheriff: Well, can you beat the women! Held for murder and worryin' about her preserves.

County Attorney: I guess before we're through she may have something more serious than preserves to worry about.

Hale: Well, women are used to worrying over trifles.

(*The two women move a little closer together.*)

County Attorney: (*with the gallantry of a young politician*) And yet, for all their worries, what would we do without the ladies? (*The women do not unbend. He goes to the sink, takes a dipperful of water from the pail and, pouring it into a basin, washes his hands. Starts to wipe them on the roller-towel, turns it for a cleaner place.*) Dirty towels! (*Kicks his foot against the pans under the sink.*) Not much of a housekeeper, would you say, ladies?

Mrs. Hale: (*stiffly*) There's a great deal of work to be done on a farm.

County Attorney: To be sure. And yet . . . (*With a little bow to her.*) . . . I know there are some Dickson county farmhouses which do not have such roller towels.

(*He gives it a pull to expose its full length again.*)

Mrs. Hale: Those towels get dirty awful quick. Men's hands aren't always as clean as they might be.

County Attorney: Ah, loyal to your sex, I see. But you and Mrs. Wright were neighbors. I suppose you were friends, too.

Mrs. Hale: *(shaking her head)* I've not seen much of her of late years. I've not been in this house—it's more than a year.

County Attorney: And why was that? You didn't like her?

Mrs. Hale: I like her all well enough. Farmers' wives have their hands full, Mr. Henderson. And then—

County Attorney: Yes—?

Mrs. Hale: *(looking about)* It never seemed a very cheerful place.

County Attorney: No—it's not cheerful. I shouldn't say she had the home-making instinct.

Mrs. Hale: Well, I don't know as Wright had, either.

County Attorney: You mean that they didn't get on very well?

Mrs. Hale: No, I don't mean anything. But I don't think a place'd be any more cheerful for John Wright's being in it.

County Attorney: I'd like to talk more of that a little later. I want to get the lay of things upstairs now.

(He goes to the left, where three steps lead to a stair door.)

Sheriff: I suppose anything Mrs. Peters does'll be all right. She was to take in some clothes for her, you know, and a few little things. We left in such a hurry yesterday.

County Attorney: Yes, but I would like to see what you take, Mrs. Peters, and keep an eye out for anything that might be of use to us.

Mrs. Peters: Yes, Mr. Henderson.

(The women listen to the men's steps on the stairs, then look about the kitchen.)

Mrs. Hale: I'd hate to have men coming into my kitchen, snooping around and criticizing.

(She arranges the pans under sink which the Lawyer had shoved out of place.)

Mrs. Peters: Of course it's no more than their duty.

Mrs. Hale: Duty's all right, but I guess that deputy sheriff that came out to make the fire might have got a little of his own. (*Gives the roller towel a pull.*) Wish I'd thought of that sooner. Seems mean to talk about her for not having things slicked up when she had to come away in such a hurry.

Mrs. Peters: (*who has gone to a small table in the left rear corner of the room, and lifted one end of a towel that covers a pan*) She had bread set.

(*Stands still.*)

Mrs. Hale: (*eyes fixed on a loaf of bread beside the bread-box, which is on a low shelf at the other side of the room. Moves slowly toward it.*) She was going to put this in there. (*Picks up loaf, then abruptly drops it. In a manner of returning to familiar things.*) It's a shame about her fruit. I wonder if it's all gone. (*Gets up on the chair and looks.*) I think there's some here that's all right, Mrs. Peters. Yes—here; (*Holding it toward the window.*) this is cherries, too. (*Looking again.*) I declare I believe that's the only one. (*Gets down, bottle in her hand. Goes to the sink and wipes it off on the outside.*) She'll feel awful bad after all her hard work in the hot weather. I remember the afternoon I put up my cherries last summer.

(*She puts the bottle on the big kitchen table, center of the room, front table. With a sigh, is about to sit down in the rocking-chair. Before she is seated realizes what chair it is; with a slow look at it, steps back. The chair which she has touched rocks back and forth.*)

Mrs. Peters: Well, I must get those things from the front room closet. (*She goes to the door at the right, but after looking into the other room, steps back.*) You coming with me, Mrs. Hale? You could help me carry them.

(*They go in the other room; reappear Mrs. Peters carrying a dress and skirt, Mrs. Hale following with a pair of shoes.*)

Mrs. Peters: My, it's cold in there.

(*She puts the cloth on the big table, and hurries to the stove.*)

Mrs. Hale: Wright was close. I think maybe that's why she kept so much to herself. She didn't even belong to the Ladies' Aid. I suppose she felt she couldn't do her part, and then you don't enjoy things when you feel shabby. She used to wear pretty clothes and be lively, when she was Minnie Foster, one of the town girls singing in the choir. But that—oh, that was thirty years ago. This all you was to take in?

Mrs. Peters: She said she wanted an apron. Funny thing to want, for there isn't much to get you dirty in jail, goodness knows. But I suppose just to make her feel more natural. She said they was in the top drawer in this cupboard. Yes, here. And then her little shawl that always hung behind the door. (*Opens stair door and looks.*) Yes, here it is.

(*Quickly shuts door leading upstairs.*)

Mrs. Hale: (*abruptly moving toward her*) Mrs. Peters?

Mrs. Peters: Yes, Mrs. Hale?

Mrs. Hale: Do you think she did it?

Mrs. Peters: *(in a frightened voice)* Oh, I don't know.

Mrs. Hale: Well, I don't think she did. Asking for an apron and her little shawl. Worrying about her fruit.

Mrs. Peters: *(starts to speak, glances up, where footsteps are heard in the room above. In a low voice)* Mr. Peters says it looks bad for her. Mr. Henderson is awful sarcastic in a speech and he'll make fun of her sayin' she didn't wake up.

Mrs. Hale: Well, I guess John Wright didn't wake when they was slipping that rope under his neck.

Mrs. Peters: No, it's strange. It must have been done awful crafty and still. They say it was such a—funny way to kill a man, rigging it all up like that.

Mrs. Hale: That's just what Mr. Hale said. There was a gun in the house. He says that's what he can't understand.

Mrs. Peters: Mr. Henderson said coming out that what was needed for the case was a motive; something to show anger, or—sudden feeling.

Mrs. Hale: *(who is standing by the table)* Well, I don't see any signs of anger around here. *(She puts her hand on the dish towel which lies on the table, stands looking down at table, one half of which is clean, the other half messy.)* It's wiped here. *(Makes a move as if to finish work, then turns and looks at loaf of bread outside the bread-box. Drops towel. In that voice of coming back to familiar things.)* Wonder how they are finding things upstairs? I hope she had it a little more red-up up there. You know, it seems kind of sneaking. Locking her up in town and then coming out here and trying to get her own house to turn against her!

Mrs. Peters: But, Mrs. Hale, the law is the law.

Mrs. Hale: I s'pose 'tis. *(Unbuttoning her coat.)* Better loosen up your things, Mrs. Peters. You won't feel them when you go out.

(Mrs. Peters takes off her fur tippet, goes to hang it on hook at back of room, stands looking at the under part of the small corner table.)

Mrs. Peters: She was piecing a quilt. *(She brings the large sewing basket and they look at the bright pieces.)*

Mrs. Hale: It's log cabin pattern. Pretty, isn't it? I wonder if she was goin' to quilt it or just knot it?

(Footsteps have been heard coming down the stairs. The Sheriff enters, followed by Hale and the County Attorney.)

Sheriff: They wonder if she was going to quilt it or just knot it.

(The men laugh, the women look abashed.)

County Attorney: *(rubbing his hands over the stove)* Frank's fire didn't do much up there, did it? Well, let's go out to the barn and get that cleared up.

(The men go outside.)

Mrs. Hale: *(resentfully)* I don't know as there's anything go strange, our takin' up our time with little things while we're waiting for them to get the evidence. *(She sits down at the big table smoothing out a block with decision.)* I don't see as it's anything to laugh about.

Mrs. Peters: *(apologetically)* Of course they've got awful important things on their minds.

(Pulls up a chair and joins Mrs. Hale at the table.)

Mrs. Hale: *(examining another block)* Mrs. Peters, look at this one. Here, this is the one she was working on, and look at the sewing! All the rest of it has been so nice and even. And look at this! It's all over the place! Why, it looks as if she didn't know what she was about!

(After she has said this they look at each other, then start to glance back at the door. After an instant Mrs. Hale has pulled at a knot and ripped the sewing.)

Mrs. Peters: Oh, what are you doing, Mrs. Hale?

Mrs. Hale: *(mildly)* Just pulling out a stitch or two that's not sewed very good. *(Threading a needle.)* Bad sewing always made me fidgety.

Mrs. Peters: *(nervously)* I don't think we ought to touch things.

Mrs. Hale: I'll just finish up this end. *(Suddenly stopping and leaning forward.)* Mrs. Peters?

Mrs. Peters: Yes, Mrs. Hale?

Mrs. Hale: What do you suppose she was so nervous about?

Mrs. Peters: Oh—I don't know. I don't know as she was nervous. I sometimes sew awful queer when I'm just tired. *(Mrs. Hale starts to say something, looks at Mrs. Peters, then goes on sewing.)* Well, I must get these things wrapped up. They may be through sooner than we think. *(Putting apron and other things together.)* I wonder where I can find a piece of paper, and string.

Mrs. Hale: In that cupboard, maybe.

Mrs. Peters: *(looking in cupboard)* Why, here's a bird-cage. *(Holds it up.)* Did she have a bird, Mrs. Hale?

Mrs. Hale:	Why, I don't know whether she did or not—I've not been here for so long. There was a man around last year selling canaries cheap, but I don't know as she took one; maybe she did. She used to sing real pretty herself.
Mrs. Peters:	*(glancing around)* Seems funny to think of a bird here. But she must have had one, or why should she have a cage? I wonder what happened to it?
Mrs. Hale:	I s'pose maybe the cat got it.
Mrs. Peters:	No, she didn't have a cat. She's got that feeling some people have about cats—being afraid of them. My cat got in her room and she was real upset and asked me to take it out.
Mrs. Hale:	My sister Bessie was like that. Queer, ain't it?
Mrs. Peters:	*(examining the cage)* Why, took at this door. It's broke. One hinge is pulled apart.
Mrs. Hale:	*(looking too)* Looks as if some one must have been rough with it.
Mrs. Peters:	Why, yes.

(She brings the cage forward and puts it on the table.)

Mrs. Hale:	I wish if they're going to find any evidence they'd be about it. I don't like this place.
Mrs. Peters:	But I'm awful glad you came with me, Mrs. Hale. It would be lonesome for me sitting here alone.
Mrs. Hale:	It would, wouldn't it? *(Dropping her sewing.)* But I tell you what I do wish, Mrs. Peters. I wish I had come over some times when *she* was here. I—*(Looking around the room)*—wish I had.
Mrs. Peters:	But of course you were awful busy, Mrs. Hale—your house and your children.
Mrs. Hale:	I could've come. I stayed away because it weren't cheerful—and that's why I ought to have come. I—I've never liked this place. Maybe because it's down in a hollow and you don't see the road. I dunno what it is, but it's a lonesome place and always was. I wish I had come over to see Minnie Foster sometimes. I can see now—

(Shakes her head.)

Mrs. Peters:	Well, you mustn't reproach yourself, Mrs. Hale. Somehow we just don't see how it is with other folks until—something comes up.
Mrs. Hale:	Not having children makes less work—but it makes a quiet house, and Wright out to work all day, and no company when he did come in. Did you know John Wright, Mrs. Peters?

Mrs. Peters: Not to know him; I've seen him in town. They say he was a good man.

Mrs. Hale: Yes—good; he didn't drink, and kept his word as well as most, I guess, and paid his debts. But he was a hard man, Mrs. Peters. Just to pass the time of day with him. *(Shivers.)* Like a raw wind that gets to the bone. *(Pauses, her eye falling on the cage.)* I should think she would 'a wanted a bird. But what do you suppose went with it?

Mrs. Peters: I don't know, unless it got sick and died.

(She reached over and swings the broken door, swings it again, both women watch it.)

Mrs. Hale: You weren't raised round here, were you? *(Mrs. Peters shakes her head.)* You didn't know—her?

Mrs. Peters: Not till they brought her yesterday.

Mrs. Hale: She—come to think of it, she was kind of like a bird herself—real sweet and pretty, but kind of timid and—fluttery. How—she—did—change. *(Silence; then as if struck by a happy thought and relieved to get back to everyday things.)* Tell you what, Mrs. Peters, why don't you take the quilt in with you? It might take up her mind.

Mrs. Peters: Why, I think that's a real nice idea, Mrs. Hale. There couldn't possibly be any objection to it, could there? Now, just what would I take? I wonder if her patches are in here—and her things.

(They look in the sewing basket.)

Mrs. Hale: Here's some red. I expect this has got sewing things in it. (Brings out a fancy box.) What a pretty box. Looks like something somebody would give you. Maybe her scissors are in here. *(Opens box. Suddenly puts her hand to her nose.)* Why—*(Mrs. Peters bends nearer, then turns her face away.)* There's something wrapped up in this piece of silk.

Mrs. Peters: Why, this isn't her scissors.

Mrs. Hale: *(lifting the silk)* Oh, Mrs. Peters—it's—

(Mrs. Peters bends closer.)

Mrs. Peters: It's the bird.

Mrs. Hale: *(jumping up)* But, Mrs. Peters—look at it. Its neck! Look at its neck! It's all—other side to.

Mrs. Peters: Somebody—wrung—its neck.

(Their eyes meet. A took of growing comprehension, of horror. Steps are heard outside. Mrs. Hale slips box under quilt pieces, and sinks into her chair. Enter Sheriff and County Attorney. Mrs. Peters rises.)

County Attorney: *(as one turning from serious things to little pleasantries)* Well, ladies, have you decided whether she was going to quilt it or knot it?

Mrs. Peters: We think she was going to—knot it.

County Attorney: Well, that's interesting, I'm sure. *(Seeing the bird-cage.)* Has the bird flown?

Mrs. Hale: *(putting more quilt pieces over the box)* We think the cat got it.

County Attorney: *(preoccupied)* Is there a cat?

(Mrs. Hale glances in a quick covert way at Mrs. Peters.)

Mrs. Peters: Well, not now. They're superstitious, you know. *(They leave.)*

County Attorney: *(to Sheriff Peters, continuing an interrupted conversation)* No sign at all of any one having come from the outside. Their own rope. Now let's go up again and go over it piece by piece. *(They start upstairs.)* It would have to have been some one who knew just the—

(Mrs. Peters sits down. The two women sit there not looking at one another, but as if peering into something and at the same time holding back. When they talk now it if in the manner of feeling their way over strange ground, as if afraid of what they are saying, but as if they can not help saying it.)

Mrs. Hale: She liked the bird. She was going to bury it in that pretty box.

Mrs. Peters: *(in a whisper)* When I was a girl—my kitten—there was a boy took a hatchet, and before my eyes—and before I could get there—*(Covers her face an instant.)* If they hadn't held me back I would have—*(Catches herself, looks upstairs where steps are heard, falters weakly)*—hurt him.

Mrs. Hale: *(with a slow look around her)* I wonder how it would seem never to have had any children around. *(Pause.)* No, Wright wouldn't like the bird—a thing that sang. She used to sing. He killed that, too.

Mrs. Peters: *(moving uneasily)* We don't know who killed the bird.

Mrs. Hale: I knew John Wright.

Mrs. Peters: It was an awful thing was done in this house that night, Mrs. Hale. Killing a man while he slept, slipping a rope around his neck that choked the life out of him.

Mrs. Hale: His neck. Choked the life out of him.

(Her hand goes out and rests on the bird-cage.)

Mrs. Peters: *(with rising voice)* We don't know who killed him. We don't know.

Mrs. Hale: *(her own feeling not interrupted)* If there'd been years and years of nothing, then a bird to sing to you, it would be awful—still, after the bird was still.

Mrs. Peters: *(something within her speaking)* I know what stillness is. When we homesteaded in Dakota, and my first baby died—after he was two years old, and me with no other then—

Mrs. Hale: *(moving)* How soon do you suppose they'll be through, looking for the evidence?

Mrs. Peters: I know what stillness is. *(Pulling herself back.)* The law has got to punish crime, Mrs. Hale.

Mrs. Hale: *(not as if answering that)* I wish you'd seen Minnie Foster when she wore a white dress with blue ribbons and stood up there in the choir and sang. *(A look around the room.)* Oh, I wish I'd come over here once in a while. That was a crime! That was a crime! Who's going to punish that?

Mrs. Peters: *(looking upstairs)* We mustn't—take on.

Mrs. Hale: I might have known she needed help! I know how things can be— for women. I tell you, it's queer, Mrs. Peters. We live close together and we live far apart. We all go through the same things—it's all just a different kind of the same thing. *(Brushes her eyes, noticing the bottle of fruit, reaches out for it.)* If I was you I wouldn't tell her her fruit was gone. Tell her it ain't. Tell her it's all right. Take this in to prove it to her. She—she may never know whether it was broke or not.

Mrs. Peters: *(takes the bottle, looks about for something to wrap it in; takes petticoat from the clothes brought from the other room, very nervously begins winding this around the bottle. In a false voice)* My, it's a good thing the men couldn't hear us. Wouldn't they just laugh. Getting all stirred up over a little thing like a—dead canary. As if that could have anything to do with—with—wouldn't they laugh!

(The men are heard coming down stairs.)

Mrs. Hale: *(under her breath)* Maybe they would—maybe they wouldn't.

County Attorney: No, Peters, it's all perfectly clear except a reason for doing it. But you know juries when it comes to women. If there was some definite thing. Something to show—something to make a story about—a thing that would connect up with this strange way of doing it.

(The women's eyes meet for an instant. Enter Hale from outer door.)

Hale: Well I've got the team around. Pretty cold out there.

County Attorney: I'm going to stay here a while by myself. *(To the Sheriff.)* You can send Frank out for me, can't you? I want to go over everything. I'm not satisfied that we can't do better.

Sheriff: Do you want to see what Mrs. Peters is going to take in? *(The Lawyer goes so the table, picks up the apron, laughs.)*

County Attorney: Oh, I guess they're not very dangerous things the ladies have picked out. *(Moves after things about, disturbing the quilt pieces which cover the box. Steps back.)* No, Mrs. Peters doesn't need supervising. For that matter, a sheriff's wife is married to the law. Ever think of it that way, Mrs. Peters?

Mrs. Peters: Not—just that way.

Sheriff: *(chuckling)* Married to the law. *(Moves toward the other room.)* I just want you to come in here a minute, George. We ought to take a look at these windows.

County Attorney: *(scoffingly)* Oh, windows!

Sheriff: We'll be right out, Mr. Hale.

(Hale goes outside. The Sheriff follows the County Attorney into the other room. Then Mrs. Hale rises, hands tight together, looking intensely at Mrs. Peters, whose eyes makes a slow turn, finally meeting Mrs. Hale's. A moment Mrs. Hale holds her, then her own eyes point the way to where the box is concealed. Suddenly Mrs. Peters throws back quilt pieces and tries to put the box in the bag she is wearing. It is too big. She opens box, starts to take bird out, cannot touch it, goes to pieces, stands there helpless. Sound of a knob turning in the other room, Mrs. Hale snatches the box and puts it in the pocket of her big coat. Enter County Attorney: and Sheriff.)

County Attorney: *(facetiously)* Well, Henry, at least we found out that she was not going to quilt it. She was going to—what is it you call it, ladies?

Mrs. Hale: *(her hand against her pocket)* We call it—knot it. Mr. Henderson.

(Curtain)

MYTH AND HISTORY

Woman With Fire, Anonymous
Nineteenth century book illustration.

INTRODUCTION

The study of myth is central to the humanities; it is an opportunity for us to consider the connections between the "Western" humanities tradition and the ideas, beliefs, and behaviors of all human beings.

Myth is a search for truth. It has a psychological and social function, as Joseph Campbell suggests in *The Power of Myth*, that is relevant to modern life. For example, religions are valid myths if they articulate a pattern of meaning and a vision of the essential purpose of our lives. A myth is a guide to the mysterious and the hidden in human existence. It is not empirical truth, but neither is it the opposite. "Empirical truth," in the form of modern science—whether physics, or psychology, or history—is an *element* of myth-making. So, for example, Isaac Newton's powerful 17th century metaphor of the universe as a giant clock, all the parts interrelated, following precise laws of nature, was a powerful myth that shaped science and technology well into the 20th century.

Myth is a quest for eternal truth. Even Existentialists in the act of rejecting myth create their own myth. Their statement, "life is a moment to moment existence," has both a sense of the past and a sense of the future. Certainly Martin Luther King had no hesitation in taking meaning from the past and applying it to the future creating, thereby, a healthy moral tension in the present. King clearly indicates that history (the stories we create about the past) is not meaningless. It has moral influence on our choices and convictions. The study of the past, the study of political values, of the meaning of words like "democracy," "justice," "freedom," in 5th century B. C. Greece, or late 18th century America, or China at the end of the 20th century has a moral significance.

If myth is a search for truth then why do we treat the words "myth" and "history" as opposites? Historians often label another historian's work with which they disagree as a myth, i.e., false. Is it possible that one person's myth is another's history? The word "myth" comes from the Greek, *mythos*, meaning story or legend. The word "history" comes from the Greek, *historia*, a narrative, or the knowledge of a wise man, a sage. The root words are connected and meaningful to us today: one—myth—is a popular, common story (folklore); the other—history—is a formal, learned story. They are both stories.

The story is the thing which is alive and meaningful. It does make a difference that Homer's Ulysses probably never lived while America's Abraham Lincoln clearly did. Lincoln was born in a certain place, at a certain time; he also died in a certain place, on a specific and known day. But myth and history are not opposites, they are complementary struggles by man to create meaning out of life. We have a need, as individuals and as a community, for historical consciousness in order to have a moral perspective. But there is no absolute truth here. We choose what we remember and what we forget, we choose how we tell the story of the past, we choose to emphasize politics, the actions of men, and the rise and fall of "great" nations. We also choose to ignore many aspects of the past. We fail to document that these choices were *made*, that a (perhaps unconscious) decision was made to ignore the presence and influence of a particular woman (Socrates' wife?), or of a particular man (the slave Nat Turner—an American black Moses?), or of a particular belief (is faith in modern science becoming a modern version of medieval religious faith with all the dogma, rigidity, and lack of freedom to question "established" truths?), or of a particular deed (did Abraham Lincoln betray the Constitution in order to "save" it?).

Myth is a hunger and a quest for eternal truth. To pursue that quest, to recognize that hunger is a form of purification; it is our road to "bliss" as Joseph Campbell suggests. The pursuit of a historical consciousness is a quest for specific truths. It is a desire to understand particular patterns of behavior that we can connect to as individuals. The study of history allows us to expose myths which are "false": that is, repressive and psychologically damaging to the human spirit.

The readings that follow Joseph Campbell's (1904-1988) *Power of Myth* all attempt to get the reader to feel the interplay between myth and history and the power of mythic ideas in our lives. They might be categorized as follows: classic myths — *The Odyssey* and Tennyson's poem *Ulysses*; Bible myths — Milton's *Before the Fall*, Chapters 2 and 3 of the *Book of Genesis*, King David's *The Twenty-Third Psalm*; non-Western myths — poems mostly from West Africa (in particular the Yoruba myths of creation: *The Creation of Land* and *The Creation of Man*) as well as the epic poem, *Sundiata*; and finally a number of readings that are part of the "American Myth."

Note the stark contrast between the poems and statements of Red and Black Americans (Chief Seattle, Chief Sitting Bull, King Joseph, the poem *Who Are They?*, Langston Hughes' *The Negro Speaks Rivers* and *Harlem*, and Claude McKay's *America*) and the great public document of American ideals, *The Declaration of Independence*. A small portion of an earlier version of the *Declaration* is provided to remind the reader that the final words were a result of human choices and decisions, not the words of a god. The following four readings may seem out of place. Why return once again to Plato's *Republic* (a part of Book V we titled, *Unless Philosophers Become Kings*)? Why read Aristotle's *Politics* or Machiavelli's *The Morals of the Prince*? What can these past myths tell us about politics today? For both Plato and Aristotle, perhaps Machiavelli, a system of politics was based on the assumption that politics was the highest activity man could be engaged in. Western civilizations built governments and societies on this classical foundation. But do we still share these assumptions about politics, this myth that politics is the most noble of activities? Perhaps we do. After all we still kill heroes like Martin Luther King and Abraham Lincoln. The readings by and about Lincoln certainly have a mythic quality: *The Gettysburg Address* and the *Second Inaugural Address*, Walt Whitman's essay, *Death of Abraham Lincoln* and his poem *When Lilacs Last in the Dooryard Bloomed*. The poem, *Death of a Hero*, suggests that our "best" people— Socrates, Lincoln, King—can only take on mythic significance through death, untimely death. Then they teach us a moral lesson about what it means to be a human being, although the lesson is seen as if through heavily leaded glass. Perhaps, as Nietzsche suggested, we need to be careful about who we make into idols. And here is our final paradox: we search for truth, for beauty, for the Good. But once we seem to have clearly found it, it is neither so clear nor so good. John Keats (1795-1821) in *Ode on a Grecian Urn* reminds us of the limits of reason and the importance of the mysterious in our lives.

Conclusion

Human beings struggle with a tension between form and freedom; between a need for logical order and the inner cry for the freedom to be fantastic and imaginative. We rely on science and technology to make this world useful, to meet our physical needs. But we cannot abandon the tentative, the ambiguous, the mysterious in the journey of life.

For our final readings we return to the novelist Walker Percy (1916-1990), *Bluebirds and Jaybirds*, and we read a short quote from Percy's spiritual and literary mentor, Feodor Dostoyevsky (1821-1881). *Bluebirds and Jaybirds* is a brief excerpt from Percy's novel *The Thanatos Syndrome*. He asks us to consider the conflict between the doers and the dreamers, but warns us that the conflict is better than no conflict, no individual personalities, when the bluebirds and jaybirds "all turned into chickens." Like Dostoyevsky in *Notes from the Underground*, Percy worries about using science and technology to "reform" man.

We have to push along in our journey. Without logic and reason (*logos*) we cannot make sense of what we find along the way; without *mythos*, without a sense of the mysterious, we have no reason to make the journey.

JOSEPH CAMPBELL (1904-1988)

A teacher for over forty years at Sarah Lawrence College, Joseph Campbell wrote 20 books, including A Hero with a Thousand Faces *(1949). He reached millions of people through his TV series "The Power of Myth." Raised a Roman Catholic in New York City, he drifted away from formal religion as he studied Hindu, Maori, Arapaho, and Christian Gods and religious myths. He argued that the most glorious work of man is the inner struggle that results in spiritual rebirth. Our greatest fear, he says, is not that we will live our lives badly, but that we will fail to live at all. Therefore, Campbell says, "follow your bliss."*

THE POWER OF MYTH: MYTH AND THE MODERN WORLD

People say that what we're all seeking is a meaning for life. I don't think that's what we're really seeking. I think that what we're seeking is an experience of being alive, so that our life experiences on the purely physical plane will have resonances within our own innermost being and reality, so that we actually feel the rapture of being alive.

Moyers: Why myths? Why should we care about myths? What do they have to do with my life?

Campbell: My first response would be, "Go on, live your life, it's a good life—you don't need mythology." I don't believe in being interested in a subject just because it's said to be important. I believe in being caught by it somehow or other. But you may find that, with a proper introduction, mythology will catch you. And so, what can it do for you if it does catch you?

One of our problems today is that we are not well acquainted with the literature of the spirit. We're interested in the news of the day, and the problems of the hour. It used to be that the university campus was a kind of hermetically sealed-off area where the news of the day did not impinge upon your attention to the inner life and to the magnificent human heritage we have in our great tradition—Plato, Confucius, the Buddha, Goethe, and others who speak of the eternal values that have to do with the centering of our lives. When you get to be older, and the concerns of the day have all been attended to, and you turn to the inner life—well, if you don't know where it is or what it is, you'll be sorry.

Greek and Latin and biblical literature used to be part of everyone's education. Now, when these were dropped, a whole tradition of Occidental mythological information was lost. It used to be that these stories were in the minds of people. When the story is in your mind, then you see its relevance to something happening in your own life. It gives you perspective on what's happening to you. With the loss of that, we've really lost something because we don't have a comparable literature to take its place. These bits of information from ancient times, which have to do with the themes that have supported human life, built civilizations, and informed religions over the millennia, have to do with deep inner problems, inner mysteries, inner thresholds of passage, and if you don't know what the guide-signs are along the way, you have to work it out yourself. But once this subject catches you, there is such a feeling, from one or another of these traditions, of information of a deep, rich, life-vivifying sort that you don't want to give it up.

Moyers: So we tell stories to try to come to terms with the world, to harmonize our lives with reality?

Campbell: I think so, yes. Novels—great novels—can be wonderfully instructive. In my twenties and thirties and even on into my forties, James Joyce and Thomas Mann were my teachers. I read everything they wrote. Both were writing in terms of what might be called the mythological traditions. Take, for example, the story of Tonio, in Thomas Mann's *Tonio Kroger*. Tonio's father was a substantial businessman, a major citizen in his hometown. Little Tonio, however, had an artistic temperament, so he moved to Munich and joined a group of literary people who felt themselves above the mere money earners and family men.

So here is Tonio between two poles: his father, who was a good father, responsible and all of that, but who never did the thing he wanted to in all his life—and, on the other hand, the one who leaves his hometown and becomes a critic of that kind of life. But Tonio found that he really loved these hometown people. And although he thought himself a little superior in an intellectual way to them and could describe them with cutting words, his heart was nevertheless with them.

But when he left to live with the bohemians, he found that they were so disdainful of life that he couldn't stay with them, either. So he left them, and wrote a letter back to someone in the group, saying, "I admire those cold, proud beings who adventure upon the paths of great and daemonic beauty and despise 'mankind'; but I do not envy them. For if anything is capable of making a poet of a literary man, it is my hometown love of the human, the living and ordinary. All warmth derives from this love, all kindness and all humor. Indeed, to me it even seems that this must be that love of which it is written that one may 'speak with the tongues of men and of angels,'and yet, lacking love, be 'as sounding brass or a tinkling cymbal.'"

And then he says, "The writer must be true to truth. " And that's a killer, because the only way you can describe a human being truly is by describing his imperfections. The perfect human being is uninteresting—the Buddha who leaves the world, you know. It is the imperfections of life that are lovable. And when the writer sends a dart of the true word, it hurts. But it goes with love. This is what Mann called "erotic irony," the love for that which you are killing with your cruel, analytical word.

Moyers: I cherish that image: my hometown love, the feeling you get for that place, no matter how long you've been away or even if you never return. That was where you first discovered people. But why do you say you love people for their imperfections?

Campbell: Aren't children lovable because they're falling down all the time and have little bodies with the heads too big? Didn't Walt Disney know all about this when he did the seven dwarfs? And these funny little dogs that people have—they're lovable because they're so imperfect.

Moyers: Perfection would be a bore, wouldn't it?

Campbell: It would have to be. It would be inhuman. The umbilical point, the humanity, the thing that makes you human and not supernatural and immortal—that's what's lovable. That is why some people have a very hard time loving God, because there's no imperfection there. You can be in awe, but that would not be real love. It's Christ on the cross that becomes lovable.

Moyers: What do you mean?

Campbell: Suffering. Suffering is imperfection, is it not?

Moyers: The story of human suffering, striving, living—

Campbell: —and youth coming to knowledge of itself, what it has to go through.

Moyers: I came to understand from reading your books—*The Masks of God* or *The Hero with a Thousand Faces*, for example—that what human beings have in common is revealed in myths. Myths are stories of our search through the ages for truth, for meaning, for significance. We all need to tell our story and to understand our story. We all need to understand death and to cope with death, and we all need help in our passages from birth to life and then to death. We need for life to signify, to touch the eternal, to understand the mysterious, to find out who we are.

Campbell: People say that what we're all seeking is a meaning for life. I don't think that's what we're really seeking. I think that what we're seeking is an experience of being alive, so that our life experiences on the purely physical plane will have resonances within our own innermost being and reality, so that we actually feel the rapture of being alive. That's what it's all finally about, and that's what these clues help us to find within ourselves.

Moyers: Myths are clues?

Campbell: Myths are clues to the spiritual potentialities of the human life.

Moyers: What we're capable of knowing and experiencing within?

Campbell: Yes.

Moyers: You changed the definition of a myth from the *search* for meaning to the *experience* of meaning.

Campbell: Experience of *life*. The mind has to do with meaning. What's the meaning of a flower? There's a Zen story about a sermon of the Buddha in which he simply lifted a flower. There was only one man who gave him a sign with his eyes that he understood what was said. Now, the Buddha himself is called "the one thus come." There's no meaning. What's the meaning of the universe? What's the meaning of a flea? It's just there. That's it. And your own meaning is that you're there. We're so engaged in doing things to achieve purposes of outer value that we forget that the inner value, the rapture that is associated with being alive, is what it's all about.

Moyers: How do you get that experience?

Campbell: Read myths. They teach you that you can turn inward, and you begin to get the message of the symbols. Read other people's myths, not those of your own religion, because you tend to interpret your own religion in terms of facts—but if you read the other ones, you begin to get the message. Myth helps you to put your mind in touch with this experience of being alive. It tells you what the experience is. Marriage, for example. What is marriage? The myth tells you what it is. It's the reunion of the separated duad. Originally you were one. You are now two in the world, but the recognition of the spiritual identity is what marriage is. It's different from a love affair. It has nothing to do with that. It's another mythological plane of experience. When people get married because they think it's a long-time love affair, they'll be divorced very soon, because all love affairs end in disappointment. But marriage is recognition of a spiritual identity. If we live a proper life, if our minds are on the right qualities in the person of the opposite sex, we will find our proper male or female counterpart. But if we are distracted by certain sensuous interests, we'll marry the wrong person. By marrying the right person, we reconstruct the image of the incarnate God, and that's what marriage is.

Moyers: The right person? How does one choose the right person?

Campbell: Your heart tells you. It ought to.

Moyers: Your inner being.

Campbell: That's the mystery.

Moyers: You recognize your other self.

Campbell: Well, I don't know, but there's a flash that comes, and something in you knows that this is the one.

Moyers: If marriage is this reunion of the self with the self, with the male or female grounding of ourselves, why is it that marriage is so precarious in our modern society?

Campbell: Because it's not regarded as a marriage. I would say that if the marriage isn't a first priority in your life, you're not married. The marriage means the two that are one, the two become one flesh. If the marriage lasts long enough, and if you are acquiescing constantly to it instead of to individual personal whim, you come to realize that that is true—the two really are one.

Moyers: One not only biologically but spiritually.

Campbell: *Primarily* spiritually. The biological is the distraction which may lead you to the wrong identification.

Moyers: Then the necessary function of marriage, perpetuating ourselves in children, is not the primary one.

Campbell: No, that's really just the elementary aspect of marriage. There are two completely different stages of marriage. First is the youthful marriage following the wonderful impulse that nature has given us in the interplay of the sexes biologically in order to produce children. But there comes a time when the child graduates from the family and the couple is left. I've been amazed at the number of my friends who in their forties or fifties go apart. They have had a perfectly decent life together with the child, but they interpreted their union in terms of their relationship through the child. They did not interpret it in terms of their own personal relationship to each other.

Marriage is a relationship. When you make the sacrifice in marriage, you're sacrificing not to each other but to unity in a relationship. The Chinese image of the Tao, with the dark and light interacting—that's the relationship of yang and yin, male and female, which is what a marriage is. And that's what you have become when you have married. You're no longer this one alone; your identity is in a relationship. Marriage is not a simple love affair, it's an ordeal, and the ordeal is the sacrifice of ego to a relationship in which two have become one.

Moyers: So marriage is utterly incompatible with the idea of doing one's own thing.

Campbell: It's not simply one's own thing, you see. It is, in a sense, doing one's own thing, but the one isn't just you, it's the two together as one. And that's a purely mythological image signifying the sacrifice of the visible entity for a transcendent good. This is something that becomes beautifully realized in the second stage of marriage, what I call the alchemical stage, of the two experiencing that they are one. If they are still living as they were in the primary stage of marriage, they will go apart when their children leave. Daddy will fall in love with some little nubile girl and run off, and Mother will be left with an empty house and heart, and will have to work it out on her own, in her own way.

Moyers: That's because we don't understand the two levels of marriage.

Campbell: You don't make a commitment.

Moyers: We presume to—we make a commitment for better or for worse.

Campbell: That's the remnant of a ritual.

Moyers: And the ritual has lost its force. The ritual that once conveyed an inner reality is now merely form. And that's true in the rituals of society and in the personal rituals of marriage and religion.

Campbell: How many people before marriage receive spiritual instruction as to what the marriage means? You can stand up in front of a judge and in ten minutes get married. The marriage ceremony in India lasts three days. That couple is glued.

Moyers: You're saying that marriage is not just a social arrangement, it's a spiritual exercise.

Campbell: It's primarily a spiritual exercise, and the society is supposed to help us have the realization. Man should not be in the service of society, society should be in the service of man. When man is in the service of society, you have a monster state, and that's what is threatening the world at this minute.

Moyers: What happens when a society no longer embraces a powerful mythology?

Campbell: What we've got on our hands. If you want to find out what it means to have a society without any rituals, read the New York *Times*.

Moyers: And you'd find?

Campbell: The news of the day, including destructive and violent acts by young people who don't know how to behave in a civilized society.

Moyers: Society has provided them no rituals by which they become members of the tribe, of the community. All children need to be twice born, to learn to function rationally in the present world, leaving childhood behind. I think of that passage in the first book of Corinthians: "When I was a child, I spoke as a child, I understood as a child, I thought as a child: but when I became a man, I put away childish things."

Campbell: That's exactly it. That's the significance of the puberty rites. In primal societies, there are teeth knocked out, there are scarifications, there are circumcisions, there are all kinds of things done. So you don't have your little baby body anymore, you're something else entirely.

When I was a kid, we wore short trousers, you know, knee pants. And then there was a great moment when you put on long pants. Boys now don't get that. I see even five-year-olds walking around with long trousers. When are they going to know that they're now men and must put aside childish things?

Moyers: Where do the kids growing up in the city on 125th and Broadway, for example—where do these kids get their myths today?

Campbell: They make them up themselves. This is why we have graffiti all over the city. These kids have their own gangs and their own initiations and their own morality, and they're doing the best they can. But they're dangerous because their own laws are not those of the city. They have not been initiated into our society.

Moyers: Rollo May says there is so much violence in American society today because there are no more great myths to help young men and women relate to the world or to understand that world beyond what is seen.

Campbell: Yes, but another reason for the high level of violence here is that America has no ethos.

Moyers: Explain.

Campbell: In American football, for example, the rules are very strict and complex. If you were to go to England, however, you would find that the rugby rules are not that strict. When I was a student back in the twenties, there were a couple of young men who constituted a marvelous forward-passing pair. They went to Oxford on scholarship and joined the rugby team and one day they introduced the forward pass. And the English players said, "Well, we have no rules for this, so please don't. We don't play that way."

Now, in a culture that has been homogeneous for some time, there are a number of understood, unwritten rules by which people live. There is an ethos there, there is a mode, an understanding that "we don't do it that way."

Moyers: A mythology.

Campbell: An unstated mythology, you might say. This is the way we use a fork and knife, this is the way we deal with people, and so forth. It's not all written down in books. But in America we have people from all kinds of backgrounds, all in a cluster, together, and consequently law has become very important in this country. Lawyers and law are what hold us together. There is no ethos. Do you see what I mean?

Moyers: Yes. It's what De Tocqueville described when he first arrived here a hundred and sixty years ago to discover "a tumult of anarchy."

Campbell: What we have today is a demythologized world. And, as a result, the students I meet are very much interested in mythology because myths bring them messages. Now, I can't tell you what the messages are that the study of mythology is bringing to young people today. I know what it did for me. But it is doing something for them. When I go to lecture at any college, the room is bursting with students who have come to hear what I have to say. The faculty very often assigns me to a room that's a little small—smaller than it should have been because they didn't know how much excitement there was going to be in the student body.

Moyers: Take a guess. What do you think the mythology, the stories they're going to hear from you, do for them?

Campbell: They're stories about the wisdom of life, they really are. What we're learning in our schools is not the wisdom of life. We're learning technologies, we're getting information. There's a curious reluctance on the part of faculties to indicate the life values of their subjects. In our sciences today—and this includes anthropology, linguistics, the study of religions, and so forth—there is a tendency to specialization. And when you know how much a specialist scholar has to know in order to be a competent specialist, you can understand this tendency. To study Buddhism, for instance, you have to be able to handle not only all the European languages in which the discussions of the Oriental come, particularly French, German, English, and Italian, but also Sanskrit, Chinese, Japanese, Tibetan, and several other languages. Now, this is a tremendous task. Such a specialist can't also be wondering about the difference between the Iroquois and Algonquin.

Specialization tends to limit the field of problems that the specialist is concerned with. Now, the person who isn't a specialist, but a generalist like myself, sees something over here that he has learned from one specialist, something over there that he has learned from another specialist—and neither of them has considered the problem of why this occurs here and also there. So the generalist—and that's a derogatory term, by the way, for academics—gets into a range of other problems that are more genuinely human, you might say, than specifically cultural.

Moyers: Then along comes the journalist who has a license to explain things he doesn't understand.

Campbell: That is not only a license but something that is put upon him—he has an obligation to educate himself in public. Now, I remember when I was a young man going to hear Heinrich Zimmer lecture. He was the first man I know of to speak about myths as though they had messages that were valid for life, not just interesting things for scholars to fool around with. And that confirmed me in a feeling I had had ever since boyhood.

Moyers: Do you remember the first time you discovered myth? The first time the story came alive in you?

Campbell: I was brought up as a Roman Catholic. Now, one of the great advantages of being brought up a Roman Catholic is that you're taught to take myth seriously and to let it operate on your life and to live in terms of these mythic motifs. I was brought up in terms of the seasonal relationships to the cycle of Christ's coming into the world, teaching in the world, dying, resurrecting, and returning to heaven. The ceremonies all through the year keep you in mind of the eternal core of all that changes in time. Sin is simply getting out of touch with that harmony.

And then I fell in love with American Indians because Buffalo Bill used to come to Madison Square Garden every year with his marvelous Wild West Show. And I wanted to know more about Indians. My father and mother were very generous parents and found what books were being written for boys about Indians at that time. So I began to read American Indian myths, and it wasn't long before I found the same motifs in the American Indian stories that I was being taught by the nuns at school.

Moyers: Creation—

Campbell: —creation, death and resurrection, accession to heaven, virgin births—I didn't know what it was, but I recognized the vocabulary. One after another.

Moyers: And what happened?

Campbell: I was excited. That was the beginning of my interest in comparative mythology.

Moyers: Did you begin by asking, "Why does it say it this way while the Bible says it that way?"

Campbell: No, I didn't start the comparative analysis until many years later.

Moyers: What appealed to you about the Indian stories?

Campbell: In those days there was still American Indian lore in the air. Indians were still around. Even now, when I deal with myths from all parts of the world, I find the American Indian tales and narratives to be very rich, very well developed.

And then my parents had a place out in the woods where the Delaware Indians had lived, and the Iroquois had come down and fought them. There was a big ledge where we could dig for Indian arrowheads and things like that. And the very animals that play the role in the Indian stories were there in the woods around me. It was a grand introduction to this material.

Moyers: Did these stories begin to collide with your Catholic faith?

Campbell: No, there was no collision. The collision with my religion came much later in relation to scientific studies and things of that kind. Later I became interested in Hinduism, and there were the same stories again. And in my graduate work I was dealing with the Arthurian medieval material, and there were the same stories again. So you can't tell me that they're not the same stories. I've been with them all my life.

Moyers: They come from every culture but with timeless themes.

Campbell: The themes are timeless, and the inflection is to the culture.

Moyers: So the stories may take the same universal theme but apply it slightly differently, depending upon the accent of the people who are speaking?

Campbell: Oh, yes. If you were not alert to the parallel themes, you perhaps would think they were quite different stories, but they're not.

Moyers: You taught mythology for thirty-eight years at Sarah Lawrence. How did you get these young women, coming to college from their middle-class backgrounds, from their orthodox religions—how did you get them interested in myths?

Campbell: Young people just grab this stuff. Mythology teaches you what's behind literature and the arts, it teaches you about your own life. It's a great, exciting, life-nourishing subject. Mythology has a great deal to do with the stages of life, the initiation ceremonies as you move from childhood to adult responsibilities, from the unmarried state into the married state. All of those rituals are mythological rites. They have to do with your recognition of the new role that you're in, the process of throwing off the old one and coming out in the new, and entering into a responsible profession. When a judge walks into the room, and everybody stands up, you're not standing up to that guy, you're standing up to the robe that he's wearing and the role that he's going to play. What makes him worthy of that role is his integrity, as a representative of the principles of that role, and not some group of prejudices of his own. So what you're standing up to is a mythological character. I imagine some kings and queens are the most stupid, absurd, banal people you could run into, probably interested only in horses and women, you know. But you're not responding to them as personalities, you're responding to them in their mythological roles. When someone becomes a judge, or President of the United States, the man is no longer that man, he's the representative of an eternal office; he has to sacrifice his personal desires and even life possibilities to the role that he now signifies.

Moyers: So there are mythological rituals at work in our society. The ceremony of marriage is one. The ceremony of the inauguration of a President or judge is another. What are some of the other rituals that are important to society today?

Campbell: Joining the army, putting on a uniform, is another. You're giving up your personal life and accepting a socially determined manner of life in the service of the society of which you are a member. This is why I think it is obscene to judge people in terms of civil law for performances that they rendered in time of war. They were acting not as individuals, they were acting as agents of something above them and to which they had by dedication given themselves. To judge them as though they were individual human beings is totally improper.

Moyers: You've seen what happens when primitive societies are unsettled by white man's civilization. They go to pieces, they disintegrate, they become diseased. Hasn't the same thing been happening to us since our myths began to disappear?

Campbell: Absolutely, it has.

Moyers: Isn't that why conservative religions today are calling for the old-time religion?

Campbell: Yes, and they're making a terrible mistake. They are going back to something that is vestigial, that doesn't serve life.

Moyers: But didn't it serve us?

Campbell: Sure it did.

Moyers: I understand the yearning. In my youth I had fixed stars. They comforted me with their permanence. They gave me a known horizon. And they told me there was a loving, kind, and just father out there looking down on me, ready to receive me, thinking of my concerns all the time. Now, Saul Bellow says that science has made a housecleaning of beliefs. But there was value in these things for me. I am today what I am because of those beliefs. I wonder what happens to children who don't have those fixed stars, that known horizon—those myths?

Campbell: Well, as I said, all you have to do is read the newspaper. It's a mess. On this immediate level of life and structure, myths offer life models. But the models have to be appropriate to the time in which you are living, and our time has changed so fast that what was proper fifty years ago is not proper today. The virtues of the past are the vices of today. And many of what were thought to be the vices of the past are the necessities of today. The moral order has to catch up with the moral necessities of actual life in time, here and now. And that is what we are not doing. The old-time religion belongs to another age, another people, another set of human values, another universe. By going back you throw yourself out of sync with history. Our kids lose their faith in the religions that were taught to them, and they go inside.

Moyers: Often with the help of a drug.

Campbell: Yes. The mechanically induced mystical experience is what you have there. I have attended a number of psychological conferences dealing with this whole problem of the difference between the mystical experience and the psychological crack-up. The difference is that the one who cracks up is drowning in the water in which the mystic swims. You have to be prepared for this experience.

Moyers: You talk about this peyote culture emerging and becoming dominant among Indians as a consequence of the loss of the buffalo and their earlier way of life.

Campbell: Yes. Ours is one of the worst histories in relation to the native peoples of any civilized nation. They are nonpersons. They are not even reckoned in the statistics of the voting population of the United States. There was a moment shortly after the American Revolution when there were a number of distinguished Indians who actually participated in American government and life. George Washington said that Indians should be incorporated as members of our culture. But instead, they were turned into vestiges of the past. In the nineteenth century, all the Indians of the southeast were put into wagons and shipped under military guard out to what was then called Indian Territory, which was given to the Indians in perpetuity as their own world—then a couple of years later was taken away from them.

Recently, anthropologists studied a group of Indians in northwestern Mexico who live within a few miles of a major area for the natural growth of peyote. Peyote is their animal—that is to say, they associate it with the deer. And they have very special missions to go collect peyote and bring it back.

These missions are mystical journeys with all of the details of the typical mystical journey. First, there is disengagement from secular life. Everybody who is going to go on this expedition has to make a complete confession of all the faults of his or her recent living. And if they don't, the magic is not going to work. Then they start on the journey. They even speak a special language, a negative language. Instead of saying yes, for example, they say no, or instead of saying, "We are going," they say, "We are coming." They are in another world.

Then they come to the threshold of the adventure. There are special shrines that represent stages of mental transformation on the way. And then comes the great business of collecting the peyote. The peyote is killed as though it were a deer. They sneak up on it, shoot a little arrow at it, and then perform the ritual of collecting the peyote. The whole thing is a complete duplication of the kind of experience that is associated with the inward journey, when you leave the outer world and come into the realm of spiritual beings. They identify each little stage as a spiritual transformation. They are in a sacred place all the way.

Moyers: Why do they make such an intricate process out of it?

Campbell: Well, it has to do with the peyote being not simply a biological, mechanical, chemical effect but one of spiritual transformation. If you undergo a spiritual transformation and have not had preparation for it, you do not know how to evaluate what has happened to you, and you get the terrible experiences of a bad trip, as they used to call it with LSD. If you know where you are going, you won't have a bad trip.

Moyers: So this is why it is a psychological crisis if you are drowning in the water where—

Campbell: —where you ought to be able to swim, but you weren't prepared. That is true of the spiritual life, anyhow. It is a terrifying experience to have your consciousness transformed.

Moyers: You talk a lot about consciousness.

Campbell: Yes.

Moyers: What do you mean by it?

Campbell: It is a part of the Cartesian mode to think of consciousness as being something peculiar to the head, that the head is the organ originating consciousness. It isn't. The head is an organ that inflects consciousness in a certain direction, or to a certain set of purposes. But there is a consciousness here in the body. The whole living world is informed by consciousness. I have a feeling that consciousness and energy are the same thing somehow. Where you really see life energy, there's consciousness. Certainly the vegetable world is conscious. And when you live in the woods, as I did as a kid, you can see all these different consciousnesses relating to themselves. There is a plant consciousness and there is an animal consciousness, and we share both these things. You eat certain foods, and the bile knows whether there's something there for it to go to work on. The whole process is consciousness. Trying to interpret it in simply mechanistic terms won't work.

Moyers: How do we transform our consciousness?

Campbell: That's a matter of what you are disposed to think about. And that's what meditation is for. All of life is a meditation, most of it unintentional. A lot of people spend most of life in meditating on where their money is coming from and where it's going to go. If you have a family to bring up, you're concerned for the family. These are all very important concerns, but they have to do with physical conditions, mostly. But how are you going to communicate spiritual consciousness to the children if you don't have it yourself? How do you get that? What the myths are for is to bring us into a level of consciousness that is spiritual.

Just for example: I walk off Fifty-first Street and Fifth Avenue into St. Patrick's Cathedral. I've left a very busy city and one of the most economically inspired cities on the planet. I walk into that cathedral, and everything around me speaks of spiritual mysteries. The mystery of the cross, what's that all about there? The stained glass windows, which bring another atmosphere in. My consciousness has been brought up onto another level altogether, and I am on a different platform. And then I walk out, and I'm back on the level of the street again. Now, can I hold something from the cathedral consciousness? Certain prayers or meditations are designed to hold your consciousness on that level instead of letting it drop down here all the way. And then what you can finally do is to recognize that this is simply a lower level of that higher consciousness. The mystery that is expressed there is operating in the field of your money, for example. All money is congealed energy. I think that that's the clue to how to transform your consciousness.

Moyers: Don't you sometimes think, as you consider these stories, that you are drowning in other people's dreams?

Campbell: I don't listen to other people's dreams.

Moyers: But all of these myths are other people's dreams.

Campbell: Oh, no, they're not. They are the world's dreams. They are archetypal dreams and deal with great human problems. I know when I come to one of these thresholds now. The myth tells me about it, how to respond to certain crises of disappointment or delight or failure or success. The myths tell me where I am.

Moyers: What happens when people become legends? Can you say, for example, that John Wayne has become a myth?

Campbell: When a person becomes a model for other people's lives, he has moved into the sphere of being mythologized.

Moyers: This happens so often to actors in films, where we get so many of our models.

Campbell: I remember, when I was a boy, Douglas Fairbanks was the model for me. Adolphe Menjou was the model for my brother. Of course those men were playing the roles of mythic figures. They were educators toward life.

Moyers: No figure in movie history is more engaging to me than Shane. Did you see the movie *Shane*?

Campbell: No, I didn't.

Moyers: It is the classic story of the stranger who rides in from outside and does good for others and rides away, not waiting for his reward. Why is it that films affect us this way?

Campbell: There is something magical about films. The person you are looking at is also somewhere else at the same time. That is a condition of the god. If a movie actor comes into the theater, everybody turns and looks at the movie actor. He is the real hero of the occasion. He is on another plane. He is a multiple presence.

            What you are seeing on the screen really isn't he, and yet the "he" comes. Through the multiple forms, the form of forms out of which all of this comes is right there.

Moyers: Movies seem to create these large figures, while television merely creates celebrities. They don't become models as much as they do objects of gossip.

Campbell: Perhaps that's because we see TV personalities in the home instead of in a special temple like the movie theater.

Moyers: I saw a photograph yesterday of this latest cult figure from Hollywood, Rambo, the Vietnam veteran who returns to rescue prisoners of war, and through violent swaths of death and destruction he brings them back. I understand it is the most popular movie in Beirut. The photograph showed the new Rambo doll that has been created and is being sold by the same company that produces the Cabbage Patch dolls. In the foreground is the image of a sweet, lovable Cabbage Patch doll, and behind it, the brute force, Rambo.

Campbell: Those are two mythic figures. The image that comes to my mind now is of Picasso's *Minotauromachy*, an engraving that shows a great monster bull approaching. The philosopher is climbing up a ladder in terror to get away. In the bullring there is a horse, which has been killed, and on the sacrificed horse lies a female matador who has also been killed. The only creature facing this terrific monster is a little girl with a flower. Those are the two figures you have just spoken of—the simple, innocent, childlike one, and the terrific threat. You see the problems of the modern day.

Moyers: The poet Yeats felt we were living in the last of a great Christian cycle. His poem "The Second Coming" says, "Turning and turning in the widening gyre/The falcon cannot hear the falconer;/Things fall apart; the centre cannot hold;/Mere anarchy is loosed upon the world,/The blood-dimmed tide is loosed, and everywhere/The ceremony of innocence is drowned." What do you see slouching "towards Bethlehem to be born"?

Campbell: I don't know what's coming, any more than Yeats knew, but when you come to the end of one time and the beginning of a new one, it's a period of tremendous pain and turmoil. The threat we feel, and everybody feels—well, there is this notion of Armageddon coming, you know.

Moyers: "I have become Death, the Destroyer of worlds," Oppenheimer said when he saw the first atomic bomb explode. But you don't think that will be our end, do you?

Campbell: It won't be the end. Maybe it will be the end of life on this planet, but that is not the end of the universe. It is just a bungled explosion in terms of all the explosions that are going on in all the suns of the universe. The universe is a bunch of exploding atomic furnaces like our sun. So this is just a little imitation of the whole big job.

Moyers: Can you imagine that somewhere else other creatures can be sitting, investing their transient journey with the kind of significance that our myths and great stories do?

Campbell: No. When you realize that if the temperature goes up fifty degrees and stays there, life will not exist on this earth, and that if it drops, let's say, another hundred degrees and stays there, life will not be on this earth; when you realize how very delicate this balance is, how the quantity of water is so important—well, when you think of all the accidents of the environment that have fostered life, how can you think that the life we know would exist on any other particle of the universe, no matter how many of these satellites around stars there may be?

Moyers: This fragile life always exists in the crucible of terror and possible extinction. And the image of the Cabbage Patch doll juxtaposed with the vicious Rambo is not at odds with what we know of life through mythology?

Campbell: No, it isn't.

Moyers: Do you see some new metaphors emerging in a modern medium for the old universal truths?

Campbell: I see the possibility of new metaphors, but I don't see that they have become mythological yet.

Moyers: What do you think will be the myths that will incorporate the machine into the new world?

Campbell: Well, automobiles have gotten into mythology. They have gotten into dreams. And airplanes are very much in the service of the imagination. The flight of the airplane, for example, is in the imagination as the release from earth. This is the same thing that birds symbolize in a certain way. The bird is symbolic of the release of the spirit from bondage to the earth, just as the serpent is symbolic of the bondage to the earth. The airplane plays that role now.

Moyers: Any others?

Campbell: Weapons, of course. Every movie that I have seen on the airplane as I traveled back and forth between California and Hawaii shows people with revolvers. There is the Lord Death, carrying his weapon. Different instruments take over the roles that earlier instruments now no longer serve. But I don't see any more than that.

Moyers: So the new myths will serve the old stories. When I saw *Star Wars*, I remembered the phrase from the apostle Paul, "I wrestle against principalities and powers." That was two thousand years ago. And in the caves of the early Stone Age hunter, there are scenes of wrestling against principalities and powers. Here in our modern technological myths we are still wrestling.

Campbell: Man should not submit to the powers from outside but command them. How to do it is the problem.

Moyers: After our youngest son had seen *Star Wars* for the twelfth or thirteenth time, I said, "Why do you go so often?" He said, "For the same reason you have been reading the Old Testament all of your life." He was in a new world of myth.

Campbell: Certainly *Star Wars* has a valid mythological perspective. It shows the state as a machine and asks, "Is the machine going to crush humanity or serve humanity?" Humanity comes not from the machine but from the heart. What I see in *Star Wars* is the same problem that Faust gives us: Mephistopheles, the machine man, can provide us with all the means, and is thus likely to determine the aims of life as well. But of course the characteristic of Faust, which makes him eligible to be saved, is that he seeks aims that are not those of the machine.

Now, when Luke Skywalker unmasks his father, he is taking off the machine role that the father has played. The father was the uniform. That is power, the state role.

Moyers: Machines help us to fulfill the idea that we want the world to be made in our image, and we want it to be what we think it ought to be.

Campbell: Yes. But then there comes a time when the machine begins to dictate to you. For example, I have bought this wonderful machine—a computer. Now I am rather an authority on gods, so I identified the machine—it seems to me to be an Old Testament god with a lot of rules and no mercy.

Moyers: There is a fetching story about President Eisenhower and the first computers—

Campbell: Eisenhower went into a room full of computers. And he put the question to these machines, "Is there a God?" And they all start up, and the lights flash, and the wheels turn, and after a while a voice says, "*Now* there is."

Moyers: But isn't it possible to develop toward your computer the same attitude of the chieftain who said that all things speak of God? If it isn't a special, privileged revelation, God is everywhere in his work, including the computer.

Campbell: Indeed so. It's a miracle, what happens on that screen. Have you ever looked inside one of those things?

Moyers: No, and I don't intend to.

Campbell: You can't believe it. It's a whole hierarchy of angels—all on slats. And those little tubes—those are miracles.

I have had a revelation from my computer about mythology. You buy a certain software, and there is a whole set of signals that lead to the achievement of your aim. If you begin fooling around with signals that belong to another system of software, they just won't work.

Similarly, in mythology—if you have a mythology in which the metaphor for the mystery is the father, you are going to have a different set of signals from what you would have if the metaphor for the wisdom and mystery of the world were the mother. And they are two perfectly good metaphors. Neither one is a fact. These are metaphors. It is as though the universe were my father. It is as though the universe were my mother. Jesus says, "No one gets to the father but by me." The father that he was talking about was the biblical father. It might be that you can get to the father only by way of Jesus. On the other hand, suppose you are going by way of the mother. There you might prefer Kali, and the hymns to the goddess, and so forth. That is simply another way to get to the mystery of your life. You must understand that each religion is a kind of software that has its own set of signals and will work.

If a person is really involved in a religion and really building his life on it, he better stay with the software that he has got. But a chap like myself, who likes to play with the software—well, I can run around, but I probably will never have an experience comparable to that of a saint.

Moyers: But haven't some of the greatest saints borrowed from anywhere they could? They have taken from this and from that, and constructed a new software.

Campbell: That is what is called the development of a religion. You can see it in the Bible. In the beginning, God was simply the most powerful god among many. He is just a local tribal god. And then in the sixth century, when the Jews were in Babylon, the notion of a world savior came in, and the biblical divinity moved into a new dimension.

You can keep an old tradition going only by renewing it in terms of current circumstances. In the period of the Old Testament, the world was a little three-layer cake, consisting of a few hundred miles around the Near Eastern centers. No one had ever heard of the Aztecs, or even of the Chinese. When the world changes, then the religion has to be transformed.

Moyers: But it seems to me that is in fact what we are doing.

Campbell: That is in fact what we had better do. But my notion of the real horror today is what you see in Beirut. There you have the three great Western religions, Judaism, Christianity, and Islam—and because the three of them have three different names for the same biblical god, they can't get on together. They are stuck with their metaphor and don't realize its reference. They haven't allowed the circle that surrounds them to open. It is a closed circle. Each group says, "We are the chosen group, and we have God."

Look at Ireland. A group of Protestants was moved to Ireland in the seventeenth century by Cromwell, and it never has opened up to the Catholic majority there. The Catholics and Protestants represent two totally different social systems, two different ideals.

Moyers: Each needs a new myth.

Campbell: Each needs its own myth, all the way. Love thine enemy. Open up. Don't judge. All things are Buddha things. It is there in the myth. It is already there.

Moyers: You tell a story about a local jungle native who once said to a missionary, "Your god keeps himself shut up in a house as if he were old and infirm. Ours is in the forest and in the fields and on the mountains when the rain comes." And I think that is probably true.

Campbell: Yes. You see, this is a problem you get in the book of Kings and in Samuel. The various Hebrew kings were sacrificing on the mountain-tops. And they did wrong in the sight of Yahweh. The Yahweh cult was a specific movement in the Hebrew community, which finally won. This was a pushing through of a certain temple-bound god against the nature cult, which was celebrated all over the place.

            And this imperialistic thrust of a certain in-group culture is continued in the West. But it has got to open to the nature of things now. If it can open, all the possibilities are there.

Moyers: Of course, we moderns are stripping the world of its natural revelations, of nature itself. I think of that pygmy legend of the little boy who finds the bird with the beautiful song in the forest and brings it home.

Campbell: He asks his father to bring food for the bird, and the father doesn't want to feed a mere bird, so he kills it. And the legend says the man killed the bird, and with the bird he killed the song, and with the song, himself. He dropped dead, completely dead, and was dead forever.

Moyers: Isn't that a story about what happens when human beings destroy their environment? Destroy their world? Destroy nature and the revelations of nature?

Campbell: They destroy their own nature, too. They kill the song.

Moyers: And isn't mythology the story of the song?

Campbell: Mythology is the song. It is the song of the imagination, inspired by the energies of the body. Once a Zen master stood up before his students and was about to deliver a sermon. And just as he was about to open his mouth, a bird sang. And he said, "The sermon has been delivered."

Moyers: I was about to say that we are creating new myths, but you say no, every myth we tell today has some point of origin in our past experience.

Campbell: The main motifs of the myths are the same, and they have always been the same. If you want to find your own mythology, the key is with what society do you associate? Every mythology has grown up in a certain society in a bounded field. Then they come into collision and relationship, and they amalgamate, and you get a more complex mythology.

But today there are no boundaries. The only mythology that is valid today is the mythology of the planet—and we don't have such a mythology. The closest thing I know to a planetary mythology is Buddhism, which sees all beings as Buddha beings. The only problem is to come to the recognition of that. There is nothing to do. The task is only to know what is, and then to act in relation to the brotherhood of all of these beings.

Moyers: Brotherhood?

Campbell: Yes. Now brotherhood in most of the myths I know of is confined to a bounded community. In bounded communities, aggression is projected outward.

For example, the ten commandments say, "Thou shalt not kill." Then the next chapter says, "Go into Canaan and kill everybody in it." That is a bounded field. The myths of participation and love pertain only to the in-group, and the out-group is totally other. This is the sense of the word "gentile"—the person is not of the same order.

Moyers: And unless you wear my costume, we are not kin.

Campbell: Yes. Now, what is a myth? The dictionary definition of a myth would be stories about gods. So then you have to ask the next question: What is a god? A god is a personification of a motivating power or a value system that functions in human life and in the universe—the powers of your own body and of nature. The myths are metaphorical of spiritual potentiality in the human being, and the same powers that animate our life animate the life of the world. But also there are myths and gods that have to do with specific societies or the patron deities of the society. In other words, there are two totally different orders of mythology. There is the mythology that relates you to your nature and to the natural world, of which you're a part. And there is the mythology that is strictly sociological, linking you to a particular society. You are not simply a natural man, you are a member of a particular group. In the history of European mythology, you can see the interaction of these two systems. Usually the socially oriented system is of a nomadic people who are moving around, so you learn that's where your center is, in that group. The nature-oriented mythology would be of an earth-cultivating people.

Now, the biblical tradition is a socially oriented mythology. Nature is condemned. In the nineteenth century, scholars thought of mythology and ritual as an attempt to control nature. But that is magic, not mythology or religion. Nature religions are not attempts to control nature but to help you put yourself in accord with it. But when nature is thought of as evil, you don't put yourself in accord with it, you control it, or try to, and hence the tension, the anxiety, the cutting down of forests, the annihilation of native people. And the accent here separates us from nature.

Moyers: Is this why we so easily dominate or subjugate nature—because we have contempt for it, because we see it only as something to serve us?

Campbell: Yes. I will never forget the experience I had when I was in Japan, a place that never heard of the Fall and the Garden of Eden. One of the Shinto texts says that the processes of nature cannot be evil. Every natural impulse is not to be corrected but to be sublimated, to be beautified. There is a glorious interest in the beauty of nature and cooperation with nature, so that in some of those gardens you don't know where nature begins and art ends—this was a tremendous experience.

Moyers: But, Joe, Tokyo today refutes that ideal in such flagrant ways. Tokyo is a city where nature has virtually disappeared, except as contained in small gardens that are still cherished by some of the people.

Campbell: There is a saying in Japan, Rock with the waves. Or, as we say in boxing, Roll with the punches. It is only about a hundred and twenty-five years ago that Perry broke Japan open. And in that time they have assimilated a terrific load of mechanical material. But what I found in Japan was that they were holding their own head against this, and assimilating this machine world to themselves. When you go inside the buildings, then you are back in Japan. It is the outside that looks like New York.

Moyers: "Holding their own head." That is an interesting idea because, even though the cities emerge around them, within the soul, the place where the inner person dwells, they are still, as you say, in accord with nature.

Campbell: But in the Bible, eternity withdraws, and nature is corrupt, nature has fallen. In biblical thinking, we live in exile.

Moyers: As we sit here and talk, there is one story after another of car bombings in Beirut—by the Muslims of the Christians, by the Christians of the Muslims, and by the Christians of the Christians. It strikes me that Marshall McLuhan was right when he said that television has made a global village of the world—but he didn't know the global village would be Beirut. What does that say to you?

Campbell: It says to me that they don't know how to apply their religious ideas to contemporary life, and to human beings rather than just to their own community. It's a terrible example of the failure of religion to meet the modern world. These three mythologies are fighting it out. They have disqualified themselves for the future.

Moyers: What kind of new myth do we need?

Campbell: We need myths that will identify the individual not with his local group but with the planet. A model for that is the United States. Here were thirteen different little colony nations that decided to act in the mutual interest, without disregarding the individual interests of any one of them.

Moyers: There is something about that on the Great Seal of the United States.

Campbell: That's what the Great Seal is all about. I carry a copy of the Great Seal in my pocket in the form of a dollar bill. Here is the statement of the ideals that brought about the formation of the United States. Look at this dollar bill. Now here is the Great Seal of the United States. Look at the pyramid on the left. A pyramid has four sides. These are the four points of the compass. There is somebody at this point, there's somebody at that point, and there's somebody at this point.

Moyers: And to them it was the god of reason.

Campbell: Yes. This is the first nation in the world that was ever established on the basis of reason instead of simply warfare. These were eighteenth-century deists, these gentlemen. Over here we read, "In God We Trust." But that is not the god of the Bible. These men did not believe in a Fall. They did not think the mind of man was cut off from God. The mind of man, cleansed of secondary and merely temporal concerns, beholds with the radiance of a cleansed mirror a reflection of the rational mind of God. Reason puts you in touch with God. Consequently, for these men, there is no special revelation anywhere, and none is needed, because the mind of man cleared of its fallibilities is sufficiently capable of the knowledge of God. All people in the world are thus capable because all people in the world are capable of reason.

All men are capable of reason. That is the fundamental principle of democracy. Because everybody's mind is capable of true knowledge, you don't have to have a special authority, or a special revelation telling you that this is the way things should be.

Moyers: And yet these symbols come from mythology.

Campbell: Yes, but they come from a certain quality of mythology. It's not the mythology of a special revelation. The Hindus, for example, don't believe in special revelation. They speak of a state in which the ears have opened to the song of the universe. Here the eye has opened to the radiance of the mind of God. And that's a fundamental deist idea. Once you reject the idea of the Fall in the Garden, man is not cut off from his source.

Now back to the Great Seal. When you count the number of ranges on this pyramid, you find there are thirteen. And when you come to the bottom, there is an inscription in Roman numerals. It is, of course, 1776. Then, when you add one and seven and seven and six, you get twenty-one, which is the age of reason, is it not? It was in 1776 that the thirteen states declared independence. The number thirteen is the number of transformation and rebirth. At the Last Supper there were twelve apostles and one Christ, who was going to die and be reborn. Thirteen is the number of getting out of the field of the bounds of twelve into the transcendent. You have the twelve signs of the zodiac and the sun. These men were very conscious of the number thirteen as the number of resurrection and rebirth and new life, and they played it up here all the way through.

Moyers: But, as a practical matter, there were thirteen states.

Campbell: Yes, but wasn't that symbolic? This is not simply coincidental. This is the thirteen states as themselves symbolic of what they were.

Moyers: That would explain the other inscription down there, "*Novus Ordo Seclorum.*"

Campbell: "A new order of the world." This is a new order of the world. And the saying above, "*Annuit Coeptis,*" means "He has smiled on our accomplishments" or "our activities."

Moyers: He—

Campbell: He, the eye, what is represented by the eye. Reason. In Latin you wouldn't have to say "he," it could be "it" or "she" or "he." But the divine power has smiled on our doings. And so this new world has been built in the sense of God's original creation, and the reflection of God's original creation, through reason, has brought this about.

If you look behind that pyramid, you see a desert. If you look before it, you see plants growing. The desert, the tumult in Europe, wars and wars and wars—we have pulled ourselves out of it and created a state in the name of reason, not in the name of power, and out of that will come the flowerings of the new life. That's the sense of that part of the pyramid.

Now look at the right side of the dollar bill. Here's the eagle, the bird of Zeus. The eagle is the down-coming of the god into the field of time. The bird is the incarnation principle of the deity. This is the bald eagle, the American eagle. This is the American counterpart of the eagle of the highest god, Zeus.

He comes down, descending into the world of the pairs of opposites, the field of action. One mode of action is war and the other is peace. So in one of his feet the eagle holds thirteen arrows—that's the principle of war. In the other he holds a laurel leaf with thirteen leaves—that is the principle of peaceful conversation. The eagle is looking in the direction of the laurel. That is the way these realists who founded our country would wish us to be looking—diplomatic relationships and so forth. But thank God he's got the arrows in the other foot, in case this doesn't work.

Now, what does the eagle represent? He represents what is indicated in this radiant sign above his head. I was lecturing once at the Foreign Service Institute in Washington on Hindu mythology, sociology, and politics. There's a saying in the Hindu book of politics that the ruler must hold in one hand the weapon of war, the big stick, and in the other the peaceful sound of the song of cooperative action. And there I was, standing with my two hands like this, and everybody in the town laughed. I couldn't understand. And then they began pointing. I looked back, and here was this picture of the eagle hanging on the wall behind my head in just the same posture that I was in. But when I looked, I also noticed this sign above his head, and that there were nine feathers in his tail. Nine is the number of the descent of the divine power into the world. When the Angelus rings, it rings nine times.

Now, over on the eagle's head are thirteen stars arranged in the form of a Star of David.

Moyers: This used to be Solomon's Seal.

Campbell: Yes. Do you know why it's called Solomon's Seal?

Moyers: No.

Campbell: Solomon used to seal monsters and giants and things into jars. You remember in the *Arabian Nights* when they'd open the jar and out would come the genie? I noticed the Solomon's Seal here, composed of thirteen stars and then I saw that each of the triangles was a Pythagorean tetrakys.

Moyers: The tetrakys being?

Campbell: This is a triangle composed of ten points, one point in the middle and four points to each side, adding up to nine: one, two, three, four/five, six, seven/eight, nine. This is the primary symbol of Pythagorean philosophy, susceptible of a number of inter-related mythological, cosmological, psychological, and sociological interpretations, one of which is the dot at the apex as representing the creative center out of which the universe and all things have come.

Moyers: The center of energy, then?

Campbell: Yes. The initial sound (a Christian might say, the creative Word), out of which the whole world was precipitated, the big bang, the pouring of the transcendent energy into and expanding through the field of time. As soon as it enters the field of time, it breaks into pairs of opposites the one becomes two. Now, when you have two, there are just three ways in which they can relate to one another: one way is of this one dominant over that; another way is of that one dominant over this; and a third way is of the two in balanced accord. It is then, finally, out of these three manners of relationship that all things within the four quarters of space derive.

There is a verse in Lao-tzu's *Tao-te Ching* which states that out of the Tao, out of the transcendent, comes the One. Out of the One come Two; out of the Two come Three; and out of the Three come all things.

So what I suddenly realized when I recognized that in the Great Seal of the United States there were two of these symbolic triangles interlocked was that we now had thirteen points, for our thirteen original states, and that there were now, furthermore, no less than six apexes, one above, one below, and four (so to say) to the four quarters. The sense of this, it seemed to me, might be that from above or below, or from any point of the compass, the creative Word might be heard, which is the great thesis of democracy. Democracy assumes that anybody from any quarter can speak, and speak truth, because his mind is not cut off from the truth. All he has to do is clear out his passions and then speak.

So what you have here on the dollar bill is the eagle representing this wonderful image of the way in which the transcendent manifests itself in the world. That's what the United States is founded on. If you're going to govern properly, you've got to govern from the apex of the triangle, in the sense of the world eye at the top.

Now, when I was a boy, we were given George Washington's farewell address and told to outline the whole thing, every single statement in relation to every other one. So I remember it absolutely. Washington said, "As a result of our revolution, we have disengaged ourselves from involvement in the chaos of Europe. " His last word was that we not engage in foreign alliances. Well, we held on to his words until the First World War. And then we canceled the Declaration of Independence and rejoined the British conquest of the planet. And so we are now on one side of the pyramid. We've moved from one to two. We are politically, historically, now a member of one side of an argument. We do not represent that principle of the eye up there. And all of our concerns have to do with economics and politics and not with the voice and sound of reason.

Moyers: The voice of reason—is that the philosophical way suggested by these mythological symbols?

Campbell: That's right. Here you have the important transition that took place about 500 B.C. This is the date of the Buddha and of Pythagoras and Confucius and Lao-tzu, if there was a Lao-tzu. This is the awakening of man's reason. No longer is he informed and governed by the animal powers. No longer is he guided by the analogy of the planted earth, no longer by the courses of the planets—but by reason.

Moyers: The way of—

Campbell: —the way of man. And of course what destroys reason is passion. The principal passion in politics is greed. That is what pulls you down. And that's why we're on this side instead of the top of the pyramid.

Moyers: That's why our founders opposed religious intolerance—

Campbell: That was out entirely. And that's why they rejected the idea of the Fall, too. All men are competent to know the mind of God. There is no revelation special to any people.

Moyers: I can see how, from your years of scholarship and deep immersion in these mythological symbols, you would read the Great Seal that way. But wouldn't it have been surprising to most of those men who were deists, as you say, to discover these mythological connotations about their effort to build a new country?

Campbell: Well, why did they use them?

Moyers: Aren't a lot of these Masonic symbols?

Campbell: They are Masonic signs, and the meaning of the Pythagorean tetrakis has been known for centuries. The information would have been found in Thomas Jefferson's library. These were, after all, learned men. The eighteenth-century Enlightenment was a world of learned gentlemen. We haven't had men of that quality in politics very much. It's an enormous good fortune for our nation that that cluster of gentlemen had the power and were in a position to influence events at that time.

Moyers: What explains the relationship between these symbols and the Masons, and the fact that so many of these founding fathers belonged to the Masonic order? Is the Masonic order an expression somehow of mythological thinking?

Campbell: Yes, I think it is. This is a scholarly attempt to reconstruct an order of initiation that would result in spiritual revelation. These founding fathers who were Masons actually studied what they could of Egyptian lore. In Egypt, the pyramid represents the primordial hillock. After the annual flood of the Nile begins to sink down, the first hillock is symbolic of the reborn world. That's what this seal represents.

Moyers: You sometimes confound me with the seeming contradiction at the heart of your own belief system. On the one hand, you praise these men who were inspirers and creatures of the Age of Reason, and on the other hand, you salute Luke Skywalker in *Star Wars* for that moment when he says, "Turn off the computer and trust your feelings." How do you reconcile the role of science, which is reason, with the role of faith, which is religion?

Campbell: No, no, you have to distinguish between reason and thinking.

Moyers: Distinguish between reason and thinking? If I think, am I not reasoning things out?

Campbell: Yes, your reason is one kind of thinking. But thinking things out isn't necessarily reason in this sense. Figuring out how you can break through a wall is not reason. The mouse who figures out, after it bumps its nose here, that perhaps he can get around there, is figuring something out the way we figure things out. But that's not reason. Reason has to do with finding the ground of being and the fundamental structuring of order of the universe.

Moyers: So when these men talked about the eye of God being reason, they were saying that the ground of our being as a society, as a culture, as a people, derives from the fundamental character of the universe?

Campbell: That's what this first pyramid says. This is the pyramid of the world, and this is the pyramid of our society, and they are of the same order. This is God's creation, and this is our society.

Moyers: We have a mythology for the way of the animal powers. We have a mythology for the way of the seeded earth—fertility, creation, the mother goddess. And we have a mythology for the celestial lights, for the heavens. But in modern times we have moved beyond the animal powers, beyond nature and the seeded earth. and the stars no longer interest us except as exotic curiosities and the terrain of space travel. Where are we now in our mythology for the way of man?

Campbell: We can't have a mythology for a long, long time to come. Things are changing too fast to become mythologized.

Moyers: How do we live without myths then?

Campbell: The individual has to find an aspect of myth that relates to his own life. Myth basically serves four functions. The first is the mystical function—that is the one I've been speaking about, realizing what a wonder the universe is, and what a wonder you are, and experiencing awe before this mystery. Myth opens the world to the dimension of mystery, to the realization of the mystery that underlies all forms. If you lose that, you don't have a mythology. If mystery is manifest through all things, the universe becomes, as it were, a holy picture. You are always addressing the transcendent mystery through the conditions of your actual world.

The second is a cosmological dimension, the dimension with which science is concerned—showing you what the shape of the universe is, but showing it in such a way that the mystery again comes through. Today we tend to think that scientists have all the answers. But the great ones tell us, "No, we haven't got all the answers. We're telling you how it works—but what is it?" You strike a match, what's fire? You can tell me about oxidation, but that doesn't tell me a thing.

The third function is the sociological one—supporting and validating a certain social order. And here's where the myths vary enormously from place to place. You can have a whole mythology for polygamy, a whole mythology for monogamy. Either one's okay. It depends on where you are. It is this sociological function of myth that has taken over in our world—and it is out of date.

Moyers: What do you mean?

Campbell: Ethical laws. The laws of life as it should be in the good society. All of Yahweh's pages and pages and pages of what kind of clothes to wear, how to behave to each other, and so forth, in the first millennium B.C.

But there is a fourth function of myth, and this is the one that I think everyone must try today to relate to—and that is the pedagogical function, of how to live a human lifetime under any circumstances. Myths can teach you that.

Moyers: So the old story, so long known and transmitted through the generations, isn't functioning, and we have not yet learned a new one?

Campbell: The story that we have in the West, so far as it is based on the Bible, is based on a view of the universe that belongs to the first millennium B.C. It does not accord with our concept either of the universe or of the dignity of man. It belongs entirely somewhere else.

We have today to learn to get back into accord with the wisdom of nature and realize again our brotherhood with the animals and with the water and the sea. To say that the divinity informs the world and all things is condemned as pantheism. But pantheism is a misleading word. It suggests that a personal god is supposed to inhabit the world, but that is not the idea at all. The idea is trans-theological. It is of an undefinable, inconceivable mystery, thought of as a power, that is the source and end and supporting ground of all life and being.

Moyers: Don't you think modern Americans have rejected the ancient idea of nature as a divinity because it would have kept us from achieving dominance over nature? How can you cut down trees and uproot the land and turn the rivers into real estate without killing God?

Campbell: Yes, but that's not simply a characteristic of modern Americans, that is the biblical condemnation of nature which they inherited from their own religion and brought with them, mainly from England. God is separate from nature, and nature is condemned of God. It's right there in Genesis: we are to be the masters of the world.

But if you will think of ourselves as coming out of the earth, rather than having been thrown in here from somewhere else, you see that we are the earth, we are the consciousness of the earth. These are the eyes of the earth. And this is the voice of the earth.

Moyers: Scientists are beginning to talk quite openly about the Gaia principle.

Campbell: There you are, the whole planet as an organism.

Moyers: Mother Earth. Will new myths come from this image?

Campbell: Well, something might. You can't predict what a myth is going to be any more than you can predict what you're going to dream tonight. Myths and dreams come from the same place. They come from realizations of some kind that have then to find expression in symbolic form. And the only myth that is going to be worth thinking about in the immediate future is one that is talking about the planet, not the city, not these people, but the planet, and everybody on it. That's my main thought for what the future myth is going to be.

And what it will have to deal with will be exactly what all myths have dealt with— the maturation of the individual, from dependency through adulthood, through maturity, and then to the exit; and then how to relate to this society and how to relate this society to the world of nature and the cosmos. That's what the myths have all talked about, and what this one's got to talk about. But the society that it's got to talk about is the society of the planet. And until that gets going, you don't have anything.

Moyers: So you suggest that from this begins the new myth of our time?

Campbell: Yes, this is the ground of what the myth is to be. It's already here: the eye of reason, not of my nationality; the eye of reason, not of my religious community; the eye of reason, not of my linguistic community. Do you see? And this would be the philosophy for the planet, not for this group, that group, or the other group.

When you see the earth from the moon, you don't see any divisions there of nations or states. This might be the symbol, really, for the new mythology to come. That is the country that we are going to be celebrating. And those are the people that we are one with.

Moyers: No one embodies that ethic to me more clearly in the works you have collected than Chief Seattle.

Campbell: Chief Seattle was one of the last spokesmen of the Paleolithic moral order. In about 1852, the United States Government inquired about buying the tribal lands for the arriving people of the United States, and Chief Seattle wrote a marvelous letter in reply. His letter expresses the moral, really, of our whole discussion.

"The President in Washington sends word that he wishes to buy our land. But how can you buy or sell the sky? The land? The idea is strange to us. If we do not own the freshness of the air and the sparkle of the water, how can you buy them?

"Every part of this earth is sacred to my people. Every shining pine needle, every sandy shore, every mist in the dark woods, every meadow, every humming insect. All are holy in the memory and experience of my people.

"We know the sap which courses through the trees as we know the blood that courses through our veins. We are part of the earth and it is part of us. The perfumed flowers are our sisters. The bear, the deer, the great eagle, these are our brothers. The rocky crests, the juices in the meadow, the body heat of the pony, and man, all belong to the same family.

"The shining water that moves in the streams and rivers is not just water, but the blood of our ancestors. If we sell you our land, you must remember that it is sacred. Each ghostly reflection in the clear waters of the lakes tells of events and memories in the life of my people. The water's murmur is the voice of my father's father.

"The rivers are our brothers. They quench our thirst. They carry our canoes and feed our children. So you must give to the rivers the kindness you would give any brother.

"If we sell you our land, remember that the air is precious to us, that the air shares its spirit with all the life it supports. The wind that gave our grandfather his first breath also receives his last sigh. The wind also gives our children the spirit of life. So if we sell you our land, you must keep it apart and sacred, as a place where man can go to taste the wind that is sweetened by the meadow flowers.

"Will you teach your children what we have taught our children? That the earth is our mother? What befalls the earth befalls all the sons of the earth.

"This we know: the earth does not belong to man, man belongs to the earth. All things are connected like the blood that unites us all. Man did not weave the web of life, he is merely a strand in it. Whatever he does to the web, he does to himself.

"One thing we know: our god is also your god. The earth is precious to him and to harm the earth is to heap contempt on its creator.

"Your destiny is a mystery to us. What will happen when the buffalo are all slaughtered? The wild horses tamed? What will happen when the secret corners of the forest are heavy with the scent of many men and the view of the ripe hills is blotted by talking wires? Where will the thicket be? Gone! Where will the eagle be? Gone! And what is it to say goodbye to the swift pony and the hunt? The end of living and the beginning of survival.

"When the last Red Man has vanished with his wilderness and his memory is only the shadow of a cloud moving across the prairie, will these shores and forests still be here? Will there be any of the spirit of my people left?

"We love this earth as a newborn loves its mother's heartbeat. So, if we sell you our land, love it as we have loved it. Care for it as we have cared for it. Hold in your mind the memory of the land as it is when you receive it. Preserve the land for all children and love it, as God loves us all.

"As we are part of the land, you too are part of the land. This earth is precious to us. It is also precious to you. One thing we know: there is only one God. No man, be he Red Man or White Man, can be apart. We are brothers after all."

HOMER (8th-7th c. B.C.)

Homer is the poet credited with the two great epic poems of the Trojan War: The Iliad, *which describes the ten-year war, and* The Odyssey, *which recounts Odysseus' (Ulysses') ten-year journey back to Ithaca. Scholars disagree about whether Homer actually wrote these poems, which were handed down orally before being written. Indeed, they disagree about whether Homer actually lived — but assuming he did, they generally place him in the eighth or seventh century B.C.*

THE ODYSSEY

The Odyssey, written in 24 books, begins in medias res *(in the middle of things), with Ulysses (Odysseus) held captive by Calypso. The poet first calls on the Muse to inspire his song, then begins the narration with a council of the gods, in which Minerva (Athena) intercedes with Jove (Zeus) to aid Odysseus in his journey home. (The names Jove and Minerva are Roman names for Zeus and Athena.) Following is a summary outline of the epic, book by book:*

1.	*Minerva appears to Telemachus.*	*13.*	*Phoenicians leave Ulysses on Ithaca shore, sleeping*
2.	*Telemachus defies the suitors.*		
3.	*Telemachus visits Nestor.*	*14.*	*Minerva disguises Ulysses, who visits Eumaeus.*
4.	*Telemachus visits Menelaus.*	*15.*	*Minerva calls Telemachus home.*
5.	*Calypso releases Ulysses.*	*16-20*	*Ulysses joins the suitors at feast, as a beggar.*
6.	*Ulysses is shipwrecked.*	*21.*	*Penelope brings Ulysses' bow and leaves; he shoots it.*
7-8	*Ulysses tells his story to the Phoenicians at feast.*		
9-12	*Ulysses continues his story: Cyclops, Circe, visit to Hades, etc.*	*22.*	*Ulysses slays the suitors.*
		23-24.	*Ulysses is reunited with Penelope and Laertes.*

Book I

Tell me, O Muse, of that ingenious hero who travelled far and wide after he had sacked the famous town of Troy. Many cities did he visit, and many were the nations with whose manners and customs he was acquainted; moreover he suffered much by sea while trying to save his own life and bring his men safely home; but do what he might he could not save his men, for they perished through their own sheer folly in eating the cattle of the Sun-god Hyperion; so the god prevented them from ever reaching home. Tell me, too, about all these things, O daughter of Jove, from whatsoever source you may know them.

So now all who escaped death in battle or by shipwreck had got safely home except Ulysses, and he, though he was longing to return to his wife and country, was detained by the goddess Calypso, who had got him into a large cave and waited to marry him. But as years went by, there came a time when the gods settled that he should go back to Ithaca; even then, however, when he was among his own people, his troubles were not yet over; nevertheless all the gods had now begun to pity him except Neptune, who still persecuted him without ceasing and would not let him get home.

Now Neptune had gone off to the Ethiopians, who are at the world's end, and lie in two halves, the one looking West and the other East. He had gone there to accept a hecatomb of sheep and oxen, and was enjoying himself at his festival; but the other gods met in the house of Olympian Jove, and the sire of gods and men spoke first. At that moment he was thinking of Ægisthus, who had been killed by Agamemnon's son Orestes; so he said to the other gods:

"See now, how men lay blame upon us gods for what is after all nothing but their own folly. Look at Ægisthus; he must needs make love to Agamemnon's wife unrighteously and then kill Agamemnon, though he knew it would be the death of him; for I sent Murcury to warn him not to do either of these things, inasmuch as Orestes would be sure to take his revenge when he grew up and wanted to return home. Murcury told him this in all good will but he would not listen, and now he has paid for everything in full."

Then Minerva said, "Father, son of Saturn, King of kings, it served Ægisthus right, and so it would any one else who does as he did; but Ægisthus is neither here nor there; it is for Ulysses that my heart bleeds, when I think of his sufferings in that lonely sea-girt island, far away, poor man, from all his friends. It is an island covered with frost, in the very middle of the sea, and a goddess lives there, daughter of the magician Atlas, who looks after the bottom of the ocean, and carries the great columns that keep heaven and earth asunder. This daughter of Atlas has got hold of poor unhappy Ulysses, and keeps trying by every kind of blandishment to make him forget his home, so that he is tired of life, and thinks of nothing but how he may once more see the smoke of his own chimneys. You, sir, take no heed of this, and yet when Ulysses was before Troy did he not propitiate you with many a burnt sacrifice? Why then should you keep on being so angry with him?"

And Jove said, "My child, what are you talking about? How can I forget Ulysses than who there is no more capable man on earth, nor more liberal in his offerings to the immortal gods that live in heaven? Bear in mind, however, that Neptune is still furious with Ulysses for having blinded an eye of Polyphemus king of the Cyclopes. Polyphemus is son to Neptune by the nymph Thoosa, daughter to the sea-king Phorcys; therefore though he will not kill Ulysses outright, he torments him by preventing him from getting home. Still, let us lay our heads together and see how we can help him to return; Neptune will then by pacified, for if we are all of a mind he can hardly stand out against us."

And Minerva said, "Father, son of Saturn, King of kings, if, then, the gods now mean that Ulysses should get home, we should first send Mercury to the Ogygian island to tell Calypso that we have made up our minds and that he is to return. In the meantime I will go to Ithaca, to put heart into Ulysses' son Telemachus; I will embolden him to call the Achæans in assembly, and speak out to the suitors of his mother Penelope, who persist in eating up any number of his sheep and oxen; I will also conduct him to Sparta and to Pylos, to see if he can hear anything about the return of his dead father—for this will make people speak well of him."

So saying she bound on her glittering golden sandals, imperishable, with which she can fly like the wind over land or sea; she grasped the redoubtable bronze-shod spear, so stout and sturdy and strong, wherewith she quells the ranks of heroes who have displeased her, and down she darted from the topmost summits of Olympus, whereon forthwith she was in Ithaca, at the gateway of Ulysses' house, disguised as a visitor, Mentes, chief of the Taphians, and she held a bronze spear in her hand. There she found the lordly suitors seated on hides of the oxen which they had killed and eaten, and playing draughts in front of the house. Men-servants and pages were bustling about to wait upon them, some mixing wine with water in the mixing bowls, some cleaning down the tables with wet sponges and laying them out again, and some cutting up great quantities of meat.

Telemachus saw her long before any one else did. He was sitting moodily among the suitors thinking about his brave father, and how he would send them flying out of the house, if he were to come to his own again and be honoured as in days gone by. Thus brooding as he sat among them, he caught sight of Minerva and went straight to the gate, for he was vexed that a stranger should be kept waiting for admittance. He took her right hand in his own, and bade her give him her spear. "Welcome," said he, "to our house, and when you have partaken of food you shall tell us what you have come for."

He led the way as he spoke, and Minerva followed him. When they were within he took her spear and set it in the spear sand against a strong bearing-post along with the many other spears of his unhappy father, and he conducted her to a richly decorated seat under which he threw a cloth of damask. There was a footstool also for her feet, and he set another seat near her for himself, away from the suitors, that she might not be annoyed while eating by their noise and insolence, and that he might ask her more freely about his father.

A maid servant then brought them water in a beautiful golden ewer and poured it into a silver basin for them to wash their hands, and she drew a clean table beside them. An upper servant brought them bread, and offered them many good things of what there was in the house, the carver fetched them plates of all manner of meats and set coups of gold by their side, and a manservant brought them wine and poured it out for them.

Then the suitors came in and took their places on the benches and seats. Forthwith men servants poured water over their their hands, maids went round with the bread-baskets, pages filled the mixing-bowls with wine and water, and they laid their hands upon the good things that were before them. As soon as they had had enough to eatand drink they wanted music and dancing, which are the crowning embellishments of a banquet, so a servant brought a lyre to Pehmius, whom they compelled perforce to sing to them. As soon as he touched his lyre and began to sing Telemachus spoke low to Minerva, with his head close to hers that no man might hear.

"I hope, sir," said he, "that you will not be offended with what I am going to say. Singing comes cheap to those who do not pay for it, and all this is done at the cost of one whose bones lie rotting in some wilderness or grinding to powder in the surf. If these men were to see my father come back to Ithaca they would pray for longer legs rather than a longer purse, for money would not serve them; but he, alas, has fallen on an ill fate, and even when people do sometimes say that he is coming, we no longer heed them; we shall never see him again. And now, sir, tell me and tell me true, who you are and where you come from. Tell me of your town and parents, what manner of ship you came in, how your crew brought you to Ithica, and of what nation they declared themselves to be—for you cannot have come by land. Tell me also truly, for I want to know, are you a stranger to this house, or have you been here in my father's time? In the old days we had many visitors for my father went about much himself."

And Minerva answered, "I will tell you truly and particularly all about it. I am Mentes, son of Anchialus, and I am King of the Taphians. I have come here with my ship and crew, on a voyage to men of a foreign tongue being bound for Temesa with a cargo for iron, and I shall bring back copper. As for my ship, it lies over yonder off the open country way from the town, in the harbour Rheithron under the wooded mountain Neritum. Our fathers were friends before us, as old Lærtes will tell you, if you will go and ask him. They say, however, that he never comes to town now, and lives by himself in the country, faring hardly, with an old woman to look after him and get his dinner for him, when he comes in tired from pottering about his vineyard. They told me your father was at home again, and that was why I came, but it seems the gods are still keeping him back, for he is not dead yet—not on the mainland. it is more likely he is on some sea-gird island in mid ocean, or a prisoner among savages who are detaining him against his will. I am no prophet, and know very little about omens, but I speak as it is borne in upon me from heaven, and assure you that he will not be away much longer; for he is a man of such resource that even though her were in chains of iron he would find some means of getting home again. But tell me, and tell me true, can Ulysses really have such a fine looking fellow for a son? You are indeed wonderfully like him about the head and eyes, for we were close friends before he set sail for Troy where the flower of all the Argives went also. Since that time we have never either of us seen the other."

"My mother," answered Telemachus, "tells me I am son to Ulysses, but it is a wise child that knows his own father. Would that I were son to one who had grown old upon his own estates, for, since you ask me, there is no more ill-starred man under heaven than he who they tell me is my father."

And Minerva said, "There is no fear of your race dying out yet, while Penelope has such a fine son as you are. But tell me, and tell me true, what is the meaning of all this feasting, and who are these people? What is it all about? Have you some banquet, or is there a wedding in the family—for no one seems to be bringing any provisions of his own? And the guests—how atrociously they are behaving; what riot they make over the whole house; it is enought to disgust any respectable person who comes near them."

"Sir," said Telemachus, "as regards your question, so long as my father was here it was well with us and with the house, but the gods in their displeasure have willed it otherwise, and have hidden him away more closely than modern man was ever yet hidden. I could have borne it better even though he were dead, if he had fallen with his men before Troy, or had died with his friends around him when the days of his fighting were done; for then the Achæans would have built a mound over his ashes, and I should myself have been heir to his renown; but now the storm-winds have spirited him away we know not whither; he is gone without leaving so much of a trace behind him, and I inherit nothing but dismay. Nor does the matter end simply with grief for the loss of my father; heaven has laid sorrows on me of another kind; for the chiefs from all our islands,Dulichium, Same, and the woodland island of Zacynthus, as also all the principal men of Ithaca itself, are eating up my house under the pretext of paying court to my mother, who will neither point blank say that she will not marry, nor yet bring matters to an end; so they are making havoc of my estate, and before long will do so also with myself."

"Is that so," exclaimed Minerva, "then you do indeed want Ulysses home again. Give him his helmet, shield, and a couple of lances, and if he is the man he was when I first knew him in our house, drinking and making merry, he would soon lay his hands about these rascally suitors, were he to stand once more upon his threshold. He was then coming from Ephyra, where he had been to beg poison for his arrows from Ilus, son of Mermerus. Ilus feared the ever-living gods and would not give him any, but my father let him have some, for he was very fond of him. If Ulysses is the man he then was these suitors will have a short shrift and a sorry wedding.

"But there! It rests with heaven to determine whether he is to return, and take his revenge in his own house or no; I would, however, urge you to set about trying to get rid of these suitors at once. Take my advice, call the Achæan heroes in assembly to-morrow morning—lay your case before them, and call heaven to bear you witness. Bid the suitors take themselves off, each to his own place, and if your a monther's mind is set on marrying again, let her go back to her father, who will find her a husband and provide her with all the marriage gifts that so dear a daughter may expect. As for yourself, let me prevail upon you to take the best ship you can get, with a crew of twenty men, and go in quest of your father who has so long been missing. Some one may tell you something, or (and people often hear things in this way) some heaven-sent message may direct you. First go to Pylos and ask Nestor; thence go on to Sparta and visit Menelaus, for he got home last of all the Achæans; if you hear that your father is alive and on his way home, you can put up with the waste these suitors will make for yet another twelve months. If on the other hand you hear of his death, come home at once, celebrate his funeral rites with all due pomp, build a barrow to his memory, and make your mother marry again. Then, having done all this, think it well over in your mind how, by fair means or foul, you may kill these suitors in your own house. You are too old to plead infancy any longer; have you not heard how people are singing Orestes's praises for having killed his father's murderer Ægisthus? You are a fine, smart looking fellow; show your mettle, then, and make yourself a name in story. Now, however, I must go back to my ship and to my crew, who will be impatient if I keep them waiting longer; think the matter over for yourself, and remember what I have said to you."

"Sir," answered Telemachus, "it has been very kind of you to talk to me in this way, as though I were your own son, and I will do all you tell me; I know you want to be getting on with your voyage, but stay a little longer till you have taken a bath and refreshed yourself. I will then give you a present, and you shall go on your way rejoicing; I will give you one of great beauty and value—a keepsake such as only dear friends give to one another."

Minerva answered, "Do not try to keep me, for I would be on my way at once. As for any present you may be disposed to make me, keep it till I come again, and I will take it home with me. You shall give me a very good one, and I will give you one of no less value in return."

With these words she flew away like a bird into the air, but she had given Telemachus courage, and had made him think more than ever about his father. He felt the change, wondered at it, and knew that the stranger had been a god, so he went straight to where the suitors were sitting.

Phemius was still singing, and his hearers sat rapt in silence as he told the sad tale of the return from Troy, and the ills Minerva had laid upon the Achæans. Penelope, daughter of Icarius, heard his song from her room upstairs, and came down by the great staircase, not alone, but attended by two of her handmaids. When she reached the suitors she stood by one of the bearing posts that supported the roof of the cloisters with a staid maiden on either side of her. She held a veil, moreover, before her face, and was weeping bitterly.

"Phemius," she cried, "you know many another feat of gods and heroes, such as poets love to celebrate. Sing the suitors some one of these, and let them drink their wine in silence, but cease this sad tale, for it breaks my sorrowful heart, and reminds me of my lost husband whom I mourn ever without ceasing, and whose name was great over all Hellas and middle Argos."

"Mother," answered Telemachus, "let the bard sing what he has a mind to; bards do not make the ills they sing of; it is Jove, not they, who makes them, and who sends weal or woe upon mankind according to his own good pleasure. This fellow means no harm by singing the ill-fated return of the Danaans, for people always applaud the latest songs most warmly. Make up your mind to it and bear it; Ulysses is not the only man who never came back from Troy, but many another went down as well as he. Go, then, within the house and busy yourself with your daily duties, your loom, your distaff, and the ordering of your servants; for speech is man's matter, and mine above all others—for it is I who am master here."

She went wondering back into the house, and laid her son's saying in her heart. Then, going upstairs with her handmaids into her room, she mourned her dear husband till Minerva shed sweet sleep over her eyes. But the suitors were clamorous throughout the covered cloisters, and prayed each one that he might be her bed fellow.

Then Telemachus spoke, "Shameless," he cried, [and insolent suitors, let us feast at our pleasure now, and let there be no brawling, for it is a rare thing to hear a man with such a divine voice as Phemius has; but in the morning meet me in full assembly that I may give you formal notice to depart, and feast at one another's houses, turn and turn about, at your own cost. If on the other hand you choose to persist in spunging upon one man, heaven help me, but Jove shall reckon with you in full, and when you fall in my father's house there shall be no man to avenge you."

The suitors bit their lips as they heard him, and marvelled at the boldness of his speech. Then, Antinous, son of Eupeithes, said, "The gods seem to have given you lessons in bluster and tall talking; may Jove never grant you to be chief in Ithaca as your father was before you."

Telemachus answered, "Antinous, do not chide with me, but, god willing, I will be chief too if I can. Is this the worst fate you can think of for me? It is no bad thing to be a chief, for it brings both riches and honour. Still, now that Ulysses is dead there are many great men in Ithaca both old and young, and some other may take the lead among them; nevertheless I will be chief in my own house, and will rule those whom Ulysses has won for me."

Then Eurymachus, son of Polybus, answered, "It rests with heaven to decide who shall be chief among us, but you shall be master in your own house and over your own possessions; no one while there is a man in Ithaca shall do you violence nor rob you. And now, my good fellow, I want to know about this stranger. What country does he come from? Of what family is he, and where is his estate? Has he brought you news about the return of your father, or was he on business of his own? He seemed a well-to-do man, but he hurried off so suddenly that he was gone in a moment before we could get to know him."

"My father is dead and gone," answered Telemachus, "and even if some rumour reaches me I put no more faith in it now. My mother does indeed sometimes send for a soothsayer and question him, but I give his prophecyings no heed. As for the stranger, he was Mentes, son of Anchialus, chief of the Taphians, an old friend of my father's." But in his heart he knew that it had been the goddess.

The suitors then returned to their singing and dancing until the evening; but when night fell upon their pleasuring they went home to bed each in his own abode. Telemachus's room was high up in a tower that looked on to the outer court; hither, then, he hied, brooding and full of thought. A good old woman, Euryclea, daughter of Ops, the son of Pisenor, went before him with a couple of blazing torches. Lærtes had bought her with his own money when she was quite young; he gave the worth of twenty oxen for her, and shewed as much respect to her in his household as he did to his own wedded wife, but he did not take her to his bed for he feared his wife's resentment. She it was who now lighted Telemachus to his room, and she loved him better than any of the other women in the house did, for she had nursed him when he was a baby. He opened the door of his bed room and sat down upon the bed; as he took off his shirt he gave it to the good old woman, who folded it tidily up, and hung it for him over a peg by his bed side, after which she went out, pulled the door to by a silver catch, and drew the bolt home by means of the strap. But Telemachus as he lay covered with a woollen fleece kept thinking all night through of his intended voyage and of the counsel that Minerva had given him.

Book XIV

Ulysses now left the haven, and took the rough track up through the wooded country and over the crest of the mountain till he reached the place where Minerva had said that he would find the swineherd, who was the most thrifty servant he had. He found him sitting in front of his hut, which was by the yards that he had built on a site which could be seen from far. He had made them spacious and fair to see, with a free run for the pigs all round them; he had built them during his master's absence, of stones which he had gathered out of the ground, without saying anything to Penelope or Lærtes, and he had fenced them on top with thorn bushes. Outside the yard he had run a strong fence of oaken posts, split, and set pretty close together, while inside he had built twelve sties near one another for the sows to lie in. There were fifty pigs wallowing in each sty, all of them breeding sows; but the boars slept outside and were much fewer in number, for the suitors kept on eating them, and the swinchered had to send them the best he had continually. There were three hundred and sixty boar pigs, and the herdsman's four hounds, which were as fierce as wolves, slept always with them. The swineherd was at that moment cutting out a pair of sandals from a good stout ox hide. Three of his men were out herding the pigs in one place or another, and he had sent the fourth to town with a boar that he had been forced to send the suitors that they might sacrifice it and have their fill of meat.

When the hounds saw Ulysses they set up a furious barking and flew at him, but Ulysses was cunning enough to sit down and loose his hold of the stick that he had in his hand: still, he would have been torn by them in his own homestead had not the swineherd dropped his ox hide, rushed full speed through the gate of the yard and driven the dogs off by shouting and throwing stones at them. Then he said to Ulysses, "Old man, the dogs were likely to have made short work of you, and then you would have got me into trouble. The gods have given me quite enough worries without that, for I have lost the best of masters, and am in continual grief on his account. I have to attend swine for other people to eat, while he, if he yet lives to see the light of day, is starving in some distant land. But come inside, and when you have had your fill of bread and wine, tell me where you come from, and all about your misfortunes."

On this the swineherd led the way into the hut and bade him sit down. He strewed a good thick bed of rushes upon the floor, and on the top of this he threw the shaggy chamois skin—a great thick one—on which he used to sleep by night. Ulysses was pleased at being made thus welcome, and said "May Jove, sir, and the rest of the gods grant you your heart's desire in return for the kind way in which you have received me."

To this you answered, O swineherd Eumæus, "Stranger, though a still poorer man should come here, it would not be right for me to insult him, for all strangers and beggars are from Jove. You must take what you can get and be thankful, for servants live in fear when they have young lords for their masters; and this is my misfortune now, for heaven has hindered the return of him who would have been always good to me and given me something of my own—a house, a piece of land, a good looking wife, and all else that a liberal master allows a servant who has worked hard for him, and whose labour the gods have prospered as they have mine in the situation which I hold. If my master had grown old here he would have done great things by me, but he is gone, and I wish that Helen's whole race were utterly destroyed, for she has been the death of many a good man. It was this matter that took my master to Ilius, the land of noble steeds, to fight the Trojans in the cause of king Agamemnon."

As he spoke he bound his girdle round him and went to the sties where the young sucking pigs were penned. He picked out two which he brought back with him and sacrificed. He singed them, cut them up, and spitted them; when the meat was cooked he brought it all in and set it before Ulysses, hot and still on the spit, whereon Ulysses sprinkled it over with white barley meal. The swineherd then mixed wine in a bowl of ivy-wood, and taking a seat opposite Ulysses told him to begin.

"Fall to, stranger," said he, "on a dish of servant's pork. The fat pigs have to go to the suitors, who eat them up without shame or scruple; but the blessed gods love not such shameful doings, and respect those who do what is lawful and right. Even the fierce free-booters who go raiding on other people's land, and Jove gives them their spoil—even they, when they have filled their ships and got home again live conscience-stricken, and look fearfully for judgement; but some god seems to have told these people that Ulysses is dead and gone; they will not, therefore, go back to their own homes and make their offers of marriage in the usual way, but waste his estate by force, without fear or stint. Not a day or night comes out of heaven, but they sacrifice not one victim nor two only, and they take the run of his wine, for he was exceedingly rich. No other great man either in Ithaca or on the mainland is as rich as he was; he had as much as twenty men put together. I will tell you what he had. There are twelve herds of cattle upon the mainland, and as many flocks of sheep, there are also twelve droves of pigs, while his own men and hired strangers feed him twelve widely spreading herds of goats. Here in Ithaca he runs eleven large flocks of goats on the far end of the island, and they are in the charge of excellent goatherds. Each one of these sends the suitors the best goat in the flock every day. As for myself, I am in charge of the pigs that you see here, and I have to keep picking out the best I have and sending it to them."

This was his story, but Ulysses went on eating and drinking ravenously without a word, brooding his revenge. When he had eaten enough and was satisfied, the swineherd took the bowl from which he usually drank, filled it with wine, and gave it to Ulysses, who was pleased, and said as he took it in his hands, "My friend, who was this master of yours that bought you and paid for you, so rich and so powerful as you tell me? You say he perished in the cause of King Agamemnon; tell me who he was, in case I may have met with such a person. Jove and the other gods know, but I may be able to give you news of him, for I have travelled much."

Eumaus answered, "Old man, no traveller who comes here with news will get Ulysses's wife and son to believe his story. Nevertheless, tramps in want of a lodging keep coming with their mouths full of lies, and not a word of truth; every one who finds his way to Ithaca goes to my mistress and tells her falsehoods, whereon she takes them in, makes much of them, and asks them all manner of questions, crying all the time as women will when they have lost their husbands. And you too, old man, for a shirt and cloak would doubtless make up a very pretty story. But the wolves and birds of prey have long since torn Ulysses to pieces, or the fishes of the sea have eaten him, and his bones are lying buried deep in sand upon some foreign shore; he is dead and gone, and a bad business it is for all his friends—for me especially; go where I may I shall never find so good a master, not even if I were to go home to my father and mother where I was bred and born. I do not so much care, however, about my parents now, though I should dearly like to see them again in my own country; it is the loss of Ulysses that grieves me most; I cannot speak of him without reverence though he is here no longer, for he was very fond of me, and took such care of me that wherever he may be I shall always honour his memory."

Book XVI

Meanwhile Ulysses and the swineherd had lit a fire in the hut and were getting breakfast ready at daybreak, for they had sent the men out with the pigs. When Telemachus came up, the dogs did not bark but fawned upon him, so Ulyssess, hearing the sound of feet and noticing that the dogs did not bark said to Eumæus:

Eumæus, I hear footsteps; I suppose one of your men or some one of your acquaintance is coming up here, for the dogs are fawning upon him and not barking."

The words were hardly out of his mouth when his son stood at the door. Eumæus sprang to his feet, and the bowls in which he was mixing wine fell from his hands, as he made towards his master. He kissed his head and both his beautiful eyes, and wept for joy. A father could not be more delighted at the return of an only son, the child of his old age, after ten years' absence in a foreign country and after having gone through much hardship. He embraced him, kissed him all over as if he had come from the dead, and spoke fondly to him:

"So you have come, Telemachus, light of my eyes that you are. When I heard you had gone to Pylos I made sure I was never going to see you any more. Come in, my dear child, and sit down, that I may have a good look at you, now that you are home again; it is not very often that you come into the country to see us herdsmen; you stick pretty close to the town generally. I suppose you think it is better to keep an eye on what the suitors are doing.

"So be it old friend," said Telemachus, " but I am come now because I want to see you, and to learn if my mother is still at her old home or whether someone else has married her, so that the bed of Ulysses is without covering and covered with cobwebs."

"She is still at the house," replied Eumæus, " grieving and breaking her heart, and doing nothing but weep, both night and day continually."

As he spoke he took Telemachus' spear, whereupon he crossed the stone threshold and came inside. Ulysses rose from his seat to give him place as he entered, but Telemachus checked him;

"Sit down, stranger," said he , "I can easily find another seat, and there is one here who will lay it for me."

Ulysses went back to his own place, and Eumæus strewed some green brushwood on the floor and threw a sheepskin over it for Telemachus to sit upon. Then the swineherd brought them platters of cold meat, the remains of what they had eaten the day before, and he filled the bread baskets with bread as fast as he could. He mixed wine also in bowls of ivy-wood, and took his seat facing Ulysses. Then they laid their hands on the good things that were before them, and as soon as they had enough to eat and drink Telemachus said to Eumæus, "Old friend, where does this stranger come from? How did his crew bring him to Ithaca, and who were they?—for assuredly he did not come here by land."

To this you answered, O swineherd Eumæus, "My son, I will tell you the real truth. He says he is a Cretan and has been a great traveller. At this moment he is running away from a Thesprotian ship, and has taken refuge at my station, so I will put him into your hands. Do whatever you like with him, only remember that he is your suppliant."

"I am very much distressed, " said Telemachus, "by what you have just told me. How can I take this stranger into my house? I am as yet young, and am not strong enough to hold my own if any man attacks me. My mother cannot make up her mind whether to stay where she is and look after the house out of respect for public opinion and the memory of her husband, or whether the time is now come for her to take the best man of those who are wooing her, and the one who will make her the most advantageous offer; still, as the stranger has come to your attention I will find a cloak and shirt of good wear, with a sword and sandals, and will send him wherever he wants to go. Or if you like you can keep him here at the station, and I will send him clothes and food that he may be no burden on you and on your men; but I will not have him go near the suitors, for they are very insolent, and are sure to ill-treat him in a way that will greatly grieve me; no matter how valiant a man may be he can do nothing against numbers, for they will be too many for him."

Then Ulysses said, "Sir, it is right that I should say something myself. I am much shocked by what you have said about the insolent way in which the suitors are behaving in despite of such a man as you are. Tell me, do you submit to such treatment tamely, or has some god set your people against you? May you not complain of your brothers—for it is to these that a man may look for support however great his quarrel may be? I wish I were as young as you are and in my present mind, if I were I son to Ulysses, or, indeed, Ulysses himself, I would rather someone came and cut my head off, but I would go to the house and be the bane of every one of these men. If they were too many for me—I being single-handed—I would rather die fighting in my own house rather than see such disgraceful sights day after day, strangers grossly maltreated, and men dragging the women servants about the house in an unseemly way, wine drawn recklessly, and bread wasted all to no purpose for an end that will never be accomplished."

And Telemachus answered, "I will tell you truly everything. There is no enmity between me and my people, nor can I complain of brothers, to whom a man may look for support however great his quarrel may be. Jove has made us a race of only sons. Lærtes was the only son of Prceisius, ans Ulysses only son of Lærtes. I myself the only son of Ulysses who left me behind when he went away, so that I have never been of any use to him. Hence it comes that my house is in the hands of numberless maraudes; for the chiefs of all the neighboring islands, Dulichium, Same, Zacynthus, as also all the principal men of Ithaca itself, are eating up my house under the pretext of paying court to my mother, who will neither say point blank that she will not marry, nor yet bring matters to an end, so they are making havoc of my estate, and before long will do so with myself into the bargain. The issue, however, rests with heaven. But do you, old friend Eumæus, go at once to Penelope and tell her that I am safe and have returned from Pylos. Tell it to herself alone, and then come back here without letting anyone else know, for there are many who are plotting mischief against me."

"I understand and heed you," replied Eumæus; "you need instruct me no further, only as I am going that way say whether I had not better let poor Lærtes know that you are returned. He used to superintend the work on his farm in spite of his bitter sorrow about Ulysses, and he would eat and drink at will along with his servants; but they tell me that from the day on which you set out for Pylos he has neither eaten nor drunk as he ought to do, nor does he look after his farm, but sits weeping and wasting the flesh from off his bones."

"More's the pity," answered Telemachus, "I am sorry for him, but we must leave him to himself just now. If people could have everything their own way, the first thing I should choose would be the return of my father; but go, and give your message; then make haste back again, and do not turn out of your way to tell Lærtes. Tell my mother to send one of her women secretly with the news at once, and let him hear it from her."

Thus did he urge the swineherd; Eumæus, therefore, took his sandals, bound them to his feet, and started for the town. Minerva watched him well off the station, and then came up to it in the form of a woman—fair, stately, and wise. She stood against the side of the entry, and revealed herself to Ulysses, but Telemachus could not see her, and knew not that she was there, for the gods do not let themselves be seen by everybody. Ulysses saw her, and so did the dogs, for they did not bark, but went scared and whining off to the other side of the yards. She nodded her head and motioned to Ulysses with her eyebrows; whereon he left the hut and stood before her outside the main wall of the yards. Then she said to him:

"Ulysses, noble son of Lærtes, it is now time for you to tell your son: do not keep him in the dark any longer, but lay your plans for the destruction of the suitors, and then make for the town. I will not be long in joining you, for I too am eager for the fray."

As she spoke she touched him with her golden wand. "First she threw a fair clean shirt and cloak about his shoulders; then she made him younger and of more imposing presence; she gave him back his colour, filled out his cheeks, and let his beard become dark again. Then she went away and Ulysses came back inside the hut. His son was astounded when he saw him, and turned his eyes away for fear he might be looking upon a god.

"Stranger," said he, "how suddenly you have changed from what you were a moment or two ago. You are dressed differently and your colour is not the same. Are you some one or other of the gods that live in heaven? If so, be propitious to me till I can make you due sacrifice and offerings of wrought gold. Have mercy upon me."

And Ulysses said, "I am no god, why should you take me for one? I am your father, on whose account you grieve and suffer so much at the hands of lawless men."

As he spoke he kissed his son, and a tear fell from his cheek on to the ground, for he had restrained all tears till now. But Telemachus could not yet believe that it was his father, and said:

"You are not my father, but some god is flattering me with vain hopes that I may grieve the more hereafter; no mortal man could of himself contrive to do as you have been doing, and make yourself old and young at a monent"s notice, unless a god were with him. A second ago you were old and all in rags, and now you are like some god come down from heaven."

Ulysses answered, "Telemachus, you ought not to be so immeasurably astonished at my being really here. There is no other Ulysses who will come hereafter. Such as I am, it is I, who after long wandering and much hardship have got home in the twentieth year to my own country. What you wonder at is the work of the redoubtable goddess Minerva, who does with me whatever she will, for she can do what she pleases. At one moment she makes me like a beggar, and the next I am a young man with good clothes on my back; it is an easy matter for the gods who live in heaven to make any man look either rich or poor."

As he spoke he sat down, and Telemachus threw his arms about his father and wept. They were both so much moved that they cried aloud like eagles or vultures with crooked talons that have been robbed of their half-fledged young by peasants. Thus piteously did they weep, and the sun would have gone down upon their mourning if Telemachus had not suddenly said, "In what ship, my dear father, did your crew bring you to Ithaca? Of what nation did they declare themselves to be—for you cannot have come by land?"

"I will tell you the truth, my son," replied Ulysses. "It was the Phæacians who brought me here. They are great sailors, and are in the habit of giving escorts to any one who reaches their coasts. They took me over the sea while I was fast asleep, and landed me in Ithaca, after giving me many presents in bronze, gold, and raiment. These things by heaven's mercy are lying concealed in a cave, and I am now come here on the suggestion of Minerva that we may consult about killing our enemies. First, therefore, give me a list of the suitors, with their number, that I may learn who, and how many, they are. I can then turn the matter over in my mind, and see whether we two can fight the whole body of them ourselves, or whether we must find others to help us."

To this Telemachus answered, "Father, I have always heard of your renown both in the field and in council, but the task you talk of is a very great one: I am awed at the mere thought of it; two men cannot stand against many and brave ones. There are not ten suitors only, nor twice ten, but ten many times over; you shall learn their number at once. There are fifty-two chosen youths from Dulichium and they have six servants; from Same there are twenty-four; twenty young Achæans from Zacynthus, and twelve from Ithaca itself, all of them well born. They have with them a servant Medon, a bard, and two men who can carve at table. If we face such numbers as this, you may have bitter cause to rue your coming, and your revenge. See whether you cannot think of someone who would be willing to come and help us."

"Listen to me," replied Ulysses, "and think whether Minerva and her father Jove may seem sufficient, or whether I am to try and find some one else as well."

"Those whom you have named," answered Telemachus, "are a couple of good allies, for though they dwell high up among the clouds they have power over both gods and men."

* * *

Then Penelope resolved that she would show herself to the suitors. She knew of the plot against Telemachus for the servant Medon had overheard their counsels and had told her; she went down therefore to the court attended by her maidens, and when she reached the suitors she stood by one of the bearing-posts supporting the roof of the cloister holding a veil before her face, and rebuked Antinous saying:

"Antinous, insolent and wicked schemer, they say you are the best speaker and counsellor of any man your own age in Ithaca, but you are nothing of the kind. Madman, why should you try to compass the death of Telemachus, and take no heed of suppliants, whose witness is Jove himself? It is not right for you to plot thus against one another. Do you not remember how your father fled to this house in fear of the people, who were enraged against him for having gone with some Taphian pirates and plundered the Thesprotians who were at peace with us? They wanted to tear him in pieces and eat up everything he had, but Ulysses stayed their hands although they were infuriated, and now you devour his property without paying for it, and break my heart by wooing his wife and trying to kill his son. Leave off doing so, and stop the others also."

To this Eurymachus son of Polybus answered, "Take heart, Queen Penelope daughter of Icarius, and do not trouble yourself about these matters. The man is not yet born, nor never will be, who shall lay hands upon your son. Telemachus, while I yet live to look upon the face of the earth. I say—and it shall surely be—that my spear shall be reddened with his blood; for many a time has Ulysses taken me on his knees, held wine up to my lips to drink, and put pieces of meat into my hands. Therefore Telemachus is much the dearest friend I have, and has nothing to fear from the hands of us suitors. Of course, if death comes to him from the gods, he cannot escape it." He said this to quiet her, but in reality he was plotting against Telemachus.

Then Penelope went upstairs again and mourned her husband till Minerva shed sleep over her eyes. In the evening Eumæus got back to Ulysses and his son, who had just sacrificed a young pig of a year old and were helping one another to get supper ready; Minerva therefore came up to Ulysses, turned him into an old man with a stroke of her wand, and clad him in his old clothes again, for fear that the swineherd might recognize him and not keep the secret, but go and tell Penelope.

Book XVII

* * *

Presently Ulysses and the swineherd came up to the house and stood by it, amid a sound of music, for Phemius was just beginning to sing to the suitors. Then Ulysses took hold of the swineherd's hand, and said:

"Eumæus, this house of Ulysses is a very fine place. No matter how far you go you will find few like it. One building keeps following on after another. The outer court has a wall with battlements all round it; the doors are double folding, and of good workmanship; it would be a hard matter to take it by force of arms. I perceive, too, that there are many people banqueting within it, for there is a smell of roast meat, and I hear a sound of music, which the gods have made to go along with feasting."

Then Eumæus said, "You have perceived aright, as indeed you generally do; but let us think what will be our best course. Will you go inside first and join the suitors, leaving me here behind you, or will you wait here and let me go in first? But do not wait long, or some one may see you loitering about outside, and throw something at you. Consider this matter I pray you."

And Ulysses answered, "I understand and heed. Go in first and leave me here where I am. I am quite used to being beaten and having things thrown at me. I have been so much buffeted about in war and by sea that I am case-hardened, and this too may go with the rest. But a man cannot hide away the cravings of a hungry belly; this is an enemy which gives much trouble to all men; it is because of this that ships are fitted out to sail the seas, and to make war upon other people."

As they were thus talking, a dog that had been lying asleep raised his head and pricked up his ears. This was Argos, whom Ulysses had bred before setting out for Troy, but he had never had any work out of him. In the old days he used to be taken out by the young men when they went hunting wild goats, or deer, or hares, but now that his master was gone he was lying neglected on the heaps of mule and cow dung that lay in front of the stable doors till the men should come and draw it away to manure the great close; and he was full of fleas. As soon as he saw Ulysses standing there, he dropped his ears and wagged his tail, but he could not get close up to his master. When Ulysses saw the dog on the other side of the yard, he dashed a tear from his eyes without Eumæus seeing it, and said:

"Eumæus, what a noble hound that is over yonder on the manure heap: his build is splendid; is he as fine a fellow as he looks, or is he only one of those dogs that come begging about a table, and are kept merely for show?"

"This hound," answered Eumæus, "belonged to him who has died in a far country. If he were what he was when Ulysses left for Troy, he would soon show you what he could do. There was not a wild beast in the forest that could get away from him when he was once on its tracks. But now he has fallen on evil times, for his master is dead and gone, and the women take no care of him. Servants never do their work when their master's hand is no longer over them, for Jove takes half the goodness out of a man when he makes a slave of him."

As he spoke he went inside the buildings to the cloister where the suitors were, but Argos died as soon as he had recognized his master.

Telemachus saw Eumæus long before any one else did, and beckoned him to come and sit beside him; so he looked about and saw a seat lying near where the carver sat serving out their portions to the suitors; he picked it up, brought it to Telemachus's table, and sat down opposite him. Then the servant brought him his portion, and gave him bread from the bread-basket.

Immediately afterwards Ulysses came inside, looking like a poor miserable old beggar, leaning on his staff and with his clothes all in rags. He sat down upon the threshold of ashwood just inside the doors leading from the outer to the inner court, and against a bearing-post of cypress-wood which the carpenter had skilfully planed, and had made to join truly with rule and line. Telemachus took a whole loaf from the bread-basket, with as much meat as he could hold in his two hands, and said to Eumæus, "Take this to the stranger, and tell him to go the round of the suitors, and beg from them; a beggar must not be shamefaced."

So Eumæus went up to him and said, "Stranger, Telemachus sends you this, and says you are to go the round of the suitors begging, for beggars must not be shamefaced."

Ulysses answered, "May King Jove grant all happiness to Telemachus, and fulfil the desire of his heart."

Then with both hands he took what Telemachus had sent him, and laid it on the dirty old wallet at his feet. He went on eating it while the bard was singing, and had just finished his dinner as he left off. The suitors applauded the bard, whereon Minerva went up to Ulysses and prompted him to beg pieces of bread from each one of the suitors, that he might see what kind of people they were, and tell the good from the bad; but come what might she was not going to save a single one of them. Ulysses,therefore, went on his round, going from left to right, and stretched out his hands to beg as though he were a real beggar. Some of them pitied him, and were curious about him, asking one another who he was and where he came from; whereon the gatherd Melanthius said, "Suitors of my noble mistress, I can tell you something about him, for I have seen him before. The swineherd brought him here, but I know nothing about the man himself, nor where he comes from."

On this Antinous began to abuse the swineherd. "You precious idiot," he cried, "what have you brought this man to town for? Have we not tramps and beggars enough already to pester us as we sit at meat? Do you think it a small thing that such people gather here to waste your master's property—and must you needs bring this man as well?"

And Eumæus answered, "Antinous, your birth is good but your words evil. It was no doing of mine that he came here. Who is likely to invite a stranger from a foreign country, unless it be one of those who can do public service as a seer, a healer of hurts, a carpenter or a bard who can charm us with his singing? Such men are welcome all the world over, but no one is likely to ask a beggar who will only worry him. You are always harder on Ulysses' servants than any of the other suitors are, and above all on me, but I do not care so long as Telemachus and Penelope are alive and here."

But Telemachus said, "Hush, do not answer him; Antinous has the bitterish tongue of all the suitors, and he makes the others worse."

Then turning to Antinous he said, "Antinous, you take as much care of my interests as though I were your son. Why should you want to see this stranger turned out of the house? Heaven forbid; take something and give it him yourself; I do not grudge it; I bid you take it. Never mind my mother, nor any of the other servants in the house; but I know you will not do what I say, for you are more fond of eating things yourself than of giving them to other people."

"What do you mean, Telemachus," replied Antinous, "by this swaggering talk? If all the suitors were to give him as much as I will, he would not come here again for another three months."

Book XIX

"Madam," answered Ulysses, "who on the face of the whole earth can dare to chide with you—Your fame reaches the firmament of heaven itself; you are like some blameless king, who upholds righteousness, as the monarch over a great and valiant nation: the earth yields its wheat and barley, the trees are loaded with fruit, the ewes bring forth lambs, and the sea abounds with fish by reason of his virtues, and his people do good deeds under him. Nevertheless, as I sit here in your house, ask me some other question and do not seek to know my race and family, or you will recall memories that will yet more increase my sorrow. I am full of heaviness, but I ought not to sit weeping and wailing in another person's house nor is it well to be thus grieving continually. I shall have one of the servants or even yourself complaining of me, and saying that my eyes swim with tears because I am heavy with wine."

Then Penelope answered, "Stranger, heaven robbed me of all beauty, whether of face or figure, when the Argives set sail for Troy and my dear husband with them. If he were to return and look after my affairs I should be both more respected and should show a better presence to the world. As it is, I am oppressed with care, and with the afflictions which heaven has seen fit to heap upon me. The chiefs from all our islands—Dulichium, Same, and Zacynthus, as also from Ithaca itself, are wooing me against my will and are wasting my estate. I can therefore show no attention to strangers, no suppliants, nor to people who say that they are skilled artisans, but am all the time broken-hearted about Ulysses. They want me to marry again at once, and I have to invent stratagems in order to deceive them. In the first place heaven put it in my mind to set up a great tambour-frame in my room, and to begin working upon an enormous piece of fine needlework. Then I said to them, 'Sweethearts, Ulysses is indeed dead, still, do not press me to marry again immediately; wait—for I would not have my skill in needlework perish unrecorded—till I have finished making a pall for the hero Lærtes, to be ready against the time when death shall take him. He is very rich, and the women of the place will talk if he is laid out without a pall.' This was what I said, and they assented; whereon I used to keep working at my great web all day long, but at night I would unpick the stitches again by torch light. I fooled them in this way for three years without their finding it out, but as time wore on and I was now in my fourth year, in the waning of moons, and many days had been accomplished, those good-for-nothing hussies my maids betrayed me to the suitors, who broke in upon me and caught me; they were very angry with me, so I was forced to finish my work whether I would or no. And now I do not see how I can find any further shift for getting out of this marriage. My parents are putting great pressure upon me, and my son chafes at the ravages the suitors are making upon his estate, for he is now old enough to understand all about it and is perfectly able to look after his own affairs, for heaven has blessed him with an excellent disposition. Still, notwithstanding all this, tell me who you are and where you come from—for you must have had father and mother of some sort; you cannot be the son of an oak or of a rock."

Book XXI

Minerva now put it in Penelope's mind to make the suitors try their skill with the bow and with the iron axes, in contest among themselves, as a means of bringing about their destruction. She went upstairs and got the store room key, which was made of bronze and had a handle of ivory; she then went with her maidens into the store room at the end of the house, where her husband's treasures of gold, bronze, and wrought iron were kept, and where was also his bow, and the quiver full of deadly arrows that had been given him by a friend whom he had met in Lacedæmon—Ipitus the son of Eurytus. The two fell in with one another in Messene at the house of Ortilochus, where Ulysses was staying in order to recover a debt that was owing from the whole people; for the Messenians had carried off three hundred sheep from Ithaca, and had sailed away with them and with their shepherds. In quest of these Ulysses took a long journey while still quite young, for his father and the other chieftains sent him on a mission to recover them. Iphitus had gone there also to try and get back twelve brood mares that he had lost, and the mule foals that were running with them. These mares were the death of him in the end, for when he went to the house of Jove's son, mighty Hercules, who performed such prodigies of valour, Hercules to his shame killed him, though he was his guest, for he feared not heaven's vengeance, nor yet respected his own table which he had set before Iphitus, but killed him in spite of everything, and kept the mares himself. It was when claiming these that Iphitus met

Ulysses, and gave him the bow which on his death had been left by him to his son. Ulysses gave him in return a sword and a spear, and this was the beginning of a fast friendship, although they never visited at one another's houses, for Jove's son Hercules killed Iphitus ere they could do so. This bow, then, given him by Iphitus, had not been taken with him by Ulysses when he sailed for Troy; he had used it so long as he had been at home, but had left it behind as having been a keepsake from a valued friend.

Penelope presently reached the oak threshold of the store room; the carpenter had planed this duly, and had drawn a line on it so as to get it quite straight; he had then set the door posts into it and hung the doors. She loosed the strap from the handle of the door, put in the key, and drove it straight home to shoot back the bolts that held the doors; these flew open with a noise like a bull bellowing in a meadow, and Penelope stepped upon the raised platform, where the chests stood in which the fair linen and clothes were laid by along with fragrant herbs: reaching thence, she took down the bow with its bow case from the peg on which it hung. She sat down with it on her knees, weeping bitterly as she took the bow out of its case, and when her tears had relieved her, she went to the cloister where the suitors were, carrying the bow and the quiver, with the many deadly arrows that were inside it. Along with her came her maidens, bearing a chest that contained much iron and bronze which her husband had won as prizes. When she reached the suitors, she stood by one of the bearing-posts supporting the roof of the cloister, holding a veil before her face, and with a maid on either side of her. Then she said:

"Listen to me you suitors, who persist in abusing the hospitality of this house because its owner has been long absent, and without other pretext than that you want to marry me; this, then, being the prize that you are contending for, I will bring out the mighty bow of Ulysses, and whomsoever of you shall string it most easily and send his arrow through each one of twelve axes, him will I follow and quit this house of my lawful husband, so goodly, and so abounding in wealth. But even so I doubt, not that I shall remember it in my dreams."

But Ulysses, when he had taken it up and examined it all over, strung it as easily as a skilled bard strings a new peg of his lyre and makes the twisted gut fast at both ends. Then he took it in his right hand to prove the string, and it sang sweetly under his touch like the twittering of a swallow. The suitors were dismayed, and turned colour as they heard it; at that moment, moreover, Jove thundered loudly as a sign, and the heart of Ulysses rejoiced as he heard the omen that the son of scheming Saturn had sent him.

He took an arrow that was lying upon the table—for those which the Achæans were so shortly about to taste were all inside the quiver—he laid it on the centre-piece of the bow, and drew the notch of the arrow and the string toward him, still seated on his seat. When he had taken aim he let fly, and his arrow pierced every one of the handle-holes of the axes from the first onwards till it had gone right through them, and into the outer courtyard.

Book XXII

Then Ulysses tore off his rags, and sprang on to the broad pavement with his bow and his quiver full of arrows. He shed the arrows on to the ground at his feet and said, "The mighty contest is at an end. I will now see whether Apollo will vouchsafe it to me to hit another mark which no man has yet hit."

On this he aimed a deadly arrow at Antinous, who was about to take up a two-handled gold cup to drink his wine and already had it in his hands. He had no thought of death—who amongst all the revellers would think that one man, however brave, would stand alone among so many and kill him? The arrow struck Antinous in the throat, and the point went clean through his neck, so that he fell over and the cup dropped from his hand, while a thick stream of blood gushed from his nostrils. He kicked the table from him and upset the things on it, so that the bread and roasted meats were all soiled as they fell over on to the ground. The suitors were in an uproar when they saw that a man had been hit; they sprang in dismay one and all of them from their seats and looked everywhere towards the walls, but there was neither shield nor spear, and they rebuked Ulysses very angrily. "Stranger," said they, "you shall pay for shooting people in this way: you shall see no other contest; you are a doomed man: he whom you have slain was the foremost youth in Ithaca, and the vultures shall devour you for having killed him."

Thus they spoke, for they thought that he had killed Antinous by mistake, and did not perceive that death was hanging over the head of every one of them. But Ulysses glared at them and said:

"Dogs, did you think that I should not come back from Troy—You have wasted my substance, have forced my women servants to lie with you, and have wooed my wife while I was still living. You have feared neither God nor man, and now you shall die."

They turned pale with fear as he spoke, and every man looked round about to see whither he might fly for safety, but Eurymachus alone spoke.

"If you are Ulysses," said he, "then what you have said is just. We have done much wrong on your lands and in your house. But Antinous who was the head and front of the offending lies low already. It was all his doing. It was not that he wanted to marry Penelope; he did not so much care about that; what he wanted was something quite different, and Jove has not vouchsafed it to him; he wanted to kill your sone and to be chief man in Ithaca. Now,therefore, that he has met the death which was his due, spare the lives of your people. We will make everything good among ourselves, and pay you in full for all that we have eaten and drunk. Each one of us shall pay you a fine worth twenty oxen, and we will keep on giving you gold and bronze till your heart is softened. Until we have done this no one can complain of your being enraged against us."

Ulysses again glared at him and said, "Though you should give me all that you have in the world both now and all that you ever shall have, I will not stay my hand till I have paid all of you in full. You must fight, or fly for your lives; and fly, not a man of you shall."

Book XXIII

* * *

"My dear," answered Penelope, "I have no wish to set myself up, nor to depreciate you; but I am not struck by your appearance, for I very well remember what kind of a man you were when you set sail from Ithaca. Nevertheless, Euryclea, take his bed outside the bed chamber that he himself built. Bring the bed outside this room, and put bedding upon it with fleeces, good coverlets, and blankets."

She said this to try him, but Ulysses was very angry and said, "Wife, I am much displeased at what you have just been saying. Who has been taking my bed from the place in which I left it? He must have found it a hard task, no matter how skilled a workman he was, unless some god came and helped him to shift it. There is no man living, however strong and in his prime, who could move it from its place, for it is a marvellous curiosity which I made with my very own hands. There was a young olive growing within the precincts of the house, in full vigour, and about as thick as a bearing-post. I built my room round this with strong walls of stone and a roof to cover them, and I made the doors strong and well-fitting. Then I cut off the top boughs of the olive tree and left the stump standing. This I dressed roughly from the root upwards and then worked with carpenter's tools well and skilfully, straightening my work by drawing a line on the wood, and making it into a bed-prop. I then bored a hole down the middle, and made it the centre-post of my bed, at which I worked till I had finished it, inlaying it with gold and silver; after this I stretched a hide of crimson leather from one side of it to the other. So you see I know all about it, and I desire to learn whether it is still there, or whether any one has been removing it by cutting down the olive tree at its roots."

When she heard the sure proofs Ulysses now gave her, she fairly broke down. She flew weeping to his side, flung her arms about his neck, and kissed him. "Do not be angry with me Ulysses," she cried, "you, who are the wisest of mankind. We have suffered, both of us. Heaven has denied us the happiness of spending our youth, and of growing old, together; do not then be aggrieved or take it amiss that I did not embrace you thus as soon as I saw you. I have been shuddering all the time through fear that someone might come here and deceive me with a lying story; for there are many very wicked people going about. Jove's daughter Helen would never have yielded herself to a man from a foreign country, if she had known that the sons of Achæans would come after her and bring her back. Heaven put it in her heart to do wrong, and she gave no thought to that sin, which has been the source of all our sorrows. Now, however, that you have convinced me by showing that you know all about our bed (which no human being has ever seen but you and I and a single maid servant, the daughter of Actor, who was given me by my father on my marriage, and who keeps the doors of our room) hard of belief though I have been I can mistrust no longer."

Then Ulysses in his turn melted, and wept as he clasped his dear and faithful wife to his bosom. As the sight of land is welcome to men who are swimming towards the shore, when Neptune has wrecked their ship with the fury of his winds and waves—a few alone reach the land, and these, covered with brine, are thankful when they find themselves on firm ground and out of danger—even so was her husband welcome to her as she looked upon him, and she could not tear her two fair arms from about his neck. Indeed they would have gone on indulging their sorrow till rosy-fingered morn appeared, had not Minerva determined otherwise, and held night back in the far west, while she would not suffer Dawn to leave Oceanus, nor to yoke the two steeds Lampus and Phæthon that bear her onward to break the day upon mankind.

At last, however, Ulysses said, "Wife, we have not yet reached the end of our troubles. I have an unknown amount of toil still to undergo. It is long and difficult, but I must go through with it, for thus the shade of Teiresias prophesied concerning me, on the day when I went down into Hades to ask about my return and that of my companions. But now let us go to bed, that we may lie down and enjoy the blessed boon of sleep."

ALFRED, LORD TENNYSON (1809-1892)

The leading poet of Victorian England, Tennyson, like his contemporary Matthew Arnold, posed questions regarding man's place in the universe. In "Ulysses," Tennyson wonders how Ulysses might have adjusted to domestication after many years of adventures at sea.

ULYSSES [1]

It little profits that an idle king,
By this still hearth, among these barren crags,
Matched with an aged wife, I mete and dole
Unequal laws unto a savage race,
That hoard, and sleep, and feed, and know not
    me.
I cannot rest from travel; I will drink
Life to the lees. All times I have enjoyed

Greatly, have suffered greatly, both with those
That loved me, and alone; on shore, and when
Through scudding drifts the rainy Hyades
Vext the dim sea. I am become a name;
For always roaming with a hungry heart
Much have I seen and known — cities of men
And manners, climates, councils, governments,
Myself not least, but honored of them all;
And drunk delight of battle with my peers,
Far on the ringing plains of windy Troy.
I am a part of all that I have met;
Yet all experience is an arch wherethrough
Gleams that untraveled world, whose margin
    fades

[1] Ulysses is Odysseus, the hero in Homer's *Odyssey*. He goes through ten years of adventurous trials to return home to his wife Penelope and his son Telemachus. The story of a final journey after this return comes from Dante's *Inferno* (Canto XXVI).

For ever and for ever when I move.
How dull it is to pause, to make an end,
To rust unburnished, not to shine in use!
As though to breathe were life! Life piled on
     life
Were all too little, and of one to me
Little remains; but every hour is saved
From that eternal silence, something more,
A bringer of new things; and vile it were
For some three suns to store and hoard myself,
And this grey spirit yearning in desire
To follow knowledge like a sinking star,
Beyond the utmost bound of human thought.

This is my son, mine own Telemachus,
To whom I leave the scepter and the isle—
Well-loved of me, discerning to fulfil
This labor, by slow prudence to make mild
A rugged people, and through soft degrees
Subdue them to the useful and the good.
Most blameless is he, centered in the sphere
Of common duties, decent not to fail
In offices of tenderness, and pay
Meet adoration to my household gods,
When I am gone. He works his work, I mine.

There lies the port; the vessel puffs her sail:
There gloom the dark, broad seas. My
     mariners,
Souls that have toiled, and wrought, and
     thought with me—

That ever with a frolic welcome took
The thunder and the sunshine, and opposed
Free hearts, free foreheads—you and I are old;
Old age hath yet his honor and his toll.
Death closes all; but something ere the end,
Some work of noble note, may yet be done,
Not unbecoming men that strove with Gods.
The lights begin to twinkle from the rocks;
The long day wanes; the slow moon climbs; the
     deep
Moans round with many voices. Come, my
     friends,
'Tis not too late to seek a newer world.
Push off, and sitting well in order smite
The sounding furrows; for my purpose holds
To sail beyond the sunset, and the baths
Of all the western stars, until I die.
It may be that the gulfs will wash us down;
It may be we shall touch the Happy Isles,[2]
And see the great Achilles, whom we knew.
Though much is taken, much abides; and
     though
We are not now that strength which in old
     days
Moved earth and heaven, that which we are,
     we are:
One equal temper of heroic hearts,
Made weak by time and fate, but strong in
     will
To strive, to seek, to find and not to yield.

JOHN MILTON (1608-1674)

Before the Fall (from Paradise Lost, Book IV: 304-355)

She as a veil down to the slender waist
Her unadorned golden tresses wore
Disheveled, but in wanton ringlets waved
As the vine curls her tendrils, which implied
Subjection, but required with gentle sway,
And by her yielded, by him best received,
Yielded with coy submission, modest pride,
And sweet reluctant amorous delay.
Nor those mysterious parts were then
     concealed,
Then was not guilty shame, dishonest shame

Of nature's works, honor dishonorable,
Sin-bred, how have ye troubled all mankind

With shows instead, mere shows of seeming
     pure,
And banished from man's life his happiest life,
Simplicity and spotless innocence.
So passed they naked on, nor shunned the
     sight
Of God or angel, for they thought no ill.
So hand in hand they passed, the loveliest pair
That ever since in love's embraces met,
Adam the goodliest man of men since born
His sons, the fairest of her daughters Eve.

---

[2] The Elysian Fields, Greek paradise where
Achilles, hero of the *Iliad*, would be.

Under a tuft of shade that on a green
Stood whispering soft, by a fresh fountain side
They sat them down, and after no more toil
Of their sweet gardening labor than sufficed
To recommend cool zephyr, and made ease
More easy, wholesome thirst and appetite
More grateful, to their supper fruits they fell,
Nectarine fruits which the compliant boughs
Yielded them, sidelong as they sat recline
On the soft downy bank damasked with
    flowers:
The savory pulp they chew, and in the rind
Still as they thirsted scoop the brimming
    stream;
Nor gentle purpose, nor endearing smiles
Wanted, nor youthful dalliance as beseems
Fair couple, linked in happy nuptial league,
Alone as they. About them frisking played

All beasts of the earth, since wild, and of all
    chase
In wood or wilderness, forest or den;
Sporting the lion ramped, and in his paw
Dandled the kid; bears, tigers, ounces, pards,
Gamboled before them, the unwieldy elephant
To make them mirth used all his might, and
    wreathed
His lithe proboscis; close the serpent sly
Insinuating, wove with Gordian twine
His braided train, and of his fatal guile
Gave proof unheeded; others on the grass
Couched, and now filled with pasture gazing
    sat,
Or bedward ruminating: for the sun
Declined was hasting now with prone career
To the Ocean Isles, and in the ascending scale
Of heaven the stars that usher evening rose.

THE BOOK OF GENESIS

I: The Primeval History

Chapter I

First Story of Creation.[1] In the beginning, when God created the heavens and the earth, [2] the earth was a formless wasteland, and darkness covered the abyss, while a mighty wind swept over the waters.

[3] Then God said, "Let there be light," and there was light. [4] God saw how good the light was. God then separated the light from the darkness. [5] God called the light "day," and the darkness he called "night." Thus evening came, and morning followed — the first day.

[6] Then God said, "Let there be a dome in the middle of the waters, to separate one body of water from the other." And so it happened:[7] God made the dome, and it separated the water above the dome from the water below it. [8] God called the dome "the sky." Evening came, and morning followed — the second day.

[9] Then God said, "Let the water under the sky be gathered into a single basin, so that the dry land may appear." And so it happened: the water under the sky was gathered into its basin, and the dry land appeared. [10] God called the dry land "the earth," and the basin of the water he called "the sea." God saw how good it was. [11] Then God said, "Let the earth bring forth vegetation: every kind of plant that bears seed and every kind of fruit tree on earth that bears fruit with its seed in it." And so it happened; [12] the earth brought forth every kind of plant that bears seed and every kind of fruit tree on earth that bears fruit with its seed

---

1.1: This section introduces the whole Pentateuch. It shows how God brought an orderly universe out of primordial chaos.

1.2: *The abyss*: the primordial ocean according to the ancient Semitic cosmogony. After God's creative activity, part of this vast body forms the salt-water seas (w 9f); part of it is the fresh water under the earth as springs and fountains (Gn 7.11; 8.2; Prv 3.20). Part of it "the upper water" (Ps 148.4; Dn 3.60), is held up by the dome of the sky (Gn 1, 6f) from which rain descends on the earth (Gn 7.11; 2 Kgs 7, 2.19; Ps 104.13). A *mighty wind*: literally, "A wind of God," or "a spirit of God"; cf Gn 8.1.

1.5: In ancient Israel a day was considered to begin at sunset. According to the highly artificial

literary structure of Gn 1. 1-2, 4a, God's creative activity is divided into six days to teach the sacredness of the sabbath rest on the seventh day in the Israelite religion (2.2f).

in it. God saw how good it was.[13] Evening came, and morning followed — the third day.

[14] Then God said: "Let there be lights in the dome of the sky, to separate day from night. Let them mark the fixed times, the days and the years, [15] and serve as luminaries in the dome of the sky, to shed light upon the earth." And so it happened: [16] God made the two great lights, the greater one to govern the day, and the lesser one to govern the night; and he made the stars. [17] God set them in the dome of the sky, to shed light upon the earth, [18] to govern the day and the night, and to separate the light from the darkness. God saw how good it was. [19] Evening came, and morning followed — the fourth day.

[20] Then God said, "Let the water teem with an abundance of living creatures, and on the earth let birds fly beneath the dome of the sky." And so it happened: [21] God created the great sea monsters and all kinds of swimming creatures with which the water teems, and all kinds of winged birds. God saw how good it was, [22] and God blessed them, saying, "Be fertile, multiply, and fill the water of the seas; and let the birds multiply on the earth." [23] Evening came, and morning followed — the fifth day.

[24] Then God said, "Let the earth bring forth all kinds of living creatures: cattle, creeping things, and wild animals of all kinds." And so it happened: [25] God made all kinds of wild animals, all kinds of cattle, and all kinds of creeping things of the earth. God saw how good it was.

[26] Then God said: "Let us make man in our image, after our likeness. Let them have dominion over the fish of the sea, the birds of the air, and the cattle, and over all the wild animals and all the creatures that crawl on the ground."

[27] God created man in his image;
    in the divine image he created him;
    male and female he created them.

[28] God blessed them, saying: "Be fertile and multiply, fill the earth and subdue it. Have dominion over the fish of the sea, the birds of the air, and all the living things that move on the earth." [29] God also said: "See, I give you every seed-bearing plant all over the earth and every tree that has seed-bearing fruit on it to be your food; [30] and to all the animals of the land, all the birds of the air, and all the living creatures that crawl on the ground I give all the green plants for food." And so it happened. [31] God looked at everything he had made, and he found it very good. Evening came, and morning followed-the sixth day.

Chapter 2

[1] Thus the heavens and the earth and all their array were completed. [2] Since on the seventh day God was finished with the work he had been doing, he rested on the seventh day from all the work he had undertaken. [3] So God blessed the seventh day and made it holy, because on it he rested from all the work he had done in creation.

[4] Such is the story of the heavens and the earth at their creation.

Second Story of Creation. At the time when the LORD God made the earth and the heavens — [5] while as yet there was no field shrub on earth and no grass of the field had sprouted, for the LORD God had sent no rain upon the earth and there was no man to till the soil, [6] but a stream was welling up out of the earth and was watering all the surface of the ground — [7] the LORD God formed man out of the clay of the ground and blew into his nostrils the breath of life, and so man became a living being.

1.26: Man is here presented as the climax of God's creative activity; he resembles God primarily because of the dominion God gives him over the rest of creation.

2.4: This section is chiefly concerned with the creation of man. It is much older than the narrative of 1.1-2,

4a. Here God is depicted as creating man before the rest of his creatures, which are made for man's sake.

2.7: God is portrayed as a potter molding man's body out of clay. There is a play on words in Hebrew between *adam* ("man") and *adama* ("ground"). *Being*: literally, "soul."

[8] Then the LORD God planted a garden in Eden, in the east, and he placed there the man whom he had formed. [9] Out of the ground the LORD God made various trees grow that were delightful to look at and good for food, with the tree of life in the middle of the garden and the tree of the knowledge of good and bad.

[10] A river rises in Eden to water the garden; beyond there it divides and becomes four branches. [11] The name of the first is the Pishon; it is the one that winds through the whole land of Havilah, where there is gold. [12] The gold of that land is excellent; bdellium and lapis lazuli are also there. [13] The name of the second river is the Gihon; it is the one that winds all through the land of Cush. [14] The name of the third river is the Tigris; it is the one that flows east of Asshur. The fourth river is the Euphrates.

[15] The LORD God then took the man and settled him in the garden of Eden to cultivate and care for it. [16] The LORD God gave man this order: "You are free to eat from any of the trees of the garden [17] except the tree of knowledge of good and bad. From that tree you shall not eat; the moment you eat from it you are surely doomed to die."

[18] The LORD God said: "It is not good for the man to be alone. I will make a suitable partner for him." [19] So the LORD God formed out of the ground various wild animals and various birds of the air, and he brought them to the man to see what he would call them; whatever the man called each of them would be its name. [20] The man gave names to all the cattle, all the birds of the air, and all the wild animals; but none proved to be the suitable partner for the man.

[21] So the LORD God cast a deep sleep on the man, and while he was asleep, he took out one of his ribs and closed up its place with flesh. [22] The LORD God then built up into a woman the rib that he had taken from the man. When he brought her to the man, [23] the man said:

"This one, at last, is bone of my bones
    and flesh of my flesh;
This one shall be called 'woman,'
    for out of 'her man' this one has been
        taken."

[24] That is why a man leaves his father and mother and clings to his wife, and the two of them become one body.

[25] The man and his wife were both naked, yet they felt no shame.

Chapter 3

The Fall of Man. [1] Now the serpent was the most cunning of all the animals that the LORD God had made. The serpent asked the woman, "Did God really tell you not to eat from any of the trees in the garden?" [2] The woman answered the serpent: "We may eat of the fruit of the trees in the garden; [3] it is only about the fruit of the tree in the middle of the garden that God said, 'You shall not eat it or even touch it, lest you die.'" [4] But the serpent said to the woman: "You certainly will not die! [5] No, God knows well that the moment you eat of it your eyes will be opened and you will be like gods who know what is good and what is bad. [6] The woman saw that the tree was good for food, pleasing to the eyes, and desirable for gaining wisdom. So she took some of its fruit and ate it; and she also gave some to her husband, who

---

2.8: *Eden*: used here as the name of a region in southern Mesopotamia; the term is derived from the Sumarian word *eden*, "fertile plain." A similar-sounding Hebrew word means "delight." The *garden in Eden* could therefore be understood as the "garden of delight," so that through the Greek version, it is now known also as "paradise," literally, a "pleasure park."

2.10-14: *Rises*: in flood to overflow its banks. *Beyond There*: as one travels upstream. *Branches*: literally, "heads," i.e., upper courses. Eden is near the head of the Persian Gulf, where the Tigris and the Euphrates join with two other streams to form a single river. *The land of Cush* here and in 10.8 is not Ethiopia (Nubia) as elsewhere, but the land of the Kassites, east of Mesopotamia.

2.23: There is a play on the similar-sounding Hebrew words *ishsha* ("women") and *ishah* ("her man, her husband").

2.24: *One body*: literally "one flesh"; classical Hebrew has no specific word for "body." The sacred writer stresses the fact that conjugal union is willed by God.

3.5: *Like gods who know*; or "like God who knows."

was with her, and he ate it. ⁷ Then the eyes of both of them were opened, and they realized that they were naked; so they sewed fig leaves together and made loin-cloths for themselves.

⁸ When they heard the sound of the LORD God moving about in the garden at the breezy time of the day, the man and his wife hid themselves from the LORD God among the trees of the garden. ⁹ The LORD God then called to the man and asked him, "Where are you?" ¹⁰ He answered, "I heard you in the garden; but I was afraid, because I was naked, so I hid myself." ¹¹ Then he asked, "Who told you that you were naked? You have eaten, then, from the tree of which I had forbidden you to eat!" ¹² The man replied, "The woman whom you put here with me—she gave me fruit from the tree, and so I ate it." ¹³ The LORD God then asked the woman, "Why did you do such a thing?" The woman answered, "The serpent tricked me into it, so I ate it."

¹⁴ Then the LORD God said to the serpent:

"Because you have done this, you shall be banned
   from all the animals
   and from all the wild creatures;
On your belly shall you crawl,
   and dirt shall you eat
   all the days of your life.

¹⁵ I will put enmity between you and the woman,

and between your offspring and hers;
He will strike at your head,
   while you strike at his heel."

¹⁶ To the woman he said:

"I will intensify the pangs of your child-bearing;
   in pain shall you bring forth children.
Yet your urge shall be for your husband,
   and he shall be your master."

¹⁷ To the man he said: "Because you listened to your wife and ate from the tree of which I had forbidden you to eat,

"Cursed be the ground because of you!
   In toil shall you eat its yield
   all the days of your life.
¹⁸ Thorns and thistles shall it bring forth to you,
   as you eat of the plants of the field.
¹⁹ By the sweat of your face
   shall you get bread to eat,

Until you return to the ground,
   from which you were taken;
For you are dirt,
   and to dirt you shall return."

²⁰ The man called his wife Eve, because she became the mother of all the living.

²¹ For the man and his wife the LORD God made leather garments, with which he clothed them. ²² Then the LORD God said: "See! The man has become like one of us, knowing what is good and what is bad! Therefore, he must not be allowed to put out his hand to take fruit from the tree of life also, and thus eat of it and live forever." ²³ The LORD God therefore banished him from the garden of Eden, to till the ground from which he had been taken. ²⁴ When he expelled the man, he settled him east of the garden of Eden; and he stationed the cherubim and the fiery revolving sword, to guard the way to the tree of life.

3.8: *The breezy time of the day*: literally "the wind of the day." On most days in Palestine a cooling breeze blows from the sea shortly before sunset.

3.15: *He will strike . . . at his heel*: since the antecedent for *he* and *his* is the collective noun *offspring*, i.e. all the descendants of the woman, a more exact rendering of the sacred writer's words would be, "They will strike . . . at their heels." However, later theology saw in this passage more than unending hostility between snakes and men. The serpent was regarded as the devil (Rev. 12.9; 20.2), whose eventual defeat seems implied in the contrast between *head and heel*. Because "the Son of God appeared that he might destroy the works of the devil" (1 JN 3.8), the passage can be understood as the first promise of a Redeemer for fallen mankind.

The woman's offspring then is primarily Jesus Christ.

3.20: This verse seems to be out of place; it would fit better after v 24. The Hebrew name *hawwa* ("Eve") is related to the Hebrew word *hay* ("living").

ANONYMOUS (TRADITIONALLY ATTRIBUTED TO KING DAVID)

THE TWENTY-THIRD PSALM (KING JAMES VERSION)

The Lord is my shepherd; I shall not want.

He maketh me to lie down in green pastures: he leadeth me beside
    the still waters,
He restoreth my soul: he leadeth me in the paths of righteousness
    for his name's sake.
Yea, though I walk through the valley of the shadow of death,
    I will fear no evil: for thou art with me;
    thy rod and thy staff they comfort me.
Thou preparest a table before me in the presence of mine enemies:
    thou anointest my head with oil; my cup runneth over.
Surely goodness and mercy shall follow me all the days of my life-
    and I will dwell in the house of the Lord for ever.

YORUBA (NIGERIA) MYTHS OF CREATION

The Yoruba people of West Africa live chiefly in Southwestern Nigeria. Their art work is widely admired.

THE CREATION OF LAND

At the beginning everything was water. Then Oludumare the supreme god sent Obatala (or Orishanla) down from heaven to create the dry land. Obatala descended on a chain and he carried with him: a snail shell filled with earth, some pieces of crow and a cock. When he arrived he placed the crow on the water, spread the earth over it and placed the cock on top. The cock immediately started to scratch and thus the land spread far and wide.

When the land had been created, the other Orisha descended from heaven in order to live on the land with Obatala.

THE CREATION OF MAN

Obatala made man out of earth. After shaping men and women he gave them to Oludumare to blow in the breath of life.

One day Obatala drank palm wine. Then he started to make hunchbacks and cripples, albinos and blind men.

From that day onwards hunchbacks and albinos and all deformed persons are sacred to Obatala. But his worshipers are forbidden to drink palm wine.

Obatala is still the one who gives shape to the new babe in the mother's womb.

EFE (ZAIRE) MYTH

FORBIDDEN FRUIT

God created the first human being Ba-atsi with the help of the moon. He kneaded the body into shape, covered it with a skin, and poured in blood. When the man had thus been given life, God whispered in his ear that he, Ba-atsi, should beget children, and upon them he should impress the following prohibition: "Of all the trees of the forest you may eat, but of the Tahu tree you may not eat." Ba-atsi had many children, impressed upon them the prohibition, and then retired to heaven. At first men respected the commandment they had been given, and lived happily. But one day a pregnant woman was seized with an irresistible desire to eat of the forbidden fruit. She tried to persuade her husband to give her some of it. At first he refused, but after a time he gave way. He stole into the wood, picked a Tahu fruit, peeled it, and hid the peel among the leaves. But the moon had seen his action and reported it to God. God was so enraged over man's disobedience that as punishment he sent death among them.

YAO (MOZAMBIQUE) MYTH

MULUNGU AND THE BEASTS

In the beginning man was not, only Mulungu and his people, the beasts. They lived happily on earth.

One day a chameleon found a human pair in his fish trap. He had never seen such creatures before and he was surprised. The chameleon reported his discovery to Mulungu. Mulungu said, "Let us wait and see what the creatures will do."

The men started making fires. They set fire to the bush so that the beasts fled into the forest. Then the men set traps and killed Mulungu's people. At last Mulungu was compelled to leave the earth. Since he could not climb a tree he called for the spider.

The spider spun a thread up to the sky and down again. When he returned he said, "I have gone on high nicely, now you Mulungu go on high." And Mulungu ascended to the sky on the spider's thread to escape from the wickedness of men.

ASHANTI (GHANA) MYTH

The Ashanti population is highly unified by tradition and is respected throughout Ghana.

THE TOWER TO HEAVEN

Long, long ago Onyankopon lived on earth, or at least was very near to us. Now there was a certain old woman who used to pound her mashed yams and the pestle kept knocking up against Onyankopon, who was not then high in the sky. So Onyankopon said to the old woman: "Why do you keep doing this to me? Because of what you are doing I am going to take myself away up in the sky." And of a truth he did so.

Now the people could no longer approach Onyankopon. But the old woman thought of a way to reach him and bring him back. She instructed her children to go and search for all the mortars they could find and bring them to her. Then she told them to pile one mortar on top of another til they reached to where Onyankopon was. And her children did so, they piled up many mortars, one on top of another, til they needed only one more mortar to reach Onyankopon.

Now, since they could not find another mortar anywhere, their grandmother the old woman said to them: "Take one out from the bottom and put it on top to make them reach." So her children removed a mortar from the bottom and all the mortars rolled and fell to the ground, causing the death of many people.

DARASA (ETHIOPIA) MYTH

MAN CHOOSES DEATH IN EXCHANGE FOR FIRE

Formerly men had no fire but ate all their food raw. At that time they did not need to die for when they became old, God made them young again. One day they decided to beg God for fire. They sent a messenger to God to convey their request. God replied to the messenger that he would give him fire if he was prepared to die. The man took the fire from God, but ever since then all men must die.

KOUYATÉ MAMADOU

King Sundiata led Mali to a dominant position in West Africa in the 13th century.

SUNDIATA: AN ORAL EPIC

The Words of the Griot Mamadou Kouyaté

I am a griot. It is I. Djeli Mamadou Kouyaté, son of Bintou Kouyate and Djeli Kedian Kouyate, master in the art of eloquence. Since the time immemorial the Kouyatés have been in the service of the Keita princes of Mali; we are vessels of speech, we are the repositories which harbour secrets many centuries old. The art of eloquence has no secrets for us; without us the names of kings would vanish into oblivion, we are the memory of mankind; by the spoken word we bring to life the deeds and exploits of kings for younger generations.

I derive my knowledge from my father Djeli Kedian, who also got it from his father; history holds no mystery for us; we teach to the vulgar just as much as we want to teach to them, for it is we who keep the keys to the twelve doors of Mali.

I know the list of all the sovereigns who succeeded to the throne of Mali. I know how the black people divided into tribes, for my father bequeathed to me all his learning; I know why such is called Kamara, another Keita, and yet another Sibibé or Traoré; every name has a meaning, a secret import.

I teach kings the history of their ancestors so that the lives of the ancients might serve them as an example, for the world is old, but the future springs from the past.

My word is pure and free of all untruth; it is the word of my father; it is the word of my father's father. I will give you my father's words just as I received them; royal griots do not know what lying is. When a quarrel breaks out between tribes it is we who settle the difference, for we are the depositaries of oaths which the ancestors swore.

Listen to my word, you who want to know; by my mouth you will learn the history of Mali.

By my mouth you will get to know the story of the ancestor of great Mali, the story of him who, by his exploits, surpassed even Alexander the Great; he who from the East, shed his rays upon all the countries of the West.

Listen to the story of the son of the Buffalo, the son of the Lion. I am going to tell you of Maghan Sundiata, of Mari-Djata, of Sogolon Djata, of Naré Maghan Djata; the man of many names against whom sorcery could avail nothing.

The First Kings of Mali

Listen then, sons of Mali, children of the black people, listen to my word, for I am going to tell you of Sundiata, the father of the Bright Country, of the savanna land, the ancestor of those who draw the bow, the master of a hundred vanquished kings.

I am going to talk of Sundiata, Manding Diara, Lion of Mali, Sogolon Djata, son of Sogolon, Naré Maghan Djata, son of Naré Maghan, Sogo Sogo Simbon Salaba, hero of many names.

I am going to tell you of Sundiata, he whose exploits will astonish men for a long time yet. He was great among kings, he was peerless among men; he was beloved of God because he was the last of the great conquerors.

Right at the beginning then, Mali was a province of the Bambara kings; those who are today called Mandingo, inhabitants of Mali, are not indigenous; they come from the East. Bilali Bounama, ancestor of the Keitas, was the faithful servant of the Prophet Muhammad (may the peace of God be upon him). Bilali Bounama had seven sons of whom the eldest, Lawalo, left the Holy City and came to settle in Mali; Lawalo had Latal Kalabi for a son, Latal Kalabi had Damul Kalabi who then had Lahilatoul Kalabi.

Lahilatoul Kalabi was the first black prince to make the Pilgrimage to Mecca. On his return he was robbed by brigands in the desert; his men were scattered and some died of thirst, but God saved Lahilatoul Kalabi, for he was a righteous man. He called upon the Almighty and jinn appeared and recognized him as king. After seven years' absence Lahilatoul was able to return, by the grace of Allah the Almighty, to Mali where none expected to see him any more.

Lahilatoul Kalabi had two sons, the elder being called Kalabi Bomba and the younger Kalabi Dauman; the elder chose royal power and reigned, while the younger preferred fortune and wealth and became the ancestor of those who go from country to country seeking their fortune.

Kalabi Bomba had Mamadi Kani for a son. Mamadi Kani was a hunter king like the first kings of Mali. It was he who invented the hunter's whistle; he communicated with the jinn of the forest and bush. These spirits had no secrets from him and he was loved by Kondolon Ni Sane. His followers were so numerous that he formed them into an army which became formidable; he often gathered them together in the bush and taught them the art of hunting. It was he who revealed to hunters the medicinal leaves which heal wounds and cure diseases. Thanks to the strength of his followers, he became king of a vast country; with them Mamadi Kani conquered all the lands which stretch from the Sankarani to the Bouré. Mamadi Kani had four sons—Kani Simbon, Kamignogo Simbon, Kabala Simbon and Simbon Tagnogokelin. They were all initiated into the art of hunting and deserved the title of Simbon. It was the lineage of Bamari Tagnogokelin which held on to the power; his son was M'Bali Nènè whose son was Bello. Bello's son was called Bello Bakon and he had a son called Maghan Kon Fatta, also called Frako Maghan Keigu, Maghan the handsome.

Maghan Kon Fatta was the father of the great Sundiata and had three wives and six children—three boys and three girls. His first wife was called Sassouma Bérété, daughter of a great divine; she was the mother of King Dankaran Touman and Princess Nana Triban. The second wife, Sogolon Kedjou, was the mother of Sundiata and the two princesses Sogolon Kolonkan and Sogolon Djamarou. The third wife was one of the Kamaras and was called Namandjé; she was the mother of Manding Bory (or Manding Bakary), who was the best friend of his half-brother Sundiata.

The Buffalo Woman

Maghan Kon Fatta, the father of Sundiata, was renowned for his beauty in every land; but he was also a good king loved by all the people. In his capital of Nianiba he loved to sit often at the foot of the great silk-cotton tree which dominated his palace of Canco. Maghan Kon Fatta had been reigning a long time and his eldest son Dankaran Touman was already eight years old and often came to sit on the ox-hide beside his father.

Well now, one day when the king had taken up his usual position under the silk-cotton tree surrounded by his kinsmen he saw a man dressed like a hunter coming towards him; he wore the tight-fitting trousers of the favourites of Kondolon Ni Sané, and his blouse oversewn with cowries showed that he was a master of the hunting art. All present turned towards the unknown man whose bow, polished with frequent usage, shone in the sun. The man walked up in front of the king, whom he recognized in the midst of his courtiers. He bowed and said, "I salute you, king of Mali, greetings all you of Mali. I am a hunter chasing game and come from Sangaran; a fearless doe has guided me to the walls of Nianiba. By the grace of my master the great Simbon[3] my arrows have hit her and now she lies not far from your walls. As is fitting, oh king, I have come to bring you your portion." He took a leg from his leather sack whereupon the king's griot, Gnankouman Doua, seized upon the leg and said, "Stranger, whoever you may be you will be the king's guest because you respect custom; come and take your place on the mat beside us. The king is pleased because he loves righteous men." The king nodded his approval and all the courtiers agreed. The griot continued in a more familiar tone, "Oh you who come from the Sangaran, land of the favourites of Kondolon Ni Sane, you who have doubtless had an expert master, will you open your pouch of knowledge for us and instruct us with your conversation, for you have no doubt visited several lands."

The king, still silent, gave a nod of approval and a courtier added, "The hunters of Sangaran are the best soothsayers; if the stranger wishes we could learn a lot from him."

The hunter came and sat down near Gnankouman Doua who vacated one end of the mat for him. Then he said, "Griot of the king, I am not one of these hunters whose tongues are more dexterous than their arms; I am no spinner of adventure yarns, nor do I like playing upon the credulity of worthy folk; but, thanks to the lore which my master has imparted to me, I can boast of being a seer among seers."

He took out of his hunter's bag twelve cowries which he threw on the mat. The king and all his entourage now turned towards the stranger who was jumbling up the twelve shiny shells with his bare hand. Gnankouman Doua discreetly brought to the king's notice that the soothsayer was left-handed. The left hand is the hand of evil, but in the divining art it is said that left-handed people are the best. The hunter muttered some incomprehensible words in a low voice while he shuffled and jumbled the twelve cowries into different positions which he mused on at length. All of a sudden he looked up at the king and said, "Oh king, the world is full of mystery, all is hidden and we know nothing but what we can see. The silk-cotton tree springs from a tiny seed—that which defies the tempest weighs in its germ no more than a grain of rice. Kingdoms are like trees; some will be silk-cotton trees, others will remain dwarf palms and the powerful silk-cotton tree will cover them with its shade. Oh, who can recognize in the little child the great king to come? The great comes from the small; truth and falsehood have both suckled at the same breast. Nothing is certain, but, sire, I can see two strangers over there coming towards your city."

He fell silent and looked in the direction of the city gates for a short while. All present silently turned towards the gates. The soothsayer returned to his cowries. He shook them in his palm with a skilled hand and then threw them out.

"King of Mali, destiny marches with great strides, Mali is about to emerge from the night. Nianiba is lighting up, but what is this light that comes from the east?"

"Hunter," said Gnankouman Doua, "your words are obscure. Make your speech comprehensible to us, speak in the clear language of your savanna."[4]

---

[3] Horrific term for a great hunter; later applied to Sundiata.

[4] The language of those who live in the savannah grasslands is, like their environment, clear and bright.

"I am coming to that now, griot. Listen to my message. Listen, sire. You have ruled over the kingdom which your ancestors bequeathed to you and you have no other ambition but to pass on this realm, intact if not increased, to your descendants; but, fine king, your successor is not yet born. I see two hunters coming to your city; they have come from afar and a woman accompanies them. Oh, that woman! She is ugly, she is hideous, she bears on her back a disfiguring hump, Her monstrous eyes seem to have been merely laid on her face, but, mystery of mysteries this is the woman you must marry, sire, for she will be the mother of him who will make the name of Mali immortal for ever. The child will be the seventh star, the seventh conqueror of the earth. He will be more mighty than Alexander. But, oh king, for destiny to lead this woman to you a sacrifice is necessary; you must offer up a red bull, for the bull is powerful. When its blood soaks into the ground nothing more will hinder the arrival of your wife. There, I have said what I had to say, but everything is in the hands of the Almighty."

The hunter picked up his cowries and put them away in his bag.

"I am only passing through, king of Mali, and now I return to Sangaran. Farewell."

The hunter disappeared but neither the king, Naré Maghan, nor his griot, Gnankouman Doua, forgot his prophetic words; soothsayers see far ahead, their words are not always for the immediate present; man is in a hurry but time is tardy and everything has its season. . . .

Summary

After some time the old man's prophecy came to pass. One day two hunters came from the land of Do to present to the king a young girl who, though she was shrouded in traveling clothes, was apparently a hunchback. They related to the king and his court how the king of Do Mansa-Gnemo Dearra had promised to reward anyone who killed an astounding buffalo that had been destroying the fields in the area. Having set out themselves to find the buffalo, the two hunters had befriended an old woman who confessed that she was the Buffalo of Do. She told them how to capture and kill it on the promise that when offered the reward of a beautiful young maiden, they choose an ugly girl who would be seated in the crowd.

Events transpired as the old woman had predicted, and the hunters were laughed out of town when they chose the ugly girl, Sogolon Kedjou. Unable to possess her, the hunters only later thought to present her to the king of Mali. Recognizing the fulfillment of what the old man had foretold, Nare Maghan married Sogolon.

The Lion Child

A wife quickly grows accustomed to her state. Sogolon now walked freely in the king's great enclosure and people also got used to her ugliness. But the first wife of the king, Sassouma Bérété, turned out to be unbearable. She was restless, and smarted to see the ugly Sogolon proudly flaunting her pregnancy about the palace. What would become of her, Sassouma Bérété, if her son, already eight years old, was disinherited in favour of the child that Sogolon was going to bring into the world? All the king's attentions went to the mother-to-be. On returning from the wars he would bring her the best portion of the booty—fine loin-cloths and rare jewels. Soon, dark schemes took form in the mind of Sassouma Bérété; she determined to kill Sogolon. In great secrecy she had the foremost sorcerers of Mali come to her, but they all declared themselves incapable of tackling Sogolon. In fact, from twilight onwards, three owls came and perched on the roof of her house and watched over her. For the sake of peace and quiet Sassouma said to herself, "Very well then, let him be born, this child, and then we'll see."

Sogolon's time came. The king commanded the nine greatest midwives of Mali to come to Niani, and they were now constantly in attendance on the damsel of Do. The king was in the midst of his courtiers one day when someone came to announce to him that Sogolon's labours were beginning. He sent all his courtiers away and only Gnankouman Doua stayed by his side. One would have thought that this was the first time that he had become a father, he was so worried and agitated. The whole palace kept complete silence. Doua tried to distract the sovereign with his one-stringed guitar but in vain. He even had to stop this music as it jarred on the king. Suddenly the sky darkened and great clouds coming from the east hid the sun, although it was still the dry season. Thunder began to tumble and swift lightning rent the clouds; a few large drops of rain began to fall while a strong wind blew up. A flash of lightning accompanied by a dull rattle of thunder burst out of the east and lit up the whole sky as far as the west. Then the rain stopped and the sun appeared and it was at this very moment that a midwife came out of Sogolon's house, ran to the antechamber and announced to Naré Maghan that he was the father of a boy.

The king showed no reaction at all. He was as though in a daze. Then Doua, realizing the king's emotion, got up and signalled to two slaves who were already standing near the royal "tabala."[5] The hasty beats of the royal drum announced to Mali the birth of a son; the village tam-tams took it up and thus all Mali got the good news the same day. Shouts of joy, tam-tams and "balafons"[6] took the place of the recent silence and all the musicians of Niani made their way to the palace. His initial emotion being over, the king had got up and on leaving the antechamber he was greeted by the warm voice of Gnankouman Doua singing:

"I salute you, father; I salute you, king Naré Maghan; I salute you, Maghan Kon Fatta, Frako Maghan Keigu. The child is born whom the world awaited. Maghan, oh happy father, I salute you. The lion child, the buffalo child is born, and to announce him the Almighty has made the thunder peal, the whole sky has lit up and the earth has trembled. All hail, father, hail king Naré Maghan!"

All the griots were there and had already composed a song in praise of the royal infant. The generosity of kings makes griots eloquent, and Maghan Kon Fatta distributed on this day alone six granaries of rice among the populace. Sassouma Bérété distinguished herself by her largesses, but that deceived nobody. She was suffering in her heart but did not want to betray anything.

The name was given the eighth day after his birth. It was a great feast day and people came from all the villages of Mali while each neighbouring people brought gifts to the king. First thing in the morning a great circle had formed in front of the palace. In the middle, serving women were pounding rice which was to serve as bread, and sacrificed oxen lay at the foot of the great silk-cotton tree.

In Sogolon's house the king's aunt cut off the baby's first crop of hair while the poetesses, equipped with large fans, cooled the mother who was nonchalantly stretched out on soft cushions.

The king was in his antechamber but he came out followed by Doua. The crowd fell silent and Doua cried, "The child of Sogolon will be called Maghan after his father, and Mari Djata, a name which no Mandingo prince has ever borne. Sogolon's son will be the first of this name."

Straight away the griots shouted the name of the infant and the tam-tams sounded anew. The king's aunt, who had come out to hear the name of the child, went back into the house, and whispered the double name of Maghan and Mari Djata in the ear of the newly-born so that he would remember it.

The festivity ended with the distribution of meat to the heads of families and everyone dispersed joyfully. The near relatives one by one went to admire the newly-born.

Childhood

God has his mysteries which none can fathom. You, perhaps, will be a king. You can do nothing about it. You, on the other hand, will be unlucky, but you can do nothing about that either. Each man finds his way already marked out for him and he can change nothing of it.

---

[5] Ceremonial drum

[6] A type of xylophone in which the wooden keys are often mounted upon gourds.

Sogolon's son had a slow and difficult childhood. At the age of three he still crawled along on an fours while children of the same age were already walking. He had nothing of the great beauty of his father Naré Maghan. He had a head so big that he seemed unable to support it; he also had large eyes which would open wide whenever anyone entered his mother's house. He was taciturn and used to spend the whole day just sitting in the middle of the house. Whenever his mother went out he would crawl on all fours to rummage about in the calabashes in search of food, for he was very greedy.

Malicious tongues began to blab. What three-year-old has not yet taken his first steps? What three-year-old is not the despair of his parents through his whims and shifts of mood? What three-year-old is not the joy of his circle through his backwardness in talking.? Sogolon Djata (for it was thus that they called him, prefixing his mother's name to his), Sogolon Djata, then, was very different from others of his own age. He spoke little and his severe face never relaxed into a smile. You would have thought that he was already thinking, and what amused children of his age bored him. Often Sogolon would make some of them come to him to keep him company. These children were already walking and she hoped that Djata, seeing his companions walking, would be tempted to do likewise. But nothing came of it. Besides, Sogolon Djata would brain the poor little things with his already strong arms and none of them would come near him any more.

The king's first wife was the first to rejoice at Sogolon Djata's infirmity. Her own son, Dankaran Touman, was already eleven. He was a fine and lively boy, who spent the day running about the village with those of his own age. He had even begun his initiation in the bush. The king had had a bow made for him and he used to go behind the town to practice archery with his companions. Sassouma was quite happy and snapped her fingers at Sogolon, whose child was still crawling on the ground. Whenever the latter happened to pass by her house, she would say, "Come, my son, walk, jump, leap about. The jinn[7] didn't promise you anything out of the ordinary, but I prefer a son who walks on his two legs to a lion that crawls on the ground." She spoke thus whenever Sogolon went by her door. The innuendo would go straight home and then she would burst into laughter, that diabolical laughter which a jealous woman knows how to use so well.

Her son's infirmity weighed heavily upon Sogolon Kedjou; she had resorted to all her talent as a sorceress to give strength to her son's legs, but the rarest herbs had been useless. The king himself lost hope.

How impatient man is! Naré Maghan became imperceptibly estranged but Gnankouman Doua never ceased reminding him of the hunter's words. Sogolon became pregnant again. The king hoped for a son, but it was a daughter called Kolonkan. She resembled her mother and had nothing of her father's beauty. The disheartened king debarred Sogolon from his house and she lived in semi-disgrace for a while. Naré Maghan married the daughter of one of his allies, the king of the Kamaras. She was called Namandjé and her beauty was legendary. A year later she brought a boy into the world. When the king consulted soothsayers on the destiny of this son he received the reply that Namandje's child would be the right hand of some mighty king. The king gave the newly-born the name of Boukari. He was to be called Manding Boukari or Manding Bory later on.

Nare Maghan was very perplexed. Could it be that the stiff-jointed son of Sogolon was the one the hunter soothsayer had foretold?

"The Almighty has his mysteries," Gnankouman Doua would say and, taking up the hunter's words, added, "The silk-cotton tree emerges from a tiny seed."

One day Naré Maghan came along to the house of Nounfaïri, the blacksmith seer of Niani, He was an old, blind man. He received the king in the anteroom which served as his workshop. To the king's question he replied, "When the seed germinates growth is not always easy; great trees grow slowly but they plunge their roots deep into the ground."

---

[7] A Muslim term for invisible spirits, supernatural agencies.

"But has the seed really germinated?" said the king. "Of course," replied the blind seer. "Only the growth is not as quick as you would like it; how impatient man is."

This interview and Doua's confidence gave the king some assurance. To the great displeasure of Sassouma Bérété the king restored Sogolon to favour and soon another daughter was born to her. She was given the name of Djamarou.

However, all Niani talked of nothing else but the stiff-legged son of Sogolon. He was now seven and he still crawled to get about. In spite of all the king's affection, Sogolon was in despair. Naré Maghan aged and he felt his time coming to an end. Dankaran Touman, the son of Sassouma Bérété, was now a fine youth.

One day Naré Maghan made Mari Djata come to him and he spoke to the child as one speaks to an adult. "Mari Djata, I am growing old and soon I shall be no more among you, but before death takes me off I am going to give you the present each king gives his successor. In Mali every prince has his own griot. Doua's father was my father's griot, Doua is mine and the son of Doua, Balla Fasséké here, will be your griot. Be inseparable friends from this day forward. From his mouth you will hear the history of your ancestors, you will learn the art of governing Mali according to the principles which our ancestors have bequeathed to us. I have served my term and done my duty too. I have done everything which a king of Mali ought to do. I am handing an enlarged kingdom over to you and I leave you sure allies. May your destiny be accomplished, but never forget that Niani is your capital and Mali the cradle of your ancestors."

The child, as if he had understood the whole meaning of the king's words, beckoned Balla Fasseke to approach. He made room for him on the hide he was sitting on and then said, "Balla, you will be my griot." "Yes, son of Sogolon, if it pleases God," replied Balla Fasséké.

The king and Doua exchanged glances that radiated confidence.

The Lion's Awakening

A short while after this interview between Naré Maghan and his son the king died. Sogolon's son was no more than seven years old. The council of elders met in the king's palace. It was no use Doua's defending the king's will which reserved the throne for Mari Djata, for the council took no account of Naré Maghan's wish. With the help of Sassouma Bérété's intrigues, Dankaran Touman was proclaimed king and a regency council was formed in which the queen mother was all-powerful. A short time after, Doua died. As men have short memories, Sogolon's son was spoken of with nothing but irony and scorn. People had seen one-eyed kings, one-armed kings, and lame kings, but a stiff-legged king had never been heard tell of. No matter how great the destiny promised for Mari Djata might be, the throne could not be given to someone who had no power in his legs; if the jinn loved him, let them begin by giving him the use of his legs. Such were the remarks that Sogolon heard every day. The queen mother, Sassouma Bérété, was the source of all this gossip.

Having become all-powerful, Sassouma Bérété persecuted Sogolon because the late NarBérété Maghan had preferred her. She banished Sogolon and her son to a back yard of the palace. Mari Djata's mother now occupied an old hut which had served as a lumberroom of Sassouma's.

The wicked queen mother allowed free passage to all those inquisitive people who wanted to see the child that still crawled at the age of seven. Nearly all the inhabitants of Niani filed into the palace and the poor Sogolon wept to see herself thus given over to public ridicule. Mari Djata took on a ferocious look in front of the crowd of sightseers. Sogolon found a little consolation only in the love of her eldest daughter, Kolonkan. She was four and she could walk. She seemed to understand all her mother's miseries and already she helped her with the housework. Sometimes, when Sogolon was attending to the chores, it was she who stayed beside her sister Djamarou, quite small as yet.

Sogolon Kedjou and her children lived on the queen mother's leftovers, but she kept a little garden in the open ground behind the village. It was there that she passed her brightest moments looking after her onions and gnougous. One day she happened to be short of condiments and went to the queen mother to beg a little baobab leaf.

"Look you," said the malicious Sassouma, "I have calabash full. Help yourself, you poor woman. As for me; my son knew how to walk at seven and it was he who went and picked these baobab leaves. Take them then, since your son is unequal to mine." Then she laughed derisively with that fierce laughter which cuts through your flesh and penetrates right to the bone.

Sogolon Kedjou was dumbfounded. She had never imagined that hate could be so strong in a human being. With a lump in her throat she left Sassouma's. Outside her hut Mari Djata, sitting on his useless legs, was blandly eating out of a calabash. Unable to contain herself any longer, Sogolon burst into sobs and seizing piece of wood, hit her son.

"Oh son of misfortune, will you never walk. Through your fault I have just suffered the greatest affront of my life! What have I done, God, for you to punish me in this way?"

Mari Djata seized the piece of wood and, looking at his mother, said, "Mother, what's the matter?"

"Shut up, nothing can ever wash me clean of this insult."

"But what then?"

"Sassouma has just humiliated me over a matter of a baobab leaf. At your age her own son could walk and used to bring his mother baobab leaves."

"Cheer up, Mother, cheer up."

"No. It's too much. I can't."

"Very well then, I am going to walk today," said Mari Djata. "Go and tell my father's smiths to make me the heaviest possible iron rod. Mother, do you want just the leaves of the baobab or would you rather I brought you the whole tree?"

"Ah, my son, to wipe out this insult I want the tree and its roots at my feet outside my hut."

Balla Fasséké, who was present, ran to the mastersmith, Farakourou, to order an iron rod.

Sogolon had sat down in front of her hut. She was weeping softly and holding her head between her two hands. Mari Djata went calmly back to his calabash of rice and began eating again as if nothing had happened. From time to time he looked up discreetly at his mother who was murmuring in a low voice, "I want the whole tree, in front of my hut, the whole tree."

All of a sudden a voice burst into laughter behind the hut. It was the wicked Sassouma telling one of her serving women about the scene of humiliation and she was laughing loudly so that Sogolon could hear. Sogolon fled into the hut and hid her face under the blankets so as not to have before her eyes this heedless boy, who was more preoccupied with eating than with anything else. With her head buried in the bed-clothes Sogolon wept and her body shook violently. Her daughter, Sogolon Djamarou, had come and sat down beside her and she said, "Mother, Mother, don't cry. Why are you crying?"

Mari Djata had finished eating and, dragging himself along on his legs, he came and sat under the wall of the hut for the sun was scorching. What was he thinking about? He alone knew.

The royal forges were situated outside the walls and over a hundred smiths worked there. The bows, spears, arrows and shields of Niani's warriors came from there. When Balla Fasseke came to order the iron rod, Farakourou said to him, "The great day has arrived then?"

"Yes. Today is a day like any other, but it will see what no other day has seen."

The master of the forges, Farakourou, was the son of the old Nounfaïri, and he was a soothsayer like his father. In his workshops there was an enormous iron bar wrought by his father Nounfaïri. Everybody wondered what this bar was destined to be used for. Farakourou called six of his apprentices and told them to carry the iron bar to Sogolon's house.

When the smiths put the gigantic iron bar down in front of the hut the noise was so frightening that Sogolon, who was lying down, jumped up with a start. Then Balla Fasséké, son of Gnankouman Doua, spoke.

"Here is the great day, Mari Djata. I am speaking to you, Maghan, son of Sogolon. The waters of the Niger can efface the stain from the body, but they cannot wipe out an insult. Arise, young lion, roar, and may the bush know that from henceforth it has a master."

The apprentice smiths were still there, Sogolon had come out and everyone was watching Mari Djata. He crept on all fours and came to the iron bar. Supporting himself on his knees and one hand, with the other hand he picked up the iron bar without any effort and stood it up vertically. Now he was resting on nothing but his knees and held the bar with both his hands. A deathly silence had gripped all those present. Sogolon Djata closed his eyes, held tight, the muscles in his arms tensed. With a violent jerk he threw his weight on to it and his knees left the ground. Sogolon Kedjou was all eyes and watched her son's legs which were trembling as though from an electric shock. Djata was sweating and the sweat ran from his brow. In a great effort he straightened up and was on his feet at one go—but the great bar of iron was twisted and had taken the form of a bow!

Then Balla Fasséké sang out the "Hymn to the Bow," striking up with his powerful voice:

"Take your bow, Simbon,
Take your bow and let us go.
Take your bow, Sogolon Djata."

When Sogolon saw her son standing she stood dumb for a moment, then suddenly she sang these words of thanks to God who had given her son the use of his legs:

"Oh day, what a beautiful day,
Oh day, day of joy;
Allah Almighty, you never created a finer day.
So my son is going to walk!"

Standing in the position of a soldier at ease, Sogolon Djata, supported by his enormous rod, was sweating great beads of sweat. Balla Fasséké's song had alerted the whole palace and people came running from all over to see what had happened, and each stood bewildered before Sogolon's son. The queen mother had rushed there and when she saw Mari Djata standing up she trembled from head to foot. After recovering his breath Sogolon's son dropped the bar and the crowd stood to one side. His first steps were those of a giant. Balla Fasséké fell into step and pointing his finger at Djata, he cried:

"Room, room, make room!
The lion has walked;
Hide antelopes,
Get out of his way."

Behind Niani there was a young baobab tree and it was there that the children of the town came to pick leaves for their mothers. With all his might the son of Sogolon tore up the tree and put it on his shoulders and went back to his mother. He threw the tree in front of the hut and said, "Mother, here are some baobab leaves for you. From henceforth it will be outside your hut that the women of Niani will come to stock up."

Sogolon Djata walked. From that day forward the queen mother had no more peace of mind. But what can one do against destiny? Nothing. Man, under the influence of certain illusions, thinks he can alter the course which God has mapped out, but everything he does falls into a higher order which he barely understands. That is why Sassouma's efforts were vain against Sogolon's son, everything she did lay in the child's destiny. Scorned the day before and the object of public ridicule, now Sogolon's son was as popular as he had been despised. The multitude loves and fears strength. All Niani talked of nothing but Djata; the mothers urged their sons to become hunting companions of Djata and to share his games, as if they wanted their offspring to profit from the nascent glory of the buffalo-woman's son. The words of Doua on the name-giving day came back to men's minds and Sogolon was now surrounded with much respect; in conversation people were fond of contrasting Sogolon's modesty with the pride and malice of Sassouma Bérété. It was because the former had been an exemplary wife and mother that God had granted strength to her son's legs for, it was said, the more a wife loves and respects her husband and the more she suffers for her child, the more valorous will the child be one day. Each is the child of his mother; the child is worth no more than the mother is worth. It was not astonishing that the king Dankaran Touman was so colourless, for his mother had never shown the slightest respect to her husband and never, in the presence of the late king, did she show that humility which every wife should show before her husband. People recalled her scenes of jealousy and the spiteful remarks she circulated about her co-wife and her child, And people would conclude gravely, "Nobody knows God's mystery. The snake has no legs yet it is as swift as any other animal that has four."

Sogolon Djata's popularity grew from day to day and he was surrounded by a gang of children of the same age as himself. These were Fran Kamara, son of the king of Tabon; Kamandjan, son of the king of Sibi; and other princes whose fathers had sent them to the court of Niani. The son of Namandjé, Manding Bory, was already joining in their games. Balla Fasséké followed Sogolon Djata all the time. He was past twenty and it was he who gave the child education and instruction according to Mandingo rules of conduct. Whether in town or at the hunt, he missed no opportunity of instructing his pupil. Many young boys of Niani came to join in the games of the royal child.

He liked hunting best of all. Farakourou, master of the forges, had made Djata a fine bow, and he proved himself to be a good shot with the bow. He made frequent hunting trips with his troops, and in the evening all Niani would be in the square to be present at the entry of the young hunters. The crowd would sing the "Hymn to the Bow" which Balla Fasséké had composed, and Sogolon Djata was quite young when he received the title of Simbon, or master hunter, which is only conferred on great hunters who have proved themselves.

Every evening Sogolon Kedjou would gather Djata and his companions outside her hut. She would tell them stories about the beasts of the bush, the dumb brothers of man. Sogolon Djata learnt to distinguish between the animals; he knew why the buffalo was his mother's wraith[8] and also why the lion was the protector of his father's family. He also listened to the history of the kings which Balla Fasséké told him; enraptured by the story of Alexander the Great, the mighty king of gold and silver, whose sun shone over quite half the world. Sogolon initiated her son into certain secrets and revealed to him the names of the medicinal plants which every hunter should know. Thus, between his mother and his griot, the child got to know all that needed to be known.

Sogolon's son was now ten. The name Sogolon Djata in the rapid Mandingo language became Sundiata or Sondjata. He was a lad full or strength; his arms had the strength of ten and his biceps inspired fear in his companions. He had already that authoritative way of speaking which belongs to those who are destined to command. His brother, Manding Bory, became his best friend, and whenever Djata was seen, Manding Bory appeared too. They were like a man and his shadow. Fran Kamara and Kamandjan were the closest friends of the young princes, while Balla Fasséké followed them all like a guardian angel.

But Sundiata's popularity was so great that the queen mother became apprehensive for her son's throne. Dankaran Touman was the most retiring of men. At the age of eighteen he was still under the influence of his mother and a handful of old schemers. It was Sassouma Bérété who really reigned in his name. The queen mother wanted to put an end to this popularity by killing Sundiata and it was thus that one night she received the nine great witches of Mali. They were

---

[8] In Mandingo religion, the double of a spirit. The spirit may leave the body and reincarnate itself in other persons or animals. In this case the mother's spirit became reincarnate in the buffalo.

old women. The eldest, and the most dangerous too, was called Soumosso Konkomba. When the nine old hags had seated themselves in a semi-circle around her bed the queen mother said:

"You who rule supreme at night, nocturnal powers, oh you who hold the secret of life, you who can put an end to one life, can you help me?"

"The night is potent," said Soumosso Konkomba, "Oh queen, tell us what is to be done, on whom must we turn the fatal blade?"

"I want to kill Sundiata," said Sassouma. "His destiny runs counter to my son's and he must be killed while there is still time. If you succeed, I promise you the finest rewards. First of all I bestow on each of you a cow and her calf and from tomorrow go to the royal granaries and each of you will receive a hundred measures of rice and a hundred measures of hay on my authority."

"Mother of the king," rejoined Soumosso Konkomba, "life hangs by nothing but a very fine thread, but all is interwoven here below. Life has a cause, and death as well. The one comes from the other. Your hate has a cause and your action must have a cause. Mother of the king, everything holds together, our action will have no effect unless we are ourselves implicated, but Mari Djata has done us no wrong. It is, then, difficult for us to compass his death."

"But you are also concerned," replied the queen mother, "for the son of Sogolon will be a scourge to us all."

"The snake seldom bites the foot that does not walk," said one of the witches.

"Yes, but there are snakes that attack everybody. Allow Sundiata to grow up and we will all repent of it. Tomorrow go to Sogolon's vegetable patch and make a show of picking a few gnougou leaves. Mari Djata stands guard there and you will see how vicious the boy is. He won't have any respect for your age, he'll give you a good thrashing."

"That's a clever idea," said one of the old hags.

"But the cause of our discomfiture will be ourselves, for having touched something which did not belong to us."

"We could repeat the offence," said another, "and then if he beats us again we would be able to reproach him with being unkind, heartless. In that case we would be concerned, I think."

"The idea is ingenious," said Soumosso Konkomba. "Tomorrow we shall go to Sogolon's vegetable patch."

"Now there's a happy thought," concluded the queen mother, laughing for joy. "Go to the vegetable patch tomorrow and you will see that Sogolon's son is mean. Beforehand, present yourselves at the royal granaries where you will receive the grain I promised you; the cows and calves are already yours."

The old hags bowed and disappeared into the black night. The queen mother was now alone and gloated over her anticipated victory. But her daughter, Nana Triban, woke up.

"Mother, who were you talking to? I thought I heard voices."

"Sleep, my daughter, it is nothing. You didn't hear anything."

In the morning, as usual, Sundiata got his companions together in front of his mother's hut and said, "What animal are we going to hunt today?"

Kamandjan said, "I wouldn't mind if we attacked some elephants right now."

"Yes, I am of this opinion too," said Fran Kamara. "That will allow us to go far into the bush."

And the young band left after Sogolon had filled the hunting bags with eatables. Sundiata and his companions came back late to the village, but first Djata wanted to take a look at his mother's vegetable patch as was his custom. It was dusk. There he found the nine witches stealing gnougou leaves. They made a show of running away like thieves caught red-handed.

"Stop, stop, poor old women," said Sundiata, "what is the matter with you to run away, like this. This garden belongs to all."

Straight away his companions and he filled the gourds of the old hags with leaves, aubergines and onions.

"Each time that you run short of condiments come to stock up here without fear."

"You disarm us," said one of the old crones, and another added, "And you confound us with your bounty."

"Listen, Djata," said Soumosso Konkomba, "we had come here to test you. We have no need of condiments but your generosity disarms us. We were sent here by the queen mother to provoke you and draw the anger of the nocturnal powers upon you. But nothing can be done against a heart full of kindness. And to think that we have already drawn a hundred measures of rice and a hundred measures of millet—and the queen promises us each a cow and her calf in addition. Forgive us, son of Sogolon."

"I bear you no ill-will," said Djata. "Here, I am returning from the hunt with my companions and we have killed ten elephants, so I will give you an elephant each and there you have some meat!"

"Thank you, son of Sogolon."

"Thank you, child of Justice."

"Henceforth," concluded Soumosso Konkomba, "we will watch over you." And the nine witches disappeared into the night. Sundiata and his companions continued on their way to Niani and got back after dark.

"You were really frightened; those nine witches really scared you, eh?" said Sogolon Kolonkan, Djata's young sister.

"How do you know?" retorted Sundiata, astonished.

"I saw them at night hatching their scheme, but I knew there was no danger for you." Kolonkan was well versed in the art of witchcraft and watched over her brother without his suspecting it.

Summary

Sogolon, knowing the danger that awaited her children in the court ruled by the jealous Sassouma, decided to leave until such time that Djata could return in safety to reign over Mali. In a parting act of malice Dankaran Touman sent Djata's griot, Balla Fasséké, on an embassy to the king of Sosso, Soumaoro Kanté, thereby depriving Djata of his friend and teacher. There Balla Fasséké remained along with Nana Triban until the eve of Soumaoro's major battle with Sundiata.

Vowing to return, Sogolon's son and his family began their seven years of exile during which Sundiata would grow to manhood. After brief stops in Djedeba and Tabon, they remained for a time at the court of the Cisse's at Wagadou. There Sundiata learned much from the merchants and officials engaged in the trans-Saharan trade. After a time the Cisse king sent them on to the king of Mema, his cousin. The king of Mema's hospitality was generous, and Sundiata quickly became a favorite at the court. His first military campaigns were fought on behalf of the king of Mema, and so valorous were his exploits that he soon was named viceroy.

Soumaoro Kante, The Scorcerer King

While Sogolon's son was fighting his first campaign far from his native land, Mali had fallen under the domination of a new master, Soumaoro Kanté, king of Sosso.

When the embassy sent by Dankaran Touman arrived at Sosso, Soumaoro demanded that Mali should acknowledge itself tributary to Sosso. Balla Fasséké found delegates from several other kingdoms at Soumaoro's court. With his powerful army of smiths the king of Sosso had quickly imposed his power on everybody. After the defeat of Ghana and Diaghan no one dared oppose him any more. Soumaoro was descended from the line of smiths called Diarisso who first harnessed fire and taught men how to work iron, but for a long time Sosso had remained a little village of no significance. The powerful king of Ghana was the master of the country. Little by little the kingdom of Sosso had grown at the expense of Ghana and now the Kantés dominated their old masters. Like all masters of fire, Soumaoro Kanté was a great sorcerer. His fetishes had a terrible power and it was because of them that all kings trembled before him, for he could deal a swift death to whoever he pleased. He had fortified Sosso with a triple curtain wall and in the middle of the town loomed his palace, towering over the thatched huts of the villages. He had had an immense seven-storey tower built for himself and he lived on the seventh floor in the midst of his fetishes. This is why he was called "The Untouchable King."

Soumaoro let the rest of the Mandingo embassy return but he kept Balla Fasséké back and threatened to destroy Niani if Dankaran Touman did not make his submission. Frightened, the son of Sassouma immediately made his submission, and he even sent his sister, Nana Triban, to the king of Sosso.

One day when the king was away, Balla Fasséké managed to get right into the most secret chamber of the palace where Soumaoro safeguarded his fetishes. When he had pushed the door open he was transfixed with amazement at what he saw. The walls of the chamber were tapestried with human skins and there was one in the middle of the room on which the king sat; around an earthenware jar nine heads formed a circle; when Balla had opened the door the water had become disturbed and a monstrous snake had raised its head. Balla Fasséké, who was also well versed in sorcery, recited some formulas and everything in the room fell quiet, so he continued his inspection. He saw on a perch above the bed three owls which seemed to be asleep; on the far wall hung strangely-shaped weapons, curved sword and knives with three cutting edges. He looked at the skulls attentively and recognized the nine kings killed by Soumaoro. To the right of the door he discovered a great balafon, bigger than he had ever seen in Mali. Instinctively he pounced upon it and sat down to play. The griot always has a weakness for music, for music is the griot's soul.

He began to play. He had never heard such a melodious balafon. Though scarcely touched by the hammer, the resonant wood gave out sounds of an infinite sweetness, notes clear and as pure as gold dust; under the skilful hand of Balla the instrument had found its master. He played with all his soul and the whole room was filled with wonderment. The drowsy owls, eyes half closed, began to move their heads as though with satisfaction. Everything seemed to come to life upon the strains of this magic music. The nine skulls resumed their earthly forms and blinked at hearing the solemn "Vulture Tune"; with its head resting on the rim the snake seemed to listen from the jar. Balla Fasséké was pleased at the effect his music had had on the strange inhabitants of this ghoulish chamber, but he quite understood that this balafon was not at all like any other. It was that of a great sorcerer. Soumaoro was the only one to play this instrument. After each victory he would come and sing his own praises. No griot had ever touched it. Not all ears were made to hear that music. Soumaoro was constantly in touch with this xylophone and no matter how far away he was, one only had to touch it for him to know that someone had got into his secret chamber.

The king was not far from the town and he rushed back to his palace and climbed up to the seventh storey. Balla Fasséké heard hurried steps in the corridor and Soumaoro bounded into the room, sword in hand. "Who is there?" he roared. "It is you, Balla Fasséké!"

The king was foaming with anger and his eyes burnt fiercely like hot embers. Yet without losing his composure the son of Doua changed key and improvised a song in honour of the king:

> There he is, Soumaoro Kanté.
> All hail, you who sit on the skins of kings.
> All hail, Simbon of the deadly arrow.
> I salute you, you who wear clothes of human skin.

This improvised tune greatly pleased Soumaoro and he had never heard such fine words. Kings are only men, and whatever iron cannot achieve against them, words can. Kings, too, are susceptible to flattery, so Soumaoro's anger abated, his heart filled with joy as he listened attentively to this sweet music:

All had, you who wear clothes of human skin.
I salute you, you who sit on the skins of kings.

Balla sang and his voice, which was beautiful, delighted the king of Sosso.

"How sweet it is to hear one's praises sung by someone else; Balla Fasséké, you will nevermore return to Mali for from today you are my griot."

Thus Balla Fasséké, whom king Naré Maghan had given to his son Sundiata, was stolen from the latter by Dankaran Touman; now it was the king of Sosso, Soumaoro Kanté, who, in turn, stole the precious griot from the son of Sassouma Bérété. In this way war between Sundiata and Soumaoro became inevitable.

Summary

The second half of the epic relates Sundiata's leave-taking of Mema in response to the pleas for rescue of a search party sent to find him, and tells of his triumphal series of battles against the terrible Soumaoro.

Allied with the armies of his childhood friends and with those who had offered him sanctuary during his exile, Sundiata led a massive force that included the cavalry of Mema and Wagadou; blacksmiths and the mountain Djallonkes; and groups under Fran Kamara of Tabon Wana. A victory at the valley of Tabon was followed by the first clash with Soumaoro's magic at Negueboria. The fame of Sundiata spread until all the sons of Mali were under his banner. But even a warrior like Sundiata was challenged to the limits by Soumaoro's sorcery. He was saved by the clever escape from Sosso of Balla Fasséké and Nana Triban; on the eve of the battle of Krina it was they who revealed Soumaoro's secret taboo. Reunited with his master, the griot Balla Fasséké sang the praises and history of Mali and challenged the assembled armies to prove themselves worthy of their heritage. At Krina, Soumaoro's power and magic were dissolved by Sundiata's mighty army and his destruction of Soumaoro's protective fetish. Despite hard-driven pursuit by Sundiata and Soumaoro's nephew Fakoli, Soumaoro avoided capture and ultimately disappeared into a mountain cave, never to be seen again. The city of Sosso was destroyed, and the rest of Soumaoro's allies now in disarray were vanquished.

The final sections relate the triumphal festival, the Kouroukan Fougan or the Division of the World, and the rebuilding of Sundiata's capital at Niani.

Kouroukan Fougan or the Division of the World

Leaving Do, the land of ten thousand guns, Sundiata mended his way to Ka-ba, keeping to the river valley. All his armies converged on Ka-ba and Fakoli and Tabon Wana entered it laden with booty. Sibi Kamandjan had gone ahead of Sundiata to prepare the great assembly which was to gather at Ka-ba, a town situated on the territory belonging to the country of Sibi. . . .

To the north of the town stretches a spacious clearing and it is there that the great assembly was to foregather. King Kamandjan had the whole clearing cleaned up and a great dais was got ready. Even before Djata's arrival the delegations from all the conquered peoples had made their way to Ka-ba. Huts were hastily built to house all these people. When all the armies had reunited, camps had to be set up in the big plain lying between the river and the town. On the appointed day the troops were drawn up on the vast square that had been prepared. As at Sibi, each people was gathered round its king's pennant. Sundiata had put on robes such as are worn by a great Muslim king. Balla Fasséké, the high master of ceremonies, set the allies around Djata's great throne. Everything was in position. The sofas,[9] forming a vast semicircle bristling with spears, stood motionless. The delegations of the various peoples had been planted at the foot of the dais.

---

[9] Army troops, often of slave origin.

A complete silence reigned. On Sundiata's right, Balla Fasséké, holding his mighty spear, addressed the throng in this manner:

"Peace reigns today in the whole country; may it always be thus. . . .

"Amen," replied the crowd, then the herald continued:

"I speak to you, assembled peoples. To those of Mali I convey Maghan Sundiata's greeting; greetings to those of Do, greetings to those of Ghana, to those from Mema greetings, and to those of Fakoli's tribe. Greetings to the Bobo warriors and, finally, greetings to those of Sibi and Ka-ba. To all the peoples assembled, Djata gives greetings.

"May I be humbly forgiven if I have made any omission. I am nervous before so many people gathered together.

"Peoples, here we are, after years of hard trials, gathered around our saviour, the restorer of peace and order. From the east to the west, from the north to the south, everywhere his victorious arms have established peace. I convey to you the greetings of Soumaoro's vanquisher, Maghan Sundiata, king of Mali.

"But in order to respect tradition, I must first of all address myself to the host of us all, Kamandjan, king of Sibi; Djata greets you and gives you the floor."

Kamandjan, who was sitting close by Sundiata, stood up and stepped down from the dais. He mounted his horse and brandished his sword, crying "I salute you all, warriors of Mali, of Do, of Tabon, of Mema, of Wagadou, of Bobo, of Fakoli . . . ; warriors, peace has returned to our homes, may God long preserve it."

"Amen," replied the warriors and the crowd. The king of Sibi continued.

"In the world man suffers for a season, but never eternally. Here we are at the end of our trials. We are at peace. May God be praised. But we owe this peace to one man who, by his courage and his valiance, was able to lead our troops to victory.

"Which one of us, alone, would have dared face Soumaoro? Ay, we were all cowards. How many times did we pay him tribute? The insolent rogue thought that everything was permitted him. What family was not dishonoured by Soumaoro? He took our daughters and wives from us and we were more craven than women. He carried his insolence to the point of stealing the wife of his nephew Fakoli! We were prostrated and humiliated in front of our children. But it was in the midst of so many calamities that our destiny suddenly changed. A new sun arose in the east. After the battle of Tabon we felt ourselves to be men, we realized that Soumaoro was a human being and not an incarnation of the devil, for he was no longer invincible. A man came to us. He had heard our groans and came to our aid, like a father when he sees his son in tears. Here is that man. Maghan Sundiata, the man with two names foretold by the soothsayers.

"It is to you that I now address myself, son of Sogolon, you, the nephew of the valorous warriors of Do. Henceforth it is from you that I derive my kingdom for I acknowledge you my sovereign. My tribe and I place ourselves in your hands. I salute you, supreme chief, I salute you, Fama of Famas.[10] I salute you, Mansa!"[11]

The huzza that greeted these words was so loud that you could hear the echo repeat the tremendous clamour twelve times over. With a strong hand Kamandjan struck his spear in the ground in front of the dais and said, "Sundiata, here is my spear, it is yours."

Then he climbed up to sit in his place. Thereafter, one by one, the twelve kings of the bright savanna country got up and proclaimed Sundiata "Mansa" in their turn. Twelve royal spears were stuck in the ground in front of the dais. Sundiata had become emperor. The old tabala of Niani announced to the world that the lands of the savanna had provided themselves with one single king. When the imperial tabala had stopped reverberating, Balla Fasséké, the grand master of ceremonies, took the floor again following the crowd's ovation.

---

[10] King of Kings.

[11] Emperor.

"Sundiata, Maghan Sundiata, king of Mali, in the name of the twelve kings of the 'Bright Country,' I salute you as 'Mansa.'"

The crowd shouted "Wassa, Wassa. . . . Ayé."

It was amid such joy that Balla Fasséké composed the great hymn "Niama" which the griots still sing:

Niama, Niama, Niama,
You, you serve as a shelter for all,
All come to seek refuge under you.
And as for you, Niama,
Nothing serves you for shelter,
God alone protects you.

The festival began. The musicians of all the countries were there. Each people in turn came forward to the dais under Sundiata's impassive gaze. Then the war dances began. The sofas of all the countries had lined themselves up in six ranks amid a great clatter of bows and spears knocking together. The war chiefs were on horseback. The warriors faced the enormous dais and at a signal from Balla Fasséké, the musicians, massed on the right of the dais, struck up. The heavy war drums thundered, the bolons gave off muted notes while the griot's voice gave the throng the pitch for the "Hymn to the Bow." The spearmen, advancing like hyenas in the night, held their spears above their heads; the archers of Wagadou and Tabon, walking with a noiseless tread, seemed to be lying in ambush behind bushes. They rose suddenly to their feet and let fly their arrows at imaginary enemies. In front of the great dais the Kéké-Tigui, or war chiefs, made their horses perform dance steps under the eyes of the Mansa. The horses whinnied and reared, then, overmastered by the spurs, knelt, got up and cut little capers, or else scraped the ground with their hooves.

The rapturous people shouted the "Hymn to the Bow" and clapped their hands. The sweating bodies of the warriors glistened in the sun while the exhausting rhythm of the tam-tams wrenched from them shrill cries. But presently they made way for the cavalry, beloved by Djata. The horsemen of Mema threw their swords in the air and caught them in flight, uttering mighty shouts. A smile of contentment took shape on Sundiata's lips, for he was happy to see his cavalry manoeuvre with so much skill.

In the afternoon the festivity took on a new aspect. It began with the procession of prisoners and booty. Their hands tied behind their backs and in triple file, the Sosso prisoners made their entry into the giant circle. All their heads had been shaved. Inside the circle they turned and passed by the foot of the dais. Their eyes lowered, the poor prisoners walked in silence, abuse heaped upon them by the frenzied crowd. Behind came the kings who had remained faithful to Soumaoro and who had not intended to make their submission. They also had their heads shorn, but they were on horseback so that everyone could see them. At last, right at the back, came Sosso Balla, who had been placed in the midst of his father's fetishes. The fetishes had been loaded onto donkeys. The crowd gave loud cries of horror on seeing the inmates of Soumaoro's grisly chamber. People pointed with terror at the snake's pitcher, the magic balafon, and the king of Sosso's owls. Soumaoro's son Balla, his hands bound, was on a horse but did not dare look up at this throne, which formerly used to tremble with fear at mere talk of his father. In the crowd could be heard:

"Each in his turn, Sosso Balla; lift up your head a bit, impudent little creature!" Or else: "Did you have any idea that one day you would be a slave, you vile fellow!"

"Look at your useless fetishes. Call on them then, son of a sorcerer!"

When Sosso Balla was in front of the dais, Djata made a gesture. He had just remembered the mysterious disappearance of Soumaoro inside the mountain. He became morose, but his griot Balla Fasséké noticed it and so he spoke thus:

"The son will pay for the father, Soumaoro can thank God that he is already dead."

When the procession had finished Balla Fasséké silenced everyone. The sofas got into line and the tam-tams stopped.

Sundiata got up and a graveyard silence settled on the whole place. The Mansa moved forward to the edge of the dais. Then Sundiata spoke as Mansa. Only Balla Fasséké could hear him, for a Mansa does not speak like a town-crier.

"I greet all the peoples gathered here." And Djata mentioned them all. Pulling the spear of Kamandjan, king of Sibi, out of the ground, he said:

"I give you back your kingdom, king of Sibi, for you have deserved it by your bravery; I have known you since childhood and your speech is as frank as your heart is straightforward.

"Today I ratify for ever the alliance between the Kamaras of Sibi and the Keitas of Mali. May these two people be brothers henceforth. In future, the land of the Keitas shall be the land of the Kamaras, and the property of the Kamaras shall be henceforth the property of the Keitas.

"May there nevermore be falsehood between a Kamara and a Keita, and may the Kamaras feel at home in the whole extent of my empire."

He returned the spear to Kamandjan and the king of Sibi prostrated himself before Djata, as is done when honoured by a Fama.

Sundiata took Tabon Wana's spear and said, "Fran Kamara, my friend, I return your kingdom to you. May the Djallonkes and Mandingoes be forever allies. You received me in your own domain, so may the Djallonkes be received as friends throughout Mali. I leave you the lands you have conquered, and henceforth your children and your children's children will grow up at the court of Niani where they will be treated like the princes of Mali."

One by one all the kings received their kingdoms from the very hands of Sundiata, and each one bowed before him as one bows before a Mansa.

Sundiata pronounced all the prohibitions which still obtain in relations between the tribes. To each he assigned its land, he established the rights of each people and ratified their friendships. The Kondés of the land of Do became henceforth the uncles of the imperial family of Keita, for the latter, in memory of the fruitful marriage between Naré Maghan and Sogolon, had to take a wife in Do. The Tounkaras and the Cissés became "banter-brothers" of the Keitas. While the Cissés, Bérétés and Tourés were proclaimed great divines of the empire. No kin groups forgotten at Kouroukan Fougan; each had its share in the division. To Fakoli Koroma, Sundiata gave the kingdom of Sosso, the majority of whose inhabitants were enslaved. Fakoli's tribe, the Koromas, which others call Doumbouya or Sissoko, had the monopoly of the forge, that is, of iron working. Fakoli also received from Sundiata part of the lands situated between the Baring and Bagbé rivers. Wagadou and Mema kept their kings who continued to bear the title of Mansa, but these two kingdoms acknowledged the suzerainty of the supreme Mansa. The Konaté of Toron became the cadets of the Keitas so that on reaching maturity a Konaté could call himself Keita.

When Sogolon's son had finished distributing lands and power he turned to Balla Fasséké, his griot, and said: "As for you, Balla Fasséké, my griot, I make you grand master of ceremonies. Henceforth the Keitas will choose their griot from your tribe, from among the Kouyatés. I give the Kouyatés the right to make jokes about all the tribes, and in particular about the royal tribe of Keita."

Thus spoke the son of Sogolon at Kouroukan Fougan. Since that time his respected word has become law, the rule of conduct for all the peoples who were represented at Ka-ba.

So, Sundiata had divided the world at Kouroukan Fougan. He kept for his tribe the blessed country of Kita, but the Kamaras inhabiting the region remained masters of the soil.

If you go to Ka-ba, go and see the glade of Kouroukan Fougan and you will see a linké tree planted there, perpetuating the memory of the great gathering which witnessed the division of the world.

DELAWARE INDIAN SONG

WHO ARE THEY?

A great land and a wide land was the east land,
A land without snakes, a rich land, a pleasant
    land.
Great Fighter was chief, toward the north.
At the Straight river, River-Loving was chief.
Becoming-Fat was chief at Sassafras land . . .

Affable was chief, and made peace with all,
All were friends, all were united under this
    great chief.
Great-Beaver was chief, remaining in Sassafras
    land.
White-Body was chief on the seashore.
Peace-Maker was chief, friendly to all.
He-Makes-Mistakes was chief, hurriedly

coming. . .
Coming-as-a-Friend was chief; he went to the
    Great Lakes,
Visiting all his children, all his friends.
Cranberry-Eater was chief, friend of the
    Ottawas.
North-Walker was chief; he made festivals.
Slow-Gatherer was chief at the shore . . .

White-Crab was chief; a friend of the shore.
Watcher was chief; he looked toward the sea.
At this time, from north and south, the whites
    came.
They are peaceful; they have great things; who
    are they?

AZTEC POEM

The Aztec Indians lived in the Valley of Mexico from the 13th century and adopted the name "Mexica." In the twelfth century, they built pyramids that can still be seen near Mexico City.

LA NOCHE TRISTE

Broken spears lie in the roads,
we have torn our hair in grief.
The houses are roofless now, and their
walls are red with blood . . . .

We have pounded our hands in despair
against the adobe walls,
for our inheritance, our city, is lost and dead.
The shields of our warriors were its defense,

but they could not save it. . . .

Weep my people; know that with these
    disasters
we have lost the Mexican nation.,
The water has turned bitter; our food is bitter!
These are the acts of the Giver of Life.

ca. 1522

CHIEF JOSEPH (1840?-1904)

Chief Joseph was leader of the Nez Perce Indian tribe of the Pacific Northwest, which was decimated in war with the white man.

I AM TIRED OF FIGHTING

I am tired of fighting. The old men are all dead. My brother is dead. It is cold, and we have no blankets. The little children are freezing to death. My people, some of them, have run away to the hills. No one knows where they are. I want to have some time to look for my children and see how many I can find. Maybe I shall find them among the dead.

Hear me my chiefs. From where the sun now stands, I will fight no more forever.

1877

CHIEF SITTING BULL

Chief of the Sioux, Chief Sitting Bull led Sioux and Cheyenne to victory over Col. George Armstrong Custer in the Battle of the Little Big Horn in 1876.

DEFEAT OF THE SIOUX

Whatever you wanted of me I have obeyed. The Great Father (President) sent me word that whatever he had against me in the past had been forgiven and thrown aside, and I accepted his promises and came in. And he told me not to step aside from the white man's path, and I am doing my best to travel in that path. I sit here and look around me and I see my people starving. We want cattle to butcher. That is the way you live and we want to live the same way. When the Great Father told me to live like his people, I told him to send me six teams of mules, because that is the way the white people make a living. I asked for a horse and buggy for my children; I was advised to follow the ways of the white man and that is why I asked for those things.

1883

LANGSTON HUGHES (1902-1967)

Born in Joplin, Missouri, Hughes attended college for one year and became a seaman and a poet. By the 1930's he had become known as an activist and poet in Harlem, where he was the leading figure in the Harlem Renaissance. He wrote popular humorous newspaper sketches in the tradition of Mark Twain, but from the viewpoint of a Black character. His sensitivity to his own culture and to language are evident in his poetry.

THE NEGRO SPEAKS OF RIVERS

I've known rivers:

I've known rivers ancient as the world and
    older than the flow of human
    blood in human veins.

My soul has grown deep like the rivers.

I bathed in the Euphrates when dawns
    were young.
I built my hut near the Congo and it lulled
    me to sleep.
I looked upon the Nile and raised the

    pyramids above it.
I heard the singing of the Mississippi when
    Abe Lincoln went down
    to New Orleans, and I've seen its muddy
    bosom turn all golden in
    the sunset.

I've known rivers:
Ancient, dusky rivers.

My soul has grown deep like the rivers.

1926

HARLEM (A DREAM DEFERRED)

What happens to a dream deferred?

    Does it dry up
    like a raisin in the sun?
    Or fester like a sore—
    And then run?
    Does it stink like rotten meat?
    Or crust and sugar over—

like a syrupy sweet?

Maybe it just sags
like a heavy load.

Or does it explode?

1951

CLAUDE MCKAY (1889-1948)

Claude McKay demonstrates in his poetry the mixed feelings of a Black man toward his native America during the years of racial segregation.

AMERICA

Although she feeds me bread of bitterness,
And sinks into my throat her tiger's tooth,
Stealing my breath of life, I will confess
I love this cultured hell that tests my
    youth!
Her vigor flows like tides into my blood,
Giving me strength erect against her hate.
Her bigness sweeps my being like a flood.
Yet as a rebel fronts a king in state,

I stand within her walls with not a shred
Of terror, malice, not a word of jeer.
Darkly I gaze into the days ahead,
And see her might and granite wonders
    there,
Beneath the touch of Time's unerring hand,
Like priceless treasures sinking in the sand.

1922

THOMAS JEFFERSON (1743-1826)

Thomas Jefferson was the first Secretary of State and the third President of the United States. He was also an architect, a lawyer, a linguist, and an excellent writer. Chosen to draft the Declaration of Independence, he first included a paragraph condemning slavery. Political pressure from slave holders led the Colonial Congress to delete that paragraph.

THE DECLARATION OF INDEPENDENCE[12]

When in the course of human events, it becomes necessary for one people to dissolve the political bands which have connected them with another, and to assume among the powers of the earth, the separate and equal station to which the Laws of Nature and of Nature's God entitle them, a decent respect to the opinions of mankind requires that they should declare the causes which impel them to the separation.

We hold these truths to be self-evident, that all men are created equal, that they are endowed by their Creator with certain unalienable Rights, that among these are Life, Liberty and the pursuit of Happiness. That to secure these rights, Governments are instituted among Men, deriving their just powers from the consent of the governed. That whenever any Form of Government becomes destructive of these ends it is the Right of the People to alter or to abolish it, and to institute new Government, laying its foundation on such principles and organizing its powers in such form, as to them shall seem most likely to effect their Safety and Happiness. Prudence, indeed, will dictate that Governments long established should not be changed for light and transient causes; and accordingly all experience has shown, that mankind are more disposed to suffer, while evils are sufferable, than to right themselves by abolishing the forms to which they are accustomed. But when a long train of abuses and usurpations, pursuing invariably the same Object evinces a design to reduce them under absolute Despotism, it is their right, it is their duty, to throw off such Government, and to provide new Guards for their future security. Such has been the patient sufferance of these Colonies; and such is now the necessity which constrains them to

---

[12] Note: This text of the Declaration of Independence is taken from the reprint in the Revised Statutes of the United States, corrected by comparison with the version printed in the journal of the Continental Congress. The original manuscript can be seen in the National Archives, Washington, D. C.

alter their former Systems of Government. The history of the present King of Great Britain is a history of repeated injuries and usurpations, all having in direct object the establishment of an absolute Tyranny over these States. To prove this, let Facts be submitted to a candid world.

He has refused his Assent to Laws, the most wholesome and necessary for the public good.

He has forbidden his Governors to pass Laws of immediate and pressing importance, unless suspended in their operation till his Assent should be obtained; and when so suspended, he has utterly neglected to attend to them. He has refused to pass other Laws for the accommodation of large districts of people, unless those people would relinquish the right of Representation in the Legislature, a right inestimable to them and formidable to tyrants only.

He has called together legislative bodies at places unusual, uncomfortable, and distant from the depository of their public Records, for the sole purpose of fatiguing them into compliance with his measures.

He has dissolved Representative Houses repeatedly, for opposing with manly firmness his invasions on the rights of the people.

He has refused for a long time, after such dissolutions, to cause others to be elected; whereby the Legislative powers, incapable of Annihilation, have returned to the People at large for their exercise; the State remaining in the meantime exposed to all the dangers of invasion from without, and convulsions within.

He has endeavoured to prevent the population of these States; for that purpose obstructing the Laws for Naturalization of Foreigners; refusing to pass others to encourage their migrations hither, and raising the conditions of new Appropriations of Lands.

He has obstructed the Administration of Justice, by refusing his Assent to Laws for establishing Judiciary powers.

He has made Judges dependent on his Will alone, for the tenure of their offices, and the amount and payment of their salaries.

He has erected a multitude of New Offices, and sent hither swarms of Officers to harass our People, and eat out their substance.

He has kept among us, in times of peace, standing Armies without the Consent of our legislatures.

He has affected to render the Military independent of and superior to the Civil power.

He has combined with others to subject us to a jurisdiction foreign to our constitution, and unacknowledged by our laws; giving his Assent to their Acts of pretended Legislation:

For Quartering large bodies of armed troops among us:

For protecting them, by a mock Trial, from punishment for any Murders which they should commit on the Inhabitants of these States:

For cutting off our Trade with all parts of the world:

For imposing Taxes on us without our Consent:

For depriving us in many cases of the benefits of Trial by Jury:

For transporting us beyond Seas to be tried for pretended offences:

For abolishing the free System of English Laws in a neighbouring Province, establishing therein an Arbitrary government, and enlarging its Boundaries so as to render it at once an example and fit instrument for introducing the same absolute rule into these Colonies:

For taking away our Charters, abolishing our most valuable Laws, and altering fundamentally the Forms of our Governments:

For suspending our own Legislatures, and declaring themselves invested with power to legislate for us in all cases whatsoever.

He has abdicated Government here, by declaring us out of his Protection and waging War against us.

He has plundered our seas, ravaged our Coasts, burnt our towns, and destroyed the Lives of our people.

He is at this time transporting large Armies of foreign Mercenaries to compleat the works of death, desolation and tyranny, already begun with circumstances of Cruelty & perfidy scarcely paralleled in the most barbarous ages, and totally unworthy the Head of a civilized nation.

He has constrained our fellow Citizens taken Captive on the high Seas to bear Arms against their Country, to become the executioners of their friends and Brethren, or to fall themselves by their Hands.

He has excited domestic insurrections amongst us, and has endeavoured to bring on the inhabitants of our frontiers the merciless Indian Savages, whose known rule of warfare is an undistinguished destruction of all ages, sexes and conditions.

In every stage of these Oppressions We have Petitioned for Redress in the most humble terms: Our repeated Petitions have been answered only by repeated injury. A Prince, whose character is thus marked by every act which may define a Tyrant, is unfit to be the ruler of a free people.

Nor have We been wanting in attentions to our British brethren. We have warned them from time to time of attempts by their legislature to extend an unwarrantable jurisdiction over us. We have reminded them of the circumstances of our emigration and settlement here. We have appealed to their native justice and magnanimity, and we have conjured them by the ties of our common kindred to disavow these usurpations, which would inevitably interrupt our connections and correspondence. They too have been deaf to the voice of justice and of consanguinity. We must, therefore, acquiesce in the necessity, which denounces our Separation, and hold them, as we hold the rest of mankind, Enemies in War, in Peace Friends.

We therefore, the Representatives of the United States of America, in General Congress, Assembled, appealing to the Supreme Judge of the world for the rectitude of our intentions, do, in the Name, and by Authority of the good People of these Colonies, solemnly publish and declare, That these United Colonies are, and of Right ought to be Free and Independent States; that they are Absolved from all Allegiance to the British Crown, and that all political connection between them and the State of Great Britain, is and ought to be totally dissolved; and that as Free and Independent States, they have full Power to levy War, conclude Peace, contract Alliances, establish Commerce, and to do all other Acts and Things which Independent States may of right do. And for the support of this Declaration, with a firm reliance on the protection of divine Providence, we mutually pledge to each other our Lives, our Fortunes and our sacred Honor.

John Hancock	Button Gwinnett	Thos. Nelson Jr.
Richd. Stockton	Lyman Hall	Francis Lightfoot Lee
Jon Witherspoon	Geo. Walton	Carter Braxton
Fras. Hopkinson	Wm. Hooper	Robt. Morris
John Hart	Joseph Hewes	Benjamin Rush
Abra Clark	John Penn	Benja. Franklin
Josiah Bartlett	Edward Rutledge	John Morton
Wm. Whipple	Thos. Heyward Junr.	Geo. Clymer
Saml. Adams	Thomas Lynch Junr.	Jas. Smith
John Adams	Arthur Middleton	Geo. Taylor
Robt. Treat Paine	Samuel Chase	James Wilson
Elbridge Gerry	Wm. Paca	Geo. Ross
Step. Hopkins	Thos. Stone	Caesar Rodney
William Ellery	Charles Carroll of	Geo Read
Roger Sherman	Carrollton	Tho M. Kean
Saml. Huntington	George Wythe	Wm. Floyd
Wm. Williams	Richard Henry Lee	Phil. Livingston
Oliver Wolcott	Th. Jefferson	Frans. Lewis
Matthew Thornton	Benja. Harrison	Lewis Morris

The following paragraph, which was part of Jefferson's first draft, was omitted from the final draft:

He has waged cruel war against human nature itself, violating its most sacred rights of life & liberty in the persons of a distant people who never offended him, captivating & carrying them into slavery in another hemisphere, or to incur miserable death in their transportation thither. This piratical warfare, the opprobrium of *infidel* powers, is the warfare of the CHRISTIAN king of Great Britain. Determined to keep open a market where MEN should be bought & sold; he has prostituted his negative for suppressing every legislative attempt to prohibit or to restrain this execrable commerce: & that this assemblage of horrors might want no fact of distinguished die, he is now exciting those very people to rise in arms among us, & to purchase that liberty of which he has deprived them, by murdering the people upon whom he also obtruded them; thus paying off former crimes committed against the *liberties* of one people, with crimes which he urges them to commit against the lives of another.

PLATO

UNLESS PHILOSOPHERS BECOME KINGS

But still I must say, Socrates, that if you are allowed to go on in this way you will entirely forget the other question which at the commencement of this discussion you thrust aside: Is such an order of things possible, and how, if at all? For I am quite ready to acknowledge that the plan which you propose, if only feasible, would do all sorts of good to the State. I will add, what you have omitted, that your citizens will be the bravest of warriors, and will never leave their ranks, for they will all know one another, and each will call the other father, brother, son; and if you suppose the women to join their armies, whether in the same rank or in the rear, either as a terror to the enemy, or as auxiliaries in case of need, I know that they will then be absolutely invincible; and there are many domestic advantages which might also be mentioned and which I also fully acknowledge: but, as I admit all these advantages and as many more as you please, if only this State of yours were to come into existence, we need say no more about them; assuming then the existence of the State, let us now turn to the question of possibility and ways and means — the rest may be left.

If I loiter for a moment, you instantly make a raid upon me, I said, and have no mercy; I have hardly escaped the first and second waves, and you seem not to be aware that you are now bringing upon me the third, which is the greatest and heaviest. When you have seen and heard the third wave, I think you will be more considerate and will acknowledge that some fear and hesitation were natural respecting a proposal so extraordinary as that which I have now to state and investigate.

The more appeals of this sort which you make, he said, the more determined are we that you shall tell us how such a State is possible: speak out and at once.

Let me begin by reminding you that we found our way hither in the search after justice and injustice.

True, he replied; but what of that?

I was only going to ask whether, if we have discovered them, we are to require that the just man should in nothing fail of absolute justice; or may we be satisfied with an approximation, and the attainment in him of a higher degree of justice than is to be found in other men?

The approximation will be enough.

We were inquiring into the nature of absolute justice and into the character of the perfectly just, and into injustice and the perfectly unjust, that we might have an ideal. We were to look at these in order that we might judge of our own happiness and unhappiness according to the standard which they exhibited and the degree in which we resembled them, but not with any view of showing that they could exist in fact.

True, he said.

Would a painter be any the worse because, after having delineated with consummate art an ideal of a perfectly beautiful man, he was unable to show that any such man could ever have existed?

He would be none the worse.

Well, and were we not creating an ideal of a perfect State?

To be sure.

And is our theory a worse theory because we are unable to prove the possibility of a city being ordered in the manner described?

Surely not, he replied.

That is the truth, I said. But if, at your request, I am to try and show how and under what conditions the possibility is highest, I must ask you, having this in view, to repeat your former admissions.

What admissions?

I want to know whether ideals are ever fully realized in language? Does not the word express more than the fact, and must not the actual, whatever a man may think, always, in the nature of things, fall short of the truth? What do you say?

I agree.

Then you must not insist on my proving that the actual State will in every respect coincide with the ideal: if we are only able to discover how a city may be governed nearly as we proposed, you will admit that we have discovered the possibility which you demand; and will be contented. I am sure that I should be contented — will not you?

Yes, I will.

Let me next endeavor to show what is that fault in States which is the cause of their present maladministration, and what is the least change which will enable a State to pass into the truer form; and let the change, if possible, be of one thing only, or, if not, of two; at any rate, let the changes be as few and slight as possible.

Certainly, he replied.

I think, I said, that there might be a reform of the State if only one change were made, which is not a slight or easy though still a possible one.

What is it? he said.

Now then, I said, I go to meet that which I liken to the greatest of the waves; yet shall the word be spoken, even though the wave break and drown me in laughter and dishonor; and do you mark my words.

Proceed.

I said: "Until philosophers are kings, or the kings and princes of this world have the spirit and power of philosophy, and political greatness and wisdom meet in one, and those commoner natures who pursue either to the exclusion of the other are compelled to stand aside, cities will never have rest from their evils — no, nor the human race, as I believe — and then only will this our State have a possibility of life and behold the light of day." Such was the thought, my dear Glaucon, which I would fain have uttered if it had not seemed too extravagant; for to be convinced that in no other State can there be happiness private or public is indeed a hard thing.

Socrates, what do you mean? I would have you consider that the word which you have uttered is one at which numerous persons, and very respectable persons too, in a figure pulling off their coats all in a moment, and seizing any weapon that comes to hand, will run at you might and main, before you know where you are, intending to do heaven knows what; and if you don't prepare an answer, and put yourself in motion, you will be " pared by their fine wits," and no mistake.

You got me into the scrape, I said.

And I was quite right; however, I will do all I can to get you out of it; but I can only give you good-will and good advice, and, perhaps, I may be able to fit answers to your questions better than another — that is all. And now, having such an auxiliary, you must do your best to show the unbelievers that you are right.

I ought to try, I said, since you offer me such invaluable assistance. And I think that, if there is to be a chance of our escaping, we must explain to them whom we mean when we say that philosophers are to rule in the State; then we shall be able to defend ourselves. There will be discovered to be some natures who ought to study philosophy and to be leaders in the State; and others who are not born to be philosophers, and are meant to be followers rather than leaders.

Then now for a definition, he said.

Follow me, I said, and I hope that I may in some way or other be able to give you a satisfactory explanation.

Proceed.

I dare say that you remember, and therefore I need not remind you, that a lover, if he is worthy of the name, ought to show his love, not to some one part of that which he loves, but to the whole.

I really do not understand, and therefore beg of you to assist my memory.

Another person, I said, might fairly reply as you do; but a man of pleasure like yourself ought to know that all who are in the flower of youth do somehow or other raise a pang or emotion in a lover's breast, and are thought by him to be worthy of his affectionate regards. Is not this a way which you have with the fair: one has a snub nose, and you praise his charming face; the hook-nose of another has, you say, a royal look; while he who is neither snub nor hooked has the grace of regularity: the dark visage is manly, the fair are children of the gods; and as to the sweet " honey-pale," as they are called, what is the very name but the invention of a lover who talks in diminutives, and is not averse to paleness if appearing on the cheek of youth? In a word, there is no excuse which you will not make, and nothing which you will not say, in order not to lose a single flower that blooms in the spring-time of youth.

If you make me an authority in matters of love, for the sake of the argument, I assent.

And what do you say of lovers of wine? Do you not see them doing the same? They are glad of any pretext of drinking any wine.

Very good.

And the same is true of ambitious men; if they cannot command an army, they are willing to command a file; and if they cannot be honored by really great and important persons, they are glad to be honored by lesser and meaner people—but honor of some kind they must have.

Exactly.

Once more let me ask: Does he who desires any class of goods, desire the whole class or a part only?

The whole.

And may we not say of the philosopher that he is a lover, not of a part of wisdom only, but of the whole?

Yes, of the whole.

And he who dislikes learning, especially in youth, when he has no power of judging what is good and what is not, such a one we maintain not to be a philosopher or a lover of knowledge, just as he who refuses his food is not hungry, and may be said to have a bad appetite and not a good one?

Very true, he said.

Whereas he who has a taste for every sort of knowledge and who is curious to learn and is never satisfied, may be justly termed a philosopher? Am I not right?

Glaucon said: If curiosity makes a philosopher, you will find many a strange being will have a title to the name. All the lovers of sights have a delight in learning, and must therefore be included. Musical amateurs, too, are a folk strangely out of place among philosophers, for they are the last persons in the world who would come to anything like a philosophical discussion, if they could help, while they run about at the Dionysiac festivals as if they had let out their ears to hear every chorus; whether the performance is in town or country—that makes no difference— they are there. Now are we to maintain that all these and any who have similar tastes, as well as the professors of quite minor arts, are philosophers?

Certainly not, I replied; they are only an imitation.

He said: Who then are the true philosophers?

Those, I said, who are lovers of the vision of truth.

That is also good, he said; but I should like to know what you mean?

To another, I replied, I might have a difficulty in explaining; but I am sure that you will admit a proposition which I am about to make.

What is the proposition?

That since beauty is the opposite of ugliness, they are two?

Certainly.

And inasmuch as they are two, each of them is one?

True again.

And of just and unjust, good and evil, and of every other class, the same remark holds: taken singly, each of them is one; but from the various combinations of them with actions and things and with one another, they are seen in all sorts of lights and appear many?

Very true.

And this is the distinction which I draw between the sight-loving, art-loving, practical class and those of whom I am speaking, and who are alone worthy of the name of philosophers.

How do you distinguish them? he said.

The lovers of sounds and sights, I replied, are, as I conceive, fond of fine tones and colors and forms and all the artificial products that are made out of them, but their minds are incapable of seeing or loving absolute beauty.

True, he replied.

Few are they who are able to attain to the sight of this.

Very true.

And he who, having a sense of beautiful things, has no sense of absolute beauty, or who, if another lead him to a knowledge of that beauty, is unable to follow—of such a one I ask, Is he awake or in a dream only? Reflect: is not the dreamer, sleeping or waking, one who likens dissimilar things, who puts the copy in the place of the real object?

I should certainly say that such a one was dreaming.

But take the case of the other, who recognizes the existence of absolute beauty and is able to distinguish the idea from the objects which participate in the idea, neither putting the objects in the place of the idea nor the idea in the place of the objects, is he a dreamer, or is he awake?

He is wide awake.

And may we not say that the mind of the one who knows has knowledge, and that the mind of the other, who opines only, has opinion?

Certainly.

But suppose that the latter should quarrel with us and dispute our statement, can we administer any soothing cordial or advice to him, without revealing to him that there is sad disorder in his wits?

We must certainly offer him some good advice, he replied.

Come, then, and let us think of something to say to him. Shall we begin by assuring him that he is welcome to any knowledge which he may have, and that we are rejoiced at his having it? But we should like to ask him a question: Does he who has knowledge know something or nothing? (You must answer for him).

I answer that he knows something.

Something that is or is not?

Something that is; for how can that which is not ever be known?

And are we assured, after looking at the matter from many points of view, that absolute being is or may be absolutely known, but that the utterly non-existent is utterly unknown?

Nothing can be more certain.

Good. But if there be anything which is of such a nature as to be and not to be, that will have a place intermediate between pure being and the absolute negation of being?

Yes, between them.

And, as knowledge corresponded to being and ignorance of necessity to not-being, for that intermediate between being and not-being there has to be discovered a corresponding intermediate between ignorance and knowledge, if there be such?

Certainly.

Do we admit the existence of opinion?

Undoubtedly.

As being the same with knowledge, or another faculty?

Another faculty.

Then opinion and knowledge have to do with different kinds of matter corresponding to this difference of faculties?

Yes.

And knowledge is relative to being and knows being. But before I proceed further I will make a division.

What division?

I will begin by placing faculties in a class by themselves: they are powers in us, and in all other things, by which we do as we do. Sight and hearing, for example, I should call faculties. Have I clearly explained the class which I mean?

Yes, I quite understand.

Then let me tell you my view about them. I do not see them, and therefore the distinctions of figure, color, and the like, which enable me to discern the differences of some things, do not apply to them. In speaking of a faculty I think only of its sphere and its result; and that which has the same sphere and the same result I call the same faculty, but that which has another sphere and another result I call afferent. Would that be your way of speaking?

Yes.

And will you be so very good as to answer one more question? Would you say that knowledge is a faculty, or in what class would you place it?

Certainly knowledge is a faculty, and the mightiest of all faculties.

And is opinion also a faculty?

Certainly, he said; for opinion is that with which we are able to form an opinion.

And yet you were acknowledging a little while ago that knowledge is not the same as opinion?

Why, yes, he said: how can any reasonable being ever identify that which is infallible with that which errs?

An excellent answer, proving, I said, that we are quite conscious of a distinction between them.

Yes.

Then knowledge and opinion having distinct powers have also distinct spheres or subject-matters?

That is certain.

Being is the sphere or subject-matter of knowledge, and knowledge is to know the nature of being?

Yes.

And opinion is to have an opinion?

Yes.

And do we know what we opine? or is the subject-matter of opinion the same as the subject-matter of knowledge?

Nay, he replied, that has been already disproven; if difference in faculty implies difference in the sphere or subject-matter, and if, as we were saying, opinion and knowledge are distinct faculties, then the sphere of knowledge and of opinion cannot be the same.

Then if being is the subject-matter of knowledge, something else must be the subject-matter of opinion?

Yes, something else.

Well, then, is not-being the subject-matter of opinion? or, rather, how can there be an opinion at all about not-being? Reflect: when a man has an opinion, has he not an opinion about something? Can he have an opinion which is an opinion about nothing?

Impossible.

He who has an opinion has an opinion about some one thing?

Yes.

And not-being is not one thing, but, properly speaking, nothing?

True.

Of not-being, ignorance was assumed to be the necessary correlative; of being, knowledge?

True, he said.

Then opinion is not concerned either with being or with not-being?

Not with either.

And can therefore neither be ignorance nor knowledge?

That seems to be true.

But is opinion to be sought without and beyond either of them, in a greater clearness than knowledge, or in a greater darkness than ignorance?

In neither.

Then I suppose that opinion appears to you to be darker than knowledge, but lighter than ignorance?

Both; and in no small degree.

And also to be within and between them?

Yes.

Then you would infer that opinion is intermediate?

No question.

But were we not saying before, that if anything appeared to be of a sort which is and is not at the same time, that sort of thing would appear also to lie in the interval between pure being and absolute not-being; and that the corresponding faculty is neither knowledge nor ignorance, but will be found in the interval between them?

True.

And in that interval there has now been discovered something which we call opinion?

There has.

Then what remains to be discovered is the object which partakes equally of the nature of being and not-being, and cannot rightly be termed either, pure and simple; this unknown term, when discovered, we may truly call the subject of opinion, and assign each to their proper faculty — the extremes to the faculties of the extremes and the mean to the faculty of the mean.

True.

This being premised, I would ask the gentleman who is of opinion that there is no absolute or unchangeable idea of beauty—in whose opinion the beautiful is the manifold—he, I say, your lover of beautiful sights, who cannot bear to be told that the beautiful is one, and the just is one, or that anything is one — to him I would appeal, saying, Will you be so very kind, sir, as to tell us whether, of all these beautiful things, there is one which will not be found ugly; or of the just, which will not be found unjust; or of the holy, which will not also be unholy?

No, he replied; the beautiful will in some point of view be found ugly; and the same is true of the rest.

And may not the many which are doubles be also halves?—doubles, that is, of one thing, and halves of another?

Quite true.

And things great and small, heavy and light, as they are termed, will not be denoted by these any more than by the opposite names?

True; both these and the opposite names will always attach to all of them.

And can any one of those many things which are called by particular names be said to be this rather than not to be this?

He replied: They are like the punning riddles which are asked at feasts or the children's puzzle about the eunuch aiming at the bat, with what he hit him, as they say in the puzzle, and upon what the bat was sitting. The individual objects of which I am speaking are also a riddle, and have a double sense: nor can you fix them in your mind, either as being or not-being, or both, or neither.

Then what will you do with them? I said. Can they have a better place than between being and not-being? For they are clearly not in greater darkness or negation than not-being, or more full of light and existence than being.

That is quite true, he said.

Thus then we seem to have discovered that the many ideas which the multitude entertain about the beautiful and about all other things are tossing about in some region which is halfway between pure being and pure not-being?

We have.

Yes; and we had before agreed that anything of this kind which we might find was to be described as matter of opinion, and not as matter of knowledge; being the intermediate flux which is caught and detained by the intermediate faculty.

Quite true.

Then those who see the many beautiful, and who yet neither see absolute beauty, nor can follow any guide who points the way thither; who see the many just, and not absolute justice, and the like — such persons may be said to have opinion but not knowledge?

That is certain.

But those who see the absolute and eternal and immutable may be said to know, and not to have opinion only?

Neither can that be denied.

The one love and embrace the subjects of knowledge, the other those of opinion? The latter are the same, as I dare say you will remember, who listened to sweet sounds and gazed upon fair colors, but would not tolerate the existence of absolute beauty.

Yes, I remember.

Shall we then be guilty of any impropriety in calling them lovers of opinion rather than lovers of wisdom, and will they be very angry with us for thus describing them?

I shall tell them not to be angry; no man should be angry at what is true.

But those who love the truth in each thing are to be called lovers of wisdom and not lovers of opinion.

Assuredly.

ARISTOTLE

POLITICS

Book II

Chapter 2

There are many difficulties in the community of women. And the principle on which Socrates rests the necessity of such an institution does not appear to be established by his arguments. The end which he ascribes to the State, taken literally, is impossible, and how we are to interpret it is nowhere precisely stated. I am speaking of the premise from which the argument of Socrates proceeds, "that the greater the unity of the State the better." Is it not obvious that a State may at length attain such a degree of unity as to be no longer a State?—since the nature of a State is to be a plurality, and in tending to greater unity, from being a State, it becomes a family, and from being a family, an individual; for the family may be said to be more one than the State, and the individual than the family. So that we ought not to attain this greatest unity even if we could, for it would be the destruction of the State. Again, a State is not made up only of so many men, but of different kinds of men; for similars do not constitute a State. It is not like a military alliance, of which the usefulness depends upon its quantity even where there is no difference in quality. For in that mutual protection is the end aimed at; and the question is the same as about the scales of a balance: which is the heavier?

* * *

Chapter 9

Let us begin by considering the common definitions of oligarchy and democracy, and what is justice oligarchical and democratical. For all men cling to justice of some kind, but their conceptions are imperfect and they do not express the whole idea. For example, justice is thought by them to be, and is, equality, not, however, for all, but only for equals. And inequality is thought to be, and is, justice; neither is this for all, but only for unequals. When the persons are omitted, then men judge erroneously. The reason is that they are passing judgment on themselves, and most people are bad judges in their own case. And whereas justice implies a relation to persons as well as to things, and a just distribution, as I have already said in the "Ethics,"[13] embraces alike persons and things, they acknowledge the equality of the things, but dispute about the merit of the persons, chiefly for the reason which I have just given — because they are bad judges in their own affairs; and secondly, because both the parties to the argument are speaking of a limited and partial justice, but imagine themselves to be speaking of absolute justice. For those who are unequal in one respect, for example wealth, consider themselves to be unequal in all; and any who are equal in one respect, for example freedom, consider themselves to be equal in all. But they leave out the capital point. For if men met and associated out of regard to wealth only, their share in the State would be proportioned to their property, and the oligarchical doctrine would then seem to carry the day. It would not be just that he who paid one mina should have the same share of a hundred minae, whether of the principal or of the profits, as he who paid the remaining ninety-nine. But a State exists for the sake of a good life, and not for the sake of life only: if life only were the object, slaves and brute animals might form a State, but they cannot, for they have no share in happiness or in a life of free choice. Nor does a State exist for the sake of alliance and security from injustice, nor yet for the sake of exchange and mutual

---

[13] Nicom. Ethics, v. 3, § 4.

intercourse; for then the Tyrrhenians and the Carthaginians, and all who have commercial treaties with one another, would be the citizens of one State. True, they have agreements about imports, and engagements that they will do no wrong to one another, and written articles of alliance. But there are no magistracies common to the contracting parties who will enforce their engagements; different States have each their own magistracies. Nor does one State take care that the citizens of the other are such as they ought to be, nor see that those who come under the terms of the treaty do no wrong or wickedness at all, but only that they do no injustice to one another. Whereas, those who care for good government take into consideration [the larger question of] virtue and vice in States. Whence it may be further inferred that virtue must be the serious care of a State which truly deserves the name: for [without this ethical end] the community becomes a mere alliance which differs only in place from alliances of which the members live apart; and law is only a convention, "a surety to one another of justice," as the sophist Lycophron says, and has no real power to make the citizens good and just.

This is obvious; for suppose distinct places, such as Corinth and Megara, to be united by a wall, still they would not be one city, not even if the citizens had the right to intermarry, which is one of the rights peculiarly characteristic of States. Again, if men dwelt at a distance from one another, but not so far off as to have no intercourse, and there were laws among them that they should not wrong each other in their exchanges, neither would this be a State. Let us suppose that one man is a carpenter, another a husbandman, another a shoemaker, and so on, and that their number is ten thousand: nevertheless, if they have nothing in common but exchange, alliance, and the like, that would not constitute a State. Why is this? Surely not because they are at a distance from one another: for even supposing that such a community were to meet in one place, and that each man had a house of his own, which was in a manner his State, and that they made alliance with one another, but only against evil-doers; still an accurate thinker would not deem this to be a State, if their intercourse with one another was of the same character after as before their union. It is clear then that a State is not a mere society, having a common place, established for the prevention of crime and for the sake of exchange. These are conditions without which a State cannot exist; but all of them together do not constitute a State, which is a community of well-being in families and aggregations of families, for the sake of a perfect and self-sufficing life. Such a community can only be established among those who live in the same place and intermarry. Hence arise in cities family connections, brotherhoods, common sacrifices, amusements which draw men together. They are created by friendship, for friendship is the motive of society. The end is the good life, and these are the means towards it. And the State is the union of families and villages having for an end a perfect and self-sufficing life, by which we mean a happy and honorable life.

Our conclusion, then, is that political society exists for the sake of noble actions, and not of mere companionship. And they who contribute most to such a society have a greater share in it than those who have the same or a greater freedom or nobility of birth but are inferior to them in political virtue; or than those who exceed them in wealth but are surpassed by them in virtue.

From what has been said it will be clearly seen that all the partisans of different forms of government speak of a part of justice only.

Chapter 15

Of these forms we need only consider two, the Lacedaemonian and the absolute royalty; for most of the others lie in a region between them, having less power than the last, and more than the first. Thus the inquiry is reduced to two points: first, is it advantageous to the State that there should be a perpetual general, and if so, should the office be confined to one family, or open to the citizens in turn? Secondly, is it well that a single man should have the supreme power in all things? The first question falls under the head of laws rather than of constitutions; for perpetual generalship might equally exist under any form of government, so that this matter may be dismissed for the present. The other kind of royalty is a sort of constitution; this we have now to consider, and briefly to run over the difficulties involved in it. We will begin by inquiring whether it is more advantageous to be ruled by the best man or by the best laws.

The advocates of royalty maintain that the laws speak only in general terms, and cannot provide for circumstances; and that for any science to abide by written rules is absurd. Even in Egypt the physician is allowed to alter his treatment after the fourth day, but if sooner, he takes the risk. Hence it is argued that a government acting according to written laws is plainly not the best. Yet surely the ruler cannot dispense with the general principle which exists in law; and he is a better ruler who is free from passion than he who is passionate. Whereas the law is passionless, passion must ever sway the heart of man.

Yes, some one will answer, but then on the other hand an individual will be better able to advise in particular cases. [To whom we in turn make reply:] There must be a legislator whether you call him a king or not, and laws must be passed: but these laws will have no authority when they miss the mark, though in all other cases retaining their authority. [Yet a further question remains behind:] When the law cannot determine a point at all, or not well, should the one best man or should all decide? According to our present practice assemblies meet, sit in judgment, deliberate and decide, and their judgments all relate to individual cases. Now any member of the assembly, taken separately, is certainly inferior to the wise man. But the State is made up of many individuals. And as a feast to which all the guests contribute is better than a banquet furnished by a single man, so a multitude is a better judge of many things than any individual.

Again, the many are more incorruptible than the few; they are like the greater quantity of water which is less easily corrupted than a little. The individual is liable to be overcome by anger or by some other passion, and then his judgment is necessarily perverted; but it is hardly to be supposed that a great number of persons would all get into a passion and go wrong at the same moment. Let us assume that they are freemen, never acting in violation of the law, but filling up the gaps which the law is obliged to leave. Or, if such virtue is scarcely attainable by the multitude, we need only suppose that the majority are good men and good citizens, and ask which will be the more incorruptible, the one good ruler, or the many who are all good? Will not the many? But, you will say, there may be parties among them, whereas the one man is not divided against himself. To which we may answer that their character is as good as his. If we call the rule of many men, who are all of them good, aristocracy, and the rule of one man royalty, then aristocracy will be better for States than royalty, whether the government is supported by force or not, provided only that a number of men equal in virtue can be found.

Chapter 18

We maintain that the true forms of government are three, and that the best must be that which is administered by the best, and in which there is one man, or a whole family, or many persons, excelling in virtue, and both rulers and subjects are fitted, the one to rule, the others to be ruled, in such a manner as to attain the most eligible life. We showed at the commencement of our inquiry that the virtue of the good man is necessarily the same as the virtue of the citizen of the perfect State. Clearly then in the same manner, and by the same means through which a man becomes truly good, he will frame a State [which will be truly good] whether aristocratical, or under kingly rule, and the same education and the same habits will be found to make a good man and a good statesman and King.

Having arrived at these conclusions, we must proceed to speak of the perfect State, and describe how it comes into being and is established.

NICCOLO MACHIAVELLI (1469-1527)

A leading political philosopher, historian, playwright, and poet of Florence, Italy, Machiavelli is best known for his political writings. He insists that political morality is not bounded by the usual ethical norms. The leading modern political philosophy of "realpolitik" is based to a great extent on Machiavelli's writings.

THE MORALS OF THE PRINCE [14]

On the Reasons Why Men Are Praised or Blamed—Especially Princes

It remains now to be seen what style and principles a prince ought to adopt in dealing with his subjects and friends. I know the subject has been treated frequently before, and I'm afraid people will think me rash for trying to do so again, especially since I intend to differ in this discussion from what others have said. But since I intend to write something useful to an understanding reader, it seemed better to go after the real truth of the matter than to repeat what people have imagined. A great many men have imagined states and princedoms such as nobody ever saw or know in the real world, for there's such a difference between the way we really live and the way we ought to live that the man who neglects the real to study the ideal will learn how to accomplish his ruin, not his salvation. Any man who tries to be good all the time is bound to come to ruin among the great number who are not good. Hence a prince who wants to keep his post must learn how not to be good, and use that knowledge, or refrain from using it, as necessity requires.

Putting aside, then, all the imaginary things that are said about princes, and getting down to the truth, let me say that whenever men are discussed (and especially princes because they are prominent), there are certain qualities that bring them either praise or blame. Thus some are considered generous, others stingy (I use a Tuscan term, since "greedy" in our speech means a man who wants to take other people's goods. We call a man "stingy" who clings to his own); some are givers, others grabbers; some cruel, others merciful; one man is treacherous, another faithful; one is feeble and effeminate, another fierce and spirited; one humane, another proud; one lustful, another chaste; one straightforward, another sly; one harsh, another gentle; one serious, another playful; one religious, another skeptical, and so on. I know everyone will agree that among these many qualities a prince certainly ought to have all those that are considered good. But since it is impossible to have and exercise them all, because the conditions of human life simply do not allow it, a prince must be shrewd enough to avoid the public disgrace of those vices that would lose him his state. If he possibly can, he should also guard against vices that will not lose him his state; but if he cannot prevent them, he should not be too worried about indulging them. And furthermore, he should not be too worried about incurring blame for any vice without which he would find it hard to save his state. For if you look at matters carefully, you will see that something resembling virtue, if you follow it, may be your ruin, while something else resembling vice will lead, if you follow it, to your security and well-being.

On Liberality and Stinginess

Let me begin, then, with the first of the qualities mentioned above, by saying that a reputation for liberality is doubtless very fine; but the generosity that earns you that reputation can do you great harm. For if you exercise your generosity in a really virtuous way, as you

---

[14] From *The Prince*, a book on statecraft written for Giuliano de' Medici (1479-1516), a member of the most famous and powerful families of Renaissance Italy.

should, nobody will know of it, and you cannot escape the odium of the opposite vice. Hence if you wish to be widely known as a generous man, you must seize every opportunity to make a big display of your giving. A prince of this character is bound to use up his entire revenue in works of ostentation. Thus, in the end, if he wants to keep a name for generosity, he will have to load his people with exorbitant taxes and squeeze money out of them in every way he can. This is the first step in making him odious to his subjects; for when he is poor, nobody will respect him. Then, when his generosity has angered many and brought rewards to a few, the slightest difficulty will trouble him, and at the first approach of danger, down he goes. If by chance he foresees this, and tries to change his ways, he will immediately be labeled a miser.

Since a prince cannot use this virtue of liberality in such a way as to become known for it unless he harms his own security, he won't mind, if he judges prudently of things, being known as a miser. In due course he will be thought the more liberal man, when people see that his parsimony enables him to live on his income, to defend himself against his enemies, and to undertake major projects without burdening his people with taxes. Thus he will be acting liberally toward all those people from whom he takes nothing (and there are an immense number of them), and in a stingy way toward those people on whom he bestows nothing (and they are very few). In our times, we have seen great things being accomplished only by men who have had the name of misers; all the others have gone under. Pope Julius II, though he used his reputation as a generous man to gain the papacy, sacrificed it in order to be able to make war; the present king of France has waged many wars without levying a single extra tax on his people, simply because he could take care of the extra expenses out of the savings from his long parsimony. If the present king of Spain had a reputation for generosity, he would never have been able to undertake so many campaigns, or win so many of them.

Hence a prince who prefers not to rob his subjects, who wants to be able to defend himself, who wants to avoid poverty and contempt, and who doesn't want to become a plunderer, should not mind in the least if people consider him a miser; this is simply one of the vices that enable him to reign. Someone may object that Caesar used a reputation for generosity to become emperor, and many other people have also risen in the world, because they were generous or were supposed to be so. Well, I answer, either you are a prince already, or you are in the process of becoming one; in the first case, this reputation for generosity is harmful to you, in the second case it is very necessary. Caesar was one of those who wanted to become ruler in Rome; but after he had reached his goal, if he had lived, and had not cut down on his expenses, he would have ruined the empire itself. Someone may say: there have been plenty of princes, very successful in warfare, who have had a reputation for generosity. But I answer: either the prince is spending his own money and that of his subjects, or he is spending someone else's. In the first case, he ought to be sparing; in the second case, he ought to spend money like water. Any prince at the head of his army, which lives on loot, extortion, and plunder, disposes of other people's property, and is bound to be very generous; otherwise, his soldiers would desert him. You can always be a more generous giver when what you give is not yours or your subjects'; Cyrus, Caesar, and Alexander[15] were generous in this way. Spending what belongs to other people does no harm to your reputation, rather it enhances it; only spending your own substance harms you. And there is nothing that wears out faster than generosity; even as you practice it, you lose the means of practicing it, and you become either poor and contemptible or (in the course of escaping poverty) rapacious and hateful. The thing above all against which a prince must protect himself is being contemptible and hateful; generosity leads to both. Thus, it's much wiser to put up with the reputation of being a miser, which brings you shame without hate, than to be forced—just because you want to appear generous—into a reputation for rapacity, which brings shame on you and hate along with it.

---

[15] Persian, Roman, and Macedonian conquerors and rulers in ancient times.

On Cruelty and Clemency: Whether It Is Better to Be Loved or Feared

Continuing now with our list of qualities, let me say that every prince should prefer to be considered merciful rather than cruel, yet he should be careful not to mismanage this clemency of his. People thought Cesare Borgia[16] was cruel, but that cruelty of his reorganized the Romagna, united it, and established it in peace and loyalty. Anyone who views the matter realistically will see that this prince was much more merciful than the people of Florence, who, to avoid the reputation of cruelty, allowed Pistoria to be destroyed.[17] Thus, no prince should mind being called cruel for what he does to keep his subjects united and loyal; he may make examples of a very few, but he will be more merciful in reality than those who, in their tenderheartedness, allow disorders to occur, with their attendant murders and lootings. Such turbulence brings harm to an entire community, while the executions ordered by a prince affect only one individual at a time. A new prince, above all others, cannot possibly avoid a name for cruelty, since new states are always in danger. And Virgil, speaking through the mouth of Dido,[18] says:

> My cruel fate
> And doubts attending an unsettled state
> Force me to guard my coast from foreign foes.

Yet a prince should be slow to believe rumors and to commit himself to action on the basis of them. He should not be afraid of his own thoughts; he ought to proceed cautiously, moderating his conduct with prudence and humanity, allowing neither overconfidence to make him careless, nor overtimidity to make him intolerable.

Here the question arises: is it better to be loved than feared, or vice versa? I don't doubt that every prince would like to be both; but since it is hard to accommodate these qualities, if you have to make a choice, to be feared is much safer than to be loved. For it is a good general rule about men, that they are ungrateful, fickle, liars and deceivers, fearful of danger and greedy for gain. While you serve their welfare, they are all yours, offering their blood, their belongings, their lives, and their children's lives, as we noted above—so long as the danger is remote. But when the danger is close at hand, they turn against you. Then, any prince who has relied on their words and has made no other preparations will come to grief; because friendships that are bought at a price, and not with greatness and nobility of soul, may be paid for but they are not acquired, and they cannot be used in time of need. People are less concerned with offending a man who makes himself loved than one who makes himself feared: the reason is that love is a link of obligation which men, because they are rotten, will break any time they think doing so serves their advantage; but fear involves dread of punishment, from which they can never escape.

Still, a prince should make himself feared in such a way that, even if he gets no love, he gets no hate either; because it is perfectly possible to be feared and not hated, and this will be the result if only the prince will keep his hands off the property of his subjects or citizens, and off their women. When he does have to shed blood, he should be sure to have a strong justification and manifest cause; but above all, he should not confiscate people's property, because men are quicker to forget the death of a father than the loss of a patrimony. Besides, pretexts for confiscation are always plentiful, it never fails that a prince who starts living by plunder can find reasons to rob someone else. Excuses for proceeding against someone's life are much rarer and more quickly exhausted.

---

[16] The son of Pope Alexander VI (referred to later) and duke of Romagna, which he subjugated in 1499-1502.

[17] By unchecked rioting between opposing factions (1502).

[18] Queen of Carthage and tragic heroine of Virgil's epic, *The Aeneid*.

But a prince at the head of his armies and commanding a multitude of soldiers should not care a bit if he is considered cruel; without such a reputation, he could never hold his army together and ready for action. Among the marvelous deeds of Hannibal,[19] this was prime: that, having an immense army, which included men of many different races and nations, and which he led to battle in distant countries, he never allowed them to fight among themselves or to rise against him, whether his fortune was good or bad. The reason for this could only be his inhuman cruelty, which, along with his countless other talents, made him an object of awe and terror to his soldiers; and without the cruelty, his other qualities would never have sufficed. The historians who pass snap judgments on these matters admire his accomplishments and at the same time condemn the cruelty which was their main cause.

When I say, "His other qualities would never have sufficed," we can see that this is true from the example of Scipio,[20] an outstanding man not only among those of his own time, but in all recorded history; yet his armies revolted in Spain, for no other reason than his excessive leniency in allowing his soldiers more freedom than military discipline permits. Fabius Maximus rebuked him in the senate for this failing, calling him the corrupter of the Roman armies. When a lieutenant of Scipio's plundered the Locrians,[21] he took no action in behalf of the people, and did nothing to discipline that insolent lieutenant; again, this was the result of his easygoing nature. Indeed, when someone in the senate wanted to excuse him on this occasion, he said there are many men who knew better how to avoid error themselves than how to correct error in others. Such a soft temper would in time have tarnished the fame and glory of Scipio, had he brought it to the office of emperor; but as he lived under the control of the senate, this harmful quality of his not only remained hidden but was considered creditable.

Returning to the question of being feared or loved, I conclude that since men love at their own inclination but can be made to fear at the inclination of the prince, a shrewd prince will lay his foundations on what is under his own control, not on what is controlled by others. He should simply take pains not to be hated, as I said.

The Way Princes Should Keep Their Word

How praiseworthy it is for a prince to keep his word and live with integrity rather than by craftiness, everyone understands; yet we see from recent experience that those princes have accomplished most who paid little heed to keeping their promises, but who knew how craftily to manipulate the minds of men. In the end, they won out over those who tried to act honestly.

You should consider then, that there are two ways of fighting, one with laws and the other with force. The first is properly a human method, the second belongs to beasts. But as the first method does not always suffice, you sometimes have to turn to the second. Thus a prince must know how to make good use of both the beast and the man. Ancient writers made subtle note of this fact when they wrote that Achilles and many other princes of antiquity were sent to be reared by Chiron the centaur,[22] who trained them in his discipline. Having a teacher who is half man and half beast can only mean that a prince must know how to use both these two natures, and that one without the other has no lasting effect.

---

[19] Carthaginian general who led a massive but unsuccessful invasion of Rome in 218-203 B.C.

[20] The Roman general whose successful invasion of Carthage in 203 B.C. caused Hannibal's army to be recalled from Rome. The episode described here occurred in 206 B.C.

[21] A people of Sicily, defeated by Scipio in 205 B.C. and placed under Q. Pleminius; *Fabius Maximus*: not only a senator but a high public official and general who had fought against Hannibal in Italy.

[22] Half man and half horse, the mythical Chiron was said to have taught the arts of war and peace, including hunting, medicine, music, and prophecy; *Achilles*: foremost among the Greek heroes in the Trojan War.

Since a prince must know how to use the character of beasts, he should pick for imitation the fox and the lion. As the lion cannot protect himself from traps, and the fox cannot defend himself from wolves, you have to be a fox in order to be wary of traps, and a lion to overawe the wolves. Those who try to live by the lion alone are badly mistaken. Thus a prudent prince cannot and should not keep his word when to do so would go against his interest, or when the reasons that made him pledge it no longer apply. Doubtless if all men were good, this rule would be bad; but since they are a sad lot, and keep no faith with you, you in your turn are under no obligation to keep it with them.

Besides, a prince will never lack for legitimate excuses to explain away his breaches of faith. Modern history will furnish innumerable examples of this behavior, showing how many treaties and promises have been made null and void by the faithlessness of princes, and how the man succeeded best who knew best how to play the fox. But it is a necessary part of this nature that you must conceal it carefully; you must be a great liar and hypocrite. Men are so simple of mind, and so much dominated by their immediate needs, that a deceitful man will always find plenty who are ready to be deceived. One of many recent examples calls for mention. Alexander VI[23] never did anything else, never had another thought, except to deceive men, and he always found fresh material to work on. Never was there a man more convincing in his assertions, who sealed his promises with more solemn oaths, and who observed them less. Yet his deceptions were always successful, because he knew exactly how to manage this sort of business.

In actual fact, a prince may not have all the admirable qualities we listed, but it is very necessary that he should seem to have them. Indeed, I will venture to say that when you have them and exercise them all the time, they are harmful to you; when you just seem to have them, they are useful. It is good to appear merciful, truthful, humane, sincere, and religious; it is good to be so in reality. But you must keep your mind so disposed that, in case of need, you can turn to the exact contrary. This has to be understood: a prince, and especially a new prince, cannot possibly exercise all those virtues for which men are called "good." To preserve the state, he often has to do things against his word, against charity, against humanity, against religion. Thus he has to have a mind ready to shift as the winds of fortune and the varying circumstances of life may dictate. And as I said above, he should not depart from the good if he can hold to it, but he should be ready to enter on evil if he has to.

Hence a prince should take great care never to drop a word that does not seem imbued with the five good qualities noted above; to anyone who sees or hears him, he should appear all compassion, all honor, all humanity, all integrity, all religion. Nothing is more necessary than to seem to have this last virtue. Men in general judge more by the sense of sight than by the sense of touch, because everyone can see but only a few can test by feeling. Everyone sees what you seem to be, few know what you really are; and those few do not dare take a stand against the general opinion, supported by the majesty of the government. In the actions of all men, and especially of princes who are not subject to a court of appeal, we must always look to the end. Let a prince, therefore, win victories and uphold his state; his methods will always be considered worthy, and everyone will praise them, because the masses are always impressed by the superficial appearance of things, and by the outcome of an enterprise. And the world consists of nothing but the masses; the few have no influence when the many feel secure. A certain prince of our own time, whom it's just as well not to name, preaches nothing but peace and mutual trust, yet he is the determined enemy of both; and if on several different occasions he had observed either, he would have lost both his reputation and his throne.

---

[23] Pope from 1492 to 1503

ABRAHAM LINCOLN (1809-1865)

Lincoln's career as a self-made man, his commitment to the union, his firm opposition to the spread of slavery, and his tragic assassination earned him a central role in the moral development of the American nation. Lincoln's speeches reflect both a facility with the language and a passion for American ideals.

THE GETTYSBURG ADDRESS

Four score and seven years ago our fathers brought forth on this continent, a new nation, conceived in Liberty, and dedicated to the proposition that all men are created equal.

Now we are engaged in a great civil war, testing whether that nation, or any nation so conceived and so dedicated, can long endure. We are met on a great battlefield of that war. We have come to dedicate a portion of that field, as a final resting place for those who here gave their lives that that nation might live. It is altogether fitting and proper that we would do this.

But, in a larger sense, we can not dedicate—we can not consecrate—we can not hallow—this ground. The brave men, living and dead, who struggled here, have consecrated it, far above our poor power to add or detract. The world will little note, nor long remember what we say here, but it can never forget what they did here. It is for us the living, rather, to be dedicated here to the unfinished work which they who fought here have thus far so nobly advanced. It is rather for us to be here dedicated to the great task remaining before us—that from these honored dead we take increased devotion to that cause for which they gave the last full measure of devotion—that we here highly resolve that these dead shall not have died in vain—that this nation, under God, shall have a new birth of freedom—and that government of the people, by the people, for the people, shall not perish from the earth.

1863

SECOND INAUGURAL ADDRESS

At this second appearing to take the oath of the presidential office, there is less occasion for an extended address than there was at the first. Then a statement, somewhat in detail, of a course to be pursued, seemed fitting and proper. Now, at the expiration of four years, during which public declarations have been constantly called forth on every point and phase of the great contest which still absorbs the attention, and engrosses the energies of the nation, little that is new could be presented. The progress of our arms, upon which all else chiefly depends, is as well known to the public as to myself; and it is, I trust, reasonably satisfactory and encouraging to all. With high hope for the future, no prediction in regard to it is ventured.

On the occasion corresponding to this four years ago, all thoughts were anxiously directed to an impending civil war. All dreaded it — all sought to avert it. While the inaugural address was being delivered from this place, devoted altogether to saving the Union without war, insurgent agents were in the city seeking to *destroy* it without war — seeking to dissolve the Union, and divide effects, by negotiation. Both parties deprecated war; but one of them would make war rather than let the nation survive; and the other would *accept* war rather than let it perish. And the war came.

One-eighth of the whole population were colored slaves, not distributed generally over the Union, but localized in the Southern part of it. These slaves constituted a peculiar and powerful interest. All knew that this interest was, somehow, the cause of the war. To strengthen, perpetuate, and extend this interest was the object for which the insurgents would rend the Union, even by war; while the government claimed no right to do more than to restrict the territorial enlargement of it. Neither party expected for the war, the magnitude, or the duration, which it has already attained. Neither anticipated that the *cause* of the conflict might cease with, or even before, the conflict itself should cease. Each looked for an easier triumph, and a result less fundamental and astounding. Both read the same Bible, and pray to the same God; and each invokes His aid against the other. It may seem strange that any men should dare to ask a just God's assistance in wringing their bread from the sweat of other men's faces; but let us judge not that we be not judged. The prayers of both could not be answered; that of neither has been answered fully. The Almighty has His own purposes. "Woe unto the world because of offenses! for it must needs be that offenses come; but woe to that man by whom the offense cometh!" If we shall suppose that American slavery is one of those offenses which, in the providence of God, must needs come, but which, having continued through His appointed time, He now wills to remove, and that He gives to both North and South, this terrible war, as the woe due to those by whom the offense came, shall we discern therein any departure from those divine attributes which the believers in a Living God always ascribe to Him? Fondly do we hope—fervently do we pray—that this mightily scourge of war may speedily pass away. Yet, if God wills that it continue, until all the wealth piled by the bondman's two hundred and fifty years of unrequited toil shall be sunk, and until every drop of blood drawn with the lash, shall be paid by another drawn with the sword, as was said three thousand years ago, so still it must be said "the judgments of the Lord are true and righteous altogether."

With malice toward none; with charity for all; with firmness in the right, as God gives us to see the right, let us strive on to finish the work we are in; to bind up the nation's wounds; to care for him who shall have borne the battle, and for His widow, and his orphan—to do all which may achieve and cherish a just, and a lasting peace, among ourselves, and with all nations.

WALT WHITMAN

DEATH OF ABRAHAM LINCOLN

I shall not easily forget the first time I ever saw Abraham Lincoln. It must have been about the 18th or 19th of February, 1861. It was rather a pleasant afternoon, in New York City, as he arrived there from the West, to remain a few hours, and then pass on to Washington, to prepare for his inauguration. I saw him in Broadway, near the site of the present Post-office. He came down, I think from Canal Street, to stop at the Astor House. The broad spaces, sidewalks, and streets in the neighborhood, and for some distance, were crowded with solid masses of people, many thousands. The omnibuses and other vehicles had all been turn'd off, leaving an unusual hush in that busy part of the city. Presently two or three shabby hack barouches made their way with some difficulty through the crowd, and drew up at the Astor House entrance. A tall figure stepp'd out of the centre of these barouches, paus'd leisurely on the sidewalk, look'd up at the granite walls and looming architecture of the grand old hotel—then, after a relieving stretch of arms and legs, turn'd round for over a minute to slowly and good-humoredly scan the appearance of the vast and silent crowds. There were no speeches—no compliments—no welcome—as far as I could hear, not a word said. Still much anxiety was conceal'd in the quiet. Cautious persons had fear'd some mark'd insult or indignity to the President-elect — for he possess'd no personal popularity at all in New York City, and very little political. But it was evidently tacitly agreed that if the few political supporters of Mr. Lincoln present would entirely abstain from any demonstration on their side, the immense majority, who were anything but supporters, would abstain on their sides also. The result was a sulky, unbroken silence, such as certainly never before characterized so great a New York crowd.

Almost in the same neighborhood I distinctly remember'd seeing Lafayette on his visit to America in 1825. I had also personally seen and heard, various years afterward, how Andrew Jackson, Clay, Webster, Hungarian Kossuth, Filibuster Walker, the Prince of Wales on his visit, and other *célèbres*, native and foreign, had been welcom'd there—all that indescribable human roar and magnetism, unlike any other sound in the universe—the glad exulting thunder-shouts of countless unloos'd throats of men! But on this occasion, not a voice—not a sound. From the top of an omnibus, (driven up one side, close by, and block'd by the curbstone and the crowds), I had, I say, a capital view of it all, and especially of Mr. Lincoln, his look and gait—his perfect composure and coolness—his unusual and uncouth height, his dress of complete black, stovepipe hat push'd back on the head, dark-brown complexion, seam'd and wrinkled yet canny-looking face, black, bushy head of hair, disproportionately long neck, and his hands held behind as he stood observing the people. He look'd with curiosity upon that immense sea of faces, and the sea of faces return'd the look with similar curiosity. In both there was a dash of comedy, almost farce, such as Shakspeare puts in his blackest tragedies. The crowd that hemm'd around consisted I should think of thirty to forty thousand men, not a single one his personal friend—while I have no doubt, (so frenzied were the ferments of the time,) many an assassin's knife and pistol lurk'd in hip or breast-pocket there, ready, soon as break and riot came.

But no break or riot came. The tall figure gave another relieving stretch or two of arms and legs; then with moderate pace, and accompanied by a few unknown-looking persons, ascended the portico-steps of the Astor House, disappear'd through its broad entrance—and the dumb-show ended.

I saw Abraham Lincoln often the four years following that date. He changed rapidly and much during his Presidency—but this scene, and him in it, are indelibly stamp'd upon my recollection. As I sat on the top of my omnibus, and had a good view of him, the thought, dim and inchoate then, has since come out clear enough, that four sorts of genius, four mighty and primal hands, will be needed to the complete limning of this man's future portrait—the eyes and brains and finger-touch of Plutarch and Eschylus and Michelangelo, assisted now by Rabelais.

And now—(Mr. Lincoln passing on from this scene to Washington, where he was inaugurated, amid armed cavalry, and sharpshooters at every point—the first instance of the kind in our history—and I hope it will be the last)—now the rapid succession of well-known events, (too well-known—I believe, these days, we almost hate to hear them mention'd)—the national flag fired on at Sumter—the uprising of the North, in paroxysms of astonishment and rage—the chaos of divided councils—the call for troops—the first Bull Run—the stunning cast-down, shock, and dismay of the North—and so in full flood the Secession war. Four years of lurid, bleeding, murky, murderous war. Who paint those years, with all their scenes?—the hard-fought engagements—the defeats, plans, failures—the gloomy hours, days, when our Nationality seem'd hung in pall of doubt, perhaps death—the Mephistophelean sneers of foreign lands and attachés—the dreaded Scylla of European·interference, and the Charybdis of the tremendously dangerous latent strata of secession sympathizers throughout the free States, (far more numerous than is supposed)—the long marches in summer—the hot sweat, and many a sunstroke, as on the rush to Gettysburg in '63—the night battles in the woods, as under Hooker at Chancellorsville—the camps in winter—the military prisons—the hospitals—(alas! alas! the hospitals.)

The Secession war? Nay, let me call it the Union war. Though whatever call'd, it is even yet too near us—too vast and too closely overshadowing—its branches unform'd yet, (but certain,) shooting too far into the future—and the most indicative and mightiest of them yet ungrown. A great literature will yet arise out of the era of those four years, those scenes—era compressing centuries of native passion, first-class pictures, tempests of life and death—an inexhaustible mine for the histories, drama, romance, and even philosophy, of peoples to come—indeed the verteber[24] of poetry and art, (of personal character too,) for all future America—far more grand,

---

[24] Vertebra.

in my opinion, to the hands capable of it, than Homer's siege of Troy, or the French wars to Shakspeare.

But I must leave these speculations, and come to the theme I have assign'd and limited myself to. Of the actual murder of President Lincoln, though so much has been written, probably the facts are yet very indefinite in most persons' minds. I read from my memoranda, written at the time, and revised frequently and finally since.

The day, April 14, 1865, seems to have been a pleasant one throughout the whole land—the moral atmosphere pleasant too—the long storm, so dark, so fratricidal, full of blood and doubt and gloom, over and ended at last by the sunrise of such an absolute National victory, and utter breakdown of Secessionism—we almost doubted our own senses! Lee had capitulated beneath the apple-tree of Appomattox. The other armies, the flanges of the revolt, swiftly follow'd. And could it really be, then? Out of all the affairs of this world of woe and failure and disorder, was there really come the confirm'd, unerring sign of plan, like a shaft of pure light—of rightful rule—of God? So the day, as I say, was propitious. Early herbage, early flowers, were out. (I remember where I was stopping at the time, the season being advanced, there were many lilacs in full bloom. By one of those caprices that enter and give tinge to events without being at all a part of them, I find myself always reminded of the great tragedy of that day by the sight and odor of these blossoms. [25] It never fails.)

But I must not dwell on accessories. The deed hastens. The popular afternoon paper of Washington, the little *Evening Star*, has spatter'd all over its third page, divided among the advertisements in a sensational manner, in a hundred different places, "*The President and his Lady will be at the Theatre this evening. . . .*" (Lincoln was fond of the theatre. I have myself seen him there several times. I remember thinking how funny it was that he, in some respects the leading actor in the stormiest drama known to real history's stage through centuries, should sit there and be so completely interested and absorb'd in those human jackstraws, moving about with their silly little gestures, foreign spirit, and flatulent text.)

On this occasion the theatre was crowded, many ladies in rich and gay costumes, officers in their uniforms, many well-known citizens, young folks, the usual clusters of gas-lights, the usual magnetism of so many people, cheerful, with perfumes, music of violins and flutes—(and over all, and saturating all, that vast, vague wonder, *Victory*, the nation's victory, the triumph of the Union, filling the air, the thought, the sense, with exhilaration more than all music and perfumes.)

The President came betimes, and, with his wife, witness'd the play from the large stage-boxes of the second tier, two thrown into one, and profusely drap'd with the national flag. The acts and scenes of the piece—one of those singularly written compositions which have at least the merit of giving entire relief to an audience engaged in mental action or business excitements and cares during the day, as it makes not the slightest call on either the moral, emotional, esthetic, or spiritual nature—a piece, (*Our American Cousin*,) in which, among other characters so call'd, a Yankee, certainly such a one as was never seen, or the least like it ever seen, in North America, is introduced in England, with a varied fol-de-rol of talk, plot, scenery, and such phantasmagoria as goes to make up a modern popular drama—had progress'd through perhaps a couple of its acts, when in the midst of this comedy, or non-such, or whatever it is to be call'd, and to offset it, or finish it out, as if in Nature's and the great Muse's mockery of those poor mimes, came interpolated that scene, not really or exactly to be described at all, (for on the many hundreds who were there it seems to this hour to have left a passing blur, a dream, a blotch)—and yet partially to be described as I now proceed to give it. There is a scene in the play representing a modern parlor, in which two unprecedented English ladies are inform'd by the impossible Yankee that he is not a man of fortune, and therefore undesirable for marriage-catching purposes; after which, the comments being finish'd, the dramatic trio make exit, leaving the stage clear for a moment. At this period came the murder of Abraham Lincoln. Great as all its manifold train,

---

[25] Cf. Whitman's elegy on Lincoln, "When Lilacs Last in the Dooryard Bloom'd" (1865-66), below.

circling round it, and stretching into the future for many a century, in the politics, history, art &c., of the New World, in point of fact the main thing, the actual murder, transpired with the quiet and simplicity of any commonest occurrence—the bursting of a bud or pod in the growth of vegetation, for instance. Through the general hum following the stage pause, with the change of positions, came the muffled sound of a pistol-shot, which not one-hundredth part of the audience heard at the time—and yet a moment's hush—somehow, surely, a vague startled thrill—and then, through the ornamented, draperied, starr'd and striped space-way of the President's box, a sudden figure, a man, raises himself with hands and feet, stands a moment on the railing, leaps below to the stage, (a distance of perhaps fourteen or fifteen feet), falls out of position, catching his boot-heel in the copious drapery, (the American flag,) falls on one knee, quickly recovers himself, rises as if nothing had happen'd, (he really sprains his ankle, but unfelt then)—and so the figure, Booth, the murderer, dress'd in plain black broadcloth, bare-headed, with full, glossy, raven hair, and his eyes like some mad animal's flashing with light and resolution, yet with a certain strange calmness, holds aloft in one hand a large knife—walks along not much back from the footlights—turns fully toward the audience his face of statuesque beauty, lit by those basilisk eyes, flashing with desperation, perhaps insanity—launches out in a firm and steady voice the words *Sic semper tyrannis*[26] —and then walks with neither slow nor very rapid pace diagonally across to the back of the stage, and disappears. (Had not all this terrible scene—making the mimic ones preposterous—had it not all been rehears'd, in blank, by Booth, beforehand?)

A moment's hush—a scream—the cry of *"murder"*—Mrs. Lincoln leaning out of the box, with ashy cheeks and lips, with involuntary cry, pointing to the retreating figure, *"He has kill'd the President."* And still a moment's strange, incredulous suspense—and then the deluge! then that mixture of horror, noises, uncertainty—(the sound, somewhere back, of a horse's hoofs clattering with speed)—the people burst through chairs and railings, and break them up—there is inextricable confusion and terror—women faint—quite feeble persons fall, and are trampl'd on— many cries of agony are heard—the broad stage suddenly fills to suffocation with a dense and motley crowd, like some horrible carnival—the audience rush generally upon it, at least the strong men do—the actors and actresses are all there in their play—costumes and painted faces, with mortal fright showing through the rouge—the screams and calls, confused talk—re-doubled, trebled— two or three manage to pass up water from the stage to the President's box—others try to clamber up—&c., &c.

In the midst of all this, the soldiers of the President's guard, with others, suddenly drawn to the scene, burst in—(some two hundred altogether)—they storm the house, through all the tiers, especially the upper ones, inflam'd with fury, literally charging the audience with fix'd bayonets, muskets, and pistols, shouting *"Clear out! clear out! you sons of—"* . . . . Such a wild scene, or a suggestion of it rather, inside the playhouse that night.

Outside, too, in the atmosphere of shock and craze, crowds of people, fill'd with frenzy, ready to seize any outlet for it, come near committing murder several times on innocent individuals. One such case was especially exciting. The infuriated crowd, through some chance, got started against one man, either for words he utter'd, or perhaps without any cause at all, and were proceeding at once to actually hang him on a neighboring lamp-post, when he was rescued by a few heroic policemen, who placed him in their midst, and fought their way slowly and amid great peril toward the station-house. It was a fitting episode of the whole affair. The crowd rushing and eddying to and fro—the night, the yells, the pale faces, many frighten'd people trying in vain to extricate themselves—the attack'd man, not yet freed from the jaws of death, looking like a corpse—the silent, resolute, half-dozen policemen, with no weapons but their little clubs, yet stern and steady through all those eddying swarms—made a fitting side-scene to the grand tragedy of the murder. They gain'd the station house with the protected man, whom they placed in security for the night, and discharged him in the morning.

---

[26] "Thus always to tyrants."

And in the midst of that pandemonium, infuriated soldiers, the audience and the crowd, the stage, and all its actors and actresses, its paint-pots, spangles, and gas-lights—the life blood from those veins, the best and sweetest of the land, drips slowly down, and death's ooze already begins its little bubbles on the lips.

Thus the visible incidents and surroundings of Abraham Lincoln's murder, as they really occur'd. Thus ended the attempted secession of these States: thus the four years' war. But the main things come subtly and invisibly afterward, perhaps long afterward—neither military, political, nor (great as those are,) historical. I say, certain secondary and indirect results, out of the tragedy of this death, are, in my opinion, greatest. Not the event of the murder itself. Not that Mr. Lincoln strings the principal points and personages of the period, like beads, upon the single string of his career. Not that his idiosyncrasy, in its sudden appearance and disappearance, stamps this Republic with a stamp more mark'd and enduring than any yet given by any one man—(more even than Washington's;)—but, join'd with these, the immeasurable value and meaning of that whole tragedy lies, to me, in senses finally dearest to a nation, (and here all our own)—the imaginative and artistic senses—the literary and dramatic ones. Not in any common or low meaning of those terms, but a meaning precious to the race, and to every age. A long and varied series of contradictory events arrives at last at its highest poetic, single, central, pictorial *dénouement*. The whole involved, baffling, multiform whirl of the secession period comes to a head, and is gather'd in one brief flash of lightning—illumination—one simple, fierce deed. Its sharp culmination, and as it were solution, of so many bloody and angry problems, illustrates those climax-moments on the stage of universal Time, where the historic Muse at one entrance, and the tragic Muse at the other, suddenly ringing down the curtain, close an immense act in the long drama of creative thought, and give it radiation, tableau, stranger than fiction. Fit radiation—fit close! How the imagination—how the student loves these things! America, too, is to have them. For not in all great deaths, not far or near—not Caesar in the Roman senate-house, or Napoleon passing away in the wild night-storm at St. Helena—not Paleologus,[27] falling, desperately fighting, piled over dozens deep with Grecian corpses—not calm old Socrates, drinking the hemlock—outvies that terminus of the secession war, in one man's life, here in our midst, in our time—that seal of the emancipation of three million slaves—that parturition and delivery of our at last really free Republic, born again, henceforth to commence its career of genuine homogeneous Union, compact, consistent with itself.

Nor will ever future American Patriots and Unionists, indifferently over the whole land, or North or South, find a better moral to their lesson. The final use of the greatest men of a Nation is, after all, not with reference to their deeds in themselves, or their direct bearing on their times or lands. The final use of a heroic-eminent life—especially of a heroic-eminent death—is its indirect filtering into the nation and the race, and to give, often at many removes, but unerringly, age after age, color and fibre to the personalism of the youth and maturity of that age, and of mankind. Then, there is a cement to the whole people, subtler, more underlying, than any thing in written constitution, or courts or armies—namely, the cement of a death identified thoroughly with that people, at its head, and for its sake. Strange, (is it not?) that battles, martyrs, agonies, blood, even assassination, should so condense—perhaps only really, lastingly condense—a Nationality.

I repeat it—the grand deaths of the race—the dramatic deaths of every nationality—are its most important inheritance-value—in some respects beyond its literature and art—(as the hero is beyond his finest portrait, and the battle itself beyond its choicest song or epic.) Is not here indeed the point underlying all tragedy? the famous pieces of the Grecian masters—and all masters? Why, if the old Greeks had had this man, what trilogies of plays—what epics—would have been made out of him! How the rhapsodies would have recited him! How quickly that quaint tall form would have enter'd into the region where men vitalize gods, and gods divinify men!

---

[27] Emperor Constantine XI, who yielded Constantinople to the Turks in 1453.

WHEN LILACS LAST IN THE DOORYARD BLOOMED

1

When lilacs last in the dooryard bloomed,
And the great star early drooped in the western sky in the night,
I mourned, and yet shall mourn with ever-returning spring.

Ever-returning spring, trinity sure to me you bring,
Lilac blooming perennial and drooping star in the west,
And thought of him I love.

2

O powerful western fallen star!
O shades of night—O moody, tearful night!
O great star disappeared—O the black murk that hides the star!
O cruel hands that hold me powerless—O helpless soul of me!
O harsh surrounding cloud that will not free my soul.

3

In the dooryard fronting an old farm-house near the white-washed palings,
Stands the lilac-bush tall growing with heart-shaped leaves of rich green,
With many a pointed blossom rising delicate, with the perfume strong I love,
With every leaf a miracle—and from this bush in the dooryard,
With delicate-colored blossoms and heart-shaped leaves of rich green,
A sprig with its flower I break.

4

In the swamp in secluded recesses,
A shy and hidden bird is warbling a song.

Solitary the thrush,
The hermit withdrawn to himself, avoiding the settlements,
Sings by himself a song.

Song of the bleeding throat,
Death's outlet song of life (for well dear brother I know,
If thou wast not granted to sing thou would'st surely die).

5

Over the breast of the spring, the land, amid cities,
Amid lanes and through old woods, where lately the violets peeped from the
        ground, spotting the gray debris,
Amid the grass in the fields each side of the lanes, passing the endless grass,
Passing the yellow-speared wheat, every grain from its shroud in the dark-brown
        fields uprisen,
Passing the apple-tree blows of white and pink in the orchards,
Carrying a corpse to where it shall rest in the grave,
Night and day journeys a coffin.

6

Coffin that passes through lanes and streets,[28]
Through day and night with the great cloud darkening the land,
With the pomp of the inlooped flags with the cities draped in black,
With the show of the States themselves as the crepe-veiled women standing,
With processions long and winding and the flambeaus of the night,
With the countless torches lit, with the silent sea of faces and the unbared heads,
With the waiting depot, the arriving coffin, and the somber faces,
With dirges through the night, with the thousand voices rising strong and solemn,
With all the mournful voices of the dirges poured around the coffin,
The dim-lit churches and the shuddering organs—where amid these you journey,
With the tolling tolling bells' perpetual clang,
Here, coffin that slowly passes,
I give you my sprig of lilac.

7

(Nor for you, for one alone,
blossoms and branches green to coffins all I bring,
For fresh as the morning, thus would I chant a song for you O sane and sacred death.
All over bouquets of roses,
O death, I cover you over with roses and early lilies,
But mostly and now the lilac that blooms the first,
Copious I break, I break the sprigs from the bushes,
With loaded arms I come, pouring for you,
For you and the coffins all of you O death.)

8

O western orb sailing the heaven,
Now I know what you must have meant as a month since I walked,
As I walked in silence the transparent shadowy night,
As I saw you had something to tell as you bent to me night after night
As you drooped from the sky low down as if to my side (while the other stars all
          looked on),
As we wandered together the solemn night (for something I know not what kept me
          from sleep),
As the night advanced, and I saw on the rim of the west how full you were of woe,
As I stood on the rising ground in the breeze in the cool transparent night,
As I watched where you passed and was lost in the netherward black of the night,
As my soul in its trouble dissatisfied sank, as where you sad orb,
Concluded, dropped in the night, and was gone.

9

Sing on there in the swamp,
O singer bashful and tender, I hear your notes, I hear your call,
I hear, I come presently, I understand you,
But a moment I linger, for the lustrous star has detained me,
The star my departing comrade holds and detains me.

---

[28] The funeral cortege stopped at many towns between Washington and Springfield, Illinois, where
Lincoln was buried.

10

O how shall I warble myself for the dead one there I loved?
And how shall I deck my song for the large sweet soul that has gone?
And what shall my perfume be for the grace of him I love?

Sea-winds blown from east to west,
Blown from the Eastern sea and blown from the Western sea, till there on the prairies
    meeting,
These and with these and the breath of my chant,
I'll perfume the grave of him I love.

11

O how shall I hang on the chamber walls?
And what shall the pictures be that I hang on the walls,
to adorn the burial-house of him I love?

Pictures of growing spring and farms and homes,
With the Fourth-month eve at sundown, and the gray smoke lucid and bright,
With floods of the yellow gold of the gorgeous, indolent, sinking sun burning,
    expanding the air,
With the fresh sweet herbage under foot, and the pale green leaves of the trees
    prolific,
In the distance the flowing glaze, the breast of the river, with a wind-dapple here and
    there,
With ranging hills on the banks, with many a line against the sky, and shadows,
And the city at hand with dwellings so dense, and stacks of chimneys,
And all the scenes of life and the workshops, and the workmen homeward returning.

12

Lo, body and soul—this land,
My own Manhattan with spires, and the sparkling and hurrying tides, and the ships,
The varied and ample land, the South and the North in the light, Ohio's shores and
    flashing Missouri,
And ever the far-spreading prairies cover'd with grass and corn.

Lo, the most excellent sun so calm and haughty,
The violet and purple morn with just-felt breezes,
The gentle soft-born measureless light,
The miracle spreading bathing all, the fulfill'd noon,
The coming eve delicious, the welcome night and the starts,
Over my cities shining all, enveloping man and land.

13

Sing on, sing on you gray-brown bird,
Sing from the swamps, the recesses, pour your chant from the bushes,
Limitless out of the dusk, out of the cedars and pines.

Sing on dearest brother, warble your reedy song,
Loud human song, with voice of uttermost woe.

O liquid and free and tender!
O wild and loose to my soul—O wondrous singer!
You only I hear—yet the star holds me, (but will soon depart,)
Yet the lilac with mastering odor holds me.

14

Now while I sat in the day and look'd forth,
In the close of the day with its light and the fields of spring, and the farmers
      preparing their crops,
In the large unconscious scenery of my land with its lakes and forests,
In heavenly aerial beauty, (after the perturb'd winds and the storms,)
Under the arching heavens of the afternoon swift passing, and the voices of children
      and women,
The many-moving sea-tides, and I saw the ships how they sail'd,
And the summer approaching with richness, and the fields all busy with labor,
And the infinite separate houses, how they all went on, each with its meals and
      minutia of daily usages,
And the streets how they throbbings throbb'd, and the cities pent—lo, then and there,

Falling upon them all and among them all, enveloping me with the rest,
Appeared the cloud, appeared the long black trail,
And I knew the death, its thought, and the sacred knowledge of death.

Then with the knowledge of death as walking one side of me,
And the thought of death close-walking the other side of me,
And I in the middle as with companions, and as holding the hands of companions,
I fled forth to the hiding receiving night that talks not,
Down to the shores of the water, the path by the swamp in the dimness,
To the solemn shadowy cedars and ghostly pines so still.

And the singer so shy to the rest received me,
The gray-brown bird I know received us comrades three,
And he sang the carol of death, and a verse for him I love.

From deep secluded recesses,
From the fragrant cedars and the ghostly pines so still,
Came the carol of the bird.

And the charm of the carol rapt me,
As I held as if by their hands my comrades in the night,
And the voice of my spirit tallied the song of the bird.

Come lovely and soothing death,
Undulate round the world, serenely arriving, arriving,
In the day, in the night, to all, to each,
Sooner or later delicate death.

Praised be the fathomless universe,
For life and joy, and for objects and knowledge curious,
And for love, sweet love—but praise! praise! praise!
For the sure-enwinding arms of cool-enfolding death.

Dark mother always gliding near with soft feet,
Have none chanted for thee a chant of fullest welcome?
Then I chanted for thee, I glorify thee above all,
I bring thee a song that when thou must indeed come, come unfalteringly.

Approach strong deliveress,
When it is so, when thou hast taken them I joyously sing the dead,
Lost in the loving floating ocean of thee,
Laved in the flood of thy bliss O death.

From me to thee glad serenades,
Dances for thee I propose saluting thee, adornments and feastings for thee,
And the signs of the open landscape and the high-spread sky are fitting,
And life and the fields, and the huge and thoughtful night.

The night in silence under many a star,
The ocean shore and the husky whispering wave whose voice I know,
And the soul turning to thee O vast and well-veiled death,
And the body gratefully nestling close to thee.

Over the tree-tops I float thee a song,
Over the rising and sinking waves, over the myriad fields and the prairies wide,
Over the dense-packed cities all and the teeming wharves and ways,
Float this carol with joy, with joy to thee O death.

15

To the tally of my soul,
Loud and strong kept up the gray-brown bird,
With pure deliberate notes spreading filling the night.

Loud in the pines and cedars dim,
Clear in the freshness moist and the swamp-perfume,
And I with my comrades there in the night.

While my sight that was bound in my eyes unclosed,
As to long panoramas of visions.

And I saw askant the armies,
I saw as in noiseless dreams hundreds of battle-flags,
Borne through the smoke of the battles and pierced with missiles I saw them,
And carried hither and yon through the smoke, and torn and bloody,
And at last but a few shreds left on the staffs (and all in silence),
And the staffs all splintered and broken.

I saw battle-corpses, myriads of them,
And the white skeletons of young men, I saw them,
I saw debris and debris of all the slain soldiers of the war,
But I saw they were not as was thought,
They themselves were fully at rest, they suffered not,
The living remained and suffered, the mother suffered,
And the wife and the child and the musing comrade suffered,
And the armies that remained suffered.

16

Passing the visions, passing the night,
Passing, unloosing the hold of my comrades' hands,
Passing the song of the hermit bird and the tallying song of my soul,
Victorious song, death's outlet song, yet varying ever-altering song,
As low and wailing, yet clear the notes, rising and falling, flooding the night,
Sadly sinking and fainting, as warning and warning, and yet again bursting with joy,
Covering the earth and filling the spread of the heaven.

As that powerful psalm in the night I heard from recesses,
Passing, I leave thee lilac with heart-shaped leaves,
I leave thee there in the door-yard, blooming, returning with spring.

I cease from my song for thee,
From my gaze on thee in the west, fronting the west, communing with thee,
O comrade lustrous with silver face in the night.

Yet each to keep and all, retrievements out of the night,
The song, the wonderous chant of the gray-brown bird,
And the tallying chant, the echo aroused in my soul,
With the lustrous and drooping star with the countenance full of woe,
With the holders holding my hand nearing the call of the bird,
Comrades mine and I in the midst, and their memory ever to keep, for the dead I
　　loved so well,
For the sweetest, wisest soul of all my days and lands—and this for his dear sake,
Lilac and star and bird twined with the chant of my soul,
There in the fragrant pines and the cedars dusk and dim.

1865-66

MIR

DEATH OF A HERO

Why are heroes fated to die?
All men die—in their time.
But heroes die in their prime.

Is this not because we fear the power and the
　　pride?
Is this not because we must kill those among us
　　who are the best?
Because they remind us life is no free ride?
Because they challenge and put us to the test?

Like Homer's wrestlers we ostracize the best.

We are afraid: of fear; of envy; of losing the
　　contest.

We kill our heroes before their time.
We kill those men who would be best.
(We kill the women with dried-up breasts)
We kill the father without the power.
(Like the mother turned sour)
We still kill heroes.
We can't stand anything but tyros.

1989

JOHN KEATS (1795-1821)

A major British Romantic poet, John Keats was inspired to write this poem by viewing a Greek vase on which scenes of pastoral life were depicted. This poem shows how art preserves beauty by freezing time.

ODE ON A GRECIAN URN

Thou still unravished bride of quietness,
    Thou foster-child of silence and slow time,
Sylvan historian, who canst thus express
    A flowery tale more sweetly than our rhyme:
What leaf-fringed legend haunts about thy shape
    Of deities or mortals, or of both,
      In Tempe or the dales of Arcady?
    What men or gods are these? What maidens loth?
What mad pursuit? What struggle to escape?
    What pipes and timbrels? What wild ecstasy?

Heard melodies are sweet, but those unheard
    Are sweeter; therefore, ye soft pipes, play on;
Not to the sensual ear, but, more endeared,
    Pipe to the spirit ditties of no tone:
Fair youth, beneath the trees, thou canst not leave
    Thy song, nor ever can those trees be bare;
      Bold Lover, never, never canst thou kiss,
Though winning near the goal—yet, do not grieve;
    She cannot fade, though thou hast not thy bliss,
For ever wilt thou love, and she be fair!

Ah, happy, happy boughs! that cannot shed
    Your leaves, nor ever bid the Spring adieu;
And, happy melodist, unwearied,
    For ever piping songs for ever new;
More happy love! more happy, happy love!
    For ever warm and still to be enjoyed,
      For ever panting, and for ever young;
All breathing human passion far above,
    That leaves a heart high-sorrowful and cloyed,
      A burning forehead, and a parching tongue.
Who are these coming to the sacrifice?
    To what green altar, O mysterious priest,
Lead'st thou that heifer lowing at the skies,
    And all her silken flanks with garlands drest?
What little town by river or sea shore,
    Or mountain-built with peaceful citadel,
      Is emptied of this folk, this pious morn?
And, little town, thy streets for evermore
    Will silent be; and not a soul to tell
      Why thou art desolate, can e'er return.
O Attic shape! Fair attitude! with brede
    Of marble men and maidens overwrought,

With forest branches and the trodden weed;
  Thou, silent form, dost tease us out of thought
As doth Eternity: Cold Pastoral!
   When old age shall this generation waste,
    Thou shalt remain, in midst of other woe
   Than ours, a friend to man, to whom thou say'st,
Beauty is truth, truth beauty,—that is all
    Ye know on earth, and all ye need to know.

WALKER PERCY (1916-1990)

Walker Percy combines Christian moral and religious concerns in all six of his novels. His first novel, The Moviegoer, *which makes use of ironic detachment, won the National Book Award in 1961. In his later novels, as in the selection which follows from the* The Thanatos Syndrome *(1987), he uses his art as a "spiritual weapon against the malaise of the age." All his novels constitute a spiritual quest--a search for meaning much in the tradition of Kierkegaard and Dostoevsky.*

BLUEBIRDS AND JAYBIRDS

What, then, to make of my patients?

Time was when I'd have tested their neurones. There's such a thing as the psyche, I discovered. I became a psyche-iatrist, as I've said, a doctor of the soul, an old-style Freudian analyst, plus a dose of Adler and Jung. I discovered that it is not sex that terrifies people. It is that they are stuck with themselves. They are frightened out of their wits that they are not doing what, according to experts, books, films, TV, they are supposed to be doing. *They*, the experts, know, don't they?

Then I became somewhat simpleminded. I developed a private classification of people, a not exactly scientific taxonomy which I find useful in working with people. It fits or fitted nearly all the people I knew, patients, neurotic people, so-called normal people.

According to my private classification, people are either blue-birds or jaybirds. Most women, it turns out, are bluebirds. Most men, by no means all, are jaybirds.

Mickey LaFaye, for example, is, or was, clearly a bluebird. She dreamed of being happy as a child in Vermont, of waiting for a visitor, a certain someone, of finding the bluebird of happiness.

Enrique Busch was a jaybird if ever I saw one. He wanted to shoot everybody in El Salvador except the generals and the fourteen families.

It is a question of being or of doing. Most of the women patients I saw were unhappy and wanted to be happy. They never doubted there was such a creature as the bluebird of happiness. Most men wanted to do this or that, take this or that, beat So-and-so out of a promotion, seduce Miss Smith, beat the Steelers, meet their quota, win the trip to Oahu, win an argument—just like a noisy jaybird. The trouble is, once you've set out to be a jaybird, there's nothing more pitiful than an unsuccessful jaybird. In my experience, that is, with patients who are not actually crazy (and even with some who are), people generally make themselves miserable for one of two reasons: They have either failed to find the bluebird of happiness or they're failed jaybirds.

It is not for me to say whether one should try to *be* happy—though it always struck me as an odd pursuit, like trying to be blue-eyed—or whether one should try to beat all the other jaybirds on the block. But it is my observation that neither pursuit succeeds very well. I only know that people who set their hearts on either usually end up seeing me or somebody like me, or having heart attacks, or climbing into a bottle.

Take a woman—and some men—who think thus: If only I could *be* with that person, or away from this person, or be in another job, or be free, or be in the South of France or on the Outer Banks, or *be* an artist or God knows what—then I'll be happy. Such a person is a bluebird in my book.

Or consider the person: What am I going to do with my no-good son, who is driving me crazy—what I want to do is knock him in the head. Or, what is the best way to take on that son of a bitch who is my boss or to get even with that other son of a bitch who slighted me? Wasn't it President Kennedy who said: Don't get mad, get even?—now, there was a royal jaybird for you. Or, I've got to have that woman—how do I get her without getting caught? Or, I think I can make a hundred thousand almost legally, and so on. Jaybirds all. B. F. Skinner, the jaybird of psychologists, put it this way: The object of life is to gratify yourself without getting arrested. Not exactly the noblest sentiment expressed in two thousand years of Western civilization, but it has a certain elementary validity. True jaybird wisdom.

But what has happened to all the bluebirds and jaybirds I knew so well?
They've all turned into chickens.

Merry Oldsmobile, Sheet Music Cover Illustration, Early Twentieth Century.

FEODOR DOSTOYEVSKY (1821-1881)

One of the greatest Russian novelists, Dostoevsky achieved renown for such novels as Crime and Punishment *and* The Brothers Karamazov. *In the latter, as in* Notes From Underground *he struggles with the meaning of existence, foreshadowing the ideas of Nietzsche.*

NOTES FROM THE UNDERGROUND

Shower upon (man) . . . every earthly blessing, drown him in a sea of happiness . . . and even then out of sheer ingratitude, sheer spite, man would deliberately desire the most fatal rubbish . . . simply to introduce into all this positive good sense his fatal fantastic element. It is just his fantastic dreams, his vulgar folly, that he will desire . . . simply in order to prove to himself . . . that men are still men and not the keys on the piano, which the laws of nature threaten to control so completely that soon one will be able to desire nothing but by the calendar.

. . . . You . . . want to cure men of their old habits and reform their will in accordance with science and good sense, but how do you know, not only that it is possible, but also that it is desirable, to reform man in that way? . . . Why are you so positively convinced that not to act against his real normal interests guaranteed by the conclusions of reason and arithmetic is certainly always advantageous for man and must always be the law for mankind? . . . It may be the law of logic, but not the law of humanity.

GLOSSARY

ABSTRACT PAINTING

Painting that is not representational, lacking recognizable images, so that the content consists in form.

AGNOSTICISM

A position that neither denies nor affirms the existence of God, based on the assumption that such knowledge cannot be attained.

ALLEGORY

A narrative that has two meanings: the literal meaning (the story itself) and the symbolic meaning. All characters and events in an allegory have symbolic meaning.

APOLLONIAN

Rational, well-ordered, and harmonious; related to Apollo, Greek god of the sun, prophecy, music, medicine, and poetry.

ARCHETYPE

An image or thematic pattern that recurs in many cultures, thus acquiring transcendent symbolic force. According to Carl Jung, these images are part of the universal, collective unconscious.

ATHEISM

Belief that there is no God (from a = without + theism).

BAROQUE

An art style of the 17th century characterized by ornate scrolls and curves; also, a style of musical composition of the same period marked by strict forms, counterpoint, and ornamentation.

BUDDHISM

The doctrine that suffering is part of existence, but inward extinction of the self and the senses through contemplation produces a state of wakeful illumination beyond both suffering and existence. Buddhism grew out of Hinduism in the 6th century B.C.

CHIAROSCURO

The use of light in painting to enhance perspective.

CLASSICAL

Looking to tradition, especially the rational order, balance, and symmetry of the classical Greeks. In music, the "classical period" is the latter half of the 18th century, the music of Mozart and Haydn, whereas "classical music" is a much broader term.

CONCERTO

A composition for an orchestra and one or more solo instruments, typically in three movements.

CUBISM

A nonrepresentational school of painting developed in Paris in the 20th century, characterized by abstract and often geometric structures.

DEISM

The belief, popular in the 18th century, that God created the universe, set it in motion, and then abandoned it, giving no supernatural revelation.

DIALECTIC

The practice of arriving at the truth by disclosing the contradictions in an opponent's argument and overcoming them.

DIONYSIAN

Spontaneous, passionate, and irrational; relating to Dionysius (called Bacchus by the Romans), god of wine, fertility, and the theater.

EPIC POEM

A long narrative poem such as *The Odyssey*, relating exploits of a national hero, usually based on myths of a culture. Often the epic poem is passed down orally before being written.

FRESCO

The art of painting on fresh, moist plaster, usually as wall or ceiling murals. Michelangelo used the technique in the Sistine Chapel.

HEBREW RELIGION

The religion of the Old Testament, practiced by the Jewish people, who are descendents of Abraham.

HINDUISM

An ancient religion predominant in India and characterized by belief in reincarnation and a supreme being of many forms and natures.

HUMANISM

A concern with human beings and their values and capacities; in particular, the movement of the Renaissance that emphasized secular classical art and literature.

HUMANITIES

Those subjects concerned with human culture, especially the arts, literature, philosophy, and history.

IMAGERY

Any verbal appeal to any of the senses; concrete as opposed to abstract language. An image suggests something that can be seen, heard, touched, smelled, or tasted.

IMPRESSIONIST PAINTING

The style of painting developed in France during the 1870's, which sought to give an impression through the use of light and unmixed colors, rather than to be purely representational.

IRONY

Language that says the opposite of what is meant or expected. Dramatic irony in a play operates in two ways: (1) Sophoclean Irony, in which the audience knows more than one of the characters, and (2) Euripedean Irony, in which the tragic ending comes as a surprise.

METAPHOR

A non-literal statement, using figurative language, such as "All the world's a stage" or "He plunged into the depths of despair."

METAPHYSICS

The branch of philosophy that examines the nature of first principles and ultimate reality.

MINIMALISM

Nonrepresentational art that simplifies by use of essential shapes and forms, often geometrical.

MOSAIC

A picture or design made by setting small colored pieces of glass, tile, or stone in mortar.

MOSLEM RELIGION (ISLAM)

Theistic religion based on the teachings of Mohammed (7th century A.D.), including belief in Allah and the Koran, the Moslem holy book. The Moslem lineage is traced to Abraham's son Ishmael.

RENAISSANCE

The humanistic revival of classical art, literature, and learning that originated in Italy in the 14th century and later spread through Europe.

REPRESENTATIONAL PAINTING

Realistic depiction of the subject. Great strides in this form were made in the Renaissance with the discovery of perspective.

ROMANTICISM

An artistic and intellectual movement dominant in the 19th century which stressed strong emotion, imagination, and freedom from classical forms in art, literature, and music.

SATIRE

An artistic or literary work that attacks human vice or folly through ridicule, wit, or humor. Hypocrisy is a common subject for satire.

SONATA

An instrumental musical composition, as for the piano, consisting of three or four movements varying in key, mood, and tempo.

SONNET

A poem of 14 lines, developing a theme according to a strict pattern of rhyme and meter: An octave (8 lines) and sestet (6 lines) in the Italian sonnet and three quatrains (4 lines) followed by a couplet (2 lines) in the Shakespearean sonnet.

SURREALISM

A 20th-century literary and artistic movement that uses fantastic imagery to express the workings of the unconscious mind.

SYMBOL

An image, object, or action that represents something else, usually an invisible abstract idea.

SYMPHONY

An extended musical composition for the orchestra, consisting of four related movements.

THEISM

The belief in God (monotheism) or in Gods (polytheism).

THEME

The underlying idea or ideas in a painting or literary work.

TRAGEDY

A literary work, especially a drama, in which the protagonist (main character) is engaged in a morally significant struggle that ends in calamity or great disappointment. Aristotle's definition called for the tragic hero to suffer and learn from a great error of his own making.

TRANSCENDENT

Pertaining to knowledge that is beyond the limits of experience.

INDEX